INFRASTRUCTUR
Lessons for future

GW01418852

Edited by Mthul
and Charles Leyeka Lufumpa

P

First published in Great Britain in 2017 by

Policy Press
University of Bristol
1-9 Old Park Hill
Bristol
BS2 8BB
UK
t: +44 (0)117 954 5940
pp-info@bristol.ac.uk
www.policypress.co.uk

North America office:
Policy Press
c/o The University of Chicago Press
1427 East 60th Street
Chicago, IL 60637, USA
t: +1 773 702 7700
f: +1 773-702-9756
sales@press.uchicago.edu
www.press.uchicago.edu

British Library Cataloguing in Publication Data
A catalogue record for this book is available from the British Library

Library of Congress Cataloging-in-Publication Data
A catalog record for this book has been requested

ISBN 978-1-4473-2664-9 paperback
ISBN 978-1-4473-2663-2 hardcover
ISBN 978-1-4473-2667-0 ePub
ISBN 978-1-4473-2668-7 Mobi
ISBN 978-1-4473-2665-6 ePdf

Cover design by Hayes Design
Front cover image: Giulia Bertuzzo
Printed and bound in Great Britain by TJ International, Padstow
Policy Press uses environmentally responsible print partners

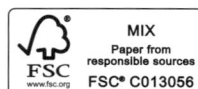

MIX
Paper from
responsible sources
FSC
www.fsc.org
FSC® C013056

Contents

Contents

Contents

List of figures

List of tables

List of boxes

Notes on contributors

Abdoulaye Adam is a statistician with more than 30 years of work experience in providing leadership on statistical capacity building, quantitative methods, analytical studies and statistical developments. Dr Adam has worked in his native Niger as the Head of the Statistics and Computer Science Division of the Institut National des Recherches Agronomiques du Niger (INRAN) and then as Director of Research. He worked for the then West Africa Rice Development Association (WARDA/ADRAO), presently Africa Rice, as th Head of the Statistics Unit in charge of providing support to WARDA's scientists and to member countries on demand in data collection (both experiments and surveys), handling, management and analysis. He also worked as Acting Head of the Training Unit and then as Acting Director of Research for some time, concurrently with his statistics duties. He moved to the African Development Bank (AfDB) to be a member of the regional team in charge of implementing the International Comparison Program (ICP) in the Africa region and handled the responsibilities of Manager of the Statistical Capacity Building Division for some time before retiring in 2010. Dr Adam is presently a senior international consultant with interest in statistical capacity building, network and regional statistical program management, price statistics, international comparison program and agricultural statistics.

Lishan Adam is a researcher and consultant specializing in Information and Communication Technologies in development, with focus on infrastructure, policies, regulations and application in different sectors. In the period 1990–2002 he worked at the United Nations Economic Commission for Africa in Addis Ababa as a programmer, trainer, network manager and regional advisor. He was one of the pioneers to introduce low-cost and internet connectivity in Africa in early 1990s. Dr Adam served as a visiting associate professor on communications policy and regulation at the Graduate School of Public and Development Management of the University of Witwatersrand (2007–10), as associate professor at the Department of Information Science of the University of Stellenbosch (2003–05) and as a course director on telecom sector planning at the University of West Indies (2006–08). Dr Adam is a member of Research ICT Africa network, with facilitating roles in eastern Africa. Since he began consulting in 2003, Dr Adam advised governments and international institutions on the broadband infrastructure, ICT applications in education, health, trade and public administration, research and academic network development, and ICT policy and telecom regulatory issues.

John C. Anyanwu is Lead Research Economist in the Development Research Department of the African Development Bank (AfDB). Prior to joining the AfDB, he was full Professor of Economics, Department of Economics and Statistics, University of Benin, Nigeria; Health Economist/Economic Adviser to Resident Representative, WHO, Lagos, Nigeria; and Consultant to the AfDB and International Health Policy Program. He had also been Chief Planning Officer in the former Strategic Planning Division of the AfDB. Professor Anyanwu holds a PhD and MSc in Economics from the University of Ibadan, Nigeria and a master's degree in Entrepreneurship and Economic Development from the University of Houston-Victoria, USA. He has taken training/executive education courses at London School of Economics, UK and Harvard University, USA, and has been a Visiting Scholar at Cornell University, USA. His research interests include natural resources, poverty/inequality reduction, economic growth/development, and good governance, among others. He is Editor of the *African Development Review*, a quarterly journal of the AfDB. Professor Anyanwu is a member of the African Finance and Economics Association (AFEA) (and a former Director and President thereof), the American Economic Association (AEA), the International Association for Energy Economics (IAEE), the National Economics Association (NEA), the International Health Economics Association (iHEA), and the Western Economic Association International (WEAI), and he belongs to a number of research networks such the Global Development Network (GDN), African Economic Research Consortium (AERC), the Institute of International Finance (IIF), and the Social Science Research Network (SSRN). He has had his papers read at more than 130 conferences/seminars/workshops worldwide. Professor Anyanwu has also authored over 100 scholarly publications in national and international journals in addition to authoring/co-authoring more than 37 book chapters and a number of books.

Zuzana Brixiova is an Adjunct Associate Professor at the University of Cape Town and Research Fellow at the Institute for the Study of Labor (IZA). Previously, she worked as Advisor to the Chief Economist and Vice President at the African Development Bank, Economic Advisor at UNDP Swaziland, and IMF Resident Representative in Belarus and Lithuania. She was the Head of the Czech Republic and

Estonia Unit in the OECD's Economics Department in 2008–09. Prior to that she was Fulbright Scholar at Addis Ababa University. She holds a PhD in Economics from the University of Minnesota, USA.

Taz Chaponda, a national of Malawi, is an Economic Adviser in the Fiscal Affairs Division of the International Monetary Fund (IMF), in Washington DC. He covers countries across Africa and Europe on fiscal policy and public investment management. Prior to joining the IMF, Taz was a Partner at Genesis Analytics where he was responsible for the infrastructure advisory practice. In this role he worked across Africa on large infrastructure projects. He was previously Head of the Budget Office in the National Treasury of South Africa. Taz holds economics degrees from Harvard University, USA and the University of Oxford, UK. He also has an MBA from INSEAD.

Mayuree Chetty is an economist currently working at McKinsey and Company as a strategy consultant. She focuses on solving problems for financial services companies and public and social sector entities across Africa. She also worked at Monitor Deloitte as an economic consultant and Genesis Analytics as a competition and regulation analyst. She holds a Business Science degree in Economics and a master's degree in Economics from the University of Cape Town, South Africa.

Oliver J.M. Chinganya is a chartered statistician with more than 28 years of experience in statistical development in Africa, at both national and international levels, of which 16 years has been at managerial level. He has a wide experience and knowledge of statistical practice across Africa at both field and management levels, and is a strong believer in the effectiveness of partnerships and coordination at country, regional and international levels for effective and sustained development programs. Mr Chinganya joined UNECA as Director of the African Centre for Statistics at the UNECA in April 2016, after having worked for the African Development Bank (AfDB) from April 2010 until end March 2016 as Manager for the Statistical Capacity Building Division in the AfDB's Statistics Department. His responsibilities among others included: managing large statistical building programs and projects involving all African countries, including resources; assessing statistical systems at regional and national levels; proposing strategies to improve statistical systems; and designing integrated statistical frameworks. Prior to joining the AfDB, he worked for the International Monetary Fund as Regional

Resident Advisor (2002–09), providing support to 21 Anglophone African countries participating in the General Data Dissemination System program. Before that, he was Deputy Director of the Zambia Central Statistical Office, and on many occasions acted as Director, where he was responsible for many surveys/projects including a census of population and housing. He also worked for the World Bank as a consultant from October 2009 to April 2010. He is a Zambian national holding an MSc in Statistics, an MBA and various other certifications, including Statistics for Strategic Resource Planning, and Leadership Skills and Competencies.

Morné Hendriksz is an economist in the competition and regulation practice of Genesis Analytics, a Johannesburg-based consultancy, where he assists both public and private sector clients. Prior to Genesis Analytics, Morné worked at the University of Stellenbosch's Department of Economics, where he tutored both economics and statistics to undergraduate students. Morné holds an economics honours degrees and a master's degree in economics, both from the University of Stellenbosch, South Africa.

George Kararach is a Senior Economist at the United Nations Economic Commission for Africa (UNECA) and Senior Consultant, Statistics Department, the African Development Bank. He has an outstanding background in policy analysis, development economics, and strategic planning. Mr Kararach has deep understandings of donor fundraising and the UN system as well as the operational activities of other agencies such as the African Capacity Building Foundation and the African Development Bank. Mr Kararach led the team members involved in the drafting of the recent UNECA governance flagship reports – *African Governance Report IV – Measuring corruption in Africa: The international dimension matters* and *African Governance Report V – Natural Resource Governance and Domestic Resource Mobilisation in Africa*. Mr Kararach is author of several books; his most recent publications include: *Rethinking Development Challenges for Public Policy: Insights from Contemporary Africa* (with Hanson, K. and Shaw, T.M. (eds), Palgrave Macmillan, 2012), *Development Policy in Africa: Mastering the Future?* (Palgrave Macmillan, 2014), *Development in Africa: Refocusing the Lens after the Millennium Development Goals* (with Besada, H. and Shaw, T.M. (eds), Policy Press, 2015), *Economic Management under Hyperinflationary Environment: The Political Economy of Zimbabwe, 1980–2008* (with Raphael Otieno (eds), Oxford University Press, 2016). George

Kararach holds a PhD in Economics from the University of Leeds, UK.

Koffi Marc Kouakou is currently the Principal Statistician-Economist on Gender at the African Development Bank (AfDB). Before joining the Office of the Special Envoy on Gender, he contributed to the success of the 2005 and 2011 International Comparison Program for Africa (ICP-Africa) at the Statistics Department of the Bank. As ICP expert, Mr Kouakou visited almost all African countries and trained more than 200 African statisticians in ICP methodology and Purchasing Power Parities (PPPs). He also contributed to the success of the Bank's Statistical Capacity Building Program Phases 1, 2 and 3. Before joining the AfDB, Mr Kouakou was working in the areas of Private Sector Competitiveness and Regional Integration respectively at the Conseil National du Patronat Ivoirien and the Bureau National d'Etudes Techniques et de Développement (BNETD), Abidjan – Côte d'Ivoire. Mr Kouakou's qualifications include an MBA in Modelling and Decision making at Laval University (Quebec – Canada) and a Masters in Statistics from Ecole Nationale Supérieure de Statistique et d'Economie Appliquée d'Abidjan – Côte d'Ivoire (ENSEA). He has published in the areas of gender and poverty measurement, private sector effectiveness, purchasing power parity (ppp), comparative incomes and price levels in African countries, and systems of national accounts.

Nirina Letsara is currently a Senior Infrastructure Data Analyst at the African Development Bank (AfDB). He has been working for more than 20 years in various areas of statistics. He worked under the frameworks of International Comparison Program for Africa (ICP-Africa) and AfDB's Statistical Capacity Building Program (SCB). His major contribution was on implementation of ICP-Africa methodology in African countries and development of a data quality assessment tool on prices and purchasing power parities. Under the SCB, his focus is on poverty and inequality statistics, data dissemination and exchange through the Open Data platform in African countries, and infrastructure statistics through the Africa Infrastructure Knowledge Program (AIKP). He has published in the areas of purchasing power parity, comparative incomes and price levels in African countries, poverty and inequality and infrastructure. Nirina obtained his BSc degree in Mathematics (1990) from the University of Madagascar and his MSc degree in Economics and Statistics (1993) as Ingénieur

Statisticien Economiste from the Ecole Nationale Supérieure de Statistique et d'Economie Appliquée (ENSEA), Côte d'Ivoire.

Duncan Lishman is an economist at Johannesburg-based consultancy Genesis Analytics. He specialises in competition and regulatory economics, assisting clients in both the public and private sector. Prior to joining Genesis, Duncan worked at the University of Cape Town's School of Economics in South Africa, where he lectured and ran the School's undergraduate writing programme. Duncan holds finance and economics honours degrees and a master's degree in economics, all from the University of Cape Town. He has a particular interest in the transport sector, and his master's dissertation focused on the economics of road pricing.

Charles Leyeka Lufumpa serves as the Director of the Statistics Department of the African Development Bank Group. He has also previously served as Officer-in-charge, Chief Economist and Vice President at the Bank. As the Director of the Statistics Department, he is in charge of overall statistical functions of the Bank, including overseeing its statistical capacity building activities that span across all African countries, sub-regional organizations and statistical training centers across Africa. Before joining the Bank, Dr Lufumpa worked on agricultural policy and planning issues with Zambia's Ministry of Agriculture and Water Development in Lusaka, Zambia. He also served as a visiting researcher in the 1980s in the Department of Economics at Iowa State University, USA, on a staff exchange program with the Zambian Government. His key research interests are in the areas of statistics, poverty, infrastructure, agriculture and environmental economic issues in Africa. His most recent book is *The Emerging Middle Class in Africa* (with Professor Mthuli Ncube (eds), Routledge, 2014). He obtained his BA degree in Economics and Statistics from the University of Zambia (1983), and his MSc degree in Agricultural Economics (1989) and PhD in Natural Resource Economics and Statistics (1991) from Iowa State University, USA.

Albert Mafusire is a macroeconomist at the African Development Bank, with special focus on countries in fragile situations. He has previously worked as a policy analyst and academic. Albert has consulted for Zimbabwean and international organizations. His research interests are mainly on macroeconomics, trade and development issues. Through his research, he has published and presented numerous papers at international and local conferences and seminars. He holds a PhD in Economics from Queensland University, Australia.

Qingwei Meng is a Research Economist in the Development Research Department of the African Development Bank where he carries out research on topics related to development economics, infrastructure development, financial inclusion, and so on. He also supports the Bank's private sector operations by conducting ex-ante assessments of additionality and development impacts. Previously, he worked as a research consultant in the Office of the Chief Economist and Vice President of the Bank, undertaking research projects on a variety of topics including fiscal and monetary policies, financial regulation, regional integration, and capital flight. He holds a PhD in Finance from the University of Birmingham, UK, and his research interests are in the area of corporate finance, corporate governance, money and banking, and financial markets.

Maurice Mubila is a Chief Statistician in the Statistics Department, African Development Bank. He has also served as Officer-in-Charge of the Economic and Social Statistics Division in the Statistics Department. Mr Mubila has over 20 years of experience at the African Development Bank, developing methodological frameworks and applying statistical methods in such areas as monitoring of Millennium Development Goals (MDGs), assessments and improvements of civil registration and vital statistics systems, poverty analysis, analysis of infrastructure statistics (transport, energy, water, ICT) and price statistics in African countries, among other things. Prior to joining the Bank, Mr Mubila spent 10 years as a professional and then Head of Price Information and Statistics Unit, at the Prices and Incomes Commission in the Zambian Government. He has contributed chapters to the edited book on *The Emerging Middle Class in Africa* (Routledge, 2014). He holds an MSc in Social Statistics, and a Postgraduate Certificate (equivalent to BSc (Hons)) in Statistics, both from the University of Southampton, UK, a BA in Economics, University of Zambia, and a College Certificate in the Design, Monitoring and Evaluation of Projects (Wye College, University of London).

Mthuli Ncube is Managing Director, Quantum Global Research Lab, Switzerland, an investment company. Prior to this he was Professor of Public Policy at Blavatnik School of Government, University of Oxford. He served as Chief Economist and Vice President at the African Development Bank Group. In this position he was responsible for the Bank's strategic economic thinking and championed the concept of 'inclusive growth' which underpinned the Bank's 10-year strategy; and supervised development research, statistics and capacity building departments. He was Dean of the Faculty of Commerce Law and Management, and also Dean and Professor of Finance at Wits Business School, in South Africa. He founded the Centre for Entrepreneurship at Wits University. He was also a Lecturer in Finance at the London School of Economics (LSE). He is Chairman of the Board of the African Economic Research Consortium (AERC) and board member of Global Development Network (GDN). Professor Ncube has published several books, papers and articles in the area of economics and political economy and finance. Some of his recent books include: *Monetary Policy and the Economy in South Africa* (Macmillan, 2013); *Quantitative Easing and its Impact on US, UK, Europe and Japan* (2013); *The Emerging Middle Class in Africa* (2014); *African Financial Markets and Monetary Policy* (2009); *Global Growth and Financial Spillovers* (2016), and *The Oxford Companion of the Economics of South Africa* (co-edited, Oxford University Press, 2015). He is on the Global Agenda Council of the World Economic Forum on "Poverty and Economic Development" and on the Advisory Council for World Economic Forum (WEF) on Sustainable Infrastructure. He is a Commissioner of the Lancet Commission on Investing Health, and member of the OECD Expect Group on Rethinking the Future of Development Aid. He is a regular commentator in media such as the BBC, *Financial Times* and *Wall Street Journal*. Professor Ncube holds a PhD in Economics (Mathematical Finance) from the University of Cambridge, UK.

Slaheddine Saidi joined the African Development Bank (AfDB) in 2008 as a statistician, with more than 20 years' various and ranging experiences in official statistics, banking, insurance, business and in the academic field. He worked under the frameworks of AfDB's Statistical Capacity Building Program (SCB). His major contribution was on data dissemination and exchange through the Open Data platform in African countries, infrastructure statistics through the Africa Infrastructure Knowledge Program (AIKP), regional integration, financial market statistics and tourism and contributed to different publication in different domain. Before joining the AfDB, Mr Saidi was a General Director of Statistics in Tunisia (the National Statistics Office). He graduated from the High School of Business (IHEC Carthage-Tunisia) and obtained an MSc degree in Economics and Statistics (1992) as Ingénieur Statisticien Economiste from the

Ecole Nationale de la Statistique et de l'Administration Economique (ENSAE), Paris, and a master's degree in Applied Mathematics in Economics (DEA Mathématiques Appliquées aux Sciences Economiques) from the University of Paris, Dauphine, Paris, France.

Ethèl Teljeur is an economist specializing in economic regulation of energy sector. Currently a partner in an economics-based consultancy firm, Genesis Analytics, she has developed energy regulation expertise through her work in both the public and private sector. Ethèl joined Genesis Analytics after seven-and-a-half years as piped gas regulator at the Energy Regulator of South Africa (NERSA). Her experience includes regulatory reform policy, design and implementation, and price and tariff-setting methodologies in network industries, particularly in the oil and gas industry and the electricity sector. She has been involved in the energy industry for over 16 years in South Africa, the EU and Southern Africa Development Community. Ms Teljeur has an MSc degree from the London School of Oriental and African Studies, a BA (Hons) from Kingston University, UK, and a propaedeuse from the Erasmus University of Rotterdam.

Tito Yepes is a researcher in the economics of infrastructure and territorial development, including transport, water and sanitation, energy, planning and competitiveness. He has developed analyses to contribute to policy making and implementation in more than 20 countries mostly from Latin America and Africa. He also advises the private sector on financial and risk structuring of investments in transport, mining and ICT. He holds a PhD in economics from Universidad Nacional de Colombia and is currently an Associated Researcher of Fedesarrollo, a top think tank of Latin America.

Acknowledgements

This book is a result of the commitment of African Development Bank to foster the infrastructure development agenda in Africa. The Bank and other research has repeatedly confirmed that infrastructure is critical for the success of its regional member countries. Africa still has massive infrastructure needs. It invests only 4% of its gross domestic product (GDP) in infrastructure, compared with 14% in China. Bridging the infrastructure gap could increase GDP growth by an estimated two percentage points a year. The Bank has made significant contributions to infrastructure development in Africa, and tens of millions of Africans are now better off thanks to Bank investments in transport, energy and water. The Bank intends to scale up infrastructure financing to the continent significantly—not just through its own lending but by leveraging its financial resources. The Infrastructure Knowledge Program (AIKP) is part and parcel of this effort. AIKP took over from where the World Bank (the Africa Infrastructure Country Diagnostics) stopped with the longer-term ambition of providing a platform for: updating the infrastructure database on African countries; providing analytic knowledge products to guide policy and funding decisions; and informing development policy and program management activities and building infrastructure statistical capacity on the continent.

To show the primacy of infrastructure in the African development discourse, the Bank is refocusing its operations to advance Africa's transformative agenda over the next 10 years or so. The Bank has sharpened its agenda by identify five high priorities. These areas are to: light up and power Africa, feed Africa, integrate Africa, industrialize Africa, and improve the quality of life for the people of Africa. These five areas, which are in line with the Bank's Ten Year Strategy 2013-2022, have been termed the "High-Fives", serving as a blueprint for African countries to embark on a course of sustainable transformation.

This volume would have not come to life without the active support of the Bank's various operational departments and associated vice-presidencies. The Office of the President was also critical in guiding the spirit that underpinned AIKP and the birth of the High-Fives. The book benefit enormously from the single-minded dedication of George Kararach in providing the leadership, management and coordination that preceded the birth of this volume. We also thank the many people who provided input both directly and indirectly—especially the team at Policy Press led by Emily Watt and Laura Vickers.

Foreword

Africa has embarked on rethinking its strategies for sustainable growth building on the recent good growth performance of about 5% per annum. At the core of this mental shift is structural transformation. African economies have to evolve in their levels of development including the associated structure of factor endowments. However, each such structure requires corresponding infrastructure (both "hard" and "soft") to circumscribe its operations and transactions.

It is now generally accepted that economic development is a continuum of change from a low-income agrarian economy to a high-income industrialized economy, not a dichotomy of two economic development levels ("poor" versus "rich" or "developing" versus "developed"). Because of historical and institutional specificities, infrastructure in African countries should not necessarily draw from infrastructure that exists in high-income countries but be fit for purpose given local realities and contexts. In essence, for any given growth/development trajectory, there is a basic mechanism for effective resource allocation. Development as a dynamic process demands "environmental" upgrading including improvements in "hard" and "soft" infrastructure at each stage. Such upgrading usually results in large externalities to firms' transaction costs and returns to capital investment. For example, there are needs for an effective market mechanism just as much as for the government to actively define the institutional parameters for infrastructure improvements.

As a number of chapters in this book show, infrastructure generally provides the physical framework for a modern, healthy, and prosperous economy. For example, telecommunications, transportation, power and water, or public buildings including schools and hospitals define the way we live and relate to each other. Infrastructure is an integral aspect of society as it shapes how people communicate, access goods and services, and look at their quality of life through research, education, and commerce. Infrastructure does not only enable the transformation of individual ideas into action but also has a critical role in either exacerbating or reducing socioeconomic inequalities. In this regard, the quality of infrastructure is very important because it defines a society's development trajectory including elements of governance, economic planning and many aspects of domestic and foreign policy.

It is estimated that Africa needs around US$93 billion annually to finance its infrastructure gap. In Africa, infrastructure priorities and projects will by necessity vary across regions. Some of African countries have opportunities to build completely new infrastructure, and in some cases, new cities, which presents an opportunity to incorporate the latest thinking in socially and environmentally sustainable design thus "leapfrogging" outdated solutions. For example, the rapid adoption of cell phones on the continent has circumvented the need for traditional telephone wires. Similar opportunities exist for leapfrogging in clean energy and efficient urban logistics among other areas.

Good infrastructure enhances effective governance whereby people are informed of developments around them and are supportive of it. If well conceived and implemented, infrastructure projects enhance people's confidence in their government, spur public willingness to pay taxes and further strengthen the demands for an accountable government. Good economic governance is critical as any infrastructure project requires the state to have sufficient administrative capabilities, be able to prevent corruption, and provide socioeconomic stability, in order for the planning process to actually attract potential investors. Good economic governance and good infrastructure relate virtuously. Infrastructure development allows people to have faith that their government is operating on their behalf. In turn, governments have to show that they are acting in the people's best interest, rather than because of elite capture. Good infrastructure is critical for social inclusion and vice versa.

There is also need to think of infrastructure as a source of services that mediate consumption. Infrastructure investments must therefore be accommodative of emerging social trends and consumer preferences. Infrastructure operators must know their customers or product consumers at all levels of the product cycle. In many instances, the long-term returns on infrastructure investments depend on the end customer who pays the bills. Despite the regulatory and political contexts, any successful infrastructure development strategy must be anchored on meeting the needs of consumers and citizens.

Unfortunately, there is a tendency among experts to consider planning, financing, and construction techniques as the difficult issues in delivering infrastructure in Africa. This list ignores completely the criticality of engaging with stakeholders and the general public at the various stages of the project cycle. Failures to consult tend to delay, let alone undermine projects. The result usually is that deadlines are missed and costs rise. The rise of social media has transformed the way much of the public gets information and react to it. Without effective consultation and engagement, negative perceptions of a new project can spread quickly and block requisite progress.

The private sector is increasingly becoming an important a source of capital for infrastructure investments in Africa, especially due to participations of the pension funds and sovereign wealth funds industries. The need for increased private sector involvement to supplement infrastructure financing is anchored on the reality that public finances in Africa have weak tax revenue collection, and more importantly, fiscal space is largely absorbed by recurrent expenditures. Currently, domestic revenue generation is around 23% of GDP and lower than the averages for other developing regions. Despite the high growth rates (averaging 5%) in the past decade, domestically raised revenues in Africa grew by less than 1.2% of GDP in the past decade. The recent decline in commodity prices has worsened the situation, with severe budget constraints on many governments—especially those of oil-exporting countries such as Angola and Nigeria. Recent experiences indicate that domestic infrastructure spending is particularly vulnerable to budget cuts during crisis and downturns.

However, the past few years have also shown that financing may not be most difficult obstacle to overcome in Africa's quest for infrastructure as part of its wider development. As this book shows, the number of institutional investors allocating assets to infrastructure has risen considerably thanks to an increased risk appetite by new players such as China and giant sovereign wealth as well as pension funds. Multilateral and development finance institutions such as the African Development Bank and Afrexim Bank are stepping up their efforts to underwrite and fund infrastructure development on the continent. The pool of capital available for infrastructure investments in Africa is getting deeper and diverse. Among infrastructure funds, institutional investors, public treasuries, development banks, commercial banks, corporations, and even retail investors, more than US$5 trillion a year is available for infrastructure investment globally.

Capital is necessary yet not sufficient to ensure success of infrastructure initiatives across Africa. Indeed, there is ample evidence to suggest that African governments could boost infrastructure productivity by US$1 trillion a year. However, such investments must focus on the right projects and be implemented judiciously. At least one of the following four ways can help infrastructure providers make good choices, namely improving project selection, streamlining delivery, and making the most of existing investments and strengthening infrastructure maintenance. None of these actions requires radical change, and successful examples exist. First, there need to effective project selection. Africa countries must overcome the common problem of not considering the larger socioeconomic objectives of the country when undertaking infrastructure initiatives. White elephants emerge when officials look at projects in isolation rather than considering how each particular project fits into the entire portfolio and especially when no evaluation is made as to whether other projects might have better returns. Second, African countries must streamline project delivery—that is, ensure the job is done as per design. Project oversight must ensure that both the supplier and the client bear responsibility for this, and in Africa, there is a tendency for both to fall short of this requirement. Unfortunately, incentives are generally structured in ways that neither the public representatives nor the contractors are rewarded for innovating and taking risk for follow-throughs. Third, countries must avoid underutilization. In essence, the cheapest and least intrusive infrastructure is that which does not have to be built. For example, "intelligent" transportation systems, which use advanced signaling to squeeze more capacity out of existing roads and rail lines, can sometimes double asset utilization at a relatively low cost. This is evident by the traffic management system on the UK's M42 motorway, which directs and controls traffic. This "smart" system has reduced travel time by 25%, accidents by 50%, pollution by 10%, and fuel consumption by 4%, from only 20% of the cost of widening the road. Yet evidence from the infrastructure sector suggests such simple fixes are underused, or non-existent in Africa, and more often, are implemented for political rather than technical reasons.

This book covers a wide range of the key issues relating to infrastructure and development in Africa. For example, we are implored to distinguish between hard and soft infrastructure; ensure integrated infrastructure; focus on more inclusive infrastructure; invest in renewable energy; and get a better understanding of how infrastructure investment supports urbanization. All these issues and more are worthy of our reflection.

Finally, African countries need to pay attention to the issues of maintenance of built infrastructure. There is absolutely no use in building a state-of-the-art infrastructure platform if it cannot be adequately maintained. It would be a quick way of wasting limited resources that Africa could put elsewhere in its quest for transformation and development.

Paul Collier
Oxford, May 2016

Introduction: Infrastructure in African development

*Mthuli Ncube, Charles Leyeka Lufumpa
and George Kararach*

Background

This book is part of a series of studies commissioned by the African Development Bank (AfDB). Since 2010, a number of *Market Studies on the Status of Infrastructure Development in Africa* have been developed by staff of the Statistics Department of the Bank and other experts. Most of these papers have been prepared under the framework of the ongoing African Infrastructure Knowledge Program (AIKP), which is a successor program to the African Infrastructure Country Diagnostic (AICD) and is being led by the AfDB. The AIKP adopts a longer-term perspective than the AICD and provides a framework for generating knowledge about infrastructure on a more sustainable basis.

The AfDB will now take the leading role in the regular collection and assessment of infrastructure indicators, the production of knowledge products and timely policy analysis of emerging infrastructure trends in the continent to guide future policy and funding decisions, and to inform development policy and program management activities, as well as building infrastructure statistical capacity on the continent. This volume is intended to fulfill the analytic knowledge products component of the program.

Infrastructure not only enhances socioeconomic growth (Dalakoglou and Harvey, 2012; Easterly and Rebelo, 1993; Estache and Goicoechea, 2005), but it is also an important driver of sustainable development. Infrastructure is a key ingredient of Africa's post-Millennium Development Goals development agenda. For example, access to safe water supplies saves time and prevents the spread of waterborne diseases—including diarrhea and cholera, which are leading causes of infant mortality. Health and education services, as well as small businesses, can be established if there is a reliable energy supply. Good road networks provide links to markets, as well as enhancing access to producer and consumer services. Information and communications technology (ICT) democratizes access to information, thus strengthening governance and inclusion, as well as reducing transport costs.

Infrastructure comprises the stock of basic facilities and capital equipment required for society to function, including roads, bridges, rail lines, airports, schools, hospitals and other public works (Srinivasu and Rao, 2013). Because of the 'negotiations' over resources that precede the construction of any new infrastructure, power games often come into play. In this regard, a political economy— or anthropological—perspective, provides a stronger basis for understanding how infrastructure and related services come into being in a particular society.

What does the literature say about infrastructure and development?

In order to understand the role of infrastructure in Africa's development, it is necessary not only to follow the various broad theories of political economy, but also to take an anthropological approach, which provides a more 'human' perspective of the issues involved.

Modernization theory, infrastructure and the birth of 'white elephants'

This theory once dominated conversations about the nature of transformation in post-colonial African economies. Broadly, the theory describes a progressive, linear transition from a 'pre-modern' or 'traditional' to a 'modern' society characterized by industrialization and mass consumption. The theory focuses on deficiencies in the poorer countries and speculates about ways to overcome these. Traditional society was viewed by modernization theorists as stagnant and non-transformative, not innovative, not progressing, not growing—due to a wide range of 'drag' factors such as the nature of governance, institutions and infrastructure. Srinivasu and Rao (ibid) note that "Infrastructure is an umbrella term for many activities such as 'Social Overhead Capital', 'Economic Overheads', 'Overhead Capital', 'Basic Economic Facilities', and so on" (pp 82-3). They report that Ragnar Nurkse (1955) elaborated on the concept of overhead capita investment as "providing the services—transport, power, and water supply, which are basic for any productive activity, cannot be imported from abroad, require large and costly installations". These investments also tend to take time to mature and are lumpy. Other development economists like Rostow and Hirschman used the notion of 'social overhead capital' to describe infrastructure.

Rostow (1960), in *Stages of Economic Growth*, outlined five stages of development: old resistances fall away; political power accrues to a group interested in promoting economic growth; the country's savings rate grows; modern technology is applied; and there is a drive to maturity (economic growth spread, integration into international markets) and high mass consumption (fruits of growth finally transferred to the bulk of the people). Infrastructure, or social overhead capital, is critical for take-off into self-sustained growth. Infrastructure investment and associated services attract entrepreneurs to invest in risk-bearing ventures. Infrastructure provides the basis for expansion of economic activities by enhancing scale economies and, in turn, profitability growth. Good infrastructure supports the emergence of an educated labor force, superstructures of communication networks, and mechanisms for the provision of energy, basic civic amenities and law and order. A conducive environment for economic growth and industrial take-off is thus created through infrastructure investment.

Hirschman (1958) sets out a broad notion of social overhead capital/ infrastructure as basic services (including all public services like transportation, communication, power, health, water supply, irrigation and drainage system) without which the primary, secondary and tertiary economic activities will not take place. This notion includes both 'hard' (transportation, communications, power and water supply) and 'soft' (law and order, education and public health, regulatory frameworks) infrastructure. According to his theory of unbalanced growth, developing countries have an insufficient endowment of resources to enable them to invest simultaneously in all sectors of the economy to achieve balanced growth and take-off; thus the need to invest strategically in selected industries or sectors to drive new investment opportunities. Growth poles need to be developed, and here infrastructure is critical because of its ability to raise productivity by opening up markets through spatial integration and creation of derived demands. For example, availability of reliable power and transportation facilities is an essential precondition for economic development. It could be said that the notion of Economic Special Zones (ESZ) is based on Hirschman's theory of unbalanced growth. A typical ESZ is characterized by a 'hard' component of industrial estate with transport, communication and such utilities to facilitate efficient linkages to the world market, and a 'soft' aspect made up of policy and regulatory architecture (Kessides, 1993). It has long been believed that the multiplier effects generated by such 'strategic' investments would lead to the industrialization of developing regions (see Rosenstein-Rodan, 1943, for example).

Hansen (1965) characterizes infrastructure by economic overhead capital (EOC) and social overhead capital (SOC). While EOC directly supports productive activities and the movement of economic goods, SOC enhances the quality of human capital and provides social services such as education, public health facilities, security, and so on. Hansen argued that the dynamic nature of infrastructure platforms can account for regional growth differentials in terms of those that are congested, intermediate, and lagging. Congested regions suffer from diseconomies of scale due to the high costs of pollution and congestion. On the other hand, intermediate regions have economically conducive environments with well-trained labor, cheap power, and raw materials. Lagging regions have low living standards due to small-scale agriculture or stagnant or declining industries. Essentially, lagging regions lack dynamism, and public infrastructure investments have little impact (Kessides, 1993; Srinivasu and Rao, 2013).

Kindleberger and Herric (1973) sought to refine the notion of social overhead capital in terms of EOC and strictly social overhead capital (SSOC). EOC is public utilities like transport, communication, roads, railways, electricity and so on, while SSOC is the plants and equipment critical for providing 'social' services such as education, health and housing. Todaro (1981) argued that capital accumulation, including all new investments in land, physical equipment and human resources, results when savings are invested to augment future output and income. Increases in physical "capital stock" partly contribute to expansion in outputs. These investments in physical capital stock are also referred to as social and economic "infrastructure": roads, electricity, water, and sanitation, communications and so on. These investments facilitate and integrate economic activities, including industrialization and the emergence of a modern economy.

Modernization theory glorified large projects as the path to development, without due consideration for the political economy constraints of a modern global economy on less developed countries. There are at least three broad factors that led to the creation of 'white elephants': the leadership in newly independent countries in Africa had few of the 'soft' or human skills critical to ensuring that infrastructure moved from being a 'thing' to a 'service'; the strategic maneuvers employed by donors to win the 'hearts and minds' of African leaders through huge infrastructure projects did not pay attention to the service delivery content (indeed, some of these tendencies sowed the seeds for kleptocratic politics, whereby politicians used major 'public' works as a means to gain support); and economic policy changes in Africa were also driven by the structural adjustment programs of the

1980s and 1990s that swept across the continent giving new impetus for the participation of the private sector in the economy. The new focus on results-based management showed that Africa had not paid sufficient attention to issues of maintenance of its infrastructure stock.

Infrastructure and the perpetuation of dependency of poor countries

Dependency theorists critiqued the modernisation theorists on the basis of the 'lived' experience of developing countries. Dependency theorists argue that the origins of persistent global poverty cannot be understood without reference to the international political economy. Investment in infrastructure alone will not propel a country towards becoming a modern industrial economy unless it 'delinks' from the broader global dynamics (Amin, 1990). The development of modern infrastructure such as roads and railways played a part in the impoverishment of many countries in Asia, Africa and Latin America, through colonialism, imperialism and primitive accumulation and extractive terms of trade within enclave economies (Thomas, 1974; Kanyenze, 2011).

Dependency theorists note that, prior to the industrial revolution, the various continents and regions were not closely connected to each other (though extensive trade networks existed). With the emergence of capitalist development in Western Europe, the ceaseless search for profit began, and the associated extraction of agricultural goods and raw materials through colonial arrangements. The colonial relationship fundamentally changed the structure of the globe, resulting in the backwaters of capitalism labelled the 'Third World' by modernisation commentators. A negative relationship thus emerged that has defined political economy ever since. Poverty in the 'Third World' is not 'traditional' or accidental but is an inherent characteristic of modern capitalist economy. Economic historians Eric Williams and Walter Rodney, for example, argue that the slave trade between Africa and the Americas was responsible for the emergence of a commercial middle class in Britain and eventually for Britain's industrial revolution. Commodities such as sugar or cotton, made profitable through the slave trade, provided the conditions that propelled Britain's industrial revolution – romanticised by W.W. Rostow in *Stages of Economic Growth: A Non-communist Manifesto* as evidence for the virtues of the free market. Colonial trade was not *free* trade. Haiti's approximately 500,000 slaves, working on the colony's 8,000-odd plantations, generated two-fifths of France's overseas trade in the latter part of the 18th century. This was a grossly unequal exchange: the Third World gave much more than it received, because of unfavourable terms of trade, but also through brute force. The exchange may have created some limited new wealth in the Third World for a small comprador class, with some infrastructure, but it also created an international system that was inherently unequal. This inequality persists up to today—and is indeed growing (Piketty, 2013, 2014).

Not all of the dependency theorists' prescriptions are anti-capitalist, and some see some good in using capitalism and protectionism to enhance national economies through creative usages of global value chains (Kaplinsky and Farooki, 2010). For example, world-systems theory, an offshoot of dependency theory, shows that a capitalist world economy began to exist as far back as the beginning of the 16th century. World-systems theorists argue that the global economy is in a constant state of flux. There are no fixed rankings and locations but cyclical rhythms of expansion and stagnation. Countries are capable of upward and downward mobility over very long periods; there is no uni-directional, progressive, development and the (re)emergence of the BRICS (Brazil, Russia, India, China and South Africa) and MINT (Mexico, Indonesia, Nigeria and Turkey) are given as evidence of these realities. Indeed, modern infrastructure (such as fibre optics and high-speed rail) is credited with being a major driver of resurgence of countries such as China and India. On the other hand, the growth in ICT has revolutionized the flow of information, making contagion, especially in financial markets, much more realizable. The development of mobile telephony in particular has made a range of services in Africa readily accessible, including banking, agricultural extension, e-governance, and wider civic engagement.

Beyond infrastructure as a "thing" to a "service": issues in soft infrastructure

A number of factors will affect Africa in the next decade or so, including a delayed demographic transition, the burden of communicable diseases such as AIDS and TB, climate change, energy security, land access and tenure. These factors will define the opportunities and constraints faced by the continent, and the role played by infrastructure. On the one hand, infrastructure services are known to raise the productivity of land, labor and other capital. On the other hand, the consumption of services by households contributes to economic welfare and livelihood security because many of these services, notably clean water and sanitation, are essential for health and create environmental amenities, while others (such as recreational transport, residential telecommunications) are valued items of consumption in their own right, but also create derived demand for other goods and services (Kessides, 1993).

Beyond the economic analysis of infrastructure, there is a burgeoning literature in cultural anthropology (Dalakoglou and Harvey, 2012). Infrastructures as 'things' allow for the possibility of exchange over space as well as time. They are platforms through which goods, ideas, waste, power, people, and finance are 'trafficked'. Infrastructures facilitate the movement of goods, knowledge, meaning, people, and power (Larkin, 2013). Indeed, infrastructure goes a long way to define the environment in which people live and which socioeconomic activities take place (Dourish and Bell, 2007; Vannini and Taggart, 2013). Graham and Marvin (2001) assert that the role of public infrastructures and new technologies in facilitating the mobility of people, goods, and utilities is only noted when old forms decay. Equally, infrastructures and associated networks themselves create new social collectivities (Larkin, 2008). Infrastructures have more roles beyond the economic, and define prominently the interactions in cultural life.

An ethnography of infrastructure is beginning to emerge in the literature (Star and Ruhleder, 1996; Star, 1999; Dewsbury, 2003; Boeck, 2011; Koch and Latham, 2012). Dourish and Bell (2007) note that infrastructures partially define how people interact and experience spaces. In reality, evolution in infrastructure alters the boundaries between material and immaterial structures (such as balance of power and institutional re-engineering or evolution), and the relationships in society, including 'people' as sources of services (Simone, 2004). An examination of infrastructure can reveal power dynamics that transcend divides between public and private, state and non-governmental organization, bringing to the fore the importance of social inclusion and participatory governance. This gives rise to a different approach from either neoliberalism or modernization theory, which have been criticized as too broad, and which fail to consider everyday political economy and practices in local contexts (Larkin, 2013). Mains (2012) criticizes neoliberalism for failing to address complex interpersonal relationships. Simone (2004, 2010) and De Boeck and Plissart (2004) argue that when the state fails, people become the key forms of infrastructure in cities such as Johannesburg and Kinshasa.

Infrastructure and macroeconomic management

The debates on infrastructure and macroeconomic management go back to the days of Keynes, wherein spending on public works has been considered a vital tool for anti-cyclical interventions. But, since the 1980s and 1990s era of structural adjustment programs in Africa, public expenditure on infrastructure has been undertaken with extreme caution due to concerns over macroeconomic destabilization arising from deficits in public budgets. The core argument has been that when infrastructure is provided by public enterprises (PEs) with inadequate cost recovery, this results in unsustainable public deficits. The two transmission mechanisms are: fiscal processes and the financial/credit markets.

Kessides (1993) argued that net transfers from government to infrastructure entities signify inappropriate policies on internal cost recovery and expenditure, and poor management by these entities or the government in general. Reforms aimed at making the entities more commercial and financially autonomous, including privatization, would reduce or eliminate many of these transfers. Subsidies often reflect socio-political rather than commercial objectives. Although some subsidies can be justified for certain infrastructure services, they must be financed without causing fiscal imbalances or rising deficits, and such funding must be properly targeted. Equally, consumer subsidies to infrastructure divert public funds which could be used more effectively on other programs to alleviate poverty, and 'crowd out' other potentially more efficient suppliers of the same services. The potential for some of the infrastructure activities to provide fiscal revenues to government is often abused by bureaucrats and other rent-seekers.

On the credit market side, the major constraints to debt/bond financing of infrastructure in developing countries are the lack of creditworthiness of many public suppliers and the 'relatively' immature domestic financial markets for long-term capital. To resolve these problems, many African countries have set up specialized financial institutions ("municipal credit institutions" or "infrastructure development funds") to mobilize funds through bond issues, government transfers, and external donor support to municipalities for housing and infrastructure investment. However, many countries are reportedly yet to develop appropriate legal and regulatory frameworks and have poor cost recovery strategies (Davey, 1988).

Explaining growth differentials and the convergence hypothesis: a variant of modernization theory

As noted earlier, some studies assert that regional differences in productivity growth are related to regional differences in public infrastructure, where the latter creates externalities which lead to increasing returns to scale and endogenous regional growth (Romer, 1986; Lucas, 1988; Calderón and Servén, 2004). Earlier authors in this tradition include Hansen (1965). Others explain regional growth differentials in terms of industrial location or cluster formation, which follow shifts in the flow of capital and labor among regions (Krugman, 1991), and allow leaders to emerge (Kararach, 2014a). Empirical studies on regional differences in the growth of manufacturing output for the US find evidence of the effects of interregional flows of capital and labor (Hulten and Schwab, 1991). These findings suggest that public capital is not a key determinant of total factor productivity growth in manufacturing.

Some of these ideas have influenced economic geographers and regional planners. The earlier theories that infrastructure could induce growth to follow planned development was reflected in efforts to create "new towns" and "growth poles" (Evans, 1990). Such investments however proved to have low returns where the underlying conditions for potential economic growth were unfavorable (Kessides, 1993).

Empirical studies of the impact of infrastructure on growth

Aschauer (1989) launched the empirical debate on the macroeconomic impact of infrastructure on the economy when he found that the elasticity of national GDP to infrastructure is high in the United States, roughly 0.4 for total public capital and 0.24 for core infrastructure. A number of studies try to estimate long-run production functions and empirical growth regressions. Infrastructure is variously measured in terms of physical stocks, spending flows, or capital stocks. Estache (2006a, 2006b), Romp and de Haan (2007) and Straub (2008) offer comprehensive surveys of this literature. The studies of developing countries show mixed results. Some find that infrastructure investment has a negative effect on productivity or growth while others show that the impact of infrastructure is positive.

Estache et al (2006) highlighted that over a 30-year period, infrastructure investments accelerated the annual growth convergence rate by over 13% in Africa. Telecommunications, roads and electricity had the strongest impact. However, evidence for a link with access to water or sanitation was weak. This result could indicate that the water sector had the highest correlation with health or education in addition to the other subsectors (UN-HABITAT, 2011).

Most of the literature records a positive long-term macroeconomic effect of infrastructure on output, productivity, or growth rate, particularly in developing countries. A meta-analysis by Calderón and Servén (2004) reports that 16 out of 17 studies of developing countries find a positive impact, as do 21 of 29 studies of high-income countries. Most of the studies deal with the growth and productivity effects of infrastructure development. Calderón (2009) provides a comprehensive assessment of the impact of infrastructure development on economic growth in African countries. Based on econometric estimates for a sample of 136 countries over the period 1960–2005, it evaluates the impact of a faster accumulation of infrastructure stocks and an enhancement in the quality of infrastructure services on economic growth across African countries over this 15-year study period. The study findings indicate that growth is positively affected by the volume of infrastructure stocks and the quality of infrastructure services. Overall, the literature supports the view that infrastructure matters, but not whether a greater or a lesser investment in infrastructure is desirable (Ayogu, 2007).

The studies show the difficulty of estimating the impact of infrastructure on growth, including those issues related to network effects, endogeneity, heterogeneity and poor-quality data. For example, infrastructure capital stocks are unreliable proxies of the growing private nature of infrastructure services, while physical indicators are inadequate to really capture the flow of services to households and firms, and optimal stocks are unlikely to be ever identifiable at the aggregation level of regions or countries (Srinivasu and Rao, 2013). This difficulty is reflected in the diverse and sometimes conflicting findings of empirical literature on infrastructure and growth.

On the microeconomic side, there is a consensus that infrastructure has major implications for a variety of development outcomes, at the household (health, education and social mobility), firm (productivity, industrial development) and global level (climate change). However, the microeconomic literature is still evolving. Using Tanzanian household survey data, Fan et al (2005) studied the impact of public investment on household level income and poverty and found very positive effects, with a ratio of one to nine in the case of public capital investment. Going beyond mere access, Gachassin et al (2010) use the second Cameroonian national household survey (Enquête Camerounaise Auprès des Ménages II, 2001) to assess the impact of road access on poverty. They report that it is not road availability per se that helps to reduce poverty, but the opportunities in terms of 'employment' in spin-off economic activities. Reinikka and Svensson (1999) use unique microeconomic firm level evidence to show the effects of poor infrastructure services on private investment in Uganda. They surveyed Ugandan firms to analyze how entrepreneurs cope with deficient public capital. They conclude that infrastructure investments result in microeconomic adjustments, with consequent implications for socioeconomic development. The micro-literature suggests that specific cases and contexts may not always provide lessons that can be generalized.

The status of infrastructure in Africa and issues of transformation

Almost all the contributions in this volume make reference to access to and quality of infrastructure services, highlighting that Africa lags well behind other developing regions. There are also variations at local and regional levels as well as across the sub-sectors. The key lesson from these studies is that weak physical infrastructure is a key factor that has prevented African countries integrating into the global trading system. Poor infrastructure is linked to the higher trade cost that Africa, especially its landlocked countries, faces compared with other regions, resulting in competitive disadvantage (UN HABITAT, 2011). To address the estimated US$90 billion plus annual funding gap, African governments should take steps to identify innovative sources of finance, and take advantage of the renewed interest shown by donors and investors in the infrastructure sectors. Significant policy reforms that will foster socially inclusive development and project design as well as implementation (Ehlers, 2014) are also needed to improve and maintain the infrastructure network over the coming decades. For example, community-centered infrastructure management and maintenance would enhance access to services. Transboundary management frameworks in water, such as the Nile Basin Initiative, already exist to be replicated in the other sub-sectors. A regional approach may also be more helpful as the infrastructure challenge varies greatly from country to country: fragile states face an impossible burden, and even resource-rich countries lag behind. Pooling resources would enhance scope and scale economies, as evident in the power pools (Kararach, 2014b).

Map of the book

Chapters are clustered around five distinct themes: spatial and demographic contexts (One, Two, Three, Four); sector-specific issues (Five, Six, Seven, Eight); regional and integrated perspectives (Nine, Ten, Eleven); financing (Twelve, Thirteen, Fourteen, Fifteen); and the conclusion (Sixteen).

Part 1: Spatial and demographic contexts

Chapter One: Infrastructure Development Index, by Charles Leyeka Lufumpa, Nirina Letsara and Slaheddine Saidi

Despite economic growth rates of over 5% per annum over the past few years, the World Economic Forum's Global Competitiveness Index 2012–2013 confirms that Africa remains the least competitive global region. Inadequate infrastructure is cited as the third most serious constraint to doing business in the continent, after access to finance and corruption. This demonstrates the close linkage between infrastructure and the region's competitiveness. Moreover, the Africa Progress Panel has ranked infrastructure development as a key priority for the advancement of the continent, and has urged the G20 leadership to continue to give it their highest support. It is against this background that the African Development Bank developed the Africa Infrastructure Development Index (AIDI) to monitor the status and progress of infrastructure development across the continent. This is intended to enhance evidence-based policymaking in Africa, with specific reference to infrastructure. The authors document the methodology and theoretical underpinnings of the AIDI.

Chapter Two: Rapid urbanization and the growing demand for urban infrastructure in Africa, by Charles Leyeka Lufumpa and Tito Yepes

This chapter highlights key elements of those institutional reforms that affect urbanization in Africa. The authors emphasize those elements that most contribute to the goals of productivity and livability in cities.

Chapter Three: Infrastructure for the growing middle class in Africa, by Maurice Mubila and Tito Yepes

The emerging middle class in Africa demands an increasing number of modern services, including infrastructure. In the absence of modern infrastructure services, the next best option would be to reach households with lower-cost, second-best solutions, such as stand-posts, improved latrines, or street lighting. However, the prevalence of such second-best solutions is surprisingly low in Africa, and those that do exist tend to cater more to the higher-income groups. The majority of Africans therefore resort instead to traditional alternatives, such as wells, unimproved latrines, or kerosene lamps. The public good nature of second-best technologies makes them more difficult to supply on a commercial basis. This chapter argues that it is important to understand the factors that lie behind this "missing middle". On the demand side, the costs of second-best alternatives may still be relatively high. Water from stand-posts, though relatively cheap to provide, is often retailed by intermediaries charging substantial mark-ups that outweigh the underlying advantages in construction costs. Improved latrines, though cheaper than flush toilets, are nonetheless substantially more expensive than unimproved latrines, and uneducated households may not be aware of the health benefits. On the supply side, their public good nature of infrastructure greatly complicates their implementation. Utility companies are reluctant to provide services like street lighting and stand-posts because of their limited scope for revenue collection, as well as the greater potential for revenue loss from clandestine connections once networks are provided.

Chapter Four: Infrastructure and rural productivity in Africa, by Maurice Mubila and Tito Yepes

Rural infrastructure—notably feeder roads and transmission lines that connect rural communities to national grids—enable individuals, households, communities, and small businesses to embark on income-generating activities thanks to improved access to electricity and links to markets. The use of renewable energy or environmentally friendly sources of energy, including solar, wind, geothermal, and hydropower—all of which Africa has in abundance—would contribute to making growth sustainable.

Part 2: Sector-specific issues

Chapter Five: Water and sanitation in Africa: current status, trends, challenges and opportunities, by George Kararach and Tito Yepes

Africa is characterized by high hydrological variability and a multiplicity of transboundary river basins, alongside poor sanitation. Substantial investments in water resource and sanitation infrastructure and institutions are needed to increase productive uses of water, to mitigate the effect of recurrent floods and droughts, and to achieve basic water security. Priority should be given to investments that focus on growth, reduce rural poverty, build climate resilience and adaptation, and foster cooperation in international river basins. Institution building and reform, improvements in water/sanitation management and operations, and strengthening of water information systems must complement improvements in infrastructure. The development of institutions is a lengthy and costly process, and adequately sequenced and balanced, it should be advanced in parallel with infrastructure investment, for example by paying particular attention to the development of river basin organizations. This chapter highlights macroeconomic and other socioeconomic correlates, drawing implications for public–private partnerships in the water and sanitation sector. Some evidence on the continent's experience to date is presented.

Chapter Six: *Africa's prospects for infrastructure development and regional integration: energy sector, by Ethèl Teljeur, Mayuree Chetty and Morné Hendriksz*

The core argument of this chapter is that energy sector development is required to enable greater regional economic integration. Regional integration is also necessary to facilitate energy trade in Africa. Enhanced integration can address problems associated with energy infrastructure investment. Regional integration will allow African nations to develop more shared energy infrastructure. In addition, regional integration facilitates trade of energy resources and services via sub-regional power pools. It is noted that actual trade within these pools is low, and the opportunity to derive efficiencies from integrated regional resource planning is missed in favor of national plans. Among the challenges facing the regional power trade is the lack of harmonization of energy policies and regulatory frameworks between neighboring countries. Different stages and design of energy market liberalization or (re-)regulation and the desire for energy self-sufficiency ("security of supply") hinder the development of bilateral or multilateral projects. Investment in interconnection capacity is required to facilitate intra-power pool trade and achieve the efficiencies associated with the pooling of demand and integrated energy planning.

Chapter Seven: *Africa's prospects for infrastructure development and regional integration: transport sector, by Taz Chaponda and Duncan Lishman*

This chapter documents the status of transport infrastructure across all four sub-sectors—road, rail, ports, and airports. Transport services sustain economic activity and enable socioeconomic progress, and require fast-tracked project development. If this does not occur, and the necessary infrastructure is not in place, Africa's growth prospects will be hampered. The chapter outlines five broad policy reform themes common to the transport sub-sectors: enhancing the role of transport corridors and regional investment, adopting an integrated approach to transport standards and policies, developing financing strategies to leverage private sector participation, promoting regulatory and institutional reforms, and building institutional capacity to execute reforms. If these reforms are to be successful, it is important that policy reform is coordinated. However, in certain reform areas, 'quick wins' should be prioritized, building confidence for tackling further, more challenging reforms.

Chapter Eight: Africa's prospects for infrastructure development and regional integration: information and communications technology sector, by Lishan Adam and Maurice Mubila

Reforms, particularly in the mobile segment of the market, have transformed the availability, quality, and cost of connectivity across the continent. Over 91% of the urban population have mobile network coverage, and coverage in rural areas is growing. However, these high overall levels hide significant variations between countries, particularly in the proportion of the populations that have access to services. Although large parts of the information and communications technology (ICT) sector have been transformed, much remains to be done. A regional approach to ICT investments would garner huge benefits and speed up access.

Part 3: Regional issues

Chapter Nine: The state of infrastructure in East Africa, by Tito Yepes and Charles Leyeka Lufumpa

This chapter reviews infrastructure from a regional perspective with a focus on East Africa. The authors note that despite a program of regional integration, infrastructural development in East Africa lags behind that of other regions of the continent in many respects.

Chapter Ten: Integrated approaches for infrastructure, by Charles Leyeka Lufumpa, Maurice Mubila and Tito Yepes

This chapter makes the case for a strategic vision and a regionally integrated approach to confront key infrastructure challenges. The two main pillars of the infrastructure agenda are: to strengthen the foundations for higher productivity in the main cities; and to ensure a more even distribution of basic living standards. The first refers to securing an appropriate level of investment in *urban infrastructure*. Firms concentrate in cities in order to lower production costs by leveraging economies of scale and network efficiencies (World Bank, 2009). By clustering, firms increase the demand for infrastructure, thereby reaping cost savings from agglomeration. On the other hand, the second pillar refers to a more even distribution of basic living conditions *in both rural and urban areas*. This entails framing agendas for both areas, in order to counter the incentives for rural–urban migration. Cities that are experiencing a growing but unmet demand for basic services from unskilled immigrants also face a long-term trend of economic deterioration, given the relatively lower contribution from those immigrants' productivity. What is needed is a broader vision of the technologies that can be deployed for service provision; the bundling of services wherever possible to increase effectiveness in peri-urban and rural areas; making use of land-planning instruments and policies to align urban expansion with service provision; and a complementary rural development strategy. An infrastructure agenda for Africa has to fully address the challenges of the 21st century by: making cities more productive and better places to live ("more livable"); integrating rural areas through the spillovers of urban growth; and finally, linking major population centers across the region. The chapter argues for an integrated approach to infrastructure in African development.

Chapter Eleven: Regional integration and infrastructure connectivity in Africa, by Maurice Mubila and Tito Yepes

Regional infrastructure is only one aspect of broader regional integration. The chapter notes that cooperation in infrastructure is easier to achieve than broad economic or political integration, because benefits are more clearly defined, and countries need to cede less sovereignty. Regional infrastructure cooperation is therefore an effective initial step on the path to broader integration. Some countries have more to gain from regional integration than others. Landlocked countries depend particularly on effective road and rail corridors to the sea, as well as on intra-continental fiber-optic backbones that link them to submarine cables. Coastal countries depend particularly on sound management of water resources upstream. Small countries benefit especially from regional power trade that reduces the costs of energy supply. As long as regional integration provides a substantial economic dividend to some of the participating countries, designing compensation mechanisms that benefit all of them should be possible.

The concept of benefit sharing is explored against the reality that financing regional public goods tends to be problematic.

Part 4: Financing issues

Chapter Twelve: Infrastructure deficit and opportunities in Africa, by Albert Mafusire, Zuzana Brixiova, John Anyanwu and Qingwei Meng

There are huge opportunities for private sector investment in Africa's infrastructure, and work to identify projects is already underway. Regulatory reforms across African countries are critical for the realization of the expected investment flows into the infrastructure sector. However, planners and policymakers need to note that there are infrastructure deficiencies in all sub-sectors, with low-income countries (LICs) facing the greatest challenge. Inefficiencies in implementing infrastructure projects account for US$17 billion annually, and improving the capacity of African countries will help minimize these costs. The donor community must play a greater role in African LICs, while innovative financing mechanisms must be the focus in the relatively richer countries of the continent. Traditional sources of finance remain important, but private investment is critical for meeting future demand.

Chapter Thirteen: Comparative analysis of costs of some selected infrastructure components across Africa, by Oliver Chinganya, Abdoulaye Adam and Marc Kouakou

A solid infrastructure and robust systems together constitute a nation's "engine of growth", and include housing, water, electricity, transportation, communication, and construction. It is postulated that the cost of doing business in Africa is much higher than in other regions, largely because of the poor quality of its infrastructure. This chapter analyzes the distribution of price levels of these economic drivers, as part of the cost of doing business in Africa. Price level indices have been calculated to provide a comparison of the cost of selected infrastructure components across African countries. The data were collected from the 2005 round of the International Comparison Program in Africa, covering 48 out of a total of 52 countries and 22 major aggregates of the national accounts.

Chapter Fourteen: Infrastructure deficit and financing needs in Africa, by Mthuli Ncube

This chapter examines the access to sources of local market finance for infrastructure development in Africa. It brings to our attention the state of infrastructure access in the continent with a special focus on constraints to infrastructure development in Africa. The author then discusses innovative local sources of infrastructure finance in the continent alongside some of the constraints and solutions to a major source that the African Development Bank has emphasized lately—infrastructure bond. The question to be answered therefore is: given the constraints and opportunities, what is the role of the African Development Bank?

Chapter Fifteen: Innovative financing for infrastructure: Africa50 Fund issues, by George Kararach

The chapter notes that increasing the rate of infrastructure delivery in Africa implies a greater focus on project preparation and project development as well as specialized financial tools to address specific market challenges. It provides a specific case study of the Africa50 Fund as a financing vehicle. The Fund aims to mobilize private financing to accelerate the speed of infrastructure delivery in Africa. Africa50 focuses on high-impact projects in the energy, transport, ICT and water sectors. In order to deliver on Africa's current infrastructure pipeline, including Program for Infrastructure Development in Africa (PIDA), Africa50 will need an equity investment of US$10 billion, as well as attracting US$100 billion worth of local and global capital. Second, to function as a commercially oriented financial institution, Africa50 will need to preserve and grow its capital base, as well as provide a return to shareholders. Finally, ownership of the Fund's equity by African countries is central to the strategy of Africa50. Such ownership must send a strong signal to developers and financiers about the commitment of African countries to address the continent's infrastructure challenges.

Part 5: Concluding remarks

Chapter Sixteen: Infrastructure, political economy and Africa's transformational agenda, by Mthuli Ncube, Charles Leyeka Lufumpa and George Kararach

Connectivity and logistical problems are the result of socioeconomic conditions that are peculiar to Africa, such as geology, poor economic governance and conflict. This has direct implications for the implementation of infrastructure projects and the type of public policies needed to foster strategic connectivity. Moreover, the major constraints on infrastructure are not technical but managerial, political, and 'cultural', and include the lack of specialized resources. Africa needs to find its own solutions to local capacity and development problems, with a greater involvement of local private sector partners wherever feasible. A political economy perspective is critical for an understanding of the dynamics around infrastructure deficits.

References

Amin, S. (1990) *Delinking: Towards Polycentric World*. London: Zed Press.

Aschauer, D.A. (1989a) 'Is public expenditure productive?', *Journal of Monetary Economics*, vol 23, pp 177-200.

Ayogu, M. (2007) 'Infrastructure and economic development in Africa: a review', *Journal of African Economies*, Supplement 1, pp 75-126.

Boeck, F.D. (2011) 'Inhabiting ocular ground: Kinshasa's future in the light of Congo's spectral urban politics', *Cultural Anthropology*, vol 26, no 2, pp 263-86.

Calderón, C. (2009) *Infrastructure and Growth in Africa*, Policy Research Working Paper No. 4914. Washington, DC: World Bank.

Calderón, C. and Servén, L. (2004) *The Effects of Infrastructure Development on Growth and Income Distribution*, Policy Research Working Paper No. 3400. Washington, DC: World Bank.

Calderón, C. and Servén, L. (2008) *Infrastructure and Economic Development in Sub-Saharan Africa*, Policy Research Working Paper No. 4712. Washington, DC: World Bank.

Dalakoglou, D. and Harvey, P. (2012) 'Roads and anthropology: ethnographic perspectives on space, time and (im)mobility', *Mobilities*, vol 7, no 4, pp 459-65.

De Boeck, F. and Plissart, M.-F. (2004) *Kinshasa. Tales of the Invisible City*, Gent/Tervuren: Ludion/Royal Museum of Central Africa.

Dewsbury, J. (2003) 'Witnessing space: "knowledge without contemplation"', *Environment and Planning A*, 35, pp 1907-32.

Dourish, P. and Bell, G. (2007) 'The infrastructure of experience and the experience of infrastructure: meaning and structure in everyday encounters with space', *Environment and Planning B: Planning and Design*, 34, pp 414-30.

Easterly, W. and Rebelo, S. (1993) 'Fiscal policy and economic growth: an empirical investigation', *Journal of Monetary Economics*, vol 32, no 3, pp 417-58.

Ehlers, T. (2014) *Understanding the Challenges for Infrastructure Finance*, BIS Working Paper No 454. Basel, Switzerland: BIS.

Estache A. (2006a) 'Africa's infrastructure: challenges and opportunities', Paper presented at the high-level seminar Realizing the Potential for Profitable Investment in Africa, organized by the IMF Institute and the Joint Africa Institute, Tunis, Tunisia, 28 February to 1 March, www.imf.org/external/np/seminars/eng/2006/rppia/pdf/estach.pdf.

Estache, A. (2006b) *Infrastructure: A Survey of Recent and Upcoming Issues.* Washington DC: World Bank.

Estache, A. and Goicoechea, A. (2005) *A Research Database On Infrastructure Economic Performance*, Policy Research Working Paper No. 3642. Washington, DC: World Bank.

Estache, A., Speciale, B. and Veredas, D. (2006) *How Much Does Infrastructure Matter to Growth in Sub-Saharan Africa?*. Washington, DC: World Bank.

Fan, S., Nyange, D. and Rao, N. (2005) *Public Investment and Poverty Reduction in Tanzania: Evidence from Household Survey Data*, International Food Policy Research Institute, DSGD Discussion Paper No 18. Washington, DC: IFPRI.

Gachassin, M., Najman, B. and Raballand, G. (2010) *Roads Impact on Poverty Reduction a Cameroon Case Study*, Policy Research Working Paper No. 5209. Washington, DC: World Bank.

Graham, S. and Marvin, S. (2001) *Splintering urbanism: Networked infrastructures, technological mobilities and the urban condition*. London: Routledge.

Hansen, N.M. (1965) 'Unbalanced growth and regional development', *Western Economic Journal*, vol 4, pp 3-4

Hirschman, A.O. (1958) *The Strategy of Economic Development*. New Haven, CT: Yale University Press.

Hulten, C.R. and Schwab, R.M. (1991) *Is There Too Little Public Capital? Infrastructure and Economic Growth*. College Park, MD: University of Maryland.

Kanyenze, G. (ed) (2011) *Beyond the Enclave: Towards a Pro-Poor and Inclusive Development Strategy for Zimbabwe*. Harare: Weaver Press.

Kaplinsky, R. and Farooki, M. (2010) 'Global value chains, the crisis, and the shift of markets from North to South'. in O. Cattaneo, G. Gereffi and C. Staritz (eds) *Global Value Chains in a Postcrisis World: A Development Perspective.* Washington DC: World Bank.

Kararach, G. (2014a) 'Leadership, cluster formations and effects of space on economic development in Africa', PowerPoint presentation at Royal Geographical Society Conference 2014, London.

Kararach, G. (2014b) *Development Policy in Africa: Mastering the Future?* New York, NY: Palgrave Macmillan.

Kessides, C. (1993) *The Contribution of Infrastructure to Economic Development: A Review of Experience and Policy Implications*, World Bank Discussion Paper No. 213. Washington DC: World Bank.

Kindleberger, C.P. and Herric, B. (1973) *Economic Development.* New York: McGraw Hill.

Koch, R. and Latham, A. (2012) 'Rethinking urban public space: accounts from a junction in West London', *Transactions of the Institute of British Geographers*, vol 37, no 4, 515-29.

Krugman, P. (1991) 'Increasing returns and economic geography', *Journal of Political Economy*, vol 99, no 3, pp 483-99.

Larkin, B. (2013) 'The politics and poetics of infrastructure', *Annual Review of Anthropology*, vol 42, pp 327-43.

Lucas, R.E. Jr (1988) 'On the mechanics of economic development', *Journal of Monetary Economics*, vol 22, pp 3-42.

Mains, D. (2012) 'Blackouts and progress: privatization, infrastructure, and a developmentalist state in Jimma, Ethiopia', *Cultural Anthropology*, vol 27, no 1, pp 3-27.

Nurkse, R. (1955) *Problems of Capital Formation in Underdeveloped Countries.* Oxford: Basil Blackwell.

Piketty, T. (2013, 2014 English edition) *Capital in the Twenty-First Century.* Cambridge, MA: Belknap Press.

Reinikka, R. and Svensson, J. (1999) *How Inadequate Provision of Public Infrastructure and Services Affects Private Investment*, Policy Research Working Paper No. 2262. Washington, DC: World Bank.

Rosenstein-Rodan, P.N. (1943) 'Problems of industrialization of Eastern and South-Eastern Europe', *The Economic Journal*, vol 53, no 210/211, pp 202-11.

Romer, P.M. (1986) 'Increasing returns and long-run growth', *Journal of Political Economy*, vol 94, no 5, pp 1002-37

Romp, W. and De Haan, J. (2007) 'Public capital and economic growth: a critical survey', *Perspektiven der Wirtschaftspolitik*, vol 8, issue s1, pp 6-52.

Rostow, W.W. (1960) *Stages of Economic Growth: A Non-Communist Manifesto*. Cambridge: Cambridge University Press.

Simone, A. (2004) 'People as infrastructure: intersecting fragments in Johannesburg', *Public Culture*, vol 16, no 3, pp 407–29.

Simone, A. (2010) *City Life from Jakarta to Dakar: Movements at the Crossroads*. Oxford: Routledge.

Srinivasu, B and Rao, S. (2013) 'Infrastructure development and economic growth: prospects and perspective', *Journal of Business Management & Social Sciences Research*, vol 2, no 1, pp 81–91.

Star, S.L. (1999) 'The ethnography of infrastructure', *American Behavioral Scientist*, vol 43, no 3, pp 377–91.

Star, S.L. and Ruhleder, K. (1996) 'Steps toward an ecology of infrastructure: design and access for large information spaces', *Information Systems Research*, vol 7, no 1, pp 111–34.

Straub, S, (2008) *Infrastructure and Development: A Critical Appraisal of the Macro Level Literature*, Policy Research Working Paper No. 4590. Washington, DC: World Bank.

Thomas, C. (1974) *Dependence and Transformation: The Economics of the Transition to Socialism*. New York, NY: Monthly Review Press.

Todaro, M.P. (1981) *Economic Development in the Third World* (2nd edn). New York, NY and London: Longman.

UN-HABITAT (2011) *Infrastructure for Economic Development and Poverty Reduction in Africa*. Nairobi: UN-HABITAT.

Vannini, P. and Taggart, J. (2013) 'Voluntary simplicity, involuntary complexities, and the pull of remove: the radical ruralities of off-grid lifestyles', *Environment and Planning A*, 45, pp 295–311.

World Bank (2009). *Africa's Development in a Changing Climate*. Washington DC: International Bank for Reconstruction and Development/World Bank.

Part 1: Spatial and demographic contexts

.

ONE

Infrastructure Development Index

Charles Leyeka Lufumpa, Nirina Letsara and Slaheddine Saidi

Introduction

Infrastructure development is a key driver for progress across the African continent and a critical enabler for productivity and sustainable economic growth. It contributes significantly to human development, poverty reduction, and the achievement of the Millennium Development Goals (MDGs). The Africa Infrastructure Country Diagnostic (AICD) results show that investment in infrastructure accounts for more than 50% of the recent improvement in economic growth in Africa, and that it has the potential to achieve even more.

In spite of its enormous mineral and other natural resources, Africa has the lowest productivity of any other region around the world, and this is largely attributable to serious infrastructural shortcomings across all the sub-sectors: energy, water, sanitation, transportation, and information and communications technology (ICT). The international community meeting during the G8 Summit of 2005 pledged significant support for the infrastructure sector. This was in recognition of the fact that Africa's weak physical infrastructure base was impeding the region's progress toward improved living standards, poverty reduction, domestic and international trade and investment, and socially inclusive gross domestic product (GDP) growth.

Recent research has also emphasized the catalytic effects of infrastructure development. The Commission on Growth and Development's *Growth Report: Strategies for Sustained Growth and Inclusive Development* (2008) highlighted infrastructure investment as crucial to both structural transformation and export diversification. Stern (1991) showed how adequate infrastructure is essential for productivity and growth, indicating that transport in particular is a driver of development. In the same vein, the findings of Anyanwu and Erhijakpor (2009) indicate that road infrastructure significantly reduces poverty in Africa. Recent studies by Canning and Pedroni (2008) and Égert et al (2009) also confirm the positive correlation between improved infrastructure and economic growth.

Despite robust economic growth rates of over 5% per annum in recent years, the World Economic Forum's Global Competitiveness Index 2012–2013 confirms that Africa remains the least competitive global region. Inadequate infrastructure is cited as the third most serious constraint on doing business in the continent, following two other criteria, namely access to finance and corruption. This demonstrates the close linkage between infrastructure and the region's competitiveness. Moreover, the Africa Progress Panel, composed of such distinguished members as Kofi Annan, Michel Camdessus and Peter Eigen, has ranked infrastructure development as a key priority for the advancement of the continent, and has urged the G20 leadership to continue to give it their highest support.

By taking into consideration this background, the African Development Bank (AfDB) carried out afterthoughts in order to respond to these concerns and computed a statistical indicator described as the Africa Infrastructure Development Index (AIDI) to monitor the status and progress of infrastructure development across the continent. The first edition of this index was published in April 2011 and the present bulletin continues to extend its coverage. The Infrastructure Index has now been updated and expanded to cover the period 2011–2012. This series of observations was based on data collected through the Africa Infrastructure Knowledge Program (AIKP), which is hosted by the AfDB (see www.infrastructureafrica. org), as well as on other data sources.

The AIDI is based on four major components: transport; electricity, ICT, and water and sanitation. These components are disaggregated into nine indicators that have a direct or indirect impact on productivity and economic growth (see Table 1.1). Results for these indicators for 2011–2012 are provided in the Annex to this chapter.

In the next section we look at the main objectives of the AIDI in terms of informing policymaking in the monitoring process and evaluation of infrastructure development in African countries over time.

Why do we need an Infrastructure Development Index?

The AIDI provides consolidated and comparative information on the status and progress of infrastructure development in African countries. The index is designed to serve as a tool for analysts, policymakers, and investors alike. It provides an accurate and up-to-date picture of the current situation of African infrastructure development by comparing the scores and rankings for various indicators across countries. In so doing, it sheds light on which countries are performing more strongly

Table 1.1: AIDI components and indicators

Composite index / indicator for each component	Indicator(s)	Sub-indicators
I. Transport Composite Index	*I.a Total Paved Roads (km per 10,000 inhabitants)* The country's total surface with crushed stone (macadam) and hydrocarbon binder or bituminized agents, with concrete, or with cobblestones. The indicator is measured in kilometres per 10,000 inhabitants as a proxy of access to road paved network.	
	I.b Total Road Network (km per km² of exploitable land area) The total road surface (both paved and non-paved roads) of a given country. The indicator is measured in km (per km² of exploitable land area). Exploitable land area is the total surface area of a country minus the surface area of deserts, forest, mountains and other inaccessible areas.	
II. Electricity Index: Net Generation (kWh per inhabitant)	The total electricity production of a given country, including the energy imported from abroad. This includes both private and public energy generated. The indicator is measured in millions of kilowatt-hours produced per hour and per inhabitant.	
III. ICT Composite Index	*III.a Total Phone Subscriptions (fixed line and mobiles) per 100 inhabitants* The total number of phone subscriptions in a country, both fixed telephone lines and mobile–cellular telephone subscriptions, in a given year. For the purpose of the AIDI, the indicator is per 100 inhabitants.	*III.a.1 Fixed-line Phone Subscriptions (% of population)* Active line connecting the subscriber's terminal equipment to the Public Switched Telephone Network (PSTN) and which has a dedicated port in the telephone exchange equipment.

(continued)

Table 1.1: AIDI components and indicators (continued)

Composite index / indicator for each component	Indicator(s)	Sub-indicators
III. ICT Composite Index (ICT) (contd.)	*III.b Number of Internet Users (per 100 inhabitants)* The estimated number of internet users in the total population. This includes those using the internet from any device (including mobile phones) in the past 12 months. For the purpose of the AIDI, the indicator is per 100 inhabitants. *III.c Fixed (wired) Broadband Internet Subscribers (per 100 inhabitants)* Total internet subscriptions using fixed (wired) broadband technologies to access the internet. Subscriptions that have access to data communications (including the internet) via mobile-cellular networks are excluded. For the purpose of the AIDI, the indicator is reported per 100 inhabitants.	*III.a.2 Mobile-cellular Subscriptions (% of population)* : Refers to the subscriptions to a public mobile telephone service, which provide access to the Public Switched Telephone Network (PSTN) using cellular technology. This indicator includes the number of pre-paid SIM cards active during the past three months. This indicator includes both analogue and digital cellular systems IMT-2000 (third generation, 3G) and 4G subscriptions.

(continued)

28

Composite index/ indicator for each component	Indicator(s)	Sub-indicators
III. ICT Composite Index (ICT) (contd.)	*III.d International Internet Bandwidth (Mbps)* Total capacity of international Internet bandwidth in megabits per second (Mbps). If capacity is asymmetric (i.e. more incoming than outgoing), the incoming capacity should be provided. This is measured as the sum of capacity of all Internet exchanges offering international bandwidth.	
IV. Water & Sanitation Composite Index (WSS)	*IV.a Improved Water Source (% of population with access)*: Access to an improved water source refers to the percentage of the population with reasonable access to an adequate amount of water from an improved source, such as a household connection, public standpipe, borehole, protected well or spring, and rainwater collection. Unimproved sources include vendors, tanker trucks, and unprotected wells and springs. Reasonable access is defined as the availability of at least 20 litres a person per day from a source within 1 km of the dwelling	
	IV.b Improved sanitation facilities (% of population with access) Access to improved sanitation facilities refers to the percentage of the population with at least adequate access to excreta disposal facilities that can effectively prevent human, animal, and insect contact with excreta. Improved facilities range from simple but protected pit latrines to flush toilets with a sewerage connection. To be effective, facilities must be correctly constructed and properly maintained.	

across the five infrastructure indicators, which is a relevant indication of their future economic prospects.

The AIDI has another equally important feature. It helps to inform policy and investment decisions regarding the various infrastructure components in a country, by identifying those sub-sectors where funding needs are most acute. Africa currently spends about US$45 billion each year on infrastructure, two-thirds of which is domestically financed from taxes and user charges. Most financing for capital investment is obtained from external sources. It is therefore vital that governments and external investors alike have an assessment tool to ensure that their investments are yielding positive results on the ground and providing the best returns. In this way, the AIDI assists in evidence-based planning, to strengthen national budgetary decisions and allocations supported by governments. It is also a useful tool to identify investment opportunities (for example, clean energy solutions; communications networks) for foreign or private investors.

The AIDI also fulfills a critical need in terms of monitoring and evaluation for benchmarking purposes (including for the MDGs) and to gauge the impact of ongoing infrastructural investments and interventions. By focusing on real and measurable impacts on development, the AIDI aligns to the principles of the Results Agenda, as enshrined in the Paris Declaration on Aid Effectiveness (2005) and the Accra Agenda for Action (2008), to which the AfDB adhered.

Methodology

Data for the four components of the AIDI are collected from various sources. Each component represents a different facet of infrastructure development. The following four steps are used in calculating the index:

Step 1: Normalization procedure. Since the components of the AIDI are originally measured in different units, the observations are "standardized" or "normalized" to permit averaging, with the average regarded as a composite index. The normalization procedure used is the min–max formula applied to all observed values of each component during the period 2010–2012. This procedure adjusts the "normalized component" to take values between 0 and 100 over the indicated period.

Step 2: Calculate a composite index for each component. The composite index is calculated as a weighted average of indicators for each component that comprise more than one indicator. The weights are based on the inverse of the standard deviation of each normalized component: $y_t = (\sigma_{tot}/\sigma_x) \star x_t$; where σ_{tot} is given by $1/\sigma_{tot} = \Sigma_x (1/\sigma_x)$ and σ_x is the standard deviation of the normalized component x. The rationale for step 2 is to reduce the impact of the most volatile components on the composite index and consequently the volatility of the rankings.

Step 3: Generate the AIDI composite index. The AIDI composite index is computed using the sub-indexes of the four components and using the same method described in step 2.

Step 4: Generate the sub-regional AIDI. Indices by sub-region are calculated as a weighted average of the normalized components of the countries within the sub-region. The weighting variables selected are as follows: *population size* is used for electricity, water, sanitation and ICT subscriptions (phone and internet), while the *road network size* is used for paved roads.

Main results

Country-by-country analysis

The results (scores and ranks) of the Africa Infrastructure Development Index and its components are presented below in a number of figures or graphs, and also through a long series given in Table A1.4 (in the Annex to this chapter) covering the period 2000–2012. A first look at the depiction given by Figures 1.1 and 1.2 shows a high heterogeneity in countries' distribution of index values, illustrated by quartile statistics

Figure 1.1: Africa Infrastructure Development Index 2012 (selected statistics over time)

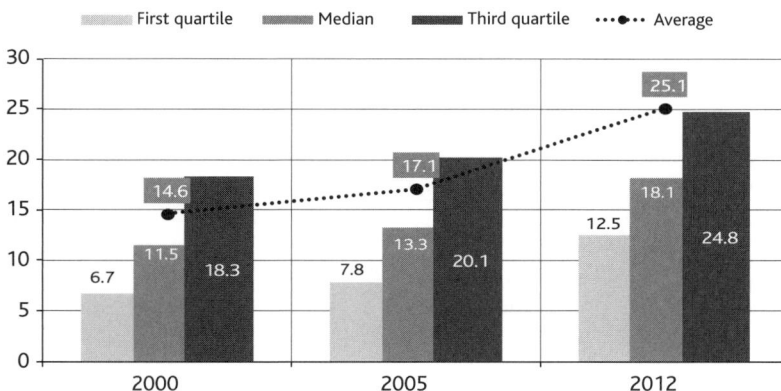

Figure 1.2: Africa Infrastructure Development Index/country scores for 2012

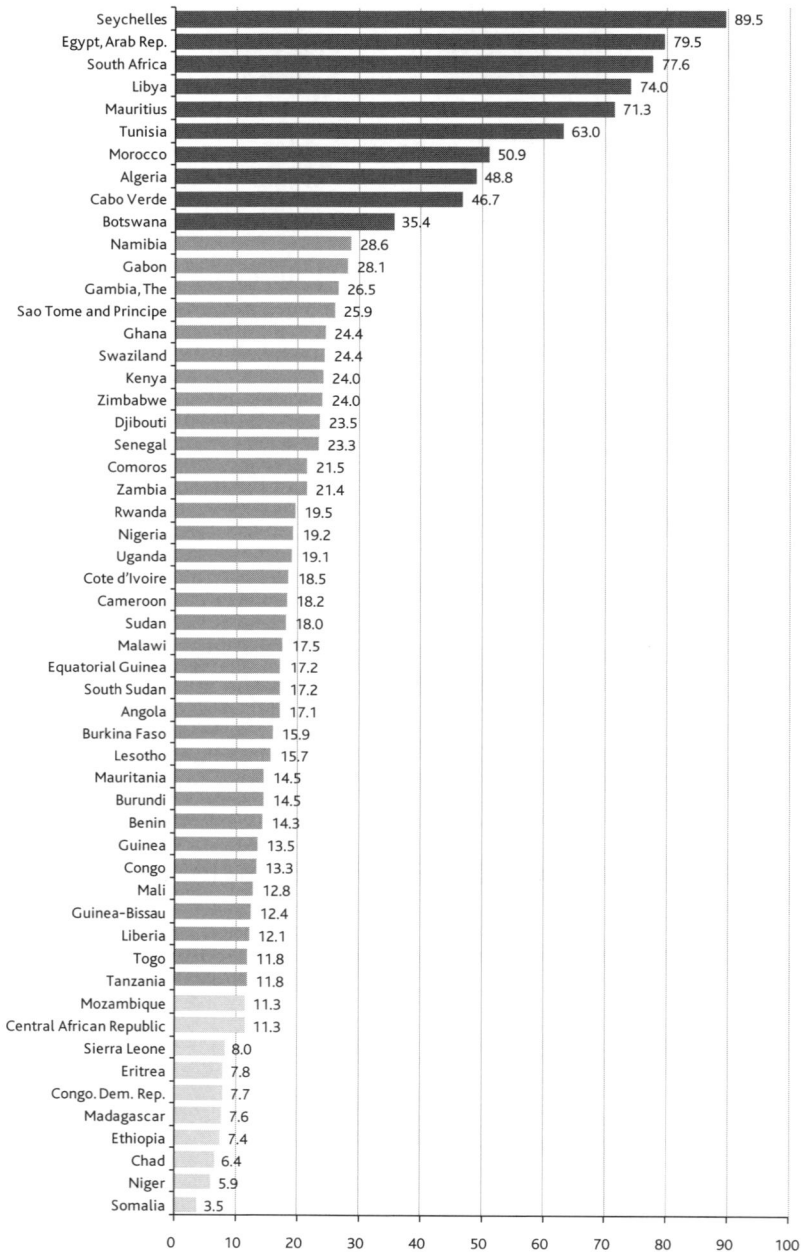

Seychelles	89.5
Egypt, Arab Rep.	79.5
South Africa	77.6
Libya	74.0
Mauritius	71.3
Tunisia	63.0
Morocco	50.9
Algeria	48.8
Cabo Verde	46.7
Botswana	35.4
Namibia	28.6
Gabon	28.1
Gambia, The	26.5
Sao Tome and Principe	25.9
Ghana	24.4
Swaziland	24.4
Kenya	24.0
Zimbabwe	24.0
Djibouti	23.5
Senegal	23.3
Comoros	21.5
Zambia	21.4
Rwanda	19.5
Nigeria	19.2
Uganda	19.1
Cote d'Ivoire	18.5
Cameroon	18.2
Sudan	18.0
Malawi	17.5
Equatorial Guinea	17.2
South Sudan	17.2
Angola	17.1
Burkina Faso	15.9
Lesotho	15.7
Mauritania	14.5
Burundi	14.5
Benin	14.3
Guinea	13.5
Congo	13.3
Mali	12.8
Guinea-Bissau	12.4
Liberia	12.1
Togo	11.8
Tanzania	11.8
Mozambique	11.3
Central African Republic	11.3
Sierra Leone	8.0
Eritrea	7.8
Congo. Dem. Rep.	7.7
Madagascar	7.6
Ethiopia	7.4
Chad	6.4
Niger	5.9
Somalia	3.5

(median, first and third quartile), reflecting typical skewness of scores' statistical distributions since one fourth of the countries still display in 2012 scores below 12.5 and one half score below 18.1 in the index value scale. Furthermore, only seven countries posted scores above 50 in the index scale for 2012 and 40 countries among 54 have a score below the average, while the exploration of annual data by country during the last decade highlights the accentuated dispersion over time in the AIDI scores between the African countries.

The top 10 ranked countries according to their scores on the AIDI in 2012 were respectively Seychelles, Egypt, South Africa, Libya, Mauritius, Tunisia, Morocco, Algeria, Cabo Verde and Botswana. Among this list, five countries are in *North Africa* and three countries in *Southern Africa*. At the same time, the top ranking also includes small island countries (Seychelles, Mauritius and Cabo Verde) where tourism constitutes particularly an important contributing sector in economic growth. These countries have therefore traditionally focused on improving infrastructure to partly attract visitors. The bottom 10 countries of AIDI in 2010 were Somalia, Niger, Chad, Ethiopia, Madagascar, Democratic Republic of Congo (DRC), Eritrea, Sierra Leone, Central African Republic and Mozambique. One shared characteristic of the bottom 10 countries is that they are mostly fragile states, involved during the past decade in some form of conflict.

Ranking and score changes over the period 2000–2012

Among the bottom 10 countries ranked in 2000, Mali and Tanzania are the only countries that moved up from this bottom rating in 2012 and significantly improved their scores and rankings over this period, as a result of enhancements in ICT (mainly increased telephone subscription coverage and improved international internet bandwidth), better access to water and sanitation, and increased construction of paved roads in the case of Mali. In general, all countries have improved their scores over time but at different rates. Countries that continue to lag behind, such as Somalia, Niger, Ethiopia, Chad and Madagascar, have registered slower improvement in comparison with the other countries and still at the bottom of ranking since 2000.

The middle 33 countries showed wide variation in their rankings over the period 2000–2012. It is important to note that although some countries moved downward in the rankings, almost all improved their scores compared with previous years. Thus, the ranking is only an indication that some countries improved their scores at a faster rate than others. Two notable high performers are:

Figure 1.3: AIDI – improving scores over 2000-2012, for the five lowest ranked countries in 2012

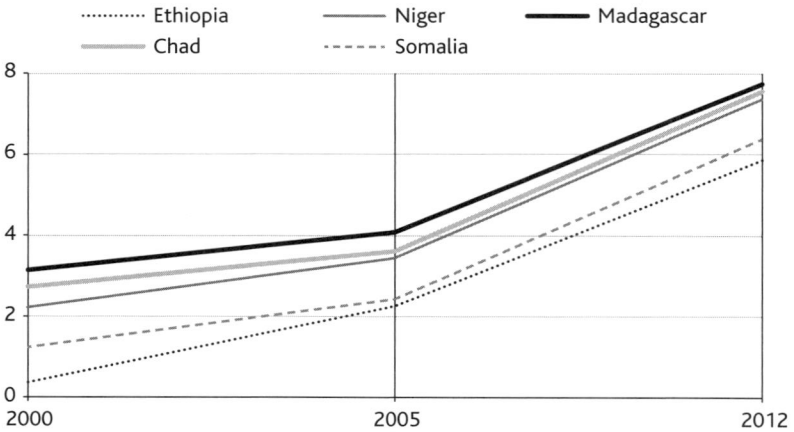

- *Kenya*, which moved from 35th to 17th position and improved its score from 7.89 in 2000 to 24.00 in 2012; and
- *Ghana*, which improved its score from 10.71 in 2000 to 24.44 in 2012 and moved up eight ranks from 29th to 15th.

At the same time, Senegal, which improved its score between 2000 and 2010, has moved down slightly since then to 20th position from the 18th rank in 2010.

Meanwhile, improvements in ranking are due generally and mainly to major progress in the ICT sector, in particular expansions in telephone subscription coverage and increased internet users from 2000 to 2010. In parallel, Ghana improved also significantly its score and its ranking for the transport indicators.

By contrast, Burundi and Lesotho dropped by 14 and nine positions respectively. In Lesotho, apart from the ICT sector, which recorded a slight improvement in the score, all the other sectors showed a decline both in scores and rankings. For Burundi, the decline is due to the slow growth in the ICT sector accompanied by a lack of progress in access to improved water and sanitation, as well as a slight decline in transport indicator performance. Also, power generation remains unchanged for Burundi.

For the top 10 countries, the rankings have changed little over time. There are two exceptions: Morocco moved up from 13th place in 2000 to seventh in 2012, while Libya dropped from the first place in 2000 to fourth in 2012. Morocco's progress is mostly attributable to greater access to improved water and sanitation and better ICT indicators. Libya's decline comes mainly from deterioration in its transport sector and, to a lesser extent, from poor progress in access to improved water and sanitation.

Sub-regional analysis

According to the AfDB's terminology, the continent comprises five geographical sub-regions: Central Africa with seven countries and a total population of over 107 million people; East Africa with 12 countries and more than 280 million population; North Africa with six countries and a total population of 170 million; Southern Africa with 12 countries and 165 million inhabitants; and West Africa with 16 countries and more than 300 million inhabitants.

The AIDI gives a fairly stable ranking for the sub-regions throughout the period of analysis, with North Africa occupying the top position, followed by Southern Africa ranked second. Central Africa held the third position from 2000 through to 2009 but then lost one place to the benefit of West Africa in 2010 (see Table 1.2 overleaf). However, East Africa has maintained its bottom position over the whole period. It should be noted that West and East Africa include a high number of low-income countries and fragile states.

Figure 1.4: AIDI sub-regional scores, 2000–2012

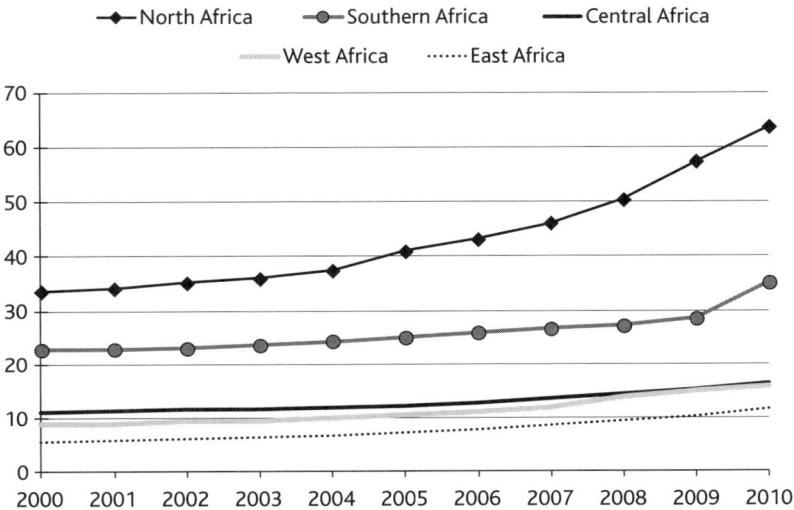

Table 1.2: Africa infrastructure development index, region scores and rankings, 2000–2010

2000		2001		2002		2003	
1 North Africa	33.6	1 North Africa	34.2	1 North Africa	35.2	1 North Africa	36.0
2 Southern Africa	22.8	2 Southern Africa	22.9	2 Southern Africa	23.0	2 Southern Africa	23.6
3 Central Africa	11.1	3 Central Africa	11.4	3 Central Africa	11.6	3 Central Africa	11.7
4 West Africa	8.7	4 West Africa	8.9	4 West Africa	9.3	4 West Africa	9.4
5 East Africa	5.6	5 East Africa	5.7	5 East Africa	6.0	5 East Africa	6.3
2004		2005		2006		2007	
1 North Africa	37.5	1 North Africa	40.99	1 North Africa	43.18	1 North Africa	46.2
2 Southern Africa	24.3	2 Southern Africa	24.99	2 Southern Africa	25.89	2 Southern Africa	26.6
3 Central Africa	12.0	3 Central Africa	12.27	3 Central Africa	12.83	3 Central Africa	13.6
4 West Africa	9.8	4 West Africa	10.42	4 West Africa	11.08	4 West Africa	11.8
5 East Africa	6.56	5 East Africa	7.04	5 East Africa	7.87	5 East Africa	8.5
2008		2009		2010			
1 North Africa	50.5	1 North Africa	57.5	1 North Africa	63.8		
2 Southern Africa	27.1	2 Southern Africa	28.5	2 Southern Africa	35.1		
3 Central Africa	14.3	3 Central Africa	15.1	3 West Africa	16.3		
4 West Africa	13.9	4 West Africa	14.9	4 Central Africa	15.7		
5 East Africa	9.3	5 East Africa	10.3	5 East Africa	11.6		

Conclusion

The AIDI is measured across four components that have an established linkage with infrastructure development. The AIDI findings indicate that the rankings for the top 10 countries have not changed significantly over 2000–2012. The AIDI results can be interpreted to identify areas of relative strength and weakness, and to assess which infrastructure components in a country need improvement in order to step up overall infrastructure development in the future.

The index computation is updated regularly on an annual basis to incorporate new data, including those generated through the AfDB's Africa Infrastructure Knowledge Program. Furthermore, it is envisioned that other indicators of infrastructure development, to cover areas such as seaports and airports (for the transport component), will be incorporated into the index as relevant data become available. This will improve both the robustness and scope of the index.

References

Anyanwu, J.C. and Erhijakpor, A.E.O. (2009) 'The impact of road infrastructure on poverty reduction in Africa', in T.W. Beasley (ed) *Poverty in Africa*. New York, NY: Nova Science Publishers.

Canning, D. and Pedroni, P. (2008) 'Infrastructure, long-run economic growth and causality tests for cointegrated panels', *Manchester School*, vol 76, no 5, pp 504-27.

Commission on Growth and Development (2008) *The Growth Report: Strategies for Sustained Growth and Inclusive Development*. Washington, DC: International Bank for Reconstruction and Development, World Bank.

Égert, B., Kozluk, T. and Sutherland, D. (2009) *Infrastructure and Growth: Empirical Evidence*, Working Paper 685. Paris: Organisation for Economic Co-operation and Development.

Stern, N. (1991) 'The determinants of growth', *Economic Journal*, vol 101, no 404, pp 122-33.

Annex: Overviews of the African International Development Index

See tables on following pages.

Table A1.1: Africa Infrastructure Development Index, country scores and rankings, 2009–2012

2009		2010		2011		2012	
Rank	Country	AIDI value	Rank	Country	AIDI value	Rank	Country	AIDI value	Rank	Country	AIDI value

2009 Rank	2009 Country	2009 AIDI value	2010 Rank	2010 Country	2010 AIDI value	2011 Rank	2011 Country	2011 AIDI value	2012 Rank	2012 Country	2012 AIDI value
1	Seychelles	77.99	1	Seychelles	84.41	1	Seychelles	85.54	1	Seychelles	89.47
2	Egypt, Arab Rep.	70.18	2	South Africa	78.97	2	Egypt, Arab Rep.	76.40	2	Egypt, Arab Rep.	79.50
3	Libya	68.96	3	Egypt, Arab Rep.	77.67	3	South Africa	73.53	3	South Africa	77.57
4	Mauritius	63.17	4	Libya	71.37	4	Libya	71.68	4	Libya	74.01
5	South Africa	59.02	5	Mauritius	67.01	5	Mauritius	68.19	5	Mauritius	71.26
6	Tunisia	52.35	6	Tunisia	59.51	6	Tunisia	60.47	6	Tunisia	62.99
7	Morocco	45.06	7	Morocco	51.81	7	Morocco	48.32	7	Morocco	50.90
8	Algeria	43.69	8	Algeria	47.78	8	Algeria	46.41	8	Algeria	48.76
9	Cabo Verde	40.45	9	Cabo Verde	44.11	9	Cabo Verde	44.59	9	Cabo Verde	46.66
10	Botswana	32.59	10	Botswana	33.50	10	Botswana	34.41	10	Botswana	35.37
11	Namibia	26.05	11	Namibia	27.83	11	Namibia	28.22	11	Namibia	28.58
12	Gabon	25.27	12	Gabon	25.90	12	Gabon	26.93	12	Gabon	28.12
13	Gambia, The	24.06	13	Sao Tome and Principe	24.75	13	Gambia, The	25.56	13	Gambia, The	26.51
14	Sao Tome and Principe	23.23	14	Zimbabwe	24.72	14	Sao Tome and Principe	25.11	14	Sao Tome and Principe	25.92
15	Zimbabwe	22.94	15	Gambia, The	24.71	15	Zimbabwe	23.63	15	Ghana	24.40
16	Djibouti	22.15	16	Djibouti	23.45	16	Swaziland	23.11	16	Swaziland	24.36
17	Swaziland	20.96	17	Swaziland	22.30	17	Djibouti	23.05	17	Kenya	24.03

(continued)

2009			2010			2011			2012		
Rank	Country	AIDI value	Rank	Country	AIDI value	Rank	Country	AIDI value	Rank	Country	AIDI value
18	Comoros	20.47	18	Senegal	21.66	18	Ghana	22.81	18	Zimbabwe	24.00
19	Senegal	20.30	19	Ghana	21.11	19	Senegal	21.92	19	Djibouti	23.54
20	Ghana	19.58	20	Comoros	20.95	20	Comoros	21.14	20	Senegal	23.30
21	Zambia	18.86	21	Zambia	20.13	21	Kenya	21.05	21	Comoros	21.47
22	Rwanda	18.07	22	Rwanda	18.65	22	Zambia	20.57	22	Zambia	21.40
23	Cote d'Ivoire	17.00	23	Kenya	18.43	23	Rwanda	18.84	23	Rwanda	19.52
24	Cameroon	16.58	24	Uganda	17.88	24	Uganda	18.13	24	Nigeria	19.25
25	Kenya	16.23	25	Cote d'Ivoire	17.75	25	Nigeria	17.94	25	Uganda	19.06
26	Uganda	16.04	26	Nigeria	17.58	26	Cote d'Ivoire	17.89	26	Cote d'Ivoire	18.51
27	Nigeria	15.94	27	Equatorial Guinea	17.30	27	Cameroon	17.50	27	Cameroon	18.25
28	Malawi	15.42	28	Cameroon	16.79	28	Equatorial Guinea	16.78	28	Sudan	18.03
29	Equatorial Guinea	14.90	29	Malawi	16.45	29	Malawi	16.73	29	Malawi	17.53
30	Lesotho	14.42	30	South Sudan	15.45	30	South Sudan	16.35	30	Equatorial Guinea	17.22
31	Burundi	14.38	31	Burkina Faso	15.33	31	Angola	15.81	31	South Sudan	17.19
32	Burkina Faso	14.25	32	Lesotho	15.11	32	Lesotho	15.36	32	Angola	17.10
33	Angola	13.75	33	Angola	14.99	33	Burkina Faso	15.31	33	Burkina Faso	15.93
34	Benin	12.29	34	Burundi	14.57	34	Sudan	15.20	34	Lesotho	15.68
35	Guinea	12.23	35	Benin	13.72	35	Burundi	14.45	35	Mauritania	14.52
36	Mauritania	11.61	36	Sudan	13.21	36	Benin	13.67	36	Burundi	14.50
37	Congo	11.29	37	Congo	13.12	37	Mauritania	13.35	37	Benin	14.32

(continued)

39

2009			2010			2011			2012		
Rank	Country	AIDI value	Rank	Country	AIDI value	Rank	Country	AIDI value	Rank	Country	AIDI value
38	Sudan	11.20	38	Mauritania	12.53	38	Guinea	12.93	38	Guinea	13.52
39	Togo	10.50	39	Guinea	12.43	39	Congo	12.73	39	Congo	13.28
40	Guinea-Bissau	10.30	40	Liberia	11.18	40	Guinea-Bissau	11.47	40	Mali	12.83
41	Central African Republic	10.19	41	Togo	10.80	41	Liberia	11.44	41	Guinea-Bissau	12.45
42	Liberia	10.07	42	Guinea-Bissau	10.61	42	Mali	11.40	42	Liberia	12.13
43	Mozambique	9.86	43	Central African Republic	10.52	43	Togo	11.12	43	Togo	11.83
44	Tanzania	9.37	44	Mozambique	10.45	44	Tanzania	10.97	44	Tanzania	11.79
45	Mali	9.17	45	Mali	10.29	45	Central African Republic	10.89	45	Mozambique	11.34
46	Eritrea	7.11	46	Tanzania	10.21	46	Mozambique	10.73	46	Central African Republic	11.31
47	Sierra Leone	6.61	47	Sierra Leone	7.55	47	Eritrea	7.52	47	Sierra Leone	8.00
48	Congo, Dem. Rep.	6.56	48	Eritrea	7.25	48	Sierra Leone	7.52	48	Eritrea	7.77
49	Madagascar	6.34	49	Congo, Dem. Rep.	6.81	49	Congo, Dem. Rep.	7.26	49	Congo, Dem. Rep.	7.73
50	Chad	5.28	50	Madagascar	6.60	50	Madagascar	7.09	50	Madagascar	7.57
51	Niger	4.69	51	Chad	5.46	51	Ethiopia	6.30	51	Ethiopia	7.37
52	Ethiopia	4.62	52	Ethiopia	5.37	52	Chad	5.90	52	Chad	6.37
53	Somalia	2.81	53	Niger	5.04	53	Niger	5.44	53	Niger	5.85
54	South Sudan	n.a	54	Somalia	2.79	54	Somalia	3.18	54	Somalia	3.53

Table A1.2: Africa Infrastructure Development Index, country scores and rankings, 2005–2008

2005			2006			2007			2008		
Rank	Country	AIDI value	Rank	Country	AIDI value	Rank	Country	AIDI value	Rank	Country	AIDI value
1	Seychelles	63.54	1	Seychelles	70.52	1	Seychelles	56.29	1	Seychelles	73.82
2	Libya	54.95	2	Libya	57.51	2	Libya	51.64	2	Libya	64.40
3	South Africa	51.70	3	South Africa	53.84	3	South Africa	48.58	3	Egypt, Arab Rep.	61.78
4	Egypt, Arab Rep.	51.19	4	Mauritius	53.25	4	Mauritius	46.19	4	Mauritius	58.92
5	Mauritius	48.75	5	Egypt, Arab Rep.	53.14	5	Egypt, Arab Rep.	45.90	5	South Africa	55.96
6	Tunisia	33.52	6	Tunisia	35.61	6	Tunisia	29.68	6	Tunisia	44.68
7	Algeria	32.73	7	Algeria	34.31	7	Algeria	28.96	7	Algeria	38.57
8	Botswana	28.98	8	Cabo Verde	32.24	8	Botswana	28.58	8	Morocco	38.47
9	Cabo Verde	28.59	9	Morocco	31.54	9	Cabo Verde	26.81	9	Cabo Verde	37.45
10	Morocco	28.15	10	Botswana	29.75	10	Namibia	25.11	10	Botswana	31.89
11	Namibia	26.29	11	Namibia	26.76	11	Morocco	21.64	11	Namibia	28.88
12	Gabon	21.91	12	Gabon	22.92	12	Zimbabwe	20.73	12	Gabon	24.85
13	Zimbabwe	21.85	13	Zimbabwe	21.45	13	Gabon	19.97	13	Gambia, The	23.64
14	Sao Tome and Principe	20.32	14	Gambia, The	20.95	14	Djibouti	19.28	14	Sao Tome and Principe	22.65
15	Gambia, The	19.95	15	Sao Tome and Principe	20.89	15	Gambia, The	19.11	15	Zimbabwe	21.81
16	Djibouti	19.74	16	Djibouti	19.84	16	Sao Tome and Principe	18.67	16	Djibouti	21.10

(continued)

2005			2006			2007			2008		
Rank	Country	AIDI value	Rank	Country	AIDI value	Rank	Country	AIDI value	Rank	Country	AIDI value
17	Comoros	19.57	17	Comoros	19.82	17	Comoros	18.64	17	Comoros	20.26
18	Swaziland	16.32	18	Zambia	17.04	18	Zambia	15.25	18	Ghana	19.37
19	Zambia	16.31	19	Swaziland	16.94	19	Swaziland	14.90	19	Swaziland	19.34
20	Rwanda	15.15	20	Senegal	15.47	20	Burundi	14.35	20	Zambia	18.07
21	Senegal	14.31	21	Rwanda	15.42	21	Rwanda	13.95	21	Senegal	18.04
22	Equatorial Guinea	14.10	22	Cote d'Ivoire	14.36	22	Equatorial Guinea	13.48	22	Rwanda	16.78
23	Burundi	13.94	23	Cameroon	14.35	23	Lesotho	13.35	23	Cote d'Ivoire	16.09
24	Cameroon	13.77	24	Equatorial Guinea	14.29	24	Cote d'Ivoire	13.22	24	Cameroon	15.74
25	Cote d'Ivoire	13.75	25	Ghana	14.20	25	Cameroon	12.86	25	Uganda	15.19
26	Lesotho	13.75	26	Burundi	13.97	26	Senegal	12.55	26	Malawi	14.81
27	Malawi	13.32	27	Malawi	13.78	27	Malawi	12.50	27	Equatorial Guinea	14.75
28	Ghana	12.96	28	Lesotho	13.68	28	Burkina Faso	12.44	28	Nigeria	14.69
29	Uganda	12.07	29	Uganda	12.50	29	Uganda	11.33	29	Lesotho	14.40
30	Burkina Faso	11.64	30	Burkina Faso	12.07	30	Ghana	11.29	30	Burundi	14.15
31	Nigeria	10.55	31	Kenya	11.49	31	Guinea	9.38	31	Burkina Faso	13.56
32	Kenya	9.91	32	Nigeria	11.25	32	Nigeria	9.17	32	Kenya	12.98
33	Guinea	9.70	33	Angola	10.41	33	Congo	9.15	33	Angola	12.58
34	Angola	9.41	34	Congo	9.85	34	Kenya	8.96	34	Guinea	11.64
35	Congo	9.32	35	Guinea	9.85	35	Benin	8.82	35	Mauritania	11.35
36	Benin	8.92	36	Benin	9.53	36	Angola	8.17	36	Benin	11.31

(continued)

2005			2006			2007			2008		
Rank	Country	AIDI value	Rank	Country	AIDI value	Rank	Country	AIDI value	Rank	Country	AIDI value
37	Central African Republic	8.49	37	Sudan	9.16	37	Central African Republic	8.00	37	Sudan	10.90
38	Liberia	8.08	38	Central African Republic	8.87	38	Sudan	7.36	38	Congo	10.82
39	Mauritania	7.83	39	Mauritania	8.76	39	Liberia	7.29	39	Guinea-Bissau	10.03
40	Guinea-Bissau	7.83	40	Guinea-Bissau	8.41	40	Togo	7.20	40	Liberia	9.63
41	Togo	7.58	41	Liberia	8.37	41	Guinea-Bissau	7.04	41	Togo	9.62
42	Sudan	7.52	42	Mozambique	8.01	42	Mauritania	6.69	42	Central African Republic	9.59
43	Mozambique	7.48	43	Togo	7.86	43	Mozambique	6.49	43	Mozambique	8.95
44	Tanzania	6.40	44	Tanzania	6.97	44	Eritrea	5.58	44	Tanzania	8.42
45	Eritrea	6.19	45	Mali	6.77	45	Tanzania	5.27	45	Mali	8.39
46	Mali	6.12	46	Eritrea	6.35	46	Sierra Leone	5.16	46	Eritrea	6.91
47	Sierra Leone	5.34	47	Congo, Dem. Rep.	5.44	47	Mali	4.89	47	Congo, Dem. Rep.	6.46
48	Congo, Dem. Rep.	5.06	48	Sierra Leone	5.22	48	Congo, Dem. Rep.	4.48	48	Sierra Leone	6.33
49	Madagascar	4.09	49	Madagascar	4.39	49	Madagascar	3.62	49	Madagascar	5.79
50	Chad	3.63	50	Chad	3.93	50	Chad	3.21	50	Chad	4.78
51	Niger	3.45	51	Niger	3.65	51	Niger	2.92	51	Niger	4.48
52	Ethiopia	2.43	52	Ethiopia	2.99	52	Somalia	1.69	52	Ethiopia	3.91
53	Somalia	2.25	53	Somalia	2.51	53	Ethiopia	1.56	53	Somalia	2.68
54	South Sudan	n.a	54	South Sudan	n.a	54	South Sudan	n.a	54	South Sudan	n.a

Table A1.3: Africa Infrastructure Development Index, country scores and rankings, 2000–2004

2000			2001			2002			2003			2004		
Rank	Country	AIDI value	Rank	Country	AIDI value	Rank	Country	AIDI value	Rank	Country	AIDI value	Rank	Country	AIDI value
1	Libya	49.73	1	Libya	49.76	1	Seychelles	50.86	1	Seychelles	56.29	1	Seychelles	59.78
2	Seychelles	47.43	2	Seychelles	48.93	2	Libya	50.86	2	Libya	51.64	2	Libya	52.54
3	South Africa	46.07	3	South Africa	45.88	3	South Africa	46.78	3	South Africa	48.58	3	South Africa	50.51
4	Egypt, Arab Rep.	43.13	4	Egypt, Arab Rep.	43.72	4	Egypt, Arab Rep.	45.08	4	Mauritius	46.19	4	Mauritius	47.26
5	Mauritius	42.10	5	Mauritius	43.29	5	Mauritius	44.51	5	Egypt, Arab Rep.	45.90	5	Egypt, Arab Rep.	46.82
6	Algeria	28.18	6	Algeria	28.15	6	Algeria	28.55	6	Tunisia	29.68	6	Tunisia	31.50
7	Tunisia	26.78	7	Tunisia	27.73	7	Botswana	28.45	7	Algeria	28.96	7	Algeria	30.43
8	Cabo Verde	24.90	8	Cabo Verde	25.58	8	Tunisia	28.37	8	Botswana	28.58	8	Botswana	28.21
9	Botswana	24.73	9	Botswana	25.18	9	Cabo Verde	26.35	9	Cabo Verde	26.81	9	Cabo Verde	27.82
10	Namibia	24.71	10	Namibia	24.81	10	Namibia	24.70	10	Namibia	25.11	10	Namibia	25.72
11	Zimbabwe	22.48	11	Zimbabwe	22.99	11	Morocco	20.80	11	Morocco	21.64	11	Morocco	24.44
12	Djibouti	19.42	12	Morocco	19.88	12	Zimbabwe	20.15	12	Zimbabwe	20.73	12	Zimbabwe	21.21
13	Morocco	19.08	13	Djibouti	19.39	13	Gabon	19.71	13	Gabon	19.97	13	Gabon	20.75
14	Gabon	18.67	14	Gabon	19.07	14	Djibouti	19.40	14	Djibouti	19.28	14	Sao Tome and Principe	19.89
15	Comoros	17.98	15	Comoros	18.15	15	Comoros	18.49	15	Gambia, The	19.11	15	Djibouti	19.45
16	Sao Tome and Principe	16.75	16	Sao Tome and Principe	17.16	16	Sao Tome and Principe	17.91	16	Sao Tome and Principe	18.67	16	Gambia, The	19.38

(continued)

	2000			2001			2002			2003			2004	
Rank	Country	AIDI value	Rank	Country	AIDI value	Rank	Country	AIDI value	Rank	Country	AIDI value	Rank	Country	AIDI value
17	Gambia, The	16.64	17	Gambia, The	17.07	17	Gambia, The	17.59	17	Comoros	18.64	17	Comoros	19.05
18	Zambia	14.42	18	Zambia	15.03	18	Zambia	15.03	18	Zambia	15.25	18	Zambia	15.65
19	Burundi	14.21	19	Burundi	14.24	19	Swaziland	14.78	19	Swaziland	14.90	19	Swaziland	15.41
20	Rwanda	13.56	20	Rwanda	13.69	20	Burundi	14.21	20	Burundi	14.35	20	Rwanda	14.98
21	Swaziland	13.22	21	Swaziland	13.63	21	Rwanda	13.96	21	Rwanda	13.95	21	Burundi	13.87
22	Lesotho	12.83	22	Cote d'Ivoire	13.03	22	Equatorial Guinea	13.25	22	Equatorial Guinea	13.48	22	Equatorial Guinea	13.71
23	Equatorial Guinea	12.82	23	Equatorial Guinea	13.02	23	Cote d'Ivoire	13.21	23	Lesotho	13.35	23	Lesotho	13.56
24	Cote d'Ivoire	12.79	24	Lesotho	12.89	24	Lesotho	13.16	24	Cote d'Ivoire	13.22	24	Senegal	13.55
25	Cameroon	11.97	25	Cameroon	12.20	25	Cameroon	12.48	25	Cameroon	12.86	25	Cameroon	13.51
26	Senegal	11.52	26	Senegal	12.02	26	Malawi	12.24	26	Senegal	12.55	26	Cote d'Ivoire	13.43
27	Malawi	11.51	27	Malawi	11.78	27	Senegal	12.16	27	Malawi	12.50	27	Malawi	12.86
28	Burkina Faso	11.36	28	Burkina Faso	11.73	28	Burkina Faso	12.00	28	Burkina Faso	12.44	28	Ghana	12.22
29	Ghana	10.71	29	Uganda	10.71	29	Uganda	11.03	29	Uganda	11.33	29	Uganda	11.58
30	Uganda	10.47	30	Ghana	10.68	30	Ghana	10.87	30	Ghana	11.29	30	Burkina Faso	11.26
31	Congo	8.68	31	Congo	8.97	31	Nigeria	9.24	31	Guinea	9.38	31	Nigeria	9.78
32	Nigeria	8.61	32	Nigeria	8.78	32	Congo	9.15	32	Nigeria	9.17	32	Guinea	9.59
33	Benin	8.25	33	Benin	8.53	33	Guinea	8.87	33	Congo	9.15	33	Kenya	9.42
34	Guinea	8.14	34	Guinea	8.51	34	Benin	8.77	34	Kenya	8.96	34	Congo	9.07
35	Kenya	7.89	35	Kenya	8.18	35	Kenya	8.53	35	Benin	8.82	35	Benin	8.68

(continued)

45

| 2000 | | | 2001 | | | 2002 | | | 2003 | | | 2004 | | |
Rank	Country	AIDI value	Rank	Country	AIDI value	Rank	Country	AIDI value	Rank	Country	AIDI value	Rank	Country	AIDI value
36	Sudan	7.30	36	Angola	7.55	36	Angola	7.96	36	Angola	8.17	36	Angola	8.54
37	Angola	7.30	37	Central African Republic	7.51	37	Central African Republic	7.76	37	Central African Republic	8.00	37	Central African Republic	8.33
38	Central African Republic	7.30	38	Sudan	7.12	38	Sudan	7.24	38	Sudan	7.36	38	Liberia	7.60
39	Liberia	6.74	39	Liberia	6.88	39	Liberia	7.02	39	Liberia	7.29	39	Guinea-Bissau	7.39
40	Togo	6.71	40	Togo	6.84	40	Togo	6.93	40	Togo	7.20	40	Sudan	7.35
41	Mozambique	5.88	41	Mozambique	6.43	41	Mozambique	6.84	41	Guinea-Bissau	7.04	41	Mauritania	7.34
42	Guinea-Bissau	5.31	42	Mauritania	5.69	42	Guinea-Bissau	6.60	42	Mauritania	6.69	42	Togo	7.32
43	Mauritania	5.18	43	Guinea-Bissau	5.61	43	Mauritania	6.39	43	Mozambique	6.49	43	Mozambique	6.82
44	Tanzania	5.17	44	Tanzania	5.23	44	Eritrea	5.33	44	Eritrea	5.58	44	Eritrea	6.07
45	Eritrea	4.76	45	Eritrea	5.02	45	Tanzania	5.27	45	Tanzania	5.27	45	Mali	5.66
46	Sierra Leone	4.51	46	Sierra Leone	4.72	46	Sierra Leone	4.90	46	Sierra Leone	5.16	46	Tanzania	5.39
47	Congo, Dem. Rep.	4.02	47	Congo, Dem. Rep.	4.12	47	Mali	4.50	47	Mali	4.89	47	Sierra Leone	5.27
48	Mali	3.94	48	Mali	4.10	48	Congo, Dem. Rep.	4.27	48	Congo, Dem. Rep.	4.48	48	Congo, Dem. Rep.	4.81
49	Madagascar	3.14	49	Madagascar	3.32	49	Madagascar	3.46	49	Madagascar	3.62	49	Madagascar	3.81
50	Chad	2.73	50	Chad	2.89	50	Chad	3.02	50	Chad	3.21	50	Chad	3.25
51	Niger	2.23	51	Niger	2.36	51	Niger	2.82	51	Niger	2.92	51	Niger	3.15
52	Somalia	1.24	52	Somalia	1.25	52	Somalia	1.55	52	Somalia	1.69	52	Somalia	2.11
53	Ethiopia	0.37	53	Ethiopia	0.65	53	Ethiopia	1.12	53	Ethiopia	1.56	53	Ethiopia	1.96
54	South Sudan	n.a	54	South Sudan	n.a	54	South Sudan	n.a	54	South Sudan	n.a	54	South Sudan	n.a

Table A1.4: Composite index for each component

I. Transport composite index (2000–2012)

	2000	2001	2002	2003	2004	2005	2006	2007	2008	2009	2010	2011	2012
Algeria	17.16	16.98	16.80	16.62	17.36	17.17	16.98	16.80	17.64	17.67	17.49	17.72	17.84
Angola	2.65	2.58	2.52	2.45	2.39	2.33	2.28	2.23	2.18	2.14	2.10	1.98	1.93
Benin	7.22	7.13	7.03	6.94	5.41	5.37	5.33	5.29	5.26	5.23	5.19	5.03	5.00
Botswana	17.21	16.97	26.10	26.91	24.40	25.00	24.68	24.35	24.03	23.72	23.43	24.51	24.40
Burkina Faso	17.36	17.18	17.00	16.83	12.41	12.37	12.32	12.28	12.24	12.20	12.17	10.99	10.95
Burundi	11.08	11.06	11.04	11.02	9.63	9.60	9.58	9.55	9.52	9.50	9.48	9.30	9.26
Cabo Verde	28.27	28.07	27.88	27.70	27.55	27.41	27.29	27.19	27.09	27.01	26.92	26.99	26.92
Cameroon	4.20	4.17	4.14	4.11	4.24	4.21	2.99	2.96	2.92	2.89	2.86	3.65	3.60
Central African Republic	2.37	2.36	2.34	2.33	2.31	2.30	2.28	2.27	2.25	2.24	2.22	2.81	2.72
Chad	0.94	0.93	0.93	0.92	0.91	1.14	1.14	1.13	1.13	1.12	1.12	1.07	1.06
Comoros	17.31	17.14	16.98	16.82	16.66	16.51	16.36	16.22	16.08	15.94	15.81	16.01	15.90
Congo	2.61	2.56	2.51	2.47	2.10	2.06	2.53	2.48	2.43	2.38	2.34	2.29	2.25
Congo, Dem. Rep.	1.65	1.64	1.63	1.62	1.57	1.56	1.56	1.55	1.54	1.54	1.53	1.53	1.53
Cote d'Ivoire	7.36	7.31	7.27	7.23	6.81	6.78	6.75	6.85	6.81	6.78	6.74	6.73	6.69
Djibouti	13.53	13.29	13.09	12.91	12.74	12.57	12.40	12.24	12.07	11.91	11.75	12.33	12.15
Egypt, Arab Rep.	50.84	50.73	50.63	50.53	50.63	54.10	54.43	54.33	57.52	55.14	55.03	57.92	57.43
Equatorial Guinea	2.67	2.66	2.66	2.65	2.64	2.64	2.63	2.62	2.62	2.61	2.61	2.61	2.61
Eritrea	1.74	1.69	1.64	1.59	1.55	1.51	1.47	1.44	1.41	1.38	1.36	1.23	1.20
Ethiopia	1.08	1.07	1.23	1.27	1.55	1.58	1.50	1.73	1.72	1.71	1.70	1.65	1.63

(continued)

	2000	2001	2002	2003	2004	2005	2006	2007	2008	2009	2010	2011	2012
Gabon	3.99	3.91	3.83	3.76	4.14	4.06	3.99	4.54	4.46	4.39	4.31	4.20	4.15
Gambia, The	6.53	6.47	6.41	8.90	8.82	8.74	8.67	8.60	8.53	8.47	8.41	8.25	8.15
Ghana	6.54	5.26	5.21	6.26	7.08	7.04	6.99	6.94	15.08	12.67	12.60	12.50	12.41
Guinea	5.87	5.82	5.77	6.62	6.57	6.53	6.49	6.44	6.39	6.34	6.29	5.94	5.88
Guinea-Bissau	4.06	4.02	5.61	5.53	5.45	5.38	5.30	5.23	5.15	5.08	5.01	4.83	4.75
Kenya	5.02	4.99	4.95	4.92	5.03	5.00	4.96	4.93	4.97	4.78	4.75	8.67	8.62
Lesotho	7.56	7.52	7.49	7.46	7.44	7.41	7.38	7.36	7.33	7.30	7.27	10.68	10.63
Liberia	3.34	3.30	3.27	3.26	3.24	3.21	3.16	3.11	3.06	3.02	2.98	2.98	2.96
Libya	58.76	57.84	56.94	56.03	55.12	54.21	53.28	52.35	51.48	50.73	50.14	52.75	52.34
Madagascar	3.54	3.48	3.42	3.36	3.31	3.26	3.21	3.16	3.11	3.06	3.02	3.03	2.99
Malawi	6.25	6.16	6.07	5.61	5.53	5.45	5.36	5.28	5.20	5.12	5.04	4.94	4.86
Mali	1.15	1.13	1.10	1.07	1.83	1.88	1.84	1.80	2.52	2.53	2.47	2.61	2.55
Mauritania	5.17	5.03	4.89	4.75	5.24	5.05	5.36	5.23	5.10	4.99	4.88	5.26	5.20
Mauritius	34.67	34.67	35.92	36.28	36.20	36.21	35.99	36.06	36.00	36.63	36.58	36.10	36.05
Morocco	8.92	8.85	8.80	8.79	8.69	9.16	9.09	9.06	9.02	9.84	9.77	9.78	9.71
Mozambique	2.15	2.11	2.06	2.02	1.98	1.95	1.91	1.88	1.99	1.95	1.92	1.86	1.82
Namibia	28.02	27.48	25.57	25.17	24.78	24.39	23.99	23.59	23.19	16.28	16.01	17.52	17.23
Niger	1.52	1.48	2.20	2.17	2.28	2.24	2.19	2.20	2.15	2.10	2.05	2.01	1.96
Nigeria	5.38	5.35	5.32	5.29	5.22	5.20	5.17	5.14	5.12	5.09	5.07	5.06	5.04
Rwanda	11.21	11.17	11.15	11.14	13.79	13.76	13.72	13.67	13.63	13.59	13.55	13.07	12.98
Sao Tome and Principe	16.19	16.05	15.92	15.79	15.68	15.56	15.44	15.33	15.21	15.09	14.97	14.25	14.07

(continued)

48

	2000	2001	2002	2003	2004	2005	2006	2007	2008	2009	2010	2011	2012
Senegal	3.71	3.65	3.59	3.26	3.21	3.16	3.41	3.35	3.30	3.43	3.38	3.52	3.46
Seychelles	36.74	36.72	36.09	48.06	48.17	52.25	52.04	52.65	51.97	51.85	51.02	50.62	50.47
Sierra Leone	4.73	4.68	4.63	4.58	4.54	4.50	4.47	4.44	4.42	4.40	4.38	4.38	4.37
Somalia	2.44	2.39	2.35	2.31	2.27	2.23	2.19	2.16	2.12	2.09	2.05	1.92	1.87
South Africa	15.04	13.64	13.54	13.44	13.35	13.27	13.19	13.12	13.05	12.99	12.94	12.72	12.66
South Sudan	n,a	n,a	n,a	n,a	n,a	n,a	n,a	n,a	n,a	n,a	0.42	0.42	0.42
Sudan	0.53	0.51	0.49	0.48	0.47	0.45	0.44	0.42	0.41	0.39	0.38	0.54	0.52
Swaziland	7.62	7.58	9.09	9.06	9.03	8.98	8.92	8.85	8.78	8.70	8.63	8.57	8.50
Tanzania	3.14	3.11	3.08	2.71	2.68	2.65	2.63	2.60	2.75	3.19	3.16	3.87	3.82
Togo	5.75	5.67	5.61	5.55	5.50	5.44	5.39	7.25	7.20	7.15	7.11	6.91	6.84
Tunisia	10.39	10.00	9.93	9.87	9.97	9.91	9.83	9.76	10.70	10.62	10.53	10.50	10.44
Uganda	10.02	9.91	9.80	9.69	9.59	9.49	9.39	9.29	9.20	9.11	9.03	8.94	8.87
Zambia	7.79	9.01	8.84	8.67	8.51	8.34	8.17	8.00	7.83	7.66	7.49	10.07	9.77
Zimbabwe	23.37	23.27	13.09	13.08	13.09	13.11	13.14	13.17	13.18	13.17	13.11	12.70	12.49

I.a *Transport*: total paved roads (km per 10,000 inhabitants)

	2000	2001	2002	2003	2004	2005	2006	2007	2008	2009	2010	2011	2012
Algeria	23.47	23.13	22.79	22.45	23.47	23.12	22.77	22.42	23.74	23.73	23.38	23.74	23.85
Angola	3.84	3.72	3.59	3.47	3.35	3.24	3.14	3.05	2.97	2.88	2.80	2.65	2.57
Benin	5.83	5.65	5.48	5.30	2.44	2.36	2.29	2.22	2.16	2.10	2.04	1.85	1.80
Botswana	30.44	29.98	47.05	48.45	43.83	44.84	44.24	43.63	43.02	42.44	41.91	42.33	41.97
Burkina Faso	12.04	11.70	11.37	11.05	2.80	2.72	2.64	2.56	2.49	2.41	2.34	0.40	0.39
Burundi	1.61	1.58	1.54	1.50	1.83	1.77	1.72	1.67	1.62	1.57	1.53	1.35	1.31
Cabo Verde	21.32	20.94	20.59	20.26	19.97	19.71	19.49	19.30	19.12	18.96	18.79	19.00	18.85
Cameroon	2.58	2.52	2.47	2.41	2.50	2.45	2.78	2.72	2.62	2.56	2.51	4.00	3.90
Central African Republic	1.77	1.74	1.71	1.69	1.66	1.63	1.61	1.58	1.55	1.52	1.49	3.12	2.95
Chad	0.32	0.31	0.30	0.29	0.28	0.33	0.32	0.31	0.30	0.29	0.29	0.26	0.26
Comoros	11.97	11.66	11.35	11.05	10.76	10.47	10.19	9.92	9.66	9.41	9.16	9.61	9.38
Congo	3.96	3.86	3.78	3.69	2.51	2.45	3.34	3.25	3.16	3.08	3.00	2.86	2.78
Congo, Dem. Rep.	0.58	0.56	0.54	0.53	0.50	0.49	0.47	0.46	0.45	0.44	0.42	0.44	0.43
Cote d'Ivoire	4.68	4.59	4.52	4.45	3.66	3.60	3.54	3.49	3.42	3.36	3.29	3.34	3.27
Djibouti	18.84	18.40	18.02	17.69	17.38	17.06	16.74	16.43	16.12	15.82	15.52	16.29	16.04
Egypt, Arab Rep.	10.66	10.47	10.28	10.09	10.27	10.79	10.68	10.49	11.64	11.26	11.07	15.96	15.70
Equatorial Guinea	0.44	0.43	0.42	0.40	0.39	0.38	0.37	0.36	0.35	0.34	0.33	0.32	0.31
Eritrea	2.38	2.29	2.20	2.11	2.02	1.95	1.88	1.82	1.77	1.71	1.66	1.47	1.43
Ethiopia	0.54	0.53	0.58	0.62	0.96	0.63	0.62	0.78	0.76	0.75	0.73	0.68	0.66
Gabon	6.78	6.63	6.49	6.36	6.97	6.83	6.70	7.71	7.57	7.43	7.29	6.90	6.74

(continued)

	2000	2001	2002	2003	2004	2005	2006	2007	2008	2009	2010	2011	2012
Gambia, The	4.02	3.91	3.79	5.10	4.95	4.81	4.67	4.54	4.42	4.30	4.18	4.17	4.04
Ghana	6.09	3.69	3.61	4.15	4.61	3.98	3.88	3.79	8.39	5.79	5.65	5.56	5.44
Guinea	6.03	5.94	5.85	4.97	4.88	4.80	4.72	4.63	4.54	4.45	4.35	3.80	3.71
Guinea-Bissau	3.65	3.58	7.49	7.34	7.20	7.06	6.92	6.78	6.64	6.50	6.37	5.94	5.80
Kenya	2.48	2.41	2.35	2.29	2.57	2.51	2.44	2.38	2.41	2.25	2.19	5.47	5.33
Lesotho	5.54	5.47	5.41	5.36	5.31	5.26	5.21	5.16	5.11	5.06	5.01	15.51	15.35
Liberia	2.31	2.24	2.19	2.16	2.12	2.07	1.98	1.89	1.80	1.71	1.65	1.61	1.57
Libya	90.97	89.27	87.57	85.89	84.19	82.48	80.75	79.01	77.39	75.99	74.89	77.98	77.32
Madagascar	3.76	3.65	3.54	3.43	3.33	3.23	3.14	3.05	2.96	2.87	2.79	2.82	2.74
Malawi	6.60	6.42	6.26	5.73	5.58	5.42	5.27	5.12	4.97	4.82	4.67	4.50	4.37
Mali	1.62	1.57	1.52	1.48	2.64	2.73	2.65	2.57	3.74	3.70	3.59	3.83	3.72
Mauritania	9.45	9.18	8.92	8.67	9.49	9.09	9.49	9.25	9.02	8.80	8.59	9.16	8.93
Mauritius	15.62	15.62	16.05	16.33	16.18	16.07	15.64	15.58	15.48	15.68	15.58	16.51	16.44
Morocco	11.29	11.16	11.05	11.03	10.87	11.73	11.62	11.54	11.46	12.94	12.81	12.89	12.71
Mozambique	3.12	3.04	2.96	2.88	2.81	2.74	2.67	2.61	2.82	2.76	2.69	2.57	2.50
Namibia	47.68	46.68	43.11	42.36	41.64	40.90	40.16	39.41	38.66	27.64	27.14	29.85	29.29
Niger	2.37	2.29	3.21	3.10	3.00	2.92	2.83	2.81	2.71	2.61	2.52	2.40	2.31
Nigeria	2.36	2.30	2.25	2.19	2.12	2.07	2.02	1.97	1.92	1.88	1.83	1.76	1.72
Rwanda	1.47	1.40	1.37	1.34	2.95	2.89	2.82	2.74	2.66	2.58	2.51	2.39	2.32
Sao Tome and Principe	15.45	15.19	14.95	14.72	14.50	14.28	14.06	13.85	13.63	13.41	13.18	11.90	11.59
Senegal	4.49	4.38	4.26	3.86	3.75	3.65	3.88	3.78	3.68	3.92	3.82	3.98	3.87

(continued)

	2000	2001	2002	2003	2004	2005	2006	2007	2008	2009	2010	2011	2012
Seychelles	38.85	38.81	37.65	53.11	53.31	57.69	56.97	57.62	56.35	56.13	54.59	53.40	53.09
Sierra Leone	2.16	2.08	2.01	1.91	1.83	1.75	1.70	1.65	1.61	1.58	1.54	1.54	1.51
Somalia	3.52	3.43	3.35	3.27	3.19	3.12	3.05	2.99	2.92	2.86	2.79	2.63	2.56
South Africa	16.42	13.80	13.61	13.43	13.26	13.11	12.96	12.83	12.70	12.59	12.50	12.13	12.03
South Sudan	n.a	n.a	n.a	n.a	n.a	n.a	n.a	n.a	n.a	n.a	0.99	0.99	0.99
Sudan	1.26	1.23	1.21	1.18	1.15	1.12	1.10	1.07	1.04	1.02	0.99	1.19	1.16
Swaziland	8.24	8.15	9.95	9.90	9.84	9.76	9.64	9.51	9.37	9.23	9.09	8.89	8.76
Tanzania	2.24	2.18	2.12	1.85	1.80	1.75	1.71	1.66	1.53	1.59	1.54	2.78	2.70
Togo	4.96	4.82	4.70	4.60	4.49	4.39	4.30	4.33	4.24	4.15	4.06	3.78	3.68
Tunisia	13.74	13.01	12.90	12.78	12.89	12.77	12.63	12.49	14.21	14.05	13.90	13.72	13.57
Uganda	6.72	6.51	6.31	6.11	5.91	5.72	5.54	5.36	5.19	5.03	4.87	4.63	4.48
Zambia	11.78	14.06	13.74	13.43	13.13	12.82	12.50	12.19	11.87	11.55	11.22	14.76	14.29
Zimbabwe	34.52	34.34	14.66	14.65	14.67	14.70	14.75	14.81	14.84	14.82	14.70	13.83	13.47

I.b *Transport*: total road network (km per km² of exploitable land area)

	2000	2001	2002	2003	2004	2005	2006	2007	2008	2009	2010	2011	2012
Algeria	2.50	2.50	2.50	2.50	2.60	2.60	2.60	2.60	2.67	2.69	2.69	2.76	2.82
Angola	0.44	0.44	0.44	0.44	0.44	0.44	0.44	0.44	0.44	0.44	0.44	0.44	0.44
Benin	2.25	2.25	2.25	2.25	2.25	2.25	2.25	2.25	2.25	2.25	2.25	2.25	2.25
Botswana	0.60	0.60	0.60	0.63	0.61	0.65	0.65	0.65	0.65	0.65	0.65	0.65	0.65
Burkina Faso	5.76	5.76	5.76	5.76	5.76	5.76	5.76	5.76	5.76	5.76	5.76	5.77	5.77
Burundi	5.40	5.40	5.40	5.40	4.59	4.59	4.59	4.59	4.59	4.59	4.59	4.59	4.59
Cabo Verde	8.82	8.82	8.82	8.82	8.82	8.82	8.82	8.82	8.82	8.82	8.82	8.82	8.82
Cameroon	1.58	1.58	1.58	1.58	1.63	1.63	0.91	0.91	0.91	0.91	0.91	0.91	0.91
Central African Republic	0.87	0.87	0.87	0.87	0.87	0.87	0.87	0.87	0.87	0.87	0.87	0.87	0.84
Chad	0.53	0.53	0.53	0.53	0.53	0.63	0.63	0.63	0.63	0.63	0.63	0.63	0.63
Comoros	5.75	5.75	5.75	5.75	5.75	5.75	5.75	5.75	5.75	5.75	5.75	5.75	5.75
Congo	0.39	0.39	0.39	0.39	0.52	0.52	0.51	0.51	0.51	0.51	0.51	0.51	0.51
Congo, Dem. Rep.	0.82	0.82	0.82	0.82	0.81	0.81	0.81	0.81	0.81	0.81	0.81	0.81	0.81
Cote d'Ivoire	2.63	2.63	2.63	2.63	2.63	2.63	2.63	2.70	2.70	2.70	2.70	2.70	2.70
Djibouti	1.91	1.91	1.91	1.91	1.91	1.91	1.91	1.91	1.91	1.91	1.91	1.91	1.91
Egypt, Arab Rep.	23.38	23.38	23.38	23.38	23.38	25.03	25.23	25.23	26.56	25.44	25.44	25.44	25.44
Equatorial Guinea	1.39	1.39	1.39	1.39	1.39	1.39	1.39	1.39	1.39	1.39	1.39	1.39	1.39
Eritrea	0.37	0.37	0.37	0.37	0.37	0.37	0.37	0.37	0.37	0.37	0.37	0.37	0.37
Ethiopia	0.54	0.54	0.61	0.62	0.67	0.77	0.73	0.81	0.81	0.81	0.81	0.81	0.81
Gabon	0.32	0.32	0.32	0.32	0.34	0.34	0.34	0.34	0.34	0.34	0.34	0.34	0.34

(continued)

	2000	2001	2002	2003	2004	2005	2006	2007	2008	2009	2010	2011	2012
Gambia, The	2.39	2.39	2.39	3.31	3.31	3.31	3.31	3.31	3.31	3.31	3.31	3.31	3.31
Ghana	1.82	1.82	1.82	2.21	2.51	2.66	2.66	2.66	5.59	5.06	5.06	5.06	5.06
Guinea	1.49	1.49	1.49	2.17	2.17	2.17	2.17	2.17	2.17	2.17	2.17	2.17	2.17
Guinea-Bissau	1.22	1.22	0.96	0.96	0.96	0.96	0.96	0.96	0.96	0.96	0.96	0.96	0.96
Kenya	2.04	2.04	2.04	2.04	2.02	2.02	2.02	2.02	2.03	1.97	1.97	5.13	5.13
Lesotho	2.50	2.50	2.50	2.50	2.50	2.50	2.50	2.50	2.50	2.50	2.50	2.50	2.50
Liberia	1.22	1.22	1.22	1.22	1.22	1.22	1.22	1.22	1.22	1.22	1.22	1.22	1.22
Libya	5.31	5.31	5.31	5.31	5.31	5.31	5.31	5.31	5.31	5.31	5.31	5.31	5.31
Madagascar	0.92	0.92	0.92	0.92	0.92	0.92	0.92	0.92	0.92	0.92	0.92	0.92	0.92
Malawi	1.54	1.54	1.54	1.44	1.44	1.44	1.44	1.44	1.44	1.44	1.44	1.44	1.44
Mali	0.28	0.28	0.28	0.28	0.35	0.35	0.35	0.35	0.40	0.42	0.42	0.42	0.42
Mauritania	0.19	0.19	0.19	0.19	0.22	0.23	0.28	0.28	0.28	0.28	0.28	0.30	0.30
Mauritius	13.69	13.69	14.21	14.32	14.32	14.36	14.36	14.41	14.41	14.68	14.68	14.68	14.68
Morocco	1.61	1.61	1.62	1.62	1.61	1.61	1.61	1.62	1.62	1.63	1.63	1.64	1.64
Mozambique	0.38	0.38	0.38	0.38	0.38	0.38	0.38	0.38	0.38	0.38	0.38	0.38	0.38
Namibia	1.42	1.42	1.42	1.42	1.42	1.42	1.42	1.42	1.42	0.90	0.90	0.93	0.93
Niger	0.26	0.26	0.38	0.39	0.48	0.48	0.48	0.49	0.49	0.49	0.49	0.49	0.49
Nigeria	2.25	2.25	2.25	2.25	2.24	2.24	2.24	2.24	2.24	2.24	2.24	2.24	2.24
Rwanda	5.50	5.50	5.50	5.50	6.42	6.42	6.42	6.42	6.42	6.42	6.42	6.42	6.42
Sao Tome and Principe	4.21	4.21	4.21	4.21	4.21	4.21	4.21	4.21	4.21	4.21	4.21	4.21	4.21
Senegal	0.81	0.81	0.81	0.75	0.75	0.75	0.82	0.82	0.82	0.82	0.82	0.83	0.83

(continued)

	2000	2001	2002	2003	2004	2005	2006	2007	2008	2009	2010	2011	2012
Seychelles	8.34	8.34	8.34	10.25	10.25	11.14	11.23	11.36	11.36	11.36	11.36	11.36	11.36
Sierra Leone	1.97	1.97	1.97	1.97	1.97	1.97	1.97	1.97	1.97	1.97	1.97	1.97	1.97
Somalia	0.42	0.42	0.42	0.42	0.42	0.42	0.42	0.42	0.42	0.42	0.42	0.42	0.42
South Africa	3.35	3.35	3.35	3.35	3.35	3.35	3.35	3.35	3.35	3.35	3.35	3.35	3.35
South Sudan	n.a	n.a	n.a	n.a	n.a	n.a	n.a	n.a	n.a	n.a	0.06	0.06	0.06
Sudan	0.06	0.06	0.06	0.06	0.06	0.06	0.06	0.06	0.06	0.06	0.06	0.06	0.06
Swaziland	1.79	1.79	2.07	2.07	2.07	2.07	2.07	2.07	2.07	2.07	2.07	2.07	2.07
Tanzania	1.14	1.14	1.14	1.02	1.02	1.02	1.02	1.02	1.13	1.34	1.34	1.38	1.38
Togo	1.73	1.73	1.73	1.73	1.73	1.73	1.73	2.67	2.67	2.67	2.67	2.67	2.67
Tunisia	1.69	1.69	1.69	1.69	1.72	1.72	1.72	1.72	1.73	1.73	1.73	1.73	1.73
Uganda	3.44	3.44	3.44	3.44	3.44	3.44	3.44	3.44	3.44	3.44	3.44	3.44	3.44
Zambia	0.90	0.90	0.90	0.90	0.90	0.90	0.90	0.90	0.90	0.90	0.90	0.90	0.90
Zimbabwe	2.65	2.65	2.83	2.83	2.83	2.83	2.83	2.83	2.83	2.83	2.83	2.83	2.83

II. *Electricity Index* - net generation (KWh per inhabitant)

	2000	2001	2002	2003	2004	2005	2006	2007	2008	2009	2010	2011	2012
Algeria	753.2	778.6	797.9	842.6	878.2	939.5	959.9	996.5	1,059.1	995.1	1,160.1	1,272.5	1,349.7
Angola	100.8	110.6	115.3	125.7	136.8	165.0	189.3	177.8	221.9	243.3	271.5	273.1	295.3
Benin	11.4	8.7	8.0	9.8	9.6	12.3	17.3	23.9	24.1	13.1	14.9	14.9	15.1
Botswana	507.1	532.4	465.6	371.4	398.9	434.5	429.4	356.3	306.7	264.9	218.1	176.2	147.5
Burkina Faso	27.4	27.4	29.7	35.1	36.2	36.5	37.6	40.9	40.2	44.0	34.6	36.2	36.2
Burundi	15.0	17.0	18.2	14.0	12.2	12.5	11.7	14.2	13.1	13.7	15.5	15.9	17.0
Cabo Verde	7,783.7	7,768.2	7,102.2	7,794.7	8,572.2	8,256.7	10,442.7	10,596.8	11,465.3	11,614.3	11,815.4	11,939.5	12,267.9
Cameroon	8.7	9.5	10.2	10.9	11.7	12.2	12.7	13.2	13.8	14.0	14.7	14.5	14.9
Central African Rep.	28.9	28.6	28.1	27.9	38.3	40.1	41.2	39.0	38.2	37.3	36.6	39.4	39.2
Chad	10.4	10.9	11.3	11.6	11.9	12.1	11.8	11.3	12.8	15.1	16.0	16.6	17.8
Comoros	36.0	51.7	55.8	57.8	71.7	74.9	77.9	69.5	66.2	61.6	60.0	61.4	58.6
Congo	93.7	103.3	119.4	116.7	113.1	119.8	121.8	106.3	116.6	131.0	184.8	297.0	363.0
Congo, Dem. Rep.	126.6	122.9	122.3	119.8	133.6	135.6	134.3	136.0	126.7	128.2	125.5	122.0	119.8
Cote d'Ivoire	285.1	285.1	303.6	288.2	307.9	311.7	305.6	300.3	304.2	304.5	302.1	302.7	302.2
Djibouti	249.0	244.0	252.5	249.0	263.8	309.0	333.9	343.1	388.8	388.1	393.3	389.8	402.5
Egypt	1,121.1	1,176.3	1,237.0	1,298.3	1,358.3	1,432.7	1,495.6	1,595.7	1,642.1	1,711.1	1,774.2	1,859.8	1,942.8
Equatorial Guinea	81.1	101.0	110.6	133.7	136.5	140.8	144.8	147.0	142.9	138.9	139.3	135.5	133.7
Eritrea	50.1	53.4	56.9	58.2	57.0	55.8	50.2	52.0	50.1	49.9	50.9	53.4	54.1
Ethiopia	25.1	29.3	28.9	31.6	33.9	37.0	41.3	43.6	45.0	46.3	56.6	57.1	61.1

(continued)

	2000	2001	2002	2003	2004	2005	2006	2007	2008	2009	2010	2011	2012
Gabon	1,041.8	1,071.5	1,111.5	1,113.2	1,101.7	1,090.8	1,133.8	1,155.4	1,194.9	1,182.2	1,144.4	1,067.7	1,055.7
Gambia, The	89.9	100.3	108.7	117.2	125.0	133.0	136.9	140.6	143.9	139.4	136.9	132.6	131.8
Ghana	378.2	400.1	358.5	281.4	281.5	311.6	373.8	299.5	351.9	369.9	408.3	439.4	457.6
Guinea	85.0	104.9	108.8	94.0	100.4	92.0	86.0	93.8	93.7	90.8	84.5	85.1	85.0
Guinea-Bissau	43.2	43.0	42.1	41.9	42.4	42.2	42.7	40.4	39.6	38.7	37.8	33.9	32.3
Kenya	129.6	143.0	144.0	150.4	156.6	163.8	172.1	172.7	170.2	167.4	179.2	181.3	183.2
Lesotho	155.2	152.3	166.5	171.2	155.3	238.3	270.6	283.3	296.1	325.6	345.5	344.9	362.2
Liberia	106.2	106.0	103.6	96.3	97.3	97.3	97.5	94.3	90.4	87.7	84.6	82.1	79.3
Libya	2,814.1	2,879.9	3,085.8	3,283.7	3,448.3	3,749.8	3,966.0	4,177.1	4,585.3	4,892.8	5,096.8	4,253.0	4,333.1
Madagascar	49.5	54.6	51.7	57.4	61.9	60.7	60.2	61.1	61.8	60.3	62.3	61.8	62.1
Malawi	106.3	105.8	107.8	107.4	115.5	117.1	116.6	115.6	124.7	118.6	132.3	133.9	137.8
Mali	38.9	38.1	37.1	38.7	38.9	38.3	38.4	37.6	37.4	36.8	36.0	36.1	35.6
Mauritania	84.8	99.6	174.1	160.2	169.5	158.6	181.0	182.0	198.4	232.4	245.2	251.2	268.6
Mauritius	1,418.6	1,509.7	1,535.7	1,636.8	1,696.0	1,768.8	1,820.0	1,902.6	1,971.8	1,982.6	2,060.6	2,127.9	2,195.1
Morocco	422.5	489.3	517.3	557.2	586.0	621.7	629.7	626.9	630.2	636.5	703.1	737.8	762.1
Mozambique	525.1	626.2	651.3	543.2	567.3	625.9	675.8	717.8	657.9	718.9	688.4	677.8	679.6
Namibia	736.6	705.0	738.9	762.2	792.2	824.9	823.0	808.5	1,003.0	788.1	663.4	714.7	704.4
Niger	16.2	13.7	14.6	14.7	14.9	16.6	15.1	14.7	14.4	15.6	17.2	18.2	18.9
Nigeria	115.0	117.7	159.9	145.9	170.8	161.3	153.8	148.9	133.1	121.1	155.7	156.5	158.5
Rwanda	223.9	233.6	226.4	233.7	248.2	258.6	254.7	256.6	266.6	264.4	259.0	254.9	255.0
Sao Tome and Principe	810.5	636.5	683.2	807.0	603.3	724.4	1,007.5	968.2	1,088.8	1,375.0	1,516.0	1,638.9	1,813.2

(continued)

	2000	2001	2002	2003	2004	2005	2006	2007	2008	2009	2010	2011	2012
Senegal	2.8	2.4	2.9	2.9	3.2	3.5	3.5	3.6	3.7	3.9	4.2	4.5	4.7
Seychelles	18,051.0	20,827.9	21,716.2	22,608.0	23,265.0	26,121.2	25,870.1	27,682.8	24,848.6	29,343.7	31,422.7	30,512.3	31,674.6
Sierra Leone	43.0	41.9	45.6	44.6	43.0	42.4	44.9	47.1	45.7	45.9	49.2	51.8	53.4
Somalia	12.1	17.2	18.9	16.8	13.6	9.2	4.5	6.4	14.8	13.8	17.2	14.6	19.8
South Africa	5.2	5.4	5.6	5.8	5.5	5.7	5.8	5.9	6.0	6.0	6.0	6.0	6.0
South Sudan	29,434.7	28,347.3	28,283.7	29,159.0	29,436.3	28,354.0	28,109.1	28,116.1	26,286.9	24,222.4	24,337.3	23,444.0	22,622.0
Sudan	107.6	114.1	119.3	124.1	124.2	132.0	149.0	159.6	169.2	194.3	227.3	244.8	270.5
Swaziland	426.8	417.8	418.6	346.5	307.8	353.1	372.9	383.3	357.9	390.2	415.7	342.4	338.3
Tanzania	71.7	77.9	78.8	71.5	75.1	89.8	84.8	98.5	102.3	99.4	109.6	110.3	116.5
Togo	34.9	24.0	28.9	33.1	33.5	33.0	37.3	32.4	20.1	20.2	20.5	21.0	19.1
Tunisia	1,043.0	1,110.0	1,142.1	1,185.7	1,235.8	1,291.0	1,307.2	1,257.7	1,299.7	1,364.9	1,424.2	1,415.9	1,439.5
Uganda	64.1	61.9	64.6	65.5	68.1	66.2	53.6	64.6	71.3	66.6	70.8	70.9	75.3
Zambia	764.1	758.6	759.3	754.7	753.4	771.2	831.7	803.6	770.5	803.4	846.4	831.6	832.2
Zimbabwe	538.9	602.4	653.7	673.8	741.4	780.5	595.5	572.0	571.7	543.7	589.2	546.2	537.7

III. ICT Composite Index (2000-2012)

	2000	2001	2002	2003	2004	2005	2006	2007	2008	2009	2010	2011	2012
Algeria	0.69	0.80	1.28	2.01	4.11	7.93	10.73	14.37	17.41	27.39	33.28	38.35	55.50
Angola	0.09	0.13	0.22	0.37	0.61	1.31	2.49	3.96	5.35	6.64	8.56	13.36	20.46
Benin	0.22	0.36	0.60	0.72	1.06	1.24	1.87	2.98	4.54	6.01	8.34	10.59	15.16
Botswana	2.80	3.55	3.50	3.90	4.21	4.69	6.19	8.31	11.18	12.88	15.18	21.93	31.64
Burkina Faso	0.08	0.14	0.18	0.33	0.46	0.63	0.98	1.61	2.45	2.98	4.43	7.06	11.81
Burundi	0.07	0.10	0.13	0.18	0.28	0.41	0.50	0.59	0.85	1.27	1.61	2.63	3.99
Cabo Verde	2.11	2.81	3.42	3.91	4.70	5.75	11.62	12.71	19.85	24.84	31.06	41.05	54.54
Cameroon	0.19	0.37	0.55	0.82	1.19	1.70	2.34	3.32	4.22	5.25	5.66	8.34	13.07
Central African Rep.	0.05	0.07	0.09	0.16	0.23	0.32	0.36	0.56	0.89	2.00	2.63	3.30	5.29
Chad	0.02	0.04	0.10	0.19	0.25	0.34	0.62	1.08	1.91	2.37	2.69	4.56	7.16
Comoros	0.20	0.29	0.35	0.52	0.81	1.17	1.54	2.07	2.64	3.15	4.14	6.28	10.16
Congo	0.24	0.45	0.65	0.89	1.05	1.46	2.27	3.07	4.14	4.89	8.23	9.85	14.30
Congo, Dem. Rep.	0.01	0.03	0.15	0.36	0.70	0.95	1.38	1.95	2.95	2.94	3.42	6.28	10.68
Cote d'Ivoire	0.45	0.65	0.85	1.03	1.26	1.64	2.85	4.58	5.98	7.66	8.62	12.37	17.59
Djibouti	0.18	0.27	0.46	0.59	0.79	0.95	1.14	1.96	3.31	5.36	7.84	10.57	16.35
Egypt	1.09	1.56	2.95	3.78	4.69	8.96	11.54	16.79	23.43	39.78	52.93	64.94	85.84
Equatorial Guinea	0.22	0.40	0.73	0.94	1.34	2.02	2.33	2.78	3.20	3.50	7.89	11.80	17.01
Eritrea	0.12	0.12	0.16	0.34	0.55	0.82	0.99	1.16	1.79	2.18	2.43	3.48	5.32
Ethiopia	0.03	0.05	0.07	0.09	0.14	0.21	0.32	0.44	0.62	0.99	2.06	3.39	5.98
Gabon	1.53	1.75	2.75	3.21	4.64	7.07	8.21	9.80	10.71	11.60	13.11	20.81	31.70

(continued)

	2000	2001	2002	2003	2004	2005	2006	2007	2008	2009	2010	2011	2012
Gambia	0.59	1.06	1.52	2.05	2.50	3.07	4.45	6.89	8.91	9.76	11.00	14.46	20.50
Ghana	0.20	0.28	0.59	0.89	1.46	2.01	3.44	4.81	6.79	7.92	10.51	17.08	24.62
Guinea	0.10	0.14	0.26	0.30	0.36	0.40	0.30	2.10	2.80	3.40	3.81	5.58	8.53
Guinea-Bissau	0.16	0.17	0.45	0.58	0.98	1.38	1.76	2.60	3.80	4.06	4.24	6.40	11.29
Kenya	0.23	0.47	0.84	1.59	1.83	2.41	4.96	5.91	7.24	13.05	16.51	26.00	46.80
Lesotho	0.26	0.42	1.10	1.24	1.78	2.19	2.78	3.32	3.87	4.21	5.49	8.42	13.24
Liberia	0.02	0.03	0.04	0.15	0.27	0.44	0.72	1.57	2.17	2.58	4.21	6.48	10.32
Libya	1.10	1.25	2.06	2.38	3.27	5.65	9.15	10.10	17.69	24.77	28.53	33.87	47.01
Madagascar	0.13	0.19	0.24	0.33	0.39	0.50	0.82	1.37	2.87	3.46	3.99	5.60	7.64
Malawi	0.11	0.14	0.19	0.25	0.34	0.50	0.67	1.18	1.30	1.95	3.05	4.44	8.17
Mali	0.09	0.12	0.15	0.32	0.47	0.73	1.40	2.01	2.89	3.49	5.12	9.14	16.00
Mauritania	0.18	0.51	0.97	1.29	1.77	2.45	3.43	4.87	6.96	7.19	9.02	12.76	19.88
Mauritius	6.00	7.35	8.56	10.52	12.07	14.21	22.18	22.87	31.27	38.56	44.95	62.89	88.39
Morocco	1.39	2.27	3.09	3.80	8.51	14.64	20.35	27.35	32.59	43.92	55.78	63.94	84.16
Mozambique	0.10	0.16	0.24	0.38	0.58	0.96	1.28	1.67	2.52	3.61	4.80	6.06	8.76
Namibia	1.47	1.88	2.14	2.73	3.13	3.91	4.65	5.53	6.68	7.77	12.35	17.96	24.47
Niger	0.02	0.05	0.10	0.13	0.20	0.32	0.45	0.75	1.44	1.86	2.50	3.74	5.61
Nigeria	0.06	0.09	0.28	0.49	1.14	2.57	4.20	5.28	10.16	12.74	15.43	21.41	31.89
Rwanda	0.08	0.17	0.21	0.28	0.37	0.49	0.59	1.50	2.93	5.08	6.42	8.31	13.35
Sao Tome and Principe	2.02	2.69	3.33	4.49	5.84	6.23	7.05	8.25	9.77	10.95	13.95	17.08	22.47
Senegal	0.56	0.84	1.09	1.79	3.14	4.19	5.90	7.50	10.36	13.63	15.68	20.39	29.49

(continued)

	2000	2001	2002	2003	2004	2005	2006	2007	2008	2009	2010	2011	2012
Seychelles	7.52	10.05	11.80	12.56	18.45	22.04	33.20	36.97	38.23	45.35	55.84	71.55	96.75
Sierra Leone	0.10	0.15	0.23	0.31	0.33	0.28	0.16	1.32	1.64	1.84	3.02	4.07	7.07
Somalia	0.12	0.16	0.18	0.45	1.01	1.00	1.05	1.09	1.11	1.11	1.10	2.44	4.61
South Africa	4.66	5.48	6.12	6.91	8.51	11.21	13.93	15.02	17.79	24.82	59.75	69.25	101.74
South Sudan	n.a	n.a	n.a	n.a	n.a	n.a	n.a	n.a	n.a	n.a	n.a	n.a	n.a
Sudan	0.10	0.18	0.37	0.56	0.82	1.08	4.23	5.49	7.27	7.75	11.33	26.64	51.26
Swaziland	0.87	1.20	1.52	1.99	2.76	3.29	3.73	4.85	7.34	9.29	10.73	16.67	23.82
Tanzania	0.11	0.17	0.26	0.58	0.79	2.33	3.44	4.48	6.10	7.62	9.14	15.51	23.26
Togo	0.46	0.58	0.73	0.94	1.20	1.45	1.95	2.83	3.54	4.91	5.48	7.62	12.42
Tunisia	1.99	2.88	3.49	5.13	7.61	10.35	14.05	18.43	30.08	43.52	56.05	81.06	104.37
Uganda	0.12	0.20	0.29	0.44	0.66	1.09	1.61	2.71	5.47	6.59	9.69	13.73	19.11
Zambia	0.22	0.25	0.35	0.62	1.18	1.85	2.90	3.96	4.84	5.79	7.80	12.38	19.74
Zimbabwe	0.49	0.70	2.01	3.05	3.25	3.99	4.80	5.62	6.22	8.18	10.84	15.06	24.00

III.a *ICT*: Total phone subscriptions (fixed line and mobiles) per 100 inhabitants

	2000	2001	2002	2003	2004	2005	2006	2007	2008	2009	2010	2011	2012
Algeria	6.05	6.39	7.63	11.05	22.75	49.36	71.39	90.34	87.43	101.02	100.66	102.41	105.92
Angola	0.65	1.06	1.48	2.82	5.23	10.36	18.53	28.85	38.18	45.34	48.28	54.29	62.41
Benin	1.64	2.74	4.06	4.22	7.19	8.81	14.39	26.66	44.77	59.99	81.45	80.96	85.21
Botswana	20.37	26.92	26.57	31.49	35.34	37.33	50.24	66.86	83.28	101.51	124.61	153.51	161.80
Burkina Faso	0.64	1.06	1.33	2.27	3.49	5.10	7.60	13.11	20.45	24.87	35.53	48.91	61.47
Burundi	0.57	0.83	1.11	1.29	1.82	2.54	3.05	3.87	6.43	10.65	14.11	20.38	22.99
Cabo Verde	17.01	21.49	24.99	27.18	29.45	32.42	37.73	46.37	71.72	73.73	89.48	96.00	100.23
Cameroon	1.26	3.26	4.95	7.00	9.50	13.40	18.20	25.75	34.20	44.01	46.82	52.73	63.81
Central African Rep.	0.39	0.53	0.56	1.27	1.77	2.74	2.98	5.10	6.18	15.82	22.36	22.39	25.28
Chad	0.19	0.38	0.52	0.85	1.44	2.28	4.82	9.16	17.40	21.39	24.29	30.60	35.58
Comoros	1.20	1.54	1.73	2.50	3.75	5.05	8.47	12.99	17.29	21.43	25.36	34.22	42.85
Congo	2.93	5.35	7.41	10.01	11.54	16.25	25.66	34.87	47.34	55.32	94.20	92.28	99.10
Congo, Dem. Rep.	0.05	0.31	1.09	2.32	3.59	4.80	7.49	10.85	15.97	14.80	17.98	24.56	30.67
Cote d'Ivoire	4.44	6.05	7.87	8.70	10.90	14.47	23.66	41.38	56.91	69.59	77.57	90.88	92.62
Djibouti	1.36	1.73	3.28	4.25	5.74	6.76	6.81	9.97	14.93	16.70	20.71	24.98	27.04
Egypt	10.12	13.77	17.51	20.33	23.58	32.48	38.23	53.71	67.85	82.37	98.96	116.06	130.52
Equatorial Guinea	2.13	4.08	7.36	8.93	12.28	17.59	20.77	24.85	28.69	30.83	58.94	68.91	70.07
Eritrea	0.83	0.82	0.90	0.92	1.37	1.74	2.14	2.54	3.01	3.72	4.56	5.07	5.96
Ethiopia	0.38	0.46	0.59	0.64	0.88	1.37	2.09	2.69	3.59	6.12	9.36	16.73	23.24
Gabon	12.87	14.82	24.13	25.69	39.28	56.60	66.88	83.97	91.92	95.39	108.96	150.10	180.85

(continued)

	2000	2001	2002	2003	2004	2005	2006	2007	2008	2009	2010	2011	2012
Gambia	3.00	6.75	10.05	13.49	14.93	19.38	29.13	53.36	74.26	80.95	88.36	83.67	88.78
Ghana	1.79	2.49	3.29	5.27	9.51	14.77	25.09	35.14	50.35	64.54	72.63	86.42	102.11
Guinea	0.80	0.96	1.36	1.57	2.04	2.37	0.82	21.57	29.05	35.97	40.25	43.71	48.93
Guinea-Bissau	0.90	0.78	0.87	0.90	3.67	7.93	11.76	21.12	34.72	38.08	39.54	45.42	63.37
Kenya	1.34	2.84	4.58	5.68	8.20	13.75	20.89	31.51	44.08	50.75	62.57	67.48	71.75
Lesotho	2.23	3.94	8.29	7.94	11.40	14.41	19.71	23.91	29.82	32.62	47.26	62.62	77.77
Liberia	0.29	0.30	0.40	1.73	3.19	5.13	8.53	16.25	23.41	28.34	39.49	49.84	57.12
Libya	12.33	13.32	14.54	15.83	22.99	49.44	82.06	90.80	134.96	169.21	190.84	180.23	169.00
Madagascar	0.77	1.30	1.36	2.04	2.26	3.37	6.38	12.39	25.58	32.15	37.92	41.13	40.47
Malawi	0.85	0.96	1.34	1.81	2.53	4.09	5.69	9.02	11.56	17.21	21.46	26.68	30.64
Mali	0.44	0.64	0.85	2.49	3.70	6.36	11.74	18.62	24.34	30.49	49.15	75.80	99.13
Mauritania	1.30	4.97	9.95	13.50	18.94	25.81	34.98	45.27	65.80	66.81	81.41	91.47	107.75
Mauritius	38.53	47.94	54.49	65.71	72.38	80.71	89.19	101.08	108.81	113.19	121.51	135.12	148.03
Morocco	13.08	20.47	24.87	28.82	35.39	45.19	56.25	72.31	82.39	91.13	111.83	125.14	130.05
Mozambique	0.75	1.28	1.78	2.60	3.87	7.56	11.32	14.48	20.08	26.48	31.26	32.32	35.29
Namibia	10.14	11.57	13.75	17.48	20.26	28.26	35.16	43.47	54.42	60.91	73.86	106.13	102.60
Niger	0.20	0.21	0.68	0.87	1.57	2.68	3.81	6.75	13.58	17.87	25.07	29.24	32.04
Nigeria	0.47	0.68	1.75	3.03	7.46	14.17	23.73	28.56	42.67	49.19	55.77	58.40	67.05
Rwanda	0.70	1.02	1.24	1.76	1.78	2.68	3.58	6.78	13.39	23.88	33.78	40.25	50.06
Sao Tome and Principe	3.27	3.79	5.73	7.96	9.84	12.49	16.79	23.99	36.34	44.06	66.60	67.15	69.22
Senegal	4.80	5.52	7.76	9.82	12.91	18.37	29.23	33.99	47.74	59.31	69.85	72.76	86.05

(continued)

	2000	2001	2002	2003	2004	2005	2006	2007	2008	2009	2010	2011	2012
Seychelles	57.42	71.34	78.81	85.07	91.71	96.80	107.59	117.60	133.17	156.64	155.54	168.31	170.49
Sierra Leone	0.75	1.15	2.02	2.93	3.15	2.49	0.93	14.72	18.54	20.78	34.32	36.70	37.26
Somalia	1.42	1.58	1.73	3.76	7.34	7.18	7.60	8.02	8.15	8.13	8.02	19.08	23.25
South Africa	29.72	34.61	40.30	46.49	54.40	80.95	91.67	95.88	100.21	102.02	108.90	132.54	139.81
South Sudan	n.a	n.a	n.a	n.a	n.a	n.a	n.a	n.a	n.a	n.a	15.11	17.36	21.22
Sudan	1.20	1.58	2.41	4.00	5.54	6.24	13.16	21.21	29.84	36.98	41.40	70.11	75.50
Swaziland	6.10	8.25	9.52	12.05	17.30	21.27	26.30	37.42	50.04	59.91	65.49	69.49	69.10
Tanzania	0.83	1.30	2.14	3.93	5.53	8.03	14.43	20.49	31.07	40.53	47.19	55.72	57.33
Togo	1.94	2.91	4.28	5.89	7.54	9.18	14.29	22.82	29.26	40.09	44.23	42.58	50.79
Tunisia	11.36	15.14	17.88	31.69	50.33	70.00	85.92	89.99	96.04	106.85	118.35	126.53	128.21
Uganda	0.78	1.36	1.74	3.14	4.49	4.93	7.21	14.37	27.84	29.71	39.36	48.83	45.87
Zambia	1.79	1.98	2.12	3.01	4.97	9.11	14.95	22.65	29.32	35.34	42.30	60.51	75.36
Zimbabwe	4.12	4.51	4.97	5.27	5.90	7.76	9.46	12.58	16.08	35.08	64.26	71.53	94.11

III.a.1 *ICT*: Fixed-line phone subscriptions (% of population)

	2000	2001	2002	2003	2004	2005	2006	2007	2008	2009	2010	2011	2012
Algeria	5.77	6.07	6.20	6.52	7.68	7.82	8.51	9.05	8.91	7.37	8.24	8.10	8.40
Angola	0.47	0.53	0.54	0.55	0.59	0.59	0.58	0.54	0.63	1.63	1.59	1.28	1.00
Benin	0.79	0.88	0.90	0.93	0.98	1.00	0.98	1.37	1.38	1.48	1.51	1.56	1.56
Botswana	7.73	8.30	8.19	7.18	7.11	7.28	6.95	7.10	7.28	6.93	6.85	7.53	8.01
Burkina Faso	0.43	0.46	0.48	0.50	0.62	0.64	0.65	0.78	0.95	0.95	0.87	0.88	0.86
Burundi	0.31	0.32	0.33	0.35	0.39	0.43	0.37	0.37	0.38	0.39	0.39	0.31	0.18
Cabo Verde	12.50	14.41	15.50	15.59	15.36	15.14	14.97	14.86	14.74	14.62	14.51	15.19	14.20
Cameroon	0.61	0.66	0.68	0.58	0.58	0.57	0.73	1.03	1.36	2.27	2.75	3.16	3.40
Central African Rep.	0.26	0.24	0.24	0.24	0.25	0.25	0.29	0.29	0.28	0.08	0.11	0.02	0.02
Chad	0.12	0.13	0.13	0.14	0.14	0.13	0.20	0.31	0.42	0.53	0.46	0.26	0.22
Comoros	1.20	1.54	1.73	2.17	2.41	2.63	2.89	3.84	4.13	4.30	2.86	3.31	3.34
Congo	0.70	0.68	0.67	0.21	0.40	0.45	0.38	0.36	0.24	0.24	0.24	0.34	0.34
Congo, Dem. Rep.	0.02	0.02	0.02	0.02	0.02	0.02	0.02	0.01	0.06	0.07	0.06	0.09	0.09
Cote d'Ivoire	1.59	1.74	1.89	1.36	1.45	1.43	1.48	1.33	1.88	1.46	1.44	1.43	1.39
Djibouti	1.33	1.32	1.32	1.30	1.40	1.31	1.37	1.68	1.74	1.93	2.08	2.18	2.32
Egypt	8.11	9.72	11.11	12.22	13.09	14.12	14.41	14.59	15.13	12.94	11.86	10.98	10.60
Equatorial Guinea	1.17	1.28	1.59	1.68	1.78	1.65	1.60	1.55	1.51	1.47	1.93	2.03	2.02
Eritrea	0.83	0.82	0.90	0.92	0.91	0.84	0.81	0.78	0.82	0.95	1.03	0.99	0.98
Ethiopia	0.35	0.42	0.51	0.57	0.67	0.82	0.95	1.13	1.13	1.13	1.10	0.93	0.87
Gabon	3.16	2.95	2.49	2.92	2.88	2.85	2.61	1.86	2.29	2.47	2.02	1.41	1.38

(continued)

	2000	2001	2002	2003	2004	2005	2006	2007	2008	2009	2010	2011	2012
Gambia	2.57	2.62	2.79	2.96	2.94	2.93	2.99	3.06	2.99	2.88	2.82	2.91	3.58
Ghana	1.11	1.25	1.37	1.41	1.48	1.49	1.61	1.66	0.62	1.12	1.14	1.15	1.12
Guinea	0.29	0.30	0.30	0.30	0.29	0.28	0.25	0.23	0.28	0.23	0.18	0.16	0.16
Guinea-Bissau	0.90	0.78	0.87	0.80	0.72	0.70	0.49	0.32	0.32	0.33	0.33	0.31	0.30
Kenya	0.93	0.96	0.98	0.97	0.86	0.81	0.80	1.24	1.68	1.68	0.94	0.67	0.58
Lesotho	1.13	1.08	1.42	1.73	1.82	2.32	2.55	2.26	1.94	1.86	1.78	1.90	2.47
Liberia	0.24	0.23	0.23	0.18	0.14	0.10	0.08	0.06	0.05	0.06	0.15	0.08	0.00
Libya	11.57	12.38	13.25	13.54	14.14	14.77	15.42	16.09	14.97	16.98	19.33	16.38	13.23
Madagascar	0.36	0.37	0.36	0.35	0.34	0.52	0.70	0.71	0.84	0.93	0.69	1.09	1.09
Malawi	0.41	0.47	0.62	0.70	0.75	0.80	0.99	1.29	0.79	0.77	1.07	1.12	1.43
Mali	0.35	0.44	0.47	0.49	0.52	0.58	0.61	0.57	0.56	0.57	0.75	0.73	0.75
Mauritania	0.72	0.91	1.13	1.32	1.32	1.35	1.11	1.25	2.32	2.20	2.07	1.95	1.71
Mauritius	23.48	25.39	26.03	28.23	28.40	28.45	28.21	28.28	28.32	29.05	29.84	30.33	28.16
Morocco	4.95	4.09	3.83	4.10	4.35	4.41	4.12	7.72	9.55	11.12	11.73	11.12	10.08
Mozambique	0.47	0.47	0.46	0.39	0.37	0.32	0.33	0.36	0.35	0.36	0.38	0.36	0.35
Namibia	5.81	6.06	6.15	6.34	6.26	6.68	6.43	6.40	6.61	6.63	6.66	7.17	7.58
Niger	0.18	0.19	0.19	0.19	0.19	0.18	0.22	0.30	0.45	0.51	0.54	0.52	0.59
Nigeria	0.45	0.47	0.54	0.67	0.75	0.87	1.18	1.07	0.87	0.96	0.66	0.44	0.25
Rwanda	0.22	0.25	0.29	0.29	0.25	0.26	0.25	0.24	0.17	0.32	0.37	0.35	0.39
Sao Tome and Principe	3.27	3.79	4.37	4.71	4.69	4.66	4.90	4.86	4.78	4.68	4.63	4.35	4.27
Senegal	2.17	2.43	2.24	2.22	2.31	2.45	2.53	2.35	2.02	2.30	2.75	2.60	2.48

(continued)

	2000	2001	2002	2003	2004	2005	2006	2007	2008	2009	2010	2011	2012
Seychelles	25.42	26.17	25.38	25.60	25.79	25.83	24.44	26.72	25.67	29.87	24.56	30.41	22.69
Sierra Leone	0.46	0.53	0.53	0.53	0.54	0.54	0.54	0.55	0.56	0.57	0.24	0.27	0.30
Somalia	0.34	0.46	0.45	1.25	1.22	1.20	1.17	1.15	1.12	1.10	1.07	0.91	0.69
South Africa	11.09	10.85	10.53	10.34	10.27	9.89	9.60	9.28	8.97	8.68	8.43	9.34	9.25
South Sudan	n.a	n.a	n.a	n.a	n.a	n.a	n.a	n.a	n.a	n.a	0.02	0.02	0.00
Sudan	1.13	1.28	1.88	2.56	2.74	1.48	1.27	0.85	0.88	0.87	0.86	1.33	1.14
Swaziland	2.99	3.14	3.24	4.24	4.06	3.17	3.93	3.88	3.82	3.77	3.71	6.26	3.70
Tanzania	0.51	0.51	0.45	0.40	0.39	0.40	0.38	0.40	0.29	0.40	0.39	0.35	0.37
Togo	0.89	0.98	1.01	1.18	1.25	1.16	1.48	1.76	2.44	3.03	3.54	0.93	0.93
Tunisia	10.10	11.06	11.92	11.97	12.26	12.69	12.66	12.57	12.09	12.34	12.30	11.32	10.10
Uganda	0.25	0.22	0.21	0.23	0.26	0.31	0.37	0.55	0.54	0.72	0.98	1.32	0.87
Zambia	0.82	0.82	0.82	0.81	0.82	0.83	0.80	0.76	0.73	0.71	0.69	0.63	0.59
Zimbabwe	1.99	2.02	2.28	2.39	2.52	2.61	2.68	2.76	2.79	3.09	3.01	2.66	2.20

III.a.2 *ICT*: Mobile-cellular subscriptions (% of population)

	2000	2001	2002	2003	2004	2005	2006	2007	2008	2009	2010	2011	2012
Algeria	0.28	0.32	1.43	4.53	15.07	41.54	62.88	81.29	78.52	93.65	92.42	94.31	97.52
Angola	0.19	0.52	0.94	2.27	4.64	9.77	17.96	28.31	37.55	43.70	46.69	53.01	61.41
Benin	0.85	1.86	3.15	3.30	6.21	7.81	13.41	25.29	43.39	58.52	79.94	79.40	83.65
Botswana	12.64	18.62	18.38	24.31	28.23	30.06	43.30	59.75	76.01	94.58	117.76	145.98	153.79
Burkina Faso	0.21	0.60	0.85	1.78	2.87	4.46	6.95	12.34	19.49	23.92	34.66	48.03	60.61
Burundi	0.26	0.51	0.78	0.94	1.43	2.11	2.68	3.50	6.05	10.26	13.72	20.07	22.81
Cabo Verde	4.51	7.08	9.49	11.60	14.09	17.28	22.76	31.51	56.97	59.11	74.97	80.81	86.03
Cameroon	0.66	2.60	4.28	6.42	8.92	12.83	17.47	24.72	32.84	41.74	44.07	49.57	60.41
Central African Rep.	0.13	0.29	0.33	1.03	1.52	2.49	2.69	4.81	5.90	15.74	22.25	22.37	25.26
Chad	0.07	0.26	0.39	0.71	1.30	2.15	4.62	8.85	16.98	20.86	23.83	30.34	35.36
Comoros	–	–	–	0.33	1.34	2.41	5.58	9.15	13.16	17.13	22.49	30.91	39.51
Congo	2.23	4.67	6.74	9.81	11.13	15.80	25.29	34.52	47.10	55.08	93.96	91.94	98.76
Congo, Dem. Rep.	0.03	0.29	1.07	2.30	3.57	4.78	7.47	10.85	15.91	14.73	17.92	24.47	30.58
Cote d'Ivoire	2.85	4.31	5.98	7.34	9.44	13.04	22.18	40.05	55.03	68.14	76.13	89.45	91.23
Djibouti	0.03	0.40	1.96	2.95	4.34	5.45	5.44	8.28	13.19	14.77	18.64	22.80	24.72
Egypt	2.01	4.06	6.41	8.11	10.49	18.37	23.82	39.11	52.71	69.44	87.11	105.08	119.92
Equatorial Guinea	0.96	2.79	5.77	7.26	10.50	15.94	19.18	23.29	27.18	29.36	57.01	66.88	68.05
Eritrea	–	–	–	–	0.46	0.90	1.33	1.76	2.20	2.77	3.53	4.08	4.98
Ethiopia	0.03	0.04	0.07	0.07	0.21	0.55	1.14	1.55	2.46	4.99	8.26	15.80	22.37
Gabon	9.71	11.87	21.64	22.77	36.41	53.74	64.27	82.11	89.64	92.93	106.94	148.69	179.47

(continued)

	2000	2001	2002	2003	2004	2005	2006	2007	2008	2009	2010	2011	2012
Gambia	0.43	4.12	7.27	10.53	11.98	16.46	26.13	50.29	71.28	78.07	85.53	80.76	85.20
Ghana	0.68	1.24	1.92	3.86	8.03	13.28	23.49	33.48	49.73	63.42	71.49	85.27	100.99
Guinea	0.50	0.66	1.05	1.28	1.74	2.09	0.57	21.34	28.77	35.74	40.07	43.55	48.77
Guinea-Bissau	–	–	–	0.10	2.94	7.23	11.27	20.80	34.40	37.76	39.21	45.11	63.07
Kenya	0.41	1.87	3.61	4.71	7.34	12.95	20.09	30.28	42.40	49.07	61.63	66.81	71.17
Lesotho	1.10	2.87	6.86	6.21	9.59	12.09	17.16	21.65	27.88	30.76	45.48	60.72	75.30
Liberia	0.05	0.07	0.17	1.56	3.05	5.03	8.45	16.19	23.36	28.29	39.34	49.76	57.12
Libya	0.76	0.94	1.29	2.29	8.85	34.66	66.64	74.71	119.99	152.24	171.52	163.85	155.77
Madagascar	0.41	0.93	1.00	1.68	1.92	2.85	5.68	11.68	24.74	31.23	37.23	40.04	39.38
Malawi	0.44	0.48	0.73	1.11	1.78	3.28	4.70	7.73	10.77	16.44	20.38	25.56	29.21
Mali	0.09	0.21	0.38	2.00	3.19	5.78	11.13	18.05	23.78	29.92	48.41	75.07	98.38
Mauritania	0.58	4.06	8.83	12.18	17.62	24.47	33.87	44.01	63.48	64.61	79.34	89.52	106.04
Mauritius	15.05	22.55	28.46	37.48	43.97	52.26	60.98	72.80	80.48	84.14	91.67	104.79	119.87
Morocco	8.13	16.38	21.05	24.72	31.04	40.78	52.13	64.59	72.84	80.01	100.10	114.02	119.97
Mozambique	0.28	0.82	1.33	2.21	3.50	7.24	10.99	14.12	19.72	26.12	30.88	31.96	34.94
Namibia	4.33	5.51	7.60	11.14	14.00	21.58	28.74	37.07	47.81	54.28	67.21	98.96	95.02
Niger	0.02	0.02	0.49	0.68	1.37	2.49	3.59	6.45	13.13	17.36	24.53	28.72	31.45
Nigeria	0.02	0.21	1.21	2.37	6.71	13.29	22.55	27.49	41.81	48.24	55.10	57.96	66.80
Rwanda	0.48	0.77	0.95	1.48	1.52	2.42	3.33	6.54	13.22	23.56	33.40	39.90	49.67
Sao Tome and Principe	–	–	1.36	3.26	5.15	7.83	11.89	19.13	31.56	39.38	61.97	62.80	64.95
Senegal	2.63	3.09	5.52	7.60	10.60	15.91	26.70	31.64	45.72	57.00	67.11	70.16	83.57

(continued)

69

	2000	2001	2002	2003	2004	2005	2006	2007	2008	2009	2010	2011	2012
Seychelles	32.00	45.17	53.43	59.47	65.92	70.97	83.14	90.88	107.50	126.77	130.99	137.90	147.80
Sierra Leone	0.29	0.62	1.49	2.39	2.62	1.95	0.38	14.17	17.98	20.21	34.09	36.43	36.96
Somalia	1.08	1.12	1.28	2.51	6.12	5.98	6.43	6.87	7.03	7.03	6.95	18.17	22.56
South Africa	18.63	23.77	29.78	36.16	44.13	71.06	82.06	86.60	91.24	93.34	100.48	123.20	130.56
South Sudan	n.a	n.a	n.a	n.a	n.a	n.a	n.a	n.a	n.a	n.a	15.09	17.34	21.22
Sudan	0.07	0.30	0.53	1.44	2.80	4.76	11.90	20.36	28.95	36.11	40.54	68.78	74.36
Swaziland	3.10	5.12	6.28	7.81	13.24	18.10	22.37	33.54	46.22	56.15	61.78	63.24	65.39
Tanzania	0.32	0.79	1.69	3.53	5.14	7.63	14.05	20.09	30.77	40.14	46.80	55.37	56.96
Togo	1.04	1.93	3.27	4.71	6.29	8.02	12.80	21.06	26.82	37.06	40.69	41.64	49.86
Tunisia	1.26	4.08	5.96	19.72	38.06	57.31	73.26	77.42	83.95	94.52	106.04	115.20	118.11
Uganda	0.52	1.13	1.52	2.91	4.23	4.63	6.84	13.83	27.30	28.99	38.38	47.50	45.00
Zambia	0.97	1.16	1.30	2.20	4.15	8.28	14.16	21.89	28.59	34.63	41.62	59.88	74.78
Zimbabwe	2.13	2.50	2.69	2.88	3.38	5.15	6.78	9.82	13.29	31.99	61.25	68.87	91.91

III.b *ICT*: Number of internet users (per 100 inhabitants)

	2000	2001	2002	2003	2004	2005	2006	2007	2008	2009	2010	2011	2012
Algeria	0.49	0.65	1.59	2.20	4.63	5.84	7.38	9.45	10.18	11.23	12.50	14.00	15.23
Angola	0.11	0.14	0.27	0.37	0.46	1.14	1.91	3.20	4.60	6.00	10.00	14.78	16.94
Benin	0.23	0.36	0.70	0.95	1.18	1.27	1.54	1.79	1.85	2.24	3.13	4.15	4.50
Botswana	2.90	3.43	3.39	3.35	3.30	3.26	4.29	5.28	6.25	6.15	6.00	8.00	11.50
Burkina Faso	0.08	0.16	0.20	0.37	0.40	0.47	0.63	0.75	0.92	1.13	2.40	3.00	3.73
Burundi	0.08	0.11	0.12	0.20	0.35	0.54	0.66	0.70	0.81	0.90	1.00	1.11	1.22
Cameroon	1.82	2.69	3.52	4.32	5.32	6.07	6.81	8.28	14.00	21.00	30.00	32.00	34.74
Cape Verde	0.25	0.28	0.36	0.59	0.98	1.40	2.03	2.93	3.40	3.84	4.30	5.00	5.70
Central African Rep.	0.05	0.08	0.13	0.15	0.22	0.27	0.31	0.38	1.00	1.80	2.00	2.20	3.00
Chad	0.04	0.05	0.17	0.32	0.36	0.40	0.58	0.85	1.19	1.50	1.70	1.90	2.10
Comoros	0.27	0.44	0.55	0.85	1.33	2.00	2.20	2.50	3.00	3.50	5.10	5.50	5.98
Congo, Dem. Rep.	0.03	0.03	0.16	0.46	1.08	1.46	2.01	2.76	4.29	4.50	5.00	5.60	6.11
Congo	0.01	0.01	0.09	0.13	0.20	0.24	0.30	0.37	0.44	0.56	0.72	1.20	1.68
Cote d'Ivoire	0.23	0.40	0.50	0.76	0.85	1.04	1.52	1.80	1.90	2.00	2.10	2.20	2.38
Djibouti	0.19	0.34	0.49	0.63	0.78	0.95	1.27	1.62	2.26	4.00	6.50	7.00	8.27
Egypt, Arab Rep.	0.64	0.84	2.72	4.04	11.92	12.75	13.66	16.03	18.01	25.69	31.42	39.83	44.00
Equatorial Guinea	0.13	0.17	0.32	0.52	0.84	1.15	1.28	1.56	1.82	2.13	6.00	11.50	13.94
Eritrea	0.14	0.16	0.23	0.07	0.12	0.19	0.29	0.41	0.47	0.54	0.61	0.70	0.80
Ethiopia	0.02	0.04	0.07	0.11	0.16	0.22	0.31	0.37	0.45	0.54	0.75	1.10	1.48
Gabon	1.22	1.35	1.94	2.66	2.98	4.89	5.49	5.77	6.21	6.70	7.23	8.00	8.62

(continued)

	2000	2001	2002	2003	2004	2005	2006	2007	2008	2009	2010	2011	2012
Gambia, The	0.92	1.34	1.80	2.44	3.31	3.80	5.24	6.21	6.88	7.63	9.20	10.87	12.45
Ghana	0.15	0.20	0.83	1.19	1.72	1.83	2.72	3.85	4.27	5.44	7.80	14.11	12.30
Guinea	0.10	0.18	0.40	0.45	0.51	0.54	0.64	0.78	0.92	0.94	1.00	1.30	1.49
Guinea-Bissau	0.23	0.30	1.02	1.35	1.81	1.90	2.06	2.21	2.35	2.30	2.45	2.67	2.89
Kenya	0.32	0.62	1.21	2.94	3.02	3.10	7.53	7.95	8.67	10.04	14.00	28.00	32.10
Lesotho	0.21	0.26	1.08	1.53	2.18	2.58	2.98	3.45	3.58	3.72	3.86	4.22	4.59
Liberia	0.02	0.03	0.03	0.03	0.03	0.10	0.24	0.55	0.53	0.51	2.30	3.00	3.79
Libya	0.19	0.37	2.24	2.81	3.53	3.92	4.30	4.72	9.00	10.80	14.00	14.00	14.00
Madagascar	0.20	0.22	0.34	0.42	0.53	0.57	0.61	0.65	1.65	1.63	1.70	1.90	2.05
Malawi	0.13	0.16	0.22	0.28	0.35	0.38	0.43	0.97	0.70	1.07	2.26	3.33	4.35
Mali	0.14	0.19	0.23	0.31	0.43	0.51	0.73	0.81	1.57	1.80	1.90	2.00	2.17
Mauritania	0.19	0.26	0.36	0.42	0.48	0.67	0.98	1.43	1.87	2.28	4.00	4.50	5.37
Mauritius	7.28	8.78	10.25	12.19	13.69	15.17	16.70	20.22	21.81	22.51	28.33	34.95	35.42
Morocco	0.69	1.37	2.37	3.35	11.61	15.08	19.77	21.50	33.10	41.30	52.00	46.11	55.42
Mozambique	0.11	0.16	0.26	0.42	0.68	0.85	0.84	0.91	1.56	2.68	4.17	4.30	4.85
Namibia	1.64	2.42	2.63	3.36	3.80	4.01	4.40	4.84	5.33	6.50	11.60	12.00	12.94
Niger	0.04	0.11	0.13	0.16	0.19	0.22	0.29	0.39	0.70	0.76	0.83	1.30	1.41
Nigeria	0.06	0.09	0.32	0.56	1.29	3.55	5.55	6.77	15.86	20.00	24.00	28.43	32.80
Rwanda	0.06	0.24	0.29	0.36	0.43	0.56	1.23	2.12	4.50	7.70	8.00	7.00	8.02
Sao Tome and Principe	4.64	6.31	7.58	10.16	13.32	13.76	14.18	14.59	15.48	16.41	18.75	20.16	21.57
Senegal	0.40	0.98	1.01	2.10	4.39	4.79	5.61	7.70	10.60	14.50	16.00	17.50	19.20

(continued)

	2000	2001	2002	2003	2004	2005	2006	2007	2008	2009	2010	2011	2012
Seychelles	7.40	11.02	14.30	14.59	24.27	25.41	34.95	38.38	40.44	40.44	41.00	43.16	47.08
Sierra Leone	0.12	0.16	0.18	0.19	0.20	0.22	0.23	0.24	0.25	0.26	0.58	0.90	1.30
Somalia	0.02	0.08	0.12	0.38	1.05	1.08	1.10	1.12	1.14	1.16	1.16	1.25	1.38
South Africa	5.35	6.35	6.71	7.01	8.43	7.49	7.61	8.07	8.43	10.00	24.00	33.97	41.00
South Sudan	n.a	n.a	n.a	n.a	n.a	n.a	n.a	n.a	n.a	n.a	n.a	n.a	n.a
Sudan	0.03	0.14	0.44	0.54	0.79	1.29	4.11	8.66	5.12	10.03	16.70	17.30	21.00
Swaziland	0.93	1.28	1.82	2.44	3.23	3.70	3.70	4.10	6.85	8.94	11.04	18.13	20.78
Tanzania	0.12	0.17	0.22	0.68	0.88	1.10	1.30	1.60	1.90	2.40	2.90	3.50	3.95
Togo	0.80	0.90	1.00	1.20	1.50	1.80	2.00	2.20	2.40	2.60	3.00	3.50	4.00
Tunisia	2.75	4.30	5.25	6.49	8.53	9.66	12.99	17.10	27.53	34.07	36.80	39.10	41.44
Uganda	0.16	0.24	0.38	0.46	0.72	1.74	2.53	3.67	7.90	9.78	12.50	13.01	14.69
Zambia	0.19	0.23	0.48	0.98	2.01	2.85	4.16	4.87	5.55	6.31	10.00	11.50	13.47
Zimbabwe	0.40	0.80	3.99	6.39	6.56	8.02	9.79	10.85	11.40	11.36	11.50	15.70	17.09

III.c *ICT*: Fixed (wired) broadband internet subscribers (per 100 inhabitants)

	2000	2001	2002	2003	2004	2005	2006	2007	2008	2009	2010	2011	2012
Algeria	0.00	0.00	0.00	0.06	0.11	0.41	0.51	0.85	1.41	2.34	2.54	2.60	3.00
Angola	0.00	0.00	0.00	0.00	0.00	0.00	0.04	0.07	0.09	0.11	0.10	0.12	0.20
Benin	0.00	0.00	0.00	0.00	0.00	0.00	0.02	0.01	0.01	0.02	0.04	0.04	0.05
Botswana	0.00	0.00	0.00	0.00	0.00	0.09	0.09	0.18	0.46	0.50	0.60	0.79	0.94
Burkina Faso	0.00	0.00	0.00	0.00	0.00	0.00	0.01	0.04	0.07	0.07	0.08	0.09	0.09
Burundi	0.00	0.00	0.00	0.00	0.00	0.00	0.00	0.00	0.00	0.00	0.00	0.00	0.00
Cabo Verde	0.00	0.00	0.00	0.00	0.06	0.20	1.56	1.51	1.66	2.43	3.22	4.35	4.02
Cameroon	0.00	0.00	0.00	0.00	0.00	0.00	0.00	0.00	0.00	0.00	0.01	0.05	0.06
Central African Rep.	0.00	0.00	0.00	0.00	0.00	0.00	0.00	0.00	0.00	0.00	0.00	0.00	0.00
Chad	0.00	0.00	0.00	0.00	0.00	0.00	0.00	0.00	0.00	0.00	0.00	0.13	0.16
Comoros	0.00	0.00	0.00	0.00	0.00	0.00	0.00	0.01	0.02	0.01	0.01	0.06	0.17
Congo, Dem. Rep.	0.00	0.00	0.00	0.00	0.00	0.00	0.00	0.00	0.00	0.01	0.01	0.00	0.01
Congo	0.00	0.00	0.00	0.00	0.00	0.00	0.00	0.00	0.00	0.00	0.00	0.01	0.01
Cote d'Ivoire	0.00	0.00	0.00	0.00	0.00	0.01	0.05	0.05	0.05	0.05	0.04	0.00	0.23
Djibouti	0.00	0.00	0.00	0.00	0.00	0.01	0.02	0.13	0.29	0.61	0.91	1.33	1.73
Egypt, Arab Rep.	0.00	0.00	0.07	0.08	0.11	0.19	0.34	0.62	0.98	1.31	1.76	2.32	2.83
Equatorial Guinea	0.00	0.00	0.00	0.00	0.00	0.03	0.03	0.03	0.03	0.03	0.17	0.19	0.20
Eritrea	0.00	0.00	0.00	0.00	0.00	0.00	0.00	0.00	0.00	0.00	0.00	0.00	0.00
Ethiopia	0.00	0.00	0.00	0.00	0.00	0.00	0.00	0.00	0.00	0.00	0.00	0.01	0.01
Gabon	0.00	0.00	0.00	0.01	0.05	0.11	0.13	0.14	0.15	0.25	0.27	0.28	0.31

(continued)

	2000	2001	2002	2003	2004	2005	2006	2007	2008	2009	2010	2011	2012
Gambia, The	0.00	0.00	0.00	0.00	0.00	0.00	0.01	0.02	0.02	0.02	0.02	0.03	0.03
Ghana	0.00	0.00	0.00	0.00	0.00	0.01	0.06	0.07	0.10	0.12	0.21	0.25	0.26
Guinea	0.00	0.00	0.00	0.00	0.00	0.00	0.00	0.00	0.00	0.00	0.01	0.01	0.01
Guinea-Bissau	0.00	0.00	0.00	0.00	0.00	0.00	0.00	0.00	0.00	0.00	0.00	0.00	0.00
Kenya	0.00	0.00	0.00	0.00	0.00	0.02	0.05	0.05	0.01	0.02	0.01	0.10	0.10
Lesotho	0.00	0.00	0.00	0.00	0.00	0.00	0.00	0.01	0.01	0.02	0.02	0.07	0.07
Liberia	0.00	0.00	0.00	0.00	0.00	0.00	0.00	0.00	0.00	0.00	0.00	0.00	0.00
Libya	0.00	0.00	0.00	0.00	0.00	0.00	0.16	0.16	0.75	1.01	1.15	1.15	1.09
Madagascar	0.00	0.00	0.00	0.00	0.00	0.00	0.01	0.01	0.02	0.02	0.03	0.03	0.04
Malawi	0.00	0.00	0.00	0.00	0.00	0.00	0.01	0.01	0.02	0.03	0.05	0.01	0.01
Mali	0.00	0.00	0.00	0.00	0.00	0.01	0.02	0.02	0.02	0.02	0.02	0.02	0.02
Mauritania	0.00	0.00	0.00	0.00	0.00	0.01	0.03	0.12	0.18	0.17	0.16	0.17	0.18
Mauritius	0.00	0.00	0.02	0.10	0.21	0.43	2.20	1.75	3.64	5.33	6.10	9.46	11.21
Morocco	0.00	0.00	0.01	0.01	0.21	0.82	1.28	1.54	1.54	1.50	1.56	1.84	2.10
Mozambique	0.00	0.00	0.00	0.00	0.00	0.00	0.00	0.03	0.05	0.05	0.06	0.09	0.08
Namibia	0.00	0.00	0.00	0.00	0.00	0.01	0.01	0.01	0.01	0.02	0.42	0.83	1.18
Niger	0.00	0.00	0.00	0.00	0.00	0.00	0.00	0.00	0.00	0.01	0.01	0.01	0.02
Nigeria	0.00	0.00	0.00	0.00	0.00	0.00	0.00	0.04	0.04	0.05	0.06	0.00	0.01
Rwanda	0.00	0.00	0.00	0.00	0.01	0.01	0.02	0.03	0.01	0.02	0.02	0.04	0.02
Sao Tome and Principe	0.00	0.00	0.00	0.00	0.00	0.00	0.08	0.20	0.24	0.28	0.34	0.40	0.41
Senegal	0.00	0.00	0.01	0.02	0.07	0.17	0.26	0.33	0.40	0.49	0.63	0.70	0.70

(continued)

	2000	2001	2002	2003	2004	2005	2006	2007	2008	2009	2010	2011	2012
Seychelles	0.00	0.00	0.00	0.00	0.42	1.14	2.94	3.36	3.20	4.56	7.26	9.80	11.03
Sierra Leone	0.00	0.00	0.00	0.00	0.00	0.00	0.00	0.00	0.00	0.00	0.00	0.00	0.00
Somalia	0.00	0.00	0.00	0.00	0.00	0.00	0.00	0.00	0.00	0.00	0.00	0.00	0.39
South Africa	0.01	0.01	0.01	0.04	0.13	0.35	0.69	0.77	0.86	0.97	1.48	1.75	2.11
South Sudan	n.a	n.a	n.a	n.a	n.a	n.a	n.a	n.a	n.a	n.a	0.00	0.00	0.00
Sudan	0.00	0.00	0.00	0.00	0.00	0.00	0.01	0.11	0.11	0.08	0.03	0.05	0.07
Swaziland	0.00	0.00	0.00	0.00	0.00	0.00	0.00	0.00	0.07	0.13	0.14	0.23	0.28
Tanzania	0.00	0.00	0.00	0.00	0.00	0.00	0.00	0.01	0.01	0.01	0.01	0.06	0.08
Togo	0.00	0.00	0.00	0.00	0.00	0.00	0.00	0.02	0.03	0.05	0.06	0.08	0.11
Tunisia	0.00	0.00	0.00	0.00	0.03	0.18	0.44	0.95	2.22	3.60	4.60	5.20	4.85
Uganda	0.00	0.00	0.00	0.00	0.00	0.00	0.00	0.01	0.02	0.02	0.16	0.10	0.11
Zambia	0.00	0.00	0.00	0.00	0.00	0.00	0.02	0.03	0.05	0.08	0.08	0.12	0.11
Zimbabwe	0.00	0.01	0.02	0.05	0.07	0.08	0.08	0.12	0.14	0.23	0.26	0.25	0.52

III.d *ICT*: International internet bandwidth (Mbps)

	2000	2001	2002	2003	2004	2005	2006	2007	2008	2009	2010	2011	2012
Algeria	9.5	86.3	156.3	156.3	156.3	156.3	156.3	156.3	3,200.0	20,000.0	36,000.0	36,000.0	108,600.0
Angola	1.1	2.0	7.0	7.0	7.0	68.0	191.0	290.0	300.0	600.0	1,200.0	1,200.0	2,000.0
Benin	2.0	2.0	2.1	47.0	47.0	47.0	47.0	155.0	155.0	205.0	622.0	622.0	1,110.6
Botswana	6.0	14.0	14.0	23.0	26.0	30.0	30.0	81.0	423.0	500.0	775.0	775.0	964.1
Burkina Faso	1.0	2.0	8.0	12.0	64.0	72.0	215.0	215.0	499.0	646.0	801.0	801.0	943.7
Burundi	0.3	0.6	4.0	4.0	4.0	4.0	4.0	10.0	15.5	124.0	152.5	152.5	520.0
Cabo Verde	1.0	2.0	3.0	8.0	10.0	14.0	68.0	68.0	155.0	310.0	465.0	465.0	697.5
Cameroon	0.3	0.3	9.0	45.0	100.0	155.0	155.0	155.0	200.0	322.0	322.0	322.0	387.5
Central African Rep.	0.5	0.5	0.5	1.0	1.5	1.5	1.5	1.5	16.0	16.0	18.0	18.0	18.8
Chad	0.3	0.3	0.5	0.5	3.5	3.5	5.5	6.0	19.0	19.2	19.2	19.2	19.3
Comoros	0.1	0.1	0.3	0.1	0.3	2.0	7.0	7.0	10.0	15.0	166.0	166.0	750.7
Congo	0.1	0.1	0.1	0.6	1.0	1.0	1.0	1.0	8.0	12.0	24.0	24.0	36.0
Congo, Dem. Rep.	2.0	2.0	5.0	5.0	5.0	5.0	5.0	5.0	13.0	17.0	110.0	110.0	321.9
Cote d'Ivoire	3.3	6.7	19.8	40.5	55.4	55.4	310.0	809.0	1,000.0	3,000.0	4,000.0	4,000.0	7,111.1
Djibouti	0.1	0.5	2.0	2.0	45.0	45.0	90.0	90.0	465.0	600.0	837.0	837.0	1,028.2
Egypt	30.6	335.0	645.0	925.0	1,240.0	3,784.0	7,897.0	13,292.0	24,665.0	63,863.0	90,558.0	90,558.0	151,147.9
Equatorial Guinea	0.1	0.1	1.0	1.0	8.4	16.8	16.8	16.8	32.0	57.0	171.0	171.0	329.5
Eritrea	0.5	1.0	2.0	2.0	6.0	6.0	8.0	12.0	24.0	30.0	30.0	30.0	32.5

(continued)

	2000	2001	2002	2003	2004	2005	2006	2007	2008	2009	2010	2011	2012
Ethiopia	1.0	2.0	10.0	10.0	42.0	58.0	118.0	245.0	500.0	897.0	3,333.0	3,333.0	7,232.3
Gabon	0.5	0.5	8.0	45.0	155.0	200.0	200.0	200.0	300.0	465.0	775.0	775.0	1,089.3
Gambia	0.1	0.1	2.0	2.1	2.1	9.0	45.0	62.0	68.0	116.0	169.0	169.0	234.5
Ghana	4.1	4.1	12.0	28.9	28.9	168.0	330.0	497.0	2,015.0	106.0	170.0	170.0	150.5
Guinea	0.1	0.1	2.0	2.0	2.0	2.0	2.0	2.0	85.0	100.0	150.0	150.0	183.8
Guinea-Bissau	0.1	0.1	0.1	0.1	0.1	0.1	2.0	2.0	2.0	2.0	2.0	2.0	2.0
Kenya	10.5	26.0	26.0	26.0	34.0	113.4	660.8	337.2	828.3	16,775.0	20,209.6	20,209.6	151,280.8
Lesotho	0.5	1.0	1.0	1.0	2.6	4.3	4.3	8.0	10.0	10.0	26.0	26.0	39.9
Liberia	0.1	0.1	0.3	0.3	0.3	0.3	0.3	0.3	6.0	14.0	55.0	55.0	133.1
Libya	2.0	2.0	6.0	6.0	40.0	100.0	124.4	310.0	500.0	9,240.0	10,000.0	10,000.0	68,540.8
Madagascar	3.0	3.0	6.0	20.0	34.0	34.0	100.0	150.0	155.0	230.0	261.0	261.0	314.8
Malawi	0.3	2.0	2.6	3.5	4.6	19.5	43.0	67.0	10.0	10.0	690.0	690.0	16,330.0
Mali	3.0	3.0	6.0	6.0	18.0	26.0	213.0	213.0	654.0	620.0	775.0	775.0	826.2
Mauritania	0.8	0.8	9.5	9.5	27.0	45.0	45.0	220.0	245.0	260.0	280.0	280.0	292.9
Mauritius	6.0	10.0	34.0	63.0	71.0	153.0	192.0	285.5	462.0	1,458.6	3,390.0	3,390.0	7,323.9
Morocco	118.0	136.0	310.0	310.0	1,240.0	7,100.0	11,500.0	25,130.0	25,130.0	51,200.0	75,000.0	75,000.0	112,556.2
Mozambique	3.0	4.5	11.5	18.5	18.5	19.0	72.0	72.0	282.0	602.0	1,280.0	1,280.0	2,244.7
Namibia	3.0	3.1	8.5	8.8	9.0	36.0	46.0	56.0	200.0	500.0	655.0	655.0	1,050.2
Niger	0.4	0.5	2.0	2.0	2.0	30.0	70.0	100.0	100.0	172.0	190.0	190.0	242.2
Nigeria	2.0	9.2	72.0	92.0	117.5	150.0	397.0	693.0	1,500.0	3,000.0	5,000.0	5,000.0	7,777.8
Rwanda	0.1	0.1	10.3	10.0	45.0	54.0	70.0	156.0	267.0	351.0	1,643.0	1,643.0	3,831.2

(continued)

	2000	2001	2002	2003	2004	2005	2006	2007	2008	2009	2010	2011	2012
Sao Tome and Principe	2.0	2.0	2.0	2.0	2.0	2.0	4.0	8.0	12.0	12.0	40.0	40.0	71.1
Senegal	36.0	48.0	79.0	310.0	465.0	775.0	1,240.0	1,705.0	2,900.0	4,660.0	4,800.0	4,800.0	5,819.1
Seychelles	2.0	6.0	6.0	6.0	14.0	23.5	26.0	44.0	74.5	149.0	185.5	185.5	262.5
Sierra Leone	0.5	0.5	0.5	0.5	0.5	0.5	0.5	0.5	0.5	0.5	170.0	170.0	18,928.4
Somalia	0.1	1.0	2.0	3.0	3.0	3.0	3.0	3.0	3.0	3.0	3.0	3.0	3.0
South Africa	348.0	475.0	564.5	625.5	881.5	881.5	2,485.0	3,380.0	9,967.0	30,000.0	130,000.0	130,000.0	361,541.5
South Sudan	n.a	n.a	n.a	n.a	n.a	n.a	n.a	n.a	n.a	n.a	n.a	n.a	n.a
Sudan	0.5	12.0	24.0	90.0	202.0	202.0	202.0	202.0	1,813.0	1,813.0	13,300.0	76,746.1	360,867.7
Swaziland	1.0	1.0	1.0	1.0	1.0	1.0	1.0	1.0	36.0	42.0	160.0	2,185.4	13,574.9
Tanzania	2.0	4.1	16.0	16.0	16.0	100.0	100.0	100.0	300.0	1,475.0	3,459.0	11,831.8	42,130.4
Togo	1.0	6.0	12.0	14.3	14.3	14.3	14.3	28.5	203.0	1,355.0	1,388.0	6,855.4	28,879.9
Tunisia	48.0	72.0	152.0	155.0	380.0	750.0	1,228.0	3,174.0	11,520.0	28,160.0	51,200.0	134,692.1	309,492.5
Uganda	1.7	5.1	7.7	10.0	60.5	60.5	133.0	344.4	369.0	1,172.0	3,608.0	8,810.8	25,541.6
Zambia	2.0	2.0	5.1	12.0	22.0	22.0	30.0	356.0	402.0	455.2	500.0	560.0	625.5
Zimbabwe	7.0	7.0	30.0	30.0	55.0	55.0	55.0	57.0	121.0	290.0	434.0	870.3	1,711.2

IV. Water & sanitation composite index (2000-2012)

	2000	2001	2002	2003	2004	2005	2006	2007	2008	2009	2010	2011	2012
Algeria	90.31	89.59	90.08	89.36	88.63	88.41	88.41	87.68	87.45	87.45	87.45	87.561	87.574
Angola	34.59	35.58	37.29	37.78	38.77	40.47	41.69	43.40	43.89	45.60	46.09	47.847	49.137
Benin	32.78	34.00	34.72	34.72	35.93	36.66	37.87	38.59	39.32	40.53	41.25	41.826	42.011
Botswana	74.93	74.93	75.92	76.41	77.62	78.12	78.61	79.60	80.09	80.58	80.58	81.122	81.280
Burkina Faso	29.43	31.37	32.81	34.75	36.69	38.13	39.35	40.80	42.73	44.67	46.12	47.615	49.185
Burundi	54.86	54.86	54.63	55.35	55.35	55.35	55.35	55.35	55.35	55.35	55.35	55.553	55.617
Cabo Verde	62.32	63.30	65.01	65.50	67.70	68.20	69.90	70.40	72.11	73.09	74.31	75.354	76.494
Cameroon	51.05	51.77	53.22	53.94	55.39	55.62	57.55	58.28	59.00	60.44	60.44	62.003	63.016
Central African Rep.	37.02	38.01	39.22	40.21	41.42	41.92	43.62	44.12	45.82	45.82	45.82	47.762	48.759
Chad	18.10	18.82	19.31	20.04	20.04	21.25	21.97	21.97	22.70	23.91	23.91	24.546	25.144
Comoros	60.93	61.42	63.13	63.63	64.84	66.55	67.04	67.04	67.04	67.04	67.04	67.282	67.378
Congo	41.09	41.81	41.81	41.32	41.32	41.32	40.83	40.83	40.83	40.83	40.83	40.664	40.578
Congo, Dem. Rep.	20.33	20.83	21.32	21.81	22.30	22.80	23.52	24.51	24.51	25.00	25.00	25.885	26.431
Cote d'Ivoire	47.14	47.86	47.86	47.86	48.58	49.07	49.07	49.07	49.07	49.07	50.29	50.006	50.279
Djibouti	69.48	69.71	69.45	68.95	69.18	69.41	69.15	69.87	68.89	68.89	68.89	68.964	68.957
Egypt	92.41	92.90	94.61	95.10	95.60	97.31	97.80	98.29	99.01	99.01	99.01	99.237	99.656
Equatorial Guinea	61.37	61.37	61.37	61.37	61.37	61.37	61.37	61.37	61.37	61.37	61.37	61.373	61.373
Eritrea	25.09	26.31	27.76	28.48	30.42	30.42	30.91	30.91	31.63	31.63	31.63	32.027	32.091
Ethiopia	6.04	7.26	9.20	11.14	12.35	14.29	16.72	18.66	19.87	22.30	22.80	25.187	26.998
Gabon	59.82	60.54	60.05	60.05	59.55	59.06	59.78	59.78	59.78	59.78	59.78	59.593	59.562

(continued)

	2000	2001	2002	2003	2004	2005	2006	2007	2008	2009	2010	2011	2012
Gambia, The	71.68	72.40	73.62	74.83	74.83	76.05	77.26	77.26	78.48	78.48	78.48	79.980	80.749
Ghana	36.89	38.33	39.55	40.76	42.21	43.65	44.37	45.10	46.31	48.25	49.70	50.129	51.267
Guinea	33.08	34.29	35.74	36.95	37.68	38.40	39.61	40.34	41.55	43.00	43.00	44.402	45.391
Guinea-Bissau	23.68	25.13	26.34	28.28	29.00	30.22	32.16	32.88	34.82	35.54	36.76	38.343	39.757
Kenya	32.03	32.52	33.24	33.24	34.46	35.18	35.90	36.40	37.12	37.84	39.06	39.231	39.897
Lesotho	50.78	50.78	50.06	50.55	50.55	49.83	49.83	49.83	50.55	49.83	49.83	49.749	49.689
Liberia	30.65	31.37	32.09	33.31	34.52	36.46	37.18	39.12	39.84	41.06	42.27	43.377	44.605
Libya	67.48	67.48	67.48	67.48	67.48	67.48	67.48	67.48	67.48	67.48	67.48	67.484	67.484
Madagascar	14.03	14.75	15.47	15.96	16.69	17.90	18.62	19.35	20.07	21.29	21.29	22.490	23.267
Malawi	48.13	49.57	51.74	53.68	55.12	57.06	59.00	60.44	62.38	63.60	65.77	67.380	69.092
Mali	22.76	23.49	25.42	26.87	28.81	30.25	31.70	33.64	34.36	36.53	37.74	39.445	41.014
Mauritania	19.91	21.35	21.85	23.06	23.78	25.00	25.72	26.94	28.87	29.60	29.60	29.554	29.620
Mauritius	96.06	96.06	96.06	96.06	96.06	96.06	96.06	96.06	96.06	96.06	96.06	96.057	96.057
Morocco	68.56	68.56	70.27	71.48	71.98	71.98	73.19	73.19	74.41	74.41	75.13	76.053	76.649
Mozambique	17.90	17.90	19.12	19.84	20.33	21.06	21.55	22.27	22.99	22.99	23.49	24.409	25.029
Namibia	52.98	54.20	55.64	56.37	58.30	59.03	60.24	61.69	62.41	63.63	63.63	65.304	66.385
Niger	14.45	15.17	15.90	16.39	17.11	18.33	19.05	19.05	20.50	20.50	20.50	21.906	22.613
Nigeria	35.71	36.43	37.15	36.66	37.38	37.61	36.89	37.61	38.34	37.84	37.84	38.366	38.508
Rwanda	51.51	52.00	53.22	52.99	52.99	53.48	54.47	54.47	54.96	55.45	54.73	55.712	56.028
Sao Tome and Principe	48.09	49.30	50.52	51.24	53.18	53.90	54.62	55.84	57.78	57.78	57.78	59.741	59.825
Senegal	50.52	51.74	51.74	52.23	53.45	53.94	54.66	55.88	55.88	57.09	58.31	58.519	59.302

(continued)

	2000	2001	2002	2003	2004	2005	2006	2007	2008	2009	2010	2011	2012
Seychelles	94.20	94.20	94.20	94.45	94.70	94.70	94.70	94.70	94.70	94.78	94.86	94.860	94.912
Sierra Leone	19.31	20.04	20.76	21.97	22.70	23.42	23.42	24.14	24.86	25.59	26.80	27.208	27.944
Somalia	7.39	7.39	8.84	8.84	9.56	10.28	11.50	12.22	12.22	12.94	12.94	13.208	13.599
South Africa	79.76	80.49	80.98	81.70	82.92	82.92	83.64	83.64	84.85	85.35	85.35	86.205	86.707
South Sudan	n.a	n.a	n.a	n.a	n.a	n.a	n.a	n.a	n.a	n.a	n.a	n.a	n.a
Sudan	38.76	37.55	37.55	37.55	36.82	36.82	36.10	36.10	36.10	35.38	35.38	35.640	35.721
Swaziland	43.86	45.30	47.24	48.46	49.90	51.84	53.29	54.73	55.95	57.88	60.05	61.337	63.019
Tanzania	24.11	24.11	24.11	24.11	24.11	24.60	24.60	23.88	23.88	23.88	23.88	24.008	23.990
Togo	26.80	27.53	27.53	28.25	28.25	28.97	28.97	29.69	30.42	31.14	31.14	31.553	32.015
Tunisia	85.61	86.83	87.55	88.53	89.26	90.47	90.47	90.47	90.47	90.47	90.47	91.914	92.257
Uganda	37.35	38.57	40.01	41.23	41.95	43.39	44.61	46.05	47.27	48.72	49.44	50.792	52.115
Zambia	42.84	43.56	43.56	44.28	45.01	46.22	45.73	46.45	47.67	48.39	48.39	49.089	49.617
Zimbabwe	58.18	58.67	58.67	58.18	58.18	58.18	57.45	58.18	58.18	57.68	58.18	57.854	57.810

IV.a WSS: improved water source (% of population with access)

	2000	2001	2002	2003	2004	2005	2006	2007	2008	2009	2010	2011	2012
Algeria	89.4	88.7	88.1	87.4	86.6	85.9	85.2	84.4	83.7	83.7	83.8	83.9	83.9
Angola	45.7	46.2	46.8	47.4	48.1	48.8	49.5	50.2	51	51.8	52.6	53.4	54.3
Benin	66.1	67	67.9	68.8	69.7	70.6	71.5	72.4	73.3	74.2	75.1	76	76.1
Botswana	94.8	95.1	95.3	95.5	95.7	95.9	96.1	96.2	96.4	96.6	96.8	96.8	96.8
Burkina Faso	59.9	61.8	63.6	65.4	67.3	69.1	71	72.8	74.6	76.4	78.2	80	81.7
Burundi	71.8	72.1	72.4	72.7	73	73.3	73.5	73.8	74.1	74.4	74.7	75	75.3
Cabo Verde	82.7	83.2	83.8	84.3	84.8	85.4	85.9	86.5	87.1	87.6	88.2	88.7	89.3
Cameroon	61.7	62.8	63.8	64.9	65.9	66.9	68	69	70	71	72.1	73.1	74.1
Central African Rep.	62.5	62.9	63.4	63.8	64.3	64.8	65.2	65.7	66.2	66.7	67.2	67.7	68.2
Chad	44.7	45.2	45.7	46.2	46.7	47.2	47.7	48.2	48.7	49.2	49.7	50.2	50.7
Comoros	92	92.5	93	93.5	94	94.6	95.1	95.1	95.1	95.1	95.1	95.1	95.1
Congo	69.2	69.5	70.1	70.6	71.2	71.7	72.2	72.8	73.3	73.8	74.3	74.8	75.3
Congo, Dem. Rep.	44	44.1	44.3	44.5	44.7	44.9	45.1	45.3	45.6	45.8	46	46.2	46.5
Côte d'Ivoire	77.5	77.7	77.9	78.1	78.3	78.6	78.8	79	79.2	79.5	79.7	79.9	80.2
Djibouti	82.3	83.3	84.2	85.2	86.1	87.1	88	88.9	89.9	90.8	91.8	92.1	92.1
Egypt	96.1	96.4	96.8	97.1	97.4	97.7	98	98.4	98.7	99	99.3	99.3	99.3
Equatorial Guinea	50.9	50.9	50.9	50.9	50.9	50.9	50.9	50.9	50.9	50.9	50.9	50.9	50.9
Eritrea	53.7	55.2	56.8	58.4	59.9	60	60	60.1	60.2	61	61	61	61
Ethiopia	29	30.9	32.7	34.6	36.5	38.4	40.3	42.1	44	45.9	47.8	49.6	51.5
Gabon	83.8	84.7	85.6	86.4	87.2	87.9	88.6	89.3	89.9	90.6	91.1	91.7	92.2

(continued)

	2000	2001	2002	2003	2004	2005	2006	2007	2008	2009	2010	2011	2012
Gambia	82.8	83.4	84.1	84.7	85.3	86	86.6	87.2	87.8	88.4	88.9	89.5	90.1
Ghana	70.8	72.3	73.7	75.2	76.6	78	79.4	80.8	82.1	83.4	84.7	85.9	87.2
Guinea	62.7	63.7	64.8	65.8	66.8	67.8	68.8	69.8	70.8	71.8	72.8	73.8	74.8
Guinea-Bissau	51.9	53.6	55.3	57.1	58.9	60.6	62.5	64.3	66.1	68	69.9	71.7	73.6
Kenya	51.8	52.7	53.5	54.4	55.2	56.1	56.9	57.7	58.5	59.3	60.1	60.9	61.7
Lesotho	79.1	79.3	79.4	79.6	79.8	80	80.2	80.4	80.6	80.8	81	81.2	81.3
Liberia	61.2	62.3	63.4	64.5	65.6	66.8	67.9	69	70.1	71.2	72.3	73.5	74.6
Libya	54.4	54.4	54.4	54.4	54.4	54.4	54.4	54.4	54.4	54.4	54.4	54.4	54.4
Madagascar	38.1	39	39.8	40.7	41.6	42.6	43.6	44.6	45.6	46.6	47.6	48.6	49.6
Malawi	62.5	64.4	66.3	68.2	70.1	71.9	73.8	75.7	77.6	79.4	81.3	83.2	85
Mali	45.5	47.3	49.1	50.9	52.7	54.5	56.3	58.1	59.9	61.7	63.6	65.4	67.2
Mauritania	40.4	41.4	42.5	43.5	44.5	45.5	46.5	47.5	48.6	49.6	49.6	49.6	49.6
Mauritius	99.2	99.3	99.3	99.4	99.4	99.5	99.5	99.6	99.6	99.7	99.7	99.8	99.8
Morocco	78.1	78.6	79.1	79.5	80	80.4	80.9	81.3	81.8	82.2	82.7	83.2	83.6
Mozambique	41.1	41.7	42.4	43.1	43.8	44.5	45.1	45.8	46.5	47.2	47.8	48.5	49.2
Namibia	79.1	80.3	81.4	82.5	83.6	84.6	85.7	86.7	87.7	88.8	89.7	90.7	91.7
Niger	42.2	43	43.8	44.6	45.4	46.2	47.1	47.9	48.8	49.6	50.5	51.4	52.3
Nigeria	54.8	55.7	56.5	57.3	58.1	58.9	59.7	60.5	61.2	61.9	62.6	63.4	64
Rwanda	66.2	66.8	67.4	67.8	68.1	68.5	68.8	69.1	69.4	69.8	70.1	70.4	70.7
Sao Tome and Principe	78.2	80	81.8	83.5	85.3	87	88.7	90.4	92.1	93.7	95.3	97	97
Senegal	66.4	67	67.6	68.3	68.9	69.5	70.2	70.8	71.5	72.1	72.8	73.4	74.1

(continued)

	2000	2001	2002	2003	2004	2005	2006	2007	2008	2009	2010	2011	2012
Seychelles	96.3	96.3	96.3	96.3	96.3	96.3	96.3	96.3	96.3	96.3	96.3	96.3	96.3
Sierra Leone	47.3	48.3	49.4	50.4	51.5	52.5	53.6	54.7	55.7	56.8	57.9	59	60.1
Somalia	23.5	24.4	25.3	26.3	27.3	28.4	29.5	30.7	30.9	31.2	31.5	31.7	32.2
South Africa	86.8	87.6	88.3	89.1	89.8	90.5	91.2	91.9	92.5	93.2	93.8	94.5	95.1
South Sudan	n.a	n.a	n.a	n.a	n.a	n.a	n.a	n.a	n.a	n.a	56.5	56.5	56.5
Sudan	62	61.3	60.6	59.9	59.1	58.4	57.7	57	56.3	55.6	54.9	55.4	55.5
Swaziland	51.9	53.7	55.5	57.4	59.2	61	62.9	64.7	66.6	68.4	70.3	72.2	74.1
Tanzania	54.3	54.3	54.2	54.1	54	53.9	53.8	53.7	53.6	53.5	53.4	53.3	53.2
Togo	53.4	53.9	54.4	54.9	55.5	56	56.6	57.1	57.7	58.3	58.8	59.4	60
Tunisia	89.4	90.1	90.8	91.5	92.1	92.8	93.4	94	94.7	95.3	95.9	96.4	96.8
Uganda	56.5	58	59.4	61	62.5	64.1	65.6	67.1	68.7	70.2	71.7	73.2	74.8
Zambia	53.1	53.9	54.8	55.7	56.6	57.5	58.3	59.2	60.1	60.9	61.7	62.5	63.3
Zimbabwe	79.5	79.6	79.6	79.6	79.6	79.7	79.7	79.7	79.7	79.8	79.8	79.9	79.9

IV.b *WSS*: improved sanitation facilities (% of population with access)

	2000	2001	2002	2003	2004	2005	2006	2007	2008	2009	2010
Algeria	92	92	93	93	93	94	94	94	95	95	95
Angola	42	44	46	47	49	51	52	54	55	57	58
Benin	9	10	10	10	11	11	12	12	12	13	13
Botswana	52	52	54	55	56	57	58	60	61	62	62
Burkina Faso	11	12	12	13	14	14	15	15	16	17	17
Burundi	45	45	46	46	46	46	46	46	46	46	46
Cameroon	49	49	49	49	49	48	49	49	49	49	49
Cape Verde	44	46	48	49	52	53	55	56	58	60	61
Central African Republic	22	24	25	27	28	29	31	32	34	34	34
Chad	10	10	11	11	11	12	12	12	12	13	13
Comoros	28	29	31	32	33	35	36	36	36	36	36
Congo	20	20	20	19	19	19	18	18	18	18	18
Congo, Democratic Republic of the	16	17	18	19	20	21	21	23	23	24	24
Côte d'Ivoire	22	22	22	22	22	23	23	23	23	23	24
Djibouti	60	59	57	56	55	54	52	52	50	50	50
Egypt	86	87	89	90	91	93	94	95	95	95	95
Equatorial Guinea	89	89	89	89	89	89	89	89	89	89	89
Eritrea	11	12	12	12	13	13	14	14	14	14	14
Ethiopia	9	10	11	12	13	14	16	17	18	20	21
Gabon	36	36	35	35	34	33	33	33	33	33	33

(continued)

86

	2000	2001	2002	2003	2004	2005	2006	2007	2008	2009	2010
Gambia	63	63	64	65	65	66	67	67	68	68	68
Ghana	10	10	11	12	12	12	12	12	13	14	14
Guinea	14	15	15	16	16	16	17	17	18	18	18
Guinea-Bissau	14	14	15	16	16	17	18	18	19	19	20
Kenya	28	29	29	29	30	30	30	31	31	31	32
Lesotho	25	25	25	26	26	26	26	26	26	26	26
Liberia	12	12	12	13	14	15	15	16	16	17	18
Libya	97	97	97	97	97	97	97	97	97	97	97
Madagascar	12	12	12	13	13	14	14	14	14	15	15
Malawi	46	46	46	47	47	48	49	49	50	51	51
Mali	18	18	19	19	20	20	20	21	21	21	22
Mauritania	21	21	22	23	23	24	24	25	26	26	26
Mauritius	89	89	89	89	89	89	89	89	89	89	89
Morocco	64	64	66	67	68	68	69	69	70	70	70
Mozambique	14	14	15	15	16	16	17	17	17	17	18
Namibia	28	29	29	29	30	30	31	31	31	32	32
Niger	7	7	7	8	8	9	9	9	9	9	9
Nigeria	34	34	34	33	33	32	32	32	32	31	31
Rwanda	47	48	49	50	50	51	53	53	54	55	55
Sao Tome and Principe	21	22	23	23	24	24	24	25	26	26	26
Senegal	45	46	46	47	48	49	49	50	50	51	52

(continued)

	2000	2001	2002	2003	2004	2005	2006	2007	2008	2009	2010
Seychelles	87	87	87	87.5	88	88	88	88	88	88	88
Sierra Leone	11	11	11	12	12	12	12	12	12	12	13
Somalia	22	22	22	22	22	22	23	23	23	23	23
South Africa	75	75	76	76	77	77	77	77	78	79	79
Sudan	27	26	26	26	26	26	26	26	26	26	26
Swaziland	52	52	53	54	54	55	55	55	56	57	57
Tanzania	9	9	9	9	9	10	10	10	10	10	10
Togo	13	13	13	13	13	13	13	13	13	13	13
Tunisia	81	82	82	84	84	85	85	85	85	85	85
Uganda	30	31	31	32	32	32	33	33	34	34	34
Zambia	47	47	47	47	47	48	47	47	48	48	48
Zimbabwe	40	41	41	40	40	40	40	40	40	39	40

TWO

Rapid urbanization and the growing demand for urban infrastructure in Africa

Charles Leyeka Lufumpa and Tito Yepes

Introduction

Achieving sustainable economic growth, as a means of lifting the continent out of poverty, is the principal objective of Africa's infrastructure agenda. The achievement of this goal relies on the productivity of firms and on ensuring better living conditions for individuals across the continent. Accordingly, strengthening the foundations for higher productivity in the main cities and ensuring a more even distribution of basic living standards may be considered as the two key pillars of an infrastructure agenda.

Firms concentrate in cities in order to benefit from agglomeration economies, namely lower production costs through leveraging economies of scale and network efficiencies.[1] By clustering, firms increase the demand for infrastructure, which will ensure that they reap cost savings from agglomeration. Roads, amenities, and services— information and communications technology (ICT), energy, and water and sanitation—are available in greater quantity and quality in cities compared with rural locations. Consequently, securing an appropriate level of investment in infrastructure will enhance the gains to be made from urban agglomeration.

While the components of a successful infrastructure agenda are already, to a greater or lesser extent, present in many African countries, they are often tainted by inefficiencies and low institutional capacity. As a consequence, productivity improvements demand an infrastructure agenda characterized by more efficient institutions, capable of providing the framework to build cost-effective and reliable infrastructure and the regulations to operate and maintain it.

The second axis for growth refers to a more even distribution in access to basic living conditions across Africa, in both rural and urban areas. An enabling strategy to enhance living conditions in cities entails framing not only a coherent urban agenda, but also a commensurate rural agenda, able to buffer the negative incentives for rural–urban migration. Cities experiencing a growing demand for basic services from unskilled immigrants face a long-term trend of economic deterioration. Their contribution to the productivity in the city is reduced while the city cannot afford to match their demands. Therefore, providing universal access to basic services across the whole urban system and its hinterland represents a macro mechanism for a healthy urbanization. This means adopting a broader vision of the type of technologies that can be utilized; the bundling of services wherever possible to increase effectiveness; making use of land planning instruments and policies that can respond to an increase in demand; and a complementary rural development strategy.

Framing an infrastructure agenda for Africa to address the challenges of the 21st century means addressing three dimensions of geographical aggregation: linking major population centers across the region; making cities more productive and better places to live ("more livable"); and finally, integrating rural areas through the spillovers of urban growth. This chapter focuses on the second level, that is, how infrastructure can be used to improve the productivity and livability of cities. It draws largely on the African Infrastructure Country Diagnostic (AICD) flagship report of 2009,[2] and its key messages on the need to improve institutional efficiency and effectiveness in order to scale up infrastructure services, and build a coherent urban agenda for sustainable economic growth.

The chapter contains four sections. The first elaborates on the idea of improving and strengthening institutions as a vehicle for increasing the productivity of firms and speeding up economic growth. The second develops in detail the elements of the urban agenda. The final section concludes the chapter by summarizing some key policy implications.

Africa's principal infrastructure challenge

Substantial investments are needed for the infrastructure agenda in Africa; however, the core issues are institutional in nature. Pouring additional funding into sectors characterized by high levels of inefficiency makes little sense. In order to promote a level of productivity among firms that is conducive to higher and sustainable economic growth, Africa needs to improve the capacity and efficiency of those institutions responsible for developing and managing infrastructure. The goal is not to reinvent existing institutions, but to reform them and support their evolution.

While the challenge varies greatly across African countries, there are three general directions in which to foster institutional advancements, namely: efficient spending; an enlarged regional approach to infrastructure investment; and an improved regulatory framework.

Regional approach to infrastructure investment for cost savings

The challenging economic geography[3] of Africa calls for a regional infrastructure perspective able to promote cross-country synergies and exploit economies of scale. There are over 20 African countries with less than five million inhabitants and almost 20 countries with economies of less than US$5 billion in gross domestic product (GDP). In addition, there are 60 international river basins and 15 landlocked countries. Therefore, what is required is a strategy that works at a regional level rather than solely within the borders of individual countries. For example, most African countries are too small to generate power efficiently and only a handful possess major hydro resources. These and other facts illustrate how upstream decisions can compromise downstream availability and underscore the urgency for regional, transboundary planning to reap cross-country synergies and efficiency.

"Thinking regionally" focuses on international transport corridors that provide maritime access for landlocked countries; regional fiber-optic networks that provide access to the internet and build the competitiveness of African industries and services; and strong regional hubs for air and sea transportation that can bolster the export potential, trade and tourism of a large number of countries.

Regional economic communities and pan-African institutions such as the New Partnership for Africa's Development (NEPAD) continue to play a vital role in this context. For example, the Program for Infrastructure Development in Africa, which is led by the African Union Commission, NEPAD Secretariat, and the African Development Bank (AfDB), is fully supported at national, regional, and international levels. Its aim is to construct a vision and strategic framework for the development of regional and continental infrastructure (energy, transportation, ICT and transboundary water resources) that will promote Africa's socioeconomic development and integration into the global economy. It also provides a framework for engagement with Africa's development partners willing to support continental infrastructure.

A regional approach is especially relevant for investments in energy and water because production in large scale is possible in countries where there is no sufficient demand, while there are countries with significant shortages of supply. With respect to energy, about 13 of 42 countries in Africa faced more than eight (the average sample) outages annually. This represents a major obstacle to doing business, curtails the continent's competitiveness, and has a negative impact on foreign direct investment flows. In some countries, power losses last approximately 13.5 hours. As a consequence, firms in Africa lose power, on average, for 7.3% of their annual sales.[4] The 48 Sub-Saharan countries with a population of 900 million by 2011 generate roughly the same amount of power as Spain (1.5 times), which has just 48 million people. Power consumption in Africa, is 317 kWh per capita annually, and excluding South Africa is 225 kWh. Recent estimates suggest that at the current pace of investment, by 2040 more than half a billion people in Africa will have no access to electricity, mainly in urban areas.[5]

For a major turnaround in the sector, the pace of investment in Sub-Saharan Africa was about 7 GW this decade of capacity per annum, and it is expected to increase to 10 GW in the 2020s and to 13 GW in 2030. This shows that the power sector is gradually expanding, but not enough to achieve the level of other developing countries. Developing cheaper energy through regional trade is one path to accelerate progress in the sector. Also, inefficiencies existing within numerous institutions have to be addressed. The direction for institutional reform should consider the international experience and a broad range of instruments including incentives, contracts, deregulation, and private sector participation. Nowadays there is substantial knowledge about what may not work; therefore it is important to avoid known mistakes.

In the water sector, a regional and multipurpose approach constitutes a promising way forward. Africa is failing to harness water for development, despite the fact that as a continent, it enjoys plentiful water resources of about 5.4 trillion cubic meters a year—yet just 3.8% of this figure has so far been developed and 300 million Africans lack access to safe drinking water. Yet only 200 cubic meters per capita of water storage is available in Africa to buffer high variability, compared with over 1,000 cubic meters per capita in most developed countries. In addition, less than 5% of agricultural land is irrigated and less than 10% of hydropower potential is captured.

Further, climate change could also have a devastating effect on water supplies in the continent, exacerbating the frequency of both droughts and floods. High population growth and increasing water scarcity is a dangerous combination, and underscore the need to increase water storage and consumption efficiency. Global warming of 2°C above pre-industrial temperatures could result in permanent reductions in annual per capita consumption of 4% to 5% for Africa.[6] Losses driven by climate change severely impact on agriculture also.

To remedy this situation, multipurpose regional infrastructure projects could involve several countries sharing both the benefits and costs. Coordination across countries is possible, provided it is based on international laws governing water-sharing to ensure equitable distribution of the benefits of common-pool water resources. The World Development Report 2010[7] on climate change comes up with the same overall conclusion. The world must act now, act together, and act differently, before costs go up and avoidable hardships are needlessly endured by poor and vulnerable people. Consequently, those living in Sub-Saharan Africa, as one the most vulnerable regions, should work together on this challenge.

Sixty of Africa's rivers cross national boundaries, making international cooperation on water resources management essential. One example of successful transboundary cooperation for water management is the Senegal River Basin Development Organization, established in 1972. It serves as a transboundary land–water management organization, covering the Senegal River basin in Mali, Mauritania, and Senegal. Its aims include: managing water for agriculture; promoting self-sufficiency in food; improving the incomes of local populations (35 million in total, of whom 12 million live in the river basin); and preserving the natural ecosystems, inter alia. Similar organizations include the Gambia River Basin Development Organization, the Komati Basin Water Authority, the Niger Basin Authority, Nile Basin Initiative, the Kagera River Basin Authority, and the Mano River Union, among others.

Improved regulatory frameworks for cost recovery

The regulatory environment is a vital part of the business-enabling environment. Clear and transparent rules and regulations can help to attract private investment and aid. On the other hand, when rules and regulations become unwieldy and unpredictable, they can represent an obstacle and even an opportunity cost for market participants. In the African context, regulatory frameworks for setting tariffs and governing competition among service providers need to be modernized. Perhaps the clearest sign of problems within regulatory frameworks in Africa is that despite the fact that infrastructure services are relatively expensive in Africa, production costs are even higher than prices. This lack of cost recovery has major detrimental effects on the sustainability and profitability of services. Under-pricing infrastructure services is estimated to cost Africa US$4.7 billion a year in revenues.

With respect to the energy sector, the existing regulatory frameworks need to be reformed to provide an enabling environment for increasing efficiency in energy investments and service delivery. In addition to a regional and coordinated investment strategy, Africa needs a redesigned subsidy scheme for the energy sector to tackle important institutional inefficiencies. Current programs use substantial resources but are ineffective in serving the poor. Another aspect of great importance is addressing flagrant deficiencies in the maintenance of assets.

As regards the regulatory frameworks governing the transportation sector in Africa, these are also sorely in need of reform. The focus should be on improving the *quality* of transportation networks and services rather than increasing physical quantity. For instance, trade facilitation measures such as one-stop border posts (OSBPs) are as important as good-quality roads for increasing transit speed and supporting the productivity of firms. The main quality concerns in Africa include a non-competitive trucking system that keeps transportation tariffs high, poor service, disconnected linkages across different transport modes, and significant safety gaps.

Seaports too—which are vital for Africa's international trade in high-volume, low-cost commodities—are badly in need of investment and regulatory reforms to remove the bottlenecks and chronic congestion problems. Ports in Africa experience institutional and regulatory constraints that create inefficiencies, hinder competition, and raise transaction costs. Furthermore, there is the specific challenge of the 15 landlocked countries that are handicapped not only by poor logistics to the hinterland, but also by cumbersome customs regulations and lengthy delays at borders. For these countries, median transport costs are almost 50% higher than the equivalent costs for coastal economies.[8]

The ICT sector has witnessed dramatic progress in Sub-Saharan Africa. Access to mobile cellular telephone increased from 12% in 2005 to 59.3% in 2012, access to broadband went from 0% to 0.2%, and the percentage of households with internet access at home went from 1.1% to 8.0% in the same period.[9] Such positive developments need to be supported by deregulation and reforms to promote intensified competition among service providers to bring down end-user prices and extend signal coverage still further. The low internet penetration rates have been accompanied by high tariffs, stemming mainly from a lack of high-capacity international networks. Africa relies on satellites and Very Small Aperture Terminal (VSAT) earth stations for most of its connectivity to the world wide web, which results in high prices.[10] Additional reforms should seek to promote private sector investment in fiber-optic backbones and competitive access to submarine cables.

Leveraging investment by improving efficiency in spending

Improving the current allocation of resources to infrastructure could help achieve substantial gains in the efficiency of infrastructure investments. Recently, external financing of infrastructure in Africa has quadrupled.[11] In order to leverage the benefits of these and future inflows of resources, efficiency considerations must be observed when developing policies for infrastructure.

According to the AICD report,[12] annual infrastructure investment needs in Africa are approximately US$93 billion, one-third of which should cover operations and maintenance. African governments, infrastructure users, the private sector, and external sources together contribute about US$45 billion a year to infrastructure. The financial gap is therefore sizable and requires appropriate management to maximize the value of local and foreign investments.[13]

Spending leakages associated with poor allocation decisions amount to nearly US$17 billion per year.[14] Such losses could be reversed by improving financial management and accountability. About US$7.5 billion could be saved by enhancing operational efficiency, while US$4.7 billion could be recovered by improved tariff setting, aiming at cost recovery. Similarly, US$3.3 billion could be recovered through improved prioritization of public projects, and about US$1.9 billion through actual spending of resources that are regularly budgeted but not executed.

While private finance tends to be limited to certain infrastructure niches, there are significant gains to be made from more efficient management, for which the private sector can contribute. Between 2001 and 2006, Africa received substantial private investments targeted to ICT (US$28 billion), thermal power generation (US$3 billion), and ports (US$3 billion). Such preferences reflect sectors where institutions are more developed and private management has made a difference with improved, more efficient services and higher-quality delivery.

Private management without complementary investment has also helped to narrow the efficiency gap in railroads, power, and water utilities, yielding significant gains to the infrastructure sector in general. Further private investment is needed in sectors such as alternative power technologies, water utilities, railroads, and highways, which often attract some portion of private financing in other regions of the world.

One of the most flagrant inefficiencies curbing sustainable economic growth is the failure to maintain infrastructure assets. Maintenance needs to be understood as an investment in asset preservation, which otherwise becomes more expensive to rebuild. Also, failing to maintain assets (such as roads) leads to deterioration of the quality of service, deterring users from the benefits they observed when the asset was built. In aggregate, where infrastructure is not maintained, the expected social and economic returns from investment erode.

Institutional reform should also go beyond utilities to strengthen relevant ministries' planning functions and address serious deficiencies in the budgetary process. As underscored in the AICD flagship report, better sector planning is needed in ministries responsible for infrastructure, to ensure that the construction of critical new assets begins early enough to come on line when needed. A cycle that will result also in better engineering designs thus better assets.

Infrastructure for more livable and productive cities

African cities are growing fast; however, due to insufficient infrastructure and poorly performing institutions, most new settlements are informal and lack access to basic services. This situation has severe consequences on health, education, incomes, market integration, and ultimately economic growth. In order to improve the living conditions of individuals across Africa, it is important to develop a coherent urban agenda that provides the right incentives for migration and proper conditions for livable and productive cities.

Improving living conditions in cities implies a strong focus on institutions. In this respect, a combination of land policy and planning, housing policies, and basic services coverage are key for a more equitable and inclusive urban expansion. The policy challenge is to harness market forces that encourage concentration and promote convergence in living standards between villages, towns, and cities. Policy decisions will be more effective if based on strategies for broad economic areas that integrate towns and cities with their surrounding rural hinterland.

This section of the chapter presents the main conclusions from the AICD analysis on facilitating urbanization.[15] First, it characterizes the typical African city development. Second, it introduces the idea that despite all the problems faced by cities, they represent the best hope for economic growth and the development of the continent. Third, it concludes that for urbanization to work, a coherent *rural* agenda also has to be developed. Fourth, rethinking the role of local governments will determine how effectively the region benefits from its cities. The differential cost of providing services across locations is strong evidence in favor of a more coherent vision for cities. Finally, the discussion reverts to a central tenet of the AICD, namely that building efficient and transparent institutions and reforming the regulatory framework are crucial to safeguarding the success of financial investments in infrastructure.

The pull of the city, urban sprawl, and informal settlements

Africa presents wide disparities in living standards across sub-regions and countries, and particularly between urban and rural areas. For household services, coverage rates in urban centers are five to 10 times higher than those in rural areas. Electricity and improved water supply (such as piped connections or standpipes) extend to the majority of the urban population, but to less than one-fifth of those living in rural areas. In addition, fewer than 40% of urban households enjoy a private water connection, a septic tank, or an improved latrine—and this proportion falls to just 5% in rural areas. Rural access to ICT services remains negligible. In almost one-half of African countries, energy coverage barely reaches 50% of the urban population and only 5% of the rural population.[16]

Such disparities boost migration towards urban settlements, where people can find better living conditions and benefit from proximity and access to bigger markets, including job markets. Between 1960 and 2015, the share of the continent's urban population increased from 19% to 40%, a trend that is expected to grow to around 47% by 2030. Rural migration accounts for one-fourth of that growth, with the remaining attributable to urban demographic growth and administrative reclassifications.[17] In several fragile states, civil war has contributed to urban expansion as people from the affected regions seek refuge and employment in cities.

The three main features of Africa's urbanization—a high concentration of people in large cities, urban sprawl, and informality—are examined in the sections that follow.

High population density in large cities

More than one-third (174.6 million) of Africa's urban population is concentrated in 56 megacities (that is, cities with more than 1 million inhabitants—see Annex for listing). Much of the remainder is spread across 232 intermediate cities of 100,000 to 1 million inhabitants and in peri-urban areas. The largest cities are growing fast, suggesting an even more concentrated urban population. However, because of insufficient infrastructure and poor institutions, most new settlements are informal and not covered by basic services.

Ensuring access to basic services for households in both urban and rural areas can improve sustainable urbanization and social equity, enhance living conditions, and prevent disproportionate flows of rural people to cities. It should be acknowledged that labor mobility can benefit both migration and destination areas when it responds to the needs of market forces, rather than to a lack of security and/ or basic services. Moreover, labor mobility can prompt convergence in living standards, as migration to denser and more productive areas balances income levels and exploits the benefits of knowledge clusters for both rural and urban locations. As rural and urban development are mutually dependent, the economic integration of rural and urban areas is the best way to produce growth and inclusive development.

Urban sprawl

The pattern of urbanization in Africa reveals strong physical growth and sprawl. This is typified by moderate and patchy densification within the inner-city core, as residential areas give way to commercial users and peripheral growth occurs in an unplanned, ad-hoc manner and at low density. Built-up areas of urban expansion are growing faster than urban populations in seven African cities, suggesting falling densities which, in turn, increase per capita infrastructure costs.[18] The highest per capita cost is found in secondary urban areas, where densities are high enough to demand better-quality solutions but still not high enough to benefit from significant economies of scale in the delivery of services.

Informality

In addition to sprawl, slums are growing faster than cities. Between 1990 and 2001, the slum population in Africa grew at an annual rate of 4.4%, faster than the total urban population. Informality characterizes land and housing markets, with about 62% of the urban population across the continent residing in slums.[19] If this trend persists, an additional 218 million Africans will be living in slums by 2020, accounting for almost one-third of the world's slum population.

Cities are the future of Africa

Cities represent the engines of growth. Their productivity is at least three times greater than that of rural areas. Rural areas contribute less than 20% of Africa's GDP while accounting for more than 60% of its population.[20] There is, though, a synergistic relationship between rural and urban areas, in that urban centers consume rural products and offer inputs for rural production, while rural areas serve as markets for goods and services produced in urban areas. So the expansion of urban markets is a key factor in raising the rural incomes in the hinterland.

In addition, cities create growth spillovers into their hinterlands. Areas within two hours' travel time of cities with at least 100,000 population seem to have diversified into non-agricultural activities.[21] Rural areas located between two and eight hours' travel time from such cities account for more than 62% of the agricultural supply and generate a surplus that can be sold to urban areas. In areas farther than eight hours from these cities, agriculture is largely for subsistence, and less than 15% of the land's agricultural potential is realized. Similarly, farmers closer to cities tend to use more and higher-quality fertilizers and pesticides and better equipment, resulting in clear improvements in productivity. Despite these dynamics, rural–urban links are constrained by inadequate transportation networks between products and markets, unreliable and costly sources of electricity and water provision, and limited coverage of ICT. Weak institutions exacerbate the impact of these constraints.

Consistent resource distribution across urban and rural areas

An African urban agenda demands adjustments to current investments to ensure a consistent resource distribution across urban and rural areas. Improving the quality and quantity of spending will maximize the complementarities between urban and rural development, counteract the failures of decentralization, and improve local authorities' revenues.

Recently, Africa has been investing around US$26 billion a year in infrastructure. Nearly 30% of these resources have gone to productive infrastructure (energy, ports, highways, and so on) which underpins the national economy, while 50% and 20% have been used to serve urban and rural areas, respectively. Most of this investment has been targeted at the energy sector to boost industrial generation and transmission. Additional spending is required to expand productive infrastructure at the national level, and to improve roads and distribution networks for basic services in rural and urban areas.

The AICD report proposes a change in emphasis from urban to rural investments. To meet its infrastructure needs, Africa would have to invest US$60 billion per year. Spatially, the split would be more evenly distributed, with 34% going to the productive infrastructure that underpins the national economy, 32% to urban areas, and 34% to rural areas.

As presented in Figure 2.1, rebalancing investment from urban to rural areas does not imply a reduction in urban spending. As discussed above, there are significant externalities and complementarities between urban and rural investments. For example, growth in urban and rural coverage of network infrastructure tends to be positively correlated. It is important to maintain connectivities to foster sustainable and balanced growth. In the figure, "national" refers to productive infrastructure underpinning the whole national economy, rather than specifically to urban or rural space (for example, the inter-urban trunk network, the national power interconnected system, major ports, and airports). "Urban" and "rural" refer to infrastructure that is primarily oriented toward servicing the needs of urban or rural inhabitants, respectively (for example, urban or rural household services, and urban or rural roads).

The role of local governments in local development

Local authorities should invest not only more, but more *wisely*. Municipal budgets are very small in relation to the total infrastructure

Figure 2.1: Spatial split of current spending versus investment needs

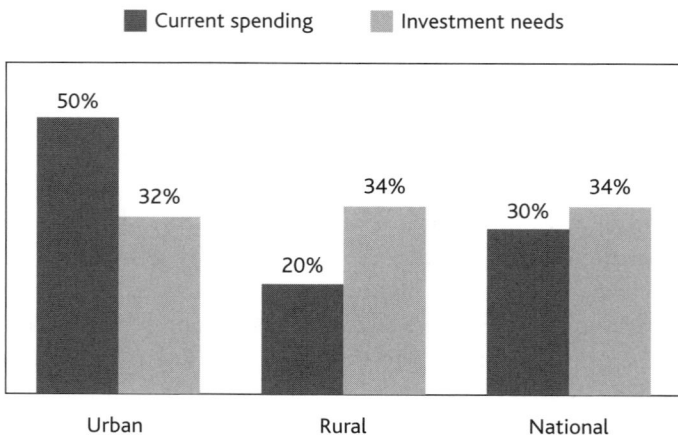

Sources: AfDB Data Portal; Foster, V. and Briceño-Garmendia, C. (eds) (2009) AICD Report, op. cit.

100

requirements occasioned by rapid urban growth. The purported benefits of decentralization have not been realized because decentralization policies have given cities more responsibilities (notably in social sectors), but without additional resources to fund them. Accordingly, municipalities lack sufficient funds to promote growth. Tax revenues, hampered by undeclared informal trade and the lack of clear property titles, are insufficient to cover investment needs. In big cities where the economic base is larger, tax receipts are often sent to central agencies, creating delays and inefficiencies in the process. Political factors often hinder the use of property taxes. Although African cities generate 80% of the national tax revenues, they receive less than 20% of the resources. They are reliant on central government for some 80% of their operating revenues. In sum, local governments lack the power and incentives to raise (and retain) their own revenue streams.

Cities need access to predictable streams of revenue; they also require the flexibility to raise additional resources in order to safeguard service provision to their populations. In addition, they need to improve their technical and managerial capacity to deal with evolving priorities in new investments, operations and maintenance, and to guide inevitable expansion. Cities should work to attract private partners and to better understand the constituency of their neighborhoods, to enable them to exploit potential synergies.

Improved and sustained revenue schemes in cities will translate into better household service coverage, which is currently quite low (as discussed later) and uncoordinated. Infrastructure investment continues to focus on sector-specific interventions rather than spatially synchronizing and concentrating the provision of different infrastructure services in larger "bundles". Access to multiple services leads to higher returns among beneficiary households compared with scenarios where services are provided individually.

Differential costs for service provision across locations

As economies of scale reduce production costs, greater concentrations facilitate increased access to basic services at lower prices. Furthermore, urban networks ease expansion toward rural areas. Evidence shows that the cost of expanding infrastructure networks in Africa is highly sensitive to population density, supporting the argument in favor of cities. As shown in Table 2.1 below, at the highest density, the cost of a bundle of high-quality services is US$325 per capita; for medium-density cities, it increases to US$665; for the rural hinterland, it is

Table 2.1: Capital cost per capita of infrastructure provision, by density (US$ per capita, unless otherwise noted)

Infrastructure type	Large cities						Secondary cities	Rural hinterland	Deep rural
Density (people/km²)	30,000	20,000	10,000	5,008	3,026	1,455	1,247	38	13
Water									
Private tap	104.2	124.0	168.7	231.8	293.6	416.4	448.5	1,825.2	3,156.2
Standpost	31.0	36.3	48.5	65.6	82.4	115.7	124.5	267.6	267.6
Borehole	21.1	21.1	21.1	21.1	21.1	21.1	21.1	53.0	159.7
Hand pump	8.3	8.3	8.3	8.3	8.3	8.3	8.3	16.7	50.4
Sanitation									
Septic tank	125.0	125.0	125.0	125.0	125.0	125.0	125.0	125.0	125.0
Improved latrine	57.0	57.0	57.0	57.0	57.0	57.0	57.0	57.0	57.0
Unimproved latrine	39.0	39.0	39.0	39.0	39.0	39.0	39.0	39.0	39.0
Power									
Grid	63.5	71.2	88.5	112.9	136.8	184.3	196.7	487.7	943.1
Mini-grid	87.6	95.2	112.5	136.9	160.8	208.3	220.7	485.8	704.2
Solar photovoltaic	92.3	92.3	92.3	92.3	92.3	92.3	92.3	92.3	92.3
Roads									
High quality	31.6	47.4	94.7	189.2	313.1	651.3	759.8	269.1	232.4
Low quality	23.6	35.4	70.7	141.2	233.8	486.3	567.3	224.3	193.6
ICT									
Constant capacity	1.1	1.7	3.3	6.6	10.9	22.8	26.6	39.8	129.7
Actual capacity	1.1	1.7	3.3	6.6	10.9	22.8	26.6	129.7	422.1
Total									
Variable quality*	325	369	480	665	879	1,031	1,061	940	836
Constant (high) quality**	325	369	480	665	879	1,400	1,557	2,837	4,879

Notes:

* For variable quality at total, technology differs by density and location as follows: (a) water—private tap in large cities, standposts in small cities, boreholes in secondary urban cities, hand pump in rural areas; (b) sanitation—septic tanks in large cities, improved latrines in small and secondary urban cities, traditional latrines in rural areas; (c) power—grid in urban areas, mini-grid in rural hinterland, solar in deep rural areas; (d) roads—high-quality scenario; (e) ICT—constant capacity in urban and rural areas.

** For constant (high) quality, the same technology—the most expensive one—applies at any density except for power (grid at any level of density).

Sources: AfDB Data Portal; Foster, V. and Briceño-Garmendia, C. (eds) (2009) AICD Report, op. cit.

US$2,837; and for isolated areas US$4,879. Countries with faster expansion of urban coverage of water and electricity also tend to have faster expansion of rural coverage, suggesting that urban customers cross-subsidize rural water networks and electrification.

Increasing infrastructure coverage in rural areas should also entail the building of complementarities across sectors. Bundling infrastructure services will increase the return of the investments and secure larger welfare gains to both rural and urban households. Such bundling maximizes the economic and social effect of services provision with improved access to economic opportunities, reducing the gap between poor and non-poor. A bundling strategy would also serve to maximize coordination and complementarities across sectors beyond the infrastructure field.

Improving the quality and quantity of infrastructure spending will forge a better path towards achieving Africa's Millennium Development Goals (MDGs), and will ensure the capability of response to the forthcoming demographic changes such as urbanization. Sub-Saharan Africa as a whole has accelerated progress on the MDGs for water supply and sanitation, but is not as close as other regions to achieving them. By 2012, Africa's access to improved water sources (excluding North Africa) increased by only 16 percentage points between 1990 and 2012, or less than one percentage point a year. Sanitation has had even smaller rates of growth, with a six percentage point increase in coverage over the past 22 years.[22]

The urban–rural divide in access to improved water source continues to be a policy challenge. Nonetheless, the proportion of rural households in Sub-Saharan Africa with access to drinking water sources increased from 54% to 65% from 1990–2006. In North Africa there was an improvement in piped water availability from 58% in 1990 to 83% in 2012.[23] Spending needed to meet what was the MDG target for water will require roughly 2.6% of Africa's annual GDP, while sanitation will require 0.9% of GDP per year.

For many countries, such spending levels are unaffordable, and current inefficiencies make them even more challenging. Spending in the water sector today totals about US$3.6 billion, one-fourth of what is required to meet the water targets. Despite such levels, nearly US$2.7 billion available to the sector is currently wasted in labor inefficiencies, under-collection of revenues, and distribution losses.

Regarding sanitation, few countries in Africa are investing in new sanitation facilities at the recommended level. Additionally, their spending on the operation and maintenance of existing facilities is inadequate.

Strengthening institutions vis-à-vis monetary investments for main cities

In many parts of Africa, formal land institutions and related legal and regulatory frameworks are still nascent. Limited land supply and high prices affect location decisions and exclude low-income households from the official land market. Land ownership is made more problematic by the extreme centralization of procedures, the costs and complexity of registering land, and ineffective land use policies and urban planning. These and other factors have encouraged the development of spontaneous settlements. Many governments have subsidized plots, but available supply is well below demand. Governments have tried to help residents excluded from land ownership and have expanded infrastructure to new settlements, but the results have been disappointing.

The limited size of the land market and the monopoly of traditional landowners lead to shortages of urban land supply and consequently to escalating prices. The lack of land titles impedes business development and the establishment of new firms. With no access to land and living in underserved and peripheral areas, the poor suffer from low levels of connectivity and access to labor markets. The resistance of landowners and lack of registries also prevent local authorities from raising revenues through taxes on urban land.

Lack of affordability and an insufficient supply of titled land make housing developments a solution restricted mostly to the middle class. Construction costs are very high, especially in landlocked countries. Cement, iron, and other materials are imported and costly to transport, making housing unaffordable. According to estimates, only one out of every five applications for new housing units is allocated to a needy household.

Land use authorization procedures are characterized by long delays and high transaction costs. Land acquisition delays are considerable in Ethiopia and Zambia. In Mozambique, businesses pay on average US$18,000 in processing fees for land, and in Nigeria, they must register land to use it as collateral, a process that can take up to two years and cost 15% of the land value.[24]

To help rectify the situation, land management institutions should include a comprehensive land registry, credible mechanisms for enforcement of land transactions and conflict resolution, flexible zoning laws, and versatile regulation of spatial subdivisions that help rather than hinder changes in land use according to the urban dynamics. Legislation that boosts land prices and excludes the poor should be revised. Lack of affordable, serviced plots and zoning policies have often excluded the poor from being integrated within the urban development.

Gender equality should also be mainstreamed into any reforms relating to land ownership, as traditionally women have been excluded in many African countries. Land rights tend to be held by men or kinship groups controlled by men, and women have access mainly through a male relative, usually a father or husband. Such access is tenuous and can be lost if, for example, the husband dies, leaving the widow landless and without a means of subsistence. In response, there is a need to introduce or strengthen laws intended to give women more secure access to land.

With respect to urban planning, this crucial function is needed to guide urban expansion and the associated infrastructure needs. When implemented properly, urban planning can prevent sprawl, deter development in precarious environmental areas, and ensure optimal delivery of affordable serviced land and infrastructure. Too often, though, urban planning is not included in the budgetary process, and master plans are rarely implemented. Because of a top-down approach and weak implementation, urban planning instruments have lost their relevance in many African cities. Urban dynamics are seldom correctly foreseen, and in most cases, decisions regarding the location of infrastructure and major developments are based on the political economy rather than coherent urban planning.

Urban planning should guide urban expansion and associated infrastructure needs. It should be flexible, participatory, and indicative (with a 10- to 15-year horizon). Urban reference maps should lay out the major roads and city services, the areas for urban expansion, and the reserves for amenities. Ideally, planning should be rooted in participatory strategies and linked to local and central budgets. Without realistic projections for resource availability, urban plans often fall into discredit. Dakar, Lagos, and Maputo are recent examples of cities where development strategies have been used as frameworks for encouraging community dialogue in discussing challenges and opportunities.

Institutional development pays off substantially, even when resources for investment are lacking. A strong "city effect" also exists. Thanks to leadership, land security, ownership, and civic participation, the inhabitants of Dakar's slums have living standards far superior to those in Nairobi, even though the latter enjoy higher incomes and education levels.[25] Learning from and expanding successful slum-upgrading programs should be used as tools to improve living standards. The Accra

District Rehabilitation Project in Ghana is an example of successful upgrading, as are several programs in Ethiopia, Kenya, and Uganda.

Elements for more productive and livable cities

The infrastructure agenda to make cities more productive and livable relies on the provision of sizable resources. However, matching the investment agenda to the goals of urbanization is a complex task, encompassing regional, national, urban, and rural dimensions which together determine the quality of the urbanization process. In this final section we highlight key elements of institutional reforms that should have a significant and positive impact on urbanization in Africa. We emphasize those recommendations that will contribute the most to the goals of productivity and livability in cities.

- *Adopt a solid analytical framework to help define priorities and sequencing.* Frameworks should integrate both urban and rural needs, specific to each area. In mostly rural areas, sound land policies and universal provision of basic services are critical goals. In areas where urbanization has accelerated, the emphasis should be on investments in connectivity. In heavily urbanized areas, targeted assistance to slum areas may be needed.

- *Recognize that the political economy influences the urban transition.* Local authorities do not have sufficient power to develop their cities because their budgets and responsibilities are restricted to basic services. Resources and decisions on other components that are crucial to the productivity of cities depend on the central government.

- *Be pragmatic.* While the long-term goal should be the achievement of well-defined property rights and land titling, some interim measures may be necessary. For example, cities need to be proactive in making land titling effective in the medium term, for example by using occupancy as a basis for land registration and taxation. Master plans will take significant time for implementation; begin with the components that are less expensive and will save investment resources in the future, such as the allocation of land for streets and network services along plots in expansion areas.

- *Focus on cities and areas important to the regional economy.* Sub-regional approaches can increase the impact of individual country efforts. To maximize the benefit from such approaches, national improvement and expenditure plans should focus first on primary economic drivers and related infrastructure, which will lead to overall growth for the sub-region.

- *Improve land policies so that markets are more flexible and can respond to the increase in demand.* A lack of clarity in land use regulation and in investment decisions across the urban space creates major uncertainties for landowners. This deters them from integrating their land into land markets, while stimulating rent-seeking behavior from those who are more influential. The aggregate effect is a market characterized by supply constraints, informality, and vacant land in the middle of dense areas.

- *Improve the fiscal soundness of cities.* Improve transparency and the predictability of transfers; strengthen and simplify local taxation; change the focus of property tax from ownership to occupancy; take advantage of cost recovery from revenue-producing services, such as markets and bus stations, as these can amount to 70% of medium-size city revenues; and use municipal contracts (between central and local governments) and establish street addresses to help local governments manage their resources.

Notes

[1] World Bank (2009) *World Development Report 2009: Reshaping Economic Geography*. Washington, DC: World Bank.

[2] Foster, V. and Briceño-Garmendia, C. (eds) (2009) *Africa's Infrastructure: A Time for Transformation* (AICD Report). Washington, DC: World Bank.

[3] "Economic geography" refers to the physical location of economic activities and population.

[4] World Bank, *Enterprise Surveys* (2015).

[5] OECD/IEA (2014) *Africa Energy Outlook: A Focus on Energy Prospects in Sub-Saharan Africa*. Paris: International Energy Agency.

[6] Nordhaus, W.D. and Boyer, J. (2000) *Warming the World: Economic Models of Global Warming*. Cambridge, MA; MIT Press. See also Stern, N. (2007) *The Economics of Climate Change* (Stern Report). London: HM Treasury.

[7] World Bank (2009) *World Development Report 2010: Development and Climate Change*. Washington, DC: World Bank.

[8] AfDB (2010) *African Development Report 2010: Ports, Logistics, and Trade in Africa*. Oxford: Oxford University Press.

[9] World Bank (2014) *The Little Data Book on Information and Communication Technology 2014*. Washington, DC: World Bank.

[10] AfDB and OECD (2009) *African Economic Outlook 2009*. Part II: Innovation and ICT in Africa, pp 81-137. Paris: Organisation for Economic Co-operation and Development.

[11] Foster, V. and Briceño-Garmendia, C. (eds) (2009) AICD Report, op. cit.

[12] Ibid.

[13] Current local investments come from taxes and tariffs and account for nearly one-third of the current annual spend.

[14] Foster, V. and Briceño-Garmendia, C. (eds) (2009) AICD Report, op. cit.

[15] Foster, V. and Briceño-Garmendia, C. (eds) (2009) AICD Report, op. cit.; see Chapter 5: Facilitating urbanization.

[16] Ibid.

[17] Farvacque-Vitkovic, C. et al (2008) *Africa's Urbanization for Development: Understanding Africa's Urban Challenges and Opportunities*. Washington, DC: World Bank.

[18] Schlomo, A., Sheppard, S.C. and Civco, D.L. (2005) *The Dynamics of Global Urban Expansion*. Washington, DC: Transport and Urban Development Department, World Bank.

[9] UN-Habitat (2013) *State of the World's Cities 2012/2013. Prosperity of Cities*. http://ww2.unhabitat.org/programmes/guo.

[20] Farvacque-Vitkovic, C. et al (2008), op. cit.

[21] Dorosh, P. et al (2008) *Crop Production and Road Connectivity in Sub-Saharan Africa: A Spatial Analysis*, Working Paper No. 19, Africa Infrastructure Country Diagnostic. Washington, DC: World Bank.

[22] UNECA, AU, AfDB and UNDP (2014) *MDG 2014 Report. Assessing Progress in Africa Toward the Millennium Development Goals*. Addis Ababa: Economic Commission for Africa

[23] *Ibid*.

[24] Kessides, C. (2006) *The Urban Transition in Sub-Saharan Africa: Implications for Economic Growth and Poverty Reduction*. Washington, DC: Cities Alliance.

[25] Gulyani, S., Debabrata, T. and Darby, J. (2008) *A Tale of Three Cities: Understanding Differences in the Provision of Modern Services*, Working Paper No. 10, Africa Infrastructure Country Diagnostic. Washington, DC: World Bank.

Annex

Table A2.1: African urban agglomerations of more than 1 million population in 2015

Country	Urban agglomeration	2015 (millions)
Algeria	El Djazaïr (Algiers)	2.59
Angola	Huambo	1.27
Angola	Luanda	5.51
Burkina Faso	Ouagadougou	2.74
Cameroon	Douala	2.94
Cameroon	Yaoundé	3.07
Chad	N'Djaména	1.26
Congo	Brazzaville	1.89
Côte d'Ivoire	Abidjan	4.86
Democratic Republic of the Congo	Kananga	1.17
Democratic Republic of the Congo	Kinshasa	11.59
Democratic Republic of the Congo	Kisangani	1.04
Democratic Republic of the Congo	Lubumbashi	2.02
Democratic Republic of the Congo	Mbuji-Mayi	2.01
Egypt	Al-Iskandariyah (Alexandria)	4.78
Egypt	Al-Qahirah (Cairo)	18.77
Ethiopia	Addis Ababa	3.24
Ghana	Accra	2.28
Ghana	Kumasi	2.60
Guinea	Conakry	1.94
Kenya	Mombasa	1.10
Kenya	Nairobi	3.91
Liberia	Monrovia	1.26
Libya	Tarabulus (Tripoli)	1.13
Madagascar	Antananarivo	2.61
Mali	Bamako	2.52
Morocco	Dar-el-Beida (Casablanca)	3.51
Morocco	Fès	1.17
Morocco	Marrakech	1.13
Morocco	Rabat	1.97
Mozambique	Maputo	1.19
Niger	Niamey	1.09
Nigeria	Abuja	2.44
Nigeria	Benin City	1.50
Nigeria	Ibadan	3.16
Nigeria	Kaduna	1.05

(continued)

Country	Urban agglomeration	2015 (millions)
Nigeria	Kano	3.59
Nigeria	Lagos	13.12
Nigeria	Onitsha	1.11
Nigeria	Port Harcourt	2.34
Rwanda	Kigali	1.26
Senegal	Dakar	3.52
Sierra Leone	Freetown	1.01
Somalia	Muqdisho (Mogadishu)	2.14
South Africa	Cape Town	3.66
South Africa	Durban	2.90
South Africa	Johannesburg	9.40
South Africa	Port Elizabeth	1.18
South Africa	Pretoria	2.06
South Africa	Vereeniging	1.16
Sudan	Al-Khartum (Khartoum)	5.13
Tunisia	Tunis	1.99
Uganda	Kampala	1.94
United Republic of Tanzania	Dar es Salaam	5.12
Zambia	Lusaka	2.18
Zimbabwe	Harare	1.50
Total		174.58

Source: United Nations (2014) *World Urbanization Prospects: The 2014 Revision.* New York, NY: United Nations.

THREE

Infrastructure for the growing middle class in Africa

Maurice Mubila and Tito Yepes

Introduction

During the first years of the century Africa experienced one of the highest growth rates in the world, even overcoming the financial crisis. The regional annual gross domestic product (GDP) growth rate climbed from 3% before 2000 to 6.5% in 2007. However during the following period and recent crisis, falling commodity prices, and lower export volumes, tinted perspectives for slower growth, which the continent seem to be managing well as real GDP growth in 2015 was 3.6%.

The African success has been accompanied with poverty reduction. The transformation suffered by Africa during recent years has reflected in an increase in trade, investment, and purchasing power of African households, as well as in the reduction of poverty. South Africa, Zambia, Ghana and Uganda were among the countries with highest poverty reductions (World Bank, 2009). In some countries poverty[1] decreased by 7% between 1990 and 2005.

Economic growth and poverty reduction entangle the growth of the middle class in all countries. In absolute terms, the middle class is defined as the population with a daily consumption between US$2 and US$20 (2005 Purchasing Parity Power [PPP]). It is composed of three different sub-classes. Individuals with consumption level between US$2 and US$4 per day, belong to the "floating class", just above the regular poverty line. Those with per capita consumption levels of US$4 to US$10 per day are the "lower-middle class" and finally the "upper-middle class" is composed of people with per capita consumption levels of US$10-US$20 per day (Mubila and Aissa, 2011). In relative terms, the middle class is composed by the population within the second, third and fourth quintile of the income or expenditure distribution.

Between 1980 and 2010 the middle class grew from 26% of the total population to 34%. The most dynamic group within the middle class is the "floating class". Not only has the "floating class" grown but the middle classes have also decreased during the past 20 years without sustained increases in the upper class. The relative high weight of the floating class implies some vulnerability of the middle class. Figure 3.1 shows the evolution of the "floating class" against the rest of the middle class. Between 1980 and 2010 the middle class reduced its participation from 15% to 13% in total population; the upper class remained at 5% after having increased to 7% by 2000, while the floating class jumped from 12% to 21%.

This represents a huge challenge for service provision because large investments have to be funded while protecting those on the verge of falling back into poverty. The growth of the middle class is associated with faster poverty reduction, the strengthening of democracy and the achievement of an inclusive growth among the population (Mubila and Aissa, 2011). Furthermore, the middle class is larger than the high-income class and has higher purchasing power in comparison to the poor class. However as the middle class has its larger component in the floating class, the contribution from charges to users is expected to be modest given the fact that they are likely to lack access.

Nevertheless, charges are important to secure sustainability of service of those with access so fresher investment resources can be devoted to expand access for those without services. As the middle class is achieving purchasing power and strength, now it is time to progress further with a longer run sustainability of living conditions. The gap in access among the middle classes to improved services like electricity or

Figure 3.1: Evolution of the floating class – the most dynamic subgroup within the middle classes of Africa

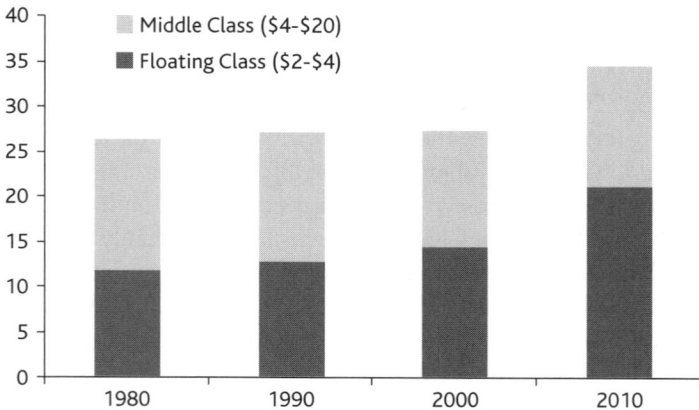

Source: Based on Mubila and Aissa, 2011

potable water should be closed rapidly as these groups can contribute to their financing. Greater contributions from the middle class through well-calibrated tariffs along with the same financial resources available today should allow for improvement in the overall sustainability of services provision. Sustainability is understood as the provision of quality services over years based on a revenue stream that is reliable and sufficient. If the revenue to operate services relies less on components tied up to economic growth like public expenditure and there is an expanded number of connections paying charges, the critical mass of revenues that make service provision sustainable can be achievable. This is a strategy that will allow households to continue benefiting from improved water or electricity even if the economy decelerates.

This chapter assesses the demand for infrastructure from the middle class of Africa. The goals are first, to inform the policy dialog on where the access gaps are and second, to understand to what extend different groups, within the middle class and across countries, can contribute further to the goal of sustainable service provision. Second, the chapter offers a characterization of accessibility conditions across sub-groups within the middle class, across countries, and across types of service provision. Third, an estimation of investment resources is presented. Fourth, the chapter reviews how much households spend on improved and alternative infrastructure services, and how many households would be able to afford subsistence consumption at cost recovery tariffs. The final section summarizes the conclusions.

Access to improved infrastructure services

Unimproved services are one of the biggest development challenges as recognized by both Millennium and Sustainable Development Goals declarations. Improved access is also linked to other development goals like health as demonstrated by the outbreak of typhoid in Zimbabwe. The Ministry of Health and Child Welfare indicated that most boreholes drilled in high-density suburbs were contaminated by bacteria that cause diarrheal diseases. Typhoid thrives in areas that do not have proper sanitation mainly through non-modern water provision facilities, such as boreholes. However, it was not the first time that waterborne diseases affected the country; in 2008 a cholera outburst killed about 4,000 people.

The picture repeats with different intensities across African countries. At present, access to improved infrastructure services in Africa is far from universal, while unimproved or moderated alternatives are widely used. On average, 25% of the population have access to electricity.

Most of the population (80%) use wood or charcoal as cooking fuel, while roughly 8% use electricity or gas cylinders. In the sanitation sector, most of the population (80%) does not have access to safe solutions while many use traditional pit latrines. In the water sector only 15% of the population have access to piped water and barely 19% have access to alternative improved sources as standposts or public taps. The remaining 64% use unimproved water sources such as wells, boreholes or surface water.

Not always lack of access is driven by supply constraints; sometimes there are cultural practices or market disincentives driving improvement decisions. For instance in the urban slums of Kisumu, Kenya, where half of the city's residents live, most landlords would rather build an extra room than a latrine; as a consequence most tenants end up using the bushes or open spaces. Due to weak regulations the rental market provides no premium for improved sanitation conditions, while it does for the number of people living in a dwelling. Further, not only does the market fail to encourage improved access but also, sometimes, signals from local public administrations are contradictory. At the Kashabo Primary School in Bukoba, Tanzania, toilets were not built until a year after its inauguration. Examples illustrating that in many instances lack of investment resources is not the main driver of the access gap.

The entanglement of supply gaps, market failures, and lack of affordability conditions results in the poorest families usually having lower access rates to improved infrastructure services. Figure 3.2 shows the dispersion and tendencies of access rates by quintile for selected infrastructure services when countries are grouped by national income. Vertical black lines establish minimum and maximum access rates for a given quintile across countries. Graphics are split into low, lower-middle or upper-middle income countries. The triangle shows the median value. Median values show the tendency of access across quintiles while minimum and maximum values determine the dispersion of these values across countries. It is worth noting that access to improved infrastructure services increases with income, unlike unimproved solutions, which have greater participation in the lowest quintiles. Large differences in coverage rates can also be observed between low-income and upper-middle income countries. However, access rates for the first quintiles are very similar across income areas, meaning that the disparities in access across quintiles are larger for richer countries.

Inequalities in access within the middle class are especially evident in access to improved water and sanitation and electricity. In low-income countries where access rates to improved services are low

Table 3.1: Access of the African middle class to infrastructure services (% of population with access by quintile)

		Q1	Q2	Q3	Q4	Q5	Total
Energy							
Electricity access	Electricity	2.26	9.23	14.65	30.30	68.18	**25.50**
Cooking fuel	Electricity	0.00	0.61	1.30	2.29	20.62	**5.31**
	LPG	0.01	1.93	6.03	9.50	21.01	**8.18**
	Kerosene/gasoline/gasoil/paraffin	0.04	1.97	3.55	6.30	8.18	**4.29**
	Wood/charcoal	99.96	93.92	87.29	78.78	48.84	**80.50**
	Residual/dung/other fuel	0.00	1.56	1.83	3.12	1.35	**1.72**
Water	Piped water	0.22	4.22	8.58	19.40	47.83	**14.90**
	Public tap/standpost	7.02	15.30	21.65	25.57	26.37	**18.55**
	Water from vendor	0.25	0.84	0.92	1.81	2.12	**1.13**
	Well/borehole	50.73	50.22	47.05	41.74	18.55	**42.38**
	Surface water	41.38	28.41	20.22	10.58	4.06	**22.07**
	Other water and sanitation	0.40	1.00	1.57	0.90	1.07	**0.97**
Sanitation	Flush toilet/septic tank	0.05	1.09	2.27	12.31	35.03	**9.19**
	Vip latrine/san plat/chemical toilet/Blair[1]	1.12	3.55	13.63	15.11	24.15	**10.84**
	Traditional pit latrine	38.68	47.29	49.49	50.07	37.43	**44.50**
	Bucket/Pan	0.05	0.47	0.11	0.27	0.28	**0.23**
	No facility/Nature/Bush	59.84	46.86	34.01	21.51	2.78	**34.75**
	Other sanitation	0.26	0.73	0.49	0.73	0.32	**0.50**

Note: Based on last data available, 2001-2008. Estimates assume a constant access rate until 2009, based on population data from 2009.

[1] The Blair Toilet (a.k.a. Blair Latrine) is a pit latrine designed in the 1970s. It was a result of large-scale projects to improve rural sanitation in Rhodesia (now Zimbabwe) under UDI at the Blair Research Institute, and then deployed further during the 1980s after Zimbabwean Independence. There was mass deployment of the toilet design in the rural areas of the country. It was developed by Dr Peter Morgan.

Source: Africa Infrastructure Knowledge Program: National Database.

Figure 3.2: Access to selected improved infrastructure services by income area

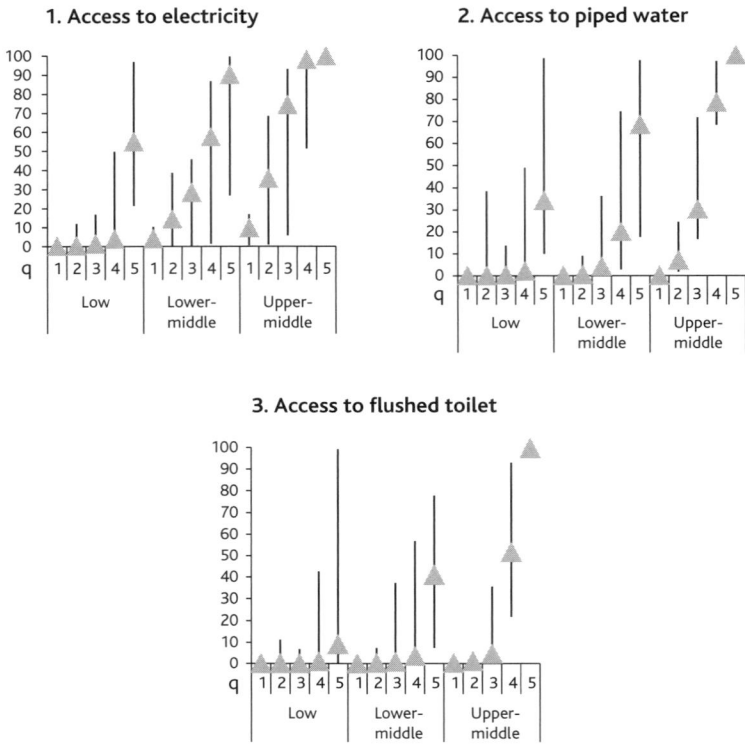

1. Access to electricity

2. Access to piped water

3. Access to flushed toilet

Source: Based on data from Africa Infrastructure Knowledge Program: National Database, African Development Bank website.

among middle classes, while in middle income countries only the upper-middle class observe high access rates. The poorest people of the middle class have low access rates to improved services. Access is strongly concentrated in the richest quintile. Rates of access to piped water vary six percentage points between quintile four and two for low-income countries, compared with 20 and 72 percentage points variation in lower-middle income and upper-middle income countries, respectively. Differences in the rates of access to flush toilets vary 85 percentage points within the middle class for the upper-middle income countries. Disparity of access to electricity is only five percentage points in low-income countries, but 40 and 60 percentage points respectively in lower- and upper-middle income countries. This can be seen in Figure 3.3 where triangles (representing the median) do not vary substantially between quintiles two, three and four in low-income countries and show greater variations for lower- and middle-income countries. Access is lower in low income countries but dispersion is lower.

Though gaps are greatly concentrated in the lower quintiles, there are still many households to be adequately served even in the higher quintiles. Despite the great disparities in access across countries and quintiles, even the richest segments of the population in the richest countries are lacking access to improved services. The highest access rate to infrastructure services in the fifth quintile is for electricity (71%), and is the only coverage rate for an improved service that is greater than 50%. For the fourth quintile all access rates to improved services are below 40%. Senegal, Cameroon, Nigeria and Côte d'Ivoire are the only lower-middle income countries to have access rates of over 70% for the middle class, and these values are only reached in access to electricity (from improved services) for all countries, and to piped water in Senegal. Within low-income countries only Rwanda and Madagascar have rates of over 70% for the fourth quintile in access to improved latrines. On the other hand, only two upper-middle income countries, Gabon and South Africa, have access rates of over 70% for the third quintile.

Alternative improved sources are largely used in the higher quintiles of low and lower-middle income countries, but barely used in upper-middle income countries. Access to alternatives to first best improved services in water and sanitation grow with income in low-income

Figure 3.3: Access to improved alternative infrastructure services in water and sanitation

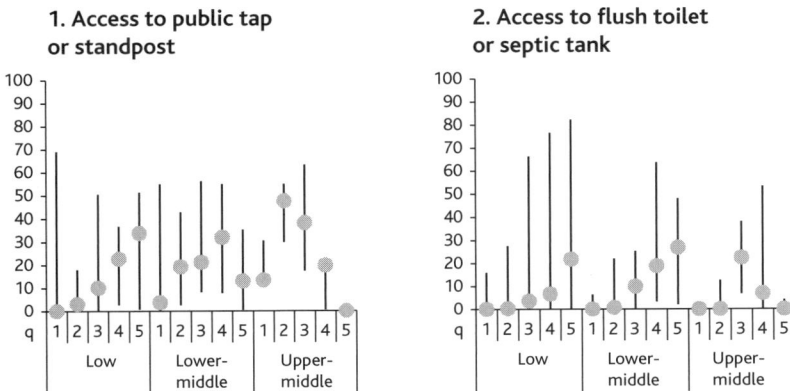

1. Access to public tap or standpost

2. Access to flush toilet or septic tank

Source: Based on data from Africa Infrastructure Knowledge Program: National Database, African Development Bank website.

countries, while decrease with income in the upper-middle income. Lower-middle income countries set a transition point between these two extremes. In these countries access rates tend to increase up until the fourth quintile, showing a sharp fall in the fifth. In the energy sector, improved services in terms of electricity and gas cylinders for cooking tend to have very low coverage rates in all income groups; high rates are only found in some countries in the fourth and fifth quintiles. Wood and charcoal tend to be the most used alternatives for all the middle class in low-income and lower-middle income countries.

In most of the regions, access rates to improved services are barely above zero for the three poorest quintiles. Results do not seem to be very dispersed except for few outliers. Figure 3.4 shows results for the minimum, maximum and median access rates by region. Triangles (which indicate median values) are placed at low levels on the vertical lines indicating that at least half of the observations are below these values. It is worth highlighting that with few exceptions, such as access to electricity in the Central region, the median values of access of the middle classes are roughly less than 10% in all improved services, especially in quintiles two and three. Of course with dispersion across countries as presented with the lines linking minimum and maximum values.

Investment requirements to provide access to the middle classes

More important than the known wide access gaps or its steep inequalities, is the potential to improve the funding coming from users to speed up expansion of coverage. But before turning to the potential contribution from the middle class, this section provides a ballpark estimate of investment requirements. Ballpark figures of the costs of closing access gaps in electricity and improved water and sanitation services are estimated by multiplying the number of missing connections by unitary costs of provision. Missing connections result from expanding access gaps by population using population projections from the United Nations World Population Prospects. Unitary costs are from Yepes (2008). Requirements for closing the gaps are estimated for three periods: the first period reflects the gaps up accumulated until 2009 by quintile, the second and third periods reflect further investment needed to keep up with population growth that will occur between 2009–2014 and 2014–2019, respectively.

Africa requires between US$19 and US$20 billion (2005 prices) per year to achieve full coverage in electricity by 2019. Covering today's

Figure 3.4: Access to selected improved infrastructure services by region

1. Access to electricity

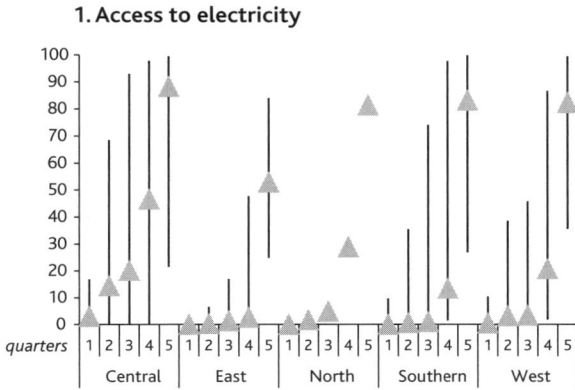

2. Access to piped water

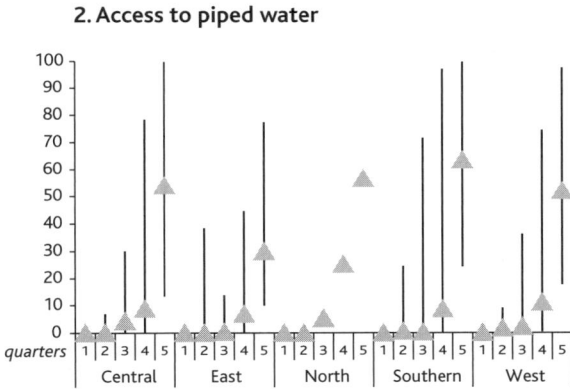

3. Access to flushed toilet

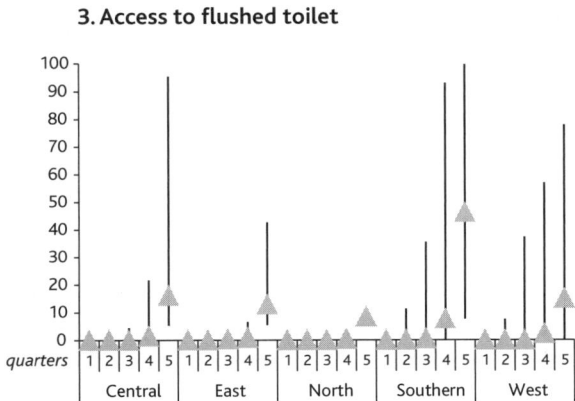

middle class requires about US$10 billion per year. Table 3.2 shows investment needs for the electricity sector. Investment gaps per quintile are estimated for the year 2009. For the years 2014 and 2019 the gap corresponds to total population growth and, therefore, investment needs are projected to be equally distributed across quintiles. On average, it will cost US$195 to connect each not serviced person according to Yepes (2008). Total investment needs to connect the African middle class to electricity are in the order of US$91 billion to US$99 billion, most of which pertain to low-income countries (US$51 billion), and the Eastern and Western regions (about US$30 billion each). An extra US$50 billion will be needed to support population growth by 2019, of which 60% corresponds to the middle class. Dividing by 10 for the years 2009 to 2019 translates into investment needs of about US$19 billion per year in total including US$10 billion only for the middle class.

Africa's supply of basic infrastructure services might fall short with the increasing demands of the growing middle class. The increase in purchasing power of the growing middle class brings an augmentation in the demand for non-food items such as houses, refrigerators, washing machines and other energy-using assets. In a recent article Gertler et al (2016) showed that households observing income increases that lead them out of poverty into the middle class use a significant share of their new budget to acquire energy-using assets such as refrigerators or washing machines. These new demands are translated into higher demand for energy both for production of appliances and their electricity consumption. Consequently, the relation between household income and its demands for infrastructure services has an "S" shape that grows faster when an income threshold is passed and stabilizes at the higher income levels.

Investment needs for access to improved water sum up to US$16 billion per year, while needs for improved sanitation reach US$17 billion to US$18 billion per year. The unitary costs used in Yepes (2008) establish provision of urban infrastructure for improved water services at US$80 per person, and US$150 for rural water and rural and urban sanitation. Table 3.3 shows investment needs for water and sanitation. In the 10-year span, investment requirements to supply the middle class with improved water services are about US$8.7 billion per year, and US$9.3 billion per year for improved sanitation. To fill the 2009 gap in access by the middle class about US$80 billion will be required for water and US$86 billion for sanitation. Because low-income countries have, on average, the smaller rates of access and concentrate a bigger share of the African population most of

Table 3.2: Investment needs for electricity connections (US$ in millions at 2005 prices)

Country	Requirements for closing access gap of 2009						Additional between 2010 and 2014	Additional between 2015 and 2019	Average per year between 2009 and 2019	
	Q1	Q2	Q3	Q4	Q5	Total	Total	Total	Middle class	Total
Central	3,825	3,268	2,837	2,244	1,365	13,539	2,783	2,903	949	1,923
East	10,651	10,527	10,259	9,549	5,150	46,136	7,576	8,021	3,345	6,173
North	6,489	6,383	6,170	4,613	1,208	24,863	2,721	2,398	1,819	2,998
Southern	6,133	5,826	5,476	4,402	1,754	23,592	3,348	3,581	1,709	3,052
West	11,091	10,025	9,532	7,313	2,884	40,846	8,102	8,858	3,026	5,781
Total	38,190	36,029	34,274	28,122	12,360	148,976	24,531	25,763	10,848	19,927

Sources: Africa Infrastructure : Knowledge Program: National Data, African Development Bank website for access rates; UN Population Projections 2010 Revision for population projections data. Data available online.

Table 3.3: Investment needs in water and sanitation connections (US$ in millions at 2005 prices)

Country	Requirements for closing access gap of 2009						Additional between 2010 and 2014 Total	Additional between 2015 and 2019 Total	Average per year between 2009 and 2019	
	Q1	Q2	Q3	Q4	Q5	Total			Middle class	Total
Improved water source										
Central	3,121	3,082	2,872	2,446	1,388	12,910	2,141	2,233	928	1,728
East	8,202	7,735	7,919	7,084	5,051	35,991	5,827	6,170	2,514	4,799
North	4,991	4,991	4,727	3,729	2,168	20,607	2,093	1,845	1,423	2,454
Southern	4,760	4,546	4,207	3,374	1,710	18,597	2,575	2,755	1,319	2,393
West	8,772	8,545	8,256	7,040	3,818	36,431	6,232	6,814	2,645	4,948
Total	29,846	28,900	27,980	23,673	14,135	124,535	18,870	19,817	8,829	16,322
Improved sanitation										
Central	3,121	3,116	3,096	2,979	2,199	14,511	2,141	2,233	1,007	1,889
East	8,199	8,198	8,162	8,025	6,801	39,386	5,827	6,170	2,679	5,138
North	4,991	4,991	4,991	4,970	4,572	24,515	2,093	1,845	1,574	2,845
Southern	4,779	4,684	4,513	3,564	2,268	19,808	2,575	2,755	1,383	2,514
West	8,786	8,688	8,386	8,057	6,258	40,175	6,232	6,814	2,774	5,322
Total	29,877	29,677	29,149	27,595	22,098	138,396	18,870	19,817	9,416	17,708

Sources: Africa Infrastructure : Knowledge Program: National Database, African Development Bank website for access rates; UN Population Projections 2010 Revision for population projections data. Data available online.

the investment needs are concentrated in this group of countries. Similarly, they are also highly concentrated in East and West Africa. The coverage rates in these regions are not the smallest but neither are they particularly high; however, each of them do concentrate about 30% percent of the population.

Household spending on infrastructure services

Low-income groups spend less on infrastructure services in absolute terms but more as a proportion of their total expenditure. Figure 3.5 shows household spending on infrastructure services by quintile. The first column shows average spending in US dollars, and the second column shows spending on infrastructure services as a percentage of

Figure 3.5: Household spending on infrastructure services by quintiles

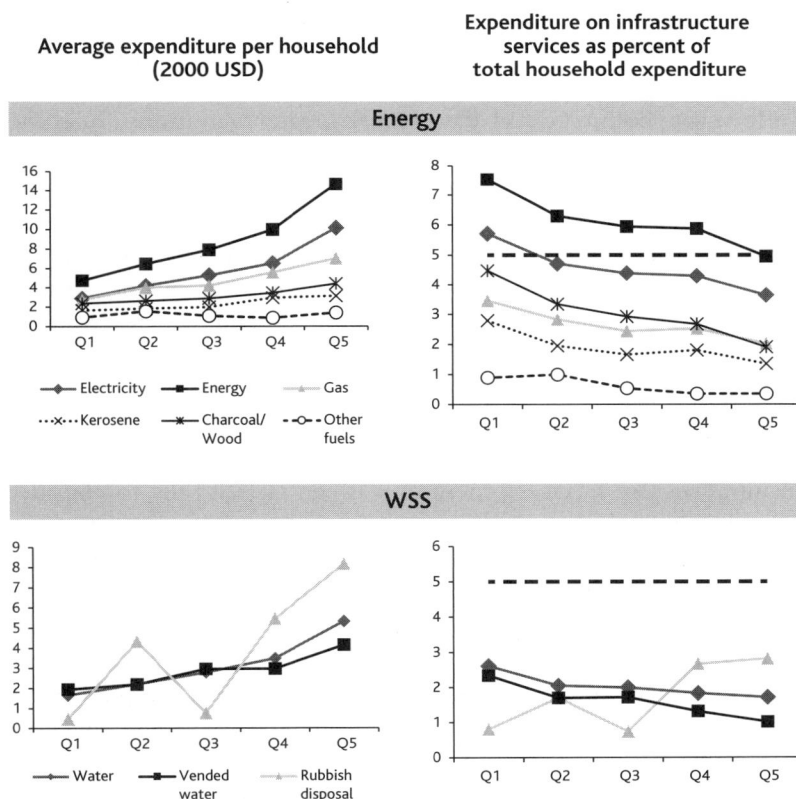

Average expenditure per household (2000 USD)

Expenditure on infrastructure services as percent of total household expenditure

Energy

WSS

Note: Based on last data available, 2001-2008. Estimates show non weighted averages.
Source: Africa Infrastructure Knowledge Program: National Data, African Development Bank.

total household spending. Except for spending on rubbish disposal, spending for all the other services is greater the higher the quintile. In the energy sector, households in the first quintile spend between US$0.92 and US$4.75 per month; this range increases, reaching US$1.38-14.67 for households in the fifth quintile. The highest spending in the sector is on electricity, followed by gas, wood/charcoal kerosene and other fuels. For comparison, the greatest household spending is on cell phones. The poorest households spend around US$2.5, while the richest spend on average US$22.2 on cell phones. Spending on water and vended water is similar in all quintiles: the poorest households spend US$1.65 and US$1.94, respectively, while the richest spend US$3.49 and US$2.97. Spending on rubbish disposal is greater the higher the quintile except for the third quintile.

With some exceptions, households do not spend more than 5% of their total expenditure on each utility service. Households spend between 5% and 8% of their total expenditure on energy, while expenditure on electricity is above the 5% threshold in the first quintile. Expenditure on water and rubbish disposal is below 3% of total spending.

However, country-level data reveal greater variations. In some countries, households spend as much as 40% on infrastructure services. In the four poorer quintiles the maximum share of total spending is found in Guinea-Bissau for energy services. Households' average spends range between 24% and 32% percent. There are 155 observations of 18 countries with expenditures in different infrastructure services that make up more than 5% percent of total spending. Fifty of these observations are greater than 10%.

Affordability conditions

In infrastructure services provision it is central not only to consider households that do not access improved services but also the extent to which such services can be financed over time after they are constructed. Excessive tariffs or low ability to pay can lead to unsustainable operation of services or low access rates; utility companies may be unable to recover their operational costs while potential consumers may not be able to afford to pay the bill. Simple lack of payment capacity has been largely documented. Evidence collected by the International Poverty Centre for Inclusive Growth shows that in some countries such as Gambia, Kenya, Guinea, Mozambique, Nigeria, Zimbabwe, and South Africa, contracts have been terminated or services disputed due to the lack of financial sustainability of the

Table 3.4: Household spending of the African middle class on infrastructure services

	Average expenditure per household (US$) (2005 prices)						Expenditure on infrastructure service as a percentage of total household expenditure					
	Q1	Q2	Q3	Q4	Q5	Total	Q1	Q2	Q3	Q4	Q5	Total
Energy												
Electricity	2.89	4.20	5.28	6.54	10.15	**5.81**	5.71	4.72	4.39	4.30	3.63	**4.55**
Energy	4.75	6.47	7.90	9.97	14.67	**8.75**	7.53	6.30	5.94	5.88	4.95	**6.12**
Gas	2.75	4.01	4.20	5.59	7.03	**4.76**	3.45	2.83	2.44	2.52	2.02	**2.64**
Kerosene	1.62	1.84	1.97	2.93	3.12	**2.30**	2.79	1.95	1.65	1.80	1.35	**1.91**
Charcoal/Wood	2.35	2.61	2.87	3.45	4.41	**3.14**	4.48	3.33	2.92	2.68	1.90	**3.06**
Other fuels	0.92	1.55	1.08	0.87	1.38	**1.16**	0.89	1.00	0.54	0.35	0.35	**0.63**
Water and sanitation services												
Water	1.65	2.20	2.79	3.49	5.33	**3.09**	2.61	2.05	2.00	1.84	1.71	**2.04**
Vended water	1.94	2.20	2.97	2.97	4.16	**2.85**	2.34	1.70	1.72	1.32	1.01	**1.62**
Rubbish disposal	0.45	4.33	0.76	5.45	8.16	**4.11**	0.80	1.71	0.74	2.67	2.82	**1.83**
Transport												
Transport	2.79	4.14	5.41	7.49	16.67	**7.30**	4.96	4.22	3.95	4.18	5.64	**4.59**

Note: Based on last data available, 2001-2008. Estimates show non-weighted averages.

Source: Africa Infrastructure Knowledge Program: National Database, African Development Bank.

local utility. For instance, a British company walked out of a water-supply contract in Zimbabwe, claiming its customers were too poor to pay for its services.

On the other hand, public protests are common in response to high tariffs introduced immediately in cases where utilities are taken over by private sector providers. Despite the fact that operational margins are already negative under the public tenure, governments expect to stop paying past inefficiencies immediately. In cases such as these, where margins under public tenure are already operating at a loss, governments expect to relinquish responsibility for past inefficiencies immediately, a situation that results in a vicious circle with users demanding on the utility company to reduce tariffs. For example, in the aftermath of reform in Nigeria electricity prices increased more than 800%, while water prices almost doubled following reforms in Guinea.

The objective of analyzing additional contributions from users is to check to what extent those with access can contribute to make utilities financially sustainable for operators while keeping tariffs affordable for consumers. There is a difficult equilibrium between contributing to the financial sustainability and being able to pay. To analyze the extent to which households can afford improved utility services, it is necessary to establish how much the household should pay to meet basic consumption needs under recovery tariffs, and what proportion of the household's total expenditure these bills constitute. A rule of thumb to determine whether households can afford the bills is to compare the share of expenditure with a threshold above which it would be unlikely that the household could pay.

There is no objective method to determine such threshold, although 5% has been considered reasonable by researchers (for example, Foster and Yepes, 2005; Banerjee et al, 2008) and has also been used by the World Health Organization. Furthermore, as pointed out earlier, on average the African middle class (quintiles 2 to 4 in each country) does not spend more than 5% on water or electricity services, which add the 5% criteria. Except for few countries (14 out of 51) spending on electricity as a proportion of total household expenditure is below 5 percent.

The cost of the bill is calculated based on minimum household consumption standards, and the minimum cost recovery tariffs. Banerjee et al (2008) establish reference points for monthly bills. For piped water, subsistence consumption ranges between 25 and 60 liters per day for a household of five. Tariffs are fixed at US$0.40 per cubic meter at operating cost recovery and at US$0.80 per cubic meter at full capital cost recovery. For electricity, minimum consumption has a lower bound of 25 kWh per month, which supports the use of two 100W light bulbs for four hours every day, and an upper bound of 50kWh per month, which supports limited use of an additional appliance, equivalent to a radio. Tariffs vary between US$0.08 and US$0.25 per kWh to reflect the different technologies used.

Taking these costs as a reference point, the purpose is to estimate the number of households that do not have access to the utility service and cannot afford to pay a tariff that recovers those costs.

Previous works have used data at the household level to estimate the fraction of African households that would not be able to pay cost-recovery tariffs. Foster and Yepes (2005) found this share to be 70%. Using a bigger sample and lower tariff bounds Banerjee et al (2008) conclude that this share is 60%. Banerjee et al (2008) also use continental quintiles to estimate the absolute expenditure at which the 5% affordability threshold would be hit. Their results show that the first quintile hits the threshold at US$4 per month, the second at US$7 per month and the remaining three quintiles reach it at US$12 per month or more, which would be enough to pay for water and electricity bills using the upper bound scenario and referring to the threshold for each infrastructure service.

However, to analyze affordability of the African middle class it is not enough to rely on continental quintiles. Continental quintiles capture the middle class defined in absolute terms, and are therefore biased by countries' income levels. For example, quintiles 2 to 4 can contain all households in a middle income country while containing no households of a high-income or low-income country.

Ideal estimations should be based on data at the household level; however, only aggregate indicators by quintile and country are available. Therefore, to estimate the unserved households that would not be able to afford the service, average household spending by

Table 3.5: Cost of infrastructure services at recovery costs

	Piped water		Electricity	
	Lower bound	Upper bound	Lower bound	Upper bound
Subsistence household consumption	4 m³	10 m³	25 kWh	50 kWh
Tariff (operating cost recovery)	US$0.40/m³	US$0.80/m³	US$0.08/kWh	US$0.25/kWh
Total monthly bill	US$2.00	US$8.00	US$2.00	US$12.00

Source: Banerjee et al (2008).

quintile and country is used as total spending for all households in each quintile and country. The result is a binomial categorization of quintiles in each country: those that would be able to afford the bills and those that would not be able to do so. Underserved households in each country that would not be able to afford the service are equal to the gap in those quintiles categorized as not able to afford the bill.

With few exceptions, the middle class would be able to afford piped water and electricity bills if the lower bounds are used. When using upper bounds, some countries would be able to pay for piped water services but fewer would be able to pay for electricity. Table 3.6 shows the results of affordability at the country level. A plus symbol means the referred quintile in that country would be able to pay the bills at the stated bound and using a 5% threshold for each service. A minus symbol reflects non-affordable. If lower bound recovery tariffs are used, only the second quintile in Mozambique would not be able to afford piped water or electricity services. However, if upper bounds are used only few quintiles within the middle class would be able to afford the subsistence consumption at recovery tariffs. For water services third and fourth quintiles would be able to afford the bills in Senegal, Republic of Congo and Madagascar. In Gabon all the middle class would be able to afford water services and electricity services. The fourth quintiles in Côte d'Ivoire and Madagascar would be able to afford piped water and electricity services, respectively.

Similar outcomes are obtained for aggregates since they mimic country-level results. When the upper bound tariffs are used most of the underserved households are not able to afford the services. However, when lower bound recovery tariffs are used, most of the lower-middle and upper-middle class are potentially profitable consumers. Table 3.7 shows the number of households that will not be able to afford recovery tariffs. Only 2,2 million middle-class households would not be able to pay lower bound tariffs, which means that almost 107,2 million middle-class households without access to piped water would be able to afford it. In electricity, 87,3 million underserved middle-class households would be able to afford lower bound recovery tariffs.

Estimates of the total underserved households in the continent, region or income group that would not be able to afford the service are the result of extrapolating the share of these households in the gap in each quintile using total continent, region or income group households in each quintile. Because Mozambique was the only country that could not afford the bills when lower bounds were used, the total households figure in Table 3.8 reflects the share of Mozambique's

Table 3.6: Quintiles that can afford piped water and electricity services at a 5% threshold of total spending, by country

By country (ordered from poorest to richest)	Lower bound					Upper bound				
	Q1	Q2	Q3	Q4	Q5	Q1	Q2	Q3	Q4	Q5
Piped water										
Congo, Dem. Rep.	+	+	+	+	+	–	–	–	–	+
Malawi	–	+	+	+	+	–	–	–	–	–
Niger	n.a.	n.a.	+	+	+	–	–	–	–	+
Mozambique	–	–	+	+	+	–	–	–	–	–
Madagascar	+	+	+	+	+	–	–	+	+	+
Uganda	–	+	+	+	+	–	–	–	–	+
Burkina Faso	+	+	+	+	+	–	–	–	–	+
Chad	+	+	+	+	+	–	–	–	–	+
Benin	+	+	+	+	+	–	–	–	–	–
Zambia	–	+	+	+	+	–	–	–	–	+
Senegal	+	+	+	+	+	–	–	+	+	+
Nigeria	–	+	+	+	+	–	–	–	–	–
Côte d'Ivoire	–	+	+	+	+	–	–	–	+	+
Cameroon	+	+	+	+	+	–	–	–	–	+
Congo, Rep.	+	+	+	+	+	–	–	+	+	+
Gabon	+	+	+	+	+	–	+	+	+	+
Electricity										
Malawi	–	+	+	+	+	–	–	–	–	–
Niger	n.a.	n.a.	+	+	+	–	–	–	–	–
Mozambique	–	–	+	+	+	–	–	–	–	–
Madagascar	+	+	+	+	+	–	–	–	+	+
Uganda	–	+	+	+	+	–	–	–	–	–
Burkina Faso	+	+	+	+	+	–	–	–	–	–
Chad	+	+	+	+	+	–	–	–	–	–
Benin	+	+	+	+	+	–	–	–	–	–
Zambia	–	+	+	+	+	–	–	–	–	–
Senegal	+	+	+	+	+	–	–	–	–	+
Nigeria	–	+	+	+	+	–	–	–	–	–
Côte d'Ivoire	+	+	+	+	+	–	–	–	–	+
Cameroon	+	+	+	+	+	–	–	–	–	–
Congo, Rep.	+	+	+	+	+	–	–	–	–	+
Gabon	+	+	+	+	+	–	+	+	+	+

Note: n.a.=not available.

Source: Authors' elaboration

Table 3.7: Underserved households that cannot afford recovery rates

Quintile	Lower bound	% of gap	Upper bound	% of gap
Piped water				
1	24,744,092	61.17	40,449,576	100.00
2	2,238,353	5.68	39,236,284	99.64
3	0	0.00	34,600,500	92.87
4	0	0.00	29,681,516	90.53
5	0	0.00	12,967,272	58.80
Total middle class (Q2+Q3+Q4)	**2,238,353**	**2.05**	**103,518,300**	**94.61**
Total	**26,982,445**	**15.69**	**156,935,148**	**91.28**
Electricity				
1	26,128,222	67.08	38,949,748	100.00
2	2,795,778	8.16	34,200,328	99.83
3	0	0.00	31,761,144	99.96
4	0	0.00	21,652,246	89.81
5	0	0.00	10,356,379	94.42
Total middle class (Q2+Q3+Q4)	**2,795,778**	**3.10**	**87,613,718**	**97.19**
Total	**28,924,000**	**20.65**	**136,919,845**	**97.76**

households that would not be able to afford the services over the gap in all low-income countries or Southern African countries.

Conclusions and recommendations

The most dynamic group within the middle class is the "floating class" as demonstrated by its high population growth and the slight decrease of other middle classes have had during the past 20 years. The upper class has maintained its participation. Such situation represents a substantial challenge for service provision because investments requirements may need to be funded without major contribution from charges to groups of users as to protect those facing the threat of falling back into poverty.

Notwithstanding, all financing sources should be considered jointly in order to secure sustainability while progressing towards closing the access gap. The contribution from charges to users may be modest in the beginning given the size of investment needs. However, it is important to make an effort in that front as soon as possible so service provision is financially sustainable while tariffs give the right signals to users' consumption. Delay in charging tariffs aiming to cost recovery also make it more difficult to implement reforms later on. The relief of acquiring access compared with the costs of unimproved sources

Table 3.8: Households that would not be able to afford cost recovery bills by income area and region using the lower bound scenario

	Q1	Q2	Q3	Q4	Q5	Total middle class	Total
Piped water							
By income area							
Low	7,064,689	2,341,783	0	0	0	2,341,783	9,406,472
Lower-middle	13,664,961	0	0	0	0	0	13,664,961
Upper-middle	0	0	0	0	0	0	0
By sub-region							
Central	0	0	0	0	0	0	0
East	11,003,677	0	0	0	0	0	11,003,677
North	n.a.	n.a.	n.a.	n.a.	n.a.	0	0
Southern	4,854,480	2,017,078	0	0	0	2,017,078	6,871,558
West	9,897,449	0	0	0	0	0	9,897,449
Africa	**24,744,092**	**2,238,353**	**0**	**0**	**0**	**4,034,157**	**55,545,369**
Electricity							
By income area							
Low	10,512,606	3,481,557	0	0	0	3,481,557	13,994,163
Lower-middle	11,425,007	0	0	0	0	0	11,425,007
Upper-middle	0	0	0	0	0	0	0
By sub-region							
Central	0	0	0	0	0	0	0
East	10,992,393	0	0	0	0	0	10,992,393
North	n.a.	n.a.	n.a.	n.a.	n.a.	0	0
Southern	4,722,240	1,909,845	0	0	0	1,909,845	6,632,085
West	8,200,532	0	0	0	0	0	8,200,532
Africa	**26,128,222**	**2,795,778**	**0**	**0**	**0**	**3,819,689**	**51,650,019**

Notes: Totals by income area, regions and continent are not compatible because different weights are used when extrapolating. n.a.=not available.

Source: Authors' elaboration

Table 3.9: Households that would not be able to afford cost recovery bills by income area and region using the upper bound scenario

	Q1	Q2	Q3	Q4	Q5	Total middle class	Total
Piped water							
By income area							
Low	18,161,598	18,024,296	16,003,638	15,020,604	2,524,320	49,048,538	69,734,456
Lower-middle	17,008,488	16,808,026	15,741,850	12,767,822	8,525,022	45,317,698	70,851,208
Upper-middle	5,225,493	0	0	0	0	0	5,225,493
By sub-region							
Central	4,495,401	4,423,302	4,208,985	3,947,036	0	12,579,323	17,074,723
East	11,003,677	10,966,920	10,820,595	9,691,584	0	31,479,099	42,482,776
North	n.a.	n.a.	n.a.	n.a.	n.a.	n.a	n.a.
Southern	6,863,220	6,175,718	3,392,995	2,579,830	1,249,438	12,148,542	20,261,200
West	11,547,568	11,361,485	10,907,681	9,270,693	6,667,098	31,539,859	49,754,525
Africa	**40,449,576**	**39,236,284**	**34,600,500**	**29,681,516**	**12,967,272**	**162,914,323**	**242,071,725**
Electricity							
By income area							
Low	18,150,712	18,024,316	17,897,894	14,523,192	7,888,932	50,445,402	76,485,046
Lower-middle	15,725,356	11,957,769	10,914,722	4,679,830	1,366,275	27,552,321	44,643,951
Upper-middle	4,876,184	0	0	0	0	0	4,876,184
By sub-region							
Central	4,424,553	3,892,744	3,220,169	1,949,099	933,304	9,062,012	14,419,868
East	10,992,393	10,972,294	10,878,873	10,636,687	5,402,341	32,487,854	48,882,588
North	n.a.	n.a.	n.a.	n.a.	n.a.	0	0
Southern	6,679,992	5,848,123	4,695,087	2,532,912	1,163,835	13,076,121	20,919,948
West	10,687,967	8,285,402	8,044,661	4,452,659	1,743,849	20,782,722	33,214,538
Africa	**38,949,748**	**34,200,328**	**31,761,144**	**21,652,246**	**10,356,379**	**141,755,405**	**220,454,015**

Notes: Totals by income area, regions and continent are not compatible because different weights are used when extrapolating. n.a.=not available.

Source: Authors' elaboration

fades with time establishing a new status quo people would not like to move from.

Still, one key element when reforming tariffs that integrate new users, such as the middle class, into the financing of infrastructure services is to preserve equity. If new users from the middle class, or more specifically from the floating class, are required to pay but cannot afford the charges, they will need to drop their connection. Well-calibrated charges have the advantage of recovering the maximum feasible revenue from low-income users without compromising their ability to benefit from the service.

The main equity issue arises from public investment allocated to provision of access because few benefit from it when access rates are low. The lucky few compared with the unserviced majority. An impact that however fades with access expansion, which is the main argument to implement user charges early on. On average, 25% of the African population have access to electricity. Most (80%) use wood or charcoal as cooking fuel, while roughly 8% use electricity or gas cylinders. In sanitation most of the population (80%) do not access improved solutions while many people use traditional pit latrines. In the water sector only 15% of Africans access piped water and barely 19% access alternative improved sources as standpost or public tap. The remaining 64% use unimproved water sources such as wells, boreholes or surface water.

In low-income countries very few people of the middle class have access to improved services, while in middle-income countries only the upper-middle class observe high access rates. The poorest people in the middle class have low access rates to improved services while access is strongly concentrated in the richest quintile. The use of alternative improved sources are largely used by the higher quintiles of low and lower-middle income countries, but barely used in upper-middle income countries. As income rises countries privilege first best solutions, which are however more expensive. The balance between speed in access expansion and the type of solution also plays a role in these sectors, especially when most sub-regions show access rates to improved services that are barely above zero for the three poorest quintiles.

The main issue continues to be financing. Africa requires between US$19 and US$20 billion (2005 prices) per year to achieve full coverage in electricity by 2019. Covering today's middle class requires about US$10 billion per year. Investment needs for access to improved water sum up to US$16 billion per year, while needs for improved sanitation reach US$17 to US$18 billion per year.

Some groups within the middle class can pay more. Low-income groups spend less on infrastructure services in absolute terms but more as a proportion of their total expenditure. Still with some exceptions, households do not spend more than 5% of their total expenditure in each utility service. Though country-level data reveal high variations, in some countries, households spend as much as 40 percent on infrastructure services.

With few exceptions, the middle class would be able to afford piped water and electricity bills using the lower bound scenario of tariffs. When using upper bounds, some groups would be able to pay for piped water services but fewer would be able to pay for electricity at the same time. Twenty-seven million households would not be able to afford cost-recovery water tariffs and 29 million cannot afford cost-recovery electricity tariffs. At least two-thirds are concentrated in the bottom quintile, which means that for tariffs that recover operational costs the middle class can afford the tariffs. If tariffs are designed to recover both operational and capital investments, the number of households lacking affordability conditions will multiply by five or six.

In funding the large size of investments that have been presented here to close the access gap, the middle class can contribute decisively to sustain the systems if proper revenue collection is done. However, their contribution seems to be limited to tariffs related to operational costs recovery, while full costs recovery seems harder to achieve. Anyway the recommendation is to integrate such contribution, even small as it is compared with investment requirements, in order to free up public resources currently covering operational costs that could be realigned towards those without access to improved services.

Note

[1] Poverty measured in terms of the poverty headcount ratio at $1.25 a day at Purchasing Parity Power (% of population).

References

Banerjee, S., Wodon, Q., Diallo, A., Pushak, T., Uddin, H., Tsimpo, C. and Foster, V. (2008). *Access, affordability, and alternatives: Modern infrastructure services in Africa*. Africa's Infrastructure, Background Paper No. 2, Africa Infrastructure Country Diagnostic. Washington, DC: World Bank.

Foster, V. and Yepes, T. (2005) *Is cost recovery a feasible objective for water and electricity? The Latin American experience*. Policy Research Working Paper WPS 3943. Washington, DC: World Bank.

Gertler, P.J. Shelef, O., Wolfram, C.D. and Fuchs, A. (2016) 'The demand for energy-using assets among the world's rising middle classes' *American Economic Review*, vol 106, no 6, pp 1366-1401.

Mubila, M. and Aissa, M.-S.B. (2011) *The middle of the pyramid: Dynamics of the middle class in Africa*. Market Brief. Tunis, Tunisia: African Development Bank.

World Bank (2009) *The World Bank annual report 2009*. Washington, DC: World Bank.

Yepes, T. (2008) *Investment needs for infrastructure in developing countries 2008-15*. Washington, DC: World Bank.

FOUR

Infrastructure and rural productivity in Africa

Maurice Mubila and Tito Yepes

Introduction

Rural activities remain highly relevant to the overall development process of Sub-Saharan Africa. The African population is mainly located in rural areas, ranging from 53% to 78% of the population in the Economic Community of Central African States (ECCAS) and the East African Community (EAC) respectively. Almost two-thirds of the labor force is engaged in agricultural-related activities and agriculture makes up a very significant share of gross domestic product (GDP) in all sub-regions, ranging from 13% to 32% in the Southern African Development Community (SADC) and the Economic Community of West African States (ECOWAS) respectively. The intersection of these two processes—high rural population and high agricultural activity—results in agriculture being the main source of income for 90% of the rural population in Africa (ECA, 2005).

The rural population faces extreme poverty and lack of access to services. Studies indicate that more than 1 billion people in the world live in extreme poverty, of which 415 million reside in Sub-Saharan Africa. In 2011, more than 900 million people lived in Sub-Saharan countries; 47% of them on less than US$1.25 a day and 64% in rural areas (World Bank, 2015). It is estimated that between 75% and 80% of the poor live in rural communities (IFAD, 2011). In household services, urban coverage rates are five to 10 times higher than those in rural areas (AfDB, 2011). Electricity and improved water supply such as piped connections or stand-posts extend to the majority of the urban population, but to less than one-fifth of the rural population with minimal differences across the sub-regions. Rural access to information and communications technology (ICT) services remains negligible (AfDB, 2011).

A vicious circle characterizes the relationship between agriculture and rural poverty. A high reliance on agriculture is not responsible

Figure 4.1: Rural activities and rural population

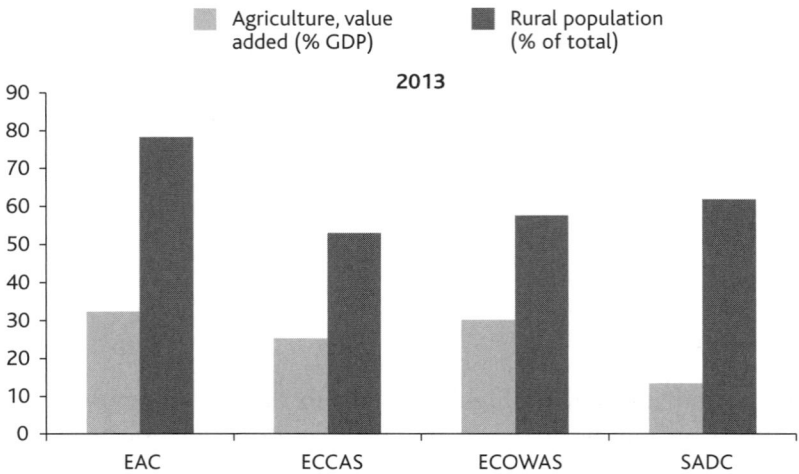

Notes: EAC: East Africa Community, ECCAS: Economic Community of Central African States, ECOWAS: Economic Community of West African States, SADC: Southern Africa Development Community.

Source: World Development Indicators.

for rural poverty; however, in order to fight poverty improving agricultural productivity is essential. Low productivity and poverty feed each other creating a vicious circle; this situation is known as the "Sahel-Syndrome". More accurately, this is a mechanism that forces poor peasants back to agricultural marginal lands for non-capital intensive exploitation.

Intensifying agricultural activities on marginal sites increases environmental degradation and damages the natural production basis, thus decreasing yields which leads to further impoverishment and stimulates an extension of the syndrome by expanding the agricultural frontier even further (Roehrig and Menz, 2005). Case studies analyzing peasant agro-ecosystems in poor countries indicate that the core mechanism of this syndrome describes the position of many poor peasants in developing countries, namely caught in the vicious circle. Breaking the circle is rather complex because some of the standard solutions for rural development may exacerbate the extent of the problem. A good example is when improving rural accessibility in areas that experience such a situation can sometimes lead to gentrification.

Challenges facing rural activities

Rural productivity in Africa ranks among the lowest in the developing world. The agricultural sector remains largely traditional and concentrated in the hands of smallholders and pastoralists (ECA, 2009a). More than 85% of the rural poor live on land of medium to high potential for increased productivity. In Eastern and Southern Africa, desert and semi-arid land make up almost 40% of the land base, where the poorest people live (IFAD, 2010). The dominance of rain-fed agriculture throughout Sub-Saharan Africa makes production vulnerable to droughts, such as the drought of 2010 in the Sahel region that had a huge impact on poverty and food security.

Furthermore, this situation also has long-term impact on ecosystems due to overgrazing and deforestation resulting from the expansion of low-productivity agricultural practices. Such outcomes can be observed currently in the Kalahari Desert. The aggregated impact is that Sub-Saharan Africa has the lowest rural productivity rate among developing regions (see Figure 4.2). Between 1990 and 2012 the ratio between the agriculture value added and the arable land, a broad measure of productivity, grew by an annual average rate of 0.79% in ECCAS and about 1.6% per annum in ECOWAS and EAC. In

Figure 4.2: Rural productivity in Sub-Saharan Africa

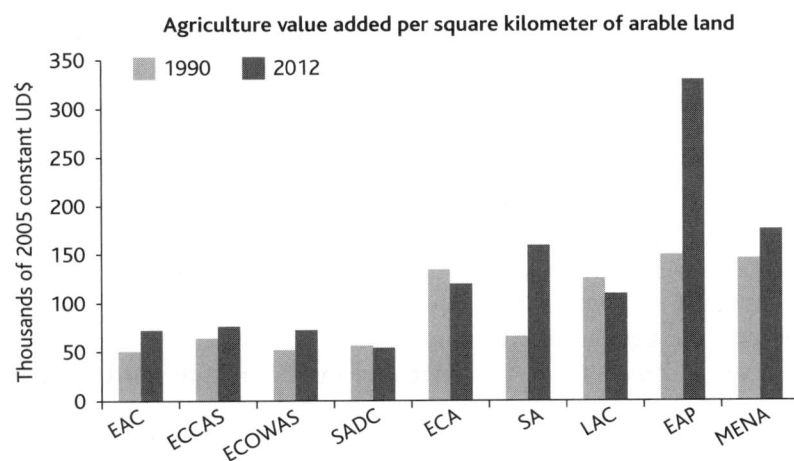

Agriculture value added per square kilometer of arable land

Notes: EAC: East Africa Community, ECCAS: Economic Central Comunitity of African States, ECOWAS: Economic Community of West African States, SADC: South African Development Community, ECA: Europe and Central Asia, SA: South Asia, LAC, Latin America & Caribbean, EAP: East Asia & Pacific, MENA: Middle East & North Africa.

Source: World Development Indicators.

the case of SADC, there was a decreasing trend equivalent to 0.17% annual average.

Rural productivity also faces huge challenges ahead, including climate change and the food crisis.

The consequences of climate change will fall disproportionately on developing countries, especially Sub-Saharan Africa. Warming of 2°C could result in a 4% to 5% permanent reduction in annual income per capita in Africa. Sub-Saharan Africa suffers from natural fragility (with two-thirds of its surface area desert or dry land) and high exposure to droughts and floods, which are forecast to increase with further climate change. In addition, the region's economies are highly dependent on natural resources. Evidence from Sub-Saharan Africa indicates that rainfall variability, projected to increase substantially, also reduces GDP and increases poverty. The prospects for crops and livestock in rain-fed semi-arid lands in Sub-Saharan Africa are bleak, even before warming reaches 2–2.5°C above pre-industrial levels (World Bank, 2010).

> Climate change related events will severely impact the productivity of Africa's agriculture. Falling agricultural productivity will be one of many factors driving the greater vulnerability. One study projects that by 2080 land with severe climate or soil constraints in Sub-Saharan Africa will increase by 26 million to 61 million hectares. That is 9 to 20 percent of the region's arable land. Greater rainfall variability and more severe droughts in semi-arid parts of Africa are expected. For instance, Southern Africa will suffer particularly severe drops in yields by 2030 without adaptation measures. (World Bank, 2010)

In the shorter term the food crisis, which is uncorrelated to climate change, is determined by low agricultural productivity. The 2011 food crisis in Africa was not caused by a supply shock but by the price shock of 2006 to 2008, therefore the required policy response should have been a supply stimulus. But African countries had few reserves and inadequate budgetary means to procure food at high prices (FAO, 2011) and they are particularly vulnerable to international shocks because 45 percent of rice and 85 percent of wheat is imported (World Bank, 2011).

There is a strong need to stimulate agricultural productivity through different programs while reducing vulnerability to price volatility. Over the longer term, the best way to lower food prices is to invest in agriculture; this will sustainably increase yields, reduce input costs, increase productivity and reduce food losses and waste. It is therefore, essential to build incentives to encourage farmers to invest in more-profitable technologies that raise their productivity and income (World Bank, 2011).

Logistics costs as a result of rural infrastructure

The overall logistics costs of Sub-Saharan Africa are among the most expensive in the world. Cross-regional analysis of the World Bank's Doing Business 2015 data indicates that on average Sub-Saharan African countries have the second longest time to export (30.5) surpassed only by South Asia, the third highest cost to export (1,922.9 US$ per container) and to import (2,117.8) surpassed only by South Asia and Europe and Central Asia, and the major number of documentation requirements for exports (8.1) and import (9.4). This means that exporting and importing a 20-foot dry container is more than double the cost of the leading region, East Asia and Pacific.

Although there is still a gap between Sub-Saharan Africa and the leading region, the Doing Business report recognized the improvement in most of the aspects related to trading across borders such as simplifying the processes for producing the inspection report (Côte d'Ivoire) and improving infrastructure at ports (Ghana).

The World Bank's Logistics Performance Index of 2014 shows how low that performance remains, compared with other developing countries (see Figure 4.3).

Despite the average improvement, there is still a gap among countries performances. Landlocked countries face the greatest logistics hurdles. Surface transportation costs and time delays are a much larger share of total export costs and time for landlocked countries, and vary substantially between the different geographic corridors within Sub-Saharan Africa. The landlocked countries in Central Africa (Chad and the Central African Republic) experience the most costly and lengthiest time to export, between two and three times over the regional average.

Still, closeness to ports does not guarantee better logistics performance. For instance in Western Africa there are shorter distances and a larger number of countries with ports, but there is better regional transport integration in the Southern African region where this is not the case (Christ and Ferrantino, 2009). One apparel producer near Nairobi, Kenya, estimated that improvements in all aspects of the transport process, including ports, roads and customs procedures, could lower total costs by 10% to 40% and significantly improve the firm's competitiveness. (USITC, 2009 cited in Christ and Ferrantino, 2009)

Figure 4.3: Logistics performance

Average logistics performance index by region, 2014

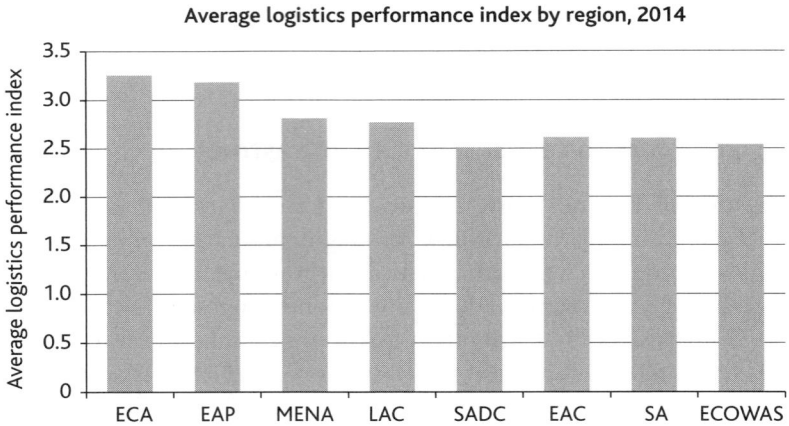

Notes: ECA: East African Community, EAP: East Asia and Pacific, MENA: Middle East and North Africa, LAC: Latin America & Caribbean, SADC: Southern African Developments Community, EAC: East African Community, SA: South Asia, ECOWAS: Economic Community of West Africa States.

Source: World Bank's Logistics Performance Index, 2014

The main determinant of high logistics costs is not necessarily just the lack of investment in physical infrastructure but also the non-physical components such as regulations. The costs that service providers face are not excessively high in Sub-Saharan Africa compared with other regions of the world; however transport prices or costs to the shipper (end-user) are high, particularly in Central Africa (Raballand and Macchi, 2009). This mainly results from official and unofficial market regulation and structure in the trucking services, and is observable most notably in West and Central Africa.

Further, Raballand and Macchi (2009) conclude that investment in infrastructure is unlikely to reduce logistics costs unless institutional issues are addressed. Since the 1970s the World Bank has actively supported the improvement of transport corridors in Africa with no clear impact on transport prices, despite the improvements resulting in lower costs for cargo trucks on the corridors. Thus, the end-users of road transport services have not fully benefitted from the lower transport costs and better quality service that the improved infrastructure has allowed.

In the SADC region, Mauritius has the best road conditions: 100% of its road network was paved by 2005 and 95% is rated to be in good condition. Botswana ranks second best with 94% of its roads regarded to be in good condition, although only 36% were paved by 2004. At the other end of the scale, Tanzania has the lowest percentage of paved roads. In some countries, despite the low percentage of paved roads, the networks are regarded as being in good condition, for example in Namibia, South Africa, Swaziland and Zambia (Mutambara, 2009).

Rural infrastructure in correlation with rural productivity

Isolation perpetuated by poor transport restrains economic progress and thus in turn traps rural people in poverty. Poor transport restricts opportunities to trade even within local markets, which leads to an increase in costs of production and distribution, reduces the profit margin on produce sales, and limits production yields to levels below their potential, partly impeding the transition from subsistence to income-producing agriculture. The economic effects of better access to, from and within rural areas can be cumulative and far reaching. Access to markets makes it worthwhile to modernize agriculture through mechanization, fertilizers and varieties with higher yields. These improvements increase demand for agricultural inputs and financial credit. However, when new roads reach remote rural areas, the economic effect can be dramatic.

Given the low quality of the road network in Sub-Saharan Africa it is not surprising that rural productivity is low. Poor logistics affects the agricultural sector more than the other sectors. Only 20% of the rural roads in Sub-Saharan Africa are in good condition and 20% are in fair condition (Carruthers et al, 2009). Hence, the remaining 60% of rural roads are in poor condition, thus requiring either rehabilitation or reconstruction, which, for the size of the area being covered, represents a tremendous financial and institutional challenge.

Productivity is greater in areas closer to urban centers and better road connectivity determines higher crop production. Agricultural production and proximity (as measured by travel time) to urban markets are highly correlated in Sub-Saharan Africa, even after taking agro-ecology into account (Dorosh et al, 2010). Total crop production relative to potential production is approximately 45% for areas within four hours' travel time from a city of 100,000 people. In contrast, it is only about 5% for areas more than eight hours' travel time from a city of 100,000 people. Therefore, better road connectivity increases crop production significantly as it reduces travel time.

The impact good rural road networks can have on rural productivity is supported by evidence from the African sub-regions. Comparing East and West Africa, reducing travel time does not significantly increase the adoption of high-input/high-yield technology in West Africa due to its already relatively well-connected road network

(Dorosh et al, 2010), whereas in East Africa reducing travel time has a significant impact on adoption: the adoption of more productive crops that use higher levels of inputs is negatively correlated with travel time to urban centers.

Longer travel time discourages the adoption of high-input/high-yield crop-production technology more than other production systems. Better road connectivity makes high-input production more profitable and therefore increases its share of production. This shift toward high-input production systems is driven by both direct and indirect channels. In the direct channel, roads increase crop production by shifting outward both the crop demand curve (through access to a larger market) and the crop supply curve (through better access to intermediate inputs and new technology). In the indirect channel, roads facilitate the adoption of high-input/high-yield crop production and therefore increase crop production by replacing low-input/low-yield crop production (Dorosh et al, 2010).

The logistics chain for buying inputs and selling produce determines the adoption of high-yield agricultural practices. Typically costs per kilometer are higher on dirt roads than on tarmac roads, and higher still where the dirt road turns into a footpath. The overall impact on input prices and marketing costs for farmers located in areas with bad accessibility is substantial.

In Bangladesh, villages with better road access are associated with higher levels of input use and agricultural production, increased incomes, better indicators of access to health services and greater wage earning opportunities (Khandker et al, 2006) A World Bank roads project in Morocco was found to have led to higher agricultural production and land productivity, increased use of agricultural inputs and extension services, and a shift towards high-value crops and off-farm employment opportunities (World Bank, 1996).

Land regulations and property rights

Among the drivers of rural productivity, no other relates as intrinsically to rural infrastructure as land regulations and property rights. The first reason is that the traditional logic for rural infrastructure provision is the political economy of land ownership. People in control of the state at any level of government face the incentive of driving investment resources in their favor, that is, their land. However, a problem arises when selected investments are in contradiction to the proposed investment agenda, such as roads being built in areas that are known to pose an environmental challenge and would be likely to face a low social return.

A second consideration regarding the role of land regulations on infrastructure provision is the changes in land use that can often arise from investment in roads. Conversely, investment in roads can sometimes turn against rural productivity due to weak land regulations. The main justification for investing in rural roads is to improve accessibility, reduce travel time, and enhance logistics. However, poor land regulations around the zones between urban and rural areas can result in gentrification and land speculation, which goes against improvements in rural productivity as agricultural land changes to other uses due to better transportation.

The minimum land regulation should trace and control urban expansion so that surrounding rural areas can continue being used for agriculture. When land regulations are non-existent or too weak, poor landowners of the improved roads will seek changes in land use towards urban activities and this will result in higher land prices that are generally inconsistent with rural activities. The resulting landscape is of vacant rural land where road improvement has been made. Furthermore, the improved accessibility incentivizes poor households to sell their land or vacate if rented, and move further into the hinterland. In these cases, the policy instrument of road improvement goes against rural productivity and further enhances the mechanisms that drive rural poverty.

On the other hand, property rights also represent a macro mechanism that drives migration and the efficient localization of population. As a matter of fact, the rural poor barely have access to land titles due to poor institutionalization, low levels of education, recent expansion of the rural frontier and weak government capacity. Land tenure laws remain vague and vary from one region to another. Given continued restrictions on land ownership and unclear regulations on land tenure, labor mobility may be hindered.

Access to land and security of tenure are the main means through which food security and sustainable development can be realized. Land tenure and wrangles over land have been growing in the past decade within the context of growing poverty, landlessness, homelessness and distress in Africa. The last few years have witnessed an increase in politics revolving around land issues and literal and physical assertion of attempts to gain land rights by some communities. The essence of the argument is that, although the land question in Africa varies across the sub-regions, there are common tendencies and empirically based data that demonstrate similar linkages between the land tenure relations on one hand, and food security and sustainable livelihoods on the other.

Sub-regional differences are substantial. In West Africa, unlike other regions, existing land problems have less to do with past land expropriation by settlers than with insecurity of tenure and the effect that this has on the effective exploitation of land (Toulmin and Longbottom, 1997, cited in ECA, 2009b). Under customary law, traditional leaders (chiefs) remain the dominant and de facto land owners. It is through them that community members obtain access to land resources. Once allocated, the land comes under the control of the community member's family in most cases. In some parts of Central Africa the scarcity of productive land is the source of conflicts and in countries like Rwanda and Burundi, scarcity of land is one of the root causes of civil unrest. According to World Bank data, with a total population of about 11 million in 2010, Rwanda is the most densely populated country in Africa after Mauritius and its population growth rate remains very high, at 3%; therefore land scarcity will continue to remain a critical issue into the future.

Unequal land access and low absolute levels of land per household have shown to be problematic for poverty reduction and growth. This is the result of the strong link between access to land and household income particularly for farm sizes below 1 ha/capita. In Africa, on average households in the highest per capita quartile control between five to 15 times more land than the lowest quartile (FAO, 2010). Landless households or those who own less than 0.1 constitute 25% of rural agricultural households. Restrained access to land limits the ability of landless groups to graduate from poverty through agricultural productivity growth (Jayne et al, 2005, cited in FAO, 2010). Expanding crop production is largely associated with issues of equitable asset distribution, yet little attention is paid to considering the implications of land inequality in relation to this and food security.

Weak or no ownership locks people to locations that could trap them in poverty. They may be better off if they are able to sell and move elsewhere. However, weak property rights may also deter them from making an efficient decision about their location. This situation is certainly exacerbated in peri-urban areas where land plots tend to be subdivided among family members as housing solutions. In these areas residents still face high travel times to urban centers and the potential exploitation of scale in agricultural production is fragmented. Better property rights may have the macro effect of allowing members with better skills for urban activities to move into cities and towns while leaving behind those more suited to rural activities.

Conclusion: an agenda for rural infrastructure

The challenge is to sequence cost-effective investments in areas that have low population density and little commercial activity. One option is to focus investments geographically to foster the development of growth poles (World Bank, 2007). The rural agenda is to enhance growth by improving small-holder competitiveness in medium and higher potential areas, where returns on investment are higher, while simultaneously ensuring the livelihoods and food security of subsistence farmers.

Improving rural productivity should not be seen as a separate or divergent agenda from that of urbanization or regional integration (urban systems integrating cities, towns and agricultural areas). The maximum efficiency in investment allocation can be obtained when the three areas (urban, regional, and rural) of spatial development are considered and are simultaneously given the functional relationships among them. In fact, rural productivity improves when it is actually bound to the growth and success of neighboring cities that represent its major market rather than through isolated rural areas that aim to produce, like extractive economies, to feed far located markets.

The best candidate areas for investment in infrastructure to improve rural productivity are those that have complementary benefits for urban areas and regional integration. The effects of infrastructure improvements to promote industrial (light industries) development and accelerate national economic growth are higher in areas where a large market is present (Lall et al, 2009). Improving infrastructure in these places provides the highest private return to public investment.

Consequently, the best alternative for improving rural productivity is in nearby areas that will benefit from the same investment in infrastructure. For instance, in a case like Uganda, the urban areas between Kampala and Jinja are likely to lead Uganda's industrial development and therefore rural activities along that corridor should form the priority of the rural productivity agenda.

Complementarities between on- and off-farm activities should be achieved. Poor road access in many cases coincides with other bottlenecks, such as poor agro-ecology, low population density, and lack of improved water and electricity services. Thus, a well-targeted program needs to take into account the interactions between geography, community and household characteristics and consider complementary investments to ease the constraints and maximize the impact of road construction and rehabilitation for market efficiency and household welfare. The package required is a more comprehensive one than simply investing in roads; it is therefore necessary to consider the feasibility of providing funding and implementation capacity. Otherwise, investing in road infrastructure in locations where those other components are missing will not yield the highest return. For instance, the combination of on- and off-farm activities is known to be a route to reduce vulnerability and poverty.

Successful diversification also appears to be associated with infrastructure variables. Households that can reach fertilizer sellers have access to motorable roads or piped water and therefore are more likely to diversify (Ariga et al, 2008). Better access to fertilizers is driving off-farm diversification because it enables adults to produce crops more efficiently and, therefore, spend more time off-farm.

The cost structure of agriculture is high in part due to high transport costs and port inefficiencies. Poor roads, particularly rural roads, raise input prices and marketing costs and thus create disincentives for farmers to behave more commercially and diversify. Useful advisory services are needed to introduce new technologies and enterprises so as to help raise overall farm productivity through increased commercialization. In general the condition of roads determines the success of households in diversifying income sources; only through better accessibility can they take part in off-farm activities.

The challenge of providing strong rural infrastructure for all is not only beyond possibility but it may be also undesirable. The challenging economic geography of Africa makes it difficult to invest in rural roads throughout. Less than 40% of rural Africans live within two kilometers of an all-season road, the lowest level of rural accessibility in the developing world. Given low population density, improving rural accessibility for all would imply doubling or tripling the length of the existing network in most countries, a level of investment beyond possibility (Gwilliam et al, 2008) for both construction and maintenance.

The rural infrastructure agenda for Africa should focus on improving and maintaining the level of current service rather than increasing the size of the network, the reason being that the current levels of road quality are too low to make it worth expanding a network that will result in even greater maintenance liabilities in the future. Funding and institutional arrangements need to be put in place to ensure the sustainability of road investments and maximize their impact. Enhance the impact of what is already in place.

Community-based maintenance contracts and labor-intensive roads maintenance are an opportunity for employment creation and improved logistics. Labor-intensive technologies are a good alternative for road maintenance given the impact on employment creation. In addition costs of infrastructure provision can be reduced if labor-intensive technologies are selected instead of equipment-intensive alternatives. Deveraux and Solomon (2006) report that some labor-intensive programs have provided up to 30% costs savings. Other authors have even identified savings of 50%. However, focusing only on reducing the overall investment amount is probably not the best criteria when considering labor-intensive technologies. Their cost structure is different from equipment-intensive provision because it should include components like training or development of institutional capacities. Therefore comparing one-to-one by days of labor versus non-labor costs can be misleading.

Investment requirements for infrastructure in Africa are huge. According to the Africa's Infrastructure Country Diagnostic (Foster and Briceño-Garmendia, 2010), annual infrastructure investment needs in Africa are approximately US$93 billion, one-third of which should cover operations and maintenance. With current spending of US$45 billion a year, the financial gap is sizable and requires appropriate management to maximize the value of local and foreign investments.

Meeting the rural accessibility standard articulated in the base scenario (75% of the rural population living within two kilometers of an all-weather road) would require a road network of more than 1.1 million km. Only a fraction of that length is provided by the regional and national road networks. The first place to look to make up the difference is the remainder of the road networks of the countries. Eleven of the 23 countries (rising to 15 under the pragmatic scenarios) would not have to add any new roads to their present official road network to reach the rural accessibility standard. What they *would* have to do to meet the standards stipulated in the scenarios is to maintain their roads in good condition. In the remaining 12 countries (or eight under the pragmatic scenario), some or all of the unclassified road network would have to be upgraded to all-weather roads and maintained in good condition and some new roads built for the rural accessibility standard to be met (Carruthers et al, 2009).

Rural roads would absorb more than 53% of the spending needed. A little more than half of that would be used to improve the existing official road network, while the remainder would be used for upgrades to the non-official network. This would add connectivity to areas representing 20% of potential agricultural output that were not already connected. Considering all of Sub-Saharan Africa together, the additional cost of adding the potential output would not be excessive (Carruthers et al, 2009).

References

AfDB (African Development Bank) (2011) *Rapid Urbanization and Growing Demands for Urban Infrastructure in Africa*. Tunis: African Development Bank.

Ariga, J., Jayne, T.S., Kibaara, B. and Nyoro, J.K. (2008) *Trends and Patterns in Fertilizer Use by Smallholder Farmers in Kenya, 1997-2007*, WPS 28/2008. Nairobi: Tegemeo Institute of Agricultural Policy and Development.

Carruthers, R., Krishnamani, R. and Murray, S. (2009) *Improving Connectivity: Investing in Transport Infrastructure in Sub-Saharan Africa*, Africa's Infrastructure. A Time for Transformation. Background Paper 7 (Phase II). Washington, DC: World Bank.

Christ, N. and Ferrantino, M. (2009) *Land Transport for Exports: The Effects of Cost, Time, and Uncertainty in Sub-Saharan Africa*, US International Trade Commission, Office of Economics Working Papers No. 2009-10-A. Washington, DC: US International Trade Commission.

Devereux, S. and Solomon, C. 2006. *Employment Creation Programmes: The International Experience*, Issues in Employment and Poverty Discussion Paper, 24. Geneva: International Labour Organization.

Dorosh, P., Wang, H., You, L. and Schmidt, E. (2010) *Crop Production and Road Connectivity in Sub-Saharan Africa. A Spatial Analysis*, Policy Research Working Paper 5385. Washington, DC: World Bank.

ECA (Economic Commission for Africa) (2005) *Economic Report on Africa 2005. Meeting the Challenges of Unemployment and Poverty in Africa*. Addis Ababa: United Nations Economic Commission for Africa.

ECA (2009a) *Economic Report on Africa 2009. Developing Africa Agriculture through Regional Value Chains*. Addis Ababa: United Nations Economic Commission for Africa.

ECA (2009b) *Land Tenure Systems and their Impacts on Food Security and Sustainable Development in Africa*. United Nations Economic Commission for Africa. Addis Ababa, Ethiopia.

FAO (Food and Agriculture Organization of the United Nations) (2010) *Africa's Changing Landscape: Securing Land Access for the Rural Poor*. Rome: FAO.

FAO (2011) *The State of Food Insecurity in the World. How does International Price Volatility Affect Domestic Economies and Food Insecurity?* Rome: FAO.

Foster, V. and Briceño-Garmendia, C. (eds) (2010) *Africa's Infrastructure Country Diagnostic. A Time for Transformation*. Washington, DC: World Bank.

Gwilliam, K., Foster, V., Archondo-Callao, R., Briceño-Garmendia, C., Nogales, A. and Sethi, K. (2008) *The Burden of Maintenance: Roads in Sub-Saharan Africa. Africa's Infrastructure*. A Time for Transformation. Background Paper 14 (Phase I). Washington, DC: World Bank.

IFAD (International Fund for Agricultural Development) (2010) *Rural poverty report 2011*. Rural Poverty Portal, www.ruralpovertyportal. org/region/home/tags/africa.

Khandker, S., Bakht, Z. and Koolwal, G. (2006) *The Poverty Impact of Rural Roads: Evidence from Bangladesh*, Policy Research Working Paper No. 3875. Washington, DC: World Bank.

Lall, S., Schoeder, E. and Schmidt, E. (2009) *Identifying Spatial Efficiency-Equity Tradeoffs in Territorial Development Policies. Evidence from Uganda*, Policy Research Working Paper No. 4966. Washington, DC: World Bank.

Mutambara, T. (2009) 'Regional transport challenges within the Southern African Development Community and their implications for economic integration and development', *Journal of Contemporary African Studies*, vol 27, no. 4, pp 501–25.

Raballand, G. and Macchi, P. (2009) *Transport Prices and Costs: The Need to Revisit Donors' Policies in Transport in Africa*, BREAD Working Paper 190. Bureau for Research and Economic Analysis of Development.

Roehrig, J. and. Menz, G. (2005) 'The determination of natural agricultural potential in Western Arica using the Fuzzy Logic Based Marginality Index', *EARSeL eProceedings*, vol 4, no 1.

World Bank (1996) *Kingdom of Morocco. Impact Evaluation Report. Socioeconomic Influence of Rural Roads. Fourth Highway Project*, World Bank Operations Evaluation Department. Report No. 15808–MOR. Washington, DC: World Bank.

World Bank (2007) *World Development Report 2008. Agriculture for Development*. Washington, DC: World Bank.

World Bank (2010) *World Development Report 2010. Development and Climate Change*. Washington, DC: World Bank.

World Bank (2011) 'The effects of high food prices in Africa', available at http://go.worldbank.org/KIFNA6OZS0 (accessed 5 November 2011).

World Bank (2015) 'World Development Indicators: Sub Saharan Africa', available at: http://data.worldbank.org/region/sub-saharan-africa.

Part 2: Sector-specific issues

Water and sanitation in Africa: current status, trends, challenges and opportunities

George Kararach and Tito Yepes

Introduction

The 21st century will prove to be of great importance to African countries, as they are confronted with the challenge of coping with an accelerated urbanization process, while simultaneously striving to take advantage of the opportunity to become one of the world's largest agricultural producers. The ability of countries to achieve certain aims requires, among other things, that they respond to the increase in demand for infrastructure endowments generated by economic growth and changes in the production structure. Demands for roads, rail, ports and airports, for electricity and information and communications technology, and especially for water and sanitation, will increase vis-à-vis productive and social needs. In this context, it is important for African countries to identify what they hope to achieve over the next 50 years, what types of investment will help them accomplish related goals, and how much this will cost them.

This chapter focuses on access to water and sanitation services in Africa. Improvements in water and sanitation are known to have huge positive effects on health and well-being. Cutler and Miller (2005) found that public investments in 13 major US cities at the beginning of the 20th century had a powerful positive effect on health, cutting total mortality by half, and infant mortality by three-quarters. Leipzinger et al (2003) also found that, apart from traditional variables (for example, income, assets, education and direct health interventions), better access to basic infrastructure services played an important role in improving child health outcomes.

The first part of the chapter outlines the urbanization and access rates trends. It then discusses the main factors underlying anticipated trends in investment needs over the next 50 years. The third part estimates the cost of these requirements. The fourth part discusses the challenges confronting the continent in terms of its ability to cope with the growing demand for water and sanitation services. Clearly articulating and documenting all these issues enables policymakers and investors to make sound decisions regarding water and sanitation investments on the continent.

Urbanization and access to water and sanitation services

Urbanization

Urbanization is still incipient in most African countries, but will be consolidated in the coming decades. The median urbanization rate by region is shown in Figure 5.1. Urbanization has reached a high rate in only few countries. For all regions considered, less than 70% of the population lives in urban areas. At the median, Eastern Africa has the lowest rate, with only 30% of the population living in urban areas; Northern and Western Africa have the highest rates, with 66% and 43% of their respective populations living in urban areas. However, according to the African Development Bank (2014), it is expected that by 2060, the median country for each region will have more than 60% of its population living in urban areas. Eastern Africa is the exception, but is not far off since 53% of its population will live in urban areas.

The most striking conclusion that will continue to be a trend across countries and across regions within countries is the heterogeneity of results. Great differences exist across countries in each region. Most of the East and West Africa countries have low urbanization rates (between 0% and 40%). Only five countries located in the Eastern, Central and Northern regions have achieved high levels of urbanization: Djibouti, Reunion, Gabon, Algeria, Libya and Western Sahara. However, by 2060, only five countries are expected to still have low urbanization rates—Burundi, Malawi, South Sudan, Swaziland and Uganda. All other countries will have urbanization rates of between 40% and 70%. More importantly, a large fraction of countries (37%) will have more than 70% of their respective populations living in urban areas. The classification of countries by their urbanization rate in years 2010 and 2060 is shown in Figure 5.2.

In the coming decades countries with low urbanization rates today may be able to take advantage of increasing economies of scale regarding water and sanitation investments to a greater extent than already urbanized countries. In most of the African countries with low urbanization rates, the urban population is highly concentrated

Figure 5.1: Percentage of urban population by region (median) – 1960–2060

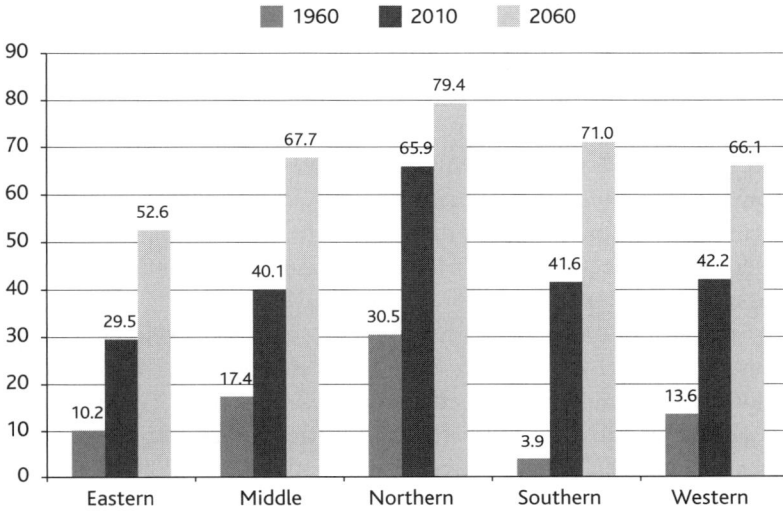

Source: Based on UNDESA (2014)

Figure 5.2: Number of countries classified by percentage of urban population

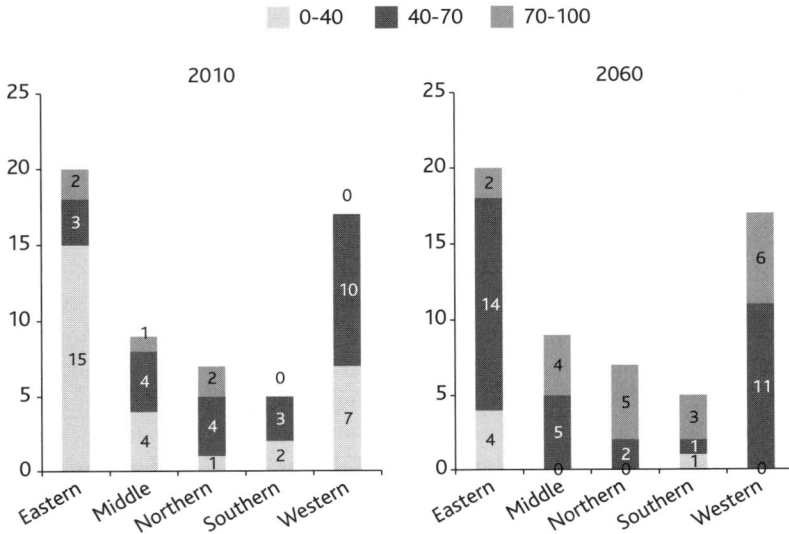

Source: Based on UNDESA (2014)

in a small number of big cities, whereas urban populations in highly urbanized countries tend to be more dispersed. Therefore, those that will urbanize in the coming decades should take advantage of less dispersion, which will allow for higher economies of scale compared to areas with more dispersed patterns of population settlement. At the median, between 30% and 50% of the urban population lives in cities with more than 1 million inhabitants, while the urban population in countries with medium urbanization rates is less spatially concentrated (Figure 5.3). Benefiting from a different pattern of location of settlements requires countries to improve their planning while avoiding to respond to scattered demands for services.

Africa should come up with a strategy for basic service provision in medium-sized cities. Africa's largest cities are mostly located in countries with low or intermediate urbanization rates. These tend to be concentrated in West and East Africa. Africa has few very large cities. Only six out of 86 African cities are in the top 100 largest cities of the world. Nearly 70 African cities can be labeled as medium-sized cities by world standards. Table 5.1 shows the distribution of cities by region and ranges of urbanization rates. The first three columns present their vertical distribution across ranges of population while the next four are horizontally distributed across regions. The bottom of the table presents cities by the level of urbanization of their respective country.

Access to water and sanitation

Most countries have high urban coverage for piped water. Other sources such as wells and surface water are used as a primary alternative by only about 20% of the urban population, most notably, in Eastern, Western and Central Africa (Figure 5.4).

These estimates are based on the results of household surveys (Demographic and Health Surveys, or DHS) collected by the United States Agency for International Development (USAID). Survey results are available for 39 countries; for each country, the last available survey is used. The DHS classifies access to sanitation and water services into different categories that cannot always be divided into improved versus unimproved sources. Instead, we classify these sources according to the African Infrastructure Country Diagnostic (AICD) definitions of modern, intermediate and basic sources. For example, water coming from wells or springs can be improved if they are protected, but will remain unimproved otherwise. Likewise, pit toilet latrines can be improved if they are ventilated improved pits, but not if they are traditional pit latrines. Detailed information is provided in Table 5.2.

Figure 5.3: Percentage of urban population in agglomerations (large cites), 2014

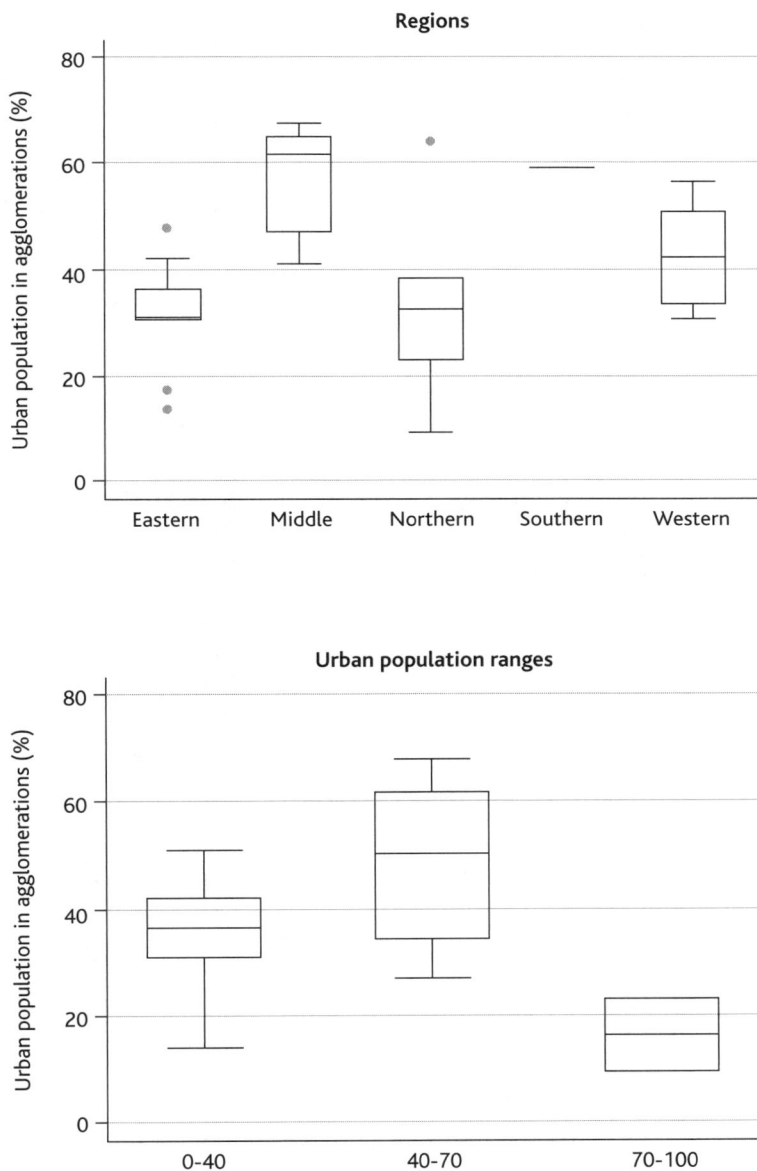

Note: Agglomerations or large cities are metropolitan areas that in 2000 had a population of more than one million people. 31 observations.

Source: Based on UNDESA (2014) and World Bank (2014)

Table 5.1: Cities by region and urbanization rate

Region	Thousand citizens — Among ranges (%)			Thousand citizens — Among regions (%)				Number of cities		
	50-500	500-1,000	1,000 or more	50-500	500-1,000	1,000 or more	Total	Total	At top world 100 largest	At top world 500 largest
Eastern	22	22	56	24	15	24	21	18	1	9
Central	22	22	56	12	7	12	10	9	1	4
Northern	13	40	47	12	22	17	17	15	1	7
Southern	40	20	40	24	7	10	12	10	1	4
Western	15	38	47	29	48	38	40	34	2	17
Total	20	31	49					86	6	41

Urbanization range	Among ranges (%)			Among urbanization ranges (%)						
	50-500	500-1,000	1,000 or more	50-500	500-1,000	1,000 or more	Total	Total	At top world 100 largest	At top world 500 largest
0-40	24	17	59	41	19	40	34	29	2	16
40-70	17	35	48	47	63	55	56	48	4	23
70-100	22	56	22	12	19	5	10	9	0	2

Source: Demographia and UN Habitat databases, 2015.

Figure 5.4: Access to modern and intermediate sources of water (median)

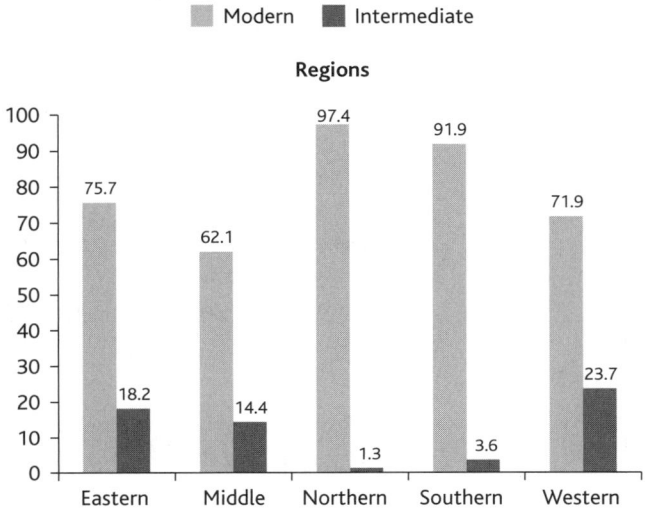

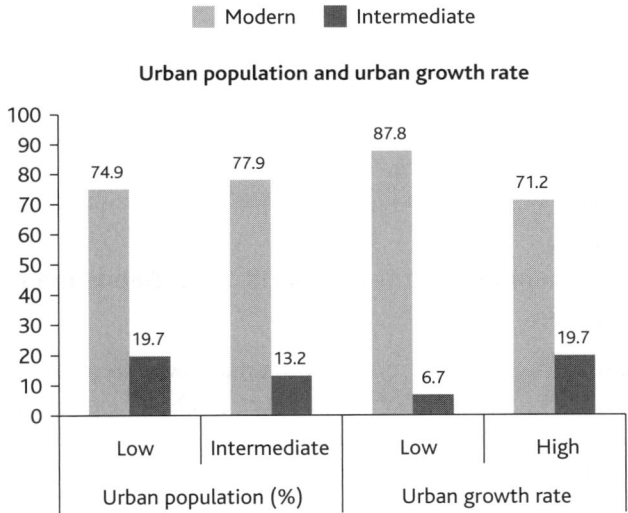

Note: Latest data available is used. Low urban population smaller than 40%, intermediate between 40% and 70%. Low urban growth rate smaller that 2.5%, high greater than 2.5%.

Source: Compiled by author from the most recent Demographic and Health Surveys databases up to 2015

Table 5.2: DHS water and sanitation categories

DHS categories	JMP category	AICD category 2
Main source of water supply		
Piped water	Improved	Modern
Bottled water/demijohn	Unimproved	Basic
Missing	–	–
Other	Unimproved	Basic
Rainwater	Improved	Intermediate
Surface water	Improved/Unimproved	Basic
Tanker truck	Improved/Unimproved	Basic
Well water	Improved/Unimproved	Intermediate
Toilet facility		
Flush toilet	Improved	Modern
Missing	–	–
No facility	Unimproved	Basic
Other	Unimproved	Basic
Pit toilet latrine	Improved/Unimproved	Intermediate

Source: Banerjee et al (2010)

Differences in access to sanitation are more prominent than in water, and tend to break down into flush toilets versus pit toilet latrines. At the median, only Northern and Southern African countries have high access to flush toilets (modern source). Eastern, Central and Western Africa countries instead mainly rely on intermediate sources. The use of intermediate sources is also dominant in countries with low urbanization rates and with high expected urban growth (Figure 5.5).

Factors influencing water and sanitation needs over the next 50 years

When considering policy actions at the urban level, four factors matter the most. The first two are the scale of any given urban area and the rate of expansion of an urban area. The scale of an urban area is important because improvements in access are strongly driven by increasing economies of scale with respect to provision—that is, it is cheaper to connect one extra household to a water or sanitation system when there are other households involved or other neighboring households are already connected. The rate at which an area grows is also important mainly because expansion poses a challenge for urban planners; rapid urban growth demands that planners react more quickly and with greater flexibly, likewise they should also ensure that there are more resources available and they are used more efficiently.

Figure 5.5: Access to modern and intermediate sanitation (median)

■ Modern ■ Intermediate

Regions

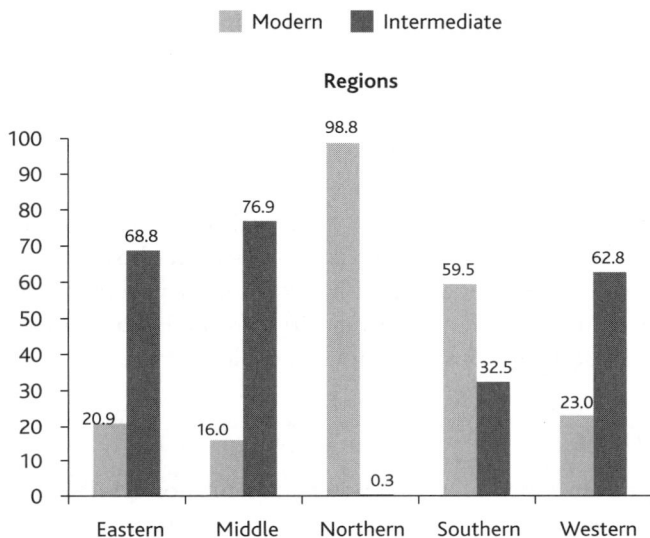

■ Modern ■ Intermediate

Urban population and urban growth rate

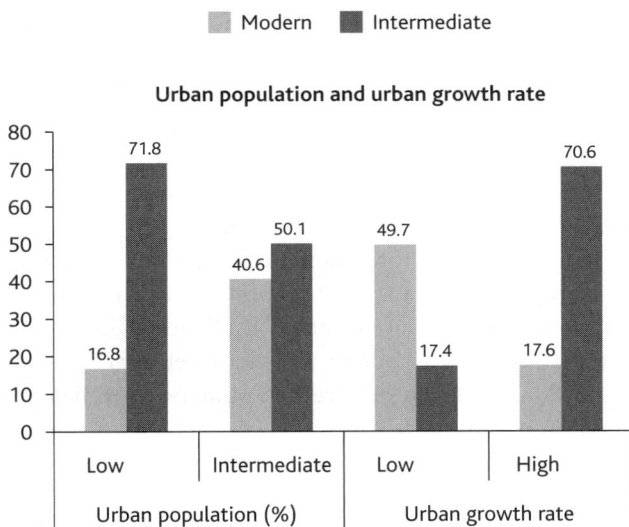

Note: Latest data available is used. Low urban population smaller than 40%, intermediate between 40% and 70%. Low urban growth rate smaller that 2.5%, high greater than 2.5%.

Source: Compiled by author from the most recent Demographic and Health Surveys databases up to 2015

Challenges in the water and sanitation sector vary within the parameters of these two dimensions, but also in relation to the current level of coverage. In general, low access rates pose a challenge for coping with the needs of households, while high urbanization rates call attention to the need to plan and react quickly to related changes.

Climate change will also affect water and sanitation needs over the following years. As such it is a third factor to be taken into account.

The fourth factor is to reduce water losses in order to save scarce water resources and increase financial sustainability in utilities. Maintenance of the systems already in place and those to be expanded over the next decades, along with better commercial management, will play a significant role in the capacity of utilities to expand coverage beyond resources from governments or donors.

Urban scale

Scale matters when providing water and sanitation services as increasing economies of scale reduce the cost of connecting new homes. Taking advantage of these economies depends on the resources available and the institutional capacity for delivering such services.

Increasing returns are stronger for sanitation than for water services. This can be partly explained in terms of the institutions involved. In general, those that provide water have been given greater priority and have had more experience. Though on the whole, access to improved services grows with urbanization, there is great diversity in this respect across countries (Figure 5.6).

In Africa, sanitation raises the greatest concern. At the regional median, the level of access to water is above 90% for all regions. By contrast, this is only true for sanitation in Northern Africa (Figure 5.7). A country-by-country assessment shows that the level of access to water in urban areas in all countries is above 50%, while for almost half of the countries (21 out of 49), the level of access for sanitation is below 50%. The levels of access to sanitation are below 40% for a large fraction of countries.[1]

Improvements are especially important in less urbanized countries. Classifying countries according to their urbanization rate and their level of access shows that 19 out of 29 countries with low levels of access to sanitation have urbanization rates below 40%; but only two of the 14 countries with high levels of access to sanitation fall within this range of urbanization. This is also true for water. The countries with the lowest levels of access are highly concentrated in countries with low urbanization rates. Fifty-three percent of the countries with

Figure 5.6: Urban population (%) versus access rate (in urban areas) by country, 2012*

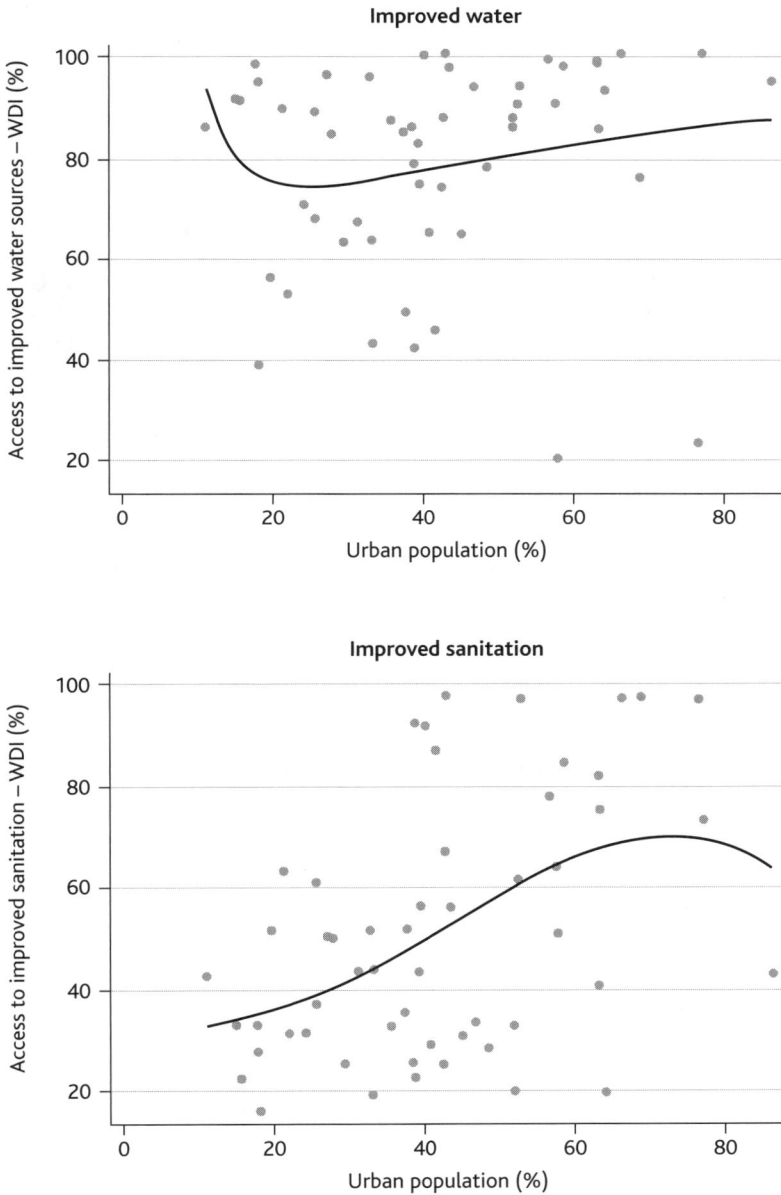

Improved water

Improved sanitation

Note: * Libya: 2001, Equatorial Guinea: 2006, Eritrea: 2008, Comoros: 2010, Somalia: 2011.

Source: Based on UNDESA (2014) and World Bank (2014)

Figure 5.7: Median access rate (urban) by region, 2012

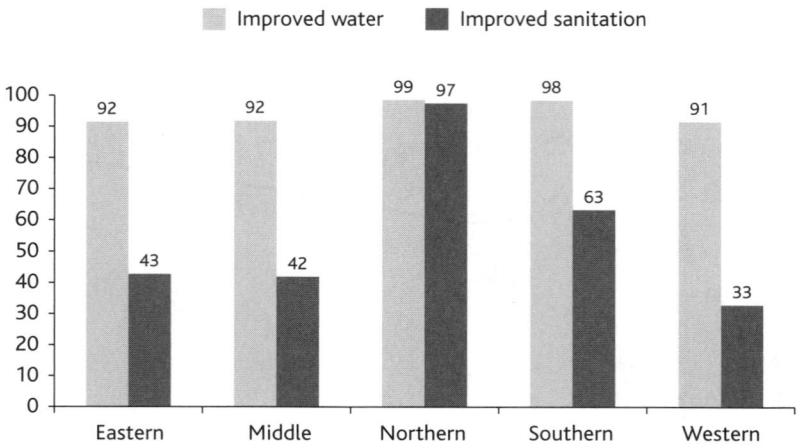

Note: Libya, Equatorial Guinea, Eritrea, Comoros and Somalia are not included because 2012 data was not available.

Source: World Bank (2012).

levels of access to water of between 50% and 80% have urbanization rates below 40%. This classification is shown in Table 5.3.

Broadly, countries with low levels of access to improved services face the challenge of coping with demand. When urbanization levels are high, they need to provide services to more people, but can take advantage of economies of scale. On the other hand, countries with high levels of access have been able to transform their institutions so as to effectively respond to demand. Furthermore, countries with high urban concentrations have already managed this transition. Intuitively, their planning institutions are more consolidated and have the experience required to respond to the needs of large urban concentrations.

How fast will cities grow?

International experiences show that it is easier to plan cities—and thus provision—when urban population growth is slower.

Urban population growth will decrease over the coming decades, but it will still pose a challenge to some countries, especially in Eastern, Central and Western Africa. Figure 5.8 shows the median of the average growth rate per decade. Eastern, Central and Western Africa will have the highest urban population growth rates, while Northern Africa's urban population will barely grow (0.5%). Middle

Table 5.3: Levels of access and urbanization (number of countries), 2012

Access ranges		Urban population ranges (%)					
		Water			Sanitation		
		0-40	40-70	70-100	0-40	40-70	70-100
Eastern	0-50	0	0	0	10	0	0
	50-80	5	0	0	5	0	1
	80-100	10	2	1	0	2	0
Central	0-50	0	0	0	2	3	1
	50-80	2	2		0	1	0
	80-100	1	3	1	1	1	0
Northern	0-50	0	0	0	1	0	0
	50-80	1	0	1	0	0	0
	80-100	0	4	0	0	4	1
Southern	0-50	0	0	0	1	0	0
	50-80	2	3	0	1	2	0
	80-100	0	0	0	0	1	0
Western	0-50	0	0	0	5	6	0
	50-80	0	2	0	0	0	0
	80-100	6	8	0	1	4	0
Total	0-50	0	0	0	19	9	1
	50-80	10	7	1	6	3	1
	80-100	17	17	2	2	12	1
Total		27	24	3	27	24	3

Source: Based on UNDESA (2014) and World Bank (2012).

and Southern Africa both have small rates, but will still see their respective urban populations grow. Thirty percent of African countries will see their urban populations grow at rates above 2.5% per year. Most of them (15) are in Eastern and Western Africa.

Countries with the highest level of unserved demands today are also those in which urban growth will pose the greatest challenge. As shown in Table 5.4, 11 of the 13 countries with intermediate access rates to water and 24 of the 29 countries with low access to improved sanitation services will experience rapid urban growth between 2010 and 2060.

Climate change

No country is immune to climate change, regardless of where they are located, or whether they contribute to it. For African countries, climate change poses two primary challenges: it affects agricultural productivity and, therefore, it accelerates urban growth.

Figure 5.8: Average urban population growth per decade, median by region (%)

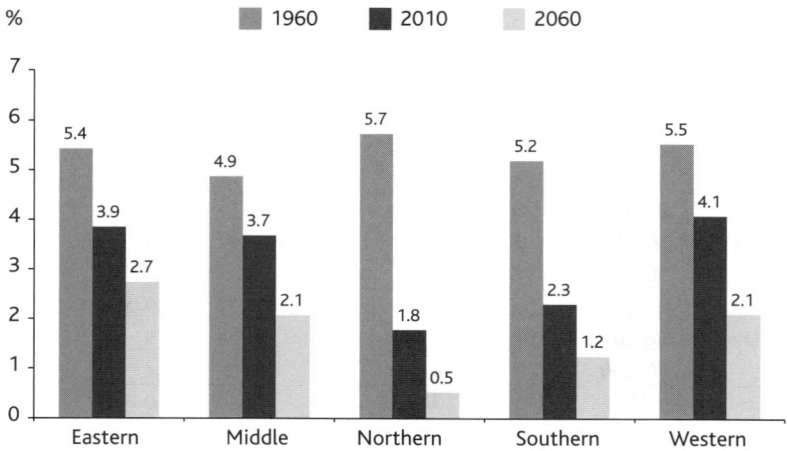

Source: Based on UNDESA (2014)

Table 5.4: Access (2012) and urban growth rates, 2010–2060

Access ranges		Urban growth rate ranges (%)			
		Water		Sanitation	
		≤2.5%	≥2.5%	≤2.5%	≥2.5%
Eastern	0-50	0	0	0	10
	50-80	0	5	2	4
	80-100	4	9	2	0
Central	0-50	0	0	2	4
	50-80	0	4	0	1
	80-100	2	3	0	2
Northern	0-50	0	0	0	1
	50-80	1	1	0	0
	80-100	4	0	5	0
Southern	0-50	0	0	1	0
	50-80	0	0	3	0
	80-100	5	0	1	0
Western	0-50	0	0	2	9
	50-80	1	1	2	3
	80-100	3	11	0	0
Total	0-50	0	0	5	24
	50-80	2	11	7	8
	80-100	18	23	8	2
Total		20	34	20	34

Source: Based on UNDESA (2014) and World Bank (2012).

Expected impacts of climate change show that Southern and Western Africa and Sudan will be severely affected by droughts, while most of Sub-Saharan Africa will be affected by floods (Figure 5.9). The World Development Report (WDR) 2010 report (World Bank, 2010) recommends that the region adopt climate-resilient technologies and practices so as to increase crop yields and protect livestock.

Unlike in other parts of the world, in Africa, climate change is one of the main drivers of urban growth. Barrios et al (2006) show that rainfall reduction is one of the main factors driving population from rural to urban areas in Africa. They explain that this is a phenomenon particular to sub-Saharan Africa due to the strong economic reliance

Figure 5.9: Exposure to climate change risks

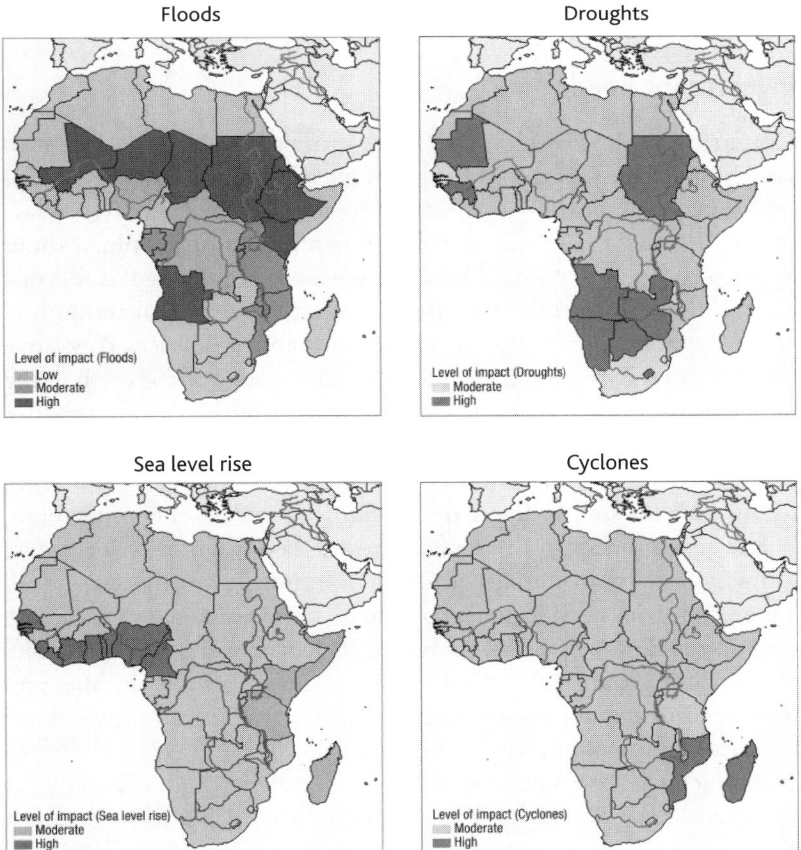

Floods

Droughts

Sea level rise

Cyclones

Source: Climate Change Strategy Background Reports: World Bank (2008e) and Washington (2008), cited in World Development Report 2010.

on rainfall. Annez et al (2010) confirm the relevance of rainfall as opposed to pro-urban policies in explaining urban growth. They add to these results by enlarging the sample and including geographical and political factors, such as dummy variables for being landlocked or resource-rich, having artificial borders, or suffering from ethnic fractionalization.

Barrios et al (2006) also explain that economies are more dependent on rainfall since agriculture accounts for more than twice the share of GDP than in other developing regions. At the same time, a much smaller proportion of cropland is irrigated, meaning that soil productivity in Africa is much more affected by drought conditions than in other parts of the world. Added to that, chronic diseases that affect labor productivity can be exacerbated by water shortages. Conflict affects migration directly, but also creates obstacles that interfere with climate change risk management (World Bank, 2010).

Investment needs

Countries can be classified into three groups based on the extent to which they have met the Millennium Development Goal (MDG) for water and sanitation. This is related to the goal that by 2015, these countries should have cut in half the percentage of people without access to both as of 1990. These three groups are defined as follows: growth in the provision of services is on target (that is, at minimum, at the expected pace); growth in the provision of services is positive but slow (that is, there is growth but at a slow pace); and growth in the provision of services is negative and slow (that is, there is no growth).

For those countries in the first group, policies aimed at increasing access to water and sanitation are proving effective. Correspondingly, future policies should focus on monitoring and maintaining them. For those countries in the second group, the provision of services is growing faster than the urban population, but slower than the ideal. These countries need some extra help or some assistance in obtaining resources and making provision more efficient. Finally, those countries in the third group have access rates that are in serious decline, and thus need to enhance institutions and programs so as to give better responses to urban population growth.

Setting goals in this manner helps us to create an MDG-like rule, as in Fay and Yepes (2003), and Yepes (2008). The MDG-like rule uses a linear trend between access as of 1990 and expected access in 2015. For countries classified as "on target" their current trend is used; for the other countries, the MDG-like rule is used to set the goal. Table 5.6

Table 5.5: MDG-trend achievement

	Water			Sanitation		
	Lagged			Lagged		
Negative	Positive	On target		Negative	Positive	On target
Eastern						
Burundi	Eritrea	Djibouti		Rwanda	Burundi	
Comoros	Madagascar	Ethiopia		Zambia	Comoros	
Kenya	Mozambique	Malawi		Zimbabwe	Kenya	
Rwanda	Seychelles	Mauritius		Eritrea	Tanzania	
Tanzania		Uganda			Madagascar	
Zambia					Mozambique	
Zimbabwe					Seychelles	
					Djibouti	
					Ethiopia	
					Malawi	
					Mauritius	
					Uganda	
Central						
Congo, DR	Congo, Rep.	Angola		Congo, DR	Central	Angola
Equatorial		Cameroon		Equatorial	African	
Guinea		Central African		Guinea	Republic	
Gabon		Republic		Gabon	Chad	
		Chad		Congo, Rep.		
				Cameroon		
Northern						
Algeria		Egypt		Algeria	Morocco	Egypt
Sudan		Morocco		Sudan		Tunisia
		Tunisia				
Southern						
Lesotho		Botswana		Lesotho	South Africa	Botswana
		Namibia		Namibia	Swaziland	
		South Africa				
		Swaziland				
Western						
Cape Verde	Côte	Benin		Cape Verde	Guinea	
Liberia	d'Ivoire	Burkina Faso		Liberia	Mauritania	
Nigeria	Guinea	Gambia, The		Nigeria	Benin	
	Mauritania	Ghana		Côte d'Ivoire	Burkina Faso	
		Guinea-Bissau		Gambia, The	Ghana	
		Mali		Guinea-	Mali	
		Niger		Bissau	Niger	
		Senegal		Sierra Leone	Senegal	
		Sierra Leone		Togo		
		Togo				

Note: Congo, DR = Democratic Republic of Congo; Congo Rep = Republic of Congo

Source: Based on World Development Indicators, http://data.worldbank.org/data-catalog/world-development-indicators.

shows investment needs in water and sanitation in urban areas. The first three columns show the distribution of total investment needs across groups, the fourth column shows the number of connections

Table 5.6: Investment need in water and sanitation in urban areas

| | Close gap in 2010 (%) | Keep up with demand Annual investment per capita | | Close gap 2010-2060 | | |
| | | | | | Annual investment | |
	2010	2035	2060	Number of connections	% GDP	% maint-enance
Water						
Region						
Eastern	19	28	36	387,586	0.15	48
Central	12	15	13	166,314	0.01	51
Northern	25	12	8	117,544	0.03	64
Southern	0	2	1	18,981	0.01	77
Western	43	42	43	509,131	0.14	50
Urbanization rate						
Low	43	48	58	644,229	0.02	48
Intermediate	43	49	41	533,346	0.04	55
High	15	3	1	21,980	0.03	70
Urban growth rate						
Low	15	23	13	207,174	0.02	64
High	85	77	87	992,381	0.03	49
Total	**100**	**100**	**100**	**1,199,555**	**0.03**	**52**
Sanitation						
Region						
Eastern	22	28	36	424,232	0.28	43
Central	17	15	13	183,503	0.01	47
Northern	6	12	7	123,919	0.07	64
Southern	2	3	1	24,553	0.03	70
Western	52	42	43	573,108	0.26	44
Urbanization rate						
Low	44	48	58	708,149	0.04	44
Intermediate	54	49	41	598,292	0.07	51
High	2	3	1	22,873	0.07	73
Urban growth rate						
Low	18	23	13	233,325	0.04	61
High	82	77	87	1,095,990	0.06	44
Total	**100**	**100**	**100**	**1,329,314**	**0.06**	**48**

Source: Author's own calculations based on data from World Development Indicators (WDI) and UN Habitat.

required, the fifth values these investment needs in terms of the GDP and the sixth column shows the percentage that should be committed to maintenance.

Supply- and demand-side constraints

Major challenges in supply and demand include making water and sanitation provision more efficient as well as setting a correct tariff structure. The next section discusses supply-side concerns, while the following section delves deeper into demand-side challenges.

Efficiency and sustainability of utilities

Infrastructure is only the first step in the provision of water and sanitation. Infrastructure is useless if, in the end, water remains unconsumed and sanitation unavailable. Two main objectives must be met in order to achieve the desired outcomes. First, tariffs must cover capital and operation and maintenance costs. Second, households should be able to afford to consume the provided services at the tariffs defined. As a price, tariffs should also be used to send price signals to users about the relationship between water use and water scarcity, and to ensure fairness in water service delivery (Cardone and Fonseca, 2003).

Utilities in Africa have difficulties to achieve both objectives. Though tariffs are designed to recover operations and maintenance (O&M) costs, there is no information concerning the collection ratio and enforcement mechanisms. Thus, it is not possible to determine whether utilities are actually raising revenues. Banerjee et al (2010) examines the AICD Water Supply and Sanitation Survey Database, which contains information on 45 water utilities from 23 countries in Africa. Findings show that the performance of African utilities is superior to that of utilities found elsewhere in the world. For instance, in Latin America and the Caribbean, which has the best record among developing countries, the degree of partial O&M cost recovery is only 38% (Foster and Yepes, 2005). In Africa, the tariff structures are designed in a manner more conducive to meeting O&M costs at the high or low ends of consumption. At the highest block levels, 80% of utilities are able to regain their operating costs.

Of 45 African utilities analyzed by Banerjee et al (2010), 17 have average tariffs (calculated at 10 m^3) higher than US$0.40/m^3 thus are expected to cover O&M costs, and only four utilities have tariffs greater than US $0.80/m^3, which is sufficiently high to cover O&M

and part of the capital cost. These four utilities—which all enforce a tariff greater than US$1—are located in South Africa, Namibia and Cape Verde—all middle-income countries.

Cost recovery is much more evident with non-residential tariffs. About 20 utilities enforce a commercial tariff greater than US$0.8/m^3 in the first block. About 95% of the utilities charge a price greater than the cost of O&M—the recovery threshold is $0.4/m^3 for an average commercial consumption level of 100 m^3.

Metering coverage is higher than expected, but many access the service without paying for it.

> In Africa, water metering is surprisingly widespread, with many utilities reporting 100 percent metering in their service areas. Nine utilities have implemented operating meters for all residential and nonresidential connections. For 35 utilities for which detailed information is available, the average metering ratio is 75 percent. Other utilities, including those in Nigeria and Sudan, have almost negligible or no metering. Most others fall somewhere in between. Those households without meters, however, can escape water utilities' enforcement mechanism, resulting in revenue losses. (Banerjee et al, 2010, p 6)

Non-payment for infrastructure services is a major issue. Among those reporting access to piped water, 31% did not report paying a bill during the month of service[2] (Banerjee et al, 2008).

However, water and sanitation utilities operate in a high-cost environment. They also have a mandate to at least partially recover their O&M costs. As a result, water tariffs are higher than in other regions of the world and households cannot afford to pay for minimum consumption. Thus, even where connections to improved water and sanitation services are available, households are not able to use them.

This mismatch between provision costs and the ability to pay for services has not been solved by subsidies. Most utilities use increasing block tariffs (IBTs) to charge for water consumption, but this hinders full cost recovery, and does not benefit to any great extent the poorest households. Banerjee et al (2010) found most African utilities are able to achieve O&M cost recovery at the highest block tariffs, but not at the first block tariffs, which are designed to provide affordable water to low-volume consumers, who are often poor. At the same time, few utilities can recover even a small part of their capital costs, even in the highest tariff blocks. Further, the equity objectives of the IBT structure are not met in many countries. The subsidy to the lowest tariff block does not benefit the poor exclusively but the majority of non-poor consumers, while the minimum consumption charge is often unaffordable for the poorest customers.

Added to that, a lack of competition in the water market implies that policymakers are never subjected to a market test of whether the tariff structure is functioning effectively; that is, consumers are unable to reject a tariff structure that has a negative impact on them (Whittington et al, 2002).

Ability of households to pay for the service

Provision costs are a key aspect of financial sustainability, but so is the ability of households to pay for services. From the demand side, the ability of consumers to pay tariffs influences the capacity of utilities to be financially capable of expanding access and ensuring quality of service.

Demand-side constraints explain up to one-third of the coverage deficit. Banerjee et al (2008) break down the unserved population into those who are not hooked up to the service, even when it is available to the community of residence, and those who live in places where the related infrastructure is not available. The latter can be thought of as being driven by supply-side constraints (that is, the network for service provision is not available), while the former can be driven by both supply-side and demand-side constraints. In these cases, supply-side constraints can become manifest because the infrastructure, though available, does not have the capacity to serve higher demand. Demand-side constraints include the inability to afford consumption, as well as a preference for other available sources. The authors make some adjustments in order to capture only that fraction of households that are unserved because of demand-side constraints. For piped water the authors found that demand-side factors account for 55-65% of the coverage deficit. However, these estimates fall substantially between 15% and 35%.

However, the capacity of most Africans to pay constitutes a great barrier to the expansion of utilities. Many poor households cannot even afford a connection to a piped water network. Foster and Yepes (2006) conclude that 70% of households in Africa will have difficulty paying internationally comparable cost-recovery tariffs. Banerjee et al (2008) extended this analysis and found that in most countries, between one- and two-thirds of the urban population will find it difficult to cover the cost of service. In eight countries, at least 70%

of urban households will be unable to afford a monthly expenditure of US$10 for water. Only in the remaining seven countries will most urban households be able to afford a monthly expenditure sufficient to allow the utility to meet costs. The affordability threshold is surpassed when more than 5% of a household's income is used to purchase a subsistence level of any given utility service (Banerjee et al, 2008).

About 60% of Africa's population cannot afford to pay full cost recovery tariffs or to extend consumption beyond the absolute minimum subsistence level.

When all African households are pooled together across countries and are grouped into a common set of quintiles based on purchasing power parity adjustments to their budgets, an average household in the three poorest quintiles hit the 5% affordability threshold at $4, $7 and $12 dollars per month. From these findings one can infer that very modest consumption baskets priced at levels compatible with recovery of operating costs would appear to be affordable across the full range of household budgets in Africa. Nevertheless, around 60 percent of the African population cannot afford to pay full cost recovery tariffs or extend consumption beyond the absolute minimum subsistence level (Banerjee et al, 2008).

As expected, these results vary across countries (see Figure 5.10 and Table 5.7). Some countries, such as Ethiopia, Democratic Republic of Congo and Malawi, have very low capacities to pay for services. In these countries, a large fraction of the urban population rapidly hit the 5% affordability threshold for low bills. For example, in Ethiopia, 40% of the urban population hits the threshold if the monthly bill is US$2, but rapidly rises to 87% of the population if the monthly bill is doubled to US$4.

> The countries are divided into three groups. At one extreme is Group 1 comprising Cape Verde, Morocco, Senegal, Cameroon, Côte d'Ivoire, Congo, and South Africa, where a majority of urban households can afford a monthly expenditure of US$12 (and indeed much higher). At the other extreme is Group 3, comprising Burundi, the Democratic Republic of Congo, Ethiopia, Guinea-Bissau, Malawi, Niger, Tanzania and Uganda, where the vast majority of urban households (at least 70 percent and in some cases over 90 percent of households) would be unable to afford a monthly expenditure of US$8 or $12 for water or electricity. All the remaining countries fall into Group 2 where a substantial share of the urban population—between

Figure 5.10: Share of average urban household budget required to purchase subsistence amounts of piped water and electricity, by continental income quintiles

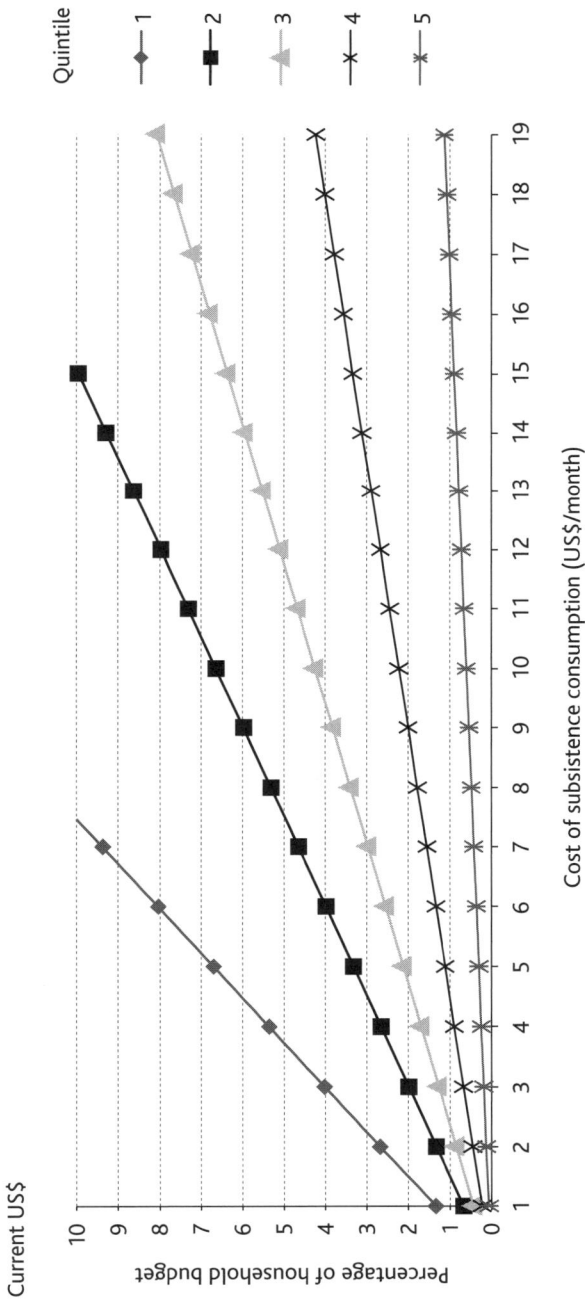

Current US$

Source: Foster and Yepes (2005)

Table 5.7: Countries by affordability ranges

Affordability	1	2	3
Region			
Eastern		3	5
Central	2	1	1
Northern	1		
Southern	1		
Western	3	5	2
Urbanization rate			
Low	5	2	
Intermediate	2	7	8
High			
Urban growth rate			
Low		5	7
High	7	4	1
Total	7	9	8

one- and two-thirds—would face difficulties covering an upper-bound monthly expenditure. (Banerjee et al, 2008)

In many countries, second-best services are a better option. For many households, stand-posts managed by utilities, donors, or private operators have emerged as an alternative to piped water. Those that are managed by utilities or that supply utility water are expected to use the formal utility tariffs, which are kept low in order to make water affordable for low-income households. The price for water resold through informal channels, however, is much more expensive than piped water. In some cases, promoting greater use of second-best alternatives may be a good way to expand access in an affordable way. Some second-best options are viable substitutes for networked services, for example shared connections or standpipes, but even access to these alternatives is still comparatively skewed toward upper-income groups, indicating that there is substantial room for growth in access to these forms of service.

Water scarcity

Water scarcity is not a major concern; the problem has to do with the provision of the infrastructure that makes access to water possible.

Sub-Saharan Africa has insufficient infrastructure, even relative to existing needs. There are few water control systems and limited water storage capacity, despite relatively abundant resources. Most rivers cross more than one country, necessitating effective cooperation across borders. Africa's 63 trans-boundary river basins together account for 90% of the continent's surface water resources. Poorly developed transport, energy, information and communication systems may also hinder adaptation. Additionally, the region's rapidly urbanizing population is vulnerable because of ill-defined property rights, weak land-use planning, and informal settlements that are often on land subject to erosion or flooding. Nearly three-quarters of the region's urban population lives in slums, and the vast majority of the 300 million additional urban residents anticipated over the next 25 years may also confront similar living conditions (World Bank, 2010).

As with the electricity sector, agreements between countries are fundamental to guaranteeing water provision in some regions.

Conclusion

Efforts should be geared towards strengthening the capabilities of governments to make the right choices of investments in infrastructure, and also posing the right regulatory mandates that help service provision to be financially sustainable. This can be nourished by prioritizing investment both in the places to invest and the types of infrastructure that are promoted.

Even if all African countries have the same resources to invest in infrastructure, results will be very heterogeneous not only because provision costs will vary, but mainly because the efficiency with which those resources are used. Setting appropriate regulatory schemes is just the first step. Guaranteeing compliance of such schemes is the biggest goal and various strategies should be taken to accomplish it. Among them, the following should be taken into account:

- *A guided transition that sets specific goals according to each country or each administrative area's capabilities.* Not all countries or places within a country have the same level of institutional strength—meaning variation in capacity to assign budgets and motor its execution correctly. Thus, there should be a guided transition to apply the regulatory scheme.

- *Monitoring processes and making the process flexible to incorporate feedback is important.*

- *Establishing communication channels across countries and places within countries to take advantage of others' experiences.* Several channels can be used, among them virtual communities to share knowledge on specific subjects, for example, how to build sustainable aqueducts. Other networks as the one promoted by the Inter-American Development Bank in Latin America can help achieve better results. The Latin American Water and Sanitation Network is a dialog mechanism between the main agents involved in decision-making processes in the region on subjects related to water resources management and utilities. Its main objective is to share and spread knowledge on best practices related to these subjects to improve regional cooperation and decision making.

- *Classifying countries by current levels of access to water and sanitation and expected population growth should be used to set priorities.* As mentioned, countries with low levels of access to improved services face the challenge of coping with demand. When urbanization levels are growing, they need to provide services to more people, but can take advantage of economies of scale. On the other hand, countries with high levels of access have been able to transform their institutions so as to effectively respond to demand. Furthermore, countries with large urban concentrations have already managed this transition. Intuitively, their planning institutions are more consolidated and have the experience required to respond to the needs of large population concentrations.

On the other hand, it is important to consider that as countries observe economic growth, household's expenditure capacity will grow—the middle-class effect. During the coming 50 years African countries have to work towards making water and sanitation consumption affordable but, at the same time, utilities financially sound. Creating a plan to transit from tariffs with universal subsidies to tariff schemes with targeted subsidies should be a priority. This transit consists of identifying and charging full cost to those who can pay for it. As shown, just a small fraction of households has those characteristics, but the capacity to pay for the services will develop with economic growth. This contribution is essential to increase everybody's access to potable water. Also, Africa should learn from experiences in other parts of the world. Though subsidies are difficult to target, more effective tariff schemes to recover at least operating cost have already been created.

To prioritize investment two factors must be taken into consideration: place and type of infrastructure. Providing water and sanitation services to small and isolated rural settlements might not be sustainable either in the short or the long term. Such settlements do not benefit from scale economies and, usually, providing the service to one household in isolated areas costs more than providing it in more families in populous areas. Despite economies of scale in water and sanitation, provision may vanish rapidly – as population increases due to investment requirements for water production and waste water treatment – gains observed at low levels of provision would make up for the difference in financial resources allocation. Hence, prioritizing investment in medium size cities and more dense urban areas *must be a must*.

The types of infrastructure provided should also be analyzed. Second-best choices can be a mid-term solution to reach good results on the impacts on health and quality of life, while having a sizeable budget restriction. In other words, it is better to provide access to second-best options to most of the population than provide first best option to a few. Piped access for everybody should be avoided as the goal.

Notes

[1] Although the countries mentioned in the figure's note were not included due to unavailability of the data and the central tendency indicator chosen (median), all of them have access to water and sanitation rates above 50%: Libya (2001): 54.2% water, 96.8% sanitation; Equatorial Guinea (2006): 65.5% water, 92.2% sanitation; Eritrea (2008): 73.7% water, 51.6% sanitation; Comoros (2010): 90.7% water, 50% sanitation; and Somalia (2011): 69.6% water, 52% sanitation.

[2] Those with access include households that are connected to the service in question, and households that are not connected but pay for the respective service.

References

African Development Bank (2014) *Tracking Africa's Progress in Figures*, Tunis: AfDB. Available at: www.afdb.org/fileadmin/uploads/afdb/Documents/Publications/Tracking_Africa%E2%80%99s_Progress_in_Figures.pdf

Annez, P., Buckley, R. and Kalarickal, J. (2010) 'African urbanization as flight? Some policy implications of geography', *Urban Forum*, 21, pp 221–34.

Banerjee, S., Foster, V., Ying, Y., Skilling, H. and Wodon, Q. (2010) *Cost Recovery, Equity, and Efficiency in Water Tariffs: Evidence from African Utilities*, Policy Research Working Paper 5384, Washington DC: The World Bank.

Banerjee, S., Wodon, Q., Diallo, A., Pushak, T., Elal Uddin, E., Tsimpo, C. and Foster, V. (2008) *Access, affordability, and alternatives: Modern infrastructure services in Africa*. Washington, DC: World Bank. Available at: https://mpra.ub.uni-muenchen.de/27740/1/MPRA_paper_27740.pdf

Barrios, S., Bertinelli, L., and Strobl, E. (2006) 'Climate change and rural urban migration: the case of Sub Saharan Africa', *Journal of Urban Economics*, 60, pp 357–71.

Cardone, R. and Fonseca, C. (2003) *Financing and Cost Recovery*. IRC thematic overview paper. Delft, the Netherlands: International Water and Sanitation Center.

Cutler, D. and Miller, G. (2005) 'The role of public health improvements in health advances: the twentieth century United States', *Demography*, 42(1), pp 1–22.

Fay, M. and Yepes, T. (2003) *Investing in Infrastructure: What is Needed from 2000 to 2010?* World Bank Policy Research Working Paper 3102. Washington, DC: World Bank.

Foster, V. and T. Yepes. (2005) *Is Cost Recovery a Feasible Objective for Water and Electricity?*, Finance, Private Sector and Infrastructure Department, Latin America and the Caribbean Region, Washington, DC: World Bank.

Leipziger, D., Fay, M., Wodon, Q. and Yepes, T. (2003) *Achieving the Millennium Development Goals: The Role of Infrastructure*, Working Paper, No. 3163, Washington, DC: World Bank.

UNDESA (United Nations, Department of Economic and Social Affairs, Population Division) (2014) *World Urbanization Prospects: The 2014 Revision, Highlights* (ST/ESA/SER.A/352). New York: UNDESA.

Whittington, D., Boland, J. and Foster, V. (2002) *Water Tariffs and Subsidies in South Asia: Understanding the Basics*. Water and Sanitation Program Paper 2. Washington DC: World Bank.

World Bank (2010) *World Development Report – development and climate change*. Washington, DC: World Bank.

World Bank (2012) *World Development Indicators*, Washington, DC: World Bank.

World Bank (2014) *World Development Indicators*. Washington, DC: World Bank.

Yepes, T. (2008) *Investment Needs for Infrastructure in Developing Countries 2008–15*. Washington DC: World Bank.

Annex

Table A5.1: African cities by world rank (in 2013)

Rank	Sub-region	Country	City	Population	Density
Cities among the top 100 largest cities in the world					
16	Northern	Egypt	Cairo	15,071,000	23,500
25	Western	Nigeria	Lagos	12,090,000	34,500
31	Central	DR of the Congo	Kinshasa	9,387,000	41,700
43	Southern	South Africa	Johannesburg-East Rand	7,426,000	7,100
64	Central	Angola	Luanda	5,425,000	18,300
70	Northern	Sudan	Khartoum	4,919,000	13,700
79	Northern	Egypt	Alexandria	4,603,000	40,700
79	Western	Côte d'Ivoire	Abidjan	4,603,000	36,800
84	Eastern	Kenya	Nairobi	4,457,000	20,700
95	Western	Ghana	Accra	3,933,000	10,800
Cities among the top 100 densest cities in the world					
16	Northern	Morocco	Fez	1,117,000	55,900
19	Central	Angola	Huambo	1,175,000	53,400
36	Central	DR of the Congo	Kananga	959,000	45,700
43	Eastern	Somalia	Mogadishu	1,637,000	44,200
46	Western	Senegal	Dakar	3,270,000	43,600
51	Central	DR of the Congo	Kinshasa	9,387,000	41,700
52	Northern	Morocco	Tangier	790,000	41,600
56	Northern	Egypt	Alexandria	4,603,000	40,700
57	Western	Côte d'Ivoire	Yamoussoukro	890,000	40,500
58	Eastern	Djibouti	Dijibouti	600,000	40,000
62	Northern	Egypt	Port Said	550,000	39,300
79	Western	Nigeria	Kano	3,636,000	37,500
85	Western	Côte d'Ivoire	Abidjan	4,603,000	36,800
86	Northern	Morocco	Casablanca	3,120,000	36,700
94	Central	DR of the Congo	Kisangani	780,000	35,500

Source: Computed by author from Demographia database

Africa's prospects for infrastructure development and regional integration: energy sector

Ethèl Teljeur, Mayuree Chetty and Morné Hendriksz

Introduction

The African energy sector lags far behind those of other developing regions. Household access to electricity is extremely low (only 29% of Africans in Sub-Saharan Africa have access); electricity supply is unreliable (African manufacturers experience power outages, on average, 56 days per year); and power is expensive (African power tariffs are significantly higher than those in other developing regions).[1,2] In addition, most people in Sub-Saharan Africa rely on traditional fuel sources such as paraffin and wood for heating and cooking.[3] Regional oil and gas infrastructure is limited, because there is little interconnectivity between national transmission and transport networks. The result is a small number of regional oil and gas pipelines (concentrated in North Africa) and many isolated national pipeline networks.[4] The lack of a sufficient and reliable supply of energy not only directly affects the quality of life of Africans, but also hinders economic growth, employment, and ultimately livelihoods.[5]

Interdependence between economic growth and energy demand

Economic growth and energy demand are interdependent: Africa requires access to energy to achieve economic growth, and greater economic growth increases energy demand, largely from industrial activities. Sufficient energy infrastructure is required to support growing African economies and to provide energy access to enable poorer African nations to grow.[6] Improving the underdeveloped energy sector has often been identified as a key to achieving greater economic growth. Currently, African businesses lie idle because power supplies are unreliable, and economic activity stagnates.[7] In addition, the lack of adequate infrastructure hinders trade and slows economic growth: African markets are inaccessible to trading partners throughout the globe, thereby reducing the world's trade with the continent.[8] Furthermore, trade between neighboring nations is limited.[9]

Uneven distribution of energy resources in Africa

Africa consists of many small, isolated economies with an uneven distribution of energy resources.[10] Windfall profits are earned by North African countries such as Libya and Algeria that capitalize on their oil and gas endowments; countries such as the Democratic Republic of the Congo (DRC) and Ethiopia[11] struggle to provide energy access for basic human needs.[12] Small national energy markets also mean that it is difficult to achieve economies of scale, which makes infrastructure investments unattractive, even when energy supplies are abundant. For example, despite Nigeria's large supplies of oil, gas and hydro energy, according to 2010 estimates from the IEA, access to electricity in the country is fairly low at 50%, and 74% of the population depend on coal and traditional biomass fuels such as wood for cooking.[13]

In addition, there is a mismatch between the geographic location of energy resources and energy demand. For example, East Africa's substantial gas reserves are far from Southern Africa, where demand for energy is high. Domestic markets in East Africa are too small to absorb the supply that will result from recent discoveries, so gas in Mozambique and Tanzania is being prepared for export to Asia.[14] The situation is similar for coal deposits in Botswana and for oil and associated gas in Nigeria, Angola and other West African nations.[15] For similar reasons, North Africa's oil and gas have traditionally been exported to Europe instead of being used to satisfy African demand.[16]

Inefficient use of energy resources and low levels of intra-African trade in energy have resulted in high fuel imports and inefficient electricity generation across the continent.[17] Economic growth in South Africa, Nigeria and other emerging economies is crucial for the development of African energy markets, as it will create energy demand and the ability to pay that make the development of energy infrastructure feasible. Regional integration of African energy markets and intra-African trade in energy are means of pooling demand and supply.[18]

Intra-African trade in energy and the regional integration of energy markets have been identified as ways to address the uneven distribution and mismatch of energy supply and demand.[19] Greater integration of electricity, oil and gas markets may create a domestic energy demand large enough to provide economic justification for and bankability of energy infrastructure development. By developing intra-African trade in energy, many nations can benefit from: exporting excess supply of power and primary energy sources; lower energy costs by relying less on imports, and possibly, less exposure to exchange rate and commodity price risk; and greater access to reliable sources.[20] Intra-African energy trade may reduce the cost of energy supply to many nations, particularly small countries that lack domestic energy resources.[21] Intra-African trade will also diversify the continent's energy mix and increase the share of green energy (for example, hydropower, and possibly, solar energy).[22] Investment in infrastructure and trade is, therefore, essential to improve energy security and reliability.[23] This, of course, has limitations—as island states and economies with fragmented population distributions will not benefit as readily from pooling of demand or supply. However, this by no means undermines the low-hanging fruit to be attained from these strategies.

Several examples demonstrate that improvements in regional energy trade and integration of infrastructure can develop African energy markets. The Republic of Mozambique Pipeline Investment Company (ROMPCO) gas pipeline, which is used to transport natural gas from Mozambique to South Africa, has benefitted both nations by creating a structural shift in Mozambique's GDP[24] and increasing the gas supply to South Africa.[25] Similarly, recent discoveries of natural gas in East Africa could stimulate intra-African trade. The Grand Inga hydropower project has the potential to generate substantial amounts of electricity to satisfy demand in Western, Central and even Southern Africa,[26] provided that the networks of the members of the Southern African Power Pool are expanded and upgraded. Regional energy infrastructure networks can reduce the cost of conducting business between African countries, improve Africa's competitiveness in global markets, and increase intra-African trade.[27]

Energy sector development and regional integration

Regional and continental integration can, under certain circumstances, be a key driver of economic growth and poverty reduction, and thus, has been identified as a priority by many African governments.[28] A regional energy infrastructure network, or more likely, an interconnected set of regional energy networks that reduce electricity costs can also reduce the cost of conducting business between African countries.[29]

Figure 6.1 provides an overview of the existing and planned power interconnector links: the South African Power Pool (SAPP, 1995); the North African power pool (COMELEC, 1998); the West African Power Pool (WAPP, 2000); the Central African Power Pool (CAPP, 2003); and the East Africa Power Pool (EAPP, 2005). These power pools aim to establish regional power markets.[30]

An interesting inter-reliant dynamic emerges as clearly energy sector development is a requirement to enable greater regional economic integration, while, simultaneously, moves towards enhanced regional integration (such as the harmonization of legal and regulatory frameworks for energy, coordination of energy infrastructure investments, and so on) are required to facilitate energy trade in Africa.[31] Enhanced integration can address problems associated with energy infrastructure investment. Regional integration will allow African nations to develop more shared energy infrastructure jointly such as the Rusumo Falls Hydroelectric Project involving Burundi, Rwanda and Tanzania and the Ethiopia–Kenya interconnector. [32, 33, 34]

Figure 6.1: Existing and planned power interconnector links in Africa

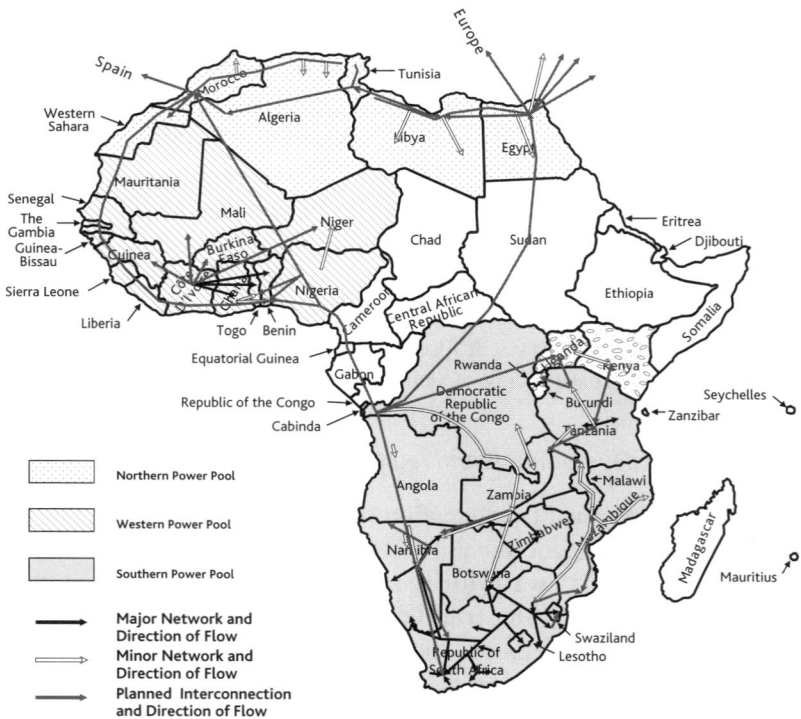

Source: Niyimbona (2005), op cit.

In addition, regional integration facilitates trade of energy resources and services via sub-regional power pools.[35]

Despite attempts to integrate regional infrastructure via power pools, actual trade within these pools is low, and the opportunity to derive efficiencies from integrated regional resource planning is missed in favor of national electricity infrastructure plans.[36]

Among the challenges facing regional power trade is the lack of harmonization of energy policies and regulatory frameworks between neighboring countries. Different stages and design of energy market liberalization or (re-)regulation and the desire for energy self-sufficiency ("security of supply") hinder the development of bilateral or multilateral projects. Investment in interconnection capacity is required to facilitate intra-power pool trade and achieve the efficiencies associated with the pooling of demand and integrated energy planning. If implemented correctly, regional power pools can enhance the security and reliability of power supply. This is in contrast to the commonly-held view that energy trade is likely to increase reliance on imported energy and reduce energy security.

Electricity: Africa's current position

Electricity is scarce in Africa. In 1980, Sub-Saharan Africa's electricity generation capacity was comparable to that of South Asia, but decades of relatively lower investment in energy infrastructure left the continent struggling to meet growing demand. The gap between the demand and the available supply has led to the development of ambitious electricity generation projects.[37] The continent is rich in natural energy resources ranging from oil, gas and uranium reserves to hydropower potential, but these resources must be converted into reliable sources of electricity.

In 2010, installed electricity capacity in Sub-Saharan Africa was approximately 78 gigawatts (GW, or 78,000 megawatts [MW]), which, in total, is similar to that of individual developed countries' installed capacity, such as the capacity of South Korea and the United Kingdom.[38] With the exclusion of South Africa, the total Sub-Saharan installed capacity is only 34 gigawatts (the same capacity as Sweden). Figure 6.2 illustrates the differences in electricity generation capacity across Africa.

The low generation capacity results from stagnant investment in, and maintenance of, infrastructure since the 1980s, which leave close to one-quarter of built capacity unavailable.[39] Many countries experience daily power outages; in Senegal outages occur, on average, 25 days

Figure 6.2: Installed generating capacity in Africa

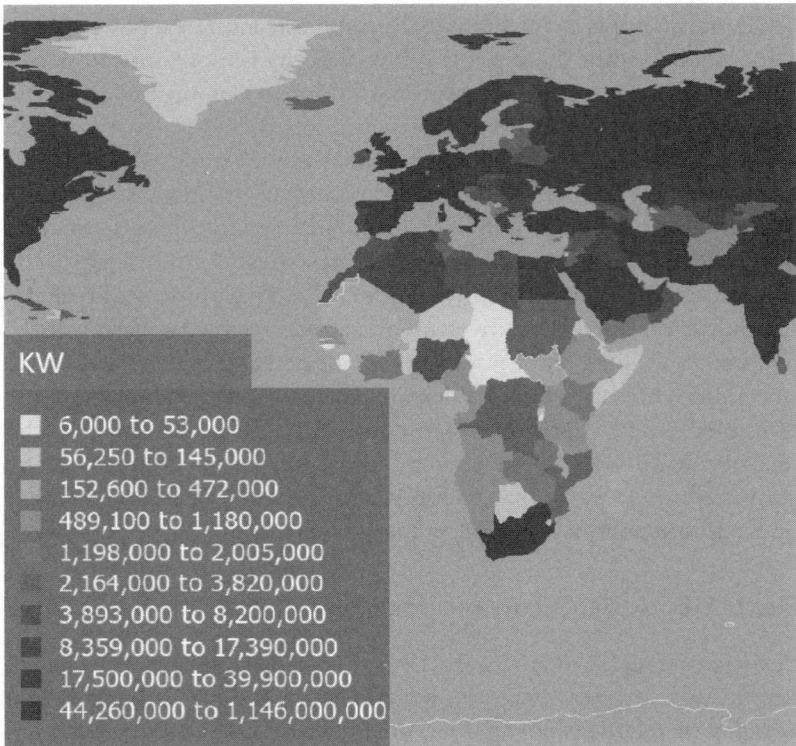

KW

- 6,000 to 53,000
- 56,250 to 145,000
- 152,600 to 472,000
- 489,100 to 1,180,000
- 1,198,000 to 2,005,000
- 2,164,000 to 3,820,000
- 3,893,000 to 8,200,000
- 8,359,000 to 17,390,000
- 17,500,000 to 39,900,000
- 44,260,000 to 1,146,000,000

Source: Mecometer.com; World Bank's World Development Indicators database

a year, while the Democratic Republic of the Congo spends about 10 days a month in the dark.[40, 41] These outages lead to substantial losses in the private sector. Costs can be as high as 16% of annual turnover for informal industries.[42]

The low generating capacity does not reflect low availability of natural energy resources; on the contrary, Africa has extensive energy resources that can be converted into electricity. Major oil and gas reserves in North and West Africa and recent discoveries of natural gas in East Africa are predicted to change the global gas market in the near future.[43] Africa's Southern region (particularly, South Africa) has large coal deposits, while hydropower potential is considerable in East, Central and West Africa.[44] Africa also has substantial uranium reserves, mainly in South Africa, Namibia and Niger, but also in other nations such as Malawi and Mauritania.[45] The potential of these resources is already apparent, with a large number of generation construction projects completed, and numerous others in the planning and execution phases.

Africa's electricity infrastructure base

The infrastructure required to convert Africa's resources into electricity and deliver it to customers varies greatly across regions. In this section, current and planned electricity infrastructure will be discussed according to the resource used to generated electricity—coal, gas, renewable energy including hydro and non-hydro sources, and nuclear.[46]

Africa's electricity generation capacity is dominated by thermal power plants, which account for 88% of total installed capacity.[47] The dominance of thermal power reflects the large installed capacities in North Africa and South Africa which use coal or oil as the primary fuel for electricity generation.[48] Hydropower stations represent most of the remaining installed capacity, particularly in Central and East Africa.

The bulk of Africa's generation capacity is found in South Africa, where coal-fired power plants are the main source of electricity. All but one of domestic utility Eskom's base load stations are coal-fired and have generation capacities exceeding 2,000 megawatts (MW) each (the exception is the nuclear power station in Koeberg).[49]

The figures below show that electrification of different regions differs by the generation technology used and in the magnitude of installed capacity.[50]

Coal-powered infrastructure

Current infrastructure

Coal-fired electricity has historically been the cheapest generation technology,[51] but because coal deposits are mainly in the southern part of the continent, it is largely confined to countries that are members of the SAPP. The installed generation capacity in the SAPP was approximately 56,321 MW in 2011, 78% of which is attributable to the South African power utility, Eskom.[52] Coal-fired plants generate 93% of Southern Africa's electricity; in the other regions, the role of coal is negligible, as none is used in the CAPP, and it accounts for 0.2% of electricity generation in the WAPP and EAPP.[53] In North Africa, oil, gas and hydropower are used to generate electricity.

Coal-fired generation has been the technology of choice in Southern Africa because of the availability of coal from Botswana and

Figure 6.3: Electricity production in Africa from coal sources

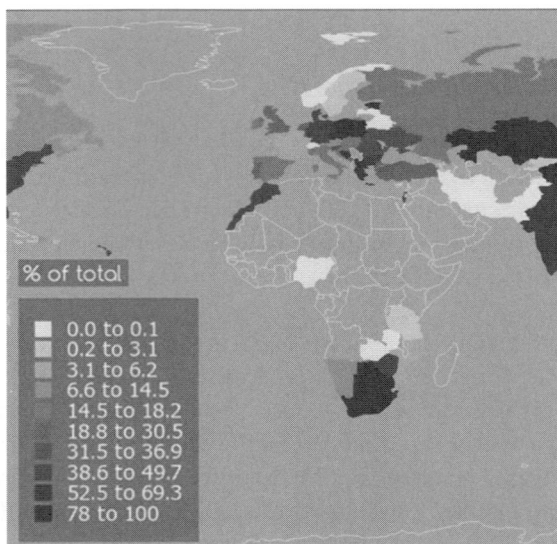

Source: Mecometer.com; World Bank's World Development Indicators database

Figure 6.4: Electricity production in Africa from oil sources

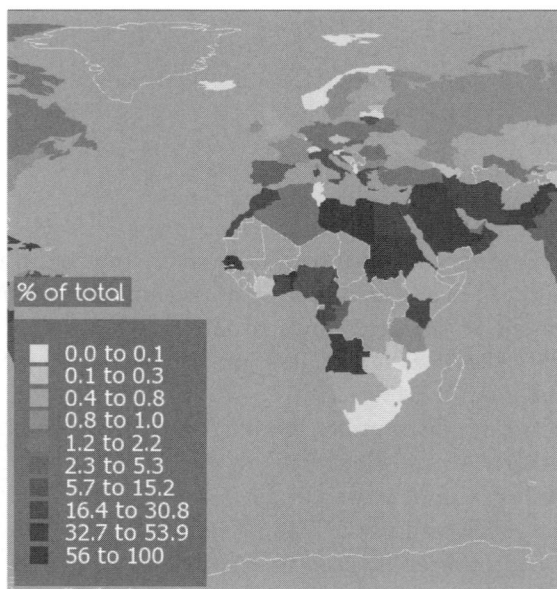

Source: Mecometer.com; World Bank's World Development Indicators database

Figure 6.5: Electricity production in Africa from natural gas sources

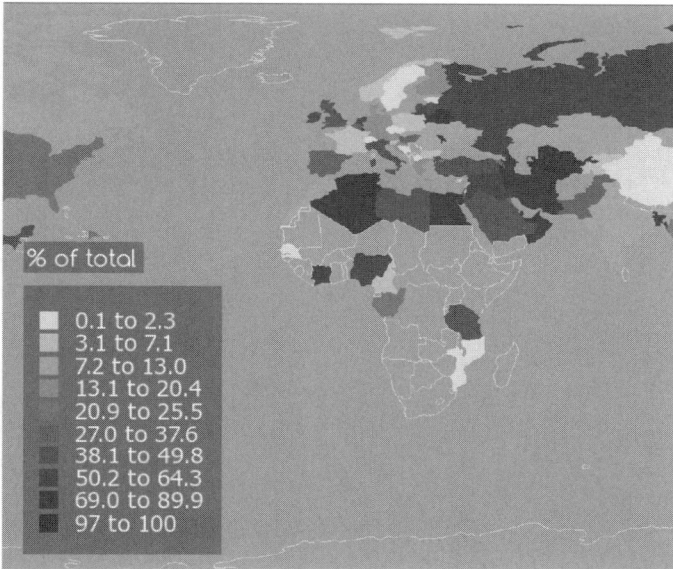

Source: Mecometer.com; World Bank's World Development Indicators database

Figure 6.6: Electricity production in Africa from renewable sources (excluding hydroelectric sources)

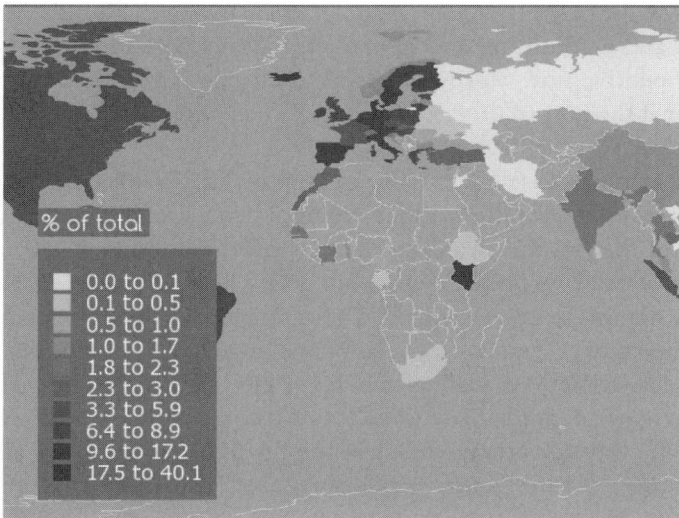

Source: Mecometer.com; World Bank's World Development Indicators database

Figure 6.7: Electricity production in Africa from hydroelectric sources

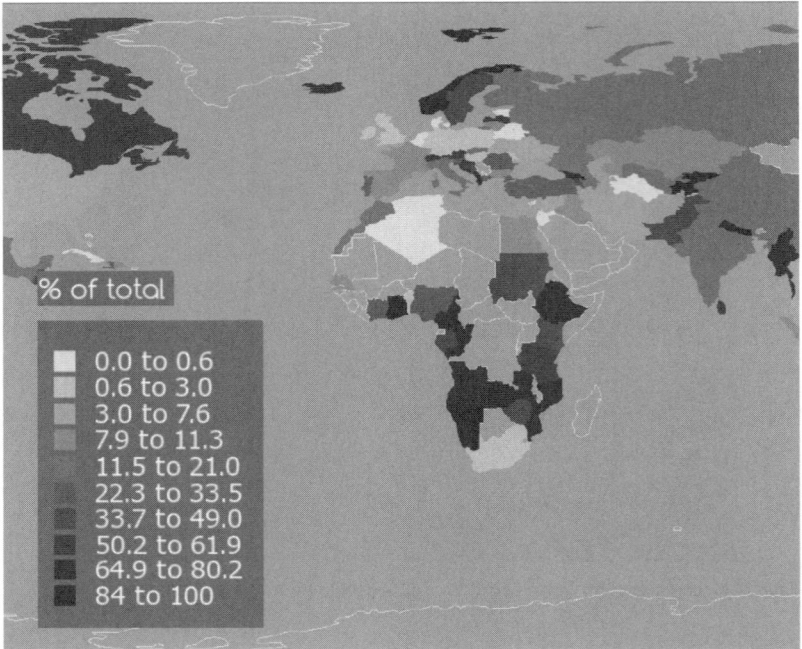

% of total

- 0.0 to 0.6
- 0.6 to 3.0
- 3.0 to 7.6
- 7.9 to 11.3
- 11.5 to 21.0
- 22.3 to 33.5
- 33.7 to 49.0
- 50.2 to 61.9
- 64.9 to 80.2
- 84 to 100

Source: Mecometer.com; World Bank's World Development Indicators database

South Africa and the relatively low cost. However, the price of coal has risen during the past few years, particularly in the South African short- and medium-term coal market.[54] While coal-fired generation is competitive now, this is expected to change if prices continue to rise, or if the cost of other technologies such as renewables continues to decline.

Eskom is the largest producer in Africa and is ranked among the top seven utilities in the world in terms of generation capacity. Eskom operates the only nuclear power plant on the continent—Koeberg Power Station in Cape Town—but relies heavily on its coal-fired power stations to meet demand. The company owns and operates 13 coal-fired power stations with a combined installed generation capacity of 34,130 MW.[55] As well as supplying electricity to South Africa, Eskom exports approximately 1,200 GWh per month to neighbouring countries through arrangements in the SAPP.[56]

Despite Eskom's large generating capacity, significant power shortages led to country-wide blackouts in 2007 and 2008.[57] One cause was delayed completion of new capacity owing to a range of factors, notably, uncertainty about the government's policy of electricity supply industry (ESI) reform, which involves vertical and horizontal unbundling of the national utility, and lack of clarity about the participation of independent power producers (IPPs) in generation infrastructure. This highlights the importance of a carefully planned and clearly communicated reform program and clarity about the funding and construction of planned infrastructure.

Planned infrastructure programs

South Africa is building two large coal-fired stations that will add 9,600 MW of generation capacity by 2015. According to the country's 2010 Integrated Resources Plan, additional coal-fired plants, totaling 6,253 MW, will be needed before 2030.[58]

The only other significant coal power station under construction in Southern Africa (outside South Africa) is in Botswana. The Mmamabula project involves the construction of a 1,200-MW plant with an integrated coal mine, an indication that the major increase in coal-fired stations is likely to occur in Southern Africa.[59]

Gas-fired power stations

Natural gas is the only fossil fuel reserve expected to grow in the next few years, because large reserves have recently been discovered or have become economically viable due to technological advances. North Africa has historically been at the forefront in natural gas reserves, but the large reserves discovered in East Africa (particularly Tanzania and Mozambique) will likely push this region into the top position.[60]

Increases in global supply have reduced the price of natural gas, making it more feasible for use in electricity generation.[61] Developing gas-fired electricity generation in Africa can be beneficial. It is a competitive technology for peak, mid-merit and even base-load generation in terms of costs. It also complements renewable energy technologies, as gas-fired generators are better suited to "load following" (generating power in response to demand fluctuations) and can supply electricity at short notice when wind or solar generation drops suddenly.[62] In many African countries, gas-fired electricity stations would be an attractive option, if the import and transmission infrastructure were available. Infrastructure investments may not be justified for relatively small volumes of gas, but technological advances have reduced the minimum efficient scale for liquefied natural gas (LNG) transport and re-gasification, so this restriction is diminishing.

Current infrastructure

To date, gas from African reserves has been destined for export rather than for direct use or electricity production in Africa. In Sub-Saharan Africa, electricity production with gas as the primary fuel is exclusive to West Africa, particularly Nigeria, where 15 natural gas power stations are fully or partially operational with a combined capacity of 7,927 MW. This amounts to about 50% of total installed capacity in the country.[63] In North Africa, Algeria and Egypt use gas-fired power to satisfy their energy needs, and there are plans for additional gas-fired power generation.[64]

In Southern Africa, South Africa has several open cycle gas turbines (OCGTs), but they largely use heavy fuel oil or diesel. Five gas turbines with a combined capacity of 2,452 MW are operational in two power stations in the Western Cape of South Africa.[65] Apart from the large capacity in North Africa and Nigeria, gas-fired power stations are sparsely distributed across the continent. In Central Africa, both Gabon and Congo Brazzaville make use of gas-fired power stations. Electricity generation in each country is approximately 210 MW and 450 MW respectively.[66, 67]

Planned infrastructure programs

A number of infrastructure programs for gas turbine power stations are planned for Nigeria. Seven stations, at different levels of development, will add a combined capacity of 2,562 MW to the national grid. They are part of the country's National Integrated Power Project, which aims to increase power generation and reduce gas flaring in the Niger Delta.[68]

South Africa's 2010 Integrated Resource Plan (IRP)[69] offers new capacity options involving both OCGT and closed cycle gas turbines (CCGTs) totaling 7,646 MW in the next 20 years. Amendments by ministerial determination in December 2011 allow for the planning of OCGT and CCGT plants interchangeably where appropriate, thereby providing scope for the introduction of LNG (or natural gas-fired) CCGTs. This signals a change in perceptions about the availability and affordability of natural gas for electricity generation and has created opportunities for CCGTs to be used for mid-merit and base-load generation rather than the more costly OCGT electricity generation run with heavy fuel oil and designated exclusively for peak use.

It is unclear if the discoveries of major gas reserves in Tanzania and Mozambique will be dedicated to the international LNG market or used to meet demand for gas and for electricity generation in the region. If it is decided that these reserves will be used for electricity generation, the member countries of the SAPP constitute a large potential market. To illustrate this point, a 532km pipeline (transporting 784 ml cubic feet of gas per day) from Mtwara to Dar es Salaam is under construction and is due to be commissioned by the end of 2014. This gas supply will be used to produce over 3,900 MW of electricity.[70]

Further along Africa's east coast, Kenya is pursuing a 700 MW gas-fired power station in Mombasa with Qatar as a strategic partner. This forms part of the Kenyan government's commitment to adding 5,000 MW of electricity capacity to its national grid.[71]

Renewable energy

Although fossil fuels are the major sources used to generate electricity, concern about climate change has directed attention to sources of renewable energy, which are abundant in Africa: hydropower in East Africa; wind and solar energy in Northern Africa; and geothermal energy in Kenya.[72]

Renewable energy: hydropower

Outside South Africa, hydropower accounts for close to 70% of generation and 50% of installed capacity (the other half is evenly divided between oil and natural gas).[73] But despite its importance (installed capacity is 24,273 MW), Africa's hydropower potential is underutilized—an estimated 93% of the continent's hydropower potential (approximately 937 terawatt hours per annum) has not been exploited.[74] Various reasons explain why this is the case. Projects require large, upfront capital investments, and often no creditworthy anchor customer exists on which to base the project, and/or the country and utility has a poor credit rating; weak project management capacity may exist for technically complex projects; and unstable political environments may impede or topple project plans.[75]

Current infrastructure

The growing importance of hydropower is apparent in the increase in the generation capacity of hydropower plants, especially in East Africa. Table 6.1 shows total installed capacity by region in 1990 and

Table 6.1: Regional comparison of hydropower generation capacity (MW)

Region	1990	2010	% change
Southern Africa	840	1,050	25
Central Africa	4,030	4,080	1
East Africa	6,300	8,700	38
West Africa	4,610	4,260	−8
North Africa	4,010	5,980	49

Source: Energy Information Administration (EIA) (2013). http://www.eia.gov/; authors' calculations

2010.[76] Hydropower generation capacity grew in all regions except West Africa.[77]

The following paragraphs describe the infrastructure in each region, specifically, the size and location of hydropower plants.

Some hydropower plants exist in Southern Africa—mainly in South Africa and Mozambique. South Africa has six active hydroelectric power stations with a combined generating capacity of 2,100 MW (about 4% of total electricity demand in the country).[78] The Ruacana Power station in Namibia has a generation capacity of 240 MW. Though there has been growth in this region, it has been off a low base. East, West and Central Africa offer the continent the greatest hydropower potential.

The largest hydropower potential is in Central Africa, particularly the Democratic Republic of Congo (DRC) and the Congo. In the DRC, the Inga I and II hydroelectric power stations have a joint generating capacity of 1,775 MW, but are operating at low capacity utilization. This is primarily due to the dams feeding the power stations falling into disrepair and requiring rehabilitation.[79] Additionally, the DRC's electrification rate is 6%, one of the lowest in the world. However, plans have been made to fully develop the hydropower potential of the Inga River under the Grand Inga Project. With its multiple dams and hydropower plants, the project is envisaged to produce a total of 42,000 MW.[80] This would be sufficient to generate enough power to provide electricity to West Africa, as well as meet a portion of Southern Africa's demand.

Hydropower infrastructure in Central Africa includes 15 hydroelectric power stations in Angola that produce approximately two-thirds of the country's electricity. Cameroon has a generation capacity of 720 MW, mostly from its Edea and Song Loulou stations. The hydroelectric power currently produced in Cameroon is estimated to be only 1% of its total potential, although hydropower accounts for 77% of all energy generated in the country.[81] These power stations constitute the majority of hydroelectric power stations in Central Africa. The region's substantial potential in this area has largely been untapped—illustrated in its marginal growth in capacity, for many of the reasons indicated above on the hurdles to infrastructure investment. Furthermore, the extent, capability and condition of the associated transmission and distribution infrastructure is unclear, but it is likely that this infrastructure is not well developed, given the low electrification rates in Angola, the DRC and Cameroon.

The greatest hydroelectric generation capacity is in East Africa, the majority of which can be found in Mozambique, Ethiopia, Kenya, Tanzania and Zambia. Several developments have led to the growth in generation capacity in the past 20 years. Mozambique's Cahora Bassa Dam has a maximum generating capacity of 2,075 MW. Most of the electricity produced by this plant is exported to South Africa, but a large part is exported back to Southern Mozambique where the country's main aluminum smelter is located.[82] The Cahora Bassa HVDC transmission system between Mozambique and South Africa is a joint venture between South Africa's Eskom and the Zambian National utility, ZAMCO, and is capable of transmitting 1,920 MWe.[83, 84]

Hydropower stations with a combined capacity of approximately 750 MW would reportedly be completed in Ethiopia during 2014.[85] The largest is the Beles Hydroelectric power plant near Lake Tana and has a generating capacity of 460 MW; the remaining capacity is provided by the Fincha and Melak Wakena power stations. The Ethiopian government has an ambitious plan that aims to double generation capacity; this includes the Grand Renaissance Dam project and the Gilgel Gibe III Dam.

In conjunction with the major plants in Mozambique and Ethiopia, the Kariba Dam (based in Zambia and Zimbabwe) contributes 1,319 MW to generating capacity in East Africa.

Although East Africa's hydropower generation capacity is by far the largest of all regions, recent droughts have cast doubt on the ability of these plants to satisfy the increasing demand.[86]

In West Africa, the largest generating capacity is in Nigeria and Ghana. West Africa relies heavily on hydropower, which accounts for 82% of total generation capacity. Nigeria has three main hydroelectric power stations—Jebba, Kainji, and Shiroro—with a combined capacity of 2,100 MW. Ghana has two main hydropower stations, the Akosombo and Kpong Dam, with a combined capacity of 1,180 MW. The former is the largest single investment in the economic development plans of Ghana and can generate 1,020 MW.[87] Other hydropower stations are located in the Côte d'Ivoire with combined capacity of 551 MW. The Manatali Dam in Mali has a capacity of 200 MW.

North Africa's hydropower generation capacity emanates largely from the Nile River—in Egypt, the Aswan Dam alone has the capacity to generate 2,100 MW. Egypt's recent political instability has hindered the development of electricity generation capacity, which lags behind demand. The problem has worsened due to declining production of natural gas in Egypt, and a foreign currency crisis limits the government's ability to pay for fuel, whether imported or produced locally by international oil companies. Egypt relies on imported fuels such as natural gas for electricity production because local production is too low.[88] In Sudan, a single hydropower station is responsible for all the electricity generated via hydropower at the Merowe Dam with an installed capacity of 1,250 MW. Although hydropower is not the primary energy source in North Africa (oil is more important), the potential exists for it to overtake other sources, especially in Sudan.

With a substantial proportion of potential still unexploited, it is difficult to envision an African future in which hydropower does not feature prominently, a view confirmed by the large-scale investments in construction of hydropower stations.

Planned infrastructure programs

Notable hydropower infrastructure plans currently under consideration are the Inga III and Grand Inga project in the DRC. Inga III has a planned electricity capacity of 4,500 MW, and the Grand Inga projects could provide between 39,000 MWe and 42,000 MWe. The combined generation capacity would be sufficient to supply 20% of the continent's total demand in 2020.[89] The Inga III project envisions interconnection of the grids in the DRC, Namibia, Angola, Botswana and South Africa. The total investment required to complete the project amounts to US$80 billion. Numerous organizations have shown interest, including the World Bank, the African Development Bank, the European Investment Bank, and South Africa's power utility company, Eskom.[90] However, although the Inga potential was identified more than two decades ago, it has not been bankable, most likely due to concern about political risk, transmission loss, and affordability.

The Grand Renaissance Dam in Ethiopia will generate over 5,000 MW and is estimated to cost nearly US$5 billion. However, the project faces technical and financial problems,[91] as well as opposition from its downstream neighbors.[92] Another major project in Ethiopia is the Gilgel Gibe Dam III, which was expected to be completed in the 2013–2015 period and to increase the country's installed capacity by 1,870 MW.[93, 94] In conjunction with the building of the dam, the required transmission infrastructure is estimated to cost around EUR35 million, and lending has been secured to complete the project.

Further infrastructure development for hydroelectric power stations is planned in Sudan. The Kajbar and Shereyk Power Stations are proposed for the banks of the Nile with generating capacities of 300 MW and 350 MW, respectively.[95] This will provide additional capacity to the large Merowe Dam already in use in Sudan. The 600-MW Karuma and the 140-MW Isimba hydropower stations are planned for Uganda, as well as the 600-MW Ayago Power Station.[96]

The 80 MW regional Rusumo Falls hydroelectric project recently achieved financial closure. It is jointly owned by Tanzania, Rwanda and Burundi.[97] In Kenya, the 700 MW High Grand Falls project is at the final design stages.[98]

Renewable energy: wind-powered electricity generation

Current infrastructure

The largest supply of wind-generated electricity is in North Africa. Egypt has wind power generation capacity of around 550 MW and is seeking to add a further 850 MW.[99] Morocco has seven wind farms with a combined generation capacity of 447 MW. Others are located on the Cape Verde Islands, where four farms with a combined capacity of 28 MW[100] have been constructed to provide the archipelago with approximately 25% of its electricity. Additionally, the small pilot Darling Wind Farm in South Africa produces 8.6 GWh annually,[101] and the 5.1 MW Ngong Wind Farm in Kenya can generate up to 14.9 GWh of energy annually.[102]

Planned infrastructure programs

Wind farm projects have been proposed in Morocco and Ethiopia.[103, 104] The Kenya Electricity Generating Company Limited (KenGen), a listed utility that was until recently owned by the state, embarked in 2009 on a project to increase its installed capacity for wind energy at Ngong to 25.5 MW.[105] In South Africa, Eskom is constructing the Sere wind farm, which will have a capacity of 100 MW. In addition, South Africa's Renewable Energy Independent Power Producers program has resulted in the licensing of 15 wind projects with a combined capacity of 1 196.5 MW.[106, 107]

Kenya relies on hydropower for about 70% of its electricity needs, but low annual rainfall has stimulated investigation of alternative sources. One project, planned for the shores of Lake Turkana where gale force winds prevail, is expected to be the largest of its kind in Africa with a generating capacity of 300 MW.[108] In Morocco, six wind farms are under construction to add to the seven that now operate in the country. The new wind farms will add approximately 1,070 MW to the Moroccan national power grid by 2017,[109] and will assist in reducing the country's reliance on oil to generate electricity.

Although wind power has gained popularity as a source of electricity, the low load factor and intermittent nature of the supply are deterrents. Investment costs are high relative to the energy generated—for every MW of installed wind power capacity, about 0.2 MW of backup capacity is required for when there is no wind.[110] Wind farms (and solar farms) also require more space per megawatt produced, so large tracts of land are necessary. Another challenge is that wind farms are usually located far from load centers, so long transmission lines are needed. Therefore, whether more significant wind generation electricity infrastructure projects will be undertaken on the continent is uncertain.

Renewable energy: solar electricity generation

Current infrastructure

Solar plants capture energy released by the sun and convert it into electricity. So far, only a few solar plants have been constructed in Africa, all in the North.

Egypt has the 20 MW Kuraymat Plant, and Morocco has the same generation capacity at its Beni Mathar Plant. These are the largest operational solar power plants on the continent, but much larger ones are under development or construction in Morocco, Tunisia and Algeria.

Planned infrastructure programs

Construction of the 160-MW Quarzazate solar power station has begun in Morocco, with plans to increase the generating capacity to 500 MW.[111] Expansion of this project is likely, because funding has been secured from the World Bank. Tunisia has plans to construct a 2,000 MW solar power plant at TuNur exclusively for domestic demand. Algeria has pledged future excess renewable energy to the European Union through the construction of solar power stations. This is part of a broader Algerian plan to generate approximately 22,000 MW of solar power by 2030.[112]

South Africa's Department of Energy hopes to add 1,650 MW of solar power generating capacity to the South African National power grid, predominantly through procurement from IPPs.[113] South Africa's Renewable Energy Independent Power Producers program has resulted in the licensing of 30 solar projects (including both concentrated solar power [CSP] and photovoltaic [PV]) with a combined capacity of 1,248.6 MW.[114]

As plans continue to be developed for North Africa, estimates indicate that as much as 470,000 MW of solar electricity could be generated if the necessary infrastructure is in place. Whether these plans will be realized is as uncertain as the ambitious hydropower plants planned for Central Africa.

Renewable energy: geothermal power

Africa's use of geothermal energy to produce electricity is slowly increasing. Kenya has several plants in operation, and the government aims to meet nearly half of the country's energy needs from geothermal power by 2018.[115] A large-scale project has begun at Mount Longonot that will help achieve this goal. Recently, the Ethiopian government announced plans to team up with Reykjavik Geothermal, a US–Icelandic private developer, to construct a 1,000 MW plant at Corbetti Caldera.[116] There are also plans to develop power stations in Zambia, Uganda, Ethiopia and Tanzania.[117, 118, 119, 120]

East Africa's Rift Valley has attracted much attention as a source of geothermal energy, and ultimately, a solution to the continent's persistent electricity shortage. The United Nations Environment Program estimates the geothermal potential of the Rift Valley at 14,000 MW. Proponents believe that 10% to 25% of the region's energy needs could be satisfied by geothermal power by 2030. Geothermal power has many advantages: it is ideal for providing the baseload because it can be harnessed to produce power regardless of the weather or the time of day; geothermal power stations are less harmful to the environment than fossil fuel alternatives; and geothermal power is relatively inexpensive to produce. On the other hand, geothermal stations have notable disadvantages: they can leak radon and other gases, and the costs of building a geothermal power station are as high as drilling for oil and may be higher than for coal power stations.[121]

Challenges associated with renewable energy technologies

Electricity generation using renewable energy sources may be promising, but renewable energy technologies (excluding hydropower) can be a large-scale benefit to African nations only in the medium to long term, because of the high costs relative to other technologies.[122] Despite concerns about the environmental effects of using fossil fuels, the pressing need for access to electricity to alleviate poverty and improve quality of life[123] is likely to strongly influence energy infrastructure decisions in many African countries. To some extent, African governments face a trade-off between protecting the environment and reducing poverty.[124]

The political economy aspects of certain renewable power projects (wind, solar and geothermal) are also important. Because these projects entail large initial capital costs, they are often constructed and operated by IPPs. Governments or the state-owned entities representing them enter into power purchase agreements (PPAs) with these IPPs, allowing for some risk-sharing. However, risk allocation can be skewed toward consumers, resulting in less predictable and, at times, higher-than-expected prices. Hence, it is not necessarily given that the growth of renewable energy in developed nations should or will be replicated in Africa. Government efforts to increase private investment in energy infrastructure are more likely to be directed to the most affordable alternatives. From a funder's perspective, the risk of non-payment increases with the price charged for the electricity generated, even where PPAs are involved, which could reduce the funds available for renewable energy projects.

However, some renewable energy options may be important for decentralized generation and rural development. Compared with conventional energy (including extending the grid to remote areas and the cost of transportation of fuel), in a remote, under-serviced area, decentralized off-grid renewable energy is an important alternative.[125] Wind power is an option for small-scale applications far from the grid,[126] and small-scale bio-gas harvesting may provide fuel for nearby villages. As technology evolves, it is expected that renewable energy will become more affordable. The relative cost of electricity has already declined for several renewable energy technologies.[127]

Hence, although renewable power (excluding hydroelectric) is not a major source of electricity in Africa, such projects offer considerable investment opportunities. Care should be taken to structure wind, solar and geothermal projects in a way that encourages private investment. The recent experience of South Africa is an example of how IPPs can be successfully introduced in a vertically integrated ESI. The South African Department of Energy is now involved in the third and final window for bids for projects to bring total renewable energy (excluding hydropower) capacity to 3,725 MW.[128] This program has already led to the licensing of 47 projects, involving 2,459.4 MW of generation capacity.[129]

Nuclear power is almost non-existent in Africa. Only one plant is located on the continent—the 1,800-MW Koeberg station in South Africa. In 2011, estimates of natural uranium reserves (for nuclear power generation) indicate that Africa has about one-fifth of the world's total. These reserves are located mainly in South Africa, Namibia, and Niger.[130]

Although nuclear power has advantages such as a stable and reliable supply of electricity, low carbon emissions and low cost of fuel transport, disadvantages have discouraged its use on the continent. These mainly relate to: the significant upfront cost of nuclear power stations; the relatively large scale of nuclear power stations; a shortage of technical expertise; reluctance to use private financing for nuclear stations due to the strategic importance and risks; and health and safety concerns regarding nuclear waste. The minimum efficient scale (usually more than 900 MW) is larger than many countries' total demand.[131]

Because nuclear power plants require scale to operate efficiently, investment makes financial sense only if relatively large plants are built. In addition, the upfront capital costs are a large share of the total cost of operation. Operation of such plants is skills-intensive, and decommissioning and waste disposal are costly.[132] Most African governments lack the capital and skills required to build and operate these plants.[133] Finally, nuclear power may not be socially acceptable.

The constrained ability of many African governments to finance construction of nuclear power plants suggests that private investment might be an alternative. However, owing to the safety and security concerns associated with nuclear power, private involvement is invariably considered inappropriate and undesirable.

Therefore, nuclear power will be a viable option for African governments only when they have the means to provide funding or guarantees for funding by state-owned companies (SOEs) for construction and operation of infrastructure. Another obstacle may be that African energy markets are at an early stage of development.

Large-scale power plants may not be feasible until regional energy markets are developed, and enough demand is pooled from various nations to absorb the substantial amounts of electricity that nuclear plants can generate.

Regulatory environment for electricity

As elsewhere, electricity infrastructure in Africa has generally been perceived to be of strategic or national importance. This led, in many cases, to the establishment of public monopolies over infrastructure, whereby state-owned utilities were the primary source of generation, transmission and distribution. This model highlighted the role of infrastructure development in economic growth and social development, and created the perception that only government could guarantee supply of electricity.[134]

By the late 1990s, the model of state-owned utilities had proved to be inefficient and led to a spate of reforms, spearheaded by the World Bank and the International Monetary Fund.[135] Electricity sector reforms, however, did not follow the standard model of "industry unbundling, privatization and competition". Instead, a hybrid emerged, in which the state-owned monopoly remained dominant, and IPPs were introduced at the margin.[136] Independent regulatory bodies were established in most Sub-Saharan African countries, and some regulatory bodies were also responsible for regulation of other sectors such as water and sanitation.[137] By 2006, most of the 24 Sub-Saharan countries had enacted "a power sector reform law, three-quarters had introduced some form of private participation, two-thirds had privatized their state-owned utilities, two-thirds had established a regulatory oversight body, and more than one-third had independent power producers".[138] Despite major electricity sector reform across Sub-Saharan Africa, state-owned utilities remained the dominant market participants, with limited interaction with independent power producers.

Independent electricity regulators are generally empowered to act in the public interest and have considerable discretion with regard to tariffs and service standards. But even with independent regulatory bodies, electricity tariffs are rarely determined without government intervention.[139] Regulatory independence remains a controversial issue, mostly unnecessarily so, as it tends to be conflated with lack of accountability or a perception of regulators being a law unto themselves. This is unfortunate as the independence refers to the ability of regulators to implement their legally bestowed mandate—arising from policymakers and the legislature—without undue influence from either the regulated industry or from politicians pursuing short-term political goals. Independence does not refer to the ability of regulators to make and alter policy decisions; it merely refers to their ability to pursue a pre-determined legal mandate without fear or favor. The independence of regulators is primarily required to provide private sector investors with sufficient regulatory certainty, and reflect a policy choice aimed at increasing private sector funding.

Regulatory reform involved in the process granting access to third-party power producers to increase electricity generation capacity, which previously had typically belonged solely to the state-owned utility. Third-party electricity generation capacity is provided by IPPs, one of the more popular private participation in infrastructure (PPI) programs in the electricity sector. More than half the PPI transactions in Africa have been IPPs, providing more than 3,000 MW of new capacity at a cost of around US$2 billion in private investment.

The most successful IPPs have been in Kenya and Côte d'Ivoire. In Kenya, sector unbundling, regulation and reform began in the 1990s, with the separation of the generator KenGen and the network operator KPLC.[140] The electricity sector was unbundled in 1998, and the Electricity Regulatory Board, which issues licenses and regulates power purchase agreements, was established. This increased IPP participation in the Kenyan electricity market and international investment in these programs. Unlike many energy IPPs in Africa, those in Côte d'Ivoire proceeded without major difficulties and partnered with commercial banks and development financial institutions such as IFC, AfDB and and the Netherlands Development Finance Company FMO [Financierings-Maatschappij voor Ontwikkelingslanden]. More than 40% of Côte d'Ivoire's installed capacity of 1,202 MW is produced by IPPs. Independent power producers CIPREL and AZITO use Ivorian domestic natural gas to create electricity at their gas-fired plants, where they generate 210 MW and 288 MW, respectively.[141]

In 2011, the South African government began a program to obtain 3,725 MW of installed renewable energy capacity from IPPs.[142] The program was estimated to have raised R47 billion (about US$4.5 billion) in private sector funding for the first window, and R28 billion (US$2.5 billion) for the second.[143] The first of these plants was commissioned in 2013. The allocation of a further 3,200 MW of renewable energy was announced in 2014, resulting in a target of total renewable energy installed capacity of 6,925 MWe by 2030.[144]

Nonetheless, most of the country's overall electricity generation additions are reserved for the state-owned incumbent, Eskom, whose new-build program has experienced construction delays, funding challenges, and cost overruns.[145] Although South Africa has an independent energy regulator, Eskom remains vertically integrated with control over the country's electricity grid and a dominant generation and distribution position. Legislation to establish an independent system and market operator has been delayed, and the country's original intention to unbundle Eskom and establish a multi-market model has been abandoned.[146] This demonstrates that without follow-through, even policies that incorporate global best-practice principles are unlikely to succeed.

Although most African countries express an intention to move toward liberalization of the electricity sector, as illustrated by the creation of independent regulatory bodies, execution has been poor. This is the result of difficulties facing independent electricity regulatory bodies, which will be discussed later in the chapter.

Gas: Africa's current position

Natural gas has attracted attention as a clean alternative to oil and coal for electricity generation and for household heating and cooking.[147] In addition, gas-fired electricity is a viable peak generation complement to renewable energy sources.[148] In the past, natural gas was considered a regional fuel, because delivery was limited to pipelines, making it difficult and expensive to transport. In the 1960s, LNG technology enabled shipping to global markets.[149] Although construction of plants and pipelines requires substantial capital investments, once they are developed, natural gas can be a relatively inexpensive source of energy.[150]

Table 6.2: Africa's proven gas reserves (trillion cubic feet)

Region	End of 1992	End of 2002	End of 2012
North Africa	179.43	244.07	291.34
East Africa	12.55	11.38	11.31
Southern Africa	3.9	2.20	2.2
West Africa	108.22	125.93	183.29
Central Africa	10.63	11.25	21.25

Note: Proved gas reserves are quantities that geological and engineering information indicates, with reasonable certainty, can be recovered from known reservoirs under existing economic and operating conditions.

Source: EIA (2013). http://www.eia.gov/

Because gas resources are not evenly distributed across the continent, current infrastructure and planned infrastructure programmes will be described by region—North, South, East, West and Central Africa.[151]

Table 6.2 shows proven reserves of natural gas by region from 1992 to 2012. "Proven reserves" are defined as those reserves that can, with reasonable certainty, be recovered and used. These amounts take time to estimate, because they are based on geological and engineering information. Therefore, proven reserves do not reflect the latest developments—notably, recent discoveries in East African countries like Mozambique and Tanzania.

An alternate measure is discoveries that may or may not result in proven reserves. The gas discoveries and developments in Mozambique and Tanzania are reflected in Table 6.3. These suggest that East Africa in particular may have reserves that are a multiple of previously proven reserve estimates, thereby drastically changing its energy mix and gas export potential.

North African countries such as Algeria, Libya and Egypt have substantial reserves of natural gas, but these reserves have been extracted mainly for export to the European Union. West Africa's natural gas production is primarily associated with large offshore oil reserves. Because markets for gas in West Africa are small, and "associated" gas volumes are relatively small, most of the gas output has been flared, which is highly inefficient.[152] Recent efforts to reduce flaring and capture natural gas for export as LNG in Nigeria and Ghana mark a change. Large oil reserves in Angola and smaller oil reserves in Cameroon, Gabon, and Equatorial Guinea have provided an opportunity for these small Central African nations to develop their gas sectors by reducing flaring and concentrating on capturing associated gas for LNG exports.[153]

Table 6.3: Natural gas developments in Mozambique and Tanzania

Country	Gas discoveries	Proposed infrastructure	Companies
Mozambique	32-65 tcf of recoverable gas resources in area 1 (Anadarko) and 75 tcf gas in place in area 4 (Eni)	LNG plant and supporting infrastructure	Anadarko and Eni
Tanzania	More than 20 tcf of recoverable gas resources in blocks 1-4	LNG plant and supporting infrastructure	BG Group, Statoil, Ophir Energy, ExxonMobil, Aminex

Notes: Information above is as of April 2013; tcf = trillion cubic feet

Source: EIA (2013) Emerging East Africa Energy. https://www.eia.gov/beta/international/analysis_includes/special_topics/East_Africa/eeae.pdf

Since 2010, new gas reserves have been discovered in the Southern and Eastern parts of the continent (as shown in Table 6.3).[154] Recent offshore discoveries in Mozambique and Tanzania have shifted the focus away from North African countries, the historically dominant forces in the continent's gas sector.[155] South Africa's shale gas beds beneath the Karoo region have been estimated to contain more than 390 tcf of shale gas, making it the 8th largest technically recoverable reserve in the world.[156] Shale gas can be extracted using well-established, yet at times controversial, hydraulic fracturing techniques. In 2011, concerns about the rapid increase in applications for and approvals of exploration licenses covering large areas of the Karoo and environmental concerns about hydraulic fracturing led the South African government to impose a moratorium on exploration. In 2012, the government lifted the moratorium on hydraulic fracturing. Shale gas discoveries in Southern Africa may change the African gas sector even further. As a result of discoveries of shale gas in the Karoo and natural gas off the coasts of Tanzania and Mozambique, Southern Africa and Eastern Africa have been described as the "next gas frontiers of the world".[157]

Global natural gas consumption is expected to increase owing to demand from China and from the transport sector, slower growth in global nuclear power and, most importantly, a substantial increase in natural gas supply.[158] This offers Africa an opportunity to use its existing and newly discovered gas resources to satisfy regional and global demand.

Africa's gas infrastructure base

For Southern and Eastern Africa to become major forces in the global gas market, it is crucial that infrastructure be in place to produce and transport gas to final consumers and to develop their energy sectors in a way that can sustain economic growth.[159] Eastern Africa could avoid the experience of Western Africa, which has not received the full benefit of its substantial gas resources because of insufficient infrastructure.[160] Nigeria, for instance, has ample oil and gas reserves and exports large quantities of oil, but has not achieved desirable levels of energy access for its population. The result has been economic stagnation, low incomes and high unemployment.[161] In addition to generating revenue from production and exports to other continents, African nations would benefit from using their gas resources to satisfy regional energy demand and to develop infrastructure so that gas markets in Africa can grow.

While gas can be transported directly to nearby regions via pipelines, it can also be liquefied and transported using LNG terminals and exported.[162] North African producers have exported significant amounts of gas to the EU and other regions instead of supplying African markets; Eastern Africa and the Western and Central parts of the continent seem to be headed in the same direction. Substantial natural gas discoveries in the Rovuma basin off the coasts of Mozambique and Tanzania are capable of supporting large LNG projects.[163] Developing gas resources in East Africa, therefore, appears to depend on LNG exports, likely to Asia, where demand, and therefore prices, will be high.[164]

Nigeria, Ghana, Angola, Cameroon, Gabon and Equatorial Guinea have recently made efforts to gear gas production toward LNG exports rather than supplying African neighbors.[165] This trend has prevailed in Africa because: gas supplies are far from potential regional markets such as South Africa; domestic demand is low due to small national economies; and regional gas infrastructure (interconnecting pipelines) is lacking. A pipeline network is economically viable only if markets are large and include major consumers (such as power plants and industrial operations).[166]

Ideally, gas-rich African nations should not export all their energy resources—the development of domestic gas markets should be seen as a means to achieve sustainable growth. Exporting gas resources helps their economies only in the short term and leaves countries with limited energy access and infrastructure.[167]

Where domestic demand is insufficient to justify investment in infrastructure, several strategies can be followed. The first is to assess and amend domestic energy and transport policies (for example, electricity and energy plans and transport fuel policies) to include use of gas to power technology or to give public transport operators an incentive to use gas as a fuel. One electricity base load station could dramatically alter the size of the market, and thereby render an infrastructure project viable. Second, regional markets could be explored, and the demand of neighboring countries pooled with domestic demand to make infrastructure projects bankable. Integration of African energy markets and the development of regional gas infrastructure, such as the ROMPCO gas pipeline in Southern Africa and the West African Gas Pipeline, can develop gas markets in Africa and enable intra-African trade in gas, allowing African nations to use their gas resources while increasing energy access across the continent. Policies and practices must support the use of resources in a manner that will enable future generations to benefit from Africa's resources.[168]

Current infrastructure

Most gas infrastructure in Africa is limited to national gas pipeline networks, but there is ample opportunity to create regional links. Figure 6.8 depicts Africa's transnational gas infrastructure pipelines.

The main regional gas pipeline network is in North Africa, home to the largest producers. Regional pipelines are used to export gas from Algeria, Libya and Egypt to different parts of Europe.[169] We address each of these countries' networks in turn below:

• Algeria: Medgaz, the most recently completed pipeline, transports gas from the Arzew refinery to southern Spain; PDF (Maghreb) transports gas directly from gas fields at Hassi R'Mel via Morocco to Spain; and the Trans-Mediterranean Pipeline transports gas from Hassi R'Mel through Tunisia to Italy.
• Libya: the Green Stream pipeline exports gas directly to Sicily, where it connects to the Italian transmission system.

Figure 6.8: Africa's natural gas pipeline network

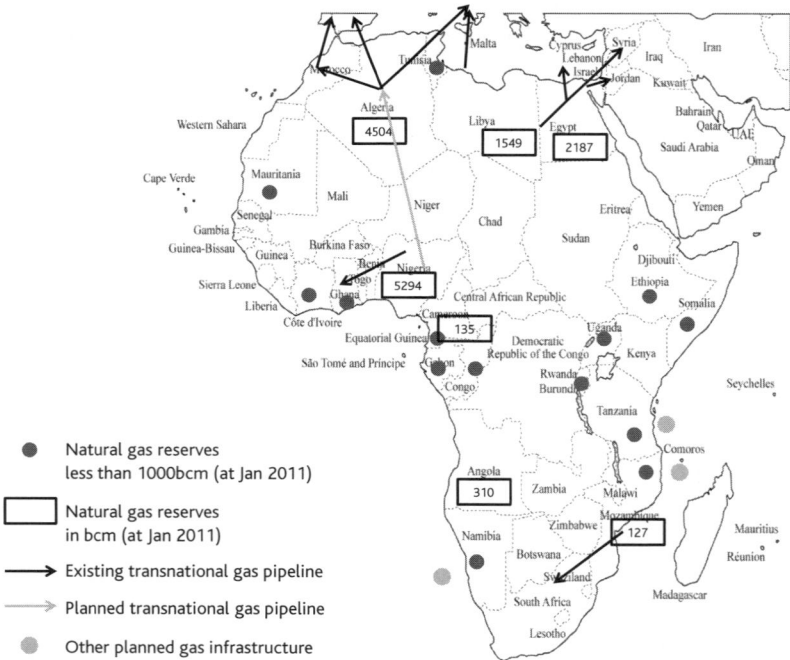

Source: Programme for Infrastructure Development in Africa (PIDA), 2011, *Africa Energy Outlook 2040*. Available at: http://www.au-pida.org/documents/ENERGIE/EOE-Energy -Outlook.pdf, p 25.

- Egypt: gas is exported by pipeline to Jordan, Syria, Lebanon and Israel, and as LNG, to Europe.

Since 2004, Mozambique has supplied South Africa with natural gas via the cross-border ROMPCO pipeline from the Pande and Temane gas fields to Sasol's synfuels plant at Secunda, near Johannesburg. The pipeline was a PPP between Sasol and the governments of Mozambique and South Africa and cost US$1.2 billion.[170] It has benefitted both nations by creating an upward shift in Mozambique's GDP and by developing the South African gas market.[171]

Africa's first regional gas transmission system, the West African Gas Pipeline (WAGP), which was commissioned in 2010, runs from Nigeria though Benin and Togo. It carries gas to two power stations in Ghana. The project has been hindered by cost overruns and security issues in Nigeria.[172] The WAGP project went into trial operations for about a month, but insurgents sabotaged the pipeline in the Nigerian delta and halted progress.[173]

Table 6.4 shows that from 2002 to 2011, production doubled in the main gas-producing regions and increased by 42.5% in Africa overall. Nonetheless, Africa's annual gross gas production is small compared with that of the Russian Federation where production in 2011 exceeded 836,000 billion cubic metres (bcm).

Planned infrastructure programs

Mozambique's offshore gas discoveries are sufficient to support large-scale LNG export projects, but the country lacks the infrastructure for gas liquefaction, transportation and processing.[174] The oil companies

Table 6.4: Africa's annual natural gas production (billion cubic meters)

Region	End of 1992	End of 2002	End of 2011	% change (2002 to 2011)
North Africa	193,648.21	255,489.40	336,763.11	31.8
East Africa	–	74.83	5,849.09	771.7
Southern Africa	49.79	3,080.44	1,596.34	−48.2*
West Africa	40,781. 53	49,249.62	87,175.19	77.1
Central Africa	5,650.27	23,789.99	41,246.71	73.4
Total Africa	240,129.8	331,684.28	472,630.44	42.5
Russia	812,451.83	716,995.98	836,465.88	16.7

Note: *The large reduction in production is due, among other factors, to the reduced production of gas feedstock for its gas-to-liquid facility by South Africa's oil and gas company (PetroSA) owing to rapid depletion of the reserve.

Source: EIA (2013). https://www.eia.gov; authors' calculations

Anadarko and ENI are building two LNG liquefaction facilities in Mozambique,[175] described as "one of the largest and most expensive LNG developments in the world".[176] These facilities are due to first deliver product by 2018.[177] Other possibilities include gas-to-liquid (GTL) production of liquid fuels.

In Tanzania, a master plan is under development, which is likely to include similar projects aimed at monetization of the large gas reserve.[178]

After being on hold since the 1970s, work on the Trans-Saharan Gas Pipeline Project resumed in 2002. The pipeline will deliver Nigerian natural gas through the Niger Republic to Algeria and Europe. The Nigerian National Petroleum Corporation has been looking at PPPs as a way to fund the project, which is expected to cost US$12 billion.[179] The Trans-Saharan gas pipeline has been identified as a way for European countries to diversify their energy mix, and thereby increase security of supply.[180] Regulatory uncertainty and the economic conditions of the past decade contributed to the delay in this project.[181] Work on the Trans-Nigeria component of the project is due to be completed by 2018.[182]

The National Petroleum Corporation of Namibia (NAMCOR), the state-owned petroleum company, and its upstream partners, Tullow Kudu Limited and CIECO E&P (Namibia) Co. Ltd, are developing the relatively small Kudu gas field (1.3 tcf), located 130km off the southwest coast.[183] This gas could be used for electricity generation at the proposed 800 MW power station in Namibia, with excess supply exported to South Africa, Zambia and other African nations.[184] Although the field was discovered in the 1970s, problems ranging from geological to political issues hindered its development.[185] Similarly, the existence of the Ibubhesi gas field off the west coast of South Africa has been known for decades, but because of its small size (0.54 tcf) and distance from the onshore market, it has not been developed. It was recently sold to an Australian firm, Sunbird Energy.[186]

Other significant infrastructure developments may be underway in South Africa, where revision of the country's Integrated Resource Plan (2010) allows for substantial gas-fired electricity generation additions— LNG import and re-gasification facilities and transmission pipelines. Large LNG import facilities may extend the gas market beyond the gas-to-power market and supply the country's GTL plant at Mossel Bay.[187]

The Galsi gas pipeline, a project that aims to transport gas from Algeria to Sardinia, has experienced delays arising from funding and technical difficulties and environmental concerns.[188] It is unclear whether the project will go ahead.[189]

Regulatory environment

Throughout the world, with the notable exception of the United States, natural gas resources found onshore or beneath territorial waters and on the continental shelf are usually owned by the state, and upstream activities in the gas sector are usually governed by legislation. In Africa, as elsewhere, interested companies require licenses, which are issued by energy ministries or other state departments or agencies, for natural gas exploration or production operations.[190] State-owned gas companies in Africa often enter production-sharing agreements (PSAs) with private companies[191] that specify how long these private companies can engage in exploration, development and production. PSAs have a profit-sharing element and contain provisions for royalties to be earned and company taxes to be paid. In some cases, the government may also require private companies to supply the domestic market.[192] The Mozambican government, for example, negotiated a 5% royalty gas allocation for domestic use to be supplied by the company that supplies South Africa with natural gas.

Downstream gas industry regulation is less uniform, because individual countries focus on country-specific concerns to be mitigated or remedied by economic regulation. Owing to the limited domestic use of gas in Africa, only a few nations have specific gas regulation.

In East Africa, Mozambique has a regulatory framework, but it primarily concerns the upstream aspects of the gas value chain. In Tanzania, the gas master plan currently under development is part of the recently published draft Natural Gas Policy, which identifies the need for a regulatory authority.[193] The National Energy Regulator of South Africa has the power to approve maximum prices for piped gas; monitor and approve gas transmission and storage tariffs; enforce third-party access; and issue licenses for construction or operation of infrastructure and for trading in gas.

In gas-rich North African countries, prices tend to be set or regulated so as to benefit local residents. In Algeria, for instance, natural gas prices are regulated by the government and its agencies— the hydrocarbon regulator and the electricity and gas regulator set and publish primary and retail gas prices, respectively. The regulatory framework for gas pricing has been criticized for setting prices too low, the result of which is unsustainable consumption patterns.[194]

In gas-rich West African countries, the industry is politicized and opaque, and prices have been low. Due to under-collection of gas revenues and weak and unenforceable supply and purchase agreements, the industry has not performed well.[195] Regulatory and legal uncertainties have delayed major projects, and unbundling of the Nigerian Gas Company Ltd into a transmission and product-marketing company has been slow. A "gas aggregator" was established to "manage the implementation of the domestic (gas) supply obligation and to act as an intermediary between suppliers and domestic purchasers".[196] This design is similar to the single-buyer model in electricity markets.

Clearly, gas policies and legislation are of limited use without concomitant implementation and enforcement. The institutional capacity to regulate downstream gas markets, in particular, is not well developed in Africa. This poses the risk of creating unsustainable consumption levels or an unattractive investment climate.

Liquid fuels

This section examines liquid fuels—oil and its derivatives.

Africa's current position

Traditionally, Africa's largest known oil reserves have been concentrated in Northern Africa (Libya, Algeria,[197] and Sudan), Western Africa (Nigeria), and Central Africa (Angola). Smaller deposits were found in Central Africa (Gabon, the Republic of Congo, Chad, Equatorial Guinea, Cameroon and the Democratic Republic of Congo) and Western Africa (Côte d'Ivoire).[198] Discoveries of oil deposits amounting to an estimated 11 billion barrels were made off the coast of Namibia in mid-2012, resulting in increased exploration along the west coast of South Africa in the Orange River basin.[199] In Uganda, successful well appraisals increased the country's proven crude oil reserves from zero in 2010 to 2.5 billion barrels as of January 1, 2013.[200]

In the past 20 years, the continent's oil reserves have grown by more than 25%, and Africa has become an important player in world oil production; production in Africa is expected to grow at 6% per annum.[201] Nonetheless, the continent's production is still dwarfed by that of major oil-producing regions, as shown in Table 6.5. At the end of 2012, total oil production in Africa was 449 million tonnes (10% of global production), compared with a staggering 1,337 million tonnes in the Middle East.

Table 6.5: Global oil production volumes (2012)

Region	Production volume (million tonnes)
Africa	449.0
South and Central America	378.0
Asia Pacific	397.3
Europe and Eurasia	836.4
North America	721.4
Middle East	1,337

Source: BP (2013) Statistical review of world energy, http://www.bp.com/content/dam/
bp-country/fr_fr/Documents/Rapportsetpublications/statistical_review_of_world_
energy_2013.pdf

Africa's liquid fuels infrastructure base

The upstream portion of the oil supply chain encompasses exploration and processing.[202] Table 6.6 indicates that from 2002 to 2012, oil production in Africa as a whole increased by 23.3%, with increases in North, West, Central and Southern Africa. Declines occurred in East Africa,[203] possibly because of the global economic downturn in 2008. Although Africa's oil production rose over the same period, most of it is exported as crude oil. The African oil scene is similar to the gas situation, with production geared toward export without development of domestic markets, because of low domestic demand, project risk, and affordability concerns. Mid- and downstream activities in the oil supply chain include refining and retail, a portion of the industry that is particularly underdeveloped in Africa.[204] African refineries have closed because of low worldwide refining margins, small local markets, high operating costs, and poor yields.[205] From 2002 to 2012, oil refinery capacity in Africa increased by only 0.5%, and refinery utilization has declined steadily since 2010.[206]

Table 6.6: Comparison of Africa's oil production over time (1992–2012)

Region	Oil production (thousands of barrels per day)			% change (2002 to 2012)
	1992	2002	2012	
North Africa	3,808	3,826	4,152	8.5
East Africa	0	241	116	−51.9
Southern Africa	140	211	181	−14.4
West Africa	1,959	2,145	2,669	24.5
Central Africa	1,165	1,712	2,912	70.0
Total	7,072	8,136	10,029	23.3

Source: EIA (2013). https://www.eia.gov; authors' calculations

Table 6.7: Comparison of Africa's oil refinery capacity over time (1992–2011)

Region	Crude oil distillation capacity (thousands of barrels per day)			% change (2002 to 2011)
	1992	2002	2011	
North Africa	1,525	1,709	1,743	2.0
East Africa	197	290	265	−8.6
Southern Africa	431	469	485	3.4
West Africa	578	601	604	0.5
Central Africa	136	134	121	−0.1
Total	2,867	3,202	3,218	0.5

Source: EIA (2013). https://www.eia.gov; authors' calculations

In addition, transportation and retail of refined petroleum products across the continent are hindered by the limited pipeline infrastructure. African pipelines are usually built for national rather than regional or continental distribution. The few regional pipelines that exist and the few infrastructure projects involving pipelines that are planned[207] are insufficient to satisfy the continent's energy demands. Currently, intra-African trade in oil is limited to trade within West Africa and North Africa;[208] trade between African oil producers and countries in Eastern and Southern Africa is minimal.[209] Infrastructure is needed to facilitate intra-African trade in oil. If domestic markets are developed and integrated, sufficient demand can be pooled to motivate oil-producing nations to refining and trade liquid fuels with other African nations.

Current infrastructure

Most petroleum pipelines are in Northern, Western and Central Africa and are used to serve national markets; regional or continental pipelines make up only a small share of liquid fuel pipelines (Figure 6.9).[210]

Southern Africa has a slightly better regional oil pipeline infrastructure. Zimbabwe and Malawi use a regional pipeline from Beira in Mozambique to Mutare/Harare in Zimbabwe to import refined products. South Africa's pipeline network is extensive, but it is limited to national distribution.[211]

In Eastern Africa, Kenya has an internal products pipeline distribution system that connects Mombasa and its refinery to Nairobi, and extends to Eldoret and Kisumu. In addition, a crude oil pipeline connects Dar es Salaam in Tanzania to Ndola in Zambia.[212]

Africa has many oil refineries—the major ones tend to be in the oil-producing regions in Western and Northern Africa. Several others located in Central and Southern Africa use imported crude oil.[213]

Figure 6.9: Africa's oil products pipeline network

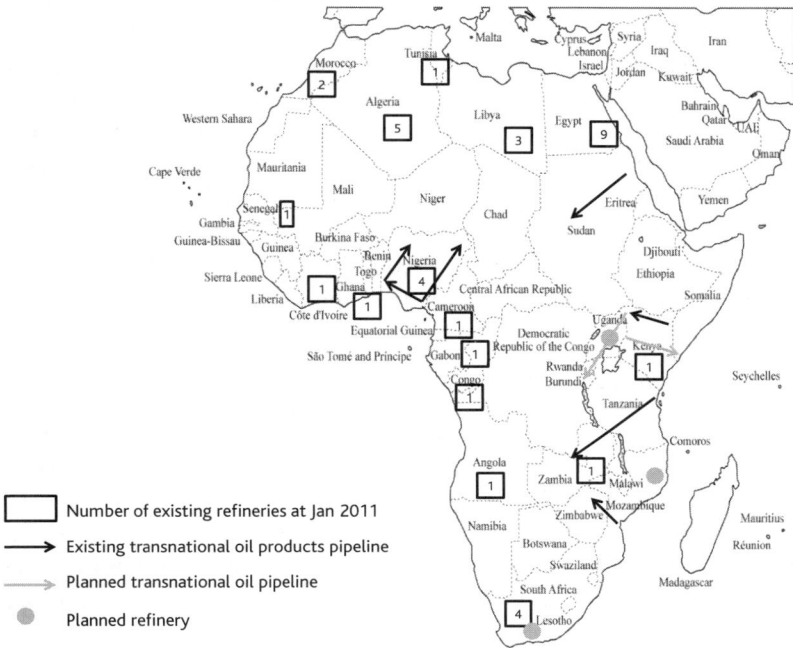

Number of existing refineries at Jan 2011

Existing transnational oil products pipeline

Planned transnational oil pipeline

Planned refinery

Source: Programme for Infrastructure Development in Africa (PIDA), 2011, *Africa Energy Outlook 2040.* Available at: http://www.au-pida.org/documents/ENERGIE/EOE-Energy -Outlook.pdf, p 26.

Planned infrastructure programs

The Ugandan government has invited bids for construction of a Kenya–Uganda Products Pipeline. The pipeline is expected to be linked with Kenya's Mombasa–Eldoret Pipeline, and later, extended to Rwanda, Burundi and Eastern Congo. The aim is to transport refined products from the proposed refinery in Uganda and the refinery in Mombasa to regional markets.[214]

Subsequent to offshore oil discoveries in Uganda in 2006, oil companies Total (France), CNOOC (China) and the Ugandan government agreed to terms for building a refinery. However, rather than building a major refinery in Uganda, Total and CNOOC intend to build a pipeline to export most of the crude oil production via Kenya's Indian Ocean coastline. The companies believe that local demand is insufficient for a refinery of the size the Ugandan government wanted.[215]

Plans are underway to develop the Mozambican Nacala refinery, which is expected to have an installed capacity of about 100,000 barrels per day (bpd). Most of the product will be exported to Malawi, Zimbabwe, and Zambia.[216] In South Africa, PetroSA plans to partner with China's Sinopec Group to develop project Mthombo, an initiative to build a crude refinery in the Coega Industrial Development Zone in the Eastern Cape. The refinery, costing US$11 billion, will have a 400,000 bpd capacity,[217] making it the largest crude refinery in Africa.[218]

The AfDB is supporting a 100,000 bpd refinery in Egypt,[219] and South Sudan is considering a crude oil pipeline to Lamu, Kenya.[220]

Regulatory environment

The regulation of oil infrastructure, as opposed to oil products, is similar to the regulation of gas, described earlier. Because oil prices are determined globally, price regulation is mainly concerned with infrastructure and refining costs rather than the global price of oil. In South Africa and many other African nations, the price of refined oil products such as petrol is regulated, based on domestic costs and the global price of (imported) oil.[221]

Energy infrastructure finance

Funding sources and financing mechanisms

The substantial funding needed to develop African infrastructure over the coming decades requires consideration of how infrastructure is currently financed and how resources may be better mobilized. As illustrated in the previous sections, Africa's energy infrastructure requires renewal and expansion. The current state is the result of the lack of governments' capacity to generate the necessary funds, small domestic markets, limited effective regulatory and legislative frameworks,[222] and the difficulty of attracting private sector investment.[223]

The PIDA Africa Energy Outlook 2040[224(i)] estimates that US$43.6 billion per year will be needed to meet forecast energy demand in Africa up to the year 2040.[224(ii)] Investment requirements are estimated at between US$42.2 billion and US$33.1 billion for generation, an upfront investment of US$5.4 billion for transmission interconnections, and US$3.7 billion to ensure access rates at a minimum of 60%. Investment requirements for gas and petroleum pipelines amount to US$1.3 billion per year.

It is imperative that all possible options be explored to close the funding gap. The following sections provide an overview of such options.

Infrastructure funding can come from a variety of public and private sources: government, development finance institutions (DFIs), overseas development assistance (ODA), foreign direct investment, capital markets, commercial banks, and institutional investors.

Financing mechanisms for infrastructure depend on the nature of the project, its characteristics, and the profile of the funder. Government funding may take the form of direct injections, soft loans, or loan guarantees. Projects may be funded by grants from DFIs or through ODA, in which case, funding is a direct injection, loan or guarantee. Donor funding is best suited to projects with high social but low financial returns, which generally do not appeal to private sector investors, given the lower prospects of cost recovery. Donor funding is attractive to governments that lack funds and the capacity to borrow funds in capital markets. Syndicated loans are generally the preserve of investment and commercial banks, and spread project risk across multiple lenders.

Traditionally, government funding has been the principal source of financing for energy infrastructure. More recently, private investors have teamed up with African governments in public–private partnerships (PPPs) to develop the energy sectors of countries like Kenya, Tanzania and Mozambique. The companies invest in order to reap commercial benefits when the power, oil and gas projects start to yield returns. Several other mechanisms that can be used to fund energy infrastructure are outlined below.

Infrastructure project bond financing

Project bond financing ("infrastructure bonds") has gained popularity in recent years. A debt instrument is issued by governments or private companies to raise funds from capital markets.[225] Typically, the coupon payments associated with infrastructure bonds are linked to cash flows generated from the project.

Although traditional loan structures are more common in project finance, particularly during the capital-intensive construction phase, infrastructure bonds have several advantages.[226] First, they are a cheaper financing method. Second, they can be tailored to have longer maturity dates, which is often useful for matching to the concession period of the project (20 to 30 years). Third, bonds can be raised in different currencies. Fourth, bonds are available for incremental funding.

Most transactions in African markets are not strictly infrastructure bonds, but rather, general government bonds with earmarking of funds for infrastructure investment. Most of Africa is in the early stage of development of infrastructure bonds. Greater uptake of this form of financing will require investors to collect more funds, borrowers to gain confidence in capital markets, and governments to create an environment that encourages the issuance of project bonds. Other emerging markets, such as Chile, Brazil and Malaysia, have used infrastructure bonds to spark investor interest and offer useful case studies for how African countries can shape their markets.

Public–private partnerships

The risk-and-reward-sharing nature of PPPs enables private sector participation in public service provision. PPPs allow private sector funds to be invested in infrastructure, thereby easing budget constraints on the public sector. They may also increase the efficiency of infrastructure provision by drawing on private sector knowledge.

However, risks are associated with PPPs. Improper structuring of the contract may result in the government absorbing an undue amount of the risk and the private sector reaping most of the profit from the infrastructure investment. African governments require professional competence in ensuring that PPPs facilitate infrastructure investment by tapping into private sector resources, while retaining a fair division of project risks and rewards.

PPPs are difficult to implement for projects which are important in facilitating community and social development but nonetheless offer relatively low financial returns (for example, increased access to electricity grids in rural areas). However, many infrastructure projects are suited to private sector investment. These projects usually involve economic infrastructure that generates an independent revenue stream, providing the private sector participant with an incentive to innovate in construction or operation. For example, extracting and processing crude oil and natural gas provides an income stream that motivates private investment in African energy infrastructure.

Independent power producers

IPPs are an additional avenue for private sector funding in the energy sector. IPPs are prevalent in electricity generation, but not in transmission and distribution. IPPs usually invest only if they receive PPAs from national utilities—it is too risky for them to invest in generation capacity without a guaranteed buyer. An improperly structured risk–and–reward allocation can be unfavorable to IPPs and discourage further investments in generation capacity, or can shift inordinate risks to electricity consumers in a captive market. This dynamic is the main rationale for the single–buyer model that has been adopted in many African countries.

Financing energy infrastructure

Electricity infrastructure in Africa has traditionally been provided by the state, but increasingly, governments are realizing that this is not feasible for funding the infrastructure required to satisfy the electricity needs of their economies.[227] Private sector participation in infrastructure has mainly been limited to the generation portion of the electricity supply chain; transmission and distribution networks are generally still owned by state utilities. Unbundling of electricity sector infrastructure has been slow, and many countries prefer to keep national energy transmission networks in state hands.[228] The share of electricity generated by private producers is small in most African countries (exceptions include Côte d'Ivoire where 40% of electricity is generated by IPPs). In South Africa, IPPs tend to be involved in electricity generation using renewable sources such as solar and wind energy. In Kenya, Nigeria, Ghana, Côte d'Ivoire and Cameroon, IPPs use gas or oil-fired generation technologies.[229] As already noted, these IPPs generally require PPAs for continued investment in generation infrastructure. If PPAs are not structured correctly, the incentive for the private sector to invest in further generation capacity can be reduced because of inequitable risk–and–reward allocation.

Gas and oil extraction and production infrastructure is more readily financed in regions with substantial reserves, because large private or state-owned oil and gas companies have sufficient financial incentives to invest.[230] For example, Anadarko Petroleum Corporation and Eni SpA plan to develop Mozambican gas fields and construct a large LNG liquefaction plant. These companies invest mostly in upstream infrastructure to extract oil and gas for export. Pipelines are financed by private companies only if they can earn returns commensurate with the risks associated with infrastructure financing. This is difficult in many parts of Africa where the markets for oil and gas are underdeveloped. Furthermore, development of oil and gas pipeline networks has high social benefits but low financial returns, so it is usually left up to African governments, whose funds are limited.

Africa50: a conceptual financing vehicle

The AfDB's recently proposed Africa50 initiative is a funding vehicle that offers various financing mechanisms and instruments to infrastructure projects across the continent.

It is envisioned as a commercially oriented financial institution with a mandate to fund high-impact national and regional infrastructure projects. The AfDB has identified transformative infrastructure projects, often with significant regional implications (including the PIDA pipeline), totaling US$150 billion. These will be financed by three broad investor groups: African countries (including sovereign wealth funds of these nations); the AfDB (preliminary commitment of US$1 billion over 10 years) and other DFIs; and institutional investors, such as pension, insurance and sovereign wealth funds. Equity capital will then be leveraged to maximize impact.

This initiative originated with the identification of two challenges to Africa's infrastructure development. First, current investors tend to channel funds to projects that are relatively advanced in terms of scope, engineering design, off-taker agreements, and so on; Africa50 is aimed at projects that have not reached similar maturity. Second, as they are currently structured, financial products do not adequately meet the continent's needs. Africa50 will establish two business lines: a *project development unit* to increase the flow of bankable infrastructure projects and reduce the time from concept to financial close to three years from the current average of seven; and a *project finance unit* that will focus on structuring and delivering the financial instruments needed to attract additional infrastructure financing. These instruments will include bridge equity; senior secured loans; credit enhancement and other risk mitigation measures; and refinancing and secondary transactions.

For several reasons, the Africa50 initiative is an innovative funding mechanism. First, it will have greater operational flexibility, because it will be a commercially, legally and financially independent entity. Second, it will have financial influence by targeting an investment-grade rating for capital raising, designing innovative financing instruments, and crowding in new sources of capital. Third, it will focus on enhancing the commercial nature (particularly bankability and risk allocation) of transformative, regional infrastructure projects. Finally, affiliation with the AfDB will attract political support, build regional consensus on infrastructure projects, and overcome many of the institutional and bureaucratic barriers that project development in Africa currently faces.

Challenges

Regulatory challenges

The mandates of regulatory bodies generally include the following elements: issuing licenses to market players (regulating entry and market structure); approving or setting prices and tariffs; enforcement of legislation and license conditions; discretionary powers concerning enquiries and investigations; third-party access enforcement or development of grid codes; service standards; and at times, safety regulation. These functions are often carried out by an independent regulator to promote private investment in public infrastructure and insulate infrastructure investment decisions from political interference. However, a number of challenges affect regulators' ability to promote the development of energy infrastructure in Africa.

Institutional capacity challenges, lack of reliable data, and the absence of a history of regulation render many regulatory entities ineffective. Moreover, regulators are often constrained by government policies and market dynamics that hinder their ability to intervene in energy markets. Electricity regulatory bodies are governed by national policy on economic development, affordability and equity concerns, capacity planning, the role of state-owned entities, and security of supply. Policymakers are hesitant to relinquish control to a regulator, who may or may not be independent, as it can be perceived as reducing government's ability to shape economic policy or direct state-owned entities. Regulatory independence, therefore, continues to be an issue in many African countries. To a large extent, the ability of regulators to achieve policy objectives depends on their legislated mandate, including freedom from political interference, enforcement powers, and their ability to make necessary decisions. Decision-making within a regulatory framework can be affected if the government alters the regulator's mandate. It is important that regulators have a clear mandate and regulatory framework that prevents political influence.

Energy regulators are entrusted with ensuring that tariffs cover the cost of supply by encouraging greater production efficiency and service quality. Unfortunately, information imbalances exist between regulators and incumbent companies about the true costs, market demand and quality of supply.[231] Incumbents who have full information about these factors can use it to exploit the regulatory process to maximize their profits. This can lead to inefficient production, lower-quality service, and higher prices for end consumers.[232]

Despite recognition of the need for reform in the electrical supply industry, many African nations are still striving to achieve it and are at different stages in the process. This makes it difficult to coordinate energy policies between countries. Some regulators have vague mandates and cannot provide clarity about their energy sector policies.

For instance, regulators may lack clear policy direction with regard to IPPs. Often, statements are made about the need for IPPs, but these are not clearly translated into policy direction for the regulator, be it via its mandate or other policy intervention such as government procurement. Giving these third-party power producers access to the national grid is an essential part of electrical supply industry reform. These IPPs are generally involved in private investment initiatives undertaken in conjunction with the larger state-owned utility to meet local market demand. Access to the national power grid is usually granted by the electricity regulator, and market competition is defined under three stages: single-buyer, wholesale, and retail.[233]

Some success has been achieved in introducing competition in the wholesale market in Kenya and Côte d'Ivoire. Most African countries have selected the single-buyer framework for regulating electricity sector IPPs. Under this arrangement, third-party producers are allowed to generate power, but a state-owned entity is the single buyer for electricity, which it transmits and distributes through the national grid. This level of market openness introduces substantial competition in electricity generation, as it provides a degree of certainty to IPPs, which attracts private investment. However, despite its success in attracting private investment to upstream activities, this approach leaves the remainder of the supply chain—transmission and distribution—under monopoly control. Therefore, the regulatory model, where state-owned utilities remain the dominant players with limited private sector participation, is likely to persist. The integration of third-party power producers, especially in renewable energy, is complicated by regulators' and policymakers' lack of expertise. They often lack the skills and experience to develop a renewable energy policy that would integrate these third-party power producers into the national grid.[234]

Cross-border energy trade is another challenge to energy regulation. Regulations are not harmonized between countries, which can hamper cross-border trade and regional integration of the transmission system. For example, tariff "pancaking" can occur when a customer is forced to pay differing cumulative rates for the transmission of energy across multiple systems.[235] Tariff pancaking is, of course, inefficient only when the stacking results in a final price that does not reflect the actual cost of providing transmission, and thereby, reduces incentives to undertake cross-border trade in energy.[236] Harmonization would mean consistent energy regulation across regions, thus avoiding issues such as regulatory barriers and prohibitively high tariffs that can deter intra-Africa energy trade.

The African energy sector also lacks coordination of licensing. Activities such as exploration and extraction require environmental approval and government authorization before they can take place, while similarly construction and operation of downstream infrastructure as well as trading in energy sources tend to be licensed separately, often involving different regulatory agencies and application requirements. Licensing should not be so onerous that it deters investment. Because long, complicated approval procedures can discourage private investment, bureaucratic requirements must be simplified and coordinated among relevant entities (for example, regulators and state departments).

Exploration and production infrastructure in Africa has traditionally been financed by private companies that can generate sufficient returns on the production of oil and gas. Africa, seen as a "reasonably mature market for oil and gas exploration and production",[237] is accustomed to private sector participation, because markets are open, and high returns can be earned from investing in infrastructure to extract and refine these commodities. For instance, in Algeria, more than 35 foreign companies currently participate in exploration and production. However, these companies gear their production toward exports; they have no incentive to develop a regional pipeline infrastructure.

Political/policy uncertainty

Most forms of infrastructure investment are exposed to political risks—"threats to the profitability of a project that derive from some form of government action or inaction rather than from changes in economic conditions in the marketplace".[238] The political risks commonly associated with Africa include violence, currency convertibility and transferability, poor labor relations, expropriation, and breach of investment agreements. Examples of these types of are the expropriation and nationalization of mines in Zimbabwe and civil unrest in Egypt, Sudan and the Central African Republic. These risks pose major challenges to attracting private investment in public infrastructure.[239] One recent development that offers opportunity to mitigate these risks is the work of the Africa Trade Insurance Agency

(ATI). ATI is a facility designed to offer political risk insurance services for projects and small to medium-sized enterprises.

Apart from political risks, regulatory bodies face policy constraints such as a lack of clear energy policy; changes in policy without concomitant changes in the legislation or mandate of the regulator; inadequate mandates of regulators; and ministerial discretion on substantive regulatory decisions. According to the African Forum for Utility Regulators, leading policy constraints faced by independent energy regulatory bodies are:[240]

- lack of experience and skills;
- lack of financial resources;
- resistance to change;
- insufficient incentives to attract new investment and private sector participation;
- lack of political will/lack of *de facto* independence;
- policies encouraging non-cost reflective tariffs;
- challenges dealing with large, resource-rich monopolies (for example, Eskom in South Africa; Nampower in Namibia).

This is a limited list of the challenges faced by regulatory bodies, as independence does not guarantee coherent and appropriate national energy policies. Ties to state-owned incumbents may result in the regulator making decisions intended to protect the interests of incumbent operators rather than those of consumers, producers and other players.

In addition, weak or non-existent institutional capacity prevents development of energy infrastructure. The lack of managerial expertise in the public sector administrations of many African countries hinders the progress of infrastructure projects. Other institutional problems such as a lack of transparency, political interference and corruption also negatively affect the public provision of infrastructure services.

A key concern in the exploitation of natural energy resources such as oil and gas is the distribution of earnings between private investors and the population to whom the nation's resource endowments actually belong.[241] Foreign investors in African oil and gas markets are expected, but generally not required, to contribute to social development.[242] But as noted earlier, these private companies usually have a strong export focus; little infrastructure is developed to increase access to energy or create long-lasting benefits for the oil-producing country and its people. Private companies have no incentive to invest in infrastructure that would improve intra-African trade and achieve social development goals, because such investments typically yield low financial returns. However, if citizens receive no benefit from their country's energy resources, the result can be social and political unrest, as happened recently in southern Tanzania where residents rioted against the development of a gas pipeline.[243]

Opposition to the commercial development of a country's natural resources is not exclusive to Africa. In Venezuela and Argentina, citizens marched in support of policies to nationalize oil and gas industries. Africans, too, are wary of how their country's resources are used and are prepared to protest if they do not perceive social benefits from the extraction and production of oil and gas. The challenge is determining how much intervention is required to ensure that social benefits will be realized. Excessive state intervention can be detrimental to oil and gas markets, and even to the economy as a whole. For example, after the Venezuelan oil and gas market was nationalized in 2007, companies such as Exxon Mobil left, further reducing the country's access to oil and gas technology and expertise.[244] In addition, the state-owned company, Petroleos de Venezuela SA (PDVSA), had to assume responsibility for the maintenance of large oil fields, which required substantial investment.[245] PDVSA's oil production has fallen steadily since nationalization. The country now has high foreign debt, inefficient maintenance, and frequent reports of political scandal and incompetence.[246]

Vandalism is another serious problem for African energy infrastructure development. It can cause widespread losses of product (oil, gas or electricity) and damage existing infrastructure. Vandalism has plagued the Nigerian oil pipeline network[247] to the extent that US$1.079 billion in product losses and pipeline repairs have been incurred over the past decade. In South Africa, electricity theft through illegal connections led to a loss of 5,850 GWh by Eskom in the 2008/2009 financial year.[248]

Political and policy uncertainty can be mitigated by developing a policy framework that takes account of the political economy of the energy industry, provides clarity on desired outcomes, and reassures investors. Staying the course during difficult times and resisting short-term, politically expedient interventions will create an atmosphere of reliability and regulatory certainty, which is critical for attracting the funds needed to upgrade and expand Africa's energy infrastructure.

Financing challenges

Development of Africa's energy infrastructure is difficult because small national markets prevent economies of scale. Thus, affordability is an issue, whether it involves electricity generation, transmission and distribution infrastructure, or oil or gas pipeline networks.[249, 250]

Most African countries have poorly developed capital markets and low sovereign credit ratings, which limits their access to international capital to fund infrastructure projects.[251] Instead, public funds must be allocated to these projects, but most African nations cannot increase their spending on infrastructure development, especially since the financial crisis of 2008.[252] Therefore, attracting private sector investment, either directly through PPIs or project bonds, is imperative. However, because private investors do not prioritize universal access, this aspect of infrastructure development is still left up to governments and utilities that lack the necessary funding.

In addition, energy infrastructure investments have high initial costs and long lifespans, which do not generate high short-term returns on the capital invested. As a result, private investors are reluctant to make such investments unless they are guaranteed a reasonable return. In the case of electricity, a reasonable return can be achieved only if tariffs are set above the levelized cost of producing the electricity, which, itself, raises affordability concerns. Furthermore, low utility performance, poor budget execution and inadequate payment collection procedures compound the uncertainty surrounding electricity infrastructure investment in Africa.[253]

Most African countries depend on revenue from resource rents and taxes, but commodity price volatility makes it difficult to predict the budget cycles of these nations. Energy infrastructure investments are large and long-term, and, in the context of macroeconomic uncertainty, it is difficult to determine future costs of investment and operations. If the expected return on energy infrastructure investment is considered too risky, private investors will raise the required return on equity or opt for more predictable returns in other industries.[254]

Even when they are interested in African infrastructure, investors often focus on ready-made projects that may not have the desired impact on the energy sector. Projects that are available to the market in a ring-fenced form are preferable to investors given that uncertainty is reduced in this situation. This often involves specific generation projects with guaranteed off-take and returns, rather than proactive policy-driven investment in network expansion in anticipation of economic growth. As a result, there is a divergence in the financing that African energy infrastructure requires and what investors are willing to fund. Furthermore, existing financial products are not sufficient to enable development of energy infrastructure that will respond to Africa's needs.[255]

Because private sector investment is imperative to closing the energy funding gap in Africa, government and regulatory objectives must be aligned with the incentives of investors, and innovative funding mechanisms must be developed to achieve desired outcomes.

Opportunities for energy infrastructure

Recent developments in energy markets across Africa offer opportunities to develop infrastructure that could improve the energy sector over the next 50 years. However, approaches that are successful in some countries may not be practical for others. For example, additional transmission facilities that provide complete coverage of a country or across different regions will contribute to energy security and sustainability, but it is not easy to implement, given the financing, regulatory and policy constraints faced by numerous African nations.

Although the development of large-scale nuclear power plants—an objective of countries such as South Africa, Nigeria and Egypt—may be desirable given Africa's uranium reserves, reduced CO_2 emissions, and the projected levelized cost,[256] it is difficult to implement owing to high upfront capital costs. In addition, there are issues relating to: the scale required for nuclear power to be efficient, which makes it less viable for smaller African markets; the skills required for operation of a nuclear power plant; and the limited prospect of using IPPs for nuclear projects.

Despite abundant solar, wind and geothermal energy resources, large-scale renewable power generation is currently too expensive to be a major source of power for the continent. Nonetheless, in the next few decades, renewable and nuclear power are likely to become more affordable, and in the case of nuclear, less scale-intensive, and so are likely to gain importance in the energy mix.

Meanwhile, decentralized generation could increase energy access. Renewable energy, in particular, can play an important role in underserviced areas where grid extension is not feasible, and displace expensive generators that use petroleum products or traditional sources. This is especially appealing, because the price of renewable energy is likely to decrease in the medium to long term as technological innovation lowers capital costs, and by extension, levelized costs of generation.

The opportunities for the development of Africa's energy sector are mainly in its resource endowments. The key is to use these resources in a way that benefits the continent as a whole.

In East and West Africa, and despite the severe 2011–2012 drought in East Africa, hydropower generation will continue to be important. This technology has great untapped potential to supply other regions in Africa. But for this potential to be harnessed, several hurdles, ranging from political uncertainty to a lack of cross-border electricity transmission capacity, must be overcome. Renewable energy is proving to be a suitable candidate for IPP involvement, and may require government and DFI funding only for less lucrative segments of the value chain, such as transmission and interconnection infrastructure.

Africa has great wealth in coal and gas. Coal-fired electricity generation is relatively cheap, and new technologies can mitigate environmental effects.[257] African nations are likely to rely on coal-fired electricity generation because of the cost advantages. Coal deposits are mainly in South Africa and Botswana, so coal-fired electricity generation will likely be confined to Southern Africa. However, extensions of the SAPP will allow trade so that the abundant supply in the South can benefit other African countries and regions. Expansion of the SAPP and greater interconnection of regional power grids are required, but because transmission and transnational systems are not attractive to the private sector, investment is more likely to come from government and DFI funding. Utilities in the region, notably those in South Africa, are reaching the limits of balance sheet funding, which creates opportunities for IPPs, PPPs and DFIs in coal-fired generation and in transnational transmission connections.

In the future, the status of coal in Africa may decline, given climate change concerns, international environmental obligations, proposed carbon taxes, and so on, and leave room for other technologies. In addition, increases in the price of coal have reduced its cost advantage. However, domestic and regional gas is or will be available, so gas-fired electricity may become the technology of choice for power generation. Discoveries in East Africa and untapped flared gas potential in Central and West Africa offer greater access to gas than ever before, and increased global supplies have resulted in lower gas prices. In addition, compared with coal, gas-fired generators can be switched on and off quickly and easily, making it a more efficient technology for mid-merit and peak generation. Renewable energy (wind and solar) power plants require back-up generators. Again, owing to the ease with which generators can be switched on and off, gas is particularly well-suited for this purpose.

With investment in gas-fired electricity generation capacity, the demand for gas will grow in Africa. Transportation infrastructure such as pipelines and LNG importation terminals will be required. Because the distance that gas pipelines can cover is limited, maritime transport of LNG is an option, even for intra-African trade. For instance, the distance between the gas fields in the Northern part of the Rovuma basin off Tanzania's shoreline and electricity demand in the Western Cape of South Africa suggests that maritime LNG transport would be preferable to pipelines.

Many infrastructure projects are too expensive for African governments and do not offer a strong business case to private investors. Involvement of DFIs like the African Development Bank in such projects can have a considerable impact on Africa's energy sector.

Opportunities for electricity infrastructure

The opportunities available to ameliorate some of the difficulties that Africa faces in closing the gap between electricity demand and supply include planned infrastructure investments, greater regional integration, and a better regulatory environment.

Future infrastructure plans and regional integration

The potential for growth in Africa's electricity generating capacity is impressive. For example, it is estimated that more than 90% of the continent's hydropower potential is yet to be exploited. Opportunities for wind energy exist in Kenya, Morocco and South Africa; for solar energy in North Africa and South Africa; and for gas in West Africa and East Africa. If these sources are harnessed effectively and efficiently, the production required to satisfy current/medium-term demand for electricity could be exceeded.

Few African countries have sufficient domestic demand to justify power plants large enough to fully exploit available potential. The only way to justify expenditures on large power plants is to extend the market beyond domestic borders through regional trade. For instance, the hydroelectric plant at the Cahora Bassa Dam in Mozambique was justified on the basis of electricity exports to South Africa.[258] Thus, the benefits of regional trade to smaller economies are not only greater electricity capacity, but also higher export revenue. Moreover, increased trade in power means that importing countries no longer have to invest in new generation capacity.

Regional trade is the optimal way to close the gap between electricity demand and supply. Countries in Africa have formed four power pools to stimulate trade: the Southern African Power Pool (SAPP), the West African Power Pool (WAPP), the East African/Nile Basin Power Pool (EAPP), and the Central African Power Pool (CAPP).[259] The SAPP was the first, and currently, most trade occurs among countries in that region. The WAPP is the second largest, followed by the EAPP and CAPP. However, they have not achieved major success, largely because the members are the incumbent electricity utilities in the various countries, which have little incentive to encourage trade, as it would entail giving competitors access to their domestic customers. Furthermore, the pools lack the mandate and means to amend regulations to encourage trade. Regulatory oversight, or at least harmonized regulatory frameworks, is needed to align the incentives of power pool members with policy objectives.

The countries involved in the power pools are at different stages of development, and so have varying regulatory and legal frameworks. A further complication is the large number of regional bodies[260] (Southern African Development Community [SADC], Common Market for Eastern and Southern Africa [COMESA], and so on) that have their own mandates for regional integration. Thus, for power pools to achieve their objectives, the respective governments should: provide a platform for national regulators to cooperate in allowing third-party access to the network; harmonize regulatory and legal frameworks; and reach political consensus on power trade across regions.[261] Greater harmonization and simplified processes will promote trade in these pools and facilitate investment generation capacity. Improved electricity infrastructure connections and trade among African countries will smooth the way for regional integration across Africa, as they will reduce costs and make it easier to do business.[262]

Beyond gains derived from cost reductions and greater ease of doing business, an economic rationale exists for regional electricity grid integration. Regional interconnection allows countries to obtain less expensive electricity from nations that have a surplus or that produce energy using a more cost-efficient input.[263] The reduction in electricity prices benefits consumers and the economy as a whole. Studies have shown that extension of the electricity grid by 1.3% "enables the addition of 3% generation capacity".[264] Regional electricity integration has also made it possible to reduce the reserves required for redundancy in each participating country (which generally entail high costs).[265] Integration of electricity grids can increase the operating efficiency of large base-load power plants, especially coal-fired and nuclear power plants.[266, 267]

Interconnection of regional grids also fosters integration of renewable energy sources into the power grid, as it allows for entry at a higher voltage. This reduces transmission losses over long distances when plants are not located close to load centers.[268] Regional grids have been established in other parts of the world, for example, the Baltic Energy Market Interconnector Plan and the North Sea grid.

Improved regulatory environment

Electricity infrastructure in Africa is largely funded by the public sector and donor agencies, but the possibility for further allocations is diminishing. Private sector participation via IPPs or PPPs and DFIs are likely to be the primary source of infrastructure funding. But given the risks, private investors have been reluctant to fund electricity infrastructure unless they are provided with extensive guarantees. Regulatory reform is, therefore, needed to reduce some of the risks that deter private participation.

The first regulatory issue that must be addressed is the introduction of IPPs in electricity generation and granting third-party access to national transmission and distribution networks. Several methods have been employed to improve competition and service delivery. These have been in the form of private participation in infrastructure (PPI), which includes management or lease contracts, concession contracts, independent power projects, and divestiture.

IPPs are among the more popular programs in the electricity infrastructure sector. Over half the PPI transactions in Africa have been in IPPs, which accounted for about 3,000 MW of new capacity and involved more than US$2 billion of private investment.[269] The most successful IPPs have been in Kenya and Côte d'Ivoire, and recently, South Africa. Kenya's electricity sector was unbundled in 1998, and the Electricity Regulatory Board, which issues licenses and regulates the power purchase agreements, was established. As a result, a growing number of IPPs participated in the Kenyan electricity market and international investment increased.

Utilities in countries with IPPs have better performance than those in countries without IPPs. Because most African nations have adopted the single-buyer framework, which makes it difficult to level the playing field for IPPs, it is important that systems are in place to ensure non-discriminatory treatment. An independent transmission system operator is appropriate under these conditions, which requires some unbundling of vertically integrated incumbents. In most cases, this allows greater integration of third-party power producers, which improves the efficiency of the state-owned entity and encourages private investment in electricity infrastructure. However, most African utilities are very small; unbundling may not improve operational efficiency in these cases. In fact, the per-unit cost of electricity is likely to increase if small utilities are unbundled. Therefore, unbundling should occur on a case-by-case basis.

Clarity is needed about cost-reflective tariffs and affordability. However, it is a misperception that subsidized rates, social tariffs or historically low prices prevent private sector participation in electricity generation. For instance, South Africa's electricity prices were comparatively low for many years, and real prices actually declined in the early 2000s, as a result of overinvestment in infrastructure that led to fully amortized and underutilized generation capacity. IPPs entering this market when new generation capacity is required would not be remunerated at the average, artificially low tariffs. Rather IPPs could enter into PPAs with the utility/single buyer to provide electricity while earning a return commensurate with the risk associated with the project. The resulting blended electricity price would increase over time. Hence, utility returns and private sector returns can co-exist, allowing for full cost recovery. Ensuring full cost recovery and a reasonable return on investment for IPPs would increase in private investment in electricity infrastructure.

Still, a balance must be struck between tariffs that are high enough to recover costs and ensuring widespread access to affordable electricity. This is particularly difficult for electricity regulators in Africa, where generation costs are significantly higher than in other developing countries.[270] If tariffs are perceived as too high, governments can employ a number of remedies such as cross-subsidization, direct subsidies to IPPs, or lifeline tariffs. Cross-subsidization occurs in many countries, among them South Africa, where large industrial users pay a premium that allows lower tariffs for low-income customers. Governments have also given direct subsidies to IPPs in Ghana and Tanzania to make them more competitive with the vertically integrated state-owned utility. Finally, with a lifeline tariff, a government supplies a limited quantity of electricity at a subsidized rate, such as providing the first 50kw per hour free in South Africa. These subsidy options allow governments and regulators to set tariffs at levels sufficient to cover costs, and to offer a reasonable return on investments, thereby encouraging private sector investment in infrastructure and expanding capacity.

Opportunities for gas infrastructure

Africa, particularly East Africa, has the potential to become a major force in the global gas market. Investment in infrastructure and export projects is key to achieving this outcome. Despite a multitude of investors,[271] in gas production on the continent, Africa has not reaped the full benefits.

Downstream opportunities for gas infrastructure investment are plentiful—gas-fired electricity generation will require pipelines, import terminals, and liquefaction and re-gasification facilities.

However, without sound governance and regulatory frameworks, national governments will struggle to achieve a climate conducive to investment,[272, 273] and the development of gas infrastructure will suffer. Increased private investment in the gas sector will generate revenue for African countries, especially in the East, and possibly in the South, if shale gas reserves are proven.

Sound governance and regulatory frameworks are also required to protect consumers in the region.[274] In fact, gas-producing countries such as Angola and Nigeria still have inadequate energy access.[275]

Because the demand for gas is not large enough to justify large projects, African nations should make efforts to increase the use of gas directly as a fuel or indirectly for electricity generation. African countries could provide incentives for the use of gas as an alternative to traditional energy sources such as oil and diesel and ensure that exploration and production concessions and licenses are tied to local market development. The use of gas as a transport fuel can be important for demand, and can be stimulated by government policies on public transport and conversion incentives.

More developed gas markets on the continent create the possibility of intra-African trade, which, in turn, makes private investments in regional pipeline networks financially feasible. This will increase energy access in Africa and reduce reliance on expensive imports of oil.

Because gas is becoming more competitive as a generation fuel, investment in gas-fired electricity generation capacity is an important step toward development of Africa's gas markets and efficient use of the continent's resources. In addition, the use of gas-fired generators for mid-merit and peak periods, as well as for back-up for renewable energy sources, has many benefits.

Opportunities for liquid fuels infrastructure

Africa's oil production has historically been concentrated in the Northern and Western parts of the continent and has generally been geared toward exports. Political unrest in North Africa (particularly Egypt and Libya) is predicted to have substantial consequences for the region's oil and gas industry. Because security of supply is threatened, European countries are seeking more stable import partners.[276] As a result, demand from Europe may diminish.

Africa could capitalize on new discoveries in Namibia and Uganda by developing refinery and export capacity in these countries. Uganda has recently taken steps to develop refinery capacity[277] and is considering export opportunities by pipeline.[278] Similarly, new refineries are considered in Namibia and Nigeria. Although it is unlikely that Africa will become a major force in global oil markets, given the colossal reserves in regions the Middle East and North America, oil-producing nations in Africa have opportunities for efficient utilization of their resources.

Over the past decade, oil production in Africa has grown, but without changes to domestic oil infrastructure, the continent's access to energy is unlikely to improve, as most of the production is exported as crude oil.

Conclusion

Given the relationship between economic growth and energy demand, investment in African energy infrastructure is imperative. The mismatch between the geographic distribution of energy resources and demand creates an opportunity for trade. This, in turn, makes transnational energy infrastructure and regional integration priorities, in that they would unlock this potential for regional trade. Moreover, by pooling demand from smaller economies, greater energy interconnection between African countries or regions would provide the much-needed minimum demand to anchor infrastructure projects.

The key to developing Africa's energy infrastructure is identifying projects in which to invest. It is unlikely that over the next 50 years a continental network of electricity grids and pipelines that ensures energy supplies for the entire continent will develop spontaneously. The focus for the next few decades should be to invest in: electricity generation capacity close to resources such as coal and gas; interconnections of existing grids to enable power trade; and transnational pipelines connecting national and regional pipelines and liquefied natural gas import terminals.

Investment opportunities arise in the following areas:

- coal- and gas-fired electricity generation capacity in Southern Africa;
- expansion of regional power pools;
- increasing interconnectivity of regional power pools;
- increasing gas-fired electricity generation plants in South, East, West, North and Central Africa;
- increasing interconnectivity between gas suppliers and customers, via gas pipelines or liquefied natural gas export and import terminals;
- decentralized renewable energy applications for rural areas;
- energy sources and technologies that increase access in poor areas, create employment, and provide opportunities to trade with the rest of the world;
- research and development regarding methods to increase access to power for the poor (for instance, decentralized distribution, incubators, and smart grids).

Development of Africa's energy infrastructure is hindered by regulatory challenges, political uncertainty, and affordability. Affordability is the key issue associated with the development of energy infrastructure. To tackle this issue, African nations should explore innovative funding mechanisms such as PPPs and IPPs. The proposed Africa50 funding vehicle can be used for energy infrastructure development across the continent.

Notes

[1] Although technically "tariffs" refer to charges for network infrastructure, and "prices," to the price of the supply of energy, the terminology of the source documents in question that refer to tariffs as the sum of all charges has been adopted.

[2] Eberhard, A., Rosnes, O., Shkaratan, M. and Vennemo, H. (2011) *Africa's Power Infrastructure – Investment, Integrity, Efficiency*. Washington, DC: World Bank. Available at www.ppiaf.org/sites/ppiaf.org/files/publication/Africas-Power-Infrastructure-2011.pdf.

[3] IEA (International Energy Agency) (2012) *World Energy Outlook*. Chapter 18: Measuring progress towards energy for all, Table 18.1. http://www.iea.org/publications/freepublications/publication/world-energy-outlook-2012.htm

[4] PIDA (Programme for Infrastructure Development in Africa) (2011) *Africa Energy Outlook 2040*. Available at: http://www.au-pida.org/documents/ENERGIE/EOE-Energy-Outlook.pdf

[5] World Economic Forum (2012) *Energy for Economic Growth*. http://www3.weforum.org/docs/WEF_EN_EnergyEconomicGrowth_IndustryAgenda_2012.pdf

[6] Deloitte (2012) 'Addressing Africa's infrastructure challenges', available at www.deloitte.com/assets/Dcom-SouthAfrica/Local%20Assets/Documents/infrastructure_brochure.pdf.

[7] Eberhard, A., Rosnes, O., Shkaratan, M. and Vennemo, H. (2011) Op. cit.

[8] Deloitte (2012) Op. cit.

[9] www.issafrica.org/iss-today/realising-the-dream-of-greater-intra-african-trade

[10] Eberhard, A., Rosnes, O., Shkaratan, M. and Vennemo, H. (2011) Op. cit.

[11] IEA (2012) Op. cit.

[12] United Nations Economic and Social Council (2013) *Report on Africa's Regional Integration Agenda* http://repository.uneca.org/bitstream/handle/10855/22134/b10696118.pdf?sequence=1; Eberhard, A., Rosnes, O., Shkaratan, M. and Vennemo, H. 2011. Op cit.

[13] IEA (2012) Op. cit.

[14] Hafner, M. and Tagliapietra, S. (2013) 'East Africa, the next game changer for the global gas markets', available at http://papers.ssrn.com/sol3/papers.cfm?abstract_id=2249723

[15] Ernst & Young (2012) 'Natural gas in Africa', available at www.ey.com/Publication/vwLUAssets/ Natural_gas_in_Africa_frontier_of_the_Golden_Age/$FILE/Natural_Gas%20in_Africa.pdf and Reuters (2013). 'Botswana aims to export 115 mln tonnes thermal coal'. 12 March 2013, available at: http://www.reuters.com/article/botswana-coal-idUSL6N0C47C620130312.

[16] Ernst & Young (2012) Op. cit.

[17] Such as diesel-fuelled generators, which are extremely expensive to operate. Eberhard, A., Rosnes, O., Shkaratan, M. and Vennemo, H. (2011). Op. cit; World Economic Forum (2012) *Energy for Economic Growth*. http://www3.weforum.org/docs/WEF_EN_EnergyEconomicGrowth_IndustryAgenda_2012.pdf

[18] www.afdb.org/en/blogs/integrating-africa/post/africas-energy-security-contingent-on-energy-sector-integration-12040/

[19] AfDB (African Development Bank) (2012) 'Energy sector policy of the AfDB Group', available at www.afdb.org/fileadmin/uploads/afdb/Documents/Policy-Documents/Energy_Sector_Policy_of_the_AfDB_Group.pdf (accessed 9 April 2015).

[20] Eberhard, A., Rosnes, O., Shkaratan, M. and Vennemo, H. (2011) Op. cit.

[21] AfDB (2012) Op. cit.; Eberhard, A., Rosnes, O., Shkaratan, M. and Vennemo, H. (2011) Op. cit.

[22] AfDB (2012) Op. cit.; Eberhard, A., Rosnes, O., Shkaratan, M. and Vennemo, H. (2011) Op. cit.

[23] AfDB (2012) Op. cit.

[24] Sasol investor presentation, S. Babbar; www.sasol.com/media-centre/media-releases/first-natural-gas-mozambique-arrives-secunda.

[25] Sasol investor presentation, S. Babbar.

[26] As we identify later, Grand Inga projects could provide 39,000 MWe in total.

[27] United Nations Economic and Social Council (2013) *Report on Africa's Regional Integration Agenda*, available at http://repository.uneca.org/bitstream/handle/10855/22134/b10696118.pdf?sequence=1

[28] Ibid.

[29] Ibid.

[30] Niyimbona, P. (2005) 'The challenges of operationalizing power pools in Africa', UNDESA Seminar on Electricity Interconnection, 19–21 June, Eqypt, UN Economic Commission for Africa, available at http://sustainabledevelopment.un.org/content/documents/3214interconnection_powerpools.pdf.

[31] AfDB (2012) Op. cit.

[32] Ibid.

[33] www.worldbank.org/en/news/press-release/2013/08/06/world-bank-approves-rusumo-falls-hydropower-plant

[34] www.africanreview.com/energy-a-power/power-generation/ethiopia-kenya-power-project-to-be-launched-soon

[35] AfDB (2012) Op. cit.

[36] Opalo, K. (2013) 'Africa's energy security contingent on energy sector integration', available at www.afdb.org/en/blogs/integrating-africa/post/africas-energy-security-contingent-on-energy-sector-integration-12040.

[37] Foster, V. and Briceño-Garmendia, C. (eds) (2009) *Africa's Infrastructure: A Time for Transformation*. Washington, DC: World Bank..

[38] South Korea and the United Kingdom had installed electricity capacity of 84 gigawatts and 93 gigawatts, respectively; EIA (2013). Electricity data browser. http://www.eia.gov/electricity/data/browser/

[39] Eberhard, A., Rosnes, O., Shkaratan, M. and Vennemo, H. (2011) Op. cit.

[40] Eberhard, A., Rosnes, O., Shkaratan, M. and Vennemo, H. (2011) Op. cit.

[41] Wolters, S. (2012) 'Harnessing the Congo River could light up Half of Africa', *Africa in Fact* (Issue 4), available at *gga.org/publications/africa-in-fact-september-2012*.

[42] Eberhard, A., Rosnes, O., Shkaratan, M. and Vennemo, H. (2011) Op. cit.

[43] http://ambriefonline.com/mining/index.php?option=com_content&view=article&id=804:awakening-the-sleeping-gas-giants-of-africa&catid=58:press-releases&Itemid=29

[44] PIDA (2011) *Africa Energy Outlook 2040*. Available at: http://www.au-pida.org/documents/ENERGIE/EOE-Energy-Outlook.pdf

[45] www.world-nuclear.org/info/Country-Profiles/Others/Uranium-in-Africa

[46] The five regions of Africa are according to United Nations definitions (see Appendix): http://millenniumindicators.un.org/unsd/methods/m49/m49regin.htm.

[47] A thermal power station is a heat- (steam-)driven power plant.

[48] Eberhard, A., Rosnes, O., Shkaratan, M. and Vennemo, H. (2011) Op. cit.

[49] Eskom (2013) 'Eskom Power Stations'. Available at www.eskom.co.za/c/12/power-stations.

[50] Because nuclear generation is found only in South Africa, this map has been omitted.

[51] www.worldcoal.org/resources/ecoal-archive/ecoal-current-issue/costs-of-coal-fired-electricity/

[52] KPMG (2012) 'Sub-Saharan power outlook', available at www.kpmg.com/ZA/en/IssuesAndInsights/ArticlesPublications/General-Industries-Publications/Documents/Sub-Saharan%20Electricity%20Outlook%20Brochure.pdf.

[53] Eberhard, A., Rosnes, O., Shkaratan, M. and Vennemo, H. (2011) Op. cit.

[54] www.engineeringnews.co.za/article/eskom-concerned-that-domestic-coal-prices-may-migrate-to-export-levels-2013-04-24

[55] Eskom (2016) 'Eskom power stations'. Available at: http://www.eskom.co.za/OurCompany/MediaRoom/Documents/EskomGenerationDivMapREV8.pdf

[56] Eskom (2014) Eskom Integrated Report 2014. Available at: http://integratedreport.eskom.co.za/abt-esk-eskom.php.

[57] The shortage was a result of poor coal stock management and high rainfall; high planned and unplanned maintenance; and delays in the completion of new generating capacity and in returning mothballed stations to service; NERSA (National Energy Regulator of South Africa) (2008) 'Inquiry into the national electricity supply shortage and load shedding' Report of the Energy Regulator, 12 May 2008. The supply shortages were alleviated by the global economic downturn between 2008 and 2012, but may recur in 2014/2015 because of delays in the construction of two new coal-fired plants in South Africa, according to Brian Dames in Medupi Power Station's Completion Delay; http://mg.co.za/article/2013-07-08-medupi-power-stations-completion-delayed.

[58] www.energy.gov.za/IRP/irp%20files/IRP2010_2030_Final_Report_20110325.pdf

[59] Aurecon (2013) 'Mmamabula Power Project, Botswana', available at www.aurecongroup.co.za/en/projects/energy/mmamabula-energy-project.aspx

[60] Ernst & Young (2012) Op. cit.

[61] www.worldcoal.org/resources/ecoal-archive/ecoal-current-issue/costs-of-coal-fired-electricity

[62] www.naturalgas.org/overview/uses_eletrical.asp

[63] Eberhard, A., Rosnes, O., Shkaratan, M. and Vennemo, H. (2011) Op. cit.

[64] www.worldbank.org/en/news/press-release/2013/06/27/world-bank-supports-boosting-much-needed-electricity-generation-capacity-across-egypt and http://gastopowerjournal.com/projectsafinance/item/2261-ge-signs-$27-billion-gas-turbine-contracts-in-algeria#axzz2h1a8V3DH

[65] South African Presidency (2007) 'Gourikwa and Ankerlig Power Stations opening', available at www.polity.org.za/article/sa-mlambongcuka-gourikwa-and-ankerlig-power-stations-opening-01102007-2007-10-01.

[66] Mbendi (2014) 'Electrical power in Gabon: overview', available at www.mbendi.com/indy/powr/af/ga/p0005.htm (accessed 10 April 2015)

[67] EIA (Energy Information Agency) (2014) 'Congo Brazzaville overview', 29 January, available at www.eia.gov/countries/cab.cfm?fips=CF (accessed 10 April 2015).

[68] www.nidelpower.com/main/index.php

[69] South African Department of Energy (2011) 'Integrated Resource Plan for Electricity 2010-2030'. Government Gazette No. 34263, 6 May 2011. Available at: http://www.energy.gov.za/IRP/2010/IRP_2010.pdf

[70] http://pipelinesinternational.com/news/tanzanian_pipeline_construction_inaugurated/077220

[71] Ventures Africa (2014) 'KenGen, Qatari firm to build 500MW power plant in Kenya', 30 April, available at www.ventures-africa.com/2014/04/kengen-qatari-firm-to-build-500mw-power-plant-in-kenya (accessed 10 April 2015).

[72] Eberhard, A., Rosnes, O., Shkaratan, M. and Vennemo, H. (2011) Op. cit.

[73] Ibid.

[74] PIDA (2011) *Africa Energy Outlook 2040*. Available at: http://www.au-pida.org/documents/ENERGIE/EOE-Energy-Outlook.pdf

[75] PIDA (2011) *Africa Energy Outlook 2040*, p 65. Available at: http://www.au-pida.org/documents/ENERGIE/EOE-Energy-Outlook.pdf

[76] The regions are defined according to the UN geographical regions.

[77] That West Africa's hydropower generation capacity declined between 1990 and 2010 may appear peculiar at first blush. However, even durable, fixed investments like power stations are susceptible to obsolescence as technologies change or may require decommissioning once the end of their useful lives is reached.

[78] Eskom (nd) 'COP17 Fact Sheet – Renewable energy: Hydroelectric power stations', available at: http://www.eskom.co.za/OurCompany/SustainableDevelopment/ClimateChangeCOP17/Documents/Renewable_energy_-_Hydroelectric_power_stations.pdf

[79] International Rivers (2014.) 'Inga 1 and Inga 2 dams', available at www.internationalrivers.org/resources/inga-1-and-inga-2-dams-3616 (accessed 10 April 2015).

[80] *Financial Times* (2014) 'Congo renews push for Grand Inga dam, an African white elephant', 8 September 8, available at www.ft.com/intl/cms/s/0/207ac48c-34ef-11e4-aa47-00144feabdc0.html#slide0 (accessed 10 April 2015).

[81] KPMG (2012) Op. cit.

[82] KPMG (2012) Op. cit.

[83] MWe stands for megawatts electric. Electricity that is transmitted is measured in kWh and is flow of electricity rather than a stock measure of installed capacity. However, reference can be made to equivalents to installed MWs, which is MWe.

[84] Compendium of HVDC schemes, available at www.e-cigre.org/bib/003.pdf

[85] Davison, W. (2014) 'Ethiopia sees output at Africa's biggest power plant by 2015', *Bloomberg Business*, available at www.bloomberg.com/news/articles/2014-03-19/ethiopia-sees-output-from-africa-s-biggest-power-plant-by-2015 (accessed 24 March 2015).

[86] KPMG (2012) Op. cit.

[87] Ghanaweb (nd) 'The history of the Akosombo Dam', available at web.archive.org/web/20110516134942/http://www.ghanaweb.com/GhanaHomePage/history/akosombo_dam.php.

[88] www.ft.com/intl/cms/s/0/82ae9418-c857-11e2-8cb7-00144feab7de.html#axzz2gytzfRnu

[89] Wolters, S. (2012) Op. cit.

[90] *BusinessDay* (2013) 'Press on with Inga', available at www.bdlive.co.za/opinion/editorials/2013/06/11/editorial-press-on-with-inga.

[91] www.globalwaterforum.org/2013/02/18/the-grand-ethiopian-renaissance-dam-and-the-blue-nile-implications-for-transboundary-water-governance

[92] http://news.nationalgeographic.com/news/2013/09/130927-grand-ethiopian-renaissance-dam-egypt-water-wars

[93] Gilgel Gibe III Project, www.gibe3.com.et/brief.html

[94] http://allafrica.com/stories/201310020132.html

[95] Phillip, D. (2012) 'Sudan's hydro headache', Engerati, available at http://news.engerati.com/2012/01/30/sudans_hydro_headache/#.Uda6SZ0aKUk.

[96] Banaabde, J. (2012) 'Energy supply in Uganda', available at www.unep.org/transport/pcfv/PDF/icct_2012/ICCT_EnergySituation_JamesBanaabe_MEMD.pdf.

[97] www.worldbank.org/en/news/press-release/2013/08/06/world-bank-approves-rusumo-falls-hydropower-plant

[98] www.constructionkenya.com/2931/high-grand-falls-dam-construction-to-start-soon/

[99] www.windpowermonthly.com/article/1185624/analysis---egypt-libya-lead-regions-wind-power-revival

[100] Cabeolica Wind Project, www.infracoafrica.com/projects-capeverde-cabeolicawind.asp

[101] www.darlingwindfarm.co.za/projectfactsheet.htm

[102] www.kengen.co.ke/index.php?page=business&subpage=wind&id=1

[103] www.invest.gov.ma/?Id=67&lang=en&RefCat=3&Ref=146

[104] http://allafrica.com/stories/201308060794.html

[105] www.kengen.co.ke/index.php?page=investor&subpage=intro

[106] www.eskom.co.za/c/12/power-stations/

[107] Sustainable Energy Society of Southern Africa (2012) 'REIPPP: 2459.4 MW of preferred bids so far', available at www.sessa.org.za/all-news/item/2-4594-mw-of-preferred-bids.

[108] Kerich. C. (2012) 'The Winds of Lake Turkana could blow away some of Kenya's reliance on hydropower', *Africa in Fact,* available at http://admin.gga.org/stories/editions/aif-4-africas-power-failure-short-circuits-growth/the-winds-of-lake-turkana-could-blow-away-some-of-kenya2019s-reliance-on-hydropower.

[109] HeliosCSP (2012) 'AfDB approved US$800 million in loans for Moroccan renewables projects', available at www.helioscsp.com/noticia.php?id_not=1309 (accessed 25 March 2015).

[110] UK Energy Research Centre (2006) 'The costs and impacts of intermittency', available at www.ukerc.ac.uk/Downloads/PDF/06/0604In termittency/0604IntermittencyReport.pdf.

[111] Coats, C. (2012) 'Solar energy facing headwinds in North Africa', *Africa in Fact.* Available: http://admin.gga.org/stories/editions/aif-4-africas-power-failure-short-circuits-growth/solar-energy-facing-headwinds-in-north-africa

[112] Ibid.

[113] South African Department of Energy (nd) 'About us', available at www.ipprenewables.co.za/#page/303.

[114] www.sessa.org.za/all-news/item/2-4594-mw-of-preferred-bids

[115] www.africa-geothermal.com

[116] www.usaid.gov/news-information/press-releases/sep-27-2013-first-power-africa-transaction-moves-forward-landmark-agreement

[117] www.bloomberg.com/news/2013-08-25/ex-kiwara-ceo-targets-zambia-geothermal-power-to-plug-gap.html

[118] www.africaelectricity.com/en/Industry-News/Uganda-geothermal/

[119] www.bdlive.co.za/indepth/AfricanPerspective/2013/03/04/full-steam-ahead-geothermal-energy-can-be-africas-game-changer

[120] www.bloomberg.com/news/2013-06-21/geothermal-power-tanzania-plans-first-steam-generation-next-year.html

[121] www.economist.com/node/12821590

[122] UNEP (2012) 'Financing renewable energy in developing countries: drivers and barriers for private finance in sub-Saharan Africa', available at www.unepfi.org?fileadmin/documents/Financing_Rewenawable_Energy _in_subSaharan_Africa.pdf.

[123] www.worldenergyoutlook.org/resources/energydevelopment/globalstatusofmodernenergyaccess

[124] thinkafricapress.com/international/fair-way-prevent-climate-change-and-end-poverty

[125] Monforti, F. (2011) 'Renewable energies in Africa; current knowledge', JRC Scientific and Technical Report, available at http://publications.jrc. ec.europa.eu/repository/bitstream/111111111/23076/1/reqno_jrc67752_final%20report%20.pdf.

[126] Good Governance Africa (2012) 'Africa's power failure short-circuits growth', *Africa in Fact*, Issue 4, September, available at http://gga.org/publications/africa-in-fact-september-2012.

[127] IRENA (2013) 'Renewable power generation costs in 2012; an overview', available at www.irena.org/DocumentDownloads/Publications/Overview_Renewable%20Power%20Generation%20Costs%20in%202012.pdf.

[128] South African Department of Energy (nd) Op cit.

[129] Sustainable Energy Society of Southern Africa (2012) Op. cit.

[130] Eberhard, A., Rosnes, O., Shkaratan, M. and Vennemo, H. (2011) Op. cit.

[131] Good Governance Africa (2012) Op. cit.

[132] www.engineeringnews.co.za/article/sa-nuclear-build-programme-needs-up-to-28-000-skilled-workers-2012-05-30

[133] www.ibtimes.com/can-africa-go-nuclear-energy-demands-battle-safety-concerns-across-continent-1359279

[134] KPMG (2012) Op. cit.

[135] It should be noted that certain countries, such as Uganda, pursued private sector participation before this, as early as the 1980s.

[136] Eberhard, A., Rosnes, O., Shkaratan, M. and Vennemo, H. (2011) Op. cit.

[137] African Forum for Utility Regulators (nd) 'Experience and difficulties encountered in electricity infrastructure regulation across Africa', available at www.energy-regulators.eu/portal/page/portal/EER_HOME/EER_INTERNATIONAL/CEER-AFUR/1st%20AFUR%20Roundtable/Experience_and_difficulties_encountered_in_electricity_infrastructure_regulation_across_Africa_Draft_One_30032.pdf.

[138] Eberhard, A., Rosnes, O., Shkaratan, M. and Vennemo, H. (2011) Op. cit.

[139] Ibid.

[140] www.kengen.co.ke/index.php?page=aboutus&subpage=milestone

[141] Shearman and Sterling (2012) 'A new landscape for the electricity sector in the Ivory Coast: opportunities for foreign investors', available at www.shearman.com/files/Publication/d917d133-587d-4aef-bb42-86089d89823f/Presentation/PublicationAttachment/64cf8e53-185e-472b-b0c6-5a6609d062b9/A-New-Landscape-for-the-Electricity-Sector-in-Ivory-Coast-Opportunities-for-Foreign-.pdf.

[142] South African Department of Energy (2012). 'Announcement of Preferred Bidders of the IPP Procurement Programme – Window 2'. Available at: http://www.ipprenewables.co.za/page/304#page/1196

[143] Creamer, T. (2012) 'Bank pleased with its share of R28bn renewables projects'. Engineering News [Online]. Available at: http://www.engineeringnews.co.za/article/bank-pleased-with-its-share-of-r28bn-renewables-projects-2012-05-21/rep_id:4136.

[144] Department of Energy (2014) 'Renewable energy IPP procurement programme (REIPPP)', available at www.ipp-projects.co.za (accessed 10 April 2015).

[145] www.eskom.co.za/c/article/1806/reipp-procurement-programme/

[146] Eberhard, A. (2005) 'From state to market and back again: South Africa's power sector reforms', available at www.gsb.uct.ac.za/files/FromStatetoMarketandBackAgain.pdf

[147] Oil and coal are the fossil fuels traditionally used for electricity generation across Africa.

[148] A. T. Kearney (2013) 'Southern Africa's oil and gas opportunity'. Available at: https://www.atkearney.com/oil-gas/ideas-insights/article/-/asset_publisher/LCcgOeS4t85g/content/southern-africas-oil-and-gas-opportunity/10192. Wind and solar units experience down periods when there is less wind or sunlight. Because gas turbines have short start-up times, they are suitable for short-term generation.

[149] Ernst & Young (2012) Op. cit.

[150] Deloitte (2013a) Deloitte Insomnia Index, www.un.org/africarenewal/magazine/october-2006/what-alternatives-oil-africa.

[151] For definitions of these five regions, see http://millenniumindicators.un.org/unsd/methods/m49/m49regin.htm.

[152] Ernst & Young (2012) Op. cit.

[153] Ibid.

[154] A. T. Kearney (2013) Op. cit.

[155] Ernst & Young (2012) Op. cit.

[156] www.eia.gov/analysis/studies/worldshalegas/

[157] http://ambrefonline.com/mining/index.php?option=com_content&view=article&id=804:awakening-the-sleeping-gas-giants-of-africa&catid=58:press-releases&Itemid=29

[158] Ernst & Young (2012) Op. cit.

[159] Hafner, M. and Tagliapietra, S. (2013) 'East Africa, the next game changer for the global gas markets', available at http://papers.ssrn.com/sol3/papers.cfm?abstract_id=2249723.

[160] Ernst & Young (2012) Op. cit.

[161] Iyawemi, A. (2008) 'Nigeria's dual energy problems: policy issues and challenges', *International Association for Energy Economics*, 4th quarter, pp 17–21.

[162] An LNG terminal offers flexibility of supply and reduces the risk of unstable supplies that could occur when gas pipelines are used. For example, when gas supply from a principal source is disrupted, or a pipeline is sabotaged, a natural gas pipeline has no alternatives; hence, gas supply is interrupted.

[163] EIA (2013) 'Emerging East Africa energy'. Available at: https://www.eia.gov/beta/international/regions-topics.cfm?RegionTopicID=EEAE

[164] Hafner, M. and Tagliapietra, S. (2013) Op. cit.

[165] Ernst & Young (2012) Op. cit.

[166] AfDB (2009) 'Oil and gas in Africa'. Available at: http://www.afdb.org/fileadmin/uploads/afdb/Documents/Publications/Oil%20and%20Gas%20in%20Africa.pdf

[167] www.greenleft.org.au/node/28922

[168] AfDB (2009) Op. cit.

[169] PIDA (2011) Op. cit.

[170] www.un.org/africarenewal/magazine/october-2007/pipeline-benefits-mozambique-south-africa

[171] Sasol investor presentations.

[172] Ernst & Young (2012) Op. cit.

[173] World Bank (2010) *Regional Energy Projects: Experience and Approaches of the World Bank Group*. Background paper for the World Bank Group Energy Strategy. Available at: http://siteresources.worldbank.org/EXTESC/Resources/Regional_energy_trade_final.pdf

[174] EIA (2013) Op. cit.

[175] A.T. Kearney (2013) Op. cit.

[176] www.ft.com/intl/cms/s/0/67553790-4b74-11e2-887b-00144feab49a.html#axzz2YS0ZrETC

[177] Mathews, C. (2014) 'Waiting to extract Mozambique's oil and gas reserves', *Financial Mail*, available at www.financialmail.co.za/coverstory/2014/05/29/waiting-to-extract-mozambique-s-oil-and-gas-reserves (accessed 24 March 2015).

[178] Ledesma, D. (2013) *East Africa Gas: Potential for Export*. Oxford: Oxford Institute for Energy Studies. Available at www.oxfordenergy.org/wpcms/wp-content/uploads/2013/03/NG-74.pdf.

[179] www.businessdayonline.com/NG/index.php/gas/51019-trans-saharan-gas-pipeline-project-still-on-track--nnpc

[180] http://uk.reuters.com/article/2009/07/03/nigeria-algeria-pipeline-idUKL345766620090703?sp=true

[181] Oyewunmi, T. (2013) 'The Nigerian gas industry: policy, law and regulatory developments', available at www.acas-law.com.

[182] Vanguard (2014) 'Nigeria mobilises $700 million for Trans-Sahara gas project – Jonathan', available www.vanguardngr.com/2014/01/nigeria-mobilises-700-million-trans-sahara-gas-project-jonathan (accessed 24 March 2015).

[183] www.economist.com.na/headlines/2986-kudu-partners-sign-development-agreement

[184] www.namcor.com.na/kudu

[185] PWC (2013) 'From promise to performance: Africa oil and gas review. Report on current developments in the oil and gas industry in Africa' available at www.pwc.com/en_NG/ng/pdf/pwc-africa-oil-and-gas-review.pdf.

[186] www.sunbirdenergy.com.au/images/ASX_Announcements/201310/091013_Ibhubesi_Transfer_of_Title_approved.pdf

[187] www.thepost.co.za/sa-may-secure-affordable-natural-gas-1.1550212

[188] www.forbes.com/sites/christophercoats/2013/02/14/galsi-pipeline-suffers-what-could-be-final-blow/

[189] http://oilprice.com/Energy/Natural-Gas/Algeria-Another-Setback-for-the-Galsi-Pipeline.html

[190] Deloitte (2013b) 'The Deloitte guide to oil and gas in East Africa: where potential lies'. Available at: https://www2.deloitte.com/content/dam/Deloitte/global/Documents/Energy-and-Resources/dttl-er-deloitte-guide-oil-gas-east-africa%20-08082013.pdf

[191] Ernst & Young (2012) Op. cit.

[192] Deloitte (2013b) Op. cit.

[193] Ledesma, D. (2013) Op. cit.

[194] Aissaouio, A. (2013) 'Algeria's natural gas policy: Beware of the Egypt syndrome!', available at www.mees.com/en/articles/7960-algeria-s-natural-gas-policy-beware-of-the-egypt-syndrome

[195] Oyewunmi, T. (2013) Op. cit.

[196] Ibid.

[197] AfDB (2009) Op. cit.

[198] Eberhard, A., Rosnes, O., Shkaratan, M., and Vennemo, H. (2011) Op cit.

[199] A.T. Kearney (2013) Op. cit.

[200] EIA (2013) Op. cit.

[201] AfDB (2009) Op. cit.

[202] Ibid.

[203] East African oil-producing countries include Sudan and South Sudan (primarily responsible for most of the production) as well as the following

countries (with very small production numbers): Zambia; Zimbabwe; Ethiopia; Malawi; and Mauritius.

[204] Oil refineries transform crude oil into fuel products, lubricating oils, bitumen, chemical feedstocks and other oil products.

[205] AfDB (2009) Op. cit.

[206] BP (2013) 'Statistical review of world energy.' Available at http://www.bp.com/content/dam/bp-country/fr_fr/Documents/Rapportsetpublications/statistical_review_of_world_energy_2013.pdf

[207] PIDA (2011) Op. cit.

[208] AfDB (2009) Op. cit.

[209] BP (2013) Op. cit.

[210] PIDA (2011) Op. cit.

[211] Ibid.

[212] Ibid.

[213] Ibid.

[214] Ibid.

[215] www.reuters.com/article/2013/04/15/uganda-oil-idUSL5N0D20HJ20130415; AfDB (2009) Op. cit.

[216] www.oilreviewafrica.com/downstream/downstream/mozambique-s-nacala-oil-refinery-project-back-on-track; AfDB (2009) Op. cit.

[217] www.sanews.gov.za/south-africa/petrosa-partners-chinas-sinopec-group-mthombo-refinery

[218] www.petrosa.co.za/building_futures/Pages/Project-Mthombo.aspx

[219] http://africaoilgasreport.com/2012/12/refining-gap/egypt-starts-construction-of-a-3-7billion-refinery-in-2013

[220] www.economist.com/news/middle-east-and-africa/21578402-east-africa-danger-throwing-away-part-its-new-found-oil

[221] www.sapia.co.za/industry-overview/fuel-industry.html

[222] PIDA (2011) Op. cit.

[223] http://africansuntimes.com/2013/05/developing-africas-infrastructure-a-catalyst-for-economic-growth/

[224] (i) PIDA (2011) http://www.au-pida.org/documents/ENERGIE/EOE-Energy-Outlook.pdf; (ii) United Nations Economic and Social Council (2013) *Report on Africa's Regional Integration Agenda*, p 8. Available at http://repository.uneca.org/bitstream/handle/10855/22134/b10696118.pdf?sequence=1

[225] Mbeng Mezui, C.A. (2010) 'Unlocking infrastructure development in Africa through infrastructure bonds', *GREAT Insights*, vol 2, no 4, May-June.

[226] Ibid.

[227] KPMG (2012) Op. cit.

[228] Muzenda, D. (2009) 'Increasing private investment in African energy infrastructure', NEPAD-OECD Africa Investment Initiative, p 43.

[229] Eberhard, A. and Gratwick, K.N. (2013) 'Contributing elements to success of IPPs in sub-Saharan Africa', available at www.proparco.fr/webdav/site/proparco/shared/PORTAILS/Secteur_prive_developpement/PDF/SPD18/SPD18_Anton_Eberhard_Katharine_Nawaal_Gratwick_UK.pdf.

[230] Ernst & Young (2012) Op. cit.

[231] Joskow, P.L. (2008) 'Incentive regulation and its application to electricity networks', available at http://economics.mit.edu/files/3623.

[232] Armstrong, M., Cowan, S. and Vickers, J. (1994) *Regulatory Reform: Economic Analysis and British Experience.* Cambridge, MA: MIT Press.

[233] For a full description of the three magnitudes of market openness, see De Vries, L.J. (2006) 'Design choices for electricity markets', available at www.worldenergy.org/documents/p000905.doc.

[234] International Renewable Energy Agency (2012) 'Policy challenges for renewable energy deployment in Pacific Island countries and territories', available at http://irena.org/DocumentDownloads/Publications/Policy_Challenges_for_Renewable_Energy_Deployment_PICTs.pdf.

[235] Melamed, A. (1999) 'Electricity restructuring', available at www.justice.gov/atr/public/testimony/2591.htm.

[236] Consortium for Electric Reliability Technology Solutions (nd) 'Relieving transmission bottlenecks by completing the transition to competitive regional wholesale electric markets', available at http://certs.lbl.gov/ntgs/main-3.pdf.

[237] Ernst & Young (2012) Op. cit.

[238] Horan, T.H. (1999) 'Political and Regulatory Risk in Infrastructure Investment in Developing Countries', available at www.dundee.ac.uk/cepmlp/journal/html/vol5/article5-6a.html.

[239] Ibid.

[240] AFUR (African Forum for Utility Regulators) (nd) 'Experience and difficulties encountered in electricity infrastructure regulation across Africa'. Available at http://www.ceer.eu/portal/page/portal/EER_HOME/ EER_INTERNATIONAL/CEER-AFUR/1st%20AFUR%20Roundtable/ Experience_and_difficulties_encountered_in_electricity_infrastructure_ regulation_across_Africa_Draft_One_30032.pdf

[241] AfDB (2009b) 'Energy sector policy'. Available at: http://www.afdb. org/fileadmin/uploads/afdb/Documents/Policy-Documents/Energy%20 Sector%20Policy%20-%20for%20consultation-30-06.pdf

[242] Ernst & Young (2012) Op. cit.

[243] www.timeslive.co.za/africa/2013/05/22/tanzanian-gas-pipeline-plan-sparks-riot--government-officials and www.reuters.com/article/2013/05/25/ tanzania-pipeline-idUSL5N0E60D620130525

[244] www.mining.com/maduros-tight-win-in-venezuelas-presidential-election-leaves-country-and-mining-companies-in-limbo-87948

[245] www.ogj.com/articles/print/volume-111/issue-3a/general-interest/ watching-government-venezuela-after.html

[246] www.economist.com/blogs/americasview/2012/08/venezuelas-oil-industry

[247] www.nnpcgroup.com/PublicRelations/NNPCinthenews/tabid/92/ articleType/ArticleView/articleId/68/How-Pipeline-Vandals-Cripple-Fuel-Supply--NNPCIncurs-over-N174-billion-in-products-losses-pipeline-repairs.aspx

[248] www.fin24.com/Economy/R4bn-lost-to-electricity-theft-20100323

[249] www.afdb.org/en/blogs/integrating-africa/post/africas-energy-security-contingent-on-energy-sector-integration-12040

[250] www.afdb.org/en/blogs/integrating-africa/post/africas-energy-security-contingent-on-energy-sector-integration-12040

[251] Muzenda, D. (2009) Op. cit.

[252] Eberhard, A., Rosnes, O., Shkaratan, M. and Vennemo, H. (2011) Op cit.

[253] Ibid, pp 158-63.

[254] Deloitte (2013a) Op. cit.

[255] AfDB (2013) Africa50 – Concept Note, African Development Bank, Tunis, Tunisia.

[256] The levelized cost of energy is the cost to build and operate a power-generating asset over its lifetime divided by the total power output of the asset over the corresponding time period.

[257] www.worldcoal.org/resources/ecoal-archive/ecoal-current-issue/costs-of-coal-fired-electricity

[258] Eberhard, A., Rosnes, O., Shkaratan, M. and Vennemo, H. (2011) Op. cit.

[259] For a full list of the power pool members, see KPMG (2012) Op. cit, pp 20-3.

[260] Some of these complications include overlapping membership, different stages of integration and integration goals are subject to different timelines.

[261] Eberhard, A., Rosnes, O., Shkaratan, M. and Vennemo, H. (2011) Op. cit.; KPMG (2012) Op. cit.

[262] United Nations Economic and Social Council (2013) *Report on Africa's Regional Integration Agenda*, p 8. Available at http://repository.uneca.org/bitstream/handle/10855/22134/b10696118.pdf?sequence=1

[263] Blumsack, S. (2007) 'Measuring the benefits and costs of regional electric grid integration', available at http://felj.org/docs/elj281/147-184.pdf.

[264] World Nuclear Association (2013) 'Electricity transmission grids', available at http://world-nuclear.org/info/Current-and-Future-Generation/Electricity-Transmission-Grids/#.UeFAgZ0aKUm.

[265] Alstom (nd) 'GCCIA Phase 1: Making interconnection in the Gulf a reality'. Available at: https://www.gegridsolutions.com/alstomenergy/grid/Global/Grid/Resources/Documents/GCCIA%20Phase%201%20Making%20interconnection%20in%20the%20Gulf%20a%20reality-epslanguage=en-GB.pdf

[266] Blumsack, S. (2007) Op. cit.

[267] The Energy Security Analysis Inc. estimated that the regional integration of the US electricity grid led to a cost saving of US$500 million to consumers; see www.ferc.gov/eventcalendar/Files/20051128133445-ESAI%20report.pdf.

[268] World Nuclear Association (2013) Op cit.

[269] Eberhard, A., Rosnes, O., Shkaratan, M. and Vennemo, H. (2011) Op. cit., p 81.

[270] Ibid, p 14.

[271] Ernst & Young (2012) Op. cit. Investment in Africa's gas sector has been primarily from the private sector, with some investment coming from Indian,

Chinese, Malaysian, South Korean, Thai and Russian state-owned oil and gas companies.

272 East Africa, the game changer.

273 AfdB (2009b) 'Energy Sector Policy'. Available at: http://www.afdb.org/fileadmin/uploads/afdb/Documents/Policy-Documents/Energy%20Sector%20Policy%20-%20for%20consultation-30-06.pdf

274 AfdB (2009b) Op. cit.

275 http://uk.reuters.com/article/2009/07/03/nigeria-algeria-pipeline-idUKL345766620090703?sp=true

276 http://online.wsj.com/article/SB100014241278873248795045785972727759235786.html

277 Kasita, I. (2013) 'East Africa: EAC states to invest 40 percent in oil refinery', Allafrica.com, 19 September, available at http://allafrica.com/stories/201309191386.html?page=2.

278 Wachira, G. (2013) 'Why Uganda needs to rethink building a small refinery plant', *Daily Monitor*, 30 April, available at www.monitor.co.ug/Business/Prosper/Why-Uganda-needs-to-rethink-building-a-small-refinery-plant/-/688616/1761980/-/slck33/-/index.html.

SEVEN

Africa's prospects for infrastructure development and regional integration: transport sector

Taz Chaponda and Duncan Lishman

Introduction

Infrastructure is critically important in supporting economic growth and development. It aids economic activity and good quality infrastructure quickens the pace of economic and social progress. At the same time, Africa has an enormous infrastructure requirement, and the need for accelerating its development in Africa is a pressing one. Numerous studies have highlighted the infrastructure requirement, notably the African Infrastructure Country Diagnostic (AICD) and, more recently, the Program for Infrastructure Development in Africa (PIDA). Successively larger figures have been suggested as necessary to address the backlog in the continent's infrastructure. As it stands, the African Development Bank (AfDB) estimates that the infrastructure financing gap currently stands at US$50 billion per annum.[1]

As a continent, Africa lags behind its peers on a range of socioeconomic infrastructure measures.[2] Not only is the continent typified by ageing infrastructure that is inadequate for existing socioeconomic demands, but the accumulation of infrastructure stock has occurred far more slowly in Africa than other developing regions.[3] Africa presents certain unique challenges for infrastructure development. The dispersed nature of settlements in rural areas, where over one-fifth of the continent's people live, increases the cost of infrastructure provision. A different challenge exists for urban areas, where rapid urbanization strains current infrastructure resources. This aggravates attempts to address socioeconomic deficiencies on the African continent and constrains economic growth prospects. Improving infrastructure in Africa would increase economic growth rates, which are estimated to be depressed by around 2% each year because of the current state of infrastructure.[4]

Furthermore, the level of intraregional infrastructure integration is low in Africa, whether measured by road network, electricity grid, or information and communications technology backbones.[5] Correspondent to this is the high cost of infrastructure services, far above those of other developing countries.[6] Over and above the higher costs users face, inadequate infrastructure constrains doing business in Africa, particularly in low-income countries. It is estimated that inadequate infrastructure may depress firm productivity by approximately 40%.[7] This ultimately impacts on the relative living standards of African residents.

The general case for infrastructure is no different for the transport sector. Good-quality roads, railways, ports and airports, with high network connectivity, are essential for sustaining the activity and growth of many key economic sectors on the African continent including agriculture, industry, mining and tourism. Efficient transport infrastructure enables the passage of individuals and freight, often in high volumes, over vast distances and with relative ease, and—in doing so—facilitates commerce and trade, provides workers with access to labor markets, and improves access to vital social services, such as health and education.

This chapter sets out to capture the current state of infrastructure in the four major transport sub-sectors across the African continent. From the overviews of each, policy challenges and appropriate responses are extracted and presented. These are emblematic of the opportunities for improved transport infrastructure outcomes and are aimed at providing a compass for where resources should be directed in order to achieve these outcomes. Across much of the analysis, countries are aggregated at a regional level (Central, Southern, North, East and West Africa) according to the United Nations geo-scheme for Africa.[8] Often, transport infrastructure issues share regional themes and such classification therefore assists in understanding common policy challenges and opportunities.

Importance of transport infrastructure

Transport infrastructure is the group of assets that makes up the networks of road and rail straddling countries, regions and continents; the ports that agglomerate and distribute the freight that these networks bring, as well as break up and distribute the imports unloaded from cargo ships; and the airports that process domestic, regional and international passengers, as well as time-sensitive freight. The orthodox view is that the infrastructure is a result of economic activity because transport, due to its reliance on other economic activities, is a derived demand.[9]

As a result of its derived demand, transport may be described as a network service industry. Generally, these industries have similar economic characteristics. Their output is determined by use and significant investments in infrastructure are required to facilitate output. Network industries often generate external benefits (or "positive spillovers") which, tied with various scale effects, produce network economies. These economies are related to the fact that the larger number of links in a network provides a greater degree of connectivity and with this a large choice set for users. Further, the ability to channel traffic along particular corridors and through hubs, rather than directly between origin and destination, generates economies of scope and of density. Worth noting is that these transport networks can also create costs and diseconomies, particularly where congestion develops on roads or railways, or at seaport and airport hubs.[10]

Transport infrastructure commonly represents a public good (or, at least, quasi-public good). Transport infrastructure has benefits which may spill over to general society and cannot be readily captured by the private investor. Thus, in the face of positive externalities and spillovers, the investor would value the infrastructure lower than its true value to society. This would lead to sub-optimally low levels of investment and may partly explain the low levels of private investment in transport infrastructure. Coupled with governmental budgets that are generally insufficient for meeting funding needs, policy decisions and regulatory design are therefore important for ensuring infrastructure development proceeds apace with economic demands.

A driver of regional integration

Developing transport infrastructure affords the opportunity for enhanced regional integration on the continent. The regional integration agenda incorporates a range of objectives, which include improving African producers' access to regional markets; integrating markets; and encouraging the free movement of goods, services, labor, and capital. These objectives require coordinated efforts at various decision-making and operational levels, including within governmental departments and agencies, at the political level, and in regional economic communities (RECs). There are several reasons why pursuing regional integration may be desirable. First, from a broad socio-political perspective, regional integration should improve peace and security on the continent. Second, it promotes the freer movement of people, allowing migratory flows to areas of economic opportunity. Third, it promotes trade and access to markets. Given the opportunities that agriculture offers for African development, enabling rural residents with access to regional consumers and modal distribution points is desirable. Overall, integration spurs economic growth and development.

Regional integration can be facilitated by transport infrastructure which allows for ease of movement by people and goods that travel over country borders. In part this can increase the proportion of intra-Africa trade that occurs. Importantly, it is not only about integrating countries within regions, but also about integrating regions with one another. For all modes, transport demand is a function of human movement and trade patterns. Transport networks and corridors are important for linking industrial, commercial and residential areas. As African economies grow and develop, linking ports and transport hubs with industrial areas (for import of inputs and export of products), mines and agricultural areas, and urban areas (markets for imported consumer goods) will become increasingly important. These changes necessitate not only spatial development modifications but also variations in the modes of transport used as the type of traffic changes. Globally, trade between Africa and Europe has declined while it has increased with Asia and North America, and the discovery of oil and gas reserves in various places across the African continent suggests that energy exports will increase going forward.

Financing transport infrastructure in Africa

Funding sources and financing mechanisms

Adequately addressing transport infrastructure requires appropriate funding mechanisms. Estimates for the most recent PIDA study suggest that of the priority projects (termed as the "Priority Action Plan" or PAP) to be completed before 2020, transport is the second-largest funding requirement with an estimated US$25.4 billion in investment needed. This equates to approximately US$2.5 billion per annum for *priority* projects, that is, those over and above routine and periodic maintenance.[11] This formidable funding deficit for developing African infrastructure over the coming decades requires consideration of the manner in which infrastructure is currently financed and how available resources may be better mobilized.

Funding for infrastructure may emerge from a variety of public and private sources. These include government budgetary funding; development finance institutions (DFIs); overseas development assistance (ODA); foreign direct investment; capital markets; commercial banks; and institutional investors.

Financing mechanisms for infrastructure depend on the nature of the project, its associated characteristics and the profile of the funder. Government funding may be in the form of direct capital contributions, soft loans, and loan guarantees. Projects may also be funded by similar mechanism provided by DFIs or through ODA. Donor funding can be well suited to infrastructure investments with high social returns and low financial returns, as these projects generally do not appeal to private sector investors. This does depend however on how the donor structures its funding and whether funds are tied to particular projects or not. Further, it is an attractive and useful funding source for governments that lack funds and have poor access to capital markets. Syndicated loans are generally the preserve of investment and commercial banks, and serve to spread project risk across multiple lenders.

Traditionally, government funding, along with grants received from donors, has been the principal source of financing for transport infrastructure in Africa.[12] Overall, spending on transport (notably roads) is the single-largest infrastructure item in general government accounts for African countries. It ranges from about half of all general government spending on infrastructure in middle-income countries to 60% in low-income countries. Despite this apparent overwhelmingly reliance on public funds, some diversity exists in terms of suitable financing options and instruments for the transport sub-sectors. While road funding traditionally comes from the government budget and is generally the preferred choice for road financing, this is not always the case for rail, ports and airports. Each of these latter sub-sectors can operate as self-funding entities (whether partially or fully) and therefore offers scope for utilizing private sector expertise and finance in the provision of transport infrastructure.

Opportunity therefore abounds in the transport sector for the use of alternative and innovative financing arrangements including PPP and other forms of private sector participation. Several of these financing mechanisms are outlined in the next section. Each of the sub-sector reviews contains further details on project opportunities and appropriate financing mechanisms.

Infrastructure project bond financing

An alternative source of financing for infrastructure projects, which has risen in popularity in recent years, is that of infrastructure project bond financing ("infrastructure bonds"). This is where a debt instrument is issued by governments or private companies to raise funds from capital markets for infrastructure projects.[13] Typically, the coupon payments associated with infrastructure bonds are linked to cash flows generated from the underlying project.

While traditional loan structures are more common in project finance given their flexibility, particularly during the capital-intensive construction phase, infrastructure bonds hold several advantages;[14] they are a relatively cheaper financing method and they can be tailored to have longer maturity dates, which is often useful for matching to the concession period of the project (20 to 30 years).

Under the definition of an infrastructure bond, most transactions in African markets are not strictly infrastructure bonds but rather general government bonds with some earmarking of funds to be spent on infrastructure investment. Other emerging markets, such as Chile, Brazil and Malaysia, have used infrastructure bonds as a way to catalyze investor interest and offer useful case studies for how African countries can shape their markets.

The AfDB found that though a legal and regulatory framework exists for bond issuance, African countries require a clear methodology for assessing whether particular infrastructure projects are suited to the bond market, based on parameters such as credit risk, execution cost and demand and supply conditions in the market.[15]

An adaption of the infrastructure bond model is the AfDB's Africa50 initiative, a proposed commercially oriented financial institution with the mandate to reduce Africa's infrastructure financing gap by funding high-impact national and regional infrastructure projects across the continent. To this end, the AfDB has already identified transformative infrastructure projects totaling US$150 billion, which includes the PIDA pipeline, often with significant regional benefits.

The Africa50 initiative is seen as a potentially exciting development for several reasons. First, it will be provided with greater operational flexibility, as it is to be established as a commercially, legally and financially independent entity. Second, it will have significant financial clout through targeting an investment-grade rating for capital raising, designing innovative financing instruments, and crowding in new sources of capital. Third, it will provide dedicated focus on enhancing the commercial nature (particularly bankability and risk allocation) of transformative, regional infrastructure projects.

Public–private partnerships

The risk-and-reward sharing nature of public–private partnerships (PPPs) enables private sector participation in public service provision. PPPs are useful as they allow for private sector funds to be invested in infrastructure, thus easing the budget constraint on the public sector. They may also increase the efficiency of infrastructure provision by utilizing private sector knowledge.

However, PPPs can be difficult to implement where projects have high social but low financial returns (for example, extending rural road networks). In general, relatively few roads across Africa are strong candidates for tolling due to the low traffic volumes and affordability concerns on the part of road users. Moreover, implementing user–pay principles at full cost recovery is very difficult for both political and affordability reasons, which usually calls for some form of government subsidy (either in upfront capital contributions or ongoing operations and maintenance support).

Yet, there are many types of infrastructure projects that are well suited to private sector investment. These projects usually involve economic infrastructure that generates an independent revenue stream, providing the private participant with an incentive to innovate in construction or operation.

Experience with private sector participation in transport infrastructure in Africa has been mixed.[16] Broadly speaking, private sector participation has been more successful in the roads and ports sectors, while rail concessions have not performed well in many countries. There have been very few examples from the aviation sector. Drivers of success relate to a thorough assessment of demand risk (projected volumes) and a more realistic allocation of project risks. Undertaking a thorough feasibility study will ensure a better risk allocation between the public and private sectors which translates into a more sustainable project. Nevertheless, successful introduction of PPP models elsewhere in the world in a variety of sectors, including the gamut of transport infrastructure projects, suggests that much scope exists for expanding the role of PPPs on the African continent.

Road sub-sector

Contextual overview

Road infrastructure serves a critically important function in a modern market-based economy. It aids commuters in their private vehicles and those using public transport, acts as a conduit for the movement of freight to and from the ports of a country, and enables the transportation and delivery of goods within the country.

Roads dominate the transport sector in most African countries, with the mode handling 80% to 90% of all passenger and freight traffic.[17] The distribution of road infrastructure across the continent is represented in Table 7.1.

In terms of economic activity, freight transport is critical to African economies, which are often dependent on the export of relatively low value-to-weight goods such agricultural or mining commodities.[18] The cost of freight transport, however, is substantially greater in Africa than other regions. While high freight charges in Africa were initially attributed to the effects of poor infrastructure on operating costs of hauliers, more recent studies have emphasized the role of institutions (particularly freight associations) and regulations on freight charges, as explained later.

Of particular importance for freight transport are the main international trade corridors that connect landlocked countries with ports. As there are relatively few of these corridors, each is of considerable importance—they account for a combined length of just over 10,000km (less than 1% of the continent's total network) but carry approximately US$200 billion of imports and exports each year.[19]

Table 7.1: Distribution of road network in Africa

Regions	Roads (%)	Paved roads (%)
North Africa	17	49
East Africa	22	10
Southern Africa	29	27
Central Africa	8	1
Western Africa	24	13
Total	100	100

Source: UNECA [United Nations Economic Commission for Africa] (2009). *Africa Review Report on Transport.* Sixth Session of the Committee on Food Security and Sustainable Development. August 2009. Addis Ababa, Ethiopia.

Table 7.2: Selected key regional road transport routes

Region	Port of entry/exit	Countries served
Central Africa	Port of Douala (Cameroon)	Chad; Central African Republic
West Africa	Benin; Cote d'Ivoire; Tema (Ghana); Guinea; Senegal; Lome (Togo)	Burkina Faso; Mali; Niger
East Africa	Mombasa (Kenya); Dar es Salaam (Tanzania)	Kenya; Uganda; Burundi; Democratic Republic of the Congo (DRC); Rwanda; Zambia
Southern Africa	Durban (South Africa)	Zambia; western Malawi; south-eastern DRC; Botswana; Zimbabwe; South Africa

Source: Gwilliam (2011, pp 18-19) [see note 12].

Infrastructure base

Descriptive characteristics

General

Similar to rail, the road sector has two components—that relating to the provision of infrastructure and that relating to operations. While private operators generally provide transport services (either private motorists or businesses ferrying passengers and freight), the road network and associated infrastructure is usually delivered by various arms of government.

Africa's total classified road network, which includes the primary and secondary networks, is estimated to be in excess of one million kilometers (km).[20] With the addition of the unclassified network and urban road network,[21] this makes a total network of just less than 2.5 million km according to UNECA data.

Between one-fifth and one-quarter of the road network in Sub-Saharan Africa (SSA) is paved, versus more than 50% for the global average. Further, most of these surfaced roads allow for the movement of traffic in both directions.[22]

Traffic in Africa is concentrated on the main road network, which comprises primary and secondary road networks. In most African countries, over 90% of traffic flows are recorded on the main network. Rural networks generally carry very low levels of traffic, estimated to be around 10% per cent of the total traffic carried on the classified network.

Table 7.3: Length of African road network

Region	Road		
	Total km	Paved	Unpaved
Central Africa	342,292	15,429	299,676
East Africa	608,463	108,789	498,817
North Africa	389,453	260,701	128,752
Southern Africa	440,819	89,804	351,015
West Africa	683,532	75,700	650,502
Total	2,464,559	550,423	1,928,762

Note: Figures for measured road length are for 2005.

Source: UNECA (2009) [as Table 7.1]; authors' own calculations.

Density and connectivity

Absolute road length is generally not a useful performance indicator given the differing geographic size of countries and regions. Metrics that therefore measure relative density and connectivity of road networks are used. For Africa, there are large discrepancies between countries and regions in terms of road metrics, which are frequently compared using the spatial density of roads.[23]

In terms of spatial density measures, classified roads have a spatial density of around 109km per 1,000km^2. This rises to a density of 149km/1,000km^2 when one considers all road types (median values of 57 and 82 respectively). This, however, varies greatly by country, with density as low as 10 in Mauritania and as high as 993 in Mauritius.[24] Globally, the average is 944km/1,000km^2. African countries therefore lag far behind in the geographic extent of their networks, and Africa's low-income countries (LICs) are particularly far behind when using global comparators, as illustrated in Table 7.4.

Though it speaks to general differences in development, the low spatial density also reflects the low population densities of Africa; that is, the large geographic size of the continent. Road density may be thought of as a measure of connectivity. Indeed, by this metric, the continent has substantial work to do in improving connections, not only across regions but within countries.

Infrastructure performance

Road condition and quality

A well-maintained road network of adequate capacity is vital in supporting the movement of commuters and freight. For many rural communities, roads offer a vital connection to markets.[25] In terms of these communities' reliance on agriculture, connections via roadways are necessary for the supply and purchase of inputs as well as the distribution of produce. Where the condition of rural roads is poor,

Table 7.4: Comparison of paved road infrastructure in low-income countries

Paved roads	Units	African LICs	Rest of the world LICs
Density by area	km/1,000km²	10.7	37.3
Density by population	km/1,000 people	269.1	700.7
Density by GDP per capita	km/US$ billion	663.1	1,210.0

Source: Carruthers et al (2009) [see note 22].

opportunities for development of outlying communities is diminished. As a result of their relative isolation, rural areas are impeded in their ability to realize their full agricultural potential.[26]

Data on the performance of road infrastructure is not well recorded. Traffic volumes are generally not monitored and it is difficult to assess performance along efficiency measures given the nature of the asset and its users. Road condition is therefore used as a proxy measure for performance.

Monitoring road quality is important, as it gives a good indication of forward-looking infrastructure service and capacity.[27] A road network in good condition promotes traffic that moves with reasonable speed, at a relatively low cost, and in a safe manner.

Ideally, road condition should be measured over time to assess changes in maintenance routines. Further, some reference should be made to the new construction of roads, as a recent surge in this activity can skew the picture even if maintenance of existing roads remains poor. However, there is limited data to provide a comparison of road conditions over time.

In Annex 3 of this chapter, the surface condition of roads is broken down into three categories: good, fair and poor. Roads in a "poor" condition are those designated to be in need of rehabilitation.[28] There is great heterogeneity in the quality of roads across African countries, and far more countries have road networks in a generally poor condition than those with networks in a good condition. That said, there is evidence to suggest that countries are continually improving efforts to maintain higher-value paved networks to a good or fair condition.[29, 30]

Urban roads are generally paved, though quality can vary substantially. As may be expected, the condition of the rural network is substantially lower than that of urban roads. On a country-weighted average, 33% of rural roads are in good condition, 23% in fair condition, and the remaining 44 per cent are in poor condition. It has been noted that there is a strong correlation between quality of the main and rural road networks, suggesting that country-competence with main road network management spills over to the rural network.[31]

Safety

In general, road safety in Africa is poor. This reflects a number of issues, including the inadequacy of infrastructure and poor monitoring and enforcement of traffic laws by authorities. Improvements in the standard of road infrastructure and its concomitant services will go a long way to improve the safety of road users.

Regional links and transport corridors

African road networks rose in prominence in the 1960s, with large and more cost-effective vehicles offering an alternative to transportation via the continent's railways. The plans for a cross-continent highway system are encapsulated in the Trans-African Highway (TAH) network initiative. Formulated in 1970 as part of a pan-African political vision, the system consists of nine main corridors with a total length of 59,100km.[32, 33]

Establishment of the TAH network was seen as important to provide direct routes between the capitals on the continent; contribute to the political, economic and social integration and cohesion of African countries; and ensure adequate transport facilities between areas of production and consumption.[34]

The TAH Bureau was established in the 1970s to oversee the implementation of the scheme. However, it was dissolved in the 1980s and efforts to re-establish it have subsequently failed.[35] In the absence of an official bureau, RECs have taken the lead in identifying and driving regional road corridors. This has led in some instances to proposals for the realignment of certain sections of the TAH network.

Approximately one-quarter of the envisioned TAH network consists of 'missing links' —those sections of the proposed highway system that do not exist. While more than 40,000km of the networks exists, almost half is in poor condition.[36] Just over 20% of the proposed network is missing, with the overwhelming majority of this situated in Central Africa.

Table 7.5: Extent of the Trans-Africa Highway network

Route	Length (km)
Cairo–Dakar	8,640
Algiers–Lagos	4,500
Tripoli–Windhoek	9,610
Cairo–Gaborone	8,860
Dakar–N'Djamena	4,500
N'Djamena–Djibouti	4,220
Dakar–Lagos	4,010
Lagos–Mombasa	6,260
Beira–Lobito	3,520
Total gross length	54,120
Overlapping length	1,670
Total net length	**52,450**

Source: AfDB (2003, p 16) [see note 33]

Table 7.6: TAH network by region

Region	Total TAH network (km)	Paved sections of network (km)	Missing links (km)
North Africa	13,292	13,195	97
East Africa	9,932	8,201	1,731
Southern Africa	7,988	6,817	1,171
Central Africa	11,246	3,891	7,355
West Africa	11,662	10,581	1,081
Total	**54,120**	**42,685**	**11,435 (21%)**

Source: UNECA (2009) [as Table 7.1], p 8

A 2003 study estimated the cost of completing these missing links was $4.2 billion at the time of the study.[37] That the scheme has not come to fruition is partly because the necessary financing has not been forthcoming from national governments.[38] This highlights the problem of co-opting national budget frameworks to support regional public goods.

Regulatory and competition issues

Several regulatory issues affect the roads sub-sector in Africa. In terms of policy framework, the past decade has seen substantial institutional and policy reform for Africa's roads. The majority of countries now have formal policy frameworks for the sector, though many of these have not been evaluated in the past five years. Many countries have also developed associated investment programs to expand the road network.[39]

Competition among transport operators is an area of much interest for policymakers. In some parts of the continent, the road freight industry is cartelized and tightly controlled, with high profits generated despite the high cost of provision.[40] This is an outcome generated by complex regulatory and competition issues, including barriers to entry in the freight transport industry in some countries, insufficient competition from other transport modes, and the absence of sufficiently empowered competition authorities. That said, there is a degree of regional dichotomy in this respect. While in West and Central Africa transport operators are tightly regulated by freight bureaus, shippers' councils, and trade unions, the market structure of East and Southern Africa is far more competitive, bringing better-quality service and lower prices.

Lastly, poor cross-border transport impedes further regional integration. The price per tonne-km for long-distance freight destined for export markets is higher than that for domestic traffic within a country. This is the converse of findings from the rest of the world and may speak to the regulatory and bureaucratic difficulties of cross-border trade. The Southern African international transport market is a good model as it combines liberalization of entry with quality standard and load control rules.[41]

Financing and expenditure

In Africa, the fiscal burden of providing roads is relatively high. Low population densities, across vast geographic areas, require road links that traverse great distances. However, the affordability of providing such likes is hampered by the low GDP per capita in many countries. The importance of a diverse and stable set of financing sources for the infrastructure is therefore pertinent.

As it stands, public investment in African roads, which is the overwhelmingly source of finance for the asset, is highly dependent on foreign aid flows and concessional finance. The available evidence on public spending financed by ODA suggests that dependence on this foreign funding may range from 50% to 90% in some countries. Volatility in these flows therefore drives volatility in road expenditure.[42]

In an attempt to provide a stable source of funding, institutional reform in the road sector has focused on establishing dedicated "road funds". These funds generally provide ring-fenced revenues for road maintenance, often based on a user charge collected through the fuel levy. The revenue stability brought by road funds allows for the signing of long-term contracts with private sector contractors for the provision of maintenance. This also allows for performance management systems that better align the incentives of the contractor with those of the roads agency.

Notwithstanding the dominance of public funding, certain roads are capable of being self-funded through tolling mechanisms. These offer the opportunity to crowd in investment from the private sector in the form of PPPs. Since 1990, the most prolific region for these has been South Africa, where eight concessions have been introduced. Elsewhere in Africa, a toll road concession was instituted for the bridge over the Abidjan Lagoon in Côte d'Ivoire; a bridge over the Limpopo River in Zimbabwe; the Lekki–Epe Expressway in Lagos, Nigeria; and the Dakar–Diamniadio toll road in Senegal. However, low traffic volumes in Africa limit the scope for privately funded toll roads on the continent. The AICD sample of countries[43] showed that less than 9,000km had traffic levels that would make tolling financially viable (that is, in excess of 10,000 vehicles per day), with 86% of this length concentrated in South Africa, 8% in Nigeria and a few other countries with over 100km of "tollable" road.

The perennial funding challenge encompasses both required maintenance expenditure and capital investment. There is an inherent trade-off in the provision of roads, where limited funds must be spread across the construction of new roads (or significant upgrades of existing roads) and maintenance of the existing road network. As it stands, a strong capital bias exists for spending in the road sector. This is despite the finding that the split between capital investment and maintenance should be approximately fifty-fifty.[44]

Even with the degree of capital spending bias on the continent, only about half of the countries surveyed for the AICD study demonstrated sufficient expenditure levels to clear current road rehabilitation backlogs. Moreover, the capital bias means that resources allocated to routine and periodic maintenance are insufficient, causing these countries to enter a vicious cycle of an ever-expanding backlog of network rehabilitation.[45] In fact, half of African countries are not devoting adequate resources to routine and periodic maintenance of the main road network. Indeed, some 25% of countries do not even cover routine maintenance activity.[46]

The capital-maintenance differential appears most pronounced in LICs; countries with geographical environments that may be adverse for road construction (for example, mountainous terrain); and those without road funds or fuel levies. There are several possible explanations for this. First, low-income countries may dedicate more of their road budgets to capital projects simply because they have a greater requirement for building the infrastructure base whereas middle-income countries have already developed this infrastructure and are focused on maintaining it. Second, challenging geography and topography necessitates higher capital expenditure. This may include tunneling, gradient and bridge construction requirements. Third, the lack of a road fund means that the funding flows are more variable, with 'lumps' of expenditure generally provided for capital projects. Funds with a ring-fenced financing mechanism promote more stable budget allocations and provide for scheduled maintenance.

Challenges, opportunities and prospects

Challenges facing the sub-sector

Several key challenges face road infrastructure development in Africa. Failure to address certain of these issues will only serve to exacerbate the sub-optimal state of affairs that governs much of the road sector.

Challenge 1: clarity and certainty over policy and regulation

Though transport policies are in existence for most African countries, these tend to be outdated in relation to the demands of the sector. Several of the constraints to road infrastructure development may be addressed through policy reform. These include, *inter alia*, a clear and proper delineation between the respective roles of the public and private sector in terms of infrastructure asset operation and funding; and the creation of regulatory frameworks that properly define vehicle specifications and associated usage charges.

Challenge 2: need to strengthen institutional structures and capacity

Public institutions in the road sector play a critical role in various levels of road infrastructure provision and management. Consequently, the strength of these institutions and their associated capacity to carry through the required tasks is of vital importance. There are often weaknesses and inadequate technical capacity in such institutions, including the following.

- *Road funds.* While there has been a rise in the number of second-generation road funds and there have been successes achieved as a result of this, overall effectiveness has been hampered by institutional inefficiency. Further, many of the funds established are without dedicated funding mechanisms—such as fuel levies—to ensure adequate and consistent revenue streams. This aggravates efforts to tackle the maintenance backlog in a structured manner.

- *Road department operations and maintenance.* Successes gained at the road fund level have often been undone by a lack of capacity at implementing agencies. Constraints in terms of technical capacity are common, with many employees lacking the requisite skills, often due to the private sector bidding engineers away with higher salaries. Weak departments prolong the contracting process, resulting in high unit cost of road construction on the continent.[47] A lack of technical capacity may also lead to internal coordination failures among the various arms of government that are typically involved in granting regulatory approvals. More broadly, the issue of a centralized or decentralized approach to road operations and management is vexing. For rural areas, road administration is frequently devolved to local governments.[48] Several problems arise as a result of this. First, local governments have meagre financial resources, both in terms of their ability to collect their own funding and in terms of allocation from the national budget. Second, local government road networks are often too small to attract experienced consulting and contracting firms, and also do not provide the necessary economies of scale to hire and retain engineering staff. Third, a lack of technical capacity impedes the functioning of these local roads agencies. Fourth, local governments often lack the necessary political influence to lobby for adequate allocations of available funds.

• *Monitoring and enforcement of traffic rules and regulations.* Monitoring and enforcement of vehicle traffic and adherence to relevant by-laws and regulation is important for two reasons: it influences the safety of motorists on the road, and it has an impact on the road infrastructure quality over time. In terms of infrastructure quality, a major culprit of accelerated depreciation of road assets is heavy vehicles, particularly when overloaded. Without adequate monitoring and enforcement of axle load and vehicle mass restrictions, overloaded vehicles will continue to have an adverse effect on the road network for general users.

Challenge 3: constrained financing ability for road infrastructure demands

The greatest challenge that exists for road infrastructure relates to financing. This constraint has a direct impact on the quality of road infrastructure on the continent. Funding shortages aggravate maintenance programs and hold back capital investment in new roads and the rehabilitation of those in a poor state. This only results in expenditure demands growing further. While African road expenditure as a percentage of GDP is not far below that of other developing countries,[49] it does fall short of the level associated with higher economic growth rates.[50] This must be addressed for meaningful progress to be made.

Maintaining infrastructure to adequate standards has been further hamstrung by other factors. First, funding problems hamper road expenditure, both in terms of the timing issue between funding and expenditure and the lack of capacity to execute. Second, the relatively high cost of road works aggravates the funding dilemma. Cost increases and overruns in road projects have been attributed to a variety of factors, depending on the region. In some instances, a lack of effective competition between contractors has led to costs being bid above a competitive market level.[51] In others, there have been delays in project implementation which have resulted in unbudgeted project cost increases. More generally, increases in the price basket of road construction inputs (bitumen, steel, cement, aggregates, and so on) have pushed up the cost of road works. Third, certain roads are sometimes over-engineered for the level of traffic volumes they handle,[52] which depletes the meagre financial resources available. Lastly, there may be political economy issues at play, including corruption in the award of contracts or cartel behavior by tendering construction firms.

Challenge 4: need for effective implementation and management of road projects

Not only do capacity issues exist for road projects on the institutional side with authorities but often local construction companies in African countries lack the necessary skills and capacity to undertake rehabilitation and maintenance programs (even at an early, preventative stage). For the other reforms to take effect, it is necessary that countries are possessed of a capable and competitive road-contracting industry. An attendant issue in this respect is the risk of cartelization of construction companies. In this respect, strong competition authorities are required to deter, detect and break these collusive arrangements.

Challenge 5: need for a consolidated approach to regional integration

Artificial barriers to regional trade and transport are common in the road sector. Bureaucratic procedures in licensing freight haulage between countries causes cross-border transit problems. These can range from different regulatory frameworks for heavy vehicles in different countries to difficulties at moving freight through border posts.

Since the dissolution of the TAH Bureau in the 1980s, the RECs have taken up the regional integration agenda in the roads sector, establishing regional technical standards. Even so, achieving regional integration through the road network remains "a Herculean task".[53]

Policy opportunities

To avert the *status quo* situation under which many of the problems in the road sector will only be exacerbated, policy reforms that may address these challenges are detailed in this next section. The proposed reforms respond to a particular challenge identified in the previous section.

Formulate renewed policy and harmonise modal regulation

A two-pronged policy reform path is advised for the road transport sector. In terms of the road assets themselves, it is necessary that authorities provide a framework that allows for increased participation by the private sector. This is in the form of both private sector investment in roads with viable traffic volumes, as well as a commercialization of maintenance arrangements, where the private sector is permitted to operate and maintain sections of the road network.

The second leg would tackle users of the road. In those countries and regions that require it (such as West and Central Africa), a liberalization of the road haulage sector is required. This includes deregulating freight transport and allowing foreign freight hauliers to compete with domestic firms. In addition, a regulatory framework is needed for users and their interaction with the road. This includes charging fees to users that send correct price signals and incentivize multi-axle vehicles to limit road damage, establishing axle and gross mass load limits that balance preservation of road assets with the commercial incentives of hauliers, and introducing regulations that appropriately punish transgressors for overloading vehicles. On these latter points, lessons can be learnt from Australia, New Zealand, and Germany, leading jurisdictions in this regard.

Strengthen institutions and their ability to respond to road infrastructure needs

Broadly, we propose institutional reform that sets up independent and autonomous agencies to professionalize the full gamut of infrastructure provision. This will improve road infrastructure through better funding and management of the asset.

In terms of funding agencies, countries should adopt *road funds* based on the 'second generation' model. This proposal requires that the road funding function is separated from that of road service provision (construction and provision). There are several critical design features that should be incorporated for second-generation road funds to work effectively. First, these funds must be legally defined, providing a defined institutional framework within which to operate, and protecting the fund against political interference and special interest groups. Second, road funds should have dedicated funding mechanisms established so as to finance road construction and maintenance. Third, road funds must develop a rule-based approach to the allocation of funds to projects. This is necessary given the extremely limited funding in the face of project demands. Further, such allocation must take cognisance of the split between capital expenditure and maintenance.

The *operations and maintenance for road departments* should continue to shift the implementation of road works out of the traditional public sector role into independent agencies (some of which have private sector participation on the boards). The level of autonomy may differ from country to country, with some agencies possessing full responsibility for road network management (such as SANRAL in South Africa), while others are limited to executing programs mandated by the roads department/ministry. Importantly, the agency must develop the technical ability to effectively select contractors, and negotiate and monitor contracts.

An extensive study of road administration in three countries (Mexico, Uganda, and Zambia) found that decentralization tended to work best under a "devolve-and-delegate" model, whereby local government retains ownership and a state-owned enterprise or private sector firm administers the work under a contractual arrangement.[54] Alternatively, or in combination, a centralized road fund model could be used with similar effectiveness. The best option depends on local factors, including the size of the authority, nature of the network and work responsibility, and the competence of authorities.

Practically, road authorities need to ensure that roads in a fair to good condition are prevented from deteriorating to the point where they are deemed "poor". Preventive maintenance has been shown to be critically important in maintaining asset value. This has been a lesson hard learned by African countries, as it was found that losses to the value of US$45 billion for the continent's road network could have been averted if US$12 billion had been spent on preventive maintenance programs during the 1970s and 1980s.[55]

Lastly, *monitoring and enforcement* can be improved on African networks by appropriately assigning responsibility for sections of the road network and by certain authorities and agencies with traffic policing powers. Overloading is of most concern on those sections of the network that carry relatively high volumes of traffic, not only because of the externality this has on other users but also because these routes are likely to be where overloading is most prevalent. Further, focusing on main routes and corridors will allow traffic policing efforts to be targeted, raising the effectiveness of enforcement. Authorities should introduce weighbridges at key points of the network and, where appropriate, possible diversion points from the main network.

Establish dedicated and innovative financing structures for networks

Notwithstanding rising national incomes, the enormity of the construction and maintenance backlog on African roads necessitates other funding sources in order for meaningful gains to be made in infrastructure provision. Two possible funding sources are available— tolling and the fuel levy. Improved funding for roads through these dedicated funding sources deepens financing opportunities and offers more stable flows for road expenditure.

Though much of Africa's road network is typified by low traffic volumes, tolling can and should be done on those roads that can support it, even if it accounts for only a fraction of the network. Indeed, toll roads are only set to rise in prominence as population and income levels rise.[56]

Given that many countries and regions currently offer limited prospects for private sector involvement in toll roads, funding for road provision should be chiefly provided by a ring-fenced fuel levy. These revenues would ideally be disbursed through road funds but, at the least, provided for general road expenditure. Where such levies are already in existence, it would require either a redirection of funding or an additional tax on fuel (petrol and diesel).[57] Risks are, of course, present for this strategy including new propulsion technologies that are less fuel intensive. That said, growth in the middle class of African countries and general economic activity should see vehicle fleets grow faster than declines in fuel consumption rates, with a net effect of a growing fuel levy fund.

Address implementation issues

To build the skills base in local road construction sectors, authorities should encourage the involvement of foreign construction companies, which bring with them extensive experience and skills. Technical capacity may be built by establishing skills transfer programs through joint tendering with local firms such that projects have a lasting impact on the domestic industry.

The high cost of road works can be partly addressed by introducing competitive pressures to road construction projects. Formal and transparent tender procedures overseen by an independent agency (such as a competition authority) could bring better quality proposals at a lower price. Allowing foreign construction companies to participate in these would further improve the situation. In conjunction with this, cartel-busting activities by competition authorities should be enacted.

Competition authorities are being established across the continent, and these should consider measures to tackle potential collusion.[58]

In terms of the infrastructure development, project scoping and approach should be better tailored to local needs and constraints. This includes designing engineering and construction programs that better cater for the affordability and needs of the economic activity or community served. For example, in rural areas roads need not be paved with tarmac or concrete; rather, an appropriately graded gravel road can work as an effective and inexpensive substitute. This is especially true given the very low volumes of traffic on rural road networks. As one example, sealed gravel can be used instead of bitumen to lower lifecycle costs of rural roads.

Harmonise regulation and review TAH proposal to quicken regional integration

There are two key drivers of regional integration in the road sector. First, regional policies must be developed for trans-border vehicle operation. This includes the harmonization of axle loads and gross mass regulations; overloading rules (set at limits that balance private hauliers' interests and the sustainability of the network); and the removal of barriers to trade in the form of border posts and the bureaucratic and onerous procedures these entail.[59] Second, a renewed view on the TAH network is required. Though the TAH network would spur regional integration, there is no need to expend effort and resources to re-establish the TAH Bureau. Rather, a more effective approach would be to devolve responsibilities from a centralized agency to respective RECs that are able to drive agendas at a local level. A study by the AfDB on the TAH network found that the RECs have a proven capability of handling regional issues relating to technical standards and transport requirements.[60] Such a move offers the opportunity to deepen economic and political integration across the continent, further than just road infrastructure.

Prospects for the road sub-sector

Addressing the challenges that currently beset the road sector could significantly unlock the sector's potential for enabling future growth. By enacting the package of policy reforms proposed, the following three outcomes are expected for African road infrastructure.

It is anticipated that there will be faster *growth in the length of the total road network*. Positive feedback loops created by better road infrastructure will nudge economic growth higher and spur on further road development. Notably, there is the opposing force exerted by the policy proposal to reduce the capital bias in road expenditure and thus reduce new road construction projects. For policymakers, the task of balancing the reach of the road network with maintaining the infrastructure to a high quality is an important one.

As in the base case, greater affordability will be introduced through rising GDP per capita in countries. An improvement of institutional structures will notably improve quality *in general*, as opposed to isolated pockets of improvement. This will be facilitated through the establishment of road funds with a dedicated fuel levy funding mechanism and rule-based investment decisions to reduce the capital bias in African road expenditure.

More of the road network will be paved, as a result of reforms that focus on reducing the cost of road works, and target improved funding mechanisms for the road network. That said, a fairly large fraction of the network will remain unpaved. Enacting the various roadwork and construction reforms should improve the state of rural roads without necessitating a shift to formal paving. Further, a revised institutional structure should see an improvement in conditions of rural roads without dramatic increases in funding requirements.

Rail sub-sector

Contextual overview

Africa's railways are predominantly built around freight transport. This follows from historically limited inter-country trade, where the major movement of freight was the shipping of export commodities from countries through ports to Western markets.[61] Trade corridors continue to connect landlocked countries with the ports along Africa's coastline.

Railways provide important internal country links, as well as regional links over longer distances. In general, rail is the most cost-effective mode of land-based transport available for moving bulk cargo. While there are certain inherent advantages to road freight transport over rail (such as a faster, more flexible service, especially over short distances, and reduced risks of handling damage and pilferage),[62] these general advantages reduce over distance, as rail becomes increasingly competitive over longer routes. It is therefore well suited to servicing the routes between ports and commercial/industrial hubs.

There has been little rail line construction and development in the past 80 years outside of Southern Africa. The only major projects include the Tazara line built in the 1970s (linking Tanzania and Zambia), the Trans-Gabonais opened in 1987 (primarily to transport minerals), and the extensions of the Cameroon and Nigerian networks.[63]

This lacklustre development of railways in Africa owes itself to several factors. Historic development of many railway lines was based on servicing extractive industries. Fluctuating commodity prices and finite life-of-mine has meant that the decline of these railways have been linked to the decline of these sectors. Part of it is also attributable to the growth of the road system and the rise of freight trucking, particularly for the transport of higher-value general freight. The decrease in revenues resulting from the loss of volumes has meant that railway operators are ill-positioned to generate sufficient cash flows for investments in track and rolling stock maintenance and upgrades. In many instances, rail traffic has therefore become limited to bulk commodity exports and bulk imports like fuel.

Infrastructure base

Descriptive characteristics

General

Rail infrastructure may be grouped into two broad categories: underlying rail network and the rolling stock. The rail network includes the track (or "lines"), signalling equipment, consolidation yards, bridges and tunnels, and power supplies; rolling stock consists of the locomotives and wagons, complete with "bogies",[64] used to haul freight around the network.

The African rail network consists of 70,000km of track, of which only 55,000km is currently operational.[65] The only sections of the network that are not single track are those parts of Transnet Freight Rail's South African operations. Further, very little of the network is electrified outside of South Africa (42% of South Africa's network is electrified): relatively short sections in the DRC and Zimbabwe, at 858km section and 313km respectively, although the latter section is currently not in use.[66] Limited electrification of the rail network means that diesel locomotives dominate in Africa. Old steam engines are generally only in operation for tourist attraction purposes, such as in Kenya.[67]

In terms of ancillary infrastructure for the rail network, signalling and telecommunication systems for African railways tend to be old and lack the reliability required of a modern transport system.[68]

Figure 7.1: Rail network distribution across Africa

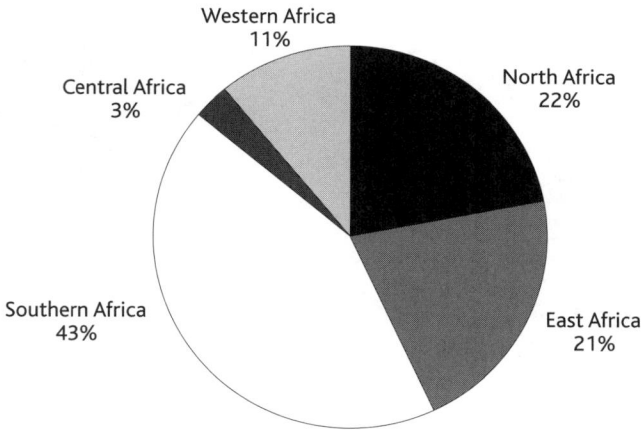

Source: UNECA (2009) [as Table 7.1], p 8

In all, there are nine different gauges used for railway lines in Africa. Three types of gauge dominate the continent—these are: *cape gauge* (measuring 1.067m), the most prolific form of gauge on the continent, representing over 60% of the total network on the continent, particularly in Southern Africa; *standard gauge* (measuring 1.435m), representing just under 15% per cent of the continent's network and dominant in North Africa; and *metre gauge* (1.000m), representing just under 20% per cent of the continent's network.[69]

There are numerous problems with the African rail track network. In general it does not enable large axle loads on the wagons and trains must move at low speeds. This is partly a function of age although the cape gauge is known to have such limitations. (For instance, cape gauge rail does not allow for the double stacking of containers.) Further, African rail infrastructure is generally undercapitalized and ill-suited to modern requirements. Limited upgrading and maintenance has taken place, and some parts of the continent's network are over 100 years old. These are major handicaps when rail is expected to compete against modern road networks. Delays in investment in track and rolling stock have seen volumes further decrease.[70]

Density and connectivity

Various lines exist across Africa, many of which make up small networks. Together, these offer low-density coverage and most lines remain isolated, with little network interconnection.[71]

Figure 7.2: Extent of rail network in Africa

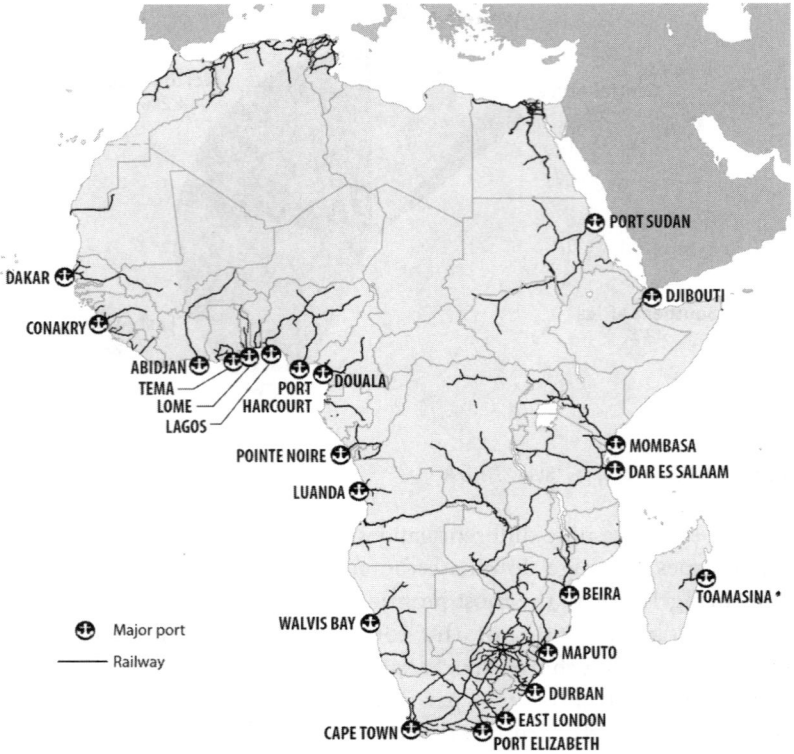

Source: Bullock, R. (2009) *Railways in Sub-Saharan Africa*. Africa Infrastructure Country Diagnostic Background Paper 17, World Bank, Washington, DC.

Similar to roads, the spatial density of the rail network in Africa is low. Most country networks range between one and six route-km per 1,000km². These measures are generally lower than larger and more sparsely populated areas (like Australia, Canada, China and Russia) and far lower than most European countries.

Infrastructure performance

Despite growth in GDP, as well as increases in trade for the continent, railways in Africa have generally failed to translate economic growth into increased volumes of freight traffic. Indeed, only five railways in Africa increased both passenger and freight traffic between 1995 and 2005.[72]

Operational performance of railways in Africa is far lower than comparators elsewhere. This owes to the generally low traffic volumes and inadequate infrastructure levels.[73]

Figure 7.3: Freight wagon productivity (traffic units/wagon)

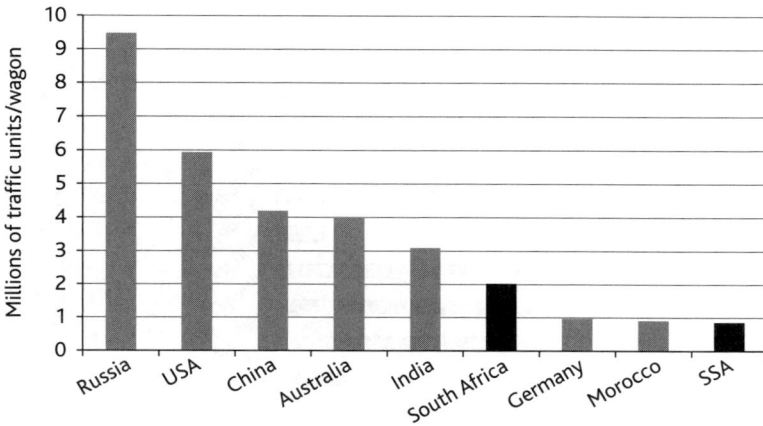

Source: Olievschi, V. N. (2013) *Rail transport: framework for improving railway sector performance in Sub-Saharan Africa.* Sub-Saharan Africa Transport Policy Program (SSATP) working paper series; no 94. Washington DC: World Bank.

Further, a clear dichotomy exists in the African rail sector, with the South African network overshadowing the rest of the continent. The country's Transnet Freight Rail (TFR) operates approximately 40% of the continent's network and carries 70% of the traffic. The continent's rail network excluding South Africa carries 1 billion traffic units (TUs) per annum; TFR carries the equivalent in just three days. Similarly, South Africa accounts for over 70% of the continent's passenger-km, predominantly due to urban commuter transport.[74]

Those railways that achieved productivity improvements in recent years have generally been private concessions; this has been driven by cuts in workforces and, to a lesser extent, moderate increases in traffic volumes.

The transportation of bulk commodities, mainly to and from ports, dominates the freight traffic of African railways, generally reflecting the underlying economic structure of countries. Additionally, import traffic generally exceeds export traffic on railways. On those few lines where this is not the case, one generally finds that these are dedicated mineral export corridors. Imports are predominantly made up of semi-finished manufactured products (for example, cement), fuel products, and general freight (such as capital equipment and final consumer goods).

In recent decades, there has been a substitution in traffic away from rail to road transport. Several factors are behind this trend. First, many commodities require specialized wagons, which means that

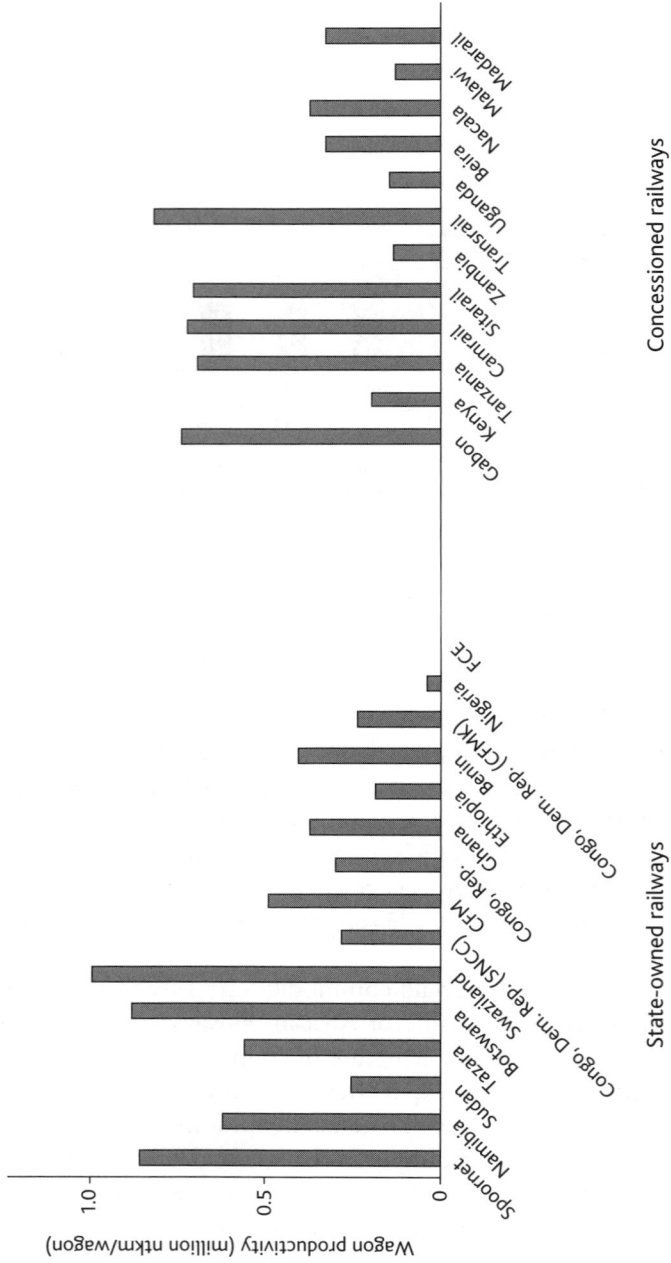

Figure 7.4: Freight wagon productivity (average, 1995–2005)

Source: Bullock (2009) [as Figure 7.2]

trains are rarely fully loaded in both directions. Road hauliers, on the other hand, tend to backload freight at a marginal cost, leaving railways to transport the remaining freight without a compensating return load. Second, the restructuring of agricultural cooperatives and central marketing structures has meant produce no longer needs to be delivered to a single point for storage and subsequent distribution. Finally, the manner in which consumer and intermediate goods are distributed has evolved over time, with general freight generally dispatched in smaller, more frequent loads (just-in-time production and distribution). This has meant road has a natural advantage over rail and has gained this share of traffic.

Regional links

Network connectivity has long been a focus area for African policymakers. In 1976, a master plan was developed by the African Railways Union for the creation of a Pan-African rail network, which included 18 projects to construct over 26,000km of new track. This plan was endorsed by the then Organization of African Unity.[75]

Envisaged as a way to unlock routes for landlocked countries and to integrate isolated networks across regions, this railway master plan initially encompassed 18 projects and 26,000km of rail construction. Since its original adoption, the plan has subsequently undergone several revisions, the most recent of which was in 2005 where the plan was simplified to cover three major transcontinental routes:

- Libya–Niger–Chad–Central African Republic–Republic of Congo–DRC–Angola–Namibia (6,500km);
- Senegal–Mali–Chad-Djibouti (7,800km);
- Kenya–Tanzania–Uganda–Rwanda–Burundi–DRC (5,600km)

Table 7.7: Extent of rail network by region

Regions	Existing lines (km)	Planned lines from 1979 master plan (km)	Total length (km)	Percentage missing
North Africa	16,012	6,484	22,496	29%
East Africa	9,341	2,299	11,640	20%
Southern Africa	33,291	4,034	37,325	11%
Central Africa	6,414	4,574	10,988	42%
Western Africa	9,715	8,971	18,686	48%
Total	74,773	26,362	101,135	26%

Source: UNECA (2009) [as Table 7.1], p 17

Most of these proposed links have not moved from the planning phase and do not show any sign of doing so imminently.

Regulation and competition issues

Railways in Africa are predominantly based on freight transport. On average, African railways carry four times as much in traffic units of freight than passengers. However, because of increasing competition from road hauliers (which is likely to increase with a focus on investment in road infrastructure), tonnage growth has been slow and, in some instances, negative.

Historically, state monopolies dominated the rail sector in many African countries before the 1990s. The poor management of these rail operators, coupled with aging and inefficient rolling stock and equipment, hampered the ability of railways to compete against a more dynamic road transport sector, largely driven by private operators.

While most railway operators were publicly owned up until the 1980s, there has been a movement toward concession contracts since the 1990s. Generally under such arrangements, the state retains ownership of some assets (typically the underlying infrastructure) and transfers others (the rolling stock) to the concessionaire. The concessionaire then assumes responsibility for the operation and maintenance of the railway.[76] Granting of concessions has necessitated regulatory changes, including economic and safety regulations to combat incentives that private operators may face (respectively, abuse of monopoly pricing power and underinvestment in safety).

Broadly, two types of private operators have been attracted to African rail concessions: those operators seeking to integrate their supply chains; and those operators specializing in managing a single type of activity.

Of the 30 African countries with state-owned railways, 14 have entered into concession arrangements; the DRC railway operates under a management contract; and four further railways are in the concession process.[77]

The track record of rail concessions in Africa has been mixed, however. Indeed, in the past year, the Rail Systems of Zambia concession was cancelled by the Zambian government and returned to state ownership and control and two others—the concession in Malawi and the Rift Valley Railway between Kenya and Uganda— were placed under review for poor performance.

Given the predominance of state-run monopolies in the sector, vertical separation of rail track and rolling stock infrastructure operations has not really been considered. With low volumes on many sections of the network, this may not be a feasible policy endeavor, as competing providers on a stretch of track necessitates relatively high volumes. However, further consideration may be warranted, as opening up competition between operators by separating the track from haulage operations may improve efficiency and shift volumes from road back to rail.

While private ownership and operation has become more prevalent in recent years, the secular trend of lost freight to the road sector has continued unabated. This speaks to the need to consider more broadly the place of rail in the continent's transport system.

Figure 7.5: Railway concessions in Africa since 1990

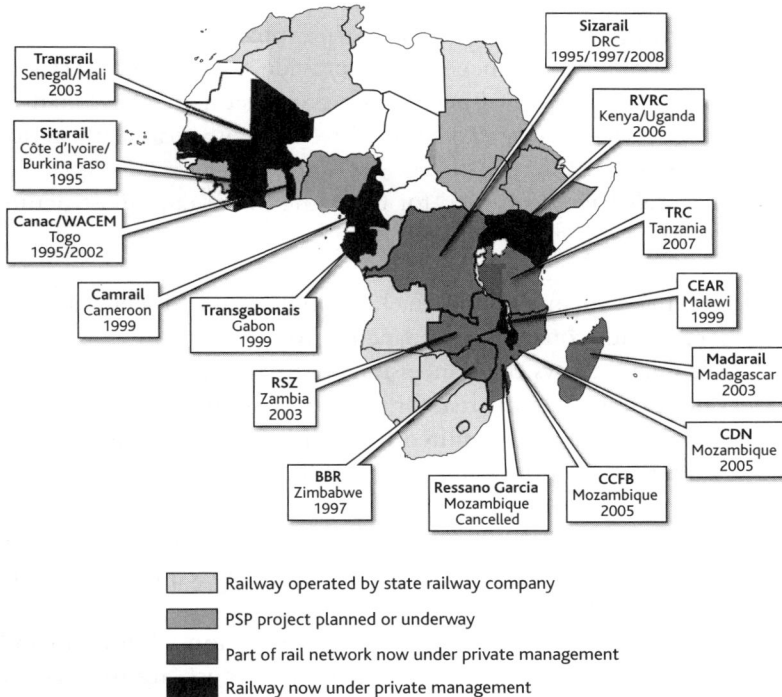

Note: BBR = Belt Bridge Railway; CDN = Corredor de Desenvolvimento do Norte; RSZ = Railway Systems of Zambia; RVRC = Rift Valley Railways Consortium; WACEM = West African Cement Company. Three different dates are given for Sitarail because the concession was relet on three occasions.

Source: Bullock (2009) [as Figure 7.2]

287

Financing and expenditure

The funding available for railways in Africa is generally insufficient to finance the modernization of track and rolling stock. Low traffic volumes hamper the profitability of African railways, rendering them hamstrung to reinvest adequately.

Investment possibilities are further aggravated by the relatively high cost of new rail infrastructure. Investment in track construction or rehabilitation is commercially viable only for lines that carry more than 2 to 3 million tonnes per annum.[78] Rehabilitation is estimated at US$200,000/km on flat terrain, but is estimated to be closer to US$350,000/km on average. Only three country railway networks in Africa, however, exceed 1 million TUs per route-km. South Africa's network averages 5 million TUs per route-km, although this falls to 2.4 million when the export iron ore and coal lines are excluded; Gabon carries 2.7 million TUs per route-km; and Cameroon's Camrail moves 1.1 million TUs per route-km.[79]

An operating model of a concessionaire provides the commercial freedom, flexibility, and incentives to provide good-quality services. There is evidence of the success that concessionaires have had in improving service quality and competitiveness with road hauliers (for example, Sitarail).[80]

Two models have been used for financing initial rail infrastructure investment:

- Government finances initial track rehabilitation and renewal costs, generally with concessional financing from DFIs.
- Government allows the concessionaire to operate and invest as it sees fit, taking the traffic risk for potential commercial reward. The concessionaire is then required to hand back the infrastructure to the government at the end of the period.

In the case of both models, governments generally agree to refund the net amount of any infrastructure investment financed by the private operator at the end of the concession period.

The funding requirement for the rehabilitation of African rail infrastructure has alone been estimated to cost approximately US$100 million per annum over 40 years. Allowing for the replacement of rolling stock and facilities and maintenance equipment, steady-state investment requirements amount to US$200 million per annum.[81] These are sizeable sums of money given the anemic performance of the rail sector in the past several decades, which generally relies on tariffs and fees charged to users for operating and investment purposes.

Challenges, opportunities and prospects

Challenges facing the sub-sector

We foresee two broad challenges to the rail sector that currently hamper the performance of rail and threaten the long-term competitiveness and viability of many routes.

Challenge 1: competition to rail freight from the road sector

Despite the natural advantage that rail has over road for the transportation of land-based freight, road freight poses a strong threat as a substitute transport form. This is as a result of several factors. First, where rail sidings are not present at the point of origin/ destination there is the additional cost of pick-up and delivery. Second, service levels are often below that which customers require, with the infrequent scheduling of trains for certain producers, repeated breakdowns of aging rolling stock, infrastructure failure, and the risk of theft all hampering operational competitiveness. Third, a lack of regional integration—through inadequate trade facilitation and cross-border coordination—further hampers the quality of service railways can offer. Fourth, pricing challenges hamper the ability of railways to compete. State-owned railways may be limited in their ability to price freight according to demand. Further, there is a fundamental mispricing between road and rail freight, where road freight is dramatically underpriced. The rail operator not only covers the costs of running its haulage operations but is also responsible for track construction and maintenance (construction and damage costs).[82] Road freight carriers, on the other hand, share few such responsibilities and costs as they are not responsible for road construction and maintenance. Fifth, certain African regions (notably West and East Africa) have several freight corridor options, placing competitive pressure on individual railways.[83]

Compared with the road sector, rail struggles to present a competitive offer to freight users. The flexibility, security and efficiency of road hauliers make road an easy choice over short distances. As distances increase, so the cost advantages of rail rise. However, the fundamental mispricing between rail and road corridors often mitigates this advantage. The overarching challenge therefore is for rail to remain competitive against road freight, and thereby generate sufficient cash flow for investment purposes.[84]

Challenge 2: difficulties presented by rail concessions

While concessions in the rail sector do offer the potential for improved performance, it should be noted that there have been a number of poorly performing projects across Sub-Saharan Africa including the Uganda-Kenya rail concession, the Nacala rail concession and the recently cancelled Zambia rail concession. The reasons for these difficulties vary from country to country. They include inadequate private sector capital investments and inadequate technical expertise on the part of investors, but also failure of governments to follow through on their contractual obligations to limit traffic growth.

Mixed performance of past concessions provides acute challenges for the future. Private operators may be hesitant to invest sufficiently in infrastructure for fear that governments will not abide fully by their commitments under the concession. Likewise, governments may be skeptical of introducing concessions for fear that they do not yield the successes expected and the public sector is therefore left burdened with significant project risks.

Policy opportunities

Reconsider overall rail policy and market structure

Market structure and ownership policy for the rail sector may be an area for policy reform. More than simply considering concessions, authorities should contemplate—where appropriate—whether vertical integration or vertical separation offers the best prospects for infrastructure development. Vertical separation, where a public entity retains track ownership and competing private operators finance and operate the rolling stock, offers the prospect of crowding in private investment and alleviating budgetary constraints where routes provide sufficient traffic volumes. Furthermore, countries should ensure that their transport policy is aligned across road and rail—the priorities and methods to achieve this must speak to each other.

Improve concession design and regulation

The experiences provided by African rail concessions suggest that greater caution and more rigorous project due diligence would be advisable in future rail concessions. The possibility of concession failure and associated fallout can be mitigated with risk guarantee measures.

There should also be greater emphasis placed in tenders on the involvement of large industrial and commercial entities that have a direct interest in rail operations such as large mining houses. This appears to be happening already in countries like Mozambique where Vale in particular is developing the rail network for coal exports.

Introduce strong and independent regulators in the rail sector

Institutionally speaking, strong regulatory authorities must be established to guide firm conduct. Such institutions need not be national; they can cover wider regions, if this makes sense from a network perspective.

In terms of the economic regulator, altering the pricing arrangement where road freight carriage was correctly priced would see relative prices increase to where rail's offering attracted greater demand. Additionally, it would provide room for rail operators to raise tariffs to levels that enable them to generate operational cash flows to finance capital expenditure programs, thereby improving operational efficiency.

This could help crowd in private sector investment, as private operators could compete, thereby funding their own rolling stock and contributing to the collective operation and maintenance of the underlying network.

Prospects for the rail sub-sector

Should policy reforms adequately address the regulatory and concession challenges in the sector, the following improvements and prospects for rail infrastructure are foreseen.

Adoption of the necessary reforms will see a revival in rail freight volumes, with benefits to operating viability. A revised pricing arrangement between road and rail freight will see a shift in freight from the former to the latter. Not only will this ease the burden on the road network but it will also bring much needed operating cash flow to rail operators. This will allow for increased investment in infrastructure, thereby improving efficiency and reliability. This may create a positive feedback loop that moves long-term rail investment to a higher steady-state level.

Better-designed concessions can tap further private capital. Improving the design on concessions will reduce the financial burden on African governments and also improve productivity. This will free up finances for other government activities.

Rail links can strengthen regional integration. Trade flow will improve, particularly between African countries and regions. This may allow for the completion of certain links in the pan-Africa rail master plan, and will bolster regional integration.

Ports sub-sector

Contextual overview

The importance of maritime transport for Africa is illustrated in the fact that 92% of the continent's international trade moves through its ports, even higher than the global average of 90%.[85]

Maritime ports are fundamental outlets for international trade, from both coastal and landlocked countries. This is because of the sheer cost advantage offered by sea-borne transport, especially for low value-for-weight items and other dry and liquid bulk items. Ready access to regular shipping services is an important enabler of trade and development. While Africa has a large number of ports that offer such services, most of these are small by global standards and unable to handle the largest ships in operation.

Shipping to and from Africa, however, remains expensive. Constraints on economies of scale, as a result of size limitations for vessel access into African ports, and the relatively small size of markets, raises the cost of shipping to and from the continent. This is aggravated by operational inefficiencies and inadequate road/rail links between ports and hinterlands. Poorly maintained port infrastructure and operational inefficiencies mean that ports often act as bottlenecks for trade.[86]

Maritime ports generally consist of three levels of activity/service provision: *infrastructure provision*, which includes the physical structure of the port; *terminal operations*, which encompass the loading and unloading of rail and road haulage and ocean-going vessels, as well as the conveyance and storage of products at the port; and *related services*, including piloting, tugging and cargo-handling.

There remains a large amount of government involvement in the ports sector in Africa. As an example, roughly half of containerized traffic passes through public ports on the continent, the highest proportion for any region in the world.[87] Internationally, however, ports handling large quantities of bulk commodities tend to have private sector involvement and report higher productivity statistics. We explain below possible reasons for this discrepancy.

Infrastructure base

Descriptive characteristics

Africa has 90 major ports, accounting for over 95% of its international trade, for its 30,725km coastline.[88]

As agglomeration points in freight transport systems, ports handle a wide variety of cargo in many forms. These are generally disaggregated into several categories: containers, dry bulk, and liquid bulk. While containers come in standard form and are therefore readily comparable, the same cannot be said for bulk cargo. Both dry and liquid bulk cargo comprise various commodities, which makes the process of measuring relative performance difficult. Nevertheless, certain conclusions about sectoral performance may be drawn.

Containerised traffic. Container traffic in Africa is still at a nascent stage of development, with much potential for growth. Average annual growth rates have been high; in the decade preceding 2005, East African container trade grew by 11% per annum, Southern Africa by 9%, and West Africa by 15%.[89]

Several factors have driven this growth. First, economic growth and rising income levels have increased demand for manufactured goods, which are generally imported in containers. Second, the decentralized globalization of manufacturing has seen trade increase between Africa and Asia (driven predominantly by the economic rise of China and India), with a concomitant rise in container traffic. Third, transport innovations have seen a greater integration of containers into logistics and distribution systems as well as shipping lines deploying increasingly larger container vessels for African trade. Fourth, institutional and regulatory reforms have seen private sector participation in the port sector with many PPPs for container-handling facilities.[90]

Still, African ports only accounted for slightly more than 2% of global container traffic in 2005, despite a far larger share of the world's population.[91] With secular trends in economic growth and income levels expected to rise, containerized traffic in Africa and the continent's share of the global market is expected to rise.

Another concern is the direction of container trade flows. There is an overwhelming dominance of containerized imports, mainly from Asia, with most containers making the trip back from Africa empty. The split of empty to loaded export containers in 2005 was 65/35 for Southern Africa, worsening to 90/10 for West Africa and 80/20 for East Africa.

Figure 7.6: Top 10 SSA container-handling ports (TEUs* per annum)

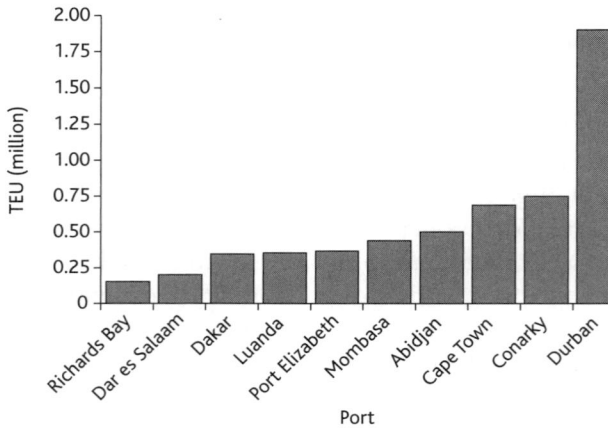

Note: *TEU = twenty-foot container equivalent unit
Source: Mundy, M. and Penfold, A. (2009) *Beyond the bottlenecks: Ports in sub-Saharan Africa.*
Background Paper 8, Africa Infrastructure Country Diagnostic. Washington, DC: World Bank.

Dry bulk. Dry bulk traffic in Africa is made up of two groupings, major bulk and minor bulk (where volume determines the groupings). Major dry bulk includes grain, iron ore, and coal, while minor bulk includes cement, aggregates, and clay.

Major dry bulk commodities tend to move through their own dedicated facilities, such as the grain terminal at Mombasa, Richards Bay Coal Terminal (RBCT) for coal exports in South Africa, and iron ore through Saldanha in South Africa.

Liquid bulk. Presently, 11 African countries are net oil exporters,[92] and Africa is a significant supplier of oil to the global market at almost 12% of world supply.[93] Recent oil and gas discoveries across the African continent suggest that the transportation of these energy products is a growth area for African ports.

Infrastructure performance

The productivity of Africa's ports is relatively low when considering global comparators, with average productivity around 30% of the international average. Poor operational efficiency tends to increase the cost of shipping. This not only has implications for the transport sector but evidence suggests that the doubling of shipping costs reduces annual economic growth rates by about half a percentage point.[94]

In terms of comparing and evaluation performance measures, there are several important metrics for considering the efficiency of port operations. These measure not only overall productivity but also the efficiency of handling various cargo types.

Vessel dwell time. The average dwell time in major African ports for shipping vessels is about 11 days, three times greater than ports in other developing regions.[95] Naturally, longer dwelling times raise costs as vessels lie idle.

Container moves per hour. Dockside container-handling performance is measured by the number of container movements per hour. Modern container terminals generally achieve between 20 and 30 moves per hour, while the African standard is somewhere below 20 moves per hour.

Larger ports with higher volumes tend to perform better as they possess highly developed container terminals, a feature not available to many African ports due to lower volumes.

Poor container-handling infrastructure is a contributing factor for the lower productivity. Many African ports do not possess purpose-built cranes for container handling and instead rely on the ships' gear.

Table 7.8: Dwell times for selected major ports in Africa

Regions and ports	Dwell time (days)
East Africa	
Djibouti (Djibouti)	10
Mombasa (Kenya)	12
Dar es Salaam (Tanzania)	15
Southern Africa	
Durban (South Africa)	5
Beira (Mozambique	10
Maputo (Mozambique)	10
Central Africa	
Douala (Cameroon)	19
Gabon	15
DRC	6
Western Africa	
Banjul (Gambia)	5
Conakry (Guinea)	15
Dakar (Senegal)	9

Source: UNECA (2009) [as Table 7.1], p 18

Table 7.9: Container terminal productivity for selected ports

Ports	Net container moves per hour
United States	
Virginia International Terminals	25-30
Ceres, Baltimore	24
Europe	
Antwerp	28
Rotterdam	27
Asia	
Singapore	33
Klang	23
Africa	
Durban	15
Cape Town	12
Mombasa	10
Abidjan	20+

Source: Mundy and Penfold (2009) [as Figure 7.6]

This type of operation generally has a far lower productivity rate, of around 8 moves per hour.

General cargo handling. General cargo handling performance usually exceeds 30 metric tonnes per hour per crane in developed countries. However, in Africa only Richards Bay and Durban approach these efficiency levels. Similar to containerized traffic, it will require modern infrastructure and handling services to increase productivity across the continent's ports.

Substantial variation in general cargo handling exists both within regions and across regions, with West Africa lagging behind other regions, particularly Southern Africa.

The presence of large volumes of bulk mining commodities may help to improve efficiency, as the loading of multiple commodities may serve to depress productivity statistics. This is, to an extent, a function of economies of scale and diseconomies of scope; insufficient

Table 7.10: General cargo productivity between African regions

Regions and ports	Tonnes moved per hour per crane
West Africa	7-15
East Africa	8-25
Southern Africa	10-25

Source: Mundy and Penfold (2009) [as Figure 7.6]

volumes for certain bulk commodities decreases productivity and raises unit costs, while catering for a wide variety of these small commodity volumes may further exacerbate the problem.

Regulatory and competition issues

Policy, planning and institutional management

Governments have several responsibilities in terms of the strategic planning of port development and management: the establishment of the roles of the public and private sectors; policies on the attraction and selection of private sector participation, if applicable; and identification of management arrangements for ports.

In most African countries, port regulation is undertaken by the ministry of transport or a port authority. Only in South Africa is there an independent regulator, the legislated Ports Regulator of South Africa.

In terms of port management, there are generally three models:[96]

- *Service port.* The port authority owns, maintains and operates all assets, and also provides the full range of services required for the functioning of the port. Most service ports are government owned, though there are some private service ports, usually dedicated to a single shipper or commodity (for example, RBCT in South Africa).

- *Landlord port.* This is a mixed public/private model, where a public sector authority acts as a regulatory body and a landlord, while operations and infrastructure are concessioned and leased to private parties. An example of this model is many of South Africa's ports, where the Transnet National Ports Authority acts as the landlord and operations are tendered out to interested parties,[97] or ports in Ghana and Nigeria.[98]

- *Whole port concessions.* The responsibility both for port management (landlord) and operations are concessioned to a private sector operator for a contracted period. Djibouti is the best example of this in Africa.

Customs procedures

Institutional failures by African governments and port authorities have meant that bureaucratic customs procedures and other formalities slow the movement of cargo, thereby driving up costs and stifling trade. Almost half the ports surveyed in the mid-2000s took more than a week to clear goods through the port, compared with one day or less for many ports in other developing countries.

Several factors have been identified as contributing to these onerous customs procedures. First, in many countries customs authorities and businesses tend not to have well-established relationships with one another; second, there are coordination difficulties due to the involvement of many agencies; third, information asymmetry exists between customs authorities and users; fourth, there is little standardisation of procedures and documentation between countries and regions; and fifth, corruption exists, especially where a lack of automation exists.[99]

Competition considerations

The relative bargaining power of African ports against shipping operators provides an interesting perspective on competitive interaction in the shipping market. The presence of a limited number of major regional ports on the continent offers a more even-handed method of competing against the bargaining power of an oligopolistic shipping industry.

Indeed, it has been suggested that Africa can only support a limited number of major regional shipping hubs. In East Africa, competition between ports in the region is already intense and collaboration is not currently considered an option.[100] The high fixed cost nature of the business means that such competition can lead to a race to the bottom in terms of fees charged to users, where only variable costs are covered in the short run and there is inadequate provision for long-run reinvestment needs.

Financing and expenditure

Port infrastructure is funded from fees and tariffs charged to the users of various port services. Whether public or private, these fees are used to continue operating the business as a going concern and fund reinvestment in the business over time.

The evolution of port management in Africa suggests a consistent rise in the role of private sector investment to fund port infrastructure, particularly through concession contracts. While the continent was slow to introduce private sector concessions for the management of ports, the decision in 2004 by the Nigerian government to embark on a wide-scale infrastructure concessioning program for its ports shows that a shift in thinking may have occurred amongst politicians and policymakers on the continent. In total, this program resulted in the concessioning of 24 ports and explains the spike in transactions around 2005/2006.[101]

Until recently, Nigerian ports experienced significant inefficiency due to excessive centralization of operations, overstaffing, and widespread corruption. Moreover, the grouping of both regulatory and operational functions within the Nigerian Ports Authority provided the incentive to increase prices rather than to improve efficiency. In 2004, the Nigerian government began to encourage private sector participation. Since then, 24 concession agreements have been signed with private parties for the management of ports. These concessions have increased the productivity of ports and reduced freight rates. Prices have fallen by 50% for containers and 25% for general cargo. Most private operators have initiated new investments in accordance with their agreements. However, the legal and institutional framework plans have not been established, which limits the effectiveness of the reform.

Concessioning out port operations can bring investment in new equipment and improvement in the management of operations, allowing substantially improved productivity. In general, concessioned African ports have higher productivity, and those which have been concessioned the longest do the best. Of the major ports in Africa, the five which perform best in terms of container-handling efficiency

Figure 7.7: Private sector involvement in African ports

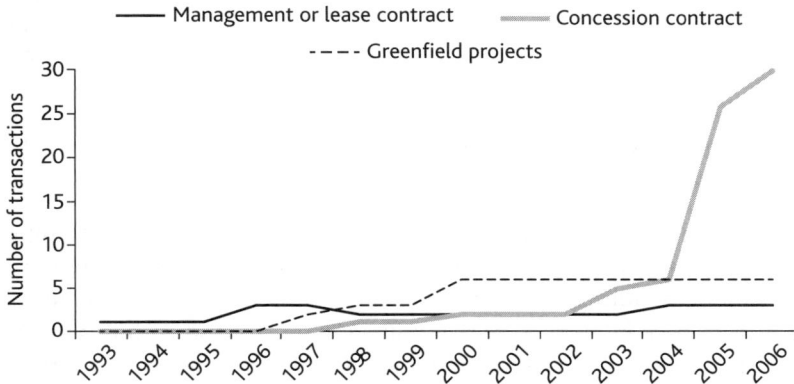

Source: World Bank (2008) *Private Participation in Infrastructure Database.* World Bank, Washington, DC. http://ppi.worldbank.org/index.aspx

are all concessions,[102] and container-handling rates, on average, at concessioned ports are double those of non-concessioned ports.[103]

Between 2000 and 2007, there were 42 major private sector transactions in the sector across 26 ports in 19 African countries, with a total investment of US$1.3 billion.

Challenges, opportunities and prospects

Challenges facing the sub-sector

Challenge 1: interaction of port authorities with different transport forms and regulators

Cargo handling at intermediary and end points of the freight logistics network is vital in a logistics system. Integration across the logistics network is therefore crucial for the efficiency and competitiveness of a nation's economy. For example, even if the privatization of ports (through concessions or greenfield developments) improves operating efficiency, problems with railway service or poor road access may induce bottlenecks further up the logistics system that have a negative impact on the overall performance of the transport system.

Challenge 2: poor operational performance and inadequate infrastructure

As noted earlier, the operating performance of African ports is generally well below that of international comparators. Where public ownership and operation dominates, outdated public management structures and bureaucratic practices by customs authorities and other agencies both contribute to operational inefficiency. With this inefficiency come higher costs and lower volumes of traffic. This result tends to hamper reinvestment efforts, meaning that laggardly ports continue to struggle.

Challenge 3: relevance of African ports given shipping trends and developments

Innovations in shipping practices continue to favor larger shipping vessels. As a result, there is a need for deep-water berths and modern container-handling facilities for these ships. Most African ports, however, have infrastructure that is ill equipped to deal with this trend.

Other developments in international shipping threaten the growth of African ports. The rise of round-the-world services may alter the role that African ports play in the route plans of major shippers. Already,

African ports are not located on the main international maritime transport routes, namely the Transpacific route (Asia–North America) and the Transatlantic route (North America–Mediterranean). This is likely to be further aggravated by the receding Arctic polar ice cap, which is predicted to open up two new major routes between Asia, North America and Europe. For Egypt, at least, these routes provide a serious risk to income generated by shipping through the Suez Canal (US$5 billion in 2011).[104]

Challenge 4: piracy concerns

According to the UNCTAD review of global maritime transport, piracy is at an all-time high.[105] It therefore remains a fundamental security issue. The majority of incidents are recorded off the coast of East Africa and in the Gulf of Guinea; the latter region has seen a surge of piracy in 2013, accounting for 31 of the 138 incidents recorded for the first half of the year worldwide.[106]

Policy opportunities

Integrate port deregulation and concessions with wider transport market reforms

For port concessions and privatization to be successful, it is necessary that any reforms enacted in the sector are coupled with wider policy reforms that ensure that feeder points in the logistics system (for example, intermodal hubs or rail operations) are capable of achieving efficiencies, and driving greater traffic volumes.

Coordinated investment across ports, railways and roads, along with other reforms to trade facilitation initiatives, would improve the operational efficiency of ports, allowing them to act as genuine gateways to and from Africa for trade.[107]

Continue to roll out private concessions

Continued roll-out of concessions will see investment levels rise with concomitant gains in port productivity. This is particularly important for container terminals, where there is expected to be a dramatic rise in containerization of traffic to and from the continent.

Privatization of port services resulted in large and rapid improvements in productivity for Columbia and other Latin American nations, with associated lower fees for port users and good commercial returns for concessionaires. Productivity levels increased in most newly privatized ports in other Latin American countries, and importantly where in many cases the ports were privatized with limited competition.

Concerns that inadequate investment would take place in the capital intensive nature of port operations has appeared unfounded, as although private operators in Latin America began with generally small investment programs, there is evidence that they later made larger investments in infrastructure expansion.[108] Importantly, these investment decisions partly speak to the quality and structure of the underlying PPP arrangements and contract. Consideration should, however, be given to concerns over inadequate investment by private operators in port *infrastructure* (the port itself). Private sector involvement will undoubtedly continue in port operations and related services, although the case for the private sector acting as a facility landlord is less clear.

It is evident that port operation privatization is not a panacea to efficiency and cost problems on its own but should rather be viewed as part of a package of reforms to improve operational competitiveness.

Additionally, allowing substantial private sector investment in port infrastructure will assist in channeling investment to high-growth areas. For example, the growth of the oil and gas industry in Africa will probably see the need for capacity expansions at port facilities based in oil-producing nations or servicing landlocked oil producers. An environment that enables private investment will see more responsive investment.

Consolidate trade flows through major regional ports

Transshipment is already fairly common for most African ports, as small local markets do not generate sufficient demand to incentivize international shipping lines to provide services to smaller ports. To counter the strength of oligopolistic shipping associations, investment should be directed to key ports that will act as regional focal points, with transshipment via smaller vessels to other, smaller ports, if needs be.

Other ports, such as either Richards Bay or Saldanha (both in South Africa), are near-dedicated facilities for a single commodity (the export of coal and iron ore, respectively) and may best be operated under private concessions by users.

Strengthen regional institutions

The problem of piracy in East and West Africa may speak to broader institutional weakness, something that the region has a whole needs to address. The importance of this is heightened considering the competition to the Suez Canal shipping route that is likely to arise from a receding Arctic toward the middle of the 21st century.

Prospects for the ports sub-sector

If this package of reforms is successfully introduced, one may expect a step-change in the performance of African ports and shipping as a consequence. This improvement will be particularly marked for non-concessioned ports.

Falling shipping costs will make imports relatively cheaper and exports more competitive, increasing trade flows. In general, there is a growing importance of ports, as rising income levels and economic activity will see a growth in trade. Demand for imports of final consumer products and inputs into industrialized processes. To lower prices for consumers and firms, productivity must be improved. This can be achieved through concession agreements—indeed, much empirical evidence exists on the successes these can bring (see Annex 2 in this chapter). Similarly, global commodity demand and African industrialization should see exports rise too. Again, productivity improvements are vital here. For both bulk and general cargo exports from Africa to be competitive on the global market, the monetary and economic costs in processing cargo must be reduced.

Regional integration will improve, though certain countries and regions stand to benefit disproportionately. The beneficiaries will overwhelmingly be the major regional ports that act as transshipment hubs and attract large vessels, with those losing out being minor ports that serve smaller markets. The proposition therefore needs to be framed correctly with country governments in order to get the requisite buy-in. That larger ports will benefit more than smaller ports does not suggest that the exercise is zero sum; instead, the policy promises to deliver greater benefits for entire regions.

Airport sub-sector

Contextual overview

Air travel is essential for opening up geographically disparate markets, facilitating economic growth and broadening development in Africa. The vast distances between centers of economic activity suggest that connectivity via air will become increasingly important. Further, the relatively poor state of Africa's land-based transport infrastructure raises the importance of air travel on the continent, particularly for the continent's 16 landlocked countries.

The African aviation industry, however, continues to lag behind the rest of the world. Despite being the second-largest and second-most populous continent, Africa's share of global air transport services was a modest 5.2% for passengers and 3.6% for freight. That said, the demand for air transport on the continent is growingly rapidly. On a disaggregated basis, the air transport market in Sub-Saharan Africa displays something of a dichotomy. In Southern and East Africa the market is growing, with three strong hubs and three major African carriers dominating international and domestic markets which are becoming increasingly concentrated.[109] In contrast, Central and West Africa have struggled with the closure of several regional airlines.

Aviation also plays an integral role in opening up the borders of African countries. Nurturing the African aviation industry therefore offers substantial opportunity to solidify regional integration on the continent. Connecting the various regions and countries across Africa via air transport may serve to drive commerce, trade and tourism. However, despite a commitment by African governments in 1999 to liberalize the aviation sector, there has been little action in the almost 14 years subsequently. Failure to fully liberalize the sector has meant reduced competitiveness and low service quality on many intra-African routes.

Infrastructure base

Descriptive characteristics and infrastructure performance

Airports and routes

It is estimated that Africa has approximately 4,000 airports, with just under 800 of these possessing paved runways. Roughly 10% of these operating scheduled services, with 53 of these airports handling 90% of the continent's air traffic.[110]

Airport infrastructure for the purposes of meeting transportation demand can be divided into two categories: *landside infrastructure* and *airside infrastructure*. Normally, the airside portion involves the infrastructure beyond security check points, which only passengers and authorized personnel can access, and is taken to include the infrastructure required to process aircraft. Landside infrastructure involves the facilities before the security check-points, including the infrastructure to process passengers or cargo as well as general terminal buildings and parking facilities.

Table 7.11: Regional distribution of airports in Africa

Region	Airports		
	Total	Paved	Unpaved
Central Africa	711	100	611
East Africa	1,342	162	1,180
North Africa	570	241	329
Southern Africa	996	182	814
West Africa	380	109	271
Total	3,999	794	3,205

Note: Figures are for 2005.
Source: UNECA (2009) [as Table 7.1]

There are three types of scheduled air traffic: intercontinental traffic; international traffic within Africa; and domestic travel. *Intercontinental traffic* in the region relies heavily on the three major hubs of Johannesburg, Nairobi and Addis Ababa. Major routes include those from South Africa to the UK and Germany (the most heavily trafficked), and North African routes between France and Morocco, Algeria, and Tunisia as well as Egypt and Germany, Russia, and the Middle East. There has also been a notable rise in the air traffic to the Middle East from various regions of the continent.[111] This is as a result of several airlines routing traffic through hubs in the region (such as Emirates, which agglomerates flights in Dubai).

As regards *international traffic*, the same three hubs of Johannesburg, Nairobi and Addis Ababa dominate, with 36% of passenger traffic moving passing through these airports. South African Airways (SAA), Kenya Airways and Ethiopian Airlines dominate these hubs respectively. Southern and East Africa have relatively well-developed networks, with many connections to domestic, regional and international destinations. In contrast, West and Central Africa only have Nigeria offering a significant number of connections.

While traffic on international routes has grown, the number of city pairs has declined sharply. Between 2001 and 2007, 229 city-pair routes were lost in Sub-Saharan Africa.[112] This is in part due to the collapse of national regional carriers in West and Central Africa.[113]

Domestic air transport and traffic volume performance vary substantially from country to country. While traffic for SSA grew by 12% across the continent between 2001 and 2007, this ranged from 67% in Nigeria to an absolute decline in volume for *half* of the countries in the AICD sample.[114]

As shown in Table 7.12, market analysis suggests that Europe will remain Africa's major route partner over the next two decades, though

Figure 7.8: Top 60 international air routes in sub-Saharan Africa (by volume)

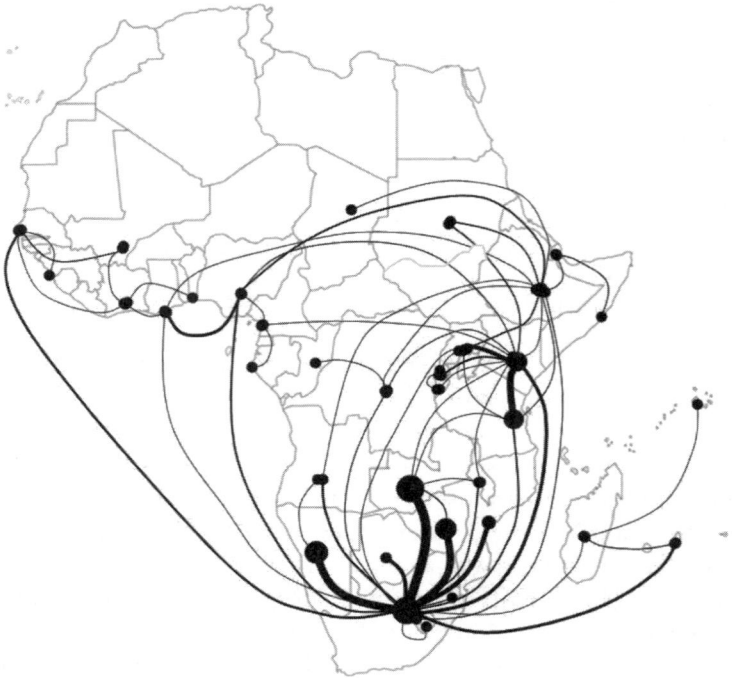

Source: Bofinger (2009) [see note 111].

all regions are expected to show strong growth. Notably, growth in revenue passenger-kilometers (RPKs) is highest for the Middle East region, which reflects the rise in importance of the hubs run by airlines in that region such as Emirates (with its hub in Dubai), Etihad (with its hub in Abu Dhabi), and Qatar Airways (with its hub in Doha).

Table 7.12: Airline passenger traffic for Africa (RPK $ in billions)

Region routes	2005	2006	2007	2008	2009	2010	2011	2012	2032	Average growth (2012-2032)
Africa–Africa	36.0	35.6	37.3	41.6	43.9	48.7	51.1	55.8	190.7	6.3%
Africa–Europe	106.4	122.0	125.3	125.6	128.2	135.5	134.1	140.5	362.1	4.8%
Africa–Middle East	16.8	20.9	23.1	24.9	32.9	36.4	39.5	49.0	208.2	7.5%
Africa–North America	3.3	4.3	4.9	6.3	8.8	11.3	11.4	12.3	38.1	5.8%
Africa–Southeast Asia	4.1	4.1	5.2	5.4	4.1	5.6	5.9	4.0	14.6	6.7%

Note: RPK is the number of fare-paying passengers multiplied by kilometres flown.
Source: Boeing Current Market Outlook 2012-2032 [see note 119].

Airside infrastructure

Almost all airports offering services have at least one paved runway. Of those airports that have been surveyed, nearly half have paved runways that are in a marginal or poor state of repair. However, airports with poor runways account for only 4% of total air traffic.[115]

Runway capacity has been found not to be a limiting factor for air traffic. Rather, capacity constraints exist with respect to the ability to enter or leave the runway via taxiways, the number of parking bays on the apron, and the terminal passenger processing capacity. Airside infrastructure capacity in these regards appears to be better in North Africa than SSA.[116]

In terms of air navigation services and air traffic control (ATC), presence of this infrastructure is unevenly distributed in SSA and tends to be concentrated in a few centers. Both South Africa and Kenya have several radar installations and are able to monitor traffic actively, while Ethiopia, home to the third largest airport in SSA, has no air traffic surveillance technology.[117] The lack of radar coverage in Africa, while concerning, is not likely to be problematic going forward. Modern air surveillance technology is migrating from radar installations towards the automatic dependent surveillance-broadcast (ADS-B) system. In this system, aircraft determine their position using global positioning system technology and transmit this to local ATC. Not only is this system more advanced but the technology is available at a lower cost.

Most airports that have capacity for more than 1 million passengers per year have an instrument landing system (ILS) to guide aircraft on their approach for landing. At smaller and less modern airports, outdated non-directional beacon systems still dominate. Satellite technology exists in this space, too, and may be a replacement option in the future.

Landside infrastructure

A more common source of capacity constraint in airport infrastructure is that of passenger terminals. As Table 7.13 indicates, many of Africa's major airports are operating significantly above stated capacity. Only Rwanda's Kigali airport and Nigeria's Kano airport exhibit excess capacity. This strongly suggest that there is a need to direct infrastructure spending towards alleviating capacity constraints at Africa's biggest and busiest airports.

Table 7.13: Airport passenger terminal capacity and volumes at selected airports

Country	City	Airport code	Reported capacity (millions)	2007 estimated seats (millions)	Capacity utilization (%)
South Africa	Johannesburg	JNB	11.9	25.3	213
Kenya	Nairobi	NBO	2.5	6.3	252
Mauritius	Mauritius	MRU	1.5	3	200
Senegal	Dakar	DKR	1	2.5	250
Tanzania	Dar es Salaam	DAR	1.5	1.9	127
Zambia	Lusaka	LUN	0.4	1.3	325
Kenya	Mombasa	MBA	0.9	1.1	122
Zimbabwe	Harare	HRE	0.5	1.1	220
Mali	Bamako	BKO	0.4	0.7	175
Djibouti	Djibouti	JIB	0.5	0.6	120
Rwanda	Kigali	KGL	4.4	0.5	11
Nigeria	Kano	KAN	0.5	0.4	80
Malawi	Lilongwe	LLW	0.2	0.4	200

Source: Adapted from Bofinger (2009) [see note 111]

Aircraft and airlines

Carriers in Africa operate a variety of aircraft, ranging from vintage Western aircraft (such as DC3s) and former USSR planes to modern Western aircraft, such as the Boeing 737 and Airbus 319. A dual trend is observable in fleet characteristics. First, average fleet age has fallen in recent years, with almost three-quarters of travel done in aircraft built in the 1980s or later, compared with only 50% in 2001. Coupled with this, the share of single-aisle aircraft has increased as airlines opt away from wide-bodied aircraft for shorter routes.[118]

African airlines are forecast to require over a thousand new planes between 2013 and 2032, worth an estimated US$130 billion.[119] For regional travel, these will predominantly be single-aisle aircraft, though wide-body aircraft will continue to be demanded for long-haul flights, particularly to Europe.[120] These new aircrafts will replace older, less efficient planes, reducing carbon emissions and lowering the cost of air travel.[121] The AICD study similarly found that in all regions wide-bodied aircraft were being replaced on regional flight routes for smaller, more efficient aircraft.[122]

In terms of the airlines themselves, the number of carriers within Africa increased between 1997 and 2007, with figures of 100 and

160 respectively.[123] Three of these carriers—SAA, Kenya Airways and Ethiopia Airlines—account for approximately 60% of the market. Across the continent, many state-owned airlines exist, often without sufficient market size and thus depending on subsidies and monopoly rights to domestic routes.

Loss in traffic volumes and reduced route networks—where these have occurred—are, in no small part, attributable to the decline and bankruptcy of several carriers in West Africa.[124] This void is being filled by SAA, Ethiopian Airlines and Kenya Airways, which has led to consolidation in the airline market.

Regulatory and competition issues

Yamoussoukro Decision

The single most important air transport policy reform was the adoption by African countries of the Yamoussoukro Decision in 1999.[125] The decision was aimed at creating an environment conducive to the development of regional and international air services that linked the continent to key centers, both at home and abroad. It called for the full liberalization of air transport services on the continent, with a gradual elimination of non-physical barriers to African air transport. This included the liberalization of scheduled and non-scheduled intra-African air services, abolishing limits on the capacity and frequency of international air services within Africa, liberalizing fares and granting universal access to the "fifth freedom of the air".[126]

Even though the decision was a pan-African agreement, the parties decided that it should be implemented by the RECs with a monitoring body to implement the decision and an execution agency to ensure fair competition. As it currently stands, the reforms under the decision are yet to be fully implemented by African states. Aviation services have not sufficiently developed on the continent as a result of this, with the consequence that in many cases air travel in Africa remains uncoordinated, erratic and of a poor service quality.

Competition between airlines

In general, air travel within Africa is considerably more expensive per mile flown than intercontinental travel, especially on routes of fewer than 4,000km. This differential arises because intercontinental routes serve larger markets than within African or domestic ones and thus have more competition among carriers.

To lower the cost of air travel in Africa, there needs to be more effective competition in the sector, and an even playing field between privately run airlines and national carrier. State-owned and supported airlines often limit the role, effectiveness and profitability of private enterprises. Commercial airline profit margins are generally relatively low; access to subsidies and monopoly route access gives state-owned airlines advantages that impinge on the ability of private airlines to compete effectively.

Financing and expenditure

Generally, the fees and charges raised by airports in Africa, particularly the larger ones, are sufficient for infrastructure requirements, often owing to the monopoly position these airports hold. Instead of being reinvested in infrastructure maintenance and expansion, however, airports are generally unable to ring-fence revenue flows which end up contributing to non-airport related budgets, such as the fiscus, or go towards subsidizing airports in the system that are not self-sufficient.

Importantly, funds need to be set aside for air traffic control and navigation technology. The installation of radar or ADS-B, as well as ILS at airports, would improve Africa's aviation safety record. Currently, however, there is little evidence that civil aviation authorities are able to garner funds for the installation (either new or as replacement) of new technologies.[127]

Despite the fact that the assets offer an attractive profile for investors, private sector participation in African airports has been limited. In most cases, involvement is in the form of concessions and management contracts, usually accompanied by relatively meagre investments. That said, there is greater scope for private investment considering that airports are essentially natural monopolies.

Challenges, opportunities and prospects

Challenges facing the sub-sector

Challenges in the aviation space are sketched in broad terms as follows.

Broad government and regulatory difficulties faced

Despite a growing understanding of the opportunities that aviation offers the African continent in terms of growth and development, the industry is often undermined by government policy. While there has been some liberalization, African governments are often reluctant to allow "open skies", given the difficulties national airlines may endure in the face of this competition. Government involvement in the aviation sector also brings a number of challenges. There are competition concerns where the state is involved in airline and airport operation,[128] and pricing concerns over the level of landing fees and passenger charges and where the fees charged for airport use do not entirely accrue to the airport. Such concerns can affect the ability of the airline industry to meet consumer demand.

Implementation challenges of Yamoussoukro Decision

Several challenges exist in implementing the "open skies" initiative for Africa. These are problems that commonly arise in the adoption of region-wide policies. The adoption of the decision is hindered by different levels of development where country self-interest often plays a role in whether support for the initiative is given. Also, airlines in various countries have different positions in the market. Those airlines with a large share of the air transport market would favor liberalization, whereas countries with "underdeveloped" airlines would be reluctant to face open competition.

Inadequate infrastructure

Although substantial progress has been made during the past decade, Africa still lags behind other regions in terms of its infrastructure. While there is evidence that runways at the region's important airports are paved, this surfacing is often in poor condition.

Further, capacity constraints are a problem in many of Africa's leading airports. While investments in airport infrastructure can substantially increase capacity, these tend to be lumpy (that is, the addition of a new terminal handling facility) and the development lifetime is long. Airport operators may approach the capacity problem in one of two ways. The airport can embark on capital projects to upgrade terminal capacity. Alternatively, pragmatic steps can be taken to alleviate the constraint in the short term, such as rescheduling arrivals and departures to allow for a greater number of flights per hour. For cash-strapped authorities, this would provide some respite, at least in the short term. However, while short-term solutions can be implemented to alleviate congestion, these are not substitutes to such investment in the longer term.

Safety and security challenges

Safety is one of the most pressing challenges facing African aviation. Almost 25% of all aviation incidents each year are recorded in Africa, despite the relatively small fraction of global air traffic that the continent constitutes. The frequency of accidents on the continent is of serious concern, given that air traffic will continue to grow. It is therefore an area that requires the urgent attention of the industry and policymakers.

Policy opportunities

Several policies are proposed to counter these challenges and improve access to air transport services on the African continent. On the whole, it is recommended that the private sector have greater involvement in both airport infrastructure and airline operation.

Complete adoption of Yamoussoukro Decision by African governments

It is important that Africa create a single market and air space to be able to benefit from economies of scale as well as achieve cost-effective management of its airspace. This should see increased connectivity through the introduction of more city pairs and a higher frequency of flights between city pairs.

Alter airport institutional arrangements to improve investment ability

Financing arrangements for airports must be redesigned so that a greater proportion of the fees and charges generated by the airport is allocated to the operation and maintenance of the airport, as well as reinvestment in the facility. Where volumes permit, concessions should be introduced as the private sector will provide access to expertise and investment capital.

Given the monopoly nature of these complexes, airports should be subject to regulation in terms of pricing and conduct. This will not only have the effect of lower prices but better regulation could assist in ensuring that fees generated from passenger throughput are used to maintain and upgrade facilities.

As it stands, 53 African airports handle 90% of the continent's air traffic. Governments, in conjunction with the private sector, should focus resources on the infrastructure of these airports and selected others that are strategically important for future growth.

Privatize airlines to optimize route allocation

State-owned airlines have generally struggled in the difficult global aviation market. As a result, some of these entities have placed a burden on the finances of African governments. These governments should investigate the option of privatizing their airlines or entering into joint ventures as seen with the highly successful case of Kenya Airways. Airlines that have set up hubs through which all long-haul flights are routed have also seemingly been successful, such as Kenya Airways and state-owned Ethiopian Airlines. These arrangements are worth examining, though demand characteristics are important and not necessarily replicable on a widespread basis.

To improve profitability of the African airline industry without comprising network connectivity (current and prospective), route prioritization needs to occur. African airlines should focus on domestic and regional routes, which tend to be profitable, and leave international routes to foreign airlines or the better-established African airlines. In this vein, there are several airline "alliances" across the globe that allow for code-sharing and the linkage of routes to long-haul destinations. A better network of flight connections will undoubtedly spur growth in air traffic.

Prospects for the airports sub-sector

By enacting a package of policy reforms, and pushing ahead with the adoption of the Yamoussoukro Decision, a number of step-changes in the aviation industry's prospects are envisaged.

The current high cost of air travel hinders further growth of the industry, with effects on wider economic development. Generally, airfares are more expensive per kilometer in Africa than anywhere else in the world. This may be a result of several factors, including market structure and high airport landing charges and passenger fees. Air travel is an increasingly costly endeavor with the rising oil price. Though the introduction of next-generation commercial aircraft will help contain these increases, close attention must be paid to the cost of air travel if the sector is to be a driver of growth and development on the continent. Liberalization of African airspace will provide more competition on routes, decreasing prices and spurring air travel. There will be concomitant benefits to economic growth and social development as a result of this.

The vast distances between countries and centers of economic activity suggest that connectivity via air will become increasingly important. A diminished involvement in the airline industry by states, while liberalizing air traffic rights, affords the private sector with the opportunity to direct resources to routes that offer profitable service. This improved connectivity will see a greater flow of people, which should serve to spur commerce and trade across Africa. Additionally, greater connectivity will see domestic and foreign airlines positioning themselves on these routes accordingly. On *domestic routes*, African airlines will provide service on domestic and shorter regional routes, while *international routes* will see foreign airlines dominate given economies of scale and other advantages. Along these routes, it is foreseen that smaller African airlines will enter into code-sharing agreements.

Certain African airports will continue to cement themselves as important hubs, and nascent hubs will form in each of the regions of Africa, with international routes being overwhelmingly directed to these hubs and then connecting flights being made to smaller centers. Adequately regulating the prices charged by airports for services rendered should see prices fall further, with the consequence of lower airfares for travelers. Ring-fencing of these revenues on behalf of airports should also improve funding for operation and maintenance of infrastructure. This particularly true for airside infrastructure, where greater spend on navigational and air traffic control can directly help improve Africa's aviation safety record.

Conclusion and recommendations

Recommendations for transport infrastructure

Transport infrastructure across all four sub-sectors—road, rail, ports, and airports—is critical for facilitating development in Africa as it provides an essential platform for accelerated economic growth. That transport services sustain economic activity and enable socioeconomic progress heightens the importance of creating an environment conducive to fast-tracked project development. If this does not occur, and necessary infrastructure is not timely constructed, Africa's growth prospects will be hampered.

There are five broad policy reform themes common to the transport sub-sectors covered in this report. The reforms proposed are an intrinsically connected package. For them to be successful in improving infrastructure development outcomes, it is important that policy reform is coordinated. However, in certain reform areas, "quick wins" should be prioritized, building confidence for tackling further, more challenging reforms.

Emphasize the role of transport corridors and regional investments

Developing transport corridors in Africa offers excellent opportunities for improving regional integration and thereby unlocking growth. Improved transport infrastructure will deepen regional integration and foster competition among firms as well as reduce inefficiencies and transport costs, which will in turn have a positive effect on intra-regional and international trade.

For both road and rail, master plans were developed several decades ago for linking the continent's major centers. Since these concepts were developed, little further work has occurred. Importantly, the development of a transport network with adequate connectivity requires that the "missing links" of networks be completed. This will allow large sections of populations to gain access to markets and essential economic and social services. Where these plans may have been too ambitious, there is a need for a re-evaluation where focus is placed on implementing the segments that make economic sense and where there is the political will at a regional level for this to be achieved (such as the North-South Corridor). For regional integration to occur in a meaningful way, local and national interests must be appropriately balanced against the interests of integration and co-operation at a regional level. RECs may be a vital mechanism to achieve this. Indeed, numerous RECs have been established to improve interregional cooperation and integration.

Alongside such initiatives is the requirement that regional and sub-regional agreements be implemented. A good example of this is the stalled Yamoussoukro Decision regarding African airspace rights. To move African aviation forward in a meaningful way requires that governments sign the accord and quicken the liberalization of the African air transport market. Framework agreements that pave the way for regional investments are an important first step in unlocking certain African infrastructure projects.

Adopt an integrated approach to transport standards and policies

Efforts are required to develop harmonized, integrated transport policies and regulations for the cross-border movement of goods and people. As trade generally entails transport through several countries, the alignment of policies, standards (such as weight, dimensions, and hygiene), certification and procedures regarding transport operations plays a major role in facilitating trade. This includes the right for foreign operators to access a national transport market for bilateral transport or cabotage,[129] the transparent allocation of road trip permits in sufficient quantities, the definition of mutually acceptable vehicle standards, and aligned policies for transit tariffs and charges.

The idea of cross-border trade and common markets may be nurtured by cross-border transport infrastructure projects. Apart from the physical infrastructure, the intangible "infrastructure" such as transport laws and regulations for border crossing (such as customs clearance and quarantine) needs to be in place. Further establishing effective institutional frameworks and strengthening existing ones are required to manage traffic effectively and ensure safety (across transport sectors), as well as ensuring that operators comply with safety and security regulations and standards. Particularly, safety improvement efforts can be improved dramatically through integrated and standardized approaches, be it piracy for maritime transport and ports or air traffic control for regional flights.

Again, the RECs may be useful for taking up what is at its heart a regional integration agenda. Indeed, in at least one instance there has been some success with this (SADC and cross-border transport markets) and the continent can learn from such practices.

Develop financing strategies to leverage private sector participation

Transport infrastructure development in Africa has a large financial requirement. Current funding mechanisms are inadequate to address infrastructure needs as they arise, let alone tackle the investment/project backlog. The private sector offers opportunities for alleviating a part of this funding constraint. The nature of infrastructure investment suggests that a carefully crafted policy and regulatory environment is necessary to encourage the emergence of private sector funding. Policymakers therefore need to do more to leverage the private sector for crowding in investment.

Currently, private sector participation in Africa is modest but growing. From under US$1 billion per annum invested in transport infrastructure in 2001, this grew to over US$4.5 billion in 2006. Similarly, the level of private sector investment for all infrastructure sectors in Africa more than tripled, to US$22 billion in 2006. Investment in transport infrastructure therefore represents just under one-quarter of private infrastructure investment.[130]

Increasingly, stakeholders realize that the mobilization of the private sector is vital to deliver infrastructure services, given the constraints faced by the public sector. An initiative that promises to tackle the infrastructure funding deficit in an innovative manner, and crowd in a mixture of public and private capital, is the Africa50 investment vehicle.

Promote regulatory and institutional reforms

Effective institutions are a key part of deepening policy reforms in the transport sector, in part with a view to attracting private sector participation. Such reform measures are necessary to strengthen regulatory mechanisms in order to create a level and well-defined playing field for participants in infrastructure development. Regulatory and institutional reform is a vital step. It is important that policy reforms balance national interests with private sector incentives while remaining mindful of regional integration imperatives. Authorities must determine the approach to a public/private split of duties and responsibilities.

First, focus should be placed on establishing effective regulatory bodies that are independent and have appropriately defined mandates. Entities that are responsible for the delivery and management of infrastructure, or the disbursement of funding to make infrastructure development possible, should also be strengthened.

Second, regulatory reforms will also grant greater oversight over the enhanced role of the private sector in infrastructure. This will promote competition in both operations and infrastructure provision. Where operators are in control of natural monopoly assets, regulators can perform an effective role of protecting and inducing pro-competitive behavior and consumer welfare.

Build institutional capacity to execute reforms

Appropriate skills in local government agencies and line ministries are often inadequate to assess and plan appropriately for the formulation, development and management of infrastructure services, as well as the enforcement of policies and regulation. This lack of technical capacity leads to a coordination failure on the part of government, across the myriad of local agencies involved in delivering transport services.

Institutional strengthening is therefore vital for the success of any major infrastructure development initiative. Many government departments, agencies and regulators in Africa are hamstrung by insufficient capacity and resources. Without addressing this, many of the initiatives proposed will not yield the expected or desired outcome. Improving the technical skills and resources available to African economies will enhance their ability to autonomously conduct project evaluation and implementation. Apart from its focus on financing instruments, Africa50 will look at ways to strengthen project preparation.

Annex 1: Overview of African transport infrastructure stocks

Table A7.1 : African transport infrastructure

Country	Road Total km	Paved	Unpaved	Rail Total km	Airports Total	Paved	Ports Unpaved	Total
Algeria	108,302	76,028	32,274	3,973	150	52	98	9
Angola	51,429	5,349	46,080	2,760	232	31	201	4
Benin	16,000	1,400	14,600	758	5	1	4	1
Botswana	25,798	8,410	17,388	884	85	11	74	Landlocked
Burkina Faso	92,495	3,857	88,638	622	33	2	31	Landlocked
Burundi	12,322	1,286	11,036	–	8	1	7	Landlocked
Cameroon	50,000	5,000	45,000	987	45	11	34	2
Cape Verde	1,350	932	418	–	8	8	–	1
Central African Republic	24,307	–	–	–	51	3	48	Landlocked
Chad	33,400	267	33,133	–	55	7	48	Landlocked
Comoros	880	603	207	–	4	4	–	2
Côte d'Ivoire	80,000	6,500	73,500	660	34	7	27	3
Democratic Republic of Congo	153,497	2,794	150,703	5,138	237	26	211	11
Djibouti	3,065	1,226	1,839	100	13	3	10	1
Egypt	92,370	74,820	17,550	5,063	88	72	16	6
Equatorial Guinea	2,880	–	–	–	5	5	–	2
Eritrea	4,010	87	3,136	306	18	4	14	2
Ethiopia	36,469	6,980	29,489	699	84	15	69	Landlocked
Gabon	9,170	937	8,233	814	53	10	43	4
Gambia, The	3,742	723	3,019	–	1	1	–	1
Ghana	62,221	9,955	52,266	953	12	7	5	1
Guinea	44,348	4,342	40,006	837	16	5	11	2
Guinea-Bissau	3,455	965	2,490	–	27	3	24	4
Kenya	63,265	8,933	54,332	2,778	225	15	210	1
Lesotho	7,091	1,404	5,687	–	28	3	25	Landlocked
Liberia	106,000	657	9,943	490	53	2	51	2
Libya	100,024	57,214	42,810	–	141	60	81	6
Madagascar	65,663	7,617	58,046	854	104	27	77	4
Malawi	15,451	6,956	8,495	797	39	6	33	Landlocked
Mali	18,709	3,368	153,411	729	29	8	21	Landlocked
Mauritania	11,066	2,966	8,100	717	25	8	17	2
Mauritius	2,028	2,028	–	–	5	2	3	1
Morocco	57,625	35,664	21,961	1,907	60	27	33	4
Mozambique	30,400	5,685	24,715	3,123	147	22	125	3
Namibia	42,237	5,406	36,831	2,382	137	21	116	2

(continued)

Country	Road Total km	Paved	Unpaved	Rail Total km	Airports Total	Paved	Unpaved	Ports Total
Niger	18,550	3,803	14,747	–	28	9	19	Landlocked
Nigeria	193,200	28,980	164,220	3,505	70	36	34	3
Republic of Congo	17,289	864	16,425	894	31	5	26	6
Rwanda	14,008	2,662	11,346	–	9	4	5	Landlocked
São Tomé and Principe	320	218	102	–	2	2	–	1
Senegal	13,576	3,972	9,604	906	20	9	11	1
Seychelles	458	440	18	–	15	9	6	1
Sierra Leone	11,300	904	10,396	–	10	1	9	3
Somalia	22,100	2,608	19,492	–	67	7	60	2
South Africa	362,099	73,506	288,593	20,872	728	146	582	8
Sudan	11,900	4,320	7,580	5,978	101	16	85	1
Swaziland	3,594	1,078	2,516	30	18	1	17	Landlocked
Tanzania	78,891	6,808	72,083	3,690	124	10	114	1
Togo	7,520	2,376	5,144	568	9	2	7	2
Tunisia	19,232	12,655	6,577	2,153	30	14	16	6
Uganda	70,746	16,272	54,474	1,244	32	5	27	Landlocked
Zambia	91,440	20,117	71,323	2,157	107	9	98	Landlocked
Zimbabwe	97,267	18,481	78,786	3,077	341	19	322	Landlocked
Total	2,464,559	550,423	1,928,762	83,405	3,999	794	3,205	116

Source: UNECA (2009) [as Table 7.1]; CIA World Factbook (https://www.cia.gov/library/publications/the-world-factbook/)

Annex 2: International evidence of successful private sector participation in the ports sector

A review of port infrastructure suggests that a multitude of models for private sector involvement exist.[131] These range from licensing, management contracts and leasing through to concessions, joint ventures and full-blown privatization. Though there is no general consensus on the relationship between port efficiency and ownership structure, case studies in port privatization suggest that greater competition leads to better outcomes. The positive international experience of private port facilities is particularly apparent in developing countries. These successes are briefly outlined below.

Colombia. Privatization took place through the establishment of separate regional port authorities for each of the country's four main ports. These authorities then contracted with private operator for the use of facilities. Together with relaxation of labor regulation, privatization of port operations was associated with efficiency increases and productivity improvements. Average waiting time per vessel fell from 10 days prior to privatization to zero days in following years, container moves per vessel per hour increased by 56%, bulk cargo tonnage per vessel per day quintupled, and operating times improved to 24 hours per day, 365 days per year.

Argentina. Initial introduction of private operators did not result in significant improvements in performance. However, with the relaxation of regulation and introduction of additional competition between 1990 and 1993, port investment and performance increased dramatically. A key reform that enabled this was the authorization of the private sector to build and operate ports for public use, which undermined the market power of existing ports.

Mexico. The concessioning of Mexico's major ports to private operators in the 1990s led to lower tariffs and improvements in efficiencies. It also generated sufficient income to end government support for ports (and, in fact, contribute tax revenues to the Mexican fiscus) and provide for investment in the modernization and expansion of port facilities.

Malaysia. The state-owned port authority of Klang, Malaysia's largest and busiest port, divested from its container operators in 1986. This resulted in an improvement in efficiency and throughput, with higher wages for employees not resulting in higher prices due to productivity gains.

Richards Bay Coal Terminal. The privately owned and operated Richards Bay Coal Terminal is a South African example of successful private terminal operation. The export coal terminal is one of the largest in the world and has undergone numerous capacity expansion projects over the years to remain ahead of the rail capacity.

Annex 3: Influences on road quality

As can be seen in Figure A7.1, the surface condition of roads is broken down into three categories: good, fair and poor. Roads in a "poor" condition are those designated to be in need of rehabilitation.[132] As can be seen, there is great heterogeneity in the quality of roads across African countries, and far more countries have road networks in a generally poor condition than those with networks in a good condition.

Gwilliam[133] identifies four proximate factors that influence road quality, which we discuss in detail below:

Figure A7.1: Condition of Africa's main road network

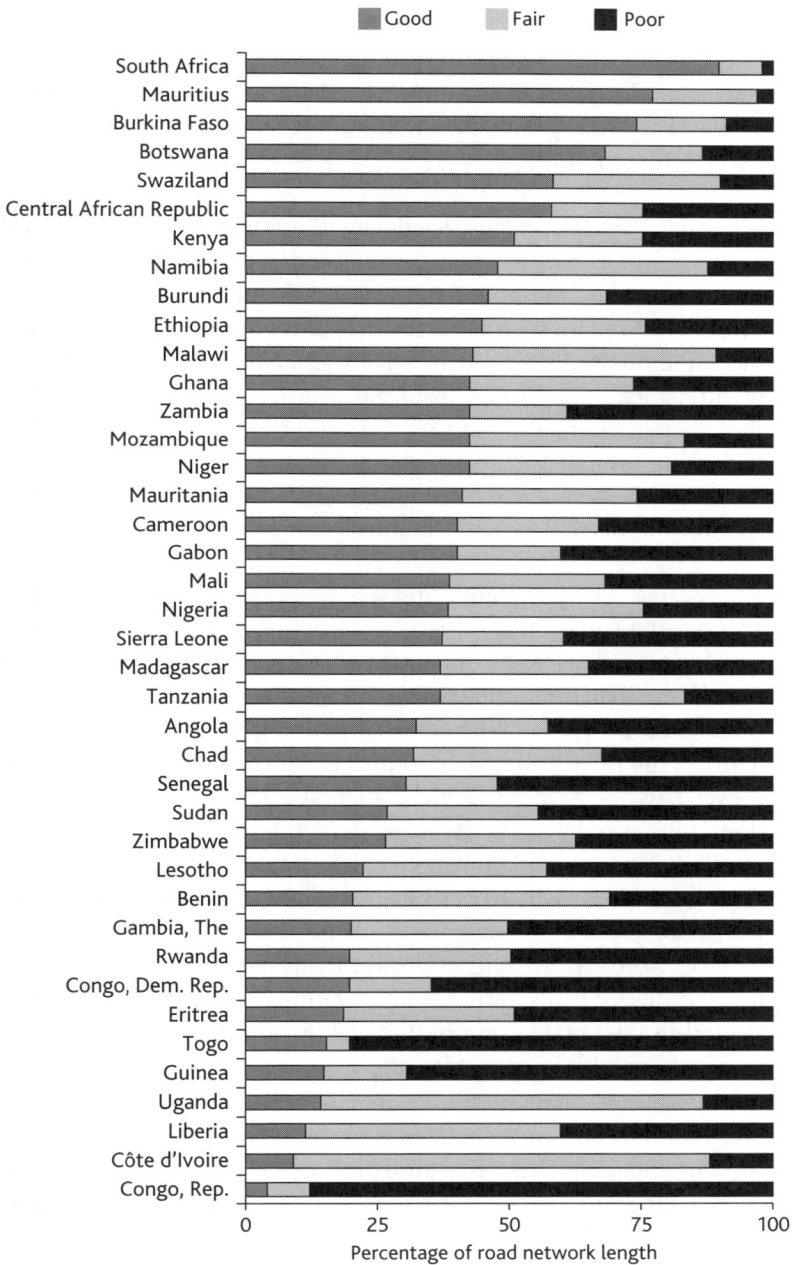

Source: Gwilliam (2011:30)

i. *GDP per capita.* Statistically significant relationship between GDP per capita and main road network condition. However, no such relationship exists with rural network. Overall, the metric explains one-third of the variation in road quality across countries. Appears one may describe this as an "affordability" metric. That said, substantial variation in road condition (for main and rural networks) exists across the LICs.

ii. *Geographic and topographic conditions.* Countries with higher and more frequent rainfall face accelerated road deterioration and therefore more frequent and serious maintenance procedures. Further, countries with large swathes of the road network crossing mountainous terrain tend to have higher road construction and maintenance costs, arising from the engineering complexities that these bring. Gwilliam[134] creates a composite climate–terrain index, indicating the relative steepness of a country's terrain and whether its rainfall is in excess of 600mm per annum. This index shows a significant correlation with the quality of road networks.

iii. *Overloading.* The prevalence and degree of vehicle overloading has an important influence on road quality. Every vehicle that travels on the road does some quantum of damage to the surface and underlying structure. Importantly, this relationship is an exponential one, based on the fourth power of the weight on each axle (axle load). This relationship is commonly referred to as the "fourth power law".[135] A heavy vehicle, such as a freight truck, therefore does substantially more damage than a light passenger vehicle. Similarly, an <u>overloaded</u> heavy vehicle imposes significantly more damage to the road than a heavy vehicle within regulated load restrictions. Gwilliam suggests that one may turn the problem on its head, so to speak, and construct roads that are better designed to carry heavy loads, citing studies on the economies of scale and operating savings that are brought about by this.[136] This may be so but it overlooks two crucially important factors. First, these roads may get increasingly cheaper to strengthen but their total cost continues to increase. This is in the face of extremely limited funding. Second, there is a mismatch in the costs and benefits of such a program. Such road strengthening comes at a social cost (postponed maintenance on other parts of the network; neglected rural network) while the benefits flow to private, profit-making entities (road hauliers). This may render the policy choice generally unpalatable.[137]

iv. *Institutional structures.* African countries that possess both road funds and road agencies, and have relatively high fuel levies that translate into maintenance expenditure, tend to have higher proportions of the main road network in fair to good condition. The limited available time series data on road condition indicates that second-generation road funds have shown improvements for the countries in which data is available.[138]

Annex 4: Role of inland water transport in Africa

Maritime ports are not the only type of "ports" in the logistics system. Inland water sources (lakes and rivers) offer great potential for relatively inexpensive, energy-efficient and environmentally friendly transport.

Twenty-nine countries have navigable bodies of inland water. While these bodies of water offer the potential for expanded transportation modes, especially in terms of access for landlocked countries, only a few of them have been adequately developed for transport services. Currently, of the total number of navigable inland waterways in Africa, five rivers and three lakes provide the bulk of the service.[139] These are listed in Table A7.1.

While these three major lakes of East and Central Africa once played an important role in transporting freight and passengers within the region, they have since declined in relative importance.

Table A7.1: Key inland waterways

Body of water	Length (km)	Surface area (km²)	Countries served
Nile River	6,650	–	Ethiopia, Sudan, Egypt, Uganda, DRC, Kenya, Tanzania, Rwanda, Burundi, South Sudan
Congo River	4,370	–	Angola, Burundi, Cameroon, Central African Republic (CAR), DRC, Gabon, Republic of the Congo, Rwanda, Tanzania, Zambia
Niger River	4,183	–	Guinea, Mali, Niger, Benin, Nigeria
Senegal River	1,790	–	Senegal, Mauritania, Mali
Zambezi River	2,574	–	Zambia, DRC, Angola, Namibia, Botswana, Zimbabwe, Mozambique, Malawi, Tanzania
Lake Victoria	–	69,000	Tanzania, Uganda, Kenya
Lake Tanganyika	–	36,000	Burundi, DRC, Tanzania, Zambia
Lake Malawi	–	29,600	Malawi, Mozambique, Tanzania

Source: UNECA (2009) [as Table 7.1]; various sources

Notes

[1] AfDB (2013) Africa50 – Concept Note, p 1. Tunis, Tunisia: African Development Bank.

[2] Yepes, T., Pierce, J. and Foster, V. (2008) *Making Sense of Sub-Saharan Africa's Infrastructure Endowment: A Benchmarking Approach*, AICD Working Paper No 1. Washington, DC: World Bank.

[3] Foster, V. (2008) *Overhauling the Engine of Growth: Infrastructure in Africa. African Infrastructure Country Diagnostic.* Draft Executive Summary of study prepared for Africa Infrastructure Country Diagnostic. Washington, DC: World Bank.

[4] AfDB (2013) Op. cit. Further, simulations suggest that increasing infrastructure to the standard of Mauritius, an economic success story, would lift African per capita growth by 2.2%. See Foster, V. and Briceño-Garmendia, C. (2010) *Africa's Infrastructure: A Time for Transformation.* Washington, DC: World Bank.

[5] Foster, V. (2008) Op. cit, p 4.

[6] Ibid, p 7.

[7] Escribano, A., Guasch, J. and Pena, J. (2008) *Impact of Infrastructure Constraints on Firm Productivity in Africa.* AICD Working Paper No 9. Washington, DC: World Bank.

[8] This is a methodology used by the United Nations Statistics Division and does not necessarily denote any political or other affiliation. See http://millenniumindicators.un.org/unsd/methods/m49/m49regin.htm for further details.

[9] There is an alternative view of the role of transport infrastructure; the development theory of unbalanced growth, shaped by economists like Albert Hirschman, suggests that investment in infrastructure such as roads on its own spurs economic development.

[10] Button, K. (2010) *Transport Economics*, 3rd edn, Cheltenham: Edward Elgar Publishing:

[11] The AICD study also found that a funding gap for the transport sector in Africa. Unlike PIDA, it argued however that there was potential for funding this gap by reallocating expenditure to the tune of US$2 billion per annum.

[12] For instance, Gwilliam, K. (2011) *Africa's Transport Infrastructure: Mainstreaming Maintenance and Management.* Washington DC: World Bank, p 314 states that about three-quarters of transport infrastructure spending is from public funds.

[13] Mbeng Mezui, C.A. (2010) 'Unlocking infrastructure development in Africa through infrastructure bonds', *GREAT Insights*, vol 2, no 4, May–June.

[14] Mbeng Mezui C.A. (2010) Ibid.

[15] AfDB (2013) Op. cit.

[16] Mbeng Mezui C.A. (2010) Op. cit.

[17] Gwilliam, K. (2011) Op. cit, p 17.

[18] Ibid, p 71.

[19] Ibid, p 18.

[20] This figure is given by the AICD technical report. See Gwilliam (2011) Op. cit.

[21] Unclassified roads are those that have not been classified according to a system of road numbering (highway, urban, and so on).

[22] Carruthers, R., Krishnamani, K., and Murray, S. (2009) *Improving Connectivity: Investing in Transport Infrastructure in Sub-Saharan Africa*, AICD Background Paper 7, Washington, DC: World Bank, p 6.

[23] Alternative measures include road-to-vehicles ratios and road surface types.

[24] There appears to be a negative correlation between road density and geographic size.

[25] Gwilliam (2011) Op. cit, p 17.

[26] Ibid, p 36.

[27] Four proximate factors have been identified as influencing road condition and quality: GDP per capita; geographical and topographical conditions; overloading; and the country's institutional structures governing roads. See Appendix 7.3 for an exploration of each of these.

[28] Gwilliam (2011) Op. cit, p 29.

[29] This is measured as the value of an existing road network as a percentage of its maximum theoretical value.

[30] Gwilliam (2011) Op. cit, p 33.

[31] Ibid.

[32] Notably, the TAH network does not cover South Africa given that the country was excluded when the scheme was formulated due to the existence of the apartheid regime. With the advent of democracy, it has been proposed that the Cairo-Gaborone section be extended to Pretoria and the Tripoli-

Windhoek link to Cape Town (UNECA [United Nations Economic Commission for Africa], 2009. *Africa Review Report on Transport*. Sixth Session of the Committee on Food Security and Sustainable Development. August 2009. Addis Ababa, Ethiopia, p 8).

[33] AfDB (2003) *Review of the Implementation status of the Trans African Highways and the Missing Links. Volume 1: Main Report, Final Report*, Stockholm: Sweco International; Nordic Consulting Group; UNICONSULT; BNEDT [consulting firms that put the report together], p 7

[34] Ibid.

[35] Ibid, p 9.

[36] Gwilliam (2011) Op. cit, pp 19-20.

[37] AfDB (2003) Op. cit, p 7.

[38] Gwilliam (2011) Op. cit, pp 19-20.

[39] Ibid, p 38.

[40] Ibid, p 17.

[41] Ibid, p 76.

[42] Ibid, p 55.

[43] These countries are: Benin, Burkina Faso, Cape Verde, Cameroon, Chad, Congo (Democratic Republic of Congo), Côte d'Ivoire, Ethiopia, Ghana, Kenya, Madagascar, Malawi, Mali, Mozambique, Namibia, Niger, Nigeria, Rwanda, Senegal, South Africa, Sudan, Tanzania, Uganda, and Zambia.

[44] Gwilliam (2011) Op. cit., p 50.

[45] Ibid, p 77.

[46] Ibid, p 59.

[47] For instance, see Gwilliam (2011) Op. cit., p 44.

[48] In the case of community roads, their "true" public ownership characteristics lead to them generally not being assigned to any organization, with no clear responsibility for maintenance.

[49] While dispersion of expenditure to GDP ratios is prevalent, the middle-income African countries are clustered around 1% of GDP; Gwilliam (2011) Op. cit., p 49.

[50] Ibid.

[51] For infrastructure more generally, the recent penalties imposed by South Africa's Competition Commission on construction firms in that country raises the spectre of collusive behaviour in civil engineering projects.

[52] See, for instance, Gwilliam (2011) Op. cit, p 63.

[53] AfDB (2003) Op. cit, p 12.

[54] See Robinson, R. and Stiedl, D. (2001) 'Decentralization of road administration: case studies in Africa and Asia', *Public Administration and Development*, vol 21, no 1, pp 53-64.

[55] Harral, C. and Faiz, A. (1988) *Road Deterioration in Developing Countries.* Washington, DC: World Bank.

[56] Though traffic volumes cannot be boosted overnight, there must be consideration of what constraints exist for traffic volumes. Lifting these volumes will improve the ability of the private sector to involve itself in providing road infrastructure. Where this is at country border posts, there must be harmonization of regulatory requirements. Where it is intra-national, other factors must be considered.

[57] From an economic theory perspective, a fuel levy is not strictly (allocatively) efficient as there is some cross-subsidization that naturally occurs, and is a sub-optimal charge to direct user fees. However, it has the advantage of recycling revenue generated by a certain class of users.

[58] Notably, Common Market for Eastern and Southern Africa (COMESA) has recently established a regional competition authority. See www.comesacompetition.org.

[59] In 2008, Southern African Development Community (SADC) mooted the implementation of a harmonized set of vehicle and transport regulations for member states. Although this has yet to be finalised, this is a positive sign of things to come.

[60] AfDB (2003) Op. cit, p 10.

[61] The dominance of this railway-port link is demonstrated in the historic institutional arrangement whereby ports and railways were commonly integrated entities.

[62] Solomon, V.E. (1983) 'Transport', in F.L. Coleman (ed) *Economic History of South Africa.* Pretoria: Haum.

[63] Gwilliam (2011) Op. cit, p 84.

[64] The bogie is the undercarriage and wheel set component of a wagon or coach.

[65] Differences do exist in the estimation of rail network length in Africa. UNECA (2009, Op. cit., p 13) suggests that the continent had a total rail network length of just over 90,000km in 2005 (though in the same report in recorded around 77,000km of rail line).

[66] Carruthers et al (2009) Op. cit, p 10.

[67] UNECA (2009) Op. cit, pp15–16.

[68] Ibid, p 16.

[69] UNECA (2009) Op. cit, p 15.

[70] Japan International Cooperation Agency (JICA) (2009) *The Research on Cross-Border Transport Infrastructure: Phase 3, Final Report, March 2009*, Tokyo, Japan: JICA, p v.

[71] Gwilliam (2011) Op. cit, pp 83, 85.

[72] Ibid, p 92.

[73] Mbangala and Perelman (1997), cited in Gwilliam (2011) Op. cit, p 116.

[74] Gwilliam (2011) Op. cit, p 92.

[75] Ibid, pp 88–9.

[76] Ibid, p 107.

[77] Ibid.

[78] Ibid, p 90.

[79] Ibid, p 87.

[80] Ibid, p 106.

[81] Ibid, p 91.

[82] Any accidents that necessitate clean–up costs have to be covered by the operator (accident costs). Further, it incurs and internalizes the effect of any congestion on its network (congestion costs). See Leiman, A. (2003) 'Efficiency and road privatisation: bidding, tolling and the "user pays" principle', *South African Journal of Economics*, vol 72, no 2; Lishman, D. (2013) 'A critical evaluation of road pricing in South Africa'. M.Com. dissertation. Available at: https://open.uct.ac.za/handle/11427/5749.

[83] Mbangala (2001), cited in Gwilliam (2011) Op. cit, p 106.

[84] By the nature of the rail business, these two factors are inextricably linked.

[85] UNECA (2009) Op. cit, p 17.

[86] Ibid, p 17.

[87] United Nations Conference on Trade and Development (UNCTAD) (2011) *Review of Maritime Transport 2011*. Geneva: United Nations, p 92.

[88] UNECA (2009) Op. cit, p 17.

[89] Gwilliam (2011) Op. cit, p 182.

[90] Ibid, p 184.

[91] Ibid, p 183.

[92] These are Nigeria, Angola, Equatorial Guinea, Sudan, the Republic of Congo, Gabon, Chad, Cameroon, Mauritania, Côte d'Ivoire, and the DRC, Nigeria and Angola (Gwilliam, 2011:193).

[93] Gwilliam (2011:193)

[94] Radelet and Sachs (1998); cited in Bell. M., and Bichou, K. (2008) *South African Network Infrastructure Review: Ports*. National Treasury: Pretoria

[95] UNECA (2009:18)

[96] World Bank (2007) *Port Reform Toolkit*, 2nd edn. Washington, DC: World Bank.

[97] This model is slightly more complicated, as the regulatory function is conducted by an independent authority, and the Transnet National Ports Authority is part of larger state–owned enterprise Transnet, which often also operates terminals through another division of the business.

[98] Swedish Maritime Administration (2010) *Shipping and the Port Sector in Sub-Sahara Africa*. Prepared for the Swedish International Development Cooperation Agency, Norkopping, Sweden: Swedish Maritime Administration, p 44

[99] McTiernan, A. (2006) *Customs and Business in Africa: A Better Way Forward Together*. London: Business Action for Improving Customs Administration in Africa.

[100] Gwilliam (2011) Op. cit, p 195.

[101] Leigland, J. and Palsson, G. (2007) "Port reform in Nigeria", *Gridlines*, Note No. 17, March.

[102] These are the ports of Abidjan (Côte D'Ivoire), Dar es Salaam (Tanzania), Doula (Cameroon), Toamasina (Madagascar), and Djibouti (Djibouti). See Mundy, M. and A. Penfold (2009) *Beyond the Bottlenecks: Ports in Sub-Saharan Africa*. Africa Infrastructure Country Diagnostic Background Paper 13, Washington, DC: World Bank.

[103] Ibid.

[104] *The Economist* (2012) 'The melting north', 16 June.

[105] UNCTAD (2011) Op. cit, p 119.

[106] Capital News (2013) 'Piracy slows worldwide but surges off west Africa', available at www.capitalfm.co.ke/news/2013/07/piracy-slows-worldwide-but-surges-off-west-africa.

[107] An example is the Maputo Corridor Development project, which targets road, rail, border posts, port and terminal facilities between the port of Maputo and South Africa, Swaziland and Zimbabwe, with positive results; see Gwilliam (2011) Op. cit, p 186.

[108] Gaviria, J. (1998) *Port Privatisation and Competition in Columbia*, Public Policy for the Private Sector, Note No 167. : Washington, DC: World Bank.

[109] The hubs are Johannesburg, Nairobi and Addis Ababa with the respective carriers from the associated countries

[110] Notably, the number of airports offering scheduled services has declined in recent years. In 2001, 318 airports offered services; by 2007, this was down to 280, with only 261 offering year-round service; see Gwilliam (2011) Op. cit, p 140.

[111] Bofinger, H.C. (2009) *Air Transport: Challenges to Growth*, Africa Infrastructure Country Diagnostic Background Paper 16. Washington, DC: World Bank.

[112] Ibid.

[113] Ibid.

[114] Ibid.

[115] Gwilliam (2011) Op. cit, p 145.

[116] Bofinger (2009) Op cit.

[117] Ibid, p 6.

[118] Gwilliam (2011) Op cit, p 162.

[119] Boeing (2013) *Current Market Outlook 2013-2032*. Chicago, IL: Boeing.

[120] Ibid.

[121] Ibid.

[122] Bofinger (2009) Op cit.

[123] Schlumberger, C. (2010) *Open Skies for Africa: Implementing the Yamoussoukro Decision*. World Bank, Washington, D.C.

[124] Notably, these include Air Afrique, Air Gabon, Ghana Airways, and Nigerian Airways; see Bofinger (2009) Op cit.

[125] The decision eventually adopted also included measures addressing safety, security and environmental issues.

[126] The regulation of international air transport is guided by the so-called eight "freedoms of the air". The first and second are technical freedoms to fly over a foreign country or to land for refueling. The third and fourth are commercial freedoms to carry passengers from a carrier's home country to another or vice versa. The fifth, sixth and seventh freedoms concern the rights to carry passengers between two foreign countries, either as an extension of a flight from the home country (fifth), through a stop in the home country (sixth), or without ongoing service to the home base (seventh). The eighth freedom is the right to carry traffic between two points in a foreign country. See International Civil Aviation Organization (ICAO) (2013) 'Freedoms of the air', available at http://legacy.icao.int/icao/en/trivia/freedoms_air.htm.

[127] Schlumberger, C. (2007) 'Emerging issues for air navigation services: a challenge for developing countries', Paper presented at Aviation Safety, Security and the Environment conference, McGill University, Montreal, 15-17 September.

[128] Where airports and the dominant carrier are both owned by a particular government, concerns may be raised about preferential treatment of the airline at airport facilities (such as access to peak flight times and parking bays).

[129] Cabotage is the transport of goods or passengers between two points in the same country by a vessel or an aircraft registered in another country.

[130] UNECA (2009), Op. cit.

[131] Bell, M. and Bichou, K. (2008) *South African Network Infrastructure Review: Ports*. Pretoria: National Treasury, p 68.

[132] Gwilliam (2011) Op. cit, p 29.

[133] Gwilliam (2011) Op. cit, pp 67-9.

[134] Ibid, p 69.

[135] Hau, T. (1992) *Economic fundamentals of road pricing: A diagrammatic analysis*, World Bank Policy Research Working Paper Series WPS 1070. Washington, DC: World Bank.

[136] Gwilliam (2011) Op. cit, p 69.

137 For further discussion on this point, see: Lishman, D. (2013) 'A critical evaluation of road pricing in South Africa', M.Com. dissertation. Available at: https://open.uct.ac.za/handle/11427/5749.

138 Gwilliam (2011) Op. cit, p 29.

139 UNECA (2009) Op. cit, p 19.

EIGHT

Africa's prospects for infrastructure development and regional integration: information and communications technology sector

Lishan Adam and Maurice Mubila

Overview of the information and communications technology ecosystem in Africa

The African information and communications technology (ICT) ecosystem is becoming a potent force for stimulating economic growth and social development. The ecosystem comprises both supply side (physical infrastructure) and demand side (application and services and its use), which require equal attention and investment.

Led by the mobile sector, the African ICT infrastructure has seen dramatic growth over the past decade. The mobile network has now bridged the voice communication gap that has been the preoccupation of African policymakers for many decades. Two-thirds (69%) of the African population had access to mobile SIM cards in 2014.[1] About half of the African population has access to mobile services, when one discounts for the ownership of multiple SIM cards and age factors.[2] Mobile footprint covers almost all population centers in the continent, but there are still pockets of rural areas that have to be connected.

The internet penetration in Africa lags very much behind mobile sector growth. Globally there are 750 million households of which 44% are connected. In Africa only one-tenth of the households are connected.[3] Individual use of the internet in Africa also lags behind the rest of the world. Internet penetration stands at 19%, five times below the world average. Figure 8.1 shows that Asia and Pacific and the Arab States have twice as much penetration by 2012.

Africa is also unable to catch up with the world gradual shift from the narrow band to the broadband and from access to "quality of access". Unlike in more mature markets, where fixed and fiber-based services

Figure 8.1: Internet penetration

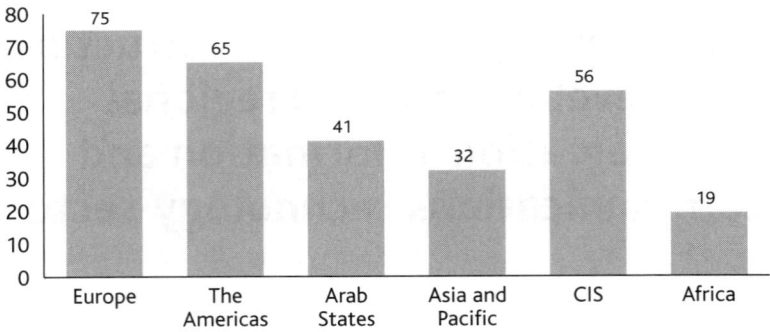

Source: International Telecommunications Union (2014) [see note 1]

are the predominant broadband platform, in Africa mobile networks provide the primary means of broadband access. Fixed broadband that often determines the quality of access at the institutional levels was 0.4% in 2014 compared with the world average of 10%. Three-quarters of consumers in developed countries have access to the smartphones and the mobile broadband. While Africa has seen considerable progress with its mobile broadband penetration, which grew from 2% in 2010 to 19% in 2014, the region still trails behind the rest of the world.

Broadband infrastructure is a new agent for change—a critical input for African prospective growth. Broadband facilitates access to economic opportunities and social welfare that were previously

Figure 8.2: Broadband penetration in 2014

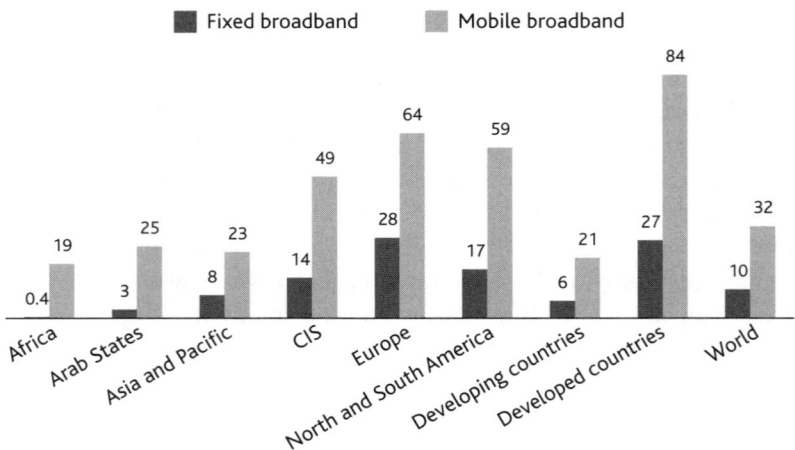

Source: International Telecommunications Union (2014) [see note 1]

inaccessible to most people in Africa. Mobile broadband has already been driving financial inclusion through mobile banking and mobile money. The delivery of public service, civic and political engagement is increasingly becoming dependent on high-speed communications. Broadband can help improve the quality and delivery of public services to people in rural and remote areas, helping youth to become more skilled and productive and earn higher income. Its role as a transformative technology is similar to the impact that electricity has had on productivity, growth and innovation.[4]

Broadband infrastructure is cross-cutting in the sense that it is not only an infrastructure by itself but also an enabler for other sectors including education, health, transport, energy and finance. The same basic broadband infrastructure can be used and reused by all sectors, thereby creating a public good with an economy of scale. Therefore the focus of ICT development over the next decade needs to pay attention to the development of broadband and its ecosystem.

The economic implication of broadband is immense. Qiang and Rossotto (2009) have estimated that a 10% increase in broadband penetration would yield a 1.21% and 1.38% increase in Gross Domestic Product (GDP) growth on average for high-income and low-/middle-income countries respectively.[5] Broadband enables economic diversification, the development of domestic ICT industries and new applications, such as services and content including new business products and applications (for example, software as a service), online services (for example, internet banking) and entertainment applications, that will create a new sets of information economy jobs for the African youth. Broadband enables trade development and integration. Recent development in national research and education networks (NRENs) indicates that broadband can transform teaching, research and learning over the next decade, ensuring Africa's improved footings in the scientific and technological innovation. Broadband can also play an important role in improving the delivery of healthcare, which can have implications of the quality of health services in the rural areas.

For broadband to make these impacts, a "critical mass" of institutions, businesses and households need to be connected. Once critical mass levels are met, and prices become sufficiently affordable, usage increases, resulting in improved social well-being and political participation. Studies show that the broadband impact threshold begins at around 30% penetration and its sizeable benefits on the social and economic growth can only be achieved through higher usage.[6] Therefore, a significant investment is required to spur Africa's broadband network over the next three decades.

While access to basic internet connection using narrowband broadband services is important, the true benefits only occur when users are able to access higher speeds that enable them to download audio visual content. The demand for high-speed connection is a moving target that requires planning for superfast speed network from the beginning. Broadband services providers in some countries have begun offering 1 Gigabit per second (Gbps) connections to the end user in order to support applications such as multiple streams of high definition TV over the internet, cloud computing and real time simulation. In effect, the major services that affect the quality of life of users, such as telemedicine, multiple education services and environmental protection, demand bandwidth in tens or thousands of Megabits per second (Mbps).

African international bandwidth per user was less than 10 Kilobits per second (Kbps) in 2013 compared with 500 Kbps of bandwidth per user in Europe.[7] The bandwidth gap can only be bridged with concerted investment by the private sector and public–private partnerships. Massive investments are required not only to build out fiber networks, but also high-speed access networks.

Applications and services

The development in applications and services did not track the available infrastructure in Africa. The government is the main driver of applications in ICT sector in the region; yet the full use of ICTs leaves much to be desired. A survey by the United Nations shows that e-government is slow to develop and uneven across the continent. While Tunisia, Mauritius, Egypt, Seychelles, Morocco and South Africa, which ranked high in providing online services to citizens, business and other institutions, made it to the top 50 countries, 16 others were listed at the bottom of the Electronic Government Development Index in 2014.[8] Growth in electronic commerce and other services has also been limited to those countries that have well-established online financial transaction systems. Overall, a lot of effort is still needed in building data centers, creating interoperable information services, and ensuring online transactions to facilitate delivery of government services to the population in Africa.

The private sector is pressing ahead with providing applications and services; yet there is a lot of room for improvement especially in tapping into the global ICT enabled services business. A.T. Kearny's Global Services Location Index lists Tunisia, Ghana, Morocco, Mauritius, Senegal and South Africa in the top 50 countries for offshoring

Table 8.1: Bandwidth requirements for different services

Upload speeds		
500 Kbps to 1 Mbps	**5 to 10 Mbps**	**100 Mbps to 1 Gbps**
• VoIP • SMS • Basic e-mail • Web browsing (simple sites) • Streaming music (caching) • Low-quality video (highly compressed)	• Telecommuting (converged services) • File sharing (large) • Internet Protocol Television (IPTV), standard definition (SD) (multiple channels) • Switched digital video • Video on demand, SD • Broadcast video, SD • Video streaming (2–3 channels) • Video downloading, high definition (HD) • Low-definition tele-presence • Medical file sharing (basic) • Remote diagnosis (basic) • Remote education	• Telemedicine • Multiple educational services • Broadcast video, full HD • Full IPTV channel support • Video on demand, HD • Remote server services for Telecommuting

Download speeds		
1 to 5 Mbps	**10 to 100 Mbps**	**1 to 10 Gbps**
• Web browsing (complex sites) • E-mail (larger attachments) • Remote surveillance • IPTV, SD (1–3 channels) • File sharing (small, medium) • Telecommuting (ordinary) • Digital broadcast video (1 channel) • Streaming music	• Telemedicine • Educational services • Broadcast video, SD and some HD • IPTV, HD • Gaming (complex) • Telecommuting (high quality video) • High-quality tele-presence • Surveillance, HD • Smart, intelligent building control	• Tele-presence using uncompressed video streams, HD • Research applications • Live event digital cinema streaming • Telemedicine remote control of scientific or medical instruments • Interactive remote visualization and virtual reality • Remote supercomputing

Source: California Broadband Task Force (2008) 'The state of connectivity. Building innovation through broadband, final report of CBTF', available at www.cio.ca.gov/broadband/pdf/CBTF_FINAL_Report.pdf

opportunities.[9] A dozen of other countries from Kenya to Namibia, and from Ethiopia to Rwanda, are establishing information technology hubs and incubation centers that have created the fertile ground for ICT applications and services. The World Bank lists 90 tech hubs that have been building applications and services with broader implications to social and economic development of the continent.

Figure 8.3: Tech hubs across Africa

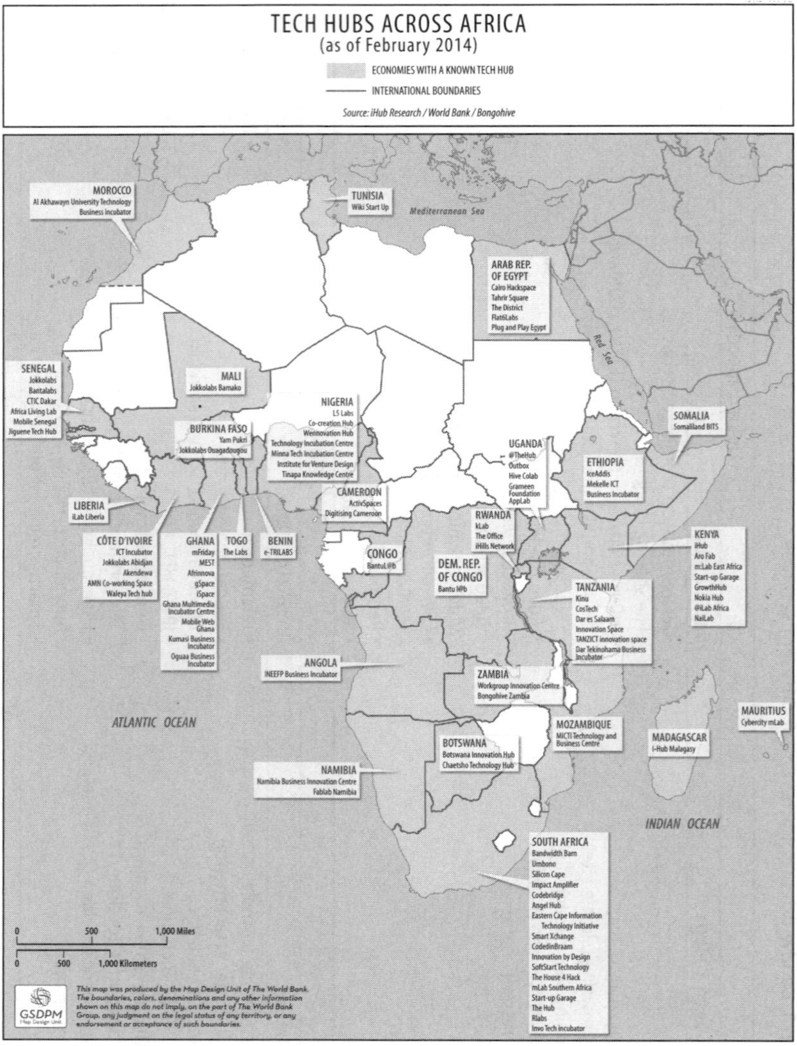

Source: Kelly, T. (2014) 'Tech hubs across Africa: Which will be the legacy-makers?', available at http://blogs.worldbank.org/ic4d/tech-hubs-across-africa-which-will-be-legacy-makers

The growing adoption of mobile services, cloud computing and social networking implies that applications and services need to be developed for the distributed networked environment. Mobile devices are becoming the main delivery platforms for applications and services. Gartner predicted that by 2013 mobile phones would overtake personal computers as the most common web access device worldwide and that by 2015 over 80% of the handsets sold in mature markets would be smartphones.[10] The efforts made in promoting applications for mobile devices will undoubtedly have greater implication on the future development of the continent.

The significant use of social network implies that huge personal and institutional data is being generated online. By 2020, the average person will maintain 130 terabytes of personal data (today it is ~128 gigabytes).[11] Data is also being made available through mobile devices, software logs, cameras, microphones, radio frequency identification readers, and wireless sensor networks. The manipulation of huge amounts of data is another frontier for the private sector along with the security of network, which has become an increasingly challenging field as the size of network grows and the sophistication and determination of those who commit cyber-crime increases.

The private sector needs to step up the development of applications and services. Universities need to establish not only advanced research and education networks but also test beds for advanced applications and services that can be deployed for solving development challenges.

The users' environment

The availability of infrastructure, applications and services is not matched by the use. A study of the Program for Infrastructure Development in Africa (PIDA) sponsored by AfDB, AUC and NEPAD shows that in 2012 only 1 Terabits per second (Tbps) (4%) of the available 25 Tbps submarine cable capacity was in use in the West African region. The situation has not improved much in the recent years.[12] There are about 200 million internet users in the continent, of which the majority live in urban areas. This leaves 81% of the population without access to the internet and unable to partake in the benefits it offers for empowerment, job creation and access to health, education and other forms of information.

There are many reasons why ICT usage is that low compared with the availability of infrastructure and services.

Lack of access to basic infrastructure like electricity and broadband network is the primary user constraint. This is exacerbated by the high costs associated with providing access to ICTs. In addition, internet use is constrained by lack of awareness among potential users of its benefits and the lack of relevant (that is, local or localized) content and services. There is also disparity between men and women, and rural and urban populations in accessing these new technologies. Women have less access to ICT services because of the underlying disparity between men and women in accessing and controlling resources including communications services. The rural/urban disparity is all too obvious due to the high costs of providing ICT services in the disproportionately high number of rural areas of the region.

The root causes of these challenges rests in the deeper social and economic problem of African countries. About three-quarters of the African population earns less than US$2 a day, an income that is not sufficient to access mobile broadband services that are generally higher than 5% of the Gross National Income (GNI) per capita. Other factors affecting low levels of ICT sector development and use include limited international and domestic backbone network, limited spectrum availability, high provider taxes and licensing fees and unfavorable market structures.

Figure 8.4: User challenges

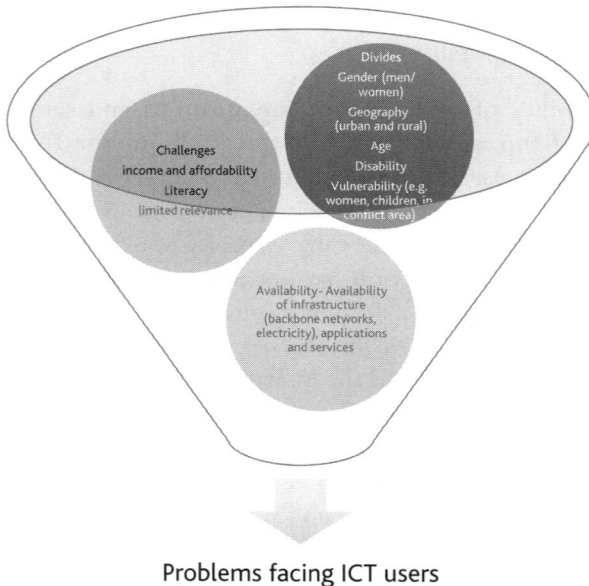

Problems facing ICT users

340

Policy and regulatory environment

The policy and regulatory environment is the main cause for the high cost of services, hefty licensing fees, spectrum unavailability, and under-resourced infrastructure development. Separate regulators have been established in over 40 countries in Africa, but the region still remains far behind the rest of the world in terms of creating legitimate, independent and capable regulatory institutions.

Furthermore, ICT sector regulation has become increasingly complex, with growing competition among players that have significant market power and new Over the Top (OTT) operators. At the customer end, there are threats to privacy, the loss of control over data, and child protection concerns. ICT systems are becoming increasingly vulnerable to cyber-security and cyber-crime. Converged regulators have been set up in Tanzania, South Africa, Kenya, Uganda and Mauritius to address these challenges, but the progress is far from adequate.

Many regulators are still grappling with the challenges of governance, and institutional independence. Policymakers are not only resistant to change, but also control regulatory decisions, making it difficult for investors to have confidence in the market. Policies are generally far behind regulatory provision and the political will to change the status quo has not been readily forthcoming in most countries. The lack of political will manifests itself in several ways, including protection of incumbents, delays in regulatory and policy approval through the legislative process and inadequate provision for financial independence of regulators.

The most dominant policy and regulatory issues revolve around extending affordable broadband access to the majority of the population, creating a level playing field for network operators and redefining universal access strategies to cover broadband access. Promoting infrastructure sharing, open access and spectrum re-farming (in-band migration) are some other areas that need to be improved in order to spur network development. Further areas that are becoming increasingly important include:

- rationalizing jurisdiction and regulatory status;
- competition and tariff regulation;
- open access and "net-neutrality";
- consumer protection and privacy;
- online content; and
- security issues.

Increasing convergence also means that there is a need for shift to open more market segments to competition and update licensing and spectrum management practices in order to foster growth in broadband networks and converged services. A rise in competition and new service providers will also require an enhanced focus on dispute resolution. The protection of intellectual property rights, transparency of regulation, and protection of privacy and personal data are becoming increasingly important.

It is evident that true progress in the ICT sector in Africa only occurs with investment in the entire ecosystem. The continent does not only require infrastructure expansion projects that extend electricity and broadband networks, but also needs investment in applications and services, e-government and in building capable and legitimate regulatory institutions.

Current investment in the African broadband ecosystem

Overview of current investment in the broadband infrastructure supply chain

The Africa region has seen a significant interest in infrastructure expansion programs over the past two decades, partly driven by mobile operators. There has also been significant attention from multilateral development banks such as the World Bank and the African Development Bank, which have increased their lending for telecommunications projects, particularly for fiber-optic networks and for the stimulation of demand for network services. The World Bank has invested over US$1 billion over the past decade through regional communication infrastructure programs (RCIPs) that cover Central, East, South and West Africa. The African Development Bank's investment in submarine cable included a senior loan of US$55 million to the Main One submarine cable project and US$15.4 million to the consortium of the East African Submarine Cable system (EASSy).

Broadband investment in the region has occurred in the whole supply chain from international access to last mile connectivity. At the top of the chain is investment in the international connectivity to provide the link to the rest of the world. The second layer is a regional network that connects countries to each other. Regional investment is important in Africa where 16 landlocked nations require access to coastal submarine cable landing stations. The third layer is a national backbone that links major population centers from which connections to the last mile can be extended.

Figure 8.5: Broadband investment supply chain

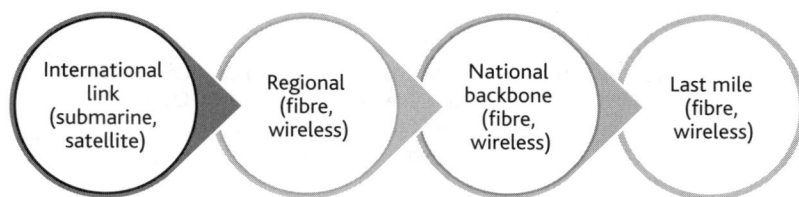

Investment in the international segment

The investment in new submarine cables was driven by lack of access to international network, especially on the eastern African coast. Apart from satellite, the SAT3/WASC/SAFE cable was the only option for connecting Africa to the rest of the world up until 2009. Submarine cable suppliers such as Alcatel were also exploring greenfield opportunities following the decline in international submarine markets. This has generated a momentum for submarine cable projects that were launched between 2004 and 2009 and entered into service between 2009 and 2012. By 2012, the private sector and a consortium drawn from traditional fixed-line and mobile operators has raised close to US$4 billion and has resulted in the availability of bandwidth in the excess of 25 Tbps.

International submarine links have thus far focused mainly on linking Africa to Europe, Asia and the Middle East. Operators have realized the importance of direct links between Africa and the Americas in recent years. Consequently, some projects have been proposed, but only the South Atlantic Cable System (SACS) is currently under construction. The SACS is a joint project of Telebras, Odebrecht and Angola Telecom and aims to connect Luanda to Sao Paulo. Commissioned in 2016, the project is expected to provide connections between Africa and South America, thus strengthening economic ties between the regions and influencing internet routing patterns by reducing the number of hops between Africa and the United States.

Investment in regional networks

Africa's cross-border network presents the main bottlenecks in extending international bandwidth to users. Figure 8.7 shows that the regional fiber network is very much concentrated in the Southern and Eastern Africa and around Nigeria in the West, but it is largely

Table 8.2: Submarine cables investment in Africa (US$ million)

Cable	Length (km)	Investment (US$)	Capacity	Region	Ownership
SAT3/SAFE	14,350	600	120 Gbps (to upgrade to 240 Gbps)	West Africa	Consortium of Operators
SEACOM	13,700	650	1.28 Tbps	East Africa	US 25% South Africa 50% Kenya 25%
Main One	7,000	240	1.92 Tbps (up to 4.96 Tbps)	West Africa	Private: individual and institutional investors
TEAMS	4,500	130	1.28 Tbps	East Africa	Consortium of operators
GLO1	9,500	800	640 Gbps (up to 2.5 Tbps)	West Africa	Telco operator
EASSy	10,000	265	3.84 Tbps	East Africa	Consortium of African operators
WACS	14,000	600	5.12 Tbps	West Africa	Consortium of Telco operators
ACE	14,000	500	5.12 Tbps	West Africa	Consortium of operators
SEAS	1,900	35	320 Gbps	Indian Ocean	Submarine Cable System (SCS), Société Réunionnaise du Radiotéléphone
LION	1,000	50	1.3 Tbps	Indian Ocean	Mauritius Teleco, Orange Madagascar
LION2	2,700	75	1.28 Tbps	Indian Ocean	Telecom Kenya Mauritius Teleco, Orange Madagascar, Emtel Ltd., Société Réunionnaise du Radiotéléphone

Source: www.manypossibilities.com and websites of cable operators

unavailable in Central Africa. Connection between North Africa and the rest of the regions is very limited.

West Africa

Substantial progress has been made in the past decade to improve connectivity within West Africa and the area has benefited from a considerable fiber network build-out by private sector operators.

Figure 8.6: Undersea cables in 2016

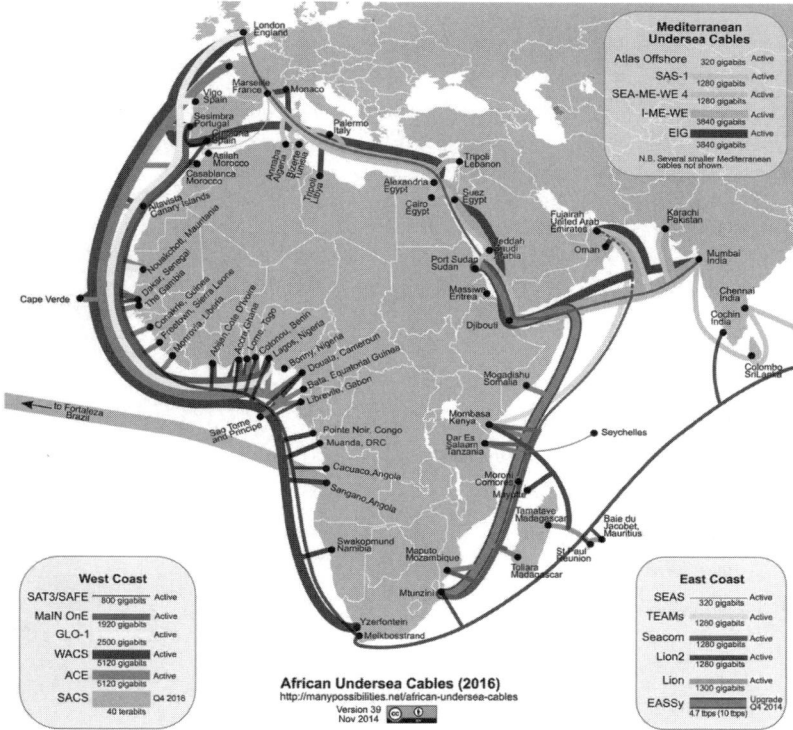

African Undersea Cables (2016)
http://manypossibilities.net/african-undersea-cables
Version 39 Nov 2014

Source: www.manypossibilities.net

Phase 3 Telecom and Suburban Telecom, Sonatel (Orange), Maroc Telecom and Globacom are the main players in the Economic Community for West Africa States (ECOWAS) region. National telecom operators, including Vodafone of Ghana, ONATEL of Burkina Faso and Togo Telecom, have also been coordinating among themselves to extend broadband connectivity across their borders. This has led to better integration of broadband networks in the region, although regulatory and interconnection issues still need to be resolved in many segments. There is also a proposal to interconnect West Africa to Algeria and Morocco through the Fientis project, as shown in Figure 8.8.

Other projects that have a significant implication to the West African regional backbone include the following.

- The ECOWAS Wide Area Network (ECOWAN) project, which aims to deploy an 8,000km terrestrial fiber and WIMAX network

Figure 8.7: Regional networks, 2012

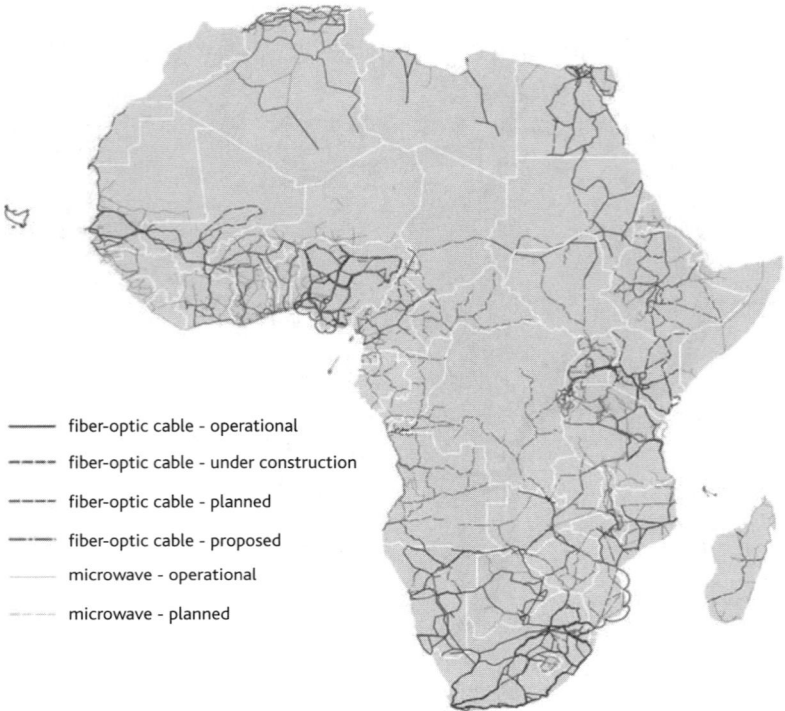

fiber-optic cable - operational

fiber-optic cable - under construction

fiber-optic cable - planned

fiber-optic cable - proposed

microwave - operational

microwave - planned

Source: World Bank (2011) 'Africa's ICT Infrastructure, Building on Mobile Revolution', http://siteresources.worldbank.org/INFORMATIONANDCOMMUNICATIONANDTECHNOLOGIES/Resources/AfricasICTInfrastructure_Building_on_MobileRevolution_2011.pdf

to connect government offices at a cost of US$366 million. The African Development Bank and the Islamic Development Bank are the major sponsors of the project, with the Islamic Development Bank providing support for Gambia and Sierra Leone.

- The West African Regional Infrastructure Program (WARCIP), a US$300 million project financed by the World Bank to support connectivity in Burkina Faso, Sierra Leone, Liberia, Guinea, Guinea Bissau, Mali, Gambia, Niger, and Togo. The first phase of the project focuses on setting up carrier-neutral landing stations. The second phase, at a cost of US$60 million, will focus on extending connectivity within Togo and Mauritania.[13]

- The West African Power Pool project, which intends to expand fiber access through the regional fiber grid.

Figure 8.8: Major players in regional broadband connectivity

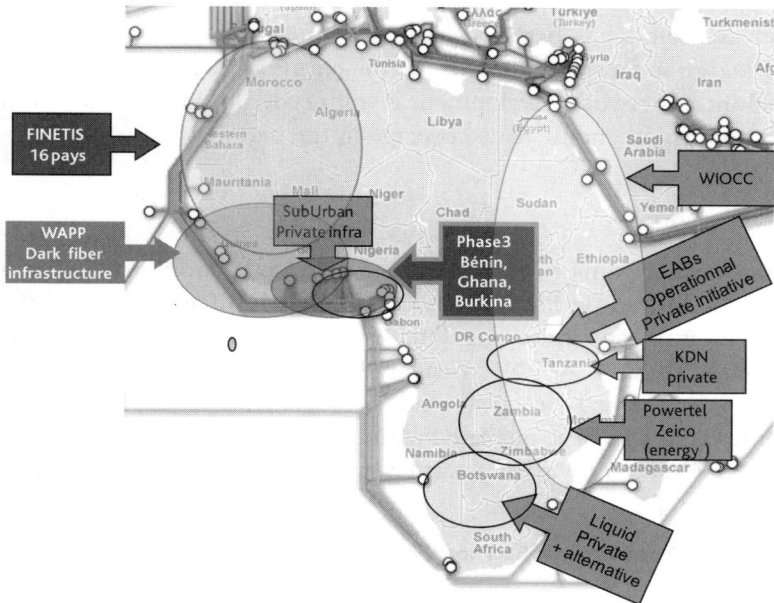

Source: PIDA Information and Communication Technology Report, unpublished

Notwithstanding progress, there are still limited competing cross-border links in West Africa; therefore the cost of access remains relatively high. The high cost of primary infrastructure such as electricity and transport across the borders, and the difficulty in obtaining right of way and cross-border permits, have not only compounded the challenges of extending connectivity but also increased the cost of the networks.

Central Africa

Central Africa does not have active private sector investment in the regional networks; therefore connectivity in the region remained far behind the rest of Sub-Saharan Africa. The launch of the Central African Backbone (CAB) project by the World Bank has brought a boost to connectivity in the region. CAB aims to develop broadband network that increases the geographic coverage and provide services at competitive rates.

The project, which is now in its fifth phase, aims to connect Central African countries beginning with Chad, Cameroon and Central African Republic, extending to other Central African countries like Congo and Gabon with ultimate connection between the Eastern,

Southern and Central African nations through the Democratic Republic of Congo, which borders many nations in the three regions, and also with a link between Chad and Sudan.

Progress so far shows that despite the efforts of CAB, a considerable amount of network development is still needed to improve access to the population and increase coverage in the region.

Eastern Africa

Cross-border connection within East Africa was coordinated within the East African Backbone Network (EAC–BIN) framework and the bilateral arrangements among different operators in the region. Mobile operators such as MTN, Vodacom and Airtel, Tanzania Telecom Company Limited have also made arrangements to establish cross-border links that have increased regional connections within the East African Community (EAC) partner states (Burundi, Kenya, Rwanda,

Figure 8.9: Central African Backbone, 2012

Source: www.arce.bf/IMG/pptx/5_Presentation_Banque_Mondiale_FRATEL_March2012.pptx

Tanzania and Uganda). Kenya Data Networks (KDN) is another player in the region and has established over 6,000km of optical fiber stretching from Kenya to the Democratic Republic of Congo with connections to Uganda and Rwanda.

Further north, Ethiopia has established connections to Sudan and Djibouti. It has begun negotiating a link to the EASSy and TEAMS cables through Kenya. Eritrea, Somalia and Southern Sudan are the only countries in the East Africa region that do not have a significant cross-border connection.

Southern Africa

Cross-border links within Southern Africa are coordinated by telecoms operators within the context of the Southern African Telecommunication Association and South African Development Community (SADC) South African Regional Information Infrastructure project. The project involves upgrading the links

Figure 8.10: The East African backbone network

EAC-BIN Fibre Route

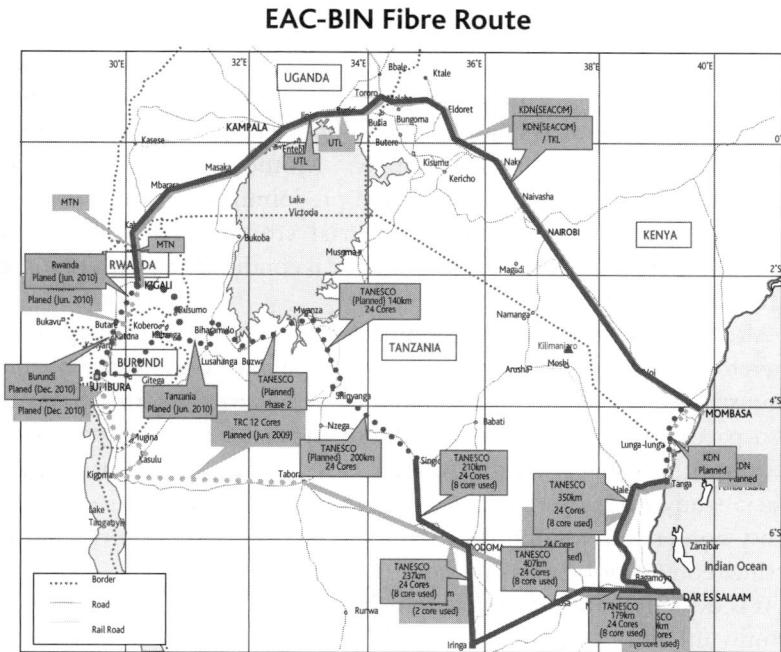

Source: East African Community, http://www.eac.int/infrastructure/index.php?option=com
_docman&Itemid=143

between South Africa and Zimbabwe, and between Zimbabwe and Botswana and Zimbabwe and Mozambique.

In addition, some of the national/regional backbone projects have taken advantage of the available electricity grids, railway lines and oil pipelines and their right of way to install fiber-optic cables within the region. The electricity parastatal Escom has been installing fiber along its grid in South Africa and in neighboring countries. In Namibia, Nampower has installed fiber-optic lines along all its new power lines. In Zimbabwe, the operator Powertel has rolled out optical ground wire infrastructure. In Zambia, the fixed-line operator Zambia Telecom has leased fiber from the Copperbelt Energy Corporation and the Zambia Energy Supply Company.

Liquid Telecom is becoming a key player in the development of a regional backbone network in Southern Africa with connection to Central Africa via the Democratic Republic of Congo (DRC). Liquid Telecom's network extends 17,000km across Uganda, Kenya, Rwanda, Zambia, Zimbabwe, Botswana, Lesotho and South Africa with a link to Lubumbashi in the DRC.

Northern Africa

Despite having good international connectivity via neighboring Europe and a relatively well-developed national backbone network, connection across Northern Africa is very limited. There is only one terrestrial fiber-optic system known as Ibn Khaldoun, which provides a regional link between Algeria, Libya, Morocco, and Tunisia. It is operated by incumbent operators and predominantly used for voice communication. There is no terrestrial cross-border connection between Libya and Egypt to expand optical continuity across all North African countries.

Alternative infrastructure spanning from Mauritania to Egypt will therefore have significant potential to increase interconnectivity within countries of the same culture and language across North Africa. It also paves a way for linking North Africa to the rest of the region. Realizing this potential, the African Development Bank has carried out a study on a North African backbone network that suggests a cross-border link among the Arab Maghreb Union countries at an estimated cost of US$203 million.

It is evident that private operators have become the main engine of bandwidth development in Africa. However there is still a substantial gap in regional cross-border networks. A study of the PIDA concludes that there is a need for various segments across Africa, shown in

Figure 8.11, to be established over the next five years at a cost of US$1.4 billion.[14]

National backbones

The development of national backbone networks is another bottleneck in extending ICT to African users. Backbone networks do not only connect major cities but also serve as a routing point for cross-border traffic. A well-designed and implemented backbone can also serve as a drop-off point for last mile connectivity using wireless and other modes of access. An example of a national backbone in Namibia, shown in Figure 8.12, indicates that a well-developed national backbone provides for last mile connectivity and cross-border links.

Figure 8.11: Cross-border, regional and national ICT infrastructure in use by operators or under construction in 2012 and expected regional link by 2012

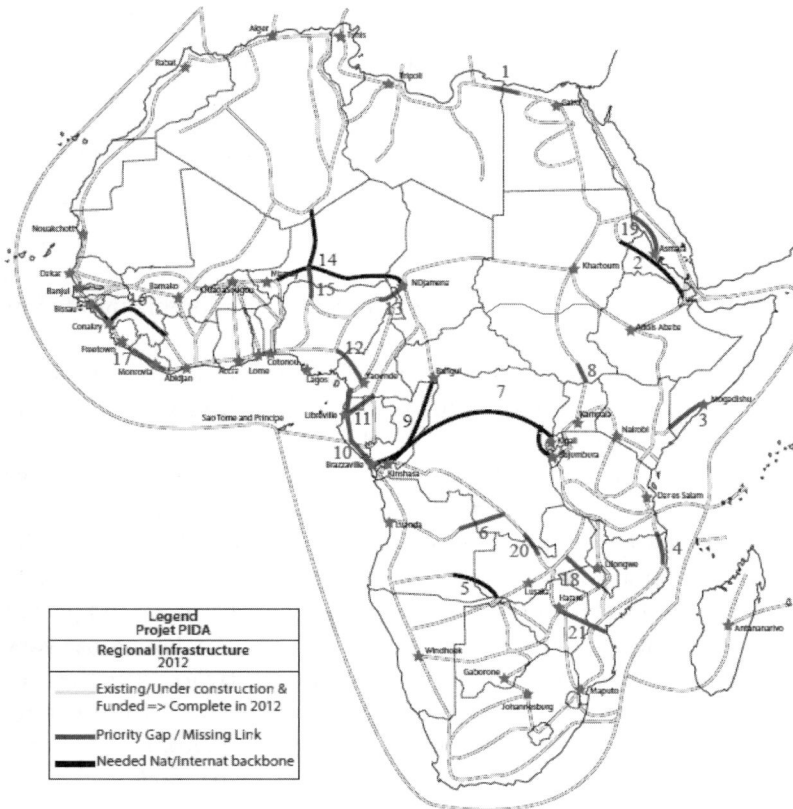

Source: PIDA Information and Communication Technology Report, unpublished

Figure 8.12: Namibia national backbone and last mile connectivity, 2010

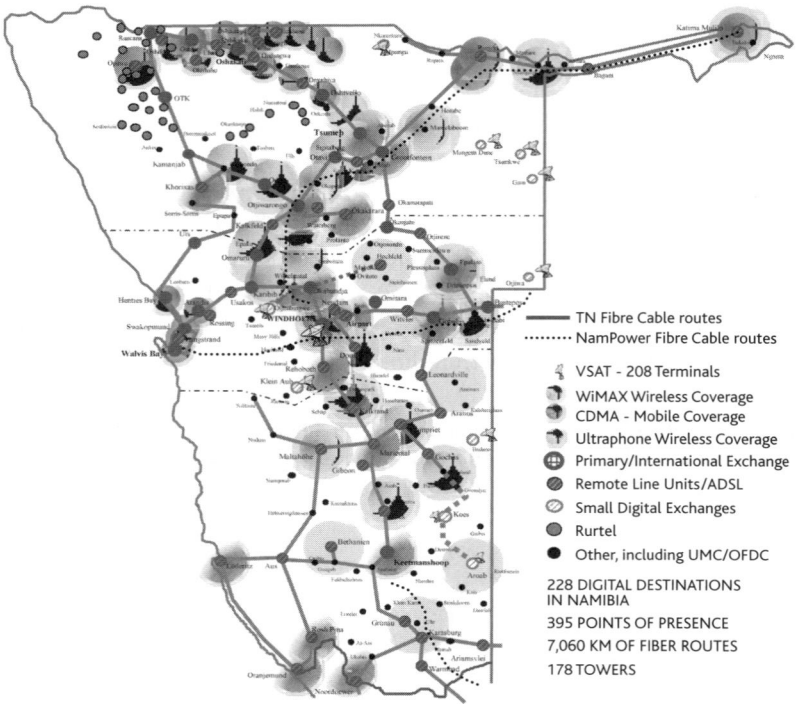

TN Fibre Cable routes
NamPower Fibre Cable routes

VSAT - 208 Terminals
WiMAX Wireless Coverage
CDMA - Mobile Coverage
Ultraphone Wireless Coverage
Primary/International Exchange
Remote Line Units/ADSL
Small Digital Exchanges
Rurtel
Other, including UMC/OFDC

228 DIGITAL DESTINATIONS IN NAMIBIA
395 POINTS OF PRESENCE
7,060 KM OF FIBER ROUTES
178 TOWERS

Source: Namibia Telecom, Annual Report, 2010

Namibia connects to Botswana, South Africa and Zambia through its backbone network.

There has been significant investment in national backbone networks throughout Africa in the recent years. Angola, Botswana, Burundi, Ethiopia, Ghana, Kenya, Malawi, Madagascar, Rwanda, Tanzania, Sudan, South Africa and Uganda are among the countries that have launched projects for the development of their national backbone networks using diverse schemes. Most countries have taken the advantages of a popular vendor credit scheme that has been readily available from China. Ethiopia, for example, has spent a good part of its US$1.5 billion vendor credit in expanding its backbone network by installing well over 10,000km fiber-optic network over the past decade. It borrowed an additional US$1.6 billion in 2013 to extend access networks. Tanzania borrowed US$170 million from the Chinese Export Import Bank in two phases to build its national backbone. Cameroon and Mali are other countries that have used vendor credit schemes, each borrowing US$45 million from the Chinese Exim

Bank. Many other countries are following suit due to more favorable loan terms with longer grace and repayment period, and lower interest rates from the Chinese Export and Import Bank.

Côte d'Ivoire and Rwanda have used local resources to extend connectivity. Côte d'Ivoire is spending US$210 million to build a 6,700km fiber backbone. The Rwanda backbone, which cost US$96 million, was funded by the government and implemented by Korean Telecom.

Private sector companies such as Orange, MTN, Vodacom and Airtel have also been building their national backbones to support mobile communications and broadband internet access. In Nigeria, for example, the terrestrial fiber backbone covers 35,000km, of which MTN owns 7,000km, Glo 1,000km, Multilinks 5,417km, Phase 3 Telecom 2,000km and Suburban Telecom 3,500km. There has also been significant investment by incumbents such the Botswana Telecommunications Corporation, Namibia Telecom, the Société Nigérienne des Télécommunications in Niger, SotelMa of Mali, Onatel of Burkina Faso, Econet Telecom of Lesotho, TDM of Mozambique, LibTelco of Liberia and the Malawi Telecom Ltd. In Burundi, incumbent operators came together to establish a Burundi Backbone System company that builds and operates a national broadband network on behalf of investors.

A significant wireless and microwave backbone also exists that provides support to mobile and other forms of communications. In 2012, the total national operational fiber route is estimated at around 500,000km. Fiber laying costs between US$100 to US$150 per meter; therefore between US$50 billion and US$75 billion has already been spent in the establishment of national backbones.

Table 8.3 shows that the deficit in national backbone is unevenly distributed among countries, with some, such as Morocco, Tunisia and South Africa, having a significant density in terrestrial network, while most of the countries in Central Africa have very limited national infrastructure. It is estimated that about 40% of African population is within a 25km radius of fiber infrastructure,[15] but actual access is lower when connection points to the last mile taken into the account. Over 30 countries in Africa have yet to build their full backbone network to support economic growth.

Last mile connectivity

The low level of fixed broadband penetration means the last mile connectivity has largely been provided by the mobile broadband

Table 8.3: National backbone in Sub-Saharan Africa

Country	Operational fiber (km)	Country	Operational fiber (km)
Algeria	65,000	Libya	13,000
Angola	7,000	Madagascar	3,300
Benin	1,694	Malawi	2,000
Botswana	5,000	Mali	3,400
Burkina Faso	1,300	Mauritius	600
Burundi	1,250	Mauritania	4,000
Cameroon	5,141	Mozambique	7,000
Cape Verde	1,500	Morocco	32,100
Central African Republic	287	Namibia	9,050
Chad	830	Niger	1,200
Comoros	160	Nigeria	35,917
Republic of Congo	1,750	Rwanda	4,200
Côte d'Ivoire	4,700	Sao Tome and Principe	400
Democratic Republic of Congo	637	Senegal	3,500
		Seychelles	200
Djibouti	122	Sierra Leone	120
Egypt	27,000	Somalia	300
Equatorial Guinea	287	South Africa	163,450
Eritrea	120	South Sudan	970
Ethiopia	16,000	Swaziland	400
Gabon	2,000	Tanzania	10,674
Gambia	500	Togo	1,300
Ghana	5,600	Tunisia	20,000
Guinea Bissau	500	Uganda	3,820
Guinea (Conakry)	100	Zambia	6,770
Kenya	13,300	Zimbabwe	4,320
Lesotho	900	Zambia	6,770
Liberia	200	Zimbabwe	4,320

Source: Various country reports

operators. Data from the International Telecommunications Union (ITU) shows that the continent's internet subscription is largely provided by mobile broadband services. Mobile broadband penetration, which was just 2% in 2010, has jumped to 19% in 2014.

The private sector is a key investor in the growing data services. Between 1998 and 2008, the private sector invested US$56 billion, which led to significant penetration of mobile network in the region.[16] Mobile operators of the Global System for Mobile communication Association (GSMA) have also announced that they are committed US$50 billion between 2007 and 2012 in new investment across the continent to expand and upgrade networks.[17] A study by the African Development Bank in 2013 found out that the private sector has actually spent that amount, which has resulted in the expansion of mobile broadband services. The investment is likely to continue to bring connectivity to a significant portion of the African population.

Last mile broadband connectivity in Africa still presents a daunting challenge in areas that are not commercially viable and among populations that cannot afford high-end mobile devices where mobile broadband is available. The lack of primary infrastructure like electricity and roads is other challenge. This implies that operators need to use a mix of technologies to reach rural and underserved areas and governments need to provide incentives to operators to invest in underserved areas.

Experiences in Latin America suggests that extending basic access to voice communication and the internet followed by improving the quality of access (increasing the bandwidth) is the best approach for achieving last mile connectivity.[18] According to the World Bank, providing the African population with voice communication and basic internet access will require an investment of US$17 billion over the next 10 years.[19] Bringing universal and affordable broadband access to well over 600 million households by the year 2050 will be a daunting project that requires enormous investment.

Investment in application and services

The public and the private sector is also investing heavily in ICT applications and services. Data on current investment in applications and services is very much unavailable, because countries lack well-established mechanisms to track ICT investments by government institutions and enterprises.

The region has seen a substantial growth of e-government projects, some driven by policymakers to attain efficiency gains, others by international development institutions like the World Bank. Typical initiatives include the design of e-government strategies that define the enterprise architecture, major e-service projects, policy and institutional frameworks, government service delivery channels and frameworks for standardization, integration and implementation. Benin, Burundi, Botswana, Ethiopia, Gabon, Kenya and Tanzania are among the countries that have developed e-government strategies.

These and many others rely on public and donor funding to implement various e-government programs. The World Bank's e-Benin, e-Ghana and e-Rwanda projects provide resources to stimulate e-government by supporting the design of e-government strategies, developing e-services and usage, promoting electronic participation, utilizing more mobile and social media tools and making government data available online.

A substantial investment has also been made to provide support for connecting schools and universities. National school networks have been linking primary and secondary schools, training teachers with new applications and tools to encourage ICTs in the teaching and learning process. Recent initiatives in national and regional research and education networking have also been on the rise. The UbuntuNet Alliance for Research and Education Network in Eastern and Southern Africa and the West African Research and Education Network (WACREN) are among the initiatives that have received international and national support to interconnect African NRENs to each other and connect them to other regional RENs and to the internet at high speeds to enable researchers, educators and students to collaborate effectively and participate in global research and education networking activities.

Efforts are also underway to establish information technology parks to stimulate ICT investment and ensure the participation of local enterprises in global IT-enabled services, including business process outsourcing and call centers. In addition to Egypt, Tunisia, Mauritius, Morocco and South Africa, which are ranked as favorable destinations for IT-enabled services, countries like Ethiopia, Ghana and Kenya are investing heavily to establish the necessary infrastructure in order to attract investment and tenants from foreign countries, facilitate the incubation of ICT enterprises and increase the contribution of ICT to the economy.

Private IT enterprises are also pushing ahead in delivery of services. The number of enterprises involved in information technology consulting, computer and network systems integration, web hosting, data processing, voice and data communications services and wired and wireless communications services is growing, along with those developing applications that have substantial impact on development at the international level. Applications such as MPESA, which is widely used for mobile money transfer in Kenya, and Ushahidi, a crowd-mapping application that is being used for reporting emergencies around the world, are good examples of the extent of growing innovation in the region.

Table 8.4: Investment in technology parks in Africa

Name of digital city	Size in hectares	Investment (US$ millions)	Purpose	Status
Ebene City (Mauritius)	70	100	100 multinational companies located, 5,000 jobs created	Operational
Konza City (Kenya)	2,000 (165 in first phase)	7,500	100,000 jobs by 2030 with 10% contribution to GDP	Under development
Ethio ICT Park (Ethiopia)	200	270	Attract investment and tenants from foreign countries, create incubation for ICT companies, increase contribution of ICT to economy	Under development
Smart Village (Egypt)	300	Undisclosed	Serve as Business Process Outsourcing (BPO) hub, attract investment and location of foreign firms, contribute to innovation and economic growth	Operational

Source: Websites of the different initiatives

Investment requirement for the ICT ecosystem over the next three decades

Prediction challenges

Africa needs superfast broadband by 2050 to attract foreign investment in the sector, to support a growing demand for e-government services, social networks and business applications, and to ensure that enterprises and individuals compete at global levels. It is difficult to predict the size of the broadband that will be required three decades on. Many uncertainties will shape the evolution of broadband demand and supply including the behavior of private companies and consumers, the economic environment and technological advances.

Broadband usage is a moving target. Experience of educational and research networks has already shown that any additional available bandwidth is likely to be consumed by users and their growing devices, tools and social networks. There are already 50 billion connected devices[20] worldwide and this is going to increase by many folds by 2050.

357

The future of the internet and broadband will be driven by the Internet of Things, networks of sensors and smart devices, embedded systems, the semantic web and cloud computing. Users' generated content in diverse formats and languages will continue to consume enormous bandwidth. The public sector will continue to provide access to a huge amount of data, with private sector also playing a key role as witnessed by Google's earth project.

Broadband is becoming an important requirement in access to education, health and e-business. Broadband will underpin future cars, smart grids, and intelligent transportation systems. The more that governments and the private sector deliver their services online by adopting the cloud computing environment, the greater the demand on broadband networks. These trends show that it is extremely difficult to predict the future of the development of the broadband ecosystem.

Lessons from the most connected country and international targets

Another possible approach for the prediction of the future of broadband is setting a forward goal based on the experience of the most connected countries. South Korea is the most connected country today, with 97% broadband penetration at the household level. According to the *State of the Internet* report from Akamai for the first quarter of 2013, the average internet speed in South Korea during the quarter was 14.2 Mbps, with a peak internet connection speed of 44.8 Mbps. Over 60% of Korea's broadband is based on fiber technology.[21]

South Africa, which featured in the Akamai report, has an average internet speed of 2 Mbps. Most of the African countries have bandwidths in the order of a few Kbps. Evidence from Korea suggests that the benefit of broadband can only accrue with such a high level of penetration; thus there is a need for setting high broadband targets for African countries.

There are already a number of proposed targets for increasing the global average internet bandwidth over the coming decades. The ITU broadband "Goal 20-20" proposes broadband internet speeds of 20 Mbps for US$20 a month, accessible to everyone in the world by 2020.[22] In September 2012, the European Commission (EC) published its broadband strategy, which that stipulates that all its citizens should have access to a basic level of broadband (2 Mbps) by 2013. As it moves towards a superfast broadband world, the EC wants to see 100% access across European households to at least 30 Mbps by 2020, and for 50% of European citizens to subscribe to 100 Mbps services by then.[23]

The United States has taken a similar step. Its broadband plan proposes that 100 million homes should have speeds of 50 Mbps download and actual upload speeds of 20 Mbps by 2015. It also suggests that "every American community should have affordable access to at least 1 gigabit per second broadband service to anchor institutions such as schools, hospitals and government buildings".[24] The United States sees institutional access points as a critical for innovation and growth, an issue often overlooked in developing countries' broadband access debates.

African has not set its broadband target for household and anchor institutions. However, it is evident from the plans in the other continents that Africa needs to reach at least 50% of its households with a broadband capacity of 100 Mbps and link all anchor institutions like government agencies, schools, universities, and so on with Gbps connections by 2050. This requires significant investment both in the underlying backbone networks and access infrastructure.

Investing in the broadband value chain

In order to achieve a higher penetration than is witnessed in most connected countries, Africa needs to invest in the broadband ecosystem—both the supply and demand aspects. This involves investment on five fronts:

- improving international bandwidth;
- bridging the regional broadband gap;
- building national backbones;
- extending connectivity to households and institutions; and
- stimulating network demand by investing in applications and services.

Improving the international bandwidth

The first wave of investment in connecting Africa through undersea cable is almost over, except for the South Atlantic Cable System, which was expected to be commissioned at the beginning of 2016. The existing undersea cables have excess fiber capacity that can be turned on when needed. As that fiber gets lit up and supply rises, prices should fall for enterprises and other users in African countries.

The demand for bandwidth is also on the rise as more countries get connected to regional fiber networks and as more users get access to smart phones that provide access to quality internet resources.

Regional demand for bandwidth is estimated to grow at least by 50% on annual basis.[25] The demand from populated countries like Ethiopia and those nations that are not well connected, like Eritrea and South Sudan, will likely to soar over the next 10 years, making the current bandwidth insufficient. Research and education networks are expected to consume most of the currently available bandwidth. For example, the Kenyan Research and Education Network alone consumes a third of the equivalent of the Ethiopian international bandwidth; therefore the demand for schools, colleges and universities will continue to flood the African international bandwidth.

A second wave of undersea cable upgrade and construction will likely to begin in the 2020s to meet growing demand. Based on the current investment cycle, it is estimated that private investment of between US$2 billion and US$3 billion is required to upgrade the network and build new fiber routes to connect Africa to the Americas and improve connectivity within the east coast of the region.

Bridging the regional broadband backhaul gap

Closing the regional broadband gap is a priority for PIDA. PIDA's candidate projects, shown in Figure 8.11, are expected to complete the immediate trans-boundary links requirements in the region. The estimated cost for the completion of the immediate trans-boundary connections is US$1.4 billion. When completed, each country would have access to multiple fiber landing stations. Landlocked countries would have access to alternative routes.

Box 8.1: PIDA key strategies

- Guarantee international access: each country to have fiber access to at least two different submarine cables.
- Guarantee of secure terrestrial route: each country to have access to its choice of submarine landing stations by at least two different terrestrial infrastructures to minimize costs and ensure reliability and security.
- Landlocked countries charter: landlocked countries to have guaranteed access to submarine landing stations in coastal countries at a similar cost enjoyed by coastal countries.
- Continental interconnectivity: each country to be connected with terrestrial fiber infrastructure to its neighbor based on the most economic criteria.

- Optimal international and national bandwidth use: each country to have a National Internet Exchange Point (IXP) and access to regional exchange points to ensure local interconnection between national operators to reduce the level of external interconnection, improve performance, encourage local applications development and build economies of scale to attract off-continent operators to peers locally, thereby reducing the need for African operators to pay any transit fees to foreign operators.
- Competitive open market: each country to have a competitive market in broadband services based on a combination of private and public infrastructure provided on an open-access, non-discriminatory approach.
- Sustainable new infrastructure: all new infrastructure needs to be have sufficient capacity (fibers) to support the medium-term vision (more than 10 years).

Source: African Development Bank, NEPAD and African Union Commission (2012) [see note 12]

Extending national backbones

While the PIDA candidate projects are expected to contribute greatly to the expansion of national networks, there is still a need for additional national backbone links to provide access to secondary cities in the continent. Over 30 countries require additional efforts to develop their national backbones in order to increase fiber penetration to their underserved areas. This implies that governments need to create incentives for the private sector to build out different segments of fiber networks in rural areas or establish public–private partnerships for extending connectivity to population centers.

Connectivity to the households and the institutions

The experience of countries in the Organisation for Economic Co-operation and Development suggests that broadband uptake at household and anchor institutions like schools, libraries and health centers is crucial for extending benefits to all. As a minimum, the continent needs to achieve broadband penetration of about 50% at household levels by 2050. Africa's population is expected to more than double, rising from 1.1 billion today to at least 2.4 billion by 2050.[26] Africa's average household size is expected to be around four by 2050. Therefore about 300 million households will need to be connected

Table 8.5: Estimated household population and broadband requirement by 2050

Penetration type	Current	2050	Current broadband penetration (%)	Broadband target by 2050 (%)	Gap (%)
Household	240 million	600 million	< 1	50	50
Population	1.1 billion	2.4 billion	19	80	20

Source: International Telecommunications Union data (http://www.itu.int/en/ITU-D/Statistics/Pages/stat/default.aspx) and Population Reference Bureau (http://www.prb.org/)

with about 100 Mbps network in 2050, a daunting task in terms of extending access networks to where people live.

Broadband availability at 50% of the African household will increase access to at least 85% of the population by 2050.

Stimulating network demand for applications and services

As discussed above, access to physical networks should be accompanied with initiatives that encourage the use of the established infrastructure for social development and economic growth. A variety of factors that constrain broadband uptake, including lack of access to computers and electricity and low levels of literacy, should be addressed along with the development of applications and services. Stimulating broadband demand includes launching government sponsored e-services, connecting schools and universities, promoting local ICT industries to participate in IT-enabled services, building national IT parks and developing skills.

The experience of the World Bank's 10-year regional communication infrastructure program (RCIP), which began in 2008, is summarized in Box 8.2, and indicates that early injection of resources for stimulation of network demand is essential to increase the impact of broadband when it is readily available. The RCIP focuses on developing access for all citizens to the information society; adapting the legal framework for ICTs; improving the quality and accessibility of public service; developing electronic administration; and stimulating a digital economy through support to enterprises.[27]

The Indian national e-government plan (NeGP) provides a useful benchmark for promoting applications and services that increase government efficiency, and promote schools and universities. The NeGP has been implemented over an eight-year period at a cost of US$4 billion (that is, US$4 per person). An investment of US$4.4 billion is therefore needed to stimulate open government, increase adoption by schools, colleges and businesses, and create the

Box 8.2: World Bank Regional Communication Infrastructure Program

Regions and cost:

- Regional Communication Infrastructure Program (Eastern and Southern Africa) US$424 million
- Central African Backbone (Central Africa) US$215 million
- West Africa Regional Communication Infrastructure Program (WARCIP I) US$305 million
- WARCIP II (Togo and Mauritania) US$60 million

Investment focus areas:

- establish terrestrial regional backbones;
- establish submarine cable landing stations and access to submarine cables;
- establish cross-border connectivity;
- create an enabling environment that would ensure public–private partnerships in ownership, management and competitive access to the infrastructure;
- increase government efficiency by deploying e-services and creating legal and regulatory frameworks;
- connect schools and universities;
- promote the local IT sector to participate in the global Information Technology Enabled Services market;
- support the creation of ICT parks, technology incubation centers, and so on;
- diversify sources of growth in knowledge-based development.

Source: World Bank, Bank's Group ICT Sector Strategy (2011) http://go.worldbank.org/VKHGDY6PY0

foundation for an information economy at the beginning, followed by additional US$8 billion for refreshing services every 10 years between 2015 and 2050.

A number of countries have already initiated information technology parks that stimulate local entrepreneurship, enable countries to tap into business process outsourcing opportunities. The African Development Bank, for example, is providing support for the development of such parks in Cape Verde and Senegal. Investment estimates for the parks range from US$100 million to US$500 million on average depending on the size of the country. The private sector plays a key role in building, operating and marketing these parks, but an initial injection of public finance may be needed in some cases to stimulate demand and ensure that key infrastructure such as land, roads, airports, water, electricity, housing and other amenities are available to these special ICT development zones.

Aggregate broadband investment by 2050

The five areas of broadband investment discussed earlier require a considerable amount of investment. Prioritization is a must for ensuring that the ICT foundations are built first. The immediate requirement in the region is largely around bridging regional connectivity, as outlined by PIDA. Bringing broadband access to households will be the next frontier that requires the bulk of the investment. Table 8.6 provides a summary of the estimated cost of broadband to Africa by 2050.

Table 8.6: Cost of the broadband ecosystem

Program		Estimated cost (US$ billions)	Source
Improving international bandwidth	Medium and long term, east coast	2.5	Private sector, operators, banks
Bridging the regional broadband gap (PIDA) priority projects	Missing trans-boundary links	1.5	Private sector, development banks, public–private partnerships
Building national backbones	30 countries, 300,000km (US$150 per metre)	4.5	Private sector, public–private partnerships
Extending connectivity (access networks to households and remote institutions)	300 million households*	135.0	Private sector, public and private partnership
Stimulating network demand, developing applications and services	Replication of some of the activities of the World Bank's Regional Communications Infrastructure Program in 40 countries**	12.4	Development banks, bilateral and multilateral donors
Total		155.9	

Note: * Based on average cost of US$450 to extend a wireless broadband link in Brazil;
** Estimates are based on NeGP, projections based on population growth

It is estimated that Africa requires around US$156 billion over the next three decade to create the necessary broadband ecosystem for its competitiveness.

The role of the private sector

The private sector will bear the primary responsibility of broadband investment. It is assumed that it will contribute 80% of the US$156 billion that is required to bring broadband, applications and services to a critical mass of African institutions, businesses and households by 2050. The private sector needs to explore public–private partnerships and other investment-sharing options to advance innovation and expend infrastructure.

The private sector has a major role in development of applications and services, in particular in supporting services and products that target specific segments and their needs, including women, rural populations, schools, libraries, and so on. It will have a prominent role in building and operating technology parks that will serve as a hub for jobs, innovation and foreign direct investment.

The role of government in stimulating broadband investment

The government has also a major role in influencing broadband deployment by creating enabling policies and regulatory frameworks. The public policies that stimulate the deployment of broadband range from the formulation of national broadband plans to the enactment of competition laws and the identification of cases where the government should intervene in order to address specific market failures.

National broadband plans are regarded as important first steps to secure government's support for the development of the ICT ecosystem. A growing number of countries have national broadband plans, policies or strategies in place. The Broadband Commission estimates that some 119 countries had broadband policies in place by mid-2012.[28]

Broadband plans are important because they outline both coverage and service targets and clear signals by policymakers and regulators of their commitment to private investment and public and private partnership. The Kenyan example cited in Box 8.3 shows that a well-thought-out plan needs to outline targets, financing mechanisms and the contribution of various players.

Box 8.3: Kenyan national broadband strategy

The national broadband strategy (NBS) of Kenya, which was adopted in 2013 at a cost of KSh257 billion (US$2.9 billion), provides a roadmap to transform Kenya into a knowledge-based society driven by a reliable high-capacity nationwide broadband network. The overall goal of the NBS is to provide quality broadband services to all Kenyans through connectivity that is always on and delivers a minimum of 40 Mbps to individuals, homes and businesses for high-speed access to voice, data, video and applications for development by 2017 and 2 Gbps by 2030. It envisages 75% of local business having an online presence, 70% of all government transactions being virtual, 40% of the population being digitally literate and 20% of Kenyan websites being in local languages. In the strategy, 5% of the national budget will be geared towards ICT annually, up from the current 0.5%.

In a move to make every part of the country connected, the strategy seeks by 2017 to have the national fiber backbone expanded by 30,000km to reach at least 80% of districts. The strategy has been regarded as critical to the achievement of Vision 2030, which recognizes the enabling role of ICT and anchors some of its key aspirations on the availability and adoption of broadband technologies.

The NBS also cites the provision of complementary infrastructure in the roads sector to allow ICT infrastructure to cross roads and railways, especially fiber-optic cables, which have to be placed underground.

The strategy will be implemented in two five-year phases. The first phase from 2013 to 2017 will cost KSh110 billion (US$1.3 billion) to implement. The government is also hoping to float an ICT bond to raise KSh70 billion (US$800 million) towards financing the project. With Kenyan telcoms companies recording huge pre-tax profits in recent years, the strategy will see companies contribute 0.5% of their annual revenues to the Universal Service Fund that will invest in the broadband network.

Source: www.balancingact-africa.com/category/newsletter/newsletter-english?page=2

Governments are also required to create a wide range of incentives to encourage private sector investment, including enabling a favorable investment climate, encouraging competition and introducing improved regulatory certainty. The policy and regulatory steps that the governments should take are very well documented in the ITU Broadband Commission's report[29] and summarized in Box 8.4.

Box 8.4: The role of government in broadband deployment

- Explore fresh approaches to spectrum management—promote spectrum sharing, limit spectrum hoarding, introduce efficient licensing framework.
- Implement "Dig Once" policies and expedite rights of way and construction permits.
- Use universal service funds and other financial mechanisms to develop broadband.
- Consider reviewing and updating ICT regulations.
- Consider a unified licensing regime.
- Consider converged regulation,
- Reduce taxes and import duties on telecommunication/ICT equipment and services.
- Stimulate the creation of local content in local languages.
- Enhance demand for broadband through e-government initiatives.
- Monitor ICT developments, based on statistical indicators.
- Incorporate sustainability principles into ICT regulations and policies.
- Promote the skills and talents necessary for broadband.

Source: Broadband Commission (2012) [see note 28]

One area where the government policy can have an immediate effect in Africa is in stimulating broadband deployment by promoting infrastructure sharing and coordinating the use of right of way between various utility agencies. Infrastructure sharing can help operators in reducing the cost of building, operating and maintaining network infrastructure.

Up to 90% cost savings can be made by using existing cabling, ducts and rights of way of energy and transport networks; therefore policymakers should pay attention to the integration of broadband in ongoing civil works. This implies that broadband roll-out needs to be fully integrated into the construction of roads, energy networks and gas pipelines. The US president's "Dig Once" order outlined in Box 8.5 shows that governments can actually play a major role in mandating coordination and information sharing during civil work to avoid multiple digging and accidental cutting of fiber networks. They can also improve legal codes that punish vandalism and theft of national broadband assets.

Box 8.5: US "Dig Once" Executive Order

US president Barack Obama issued an Executive Order in 2012 aimed at lowering governmental barriers to broadband infrastructure deployment on federal lands and along US highways. The "Dig Once" initiative is designed to help rapid deployment of broadband throughout the US by requiring federal agencies to facilitate broadband deployment activities where roads or other property are already under construction. Federal agencies are also be required to develop a consistent federal contracts process for the leasing of property and uniform steps for broadband firms to follow that will eliminate bureaucratic hurdles and make submission and approval of infrastructure projects much easier. The Executive Order also requires that federal assets and lease requirements be listed on departmental websites and that regional broadband deployment projects be listed and tracked on the US government's Federal Infrastructure Projects Dashboard (http://permits.performance.gov). The order affects all properties managed by the federal government, and includes tracts of land, roadways, and more than 10,000 buildings in the United States.

Source: The White House, Office of the Press Secretary (2012) Executive Order – Accelerating Broadband Infrastructure Deployment, https://www.whitehouse.gov/the-press-office/2012/06/14/executive-order-accelerating-broadband-infrastructure-deployment

It is evident that a significant portion of the population does not subscribe to broadband internet for reasons beyond service availability. Affordability, lack of digital literacy and other social and economic factors will continue to constrain broadband usage in the region. An understanding of these problems and their causes is critical in order to put an appropriate set of policies in place for promoting broadband adoption in the region. This requires extensive data gathering and ongoing studies that enable policymakers and regulators to monitor broadband infrastructure access, affordability, and usage patterns by individuals, businesses and public organizations.

Financing information and communications technology sector development

The private sector will bear the bulk of the financial burden by providing upfront investment in terms of equity or debt. A significant potential exists for banks, pension funds, sovereign funds and other institutional investors to participate in the broadband infrastructure expansion in Africa by issuing equity.

The ICT sector provides promising bankable projects for private equity as a result of improvements in the regulatory environment and a growing strategic vision on the part of countries to advance the sector as an engine of growth. Experience in the mobile services and international undersea cable sector has already shown that the ICT sector is one of the most attractive ventures for the private sector.

The private sector will also play a major role in the deployment of applications and services, because the capacity to implement large-e-government programs efficiently and cost-effectively is not available within the public sector in Africa. Thus a significant potential exists for designing, building, financing and operating ICT projects in the continent.

However, not all ICT projects will be bankable for the private sector. Governments need to work closely with the private sector through public–private partnerships where the private sector provides the upfront financing for the ICT infrastructure and receives payment from the public sector for providing it with a stream of services. Experience in Latin America suggests that carefully designed public–private partnership models can actually improve ICT sector growth.

Governments have also been using other financing models that are proven to work for different countries under diverse circumstances. These include the following.

- *Universal service funds.* Collected from levies on operators, these have been used to subsidize targeted infrastructure development in some countries. The funds are distributed based on analysis of the size of anticipated revenues, percentage of population coverage, or geographical coverage. Universal services funds can generate substantial amount of resources when operators' revenues are high. On the other hand, the levies can put high burdens on them that are often transferred to consumers. Thus, a careful balance should be made between encouraging investment and innovation by the private sector and collecting levies and spending them on worthwhile ICT development initiatives.

- *Infrastructure bonds.* Some countries have proposed dedicated broadband development funds by issuing bonds. Kenya, for example, aims to float ICT bonds to raise KSh70 billion

(US$800 million) for its broadband network. Infrastructure bonds have been attractive in the road sector and are expected to succeed in the ICT sector.

- *Loans.* Loans have also been used by many African governments to extend access. Loans have been available from multilateral development banks and national import and export banks such as the Chinese Exim Bank that encourage vendor credit schemes. Loans will continue to be one of the most viable sources of financing of broadband infrastructure in Africa.

Large-scale projects that are aggregated at regional levels such as those proposed by the PIDA in Africa can also attract donor financing, especially from multilateral agencies such as the European Union. Governments such as the United States have already shown keen interest to bridge the energy gaps that will facilitate an increased use of broadband in the continent.

Implications for regional cooperation

The investment in broadband network will continue to stimulate regional cooperation, raising the profiles of regional economic communities (RECs) as major advocates and promoters of ICT sector development. Broadband will stimulate regional integration through cross-border connection and the facilitation of regional trade, in particular in the movement of people, goods and finance. In Eastern Africa, for example, ICT is being used for modernizing port operations and customs, connecting border stations within the East African community partner states, thus preventing unreliable declarations and simplifying and accelerating the movement of goods across transit corridors. A single window approach to information sharing and networking among the ministries of agriculture, health, veterinary services, transport, customs and broader control is being deployed in the region to streamline transport, freight forwarding, trade logistics, customs clearance and payments. ICT is increasingly being used to provide access to trade information, forms, and online transactions throughout Africa. Electronic cargo tracking systems are being implemented in West Africa to facilitate the tracking of goods and prevent malpractice.

Electronic passports and identification documents are widely used in the region to facilitate the movement of goods, and no financial transfer can take place without some form of ICT mediation. Experience in

Asia shows that advances in the ICT sector can strengthen other high tech-sectors, leading to improved global trade and market shares.[30]

The ICT sector is one of the growing segments where actual functional cooperation between countries and institutions is occurring. The "one network" mobile roaming model across the different countries in the region and the movement of ICT labor across Africa are two examples of ICT-driven regional integration. Regional cooperation is already taking place in the area of telecommunications where access to submarine cable is granted to landlocked countries in Western, Central, Eastern and Southern Africa, creating alternative routes for access to the global network.

The increasing presence of South African ICT companies in the region, the influence of Kenyan ICT companies in East African Community partner states (Uganda, Burundi, Rwanda and Tanzania) and the ongoing use of Senegalese expertise in French-speaking Western and Central Africa are some of the early examples of regional cooperation induced by a growing broadband deployment.

Collaboration among tertiary-level institutions is another area where broadband is directly affecting regional academic collaboration. Broadband is playing a pivotal role in creation of regional research and education networks in Africa. The UbuntuNet Alliance[31] for Research and Education Network that was established in 2005 by five emerging NRENs now serves as a regional node for Eastern and Southern Africa. Through the funding from the European Union's AfricaConnect project, the UbuntuNet Alliance is building a high-speed research and education backbone that connects NRENs in Kenya, Mozambique, Sudan, Tanzania, South Africa, Zambia, Democratic Republic of Congo, Malawi, Rwanda and Uganda to the European research and education network GEANT.

Academic networking in the Western and Central African region is being spearheaded by the West and Central African Research and Education Network (WACREN),[32] whose members comprise recently established NRENs in Benin, Burkina Faso, Cameroon, Côte d'Ivoire, Gabon, Ghana, Mali, Niger, Nigeria, Senegal and Togo. There are is already an initiative to create an African research and education network (AfREN) that aims promote a regional cooperation between tertiary level institutions.

Broadband is increasing the role of RECs' participation in the ICT sector. The Common Market for Eastern and Southern Africa, Economic Community of the West African States (ECOWAS), East African Community (EAC), Economic Community of Central African States (ECCAS), Arab Maghreb Union and SADC have played

Figure 8.13: The UbuntuNet backbone to GEANT by 2015

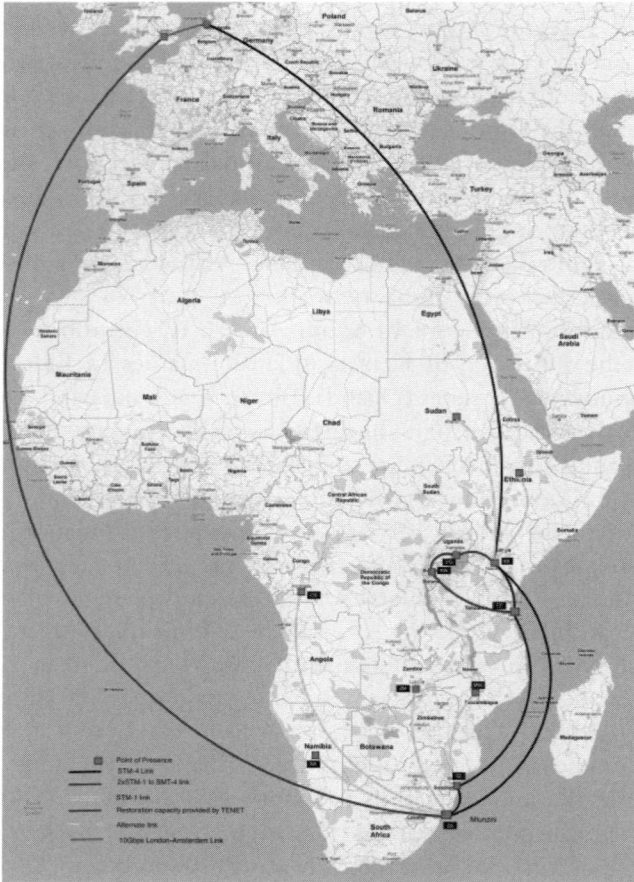

a crucial role in raising the awareness of policymakers and regulators of the importance of broadband. All RECs have been involved in the deployment of broadband infrastructure. Most notable are the ECCAS involvement in the Central African Backbone, EAC-BIN and the ECOWAS Wide Area Network (ECOWAN).

RECs have also been the key platforms for regional policy harmonization. The regulatory associations that are sponsored by the RECs, such as the East African Communications Organization, the Association of Regulators of Information and Communication of Eastern and Southern Africa, the Communications Regulators Association of Southern Africa and the West African Regulators Assembly, have played a major role in raising awareness and promoting regulatory harmonization.

Apart from trade facilitation, the RECs have not been able to tap into ICTs fully to foster cooperation in the area of health, security, agriculture and environment. It is envisaged that RECs will leverage ICTs to foster cooperation in these key areas and continue their regional coordination efforts and policy harmonization over the next three decades. The key roles of RECs are summarized in Box 8.6.

Box 8.6: Role of RECs

- Consolidation of ICT applications for trade facilitation by setting up ICT-enabled single windows and online payment systems.
- Assuring harmonization policies and regulation across countries.
- Creating platforms for applications and services including creating interoperable frameworks across regions and addressing common challenges such as cyber-security.
- Coordination of regional broadband plans that draw on regional plans.
- Providing a unified program for capacity building and developing an enabling environment for broadband.
- Provide support for the implementation of a regional cross-border connections program (PIDA) for bridging regional backbone gaps.

Conclusion

This chapter highlights investment requirement in the ICT sector in Africa centered around the broadband ecosystem. Broadband is a new agent for change—a critical input for African prospective growth. The social and economic impact of broadband is immense and its transformative potential is as high as the water, energy and transport sectors. Africa's progress in the mobile sector has been impressive, yet the continent has been unable to catch up with the global transition from narrow band to broadband and from quantity to quality of access.

The impact of broadband can only be felt with a high level of investment in the entire supply chain, both in physical infrastructure and access networks (the supply side) and in applications and services (the demand side). To achieve social and economic transformation, Africa needs to reach at least 50% of its households with a minimum of 100 Mbps connection and connect anchor institutions like hospitals, schools, public institutions with gigabits of connection by 2050. This requires investment of about US$150 billion over the next three decades.

The private sector will play a significant role in expanding broadband, but governments need to pave the way by creating an enabling investment and regulatory climate. RECs have a role to play to ensure that countries harmonize policies for competitive cross-border interconnection that spurs further regional trade and integration. Development institutions need to continue to raise awareness and finance programs that stimulate large-scale broadband investments that are led by the private sector and complemented by public– private partnerships. Without a large-scale approach, African countries will have little choice other than the painful evolution of building infrastructure over a long time, which will be detrimental to the creation of information economy jobs for the youth, the delivery of efficient public services and the growth competitive private sector.

Notes

[1] International Telecommunications Union (2014) 'ICT facts and figures 2014', available at www.itu.int/en/ITU-D/Statistics/Documents/facts/ICTFactsFigures2014-e.pdf.

[2] Cisco estimates that by 2016, a quarter of all mobile users will own more than one device and about 9% will have three or more devices. A research ICT Africa study (www.researchictafrica.net) shows a median SIM card duplication in 12 countries in Africa of about 40%.

[3] International Telecommunication Union (2014) Op. cit.

[4] Kelly, T. and Rossoto, M. (eds) (2012) *Broadband Strategies Handbook*. Washington, DC: World Bank, available at http://broadbandtoolkit.org/Custom/Core/Documents/Broadband%20Strategies%20Handbook.pdf.

[5] Qiang, C.Z. and Rossotto, C.M. (2009) 'Economic impacts of broadband', in *Information and Communications for Development 2009: Extending Reach and Increasing Impact, 35–50.* Washington, DC: World Bank.

[6] International Telecommunications Union (2012) 'The impact of broadband on the economy: regulatory and market environment', available at www.itu.int/ITU-D/treg/broadband/ITU-BB-Reports_Impact-of-Broadband-on-the-Economy.pdf.

[7] www.itu.int/en/ITU-D/Statistics/Documents/publications/mis2014/MIS2014_without_Annex_4.pdf

[8] United Nations (2014) 'E-government survey', available at http://unpan3.un.org/egovkb/Reports/UN-E-Government-Survey-2014

[9] A.T. Kearny (2014) 'Global Service Location Index, 2014', available at www.atkearney.com/web/gsli-2014/home.

[10] www.gartner.com/newsroom/id/2209615

[11] CISCO (2009) 'Top 25 technology predictions', available at www.cisco.com/web/about/ac79/docs/Top_25_Predictions_121409rev.pdf.

[12] African Development Bank, NEPAD and African Union Commission (2012) 'Report of a Study of the Programme for Infrastructure Development in Africa (PIDA), Information and Communication Technology', unpublished .

[13] www.worldbank.org/en/news/press-release/2013/05/30/world-bank-approves-funds-improve-broadband-connectivity-mauritania-togo

[14] African Development Bank, NEPAD and African Union Commission (2012) Op. cit.

[15] www.africabandwidthmaps.com/?p=3144

[16] World Bank (2011) *Transformation Ready: Using ICT to Fast Track Africa's Development Path*, Washington, DC: World Bank, available at http://siteresources.worldbank.org/INFORMATIONANDCOMMUNICATIONANDTECHNOLOGIES/Resources/WorldBank_ICT_brochure.pdf.

[17] African Development Bank (2013) 'Connecting Africa: An Assessment of Progress Towards the Connect Africa Summit Goal', http://www.afdb.org/fileadmin/uploads/afdb/Documents/Project-and-Operations/Connecting_Africa_-_An_Assessment_of_Progress_Towards_the_Connect_Africa_Summit_Goals_-_Main_Report.pdf

[18] Jordan, V. and Galperin, H. (2013) 'Broadband in Latin America, beyond connectivity', available at www.intertic.org/Policy%20Papers/StructuralChange.pdf.

[19] World Bank (2010) *Africa Infrastructure Country Diagnostic Report, 2010*, Chapter 7. ICT: A boost for African growth, available at www.infrastructureafrica.org/system/files/Africa%27s%20Infrastructure%20A%20Time%20for%20Transformation%20FULL%20TEXT.pdf.

[20] Ericson (2011) 'More than 50 billion connected devices', available at www.ericsson.com/res/docs/whitepapers/wp-50-billions.pdf.

[21] Akamai (2013) *The State of the Internet*, Volume 6, No. 1, available at www.akamai.com/dl/akamai/akamai_soti_q113.pdf.

[22] Toure, H. (2013) Speech at the 7th Meeting of the Broadband Commission, available at www.broadbandcommission.org/work/events/7thmeeting.aspx.

[23] European Commission (2010) *Digital Agenda for Europe*, available at http://ec.europa.eu/digital-agenda.

[24] US Government (2010) 'Broadband strategy', available at www.broadband.gov/plan.

[25] www.pcworld.com/article/2060120/africa-to-lead-the-world-in-international-bandwidth-demand.html

[26] Population Reference Bureau (2013) Population datasheet, available at www.prb.org/Publications/Datasheets/2013/2013-world-population-data-sheet/data-sheet.aspx.

[27] World Bank (2013) 'Regional Infrastructure Programme, Phase I and II', http://go.worldbank.org/VKHGDY6PY0

[28] Broadband Commission (2012) 'The state of broadband 2012: achieving digital inclusion for all', available at www.broadbandcommission.org/Documents/bb-annualreport2012.pdf.

[29] Ibid.

[30] Gelvanovska, N., Rogy, M. and Rossotto, C.M. (2013) *Broadband Networks in the Middle East and North Africa: Accelerating High-speed Internet Access*, Washington, DC: World Bank, available at www.worldbank.org/en/region/mena/publication/broadband-networks-in-mna.

[31] www.ubuntunet.net

[32] www.wacren.org

Part 3: Regional issues

NINE

The state of infrastructure in East Africa

Tito Yepes and Charles Leyeka Lufumpa

Introduction

This chapter outlines some of the principal ongoing infrastructure challenges faced by the East African sub-region,[1] with a particular focus on water, sanitation, energy, surface transport and information and communications technology (ICT). The progress made to date is evaluated in the light of recent studies and new data.

At the sub-regional level, in most measures, East Africa's infrastructure ranks behind that of the Southern African Development Community (SADC) and the Economic Community of West African States (ECOWAS). However, in some areas (such as water and sanitation and internet density), East African performance is comparable to that of Southern Africa.

There are significant opportunities for East Africa to improve its infrastructure, particularly in productivity-related areas, namely energy production, logistics and ICT.[2] For instance, the African Infrastructure Country Diagnostic (AICD) study (AICD, 2011) estimated that if the sub-region's overall infrastructure were raised to the level of the top-performing African country, Mauritius, gross domestic product (GDP) would grow by 6%. In this respect, increased power generation capacity would make the biggest contribution to growth.

Despite potentially huge gains to be made from boosting productive infrastructure, there remain substantial challenges across all sectors. Among these, the main is the lack of a *regional vision for infrastructure provision*, even though it remains one of the critical determinants of success. Recently, some efforts have been made towards a regional vision; however it is still too early to assess their real impact and success. For example, the East African Community developed a master plan for the energy sector aiming to achieve a regional vision that goes beyond the power system capacity supporting an institutional arrangement.

Social infrastructure: access to water and sanitation, and electricity

Water and sanitation

East Africa's overall result for access to improved water sources falls behind other economic communities. Although urban areas present a positive trend in most East African countries, there is still a significant differential between urban and rural areas (about 35 percentage points on average). On a positive note, internal disparities between lagging and leading areas within single countries are narrowing.

East Africa's overall performance for access to improved water had shown an improvement of 10 percentage points between 2005 and 2010. No other community has shown such an improvement (see Figure 9.1 and Table 9.1). Nevertheless, gaps persist. The East African region is eight percentage points below the Economic Community of West African States (ECOWAS), seven percentage points behind the Communauté Économique et Monétaire de l'Afrique Centrale (Economic and Monetary Community of Central Africa; CEMAC), and four percentage points behind SADC.

Figure 9.1: Access to improved water and sanitation (% of population)

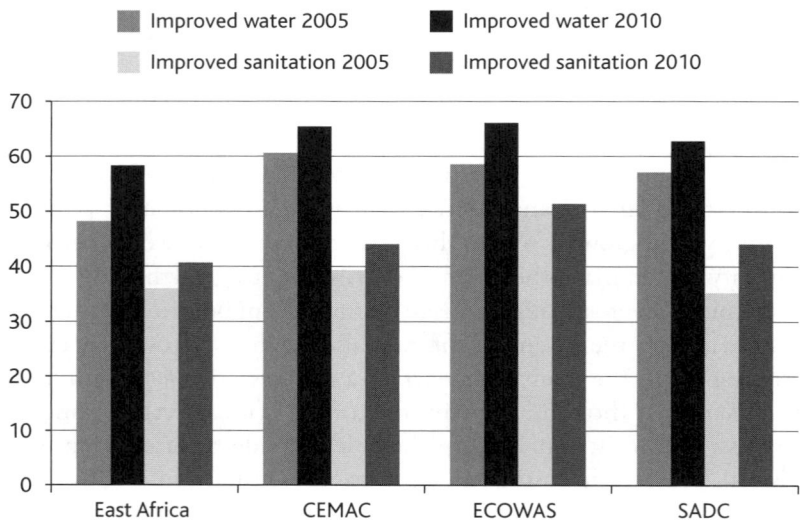

Note: Years used by each country vary according to data availability; closest year used.

Source: Demographic and Health Surveys (DHS) and Mutiple Indicators Cluster Surveys (MICS), compiled by WHO and UNICEF Joint Monitoring Program (JMP)

Table 9.1: Households with access to improved water source and improved sanitation facilities, by country

Country	Year*	Urban	Rural	Total
*Households with access to improved drinking water source (%)**				
Burundi	2010	94.9	74.7	76.9
Ethiopia	2011	94.4	41.7	50.7
Kenya	2008	89.3	53.8	61.9
Rwanda	2010	88.5	70.8	74.1
Tanzania	2010	79.5	41.2	51.3
Uganda	2011	89.8	66.8	70.3
*Households with access to improved sanitation (%)***				
Burundi	2010	84.8	60.5	63.1
Ethiopia	2011	65.0	32.2	37.8
Kenya	2008	82.8	37.1	47.7
Rwanda	2010	87.6	72.2	75.1
Tanzania	2010	47.3	11.3	20.7
Uganda	2011	81.2	49.3	54.2

Notes:
*Refers to the last year of available data.
** Improved water: tap water (house connections, public tap, standpipe), protected wells or springs, rainwater (covered cistern/tank), and other improved sources.
*** Improved sanitary: flush and pour flush, improved latrines (ventilated improved pit latrine or pit latrine with slab/covered latrine)
Source: DHS compiled by WHO and UNICEF Joint Monitoring Program.

Sanitation also shows signs of progress but comparisons between urban and rural areas show a differential as in the case of access to improved water. East African countries lag about four percentage points with SADC and CEMAC, and about 11 percentage points with ECOWAS.

A positive trend is also present in access to improved sanitation facilities but significantly lower in percentage points (4.7% from 2005 to 2010). A deep analysis into HH reports shows that in most countries access to sanitation facilities has been increasing in the last quintile while the rest of the population it has shown no progress.

Sub-Saharan Africa has been accelerating its access to improved sources of drinking water very significantly. The latest data available show that all regions have been showing an increase in access rates. East Africa, for instance, increased by 10% in the most recent period compared with the figures of the early 2000s, when no additional coverage was gained (Figure 9.2).

Nonetheless, as shown in Table 9.1, there are significant differences in the access rates of urban and rural areas. Most East African countries have attained relatively high levels of access to improved water and

Figure 9.2: Rural/urban water access

Additional access rate

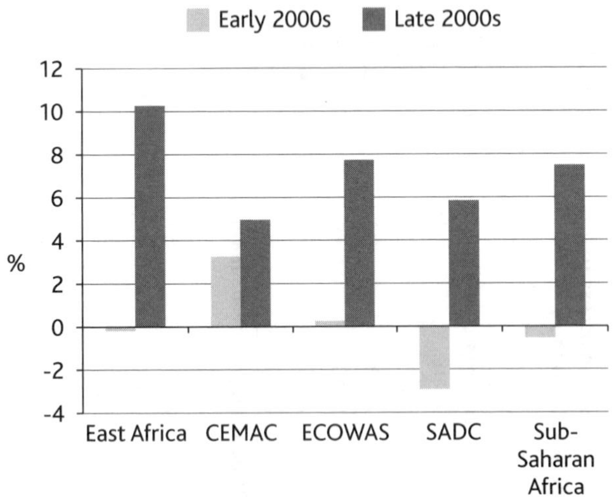

Legend: Early 2000s, Late 2000s

Access rates to improved drinking water sources

	East Africa	CEMAC	ECOWAS	SADC	Sub-Saharan Africa
Total (%)					
2000	48.2	57.3	58.3	60.0	55.9
2005	48.1	60.6	58.5	57.1	55.3
2010	58.3	65.5	66.1	62.8	62.7
Urban (%)					
2000	87.4	80.2	82.3	88.9	85.4
2005	85.1	85.0	79.7	84.6	82.6
2010	84.0	87.9	84.4	87.6	85.6
Rural (%)					
2000	39.0	41.9	43.6	44.6	42.3
2005	40.1	43.7	44.0	41.0	41.8
2010	51.3	47.1	51.8	47.0	50.0

Source: DHS and censuses processed by JMP.

sanitation in urban areas, but in many rural areas households are still without improved access. As a large majority of East Africans reside in rural areas, the national access rates are still low in some countries, such as Ethiopia and Tanzania, particularly in the area of improved sanitation.

Furthermore, access to improved water supplies is losing momentum in most East African countries (see Figure 9.3a). Whereas Kenya, Tanzania, and Uganda recorded a substantial increase in access rates during the 1990s, in the subsequent decade the growth rate declined in Rwanda and especially in Tanzania. Uganda's progress also stalled, registering only a minor decrease during the next decade, compared with its achievements in the 1990s. Ethiopia shows an important increase throughout the last decade (7% annual average), reaching levels of 50% of water access in 2011.

Tanzania's deterioration in access to improved water has been driven by excessive expenses arising from operational inefficiencies, which have curbed expansion in services. Such inefficiencies are a more significant problem in rural areas, where scale economies are not easily achievable. Another negative factor is low access to financing sources, since traditionally these only cover about half of the investment needs. In view of these constraints, countries are forced to consider adopting low-cost technologies. One counterintuitive finding is that, despite a clear financing gap, most countries in East Africa still underprice water provision for connected customers, even though these customers could afford cost-recovery tariffs. Finally, another factor for increasingly deteriorating access to improved water supply could be rapid population growth and therefore a rapidly growing demand, which outstrips supply.

On the other hand, access to improved sanitation (see Figure 9.3b) over the last two decades has shown a very positive trend in all countries, especially Tanzania during the last decade. Despite this generalized improvement, the magnitude of access rates must be taken into account.

Disparities between lagging and leading regions within each country are narrowing (see Figure 9.4). In the 1990s, the leading region in Tanzania recorded twice the level of access compared with the worst-performing region. During the 2000s though, the ratio reduced from 2 to 1.5. The same narrowing of the differentials between leading and lagging areas is observed in all other countries in East Africa in respect of improved water access, except for Ethiopia, which recorded a ratio of almost 2.5 (dividing the access rate of leading region by that of the lagging region) in the 2000s. This trend could evidence the development of territorial capabilities in some specific regions.

Figure 9.3: Changes in access rates to (a) improved water and (b) sanitation, 1990s and 2000s

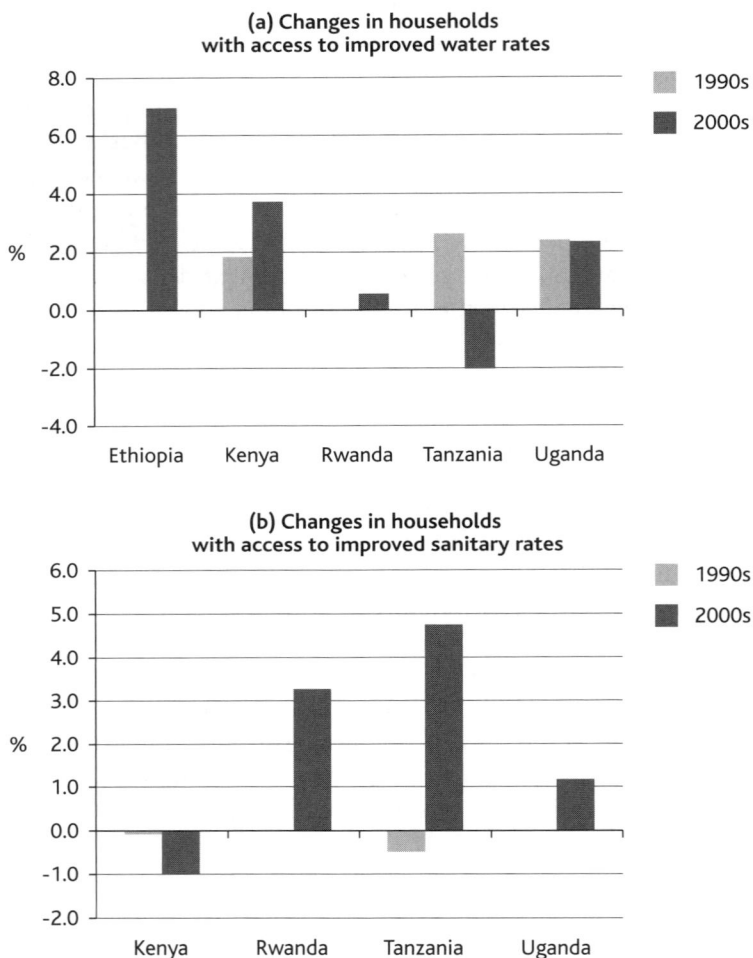

(a) Changes in households
with access to improved water rates

(b) Changes in households
with access to improved sanitary rates

Note: Improved water: Tap water (house connections, public tap, standpipe), protected wells or springs, rainwater (covered cistern/tank), and other improved sources. Improved sanitary: Flush and pour flush, improved latrines (ventilated improved pit latrine or pit latrine with slab/covered latrine). Ethiopia's 2000's average annual growth sanitary rate: 5.9%.

Source: DHS compiled by JMP.

Tanzania is lagging behind in improving access to drinking water (Figure 9.5). It observed a sharp 14% reduction in access between 1999 and 2005 and, since then, it has recovered only slightly. The national access rate was 52% in the 2002 census and 53% in the 2012 census. Both sources, the censuses and the DHSs, present a consistent

Figure 9.4: Differentiated access to improved water for lagging and leading regions within selected countries, 1990s and 2000s

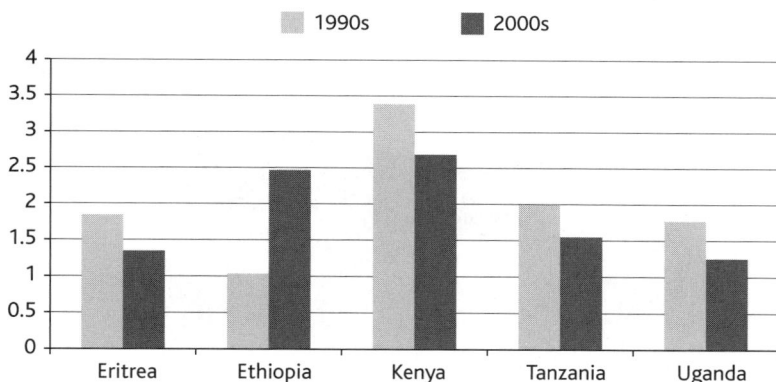

Note: Years used by each country vary according to data availability. Improved water: data on piped and well water from stat compiler.

Source: Demographic and Health Surveys

Figure 9.5: Access rates to improved drinking water sources in Tanzania

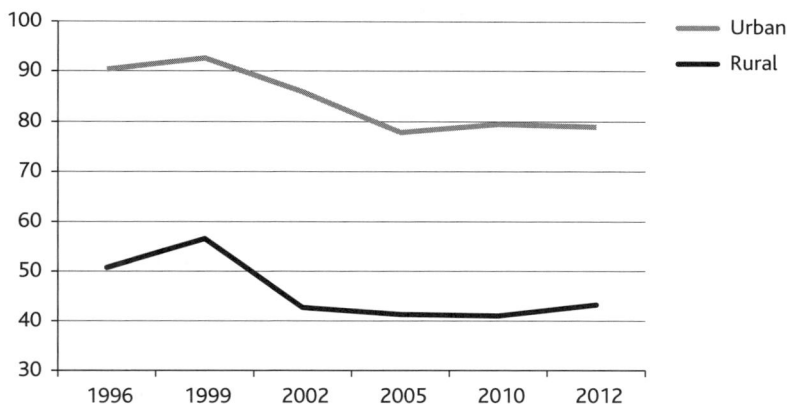

Source: DHS processed by JMP and censuses of the National Bureau of Statistics of Tanzania

history of decrease in the early 2000s and stagnation in the most recent period.

Despite those worrying trends, the number of people with access has been increasing mostly in urban areas, while it is in rural areas that the situation from 2002 to 2012 did not change significantly. Between 2002 and 2012, 3.4 million people gained access (Figure 9.6a) but the number of people without access is increasing faster (Figure 9.6b). The

Figure 9.6: Comparative access to water

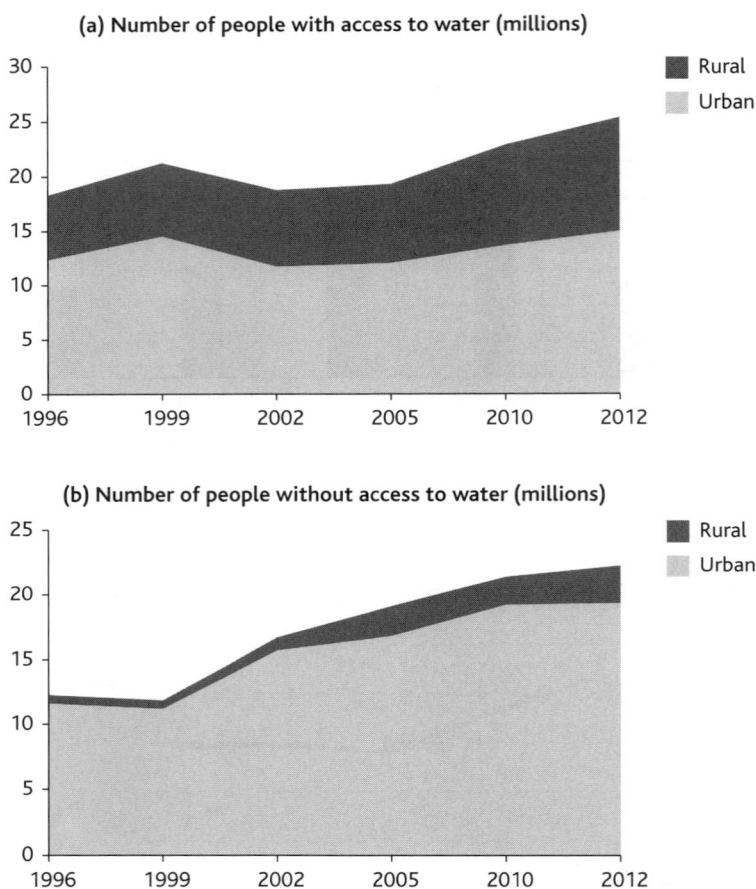

(a) Number of people with access to water (millions)

(b) Number of people without access to water (millions)

Source: DHS and censuses processed by JMP.

structural problem, though, is that the number of people without access continues to increase. In the same period, an additional 5.5 million people lacked access on top of the 11.7 million who has never had it. Furthermore, as Tanzania's urbanization rate is 27%, the number of those without access to improved drinking water in rural areas has been increasing very rapidly but it has also increased in urban areas.

The Government of Tanzania has implemented different strategies over the past decade to address the situation. In 2002, in addition to increasing investment levels, it[3] included the quest for cost recovery—in segments where affordability allows it— and institutional strengthening. In 2006, a new plan further increased financing from multi-funding sources from development partners plus a vision for integration and consistency of approaches to serve rural and urban areas and for different water sources. Despite the fact that these strategies seem to be working, they are not pointing in the direction of trend changes. According to the journalistic work of Ground Truth Project, failure in programs for rural groundwater—where the figures above show the major concentration of underserved population—is to blame.

Other usual suspects that can explain the situation are high population growth or insufficient investment resources. Data[4] contradicts these alternative explanations. Concurrently with the drop in access already discussed, public expenditure per capita increased more than twofold, passing from an average of about US$700 between 1997 and 2003 to an average of US$2,000 between 2004 and 2012. The metrics of expenditure per capita accounts for population growth. Two facts cannot be rejected: Tanzania has been investing significantly in the water sector but it has been lagging significantly behind in access rates.

Access to electricity

Access to electricity is a major problem in East Africa (Figure 9.7). While it has been improving at a steady rate in most countries, sub-regional performance as a whole falls well below the performance of the rest of the continent, with firewood and charcoal still being the most commonly used fuel for cooking.

Levels of access to electricity and other improved energy sources for cooking are extremely low in East Africa. Indeed, the sub-region

Figure 9.7: Urban households with access to electricity (%)

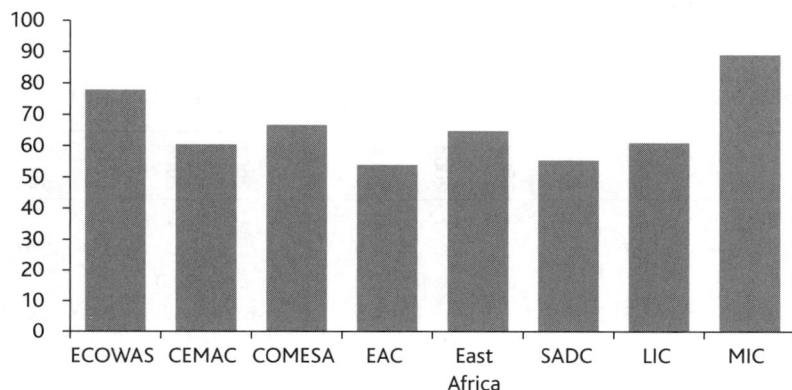

Note: Latest data available is used.

Source: World Bank and International Energy Agency (2014).

is the worst performer in the whole continent for this indicator, and this is currently the most significant social infrastructure problem. In terms of access to electricity for its urban population, the East African Community records a low rate of 54%, compared with the whole region (65%), CEMAC (60.5%), COMESA (66.8%), SADC (55.5%), and ECOWAS (77.9%) (see Table 9.2).[5]

The Demographic and Health Surveys show that electricity access has generally remained low in the East African countries (EAC) in recent years, despite an increase in Kenya, Rwanda, Tanzania, Ethiopia, and Uganda. Burundi is lagging behind, according to the surveys (see Table 9.3). The use of firewood and charcoal is almost universal across East Africa. Over the decade 2001-2011, available data reveal that the rate of utilization of these fuel sources in Ethiopia, Kenya and Rwanda has changed very little (see Table 9.4).

Table 9.2: Benchmarking access to electricity for urban households (%)

	Access (urban, % of households)	Growth in access of household to electricity, annual (%)*
CEMAC	60.5	1.5 (9.6)
COMESA	66.8	−0.1 (6.7)
EAC	54.0	3.8 (6)
East Africa	65.0	1.4 (6)
ECOWAS	77.9	0.7 (6.4)
SADC	55.5	0.6 (6.7)
Low income	61.2	1.3 (7)
Middle income	89.3	1.2 (8)

Note: *Average years within the latest and previous data for regions is shown in parenthesis. Latest data available is used for each country.
Source: DHS..

Table 9.3: Percentage of households with access to electricity, 2000–2011

	2000	2001	2003	2004	2005	2006	2007	2008	2010	2011
Burundi	...	...	...	...	...	...	...	...	5.3	...
Ethiopia	12.7	...	...	...	14.0	...	...	...	...	23.0
Kenya	...	...	16.0	...	...	...	...	23.0	...	...
Rwanda	6.2	...	...	...	4.8	...	6.0	...	9.7	...
Tanzania	...	...	...	11.4	...	...	...	...	14.8	...
Uganda	...	8.6	...	...	...	9.0	...	...	...	14.6

Note: ... indicates unavailable data.
Source: STAT compiler, DHS Project.

Table 9.4: Percentage of households using firewood or charcoal as cooking fuel, 2000–2011

	2000	2003	2004	2005	2006	2007	2008	2010	2011
Burundi	...	...	...	...	...	...	...	98.6	...
Ethiopia	79.6	...	...	87.8	...	...	...	...	87.7
Kenya	...	80.4	...	...	...	...	83.2	...	...
Rwanda	98.3	...	...	98.6	...	91.1	...	...	...
Tanzania	...	...	96.0	...	...	...	...	94.9	...
Uganda	95.9	...	...	...	95.7	...	...	...	95.5

Note: ... indicates unavailable data.
Source: STAT compiler, DHS Project.

Infrastructure to serve productive needs

Energy production

Energy deficiency is the most notable problem across all infrastructure sectors in East Africa, with a negative impact on households, industries, and businesses alike. The sub-region has the lowest generation capacity after Central Africa (see Figure 9.8) and the smallest per capita generation in the whole continent. Improving access to a reliable and affordable source of energy would do much to improve the business-enabling environment for the sub-region, stimulating trade and encouraging both domestic and foreign investment. Regional integration offers a win-win solution; however as yet there has been

Figure 9.8: Total electricity installed capacity (megawatts)

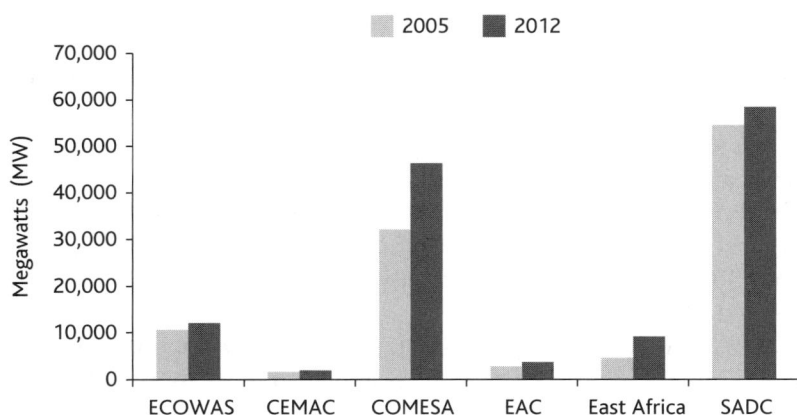

Source: U.S. Energy Information Administration (EIA), International Energy Statistics

few signs that East African countries have begun to work effectively together toward this end.

Generation capacity in the SADC region is 16 times greater than in the EAC region, while in ECOWAS it is three times greater. Although annual power outages in the region are lower than in ECOWAS, they cause greater economic loss to firms, possibly because of the nature of industry in East Africa (see Table 9.5).

On the other hand, utility performance in East Africa is comparatively better than in some of the other sub-regions despite high system losses. Its hidden costs are less serious, while it enjoys the highest cost-recovery record in Africa. In terms of pricing, the average historic costs of power in the sub-region are high—almost US$0.20 per kilowatt-hour (kWh). With the demand for power expected to increase by 70%, the expansion of power infrastructure will be critical for the economic development of the sub-region (AICD, 2011, p vii).

Power trade and regional integration

During the past decade, the demand for electricity in East Africa[6] has doubled and it is expected to rise seven times by 2040, becoming the region with the highest growth. Although in all regions the generation of electricity will meet final demand (see Table 9.6), most of the allocation problems persist due to lack of transmission and distribution lines, especially in rural areas. This lack of infrastructure makes total access to electricity in Sub-Saharan African countries more difficult to achieve, since not only must the investment required for increase generation and capacity be met, but also the investment to build distribution lines and promote the use of alternative sustainable sources.

Grid-based capacity in East Africa totals 8.1 Gigawatts (GW): hydropower is more than half, oil-fired capacity about 45% and the remainder is made up of geothermal and gas-fired capacity. This means that the region has the lowest capacity after Central Africa, a situation that does not seem to have changed over time (see Table 9.7). However, East Africa will show the second major average growth rate in capacity (7% annual average) after Central Africa (8% annual), while both South Africa and West Africa will have the lowest (4% and 5%, respectively).

In East Africa, the biggest contribution to hydropower belongs to Ethiopia with the Beles II hydropower project (460 MW), the Gilgel Gibe II (420 MW), the Gilgel Gibe III (1.87 GW, nearing completion) and the Grass Renaissance Dam (6 GW, in progress).

Table 9.5: Benchmarking power infrastructure, capacity and utility performance

Aspect	ECOWAS	CEMAC	COMESA	EAC	SADC	Low-income countries	Middle-income countries
Electricity installed capacity 2012 (MW)	12,067	1,901	46,476	3,649	58,509	20,409	46,528
Net generation per capita 2011, annual (kWh/capita/year)*	158.4	230.3	457.7	110.1	1,099.5	150.9	4,271.6
Outages annually (number/year)	133.4	202.8	59.7	86.9	50.9	107.1	27.1
Outages, value lost, annually (% of sales)	5.0	7.8	4.5	5.6	4.2	5.5	1.7
Firms with own generator (% of firms)	51.9	59.3	41.1	48.6	34.1	46.1	29.5
System losses (% of generation, 2011)*	15.5	17.6	13.6	18.0	10.6	16.7	9.4
Cost recovery ratio, historical (%)	79	45	73	69	68	100	87
Total hidden costs (% of revenue)	159	107	102	65	4	544	0
Collection rate reported by utility, electricity (% of billing)	71	93	93	94	89		91
	WAPP	CAPP	SAPP	EAPP			
Average historic cost (US$/kWh)	0.21	0.49	0.14	0.19			
Long-run marginal cost (US$/kWh)	0.18	0.09	0.07	0.12			

Notes: *Aggregate values not average. EAPP = East African Power Pool; CAPP = Central Africa Power Pool; SAPP = Southern African Power Pool; WAPP = West African Power Pool.

Source: Electricity installed capacity, net generation, and system losses (distribution losses): US Energy Information Administration data. Outages, value-lost and firms with own generation: World Bank Enterprises Surveys (latest available data is used). Cost recovery ratio, total hidden costs, collection rate reported by utility, average historic cost and long-run marginal cost: excerpt from Eberhard et al (2009) cited in AICD (2011, p 37).

Table 9.6: Electricity demand and generation by regions (TWh)

Region	2000 Demand	2000 Generation	2012 Demand	2012 Generation	2040 Demand	2040 Generation	Average annual growth (2012-2040) (%) Demand	Average annual growth (2012-2040) (%) Generation
Sub-Saharan Africa	269	307	368	440	1,297	1,541	3.4	3.4
West Africa	29	38	61	74	417	474	5.2	5.0
Central Africa	9	12	16	19	74	114	4.1	4.8
East Africa	9	11	23	29	177	229	5.5	5.6
Southern Africa	222	246	268	317	630	724	2.3	2.2

Source: The *African Energy Outlook 2014* (2014). International Energy Agency.

Table 9.7: Electrical capacity (GW), 2012–2040

Region	West Africa 2012	West Africa 2040	Central Africa 2012	Central Africa 2040	East Africa 2012	East Africa 2040	Southern Africa 2012	Southern Africa 2040
Total generation	25	113	4	36	8	55	59	181
Coal	0	9	...	...	...	7	40	69
Oil	11	11	1	2	4	7	6	11
Gas	11	50	1	12	0	6	1	26
Nuclear	...	...	...	...	...	...	2	7
Hydropower	4	24	3	20	4	20	9	29
Bioenergy	...	2	...	0	...	2	0	6
Solar PV	...	10	...	0	...	4	0	19
Other renewables	...	7	...	2	0	9	0	15

Source: The *African Energy Outlook 2014* (2014). International Energy Agency.

Thus, there is clear interest from Ethiopia in becoming an electricity supplier to neighbors such as Kenya, Burundi, Tanzania, Uganda and Rwanda. The rest of the hydropower capacity is in Sudan (the Merowe hydropower dam, 1.25 GW), as well as most of the oil-fired capacity. Kenya had the main participation in geothermal capacity with 250 MW in 2012. Naturally, most of the growth that East Africa will achieve by 2040 will be due to hydropower capacity, which is expected to grow by 6% annually, reaching 20 GW.

In addition to the increasing trade within sub-regions due to the fact that power pools support greater regional cooperation, there is also a strong trend in trade across sub-regions. East Africa and Central Africa will stand as net exporters while West and Southern Africa consolidate as net importers (see Table 9.8). Both East and Central Africa will achieve important growth in electricity generation because

Table 9.8: Electricity generation and trade (TWh), 2012–2040

Region	West Africa		Central Africa		East Africa		Southern Africa	
Year	2012	2040	2012	2040	2012	2040	2012	2040
Total Generation	74	474	19	114	29	229	317	724
Coal	1	54	...	...	...	29	246	329
Oil	22	20	3	3	8	22	7	18
Gas	35	249	2	17	...	22	3	97
Nuclear	...	...	...	...	...	...	13	47
Hydro	17	100	14	88	19	90	46	130
Bioenergy	0	12	0	1	0	10	1	27
Solar PV	0	17	...	1	0	7	0	34
Other renewables	0	21	...	4	2	50	0	42
Net imports	2	17	0	−27	0	−11	0	16

Source: The African Energy Outlook 2014 (2014). International Energy Agency.

of hydropower expansion (6.8% and 5.7% annual average growth, respectively), and the former will increase the generation of other renewables sources from 2 TWh to 50 TWh (an average rate of 12.2%).

In the East African region, Ethiopia's performance stands out, since by 2040, it will be one of the three largest net electricity exporting countries (together with Democratic Republic of Congo [DRC] and Mozambique), due to the development of large hydropower projects (IEA, 2014).

The achievement of such power development will require an important investment from all regions. In the case of East Africa, the importance of hydropower is shown by the almost 20% of total investment that the region needs for hydropower plants in contrast to the less than 10% of total investment that the region will allocate for fossil-fuelled plants (see Table 9.9). As expected, regions with more production of fossil sources (namely West Africa and Southern Africa) will need major investment in this sector.

The capacity to develop a hydropower backbone for electricity generation implies more impact on the environment through CO_2 emissions. As shown in Table 9.10, the East African region will suffer an increase in CO_2 emissions for power generation due to the use of coal and gas resources, but its emission levels will remain below those of Southern Africa and West Africa. Central Africa stands out for being the region with the lowest emission levels.

A key issue for the sector is the impact of climate change on hydropower capacity. According to Hamududu and Killingtveit (2012, cited in IEA, 2014), East Africa could increase output from hydropower because of an increase in run-off due to climate change,

Table 9.9: Cumulative investments in the power sector (US$ billions, 2013)

	West Africa		Central Africa		East Africa		Southern Africa	
	2014-2030	2031-2040	2014-2030	2031-2040	2014-2030	2031-2040	2014-2030	2031-2040
Total investment	181	210.8	51.1	52.1	100.6	109.3	282.2	262.5
Power plants	303.1	305	23	25	44.6	52.3	158.3	142.4
Hydropower plants	26.2	26.3	16.5	19.7	17.9	18.6	29.7	20.1
Fossil-fuelled plants	20.6	23.1	3.6	2.9	8	7.4	64.7	57.6
Transmission and distribution lines	103.8	125.5	28.1	27.1	56	57	123.9	120.2

Source: IEA (2014)

Table 9.10: CO$_2$ emissions for power generation (Metric tons)

Region	West Africa		Central Africa		East Africa		Southern Africa	
Year	2012	2040	2012	2040	2012	2040	2012	2040
Power generation	37	161	4	10	6	53	249	305
Coal	1	54	...	...	...	30	240	256
Oil	18	17	2	3	6	16	7	15
Gas	18	90	1	6	...	7	2	34

Source: IEA (2014)

but could show a decrease in run-off water in parts of West and Southern Africa, which will suffer a reduction in hydropower output.

Almost all the effective power demand for the East African Power Pool/Nile Basin (EAPP/NB)[7] is currently being met. The baseline total net demand for power was 100.6 terawatt-hours (TWh) in 2005, making it the second-largest power market in Sub-Saharan Africa, behind the SAPP. But power demand in the EAPP area is expected to increase by 69% over the next decade. It is estimated that power demand could reach 169 TWh by 2015, taking into account the anticipated expansion in market demand. This will be driven by economic growth in commerce and industry, and by the planned expansion of the electrification coverage from 35% to 60% of households in the sub-region.

Meeting this demand would require 26,000 MW of new generation capacity, which means more than doubling existing capacity (see Table 9.11). This could be achieved either by expanding national production or by expanding cross-border power trade within EAPP

Table 9.11: Demand and suppressed demand in EAPP (TWh)

	EAPP
Total net demand in 2005	100.6
% suppressed demand as a share of net demand (2005)	1
Market demand 2015	144.8
Social demand with national targets 2015	24.2
Total net demand 2015	169

Source: Rosnes and Vennemo (2009), cited in AICD (2011, p 38).

(AICD, 2011, p 38). There is great potential for integration in the electricity sector in East Africa.

In 2005, power trade flows in the EAPP comprised just 0.28 TWh of imports and 0.18 TWh of exports, that is, about 2.1% of the electricity generated. Although EAPP is the third most active regional power pool in Africa after SAPP and WAPP, these power volumes are very small. Under a trade expansion scenario, the volume traded has the potential to increase from 12 to 162 TWh per year. Regional power demand would be met by the most cost-effective energy resources available to the sub-region as a whole, and additional cross-border transmission capacity would be added where required, to allow power to flow from production to consumption locations.

Expanding electricity trade in the East African Power Pool/Nile Basin (EAPP/NB) would position Ethiopia, Rwanda, South Sudan, Sudan, Uganda, and Tanzania as net exporters, while Kenya, Egypt and Burundi would be net importers (see Figure 9.9). As an example, if Ethiopia and Sudan were to fully develop their hydropower potential and become the major power exporters in the region, Ethiopia could export as much as 200% and Sudan more than 100% of its domestic consumption (AICD, 2011, p 40).

As a whole, expanding trade in the Nile basin could generate US$1 billion a year. But many countries such as Ethiopia and Sudan— and to a lesser extent Rwanda, Tanzania, and Uganda—would need to develop their hydropower potential. In addition, all EAPP countries would need to invest significantly in cross-border interconnectors to allow power to flow more readily around the sub-region. To finance this, investment needs would be greater for some of the countries under the trade expansion scenario. Ethiopia, for example, would need to develop more than 6,700 MW of additional hydropower capacity to supply export markets in neighboring countries. In turn, Sudan would have to develop 3,100 MW of additional hydropower capacity (AICD, 2011, p 39).

Figure 9.9: Trade flows in EAPP/Nile Basin under the trade expansion scenario

(a)
Current
trade
integration
in EAPP/Nile
Basin

(b)
Trade flows
in EAPP/Nile
Basin under
the trade
expansion

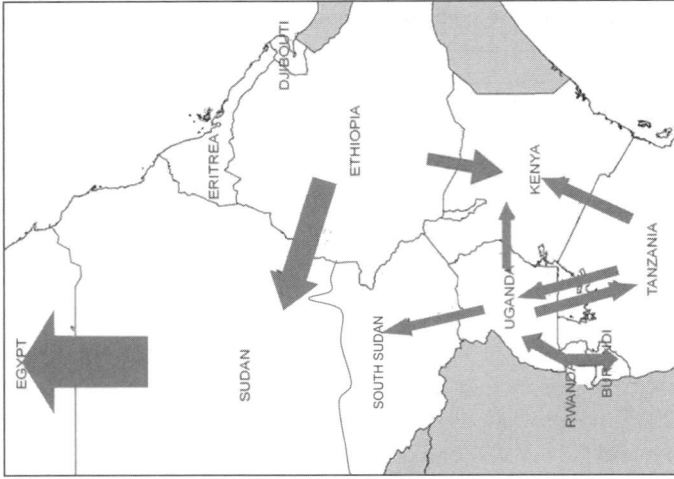

Source: Rosnes and Vennemo, 2009 in AICD, 2011, p 42.

For the EAPP, regional power trade could result in gains of more than 20% per year accruing to the power pool members. However, individual countries will experience higher returns: in some cases such as Kenya, as high as 400% (see Table 9.12). These economic gains would arise not from cost reductions but rather from an increase in power production.

Moreover, in addition to economic gains, improving regional power trade would increase reliance on hydropower and would result in significant CO_2 emission reductions, in the order of 20 million tonnes (see Table 9.13).

Table 9.12: Benefits from trade expansion in the power sector

	Unit benefit (US$/kWh)	Net power trade (TWh)	Annual benefits (US$ millions per annum)	One-time investment (US$ millions)	Rate of return (%)
Exporters					
Ethiopia	0.19	26.2	5,974	1,001	60
Rwanda	0.12	1.0	144	59	24
Sudan	0.13	13.0	2,044	1,032	20
Tanzania	0.1	2.4	288	44	66
Uganda	0.12	2.8	403	145	28
Importers					
Burundi	0.03	1.0	210	10	210
Djibouti	<0.01	<1	....	0	....
Kenya	0.01	12.0	1,200	30	400
Egypt	<0.01	123	6,165	....	...

Source: AICD (2011, p 46).

Table 9.13: Emissions savings from turning to hydropower

	WAPP	SAPP	EAPP	CAPP	Total	WAPP	SAPP	EAPP	CAPP	Total
	Production difference (TWh)					Emissions savings (per million tonnes)				
Coal	....	−41.5	0.7	....	−40.8	....	−37.8	0.6	....	−37.2
Diesel	−0.8	−0.3	0.3	....	−0.8	−0.6	−0.2	0.2	....	−0.6
Gas	−9.2	−5.3	−42.4	....	−56.8	−4.7	−2.7	−21.5	....	−28.9
HFO	0.2	....	0.4	−4.9	−4.3	0.1	....	0.3	−3.6	−3.2
Hydro	11.5	47.5	43.4	5.1	107	....	....	....	....	0
Total	1.6	0.5	2.4	0.3	4.7	−5.2	−40.7	−20.4	−3.6	−69.9

Source: Derived from Rosnes and Vennemo (2009), cited in AICD (2011, p 44).

Developing a regional approach to hydropower investment

The possibility of accelerating regional power trade in EAPP critically depends on the ability of the countries involved to deliver the necessary massive investments in hydropower. A host of technical, financial, and political challenges are making this difficult.

A recent report, *Regional Power System Master Plan and Grid Code Study* (EAPP and EAC, 2011), shows that countries in the sub-region have been planning and implementing their power systems in an isolated manner focused on the national demand for growth. While bilateral power exchange agreements between some countries in the sub-region exist, the volume exchanged is insignificant. Moreover, exporting parties have frequently failed to meet their commitments to deliver power because of deficits in their own systems.

The current demand for power is mostly being met at the power pool level, but with country variations. Additionally, power outages suppress demand at the country level. For example, in Burundi, 13% of the net demand was suppressed in 2005, in Kenya 8%, and in many of the remaining countries around 5%, whereas for the overall region, the percentage of suppressed demand as a share of net demand in 2005 was 1% (AICD, 2011, p 37). Harmonization of the national expansion plans would result in Ethiopia and Djibouti achieving a significant surplus in 10 years' time (see Table 9.14).

Table 9.14: Electricity generation according to harmonized national expansion plans (MW)

Country	Existing generation 2012	Future generation 2013	Future generation 2023	Future demand 2013	Future demand 2023	Future surplus* (%) 2013	Future surplus* (%) 2023
Burundi	49	49	269	56	204	−13	32
Djibouti	123	116	173	30	62	287	179
Ethiopia	2,179	4,890	9,140	1,964	4,912	149	86
Kenya	1,916	2,633	5,604	1,958	4,537	34	24
Rwanda	103	205	305	94	276	118	11
Sudan	3,951	3,878	7,466	2,019	5,956	92	25
Tanzania	1,205	1,423	3,573	1,213	2,479	17	44
Uganda	822	882	1,629	715	1,310	23	24

Note:*The minus sign denotes deficit.

Source: SNC Lavalin International Inc. and Parsons Brinckerhoff (2011), cited in EAPP and EAC (2011).

Surface transportation

Costs associated with logistics in East Africa are higher than in any other region in the world. This can be explained mostly by lengthy administrative and customs procedures in ports, and delays at borders and other points along the roads. Capacity constraints faced in the ports, coupled with extremely cumbersome import and export procedures, add considerable time and costs to transporting goods. This affects trade not only among countries within the sub-region, but also with other African sub-regions and with destinations in Europe and elsewhere.

The state of East African road corridors is reasonably good and has improved further over the past five years (see Figure 9.10), with the proportion of paved sections increasing (see Table 9.15). Strong differences between localities within the sub-region are noticeable, though.

Figure 9.10: Roads in good condition (%)

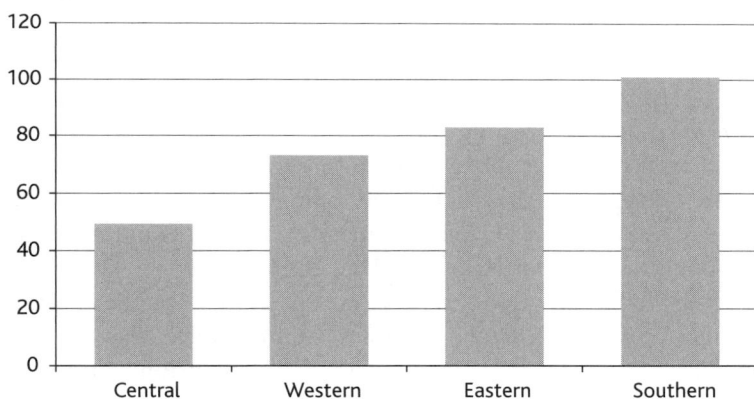

Source: Teravaninthorn and Raballand (2009) cited in AICD (2011, p 10)

Table 9.15: Key transportation corridors for international trade in Sub-Saharan Africa

Corridor	Length (km)	Road in good condition (%)	Trade density (US$ millions per km)	Implicit velocity (km/hr)	Freight tariff (US$/ tonne-km)
Central	3,280	49	4.2	6.1	0.13
Western	2,050	72	8.2	6.0	0.08
Eastern	2,845	82	5.7	8.1	0.07
Southern	5,000	100	27.9	11.6	0.05

Source: Teravaninthorn and Raballand (2009) cited in AICD (2011, p 10).

Two new bills aimed at establishing one-stop border posts and harmonized maximum vehicle loads should improve logistics on sub-region networks.

Overview

Compared with other corridors in the continent, those in East Africa perform relatively well. The road network is generally in good condition, although there are patches of poor-quality roads along some corridors and significant stretches of unpaved roads. East Africa has the second smallest trade density in all the African sub-regions, yet some of the best road conditions. While only US$5.7 million per kilometer was transported along its corridors (compared with US$8.2 million in the Western sub-region and US$27.9 million in the Southern sub-region), the implicit velocity[8] has been surpassed only by the Southern Corridor (see Table 9.15) (AICD, 2011, p 10).

Road freight tariffs average US$0.07 per tonne-kilometer, which is in the mid-range for the African sub-regions but still exceedingly high in relation to global standards. At the broader logistics level, according to the 2010 International Logistics Performance Index (LPI) (World Bank, 2010), the costs associated with logistics in East Africa are higher than in any other region in world. The domestic LPI suggests that average lead times for exports and imports in East Africa are the highest and second-highest in the developing world, respectively, while clearance times for landlocked countries are around five times higher than for those with port access (AIDC, 2011, p 10).

The slow effective velocity of freight in East Africa can be explained by lengthy customs clearance processes, administrative delays in ports, and delays at borders. In addition, roadblocks, weigh stations and random police checks that impose costs and delay trucks are pervasive (AICD, 2011, p 11). Furthermore, while overall traffic and trade flows have increased, the policy environment has shown no signs of improvement. But on a positive note, the EAC sectoral council has cleared the legal content of two bills—the One Stop Border Post Bill and the Vehicle Load Control Bill—to be introduced in the East African Legislative Assembly (Nakaweesi, 2012). These two bills will establish the operation of the planned one-stop border posts and the application of a uniform vehicle weight (axle load) limit for the region. This should speed up customs procedures and regularize truck loads across the sub-region. Regularized truck loads should also help to prevent excessive deterioration of the road networks and, therefore, reduce maintenance costs.

The trucking industry in East Africa is actually more competitive and mature in comparison with West and Central Africa. One explanation is that freight transportation rates are determined by market forces rather than by government regulations. But among logistics operators surveyed as part of the LPI study, 60–75% of the respondents from East Africa considered the port, airport, and road transportation rates to be exorbitant, while 45% of the respondents from the rest of the world found the rates high or very high. Bribes are also estimated to be in the order of US$8 million per year in the EAC alone (USAID, 2009). To gain a deeper understanding of surface transportation performance, we need to examine the national performance of the various modal components—roads, railroads, and ports.

Roads

There are a number of major corridors in East Africa. The Northern Corridor runs inland from Mombasa and is by far the most significant trading corridor in the sub-region. The Central Corridor runs through Tanzania. Further north, a corridor connects Addis Ababa with Djibouti, while another connects Addis Ababa with South Sudan. No major road routes link Ethiopia and Sudan with the EAC.

The *Northern Corridor* is the main corridor in East Africa and connects four of the five EAC countries (Kenya, Uganda, Rwanda, and Burundi) with the port of Mombasa. It also provides connections to South Sudan, Eastern DRC, and parts of Northern Tanzania (see Figures 9.12 and 9.13). It starts out in Kenya as a paved corridor, which was generally in good or fair condition as at 2008. However, the Ugandan portions of the corridor are only about three-quarters paved, with a marked decline in road infrastructure condition. In Kampala, the corridor then bifurcates towards Kigali (Rwanda) and Juba (South Sudan). The Rwandan portions are paved and reasonably maintained, while the northern portions in South Sudan remain unpaved but in reasonable condition. Further north in Ethiopia and Sudan, there is a marked absence of paving, even along routes of strategic significance.

In the south of the sub-region, the *Central Corridor* also plays an important role connecting the port of Dar es Salaam to markets in Tanzania, Burundi, Rwanda, Uganda, and the DRC (see Figure 9.13). Along the southern side of Lake Victoria, the Central Corridor route from Bujumbura to Dar es Salaam starts out in Burundi as a paved road in reasonable condition, while the Tanzanian section is only partially paved but is fairly well maintained.

Figure 9.11: East African Community Road Network Project

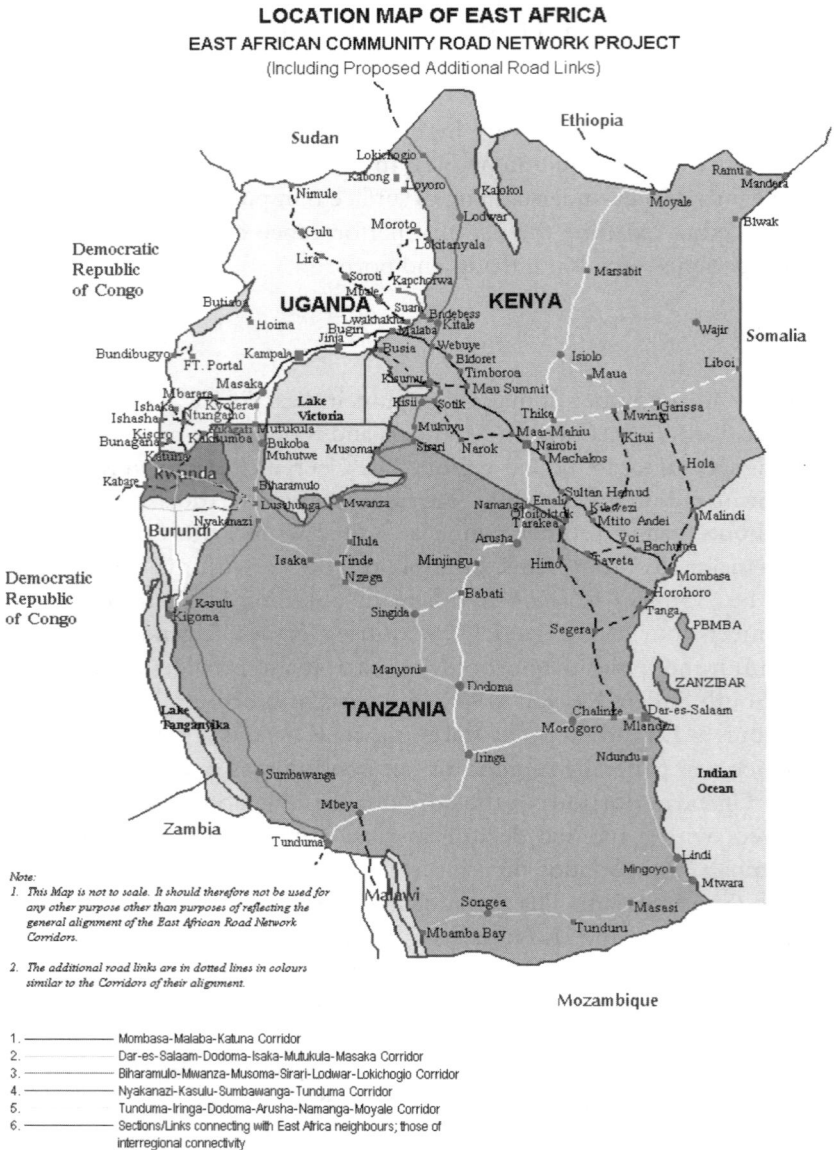

LOCATION MAP OF EAST AFRICA
EAST AFRICAN COMMUNITY ROAD NETWORK PROJECT
(Including Proposed Additional Road Links)

Note:
1. This Map is not to scale. It should therefore not be used for any other purpose other than purposes of reflecting the general alignment of the East African Road Network Corridors.

2. The additional road links are in dotted lines in colours similar to the Corridors of their alignment.

1. ——————— Mombasa-Malaba-Katuna Corridor
2. ················ Dar-es-Salaam-Dodoma-Isaka-Mutukula-Masaka Corridor
3. – – – – – Biharamulo-Mwanza-Musoma-Sirari-Lodwar-Lokichogio Corridor
4. ——————— Nyakanazi-Kasulu-Sumbawanga-Tunduma Corridor
5. Tunduma-Iringa-Dodoma-Arusha-Namanga-Moyale Corridor
6. ——————— Sections/Links connecting with East Africa neighbours; those of interregional connectivity

Source: East African Community Infrastructure (2013)

Figure 9.12: Northern Corridor

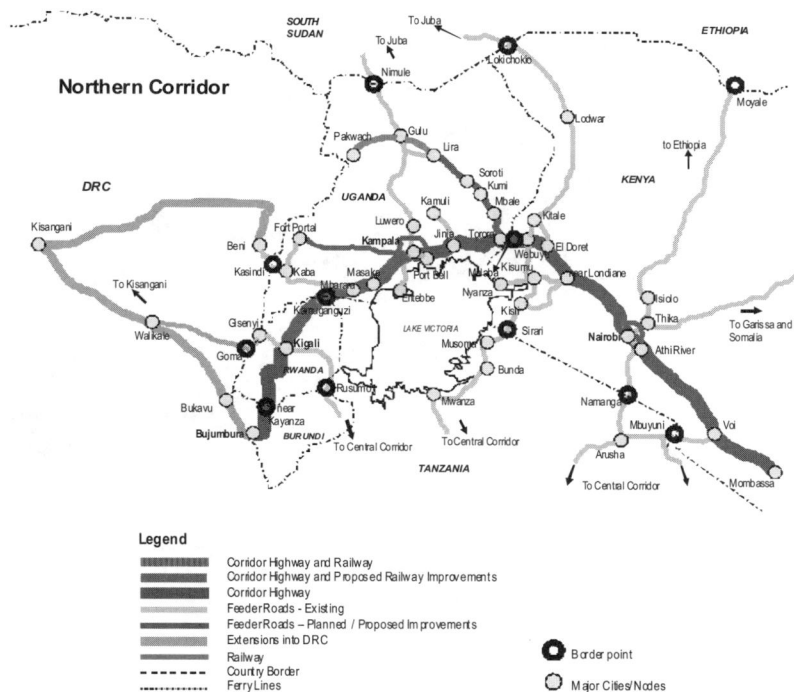

Source: EAC (2011).

The recent publication of the *Corridor Diagnostic Study of the Northern and Central Corridors of East Africa* (EAC, 2011) responded to the demand for an in-depth assessment of corridor performance and preparation of an action plan to remove identified logistical impediments.

Performance indicators in this study classify roads in levels of service, such that the best operating conditions enable free flow, high average speed, and the possibility to overtake easily. There are scant data available for the Central Corridor. However, for the Northern Corridor, the study shows that only 13% of roads are in good condition, 44% are in fair condition, and 43% in bad condition.

The only comparable statistic between the AICD 2011 report and the *Corridor Diagnostic Study* is the percentage of paved roads. The latter shows that paved roads have substantially increased along the Central Corridor. In 2006, the figure was 57%, but by 2010 it had risen to 87%. The Northern Corridor is now almost totally paved (see Table 9.16 and Figure 9.14).

Figure 9.13: Central Corridor

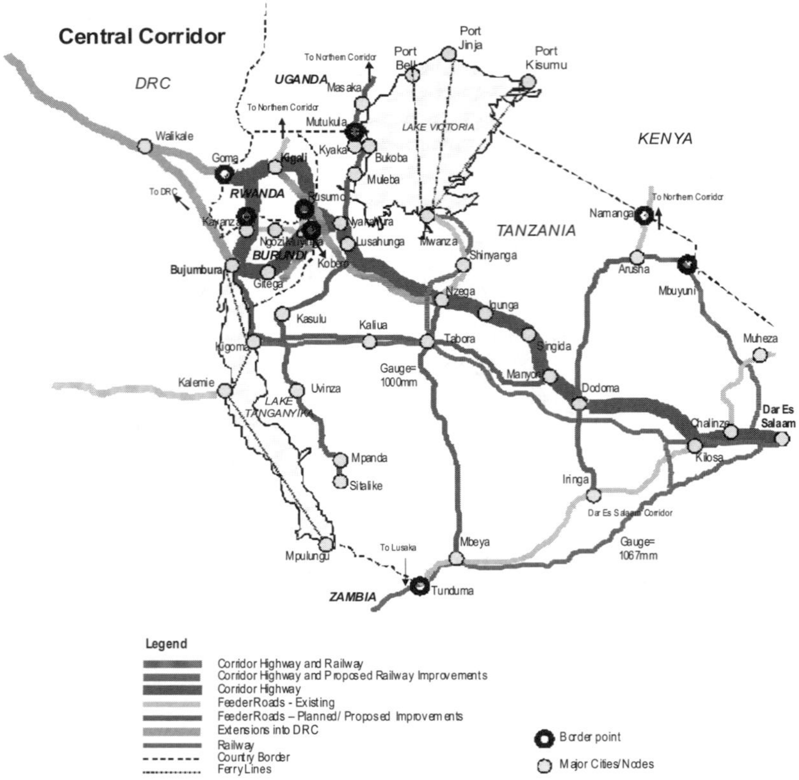

Source: EAC (2011)

Table 9.16: Status of the two main corridors in East Africa

Status	Northern Corridor		Central Corridor	
	Length in km	%	Length in km	%
1 lane	1,738	91.5	3,026	80.2
2 lanes	161	8.5	747	19.8
Paved	1,896	99.8	2,651	70.3
Unpaved	3	0.2	449	11.9
Good	259	13.4	67	1.8
Fair	849	43.8	286	7.6
Poor	831	42.9	9	0.2
Total	1,899		3,773	

Source: EAC (2011) and AICD (2011).

Figure 9.14: Comparison of paved roads between 2006 and 2011 for Northern and Central Corridors (%)

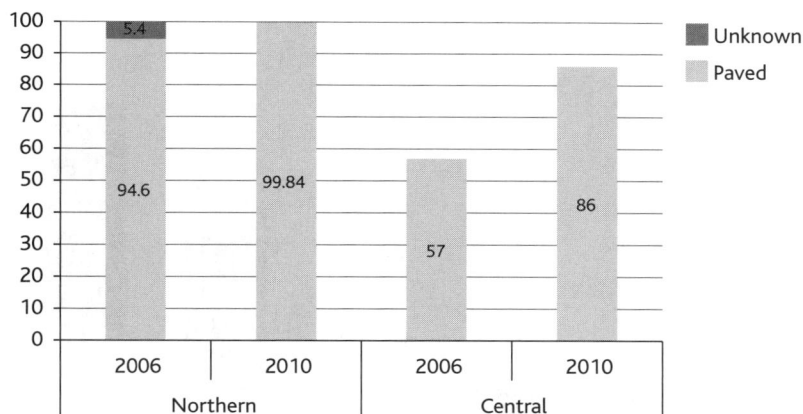

Source: EAC (2011) and AICD (2011).

The recent study also highlights the significant regional differences in the condition and types of corridors in East Africa. Between 84% and 97% of the Northern Corridor, which is by far the most significant artery in the region (connecting Kenya, Uganda, Rwanda, and South Sudan), is paved. By comparison, only 57% of the road from Dar es Salaam to Bujumbura and 23% of the road from Addis Ababa to Djibouti is paved (see Table 9.17).

The reason for the higher level of paving along the Northern Corridor is the greater concentration of traffic. As Figure 9.15 indicates,

Table 9.17: Type and condition of East African road corridors, 2011

	Condition (%)		Type (%)	
	Good	Fair	Poor	Paved
Mombasa to Nairobi to Kampala (Kenya–Uganda)	50	34	13	97
Mombasa to Nairobi to Kampala to Kigali (Kenya–Uganda–Rwanda)	40	36	11	94
Mombasa to Nairobi to Kampala to Juba (Kenya–Uganda–South Sudan)	44	48	9	84
Dar es Salaam to Bujumbura (Tanzania–Burundi)	45	36	6	57
Addis Ababa to Djibouti (Ethiopia–Djibouti)	37	17	16	23

Source: EAC (2011)

Figure 9.15: Annual average daily traffic (AADT) by corridor, 2011

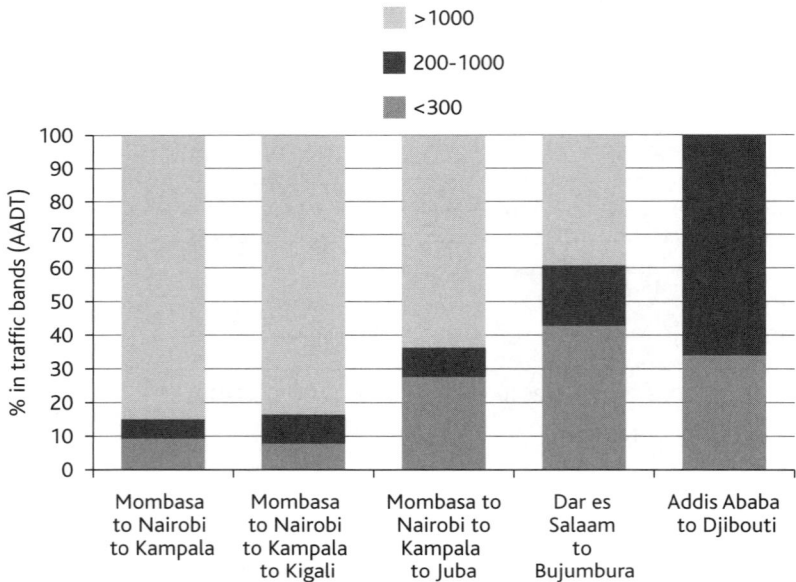

Source: EAC (2011)

most of the annual average daily traffic (AADT) is concentrated above 1,000 vehicles in the three Northern Corridor sections, compared with only 39% in the Dar es Salaam–Bujumbura corridor and the Addis Ababa–Djibouti corridor with less than 1,000 vehicles.

The competitiveness of each corridor can be gauged by aggregating the time and costs associated with transport, administrative processes (customs) in ports, and long waits along the route. The cost of moving imports (or exports) along each of these key arteries and the time taken for this movement are key elements of competitiveness for both international and intra-regional trade.

There are significant cost differences among road corridors serving landlocked countries and a strong negative correlation between lower traffic volumes and cost. As the traffic increases, the unit costs of transportation (per tonne) decrease. Costs and times are more significant for the four landlocked East African countries (Ethiopia, Burundi, Rwanda, and Uganda) due to inefficient ports, high freight rates, and delays at borders. Among the road corridors serving landlocked countries, there are significant cost differences. Based on the three main intra-regional arteries in East Africa, the cost of importing goods from a landlocked country lies in the range of US$170 to US$370 per tonne-kilometer. Overall, travel to landlocked Burundi, Rwanda, and

Box 9.1: The Nairobi–Thika superhighway: a successful interregional road project

The 50km Nairobi–Thika superhighway is a positive example of a large project undertaken jointly by different actors in order to improve regional road infrastructure. The area covered lies within the Nairobi Metropolitan and Central Province, including large sections of the city and Thika district. The superhighway is an important part of the regional and continental transport corridor from Cape Town, South Africa to Cairo, Egypt.

The total cost of the project amounted to US$360 million, of which US$180 million were provided by the African Development Bank. The Kenyan government contributed US$80 million and the Exim Bank of China, US$100 million.

The superhighway will serve approximately 1 million people who live along the road network. The main beneficiaries comprise commuters who travel daily to the Central Business District, for example, workers, students, shoppers, and traders. It will reduce the time the goods take to reach urban markets and so enhance the supply chain.

The superhighway's major impact will be to reduce transport costs and travel times in the region. The time taken to traverse Thika town and Nairobi has fallen from two to three hours to 30-45 minutes (AfDB, 2012a). The project will contribute to transform the country into an economic hub and will boost trade with other countries in the region.

The Nairobi–Thika superhighway in Kenya, which was officially opened by President Mwai Kibaki in November 2012

Photo: Xinhua: Ding Haitao

An aerial view of Thika superhighway, Nairobi, Kenya

Uganda is cheaper via the Northern Corridor than via the Central Corridor. For Burundi, the Northern Corridor has a competitive edge over the Central Corridor. This is striking because Bujumbura is closer to Dar es Salaam than to Mombasa (AICD, 2011, p 16). Port times generally constitute 50–80% of the total time required to move imports to landlocked countries. Similarly, costs in ports and high transportation rates constitute more than 90% of the total cost of importing goods (see Figures 9.16 and 9.17).

Railroads

Except for Tazara, there is no effective regional railroad network within East Africa. Furthermore, the existing rail networks are scarcely used, which hinders regional integration (Figure 9.18). The national rail networks of the East African member states are mostly independent of one another, again with the exception of Tazara, which is linked into the Southern African network. This situation provides a stark contrast to Southern Africa, where national railroad systems form a regional network that spans half a dozen countries. Further integration of East Africa's rail systems is complicated by the use of different gauges in the region. Only three East African railroad lines span more than one country.

Figure 9.16: Time required to import goods by road through alternative gateways

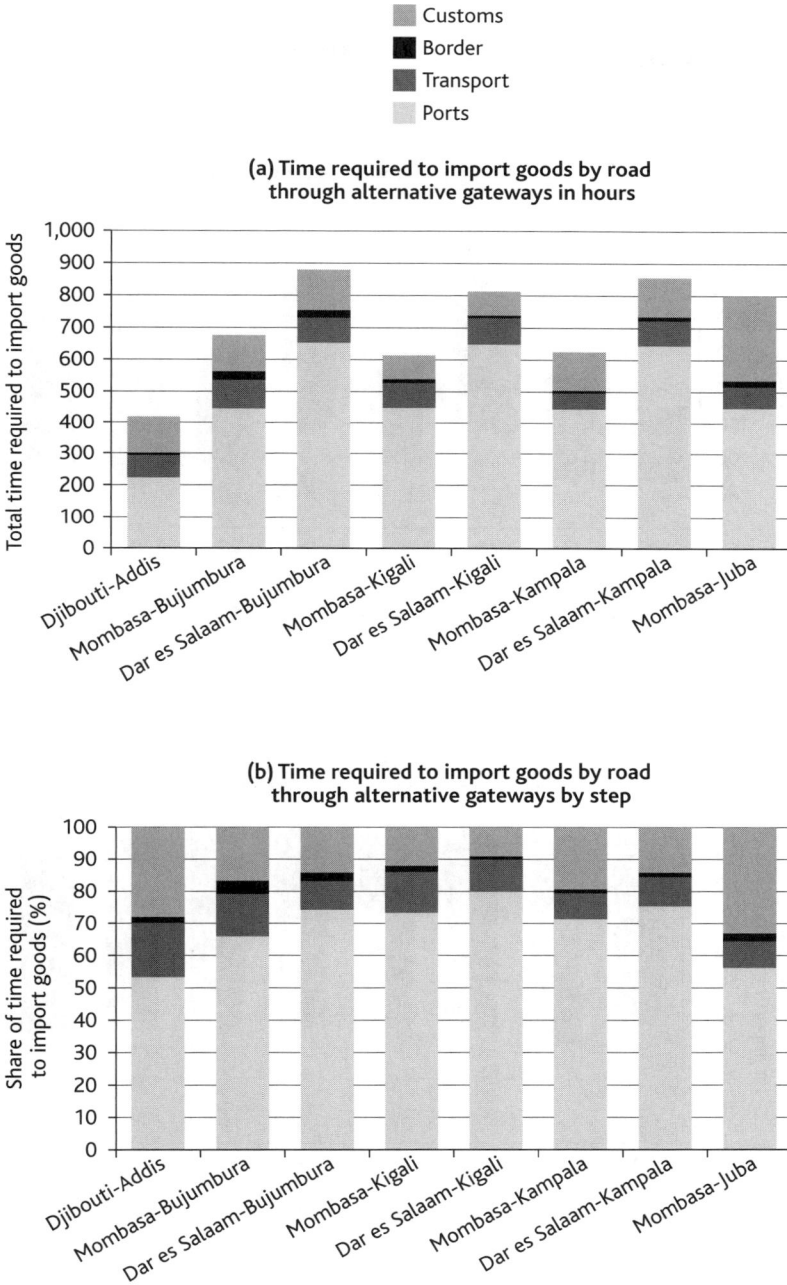

(a) Time required to import goods by road through alternative gateways in hours

(b) Time required to import goods by road through alternative gateways by step

Source: Ranganathan and Foster (2011).

Figure 9.17: Cost of importing goods by road through alternative gateways

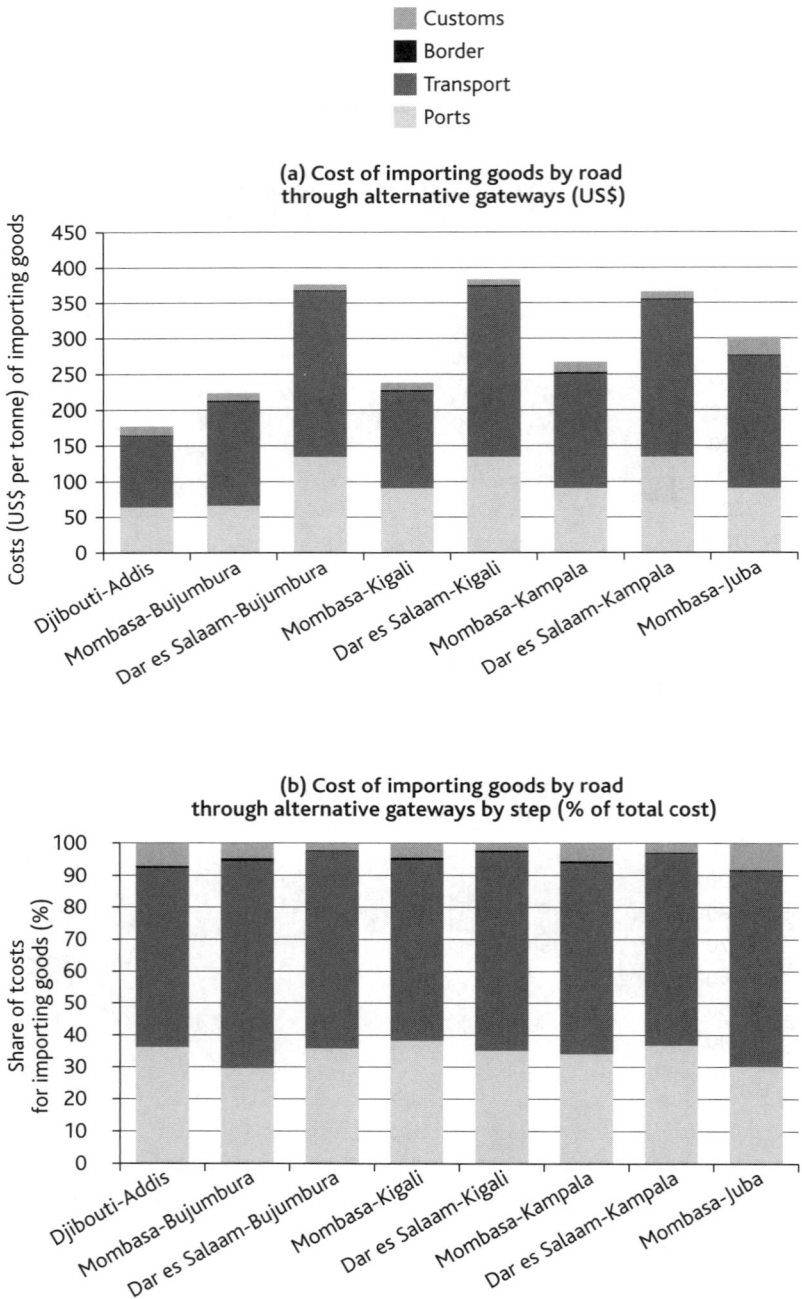

(a) Cost of importing goods by road
through alternative gateways (US$)

(b) Cost of importing goods by road
through alternative gateways by step (% of total cost)

Source: Ranganathan and Foster (2011).

Figure 9.18: EAC current rail network with proposed new lines

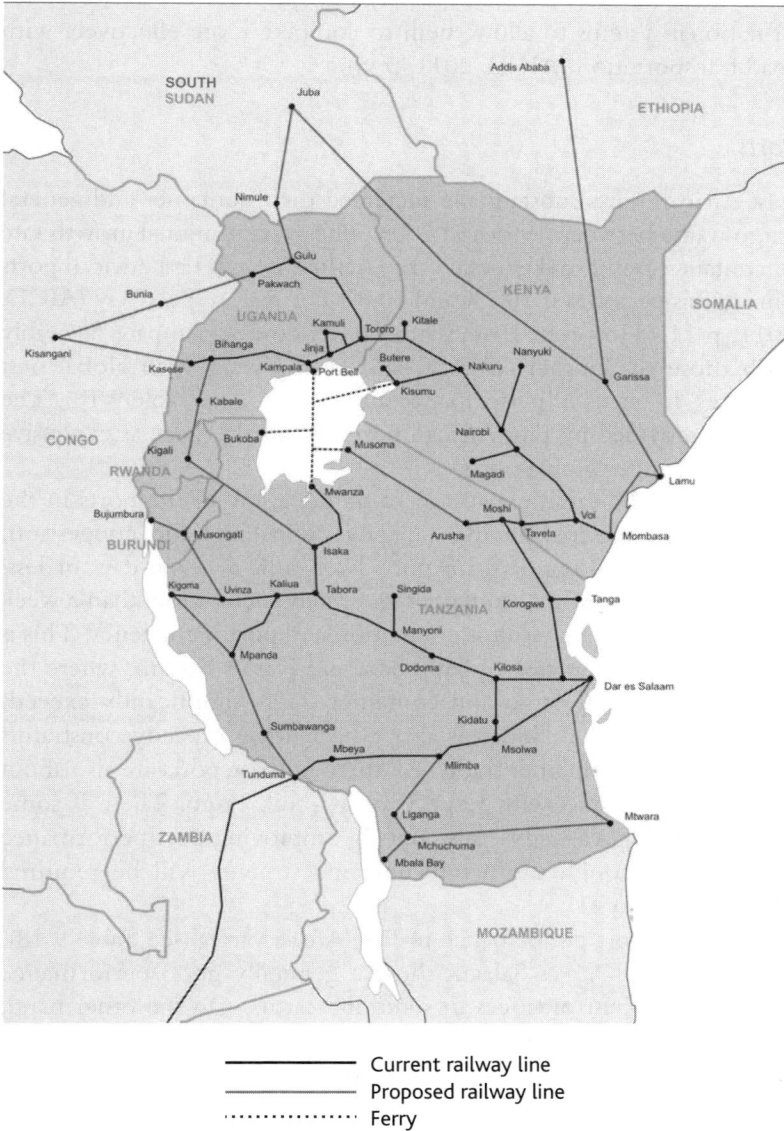

Current railway line
Proposed railway line
Ferry

Source: EAC (2013)

Poor operational performance (with the exception of Tazara and the Tanzania Railways Corporation), together with limited use of existing rail networks, makes the economic case for integration even less clear. The most pressing priority is to improve the performance of national systems to allow them to compete more effectively with road transportation (AICD, 2011, p vi).

Ports

East African ports substantially increased their container and general cargo traffic between 1995 and 2005. The average annual growth rate of container traffic and general cargo traffic through East African ports during this period was 10.7% and 10.8% per year, respectively (AICD, 2011, p 21). However, East African ports do not compare favorably with those of Southern Africa, and even less so with global best practices, in terms of performance and charges (see Table 9.18). The services provided by East African ports are nearly twice as expensive as those in other global ports.

Owing to the rapid expansion of traffic, a few of the ports in the sub-region are experiencing capacity constraints and congestion. The international standard for port dwell time is seven days or less. However in East Africa, containers routinely spend more than a week in the terminal. The result is congestion and port inefficiency. This is most notable in the case of Mombasa and Dar es Salaam, where the volume of general cargo and container traffic significantly exceeds design capacity. Port Sudan is also experiencing capacity constraints with respect to container traffic. All three of these ports are also about to reach their limits with respect to dry-bulk cargo. There is some scope for easing capacity constraints by improving port performance efficiency, although ultimately new investments will be required (AICD, 2011, p 21).

Individual port performance in East Africa varies (see Table 9.18). Mombasa and Dar es Salaam show a generally good performance within global best practices in some indicators. On the other hand, Port Sudan and Djibouti exhibit much lower port efficiency levels.

The capacity constraints faced in the ports of Mombasa and Dar es Salaam, coupled with extremely lengthy import and export procedures, considerably extend the time required to clear goods. The long detention of goods in port has become a major obstacle to distribution and a major contributor to logistics costs, thereby impeding trade.

Table 9.18: Comparative performance across East African ports and African subregions

Performance indicator	Djibouti	Mombasa	Port Sudan	Dar es Salaam	East Africa	Southern Africa	West Africa	Global best practice
Container dwell time (days)	8	5	28	7	5-28	4-8	11-30	<7
Truck processing time (hours)	12	5	24	5	4-24	2-12	6-24	1
Container crane productivity (container per hour)	17	10	8	20	8-20	8-22	7-20	20-30
Charges								
Container cargo handling charge (US$ per TEU*)	135	68	150	275	135-275	110-243	100-320	80-150
General cargo handling charge (US$ per tonne)	8	7	10	14	6-15	11-15	8-15	7-9

Note: *Twenty foot equivalent unit
Source: AICD (2011, p 24).

Information and communications technology

East Africa's ICT sector is characterized by high costs and low penetration (see Figure 9.19). However, a trend of falling prices and higher penetration has been observed, particularly where there is access to submarine cables. The most pressing issue for the sub-region is to complete the fiber-optic backbone and provide broader coverage to all East Africa. Around 3,565 kilometers of fiber-optic cable are needed to complete the network. This represents a major investment of US$96 million but it promises high rates of return, particularly for Sudan (116%) and Uganda (304%).

Overview

By 2012, East Africa had the lowest costs and highest penetration of internet services and landline telephone among the African sub-regions, while the density of mobile subscriptions was among the lowest in Africa. The EAC has 0.1 broadband subscribers, 0.3 internet subscribers, and 55.4 mobile telephone subscribers per 100 inhabitants (see Table 9.19).

Within East Africa, there is strong mobile signal coverage around Lake Victoria—spanning Rwanda, Uganda, and Kenya. Coverage in Burundi, Sudan and Tanzania is less extensive but good. Ethiopia

Figure 9.19: Internet and telephone subscriptions (2013)

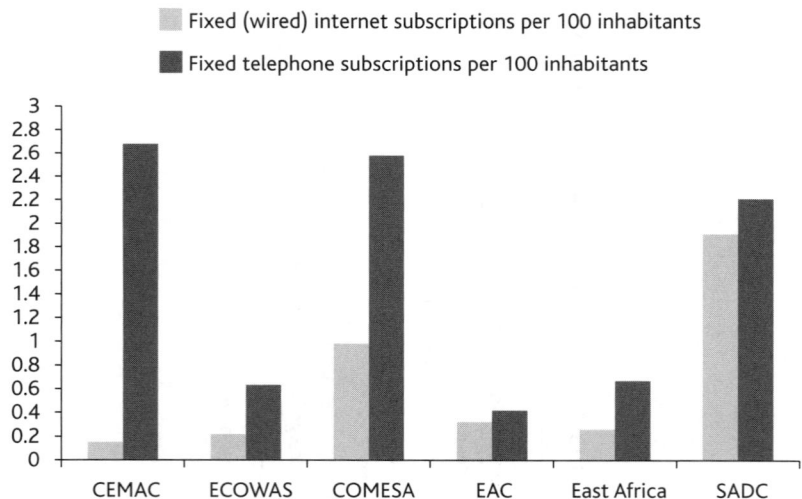

Source: International Communications Union (ICT) database (www.itu.int/en/ITU-D/Statistics/)

Table 9.19: Access and pricing in the ICT sector, by African region (2012)

Indicator	CEMAC	ECOWAS	COMESA	EAC	East Africa	SADC
Fixed (wired) broadband subscriptions (per 100 people)	0.4	0.1	0.6	0.1	0.0	0.5
International internet bandwidth (bit/s per Internet user)	1,458.0	3,959.3	5,917.9	8,481.2	6,984.0	5,575.0
Fixed (wired) internet subscriptions (mostly 2012–13, per 100 people)	0.2	0.2	1.0	0.3	0.3	1.9
Landline telephone subscriptions (per 100 people)	2.7	0.6	2.6	0.4	0.7	2.2
Mobile cellular telephone subscriptions (per 100 people)	58.1	69.7	57.5	55.4	47.0	62.9
Prices (US$)						
Price of prepaid mobile monthly sub-basket	17.6	14.6	12.5	8.8	7.4	16.9
Price of a three-minute call to US	5.68	0.83	2.2	1.37		1.5
Price of fixed-broadband sub-basket	357.8	127.7	162.9	44.6	35.3	73.3
Price of landline telephone monthly sub-basket	24.4	10.2	8.3	9.9	7.6	12.7

Notes: Mobile monthly sub-basket: standard basket of mobile monthly usage for 30 outgoing calls per month (on-net, off-net, to a landline, and for peak and off-peak times) in predetermined ratios, plus 100 SMS messages. Fixed-broadband (internet) sub-basket: based on a monthly usage of (a minimum of) 1 gigabyte. Landline telephone sub-basket: refers to the monthly price charged for subscribing to the Public Switched Telephone Network, plus the cost of 30 local calls to the same (fixed) network (15 peak and 15 off-peak calls) of three minutes each.

Source: ICT database (www.itu.int/en/ITU-D/Statistics/).

and Burundi stand out for its low mobile coverage and penetration. The density of internet and broadband subscribers, and international internet bandwidth is generally low across East Africa, but it is particularly low in Rwanda (see Table 9.20).

Prices vary widely among countries. Telecom services in Ethiopia and Sudan are generally cheaper than in the EAC countries. Most recent estimates for mobile prices range from less than US$1 per month for a standard basket of services in Ethiopia and Sudan to almost US$112 per month in Rwanda. The median price for a standard basket of services in the sub-region is around US$9. The price of broadband service reveals wide variation across countries (by up to a factor of 10), ranging from US$9.7 per month in Sudan to US$111.7 per month in Rwanda (see Table 9.21).

There are also substantial differences in call rates among countries. In the EAC, the cost of international calls to another EAC country substantially exceeds that of international calls to the US. The difference is as much as 14 cents per minute in Kenya and 19 cents in Tanzania. Internet prices also generally remain high in the EAC due to a lack of submarine cables.

The most pressing issue for the region is to complete the fiber-optic backbone to improve GSM coverage and reduce the price discrepancy between EAC and broader East Africa.

Given that landline services have largely been overtaken by mobile services in East Africa, the regional availability of roaming arrangements on mobile tariffs is in many ways much more relevant than the level of international landline tariffs. East Africa pioneered borderless mobile roaming, with free incoming calls and local tariffs. But so far only limited progress with intra-regional roaming has been achieved, particularly connecting Kenya with Tanzania, Kenya with Uganda, Uganda with Rwanda, and Uganda with Tanzania. Regional cooperation has been partly introduced through the incumbent telecoms operators. The East African Regulatory Post and Telecommunications Organization, an EAC regulatory body, is less active than similar sub-regional organizations, although it has made some progress.

Foreign investment has contributed to connectivity and service enhancement, particularly when the same investor is involved in different countries. For example, Zain offers attractive mobile prices for its subscribers roaming around Kenya, Tanzania, and Uganda. Collaboration over mobile roaming and fiber-optic connectivity between Rwandatel and Uganda Telecom has also been facilitated by common ownership (AICD, 2011, p 51).

The state of infrastructure in East Africa

Table 9.20: Access in the ICT sector, by country (2012)

Indicator	Burundi	Kenya	Rwanda	Tanzania	Uganda	Ethiopia	Sudan
Coverage of mobile network (% of population)	60	92	90	60	97	10	70
Mobile cellular telephone subscriptions (per 100 people)	22.8	71.2	49.7	57.0	45.0	22.4	74.4
Fixed (wired) internet subscriptions (mostly 2012-13, per 100 people)	0.9	0.2	0.0	0.4	0.3	0.2	0.1
Fixed (wired) broadband subscriptions (per 100 people)	0	0.1	0	0	0.1	0	0.1
International internet bandwidth (bit/s per internet user)	3,462.0	23,715.0	6,585.0	3,974.0	4,670.0	4,779.0	1,703.0
Landline telephone subscriptions (per 100 people)	0.2	0.6	0.4	0.4	0.3	0.9	1.1

Source: ICT database (www.itu.int/en/ITU-D/Statistics/).

Table 9.21: Pricing in the ICT sector, by country (US$)

Indicator	Burundi	Kenya	Rwanda	Tanzania	Uganda	Ethiopia	Sudan
Price of a prepaid mobile monthly sub-basket	...	3.6	14.7	7.7	9	3.8	5.6
Price of a three-minute call to USA	2.4	1.8	1.3	0.7	1.4	3.3	1.3
Price of fixed-broadband sub-basket	...	33.7	111.7	19.1	14	23.7	9.7
Price of landline telephone monthly sub-basket	...	12.6	9	8.9	9.2	1	4.9

Notes: Mobile monthly sub-basket: standard basket of mobile monthly usage for 30 outgoing calls per month (on-net, off-net, to a landline, and for peak and off-peak times) in predetermined ratios, plus 100 SMS messages. Fixed-broadband (internet) sub-basket: is based on a monthly usage of (a minimum of) 1 gigabyte. Landline telephone sub-basket: refers to the monthly price charged for subscribing to the Public Switched Telephone Network, plus the cost of 30 local calls to the same (fixed) network (15 peak and 15 off-peak calls) of three minutes each.

Source: World Bank (2014). Price of a three-minute call to US: AICD (2011).

Opening up the telecommunications market has also resulted in a price decrease, particularly in Kenya. This has paved the way in East Africa for the establishment of gateways with licenses for multiple mobile operators and to cheaper international call tariffs (World Economic Forum, 2007).

Submarine cable access

For years, the EAC suffered from a shortage of international connectivity, due to lack of undersea fiber-optic cables. As at 2007, most of the EAC countries did not have access to submarine cables (Ethiopia and Sudan have gained access for some time through SAS-1). However, since 2009 this situation has been changing with the advent of three new cable systems: SEACOM (South Africa–East Africa–South Asia–Fiber Optic Cable), the East African Submarine Cable System (EASSy) and the TEAMS cable, linking the United Arab Emirates and Kenya (see Figure 9.20). The installation of these new

Figure 9.20: Mediterranean undersea cable

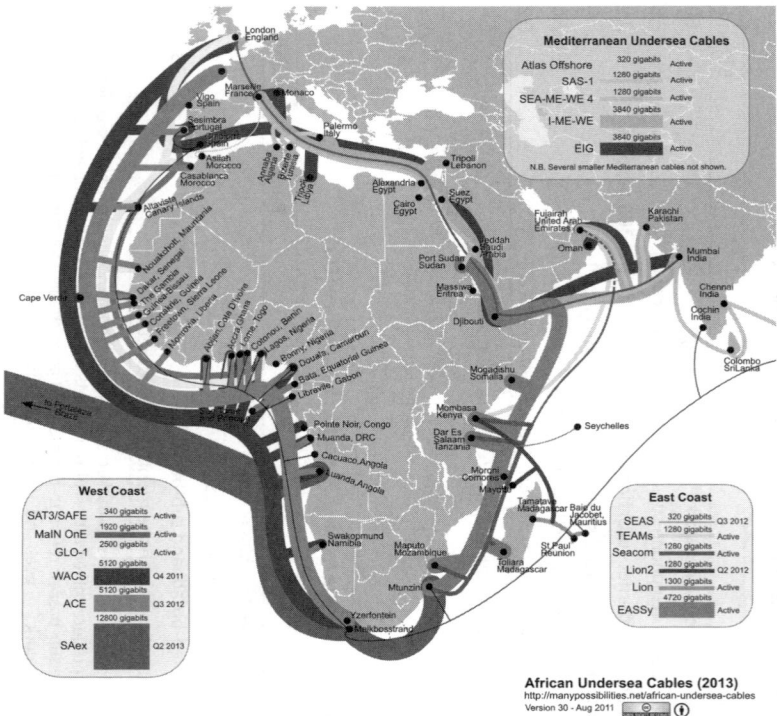

Source: www.flickr.com/photos/ssong/6025279006/in/photostream

submarine cables is spurring upgrades and the expansion of domestic backbones and cross-border agreements for onward transmission throughout the region (AICD, 2011, p 52).

The experience of Sub-Saharan Africa shows that countries with submarine cable access enjoy greater benefits, such as lower prices and improved connectivity speeds. Moreover, these become even greater if there is competitive access to the gateway (see Table 9.22). The experience of other African countries suggests that connecting a country to a submarine cable can reduce the costs of broadband internet by as much as 75%. Not only does this bring substantial savings to existing broadband users, but a substantial price reduction generally induces additional hiring of the broadband service (AICD, 2011, p 55).

Intraregional connectivity: completing the fiber-optic backbone network

To complete the regional fiber-optic backbone network in East Africa and obtain full intraregional connectivity, around 3,565 kilometers of new fiber-optic links are needed. This means a required investment of US$96 million. Tanzania and Kenya would account for 60% of the total investment needs (see Table 9.23).

The benefits of completing regional integration of ICT networks would be substantial in relation to the modest costs. The overall benefits are estimated at US$53 million per year for the sub-region, against a one-time cost of US$96 million. As shown in Table 9.24, completing East Africa's regional fiber-optic network promises high rates of return, particularly for Sudan (116%) and Uganda (304%). The

Table 9.22: Comparison of internet and phone charges in Sub-Saharan Africa, with and without access to submarine cables

	Country share (%)	Price per minute for a call within Sub-Saharan Africa (US$)	Price per minute for a call to US (US$)	Price for 20 hours per month of dial-up internet access (US$)
No access to submarine cable	67	1.34	0.86	67.95
Access to submarine cable	32	0.57	0.48	47.28
Monopoly international gateway	16	0.70	0.72	37.36
Competitive international gateways	16	0.48	0.23	36.62

Source: AICD (2011, p 53).

Table 9.23: Investment needs to complete gaps in East Africa's fiber-optic backbone

Country	Gap (km)	Investment (US$ millions)
Eastern Africa	3,565	96
Burundi	90	2
Ethiopia	408	11
Kenya	894	24
Rwanda	198	5
Sudan	670	18
Tanzania	1,220	33
Uganda	85	2

Source: AICD (2011, p 55).

Table 9.24: Expected rates of return from expanding the subregional fiber-optic network

	Broadband price (US$/month)		Broadband subscriptions ('000s)		Benefits (US$ millions/ year)	Costs (US$ millions)	Rate of return (%)
	Baseline 2008	Induced	Baseline 2008	Induced			
Burundi	...	....	0.2	....	....	2	....
Ethiopia	486.5	304.1	0.4	5.5	6	11	59
Kenya	39.8	24.9	3.3	120.9	11	24	46
Rwanda	88	55.0	4.2	6.5	2	5	42
Sudan	23.25	14.5	44.6	354.3	21	18	116
Tanzania	63.56	39.7	6.4	43.5	7	33	22
Uganda	194.37	121.5	4.8	9.1	6	2	304

Source: AICD (2011, p 56).

bulk of the benefits would derive from the addition of new broadband users. Regional integration is therefore a positive business prospect for broadband service providers (AICD, 2011, p 55).

Notes

[1] Includes the East African Community (EAC) countries of Burundi, Kenya, Rwanda, Tanzania, and Uganda, as well as Sudan and Ethiopia.

[2] "Productive infrastructure" can be defined as infrastructure that facilitates the production of goods and services, and thereby boosts a country's GDP.

[3] www.muwsa.or.tz/uploads/Tanzania_Water_Policy_Overview.pdf

[4] www.twaweza.org/uploads/files/SzW-R8-WaterFINAL25032014-EN.pdf; www.wateraid.org/~/media/Publications/national-water-sector-assessment-tanzania.pdf

[5] CEMAC = Economic and Monetary Community of Central Africa; COMESA = Common Market for Eastern and Southern Africa; SADC = Southern African Development Community; ECOWAS = Economic Community of West African States.

[6] For this section East Africa is made up of Burundi, Djibouti, Eritrea, Ethiopia, Kenya, Rwanda, Somalia, South Sudan, Sudan and Uganda. Central Africa: Cameroon, CAR, Chad, Congo, Democratic Republic of Congo, Equatorial Guinea and Gabon. Southern Africa: Angola, Botswana, Comoros, Lesotho, Madagascar, Malawi, Mauritius, Mozambique, Namibia, Seychelles, South Africa, Swaziland, United Republic of Tanzania, Zambia and Zimbabwe. West Africa: Benin, Burkina Faso, Cabo Verde, Côte d'Ivoire, Ghana, Guineas, Guinea-Bissau, Liberia, Mali, Mauritania, Niger, Nigeria, São Tomé and Príncipe, Senegal, Sierra Leone and Togo.

[7] The East African Power Pool has been expanded to include key Nile Basin trading partners Egypt, Ethiopia, and Sudan.

[8] Implicit velocity is the total distance divided by the total time taken to make the trip, including time spent stationary in ports, at border crossings, and other stops.

References

Africa Infrastructure Country Diagnostic (AICD) (2011) *East Africa's Infrastructure: A Regional Perspective*, Policy Research Working Paper No.5844. Washington, DC: World Bank, available at http://econ.worldbank.org/external/default/main?pagePK=64165259&piPK=64165421&theSitePK=469372&menuPK=64166093&entityID=000158349_20111013121848.

African Development Bank (AfDB) (2012a) 'AfDB-funded Thika superhighway: a masterpiece for East Africa: "A national pride" – President Mwai Kibaki', available at http://www.afdb.org/en/news-and-events/article/afdb-funded-thika-superhighway-a-masterpiece-for-east-africa-a-national-pride-president-mwai-kibaki-9986.

AfDB (2012b) *African Infrastructure Development Index. Draft.* AfDB:Tunis.

EAC (2011) *Corridor Diagnostic Study of the Northern and Central Corridors of East Africa*, available at www.eastafricancorridors.org/updates/actionplan/CDS%20Action%20Plan%20Vol%201%20ToC%20ExSum.pdf.

EAPP and EAC (2011) *Regional Power System Master Plan and Grid Code Study*. East African Power Pool Permanent Secretariat: Addis Ababa.

East African Community (EAC) (2013) 'Infrastructure', available at www.infrastructure.eac.int.

IEA (International Energy Agency) (2014) *Africa Energy Outlook: A Focus on Energy Prospects in Sub-Saharan Africa*. Paris: IEA.

Nakaweesi, D. (2011). "East Africa okays one stop border post Bill", *The Monitor*, 27 October, available at www.monitor.co.ug/Business/ East-Africa-okays-one-stop-border-post-Bill/-/688322/1604018/-/ jvdy16z/-/index.htm.

Ranganathan, R. and Foster, V. (2011) *East Africa's Infrastructure: A Continental Perspective*. Policy Research Working Paper 5844, Washington, DC: World Bank.

USAID (United States Agency for International Development) (2009) *Cross-Border Trade in East African Countries: Shared Issues and Priorities for Reform*. Washington, DC: USAID.

World Bank (2010) 'Logistics Performance Index 2010', in *Connecting to Compete 2010: Trade Logistics in the Global Economy*. Washington, DC: World Bank.

World Bank and International Energy Agency (2014) *Sustainable Energy for All 2013–2014: Global Tracking Framework*. Washington, DC: World Bank.

World Economic Forum, World Bank and African Development Bank (2007) *The Africa Competitiveness Report 2007*. Geneva: World Economic Forum, available at https://openknowledge.worldbank. org/handle/10986/6612.

TEN

Integrated approaches for infrastructure

Charles Leyeka Lufumpa, Maurice Mubila and Tito Yepes

Introduction

Despite significant differences between countries, in general Africa requires better quality and more infrastructure vis-à-vis its progress in other development areas. Not only is Africa's level of infrastructure endowment low, but the continent also faces higher access costs for all infrastructure services compared with other developing regions. Of all the infrastructure sub-sectors, that of energy registers the largest deficit. While total road density and access to clean water compare relatively well, they still lag behind that of other developing regions. In the area of information and communications technology (ICT), even the top five African countries are only ranked 66th to 109th against all countries.

Estimates of investment requirements for infrastructure should be used only as indications of the different emphases needed. Not as overall truth of what is actually needed because there is always space to invest more vis-à-vis the progress in other components of development. The African Infrastructure Country Diagnostic (AICD) report (Foster and Briceño-Garmendia, 2009) presents the latest detailed calculations of annual infrastructure investment needs for Africa. Given the use of these numbers for the discussion on development, it would not be necessary to update them more regularly. The total investment requirements estimated in the study amounts to US$93 billion, one-third of which is needed to cover operations and maintenance. With current spending of US$45 billion a year, the financial gap is sizable and shows the importance of appropriate management to maximize the value for the money invested. Even at the most efficient costs of provision, the region cannot afford the wrong selection of portfolio projects.

Funding the infrastructure gap is not the sole problem—the core issues are institutional in nature. Pouring additional funding into sectors characterized by high levels of inefficiency makes little sense. The region needs to improve the capacity and efficiency of those institutions responsible for developing and managing infrastructure. The goal should not be to demolish existing institutions but to reform them and support their transformations.

While the scale of the challenge varies greatly across African countries, three general strategies could help to foster institutional advancements, namely: more efficient spending; an enlarged regional approach to infrastructure investment based on a pragmatic selection of projects; and an improved regulatory framework.

More efficient spending

At the outset, when choosing infrastructure projects, adherence to a set of criteria will help to achieve efficient spending, by identifying those projects with the highest returns. When improving or expanding current infrastructure, investment should make the most of the resources at hand, since any wastage will affect the development of other projects. Service providers should ensure that they are charging cost-recovery tariffs and utilizing cost-saving technologies, in order to provide a reliable, but more importantly, a sustainable service. Reconstructing infrastructure that was paid for in the past is one of the major factors dragging behind access.

An enlarged regional approach to infrastructure

The challenging economic geography of Africa calls for a regional infrastructure perspective, able to promote cross-country synergies and exploit economies of scale. "Thinking regionally" means focusing on three key areas: international transportation corridors to provide maritime access for Africa's 16 landlocked countries; regional fiber-optic networks to provide access to the internet and build the competitiveness of African industries and services; and strong regional hubs for air and sea transportation to bolster the export potential, trade, and tourism sectors of a large number of countries. A regional approach is especially relevant for investments in energy and water.

An improved regulatory framework

The regulatory environment is a vital part of the business-enabling environment. In the African context, regulatory frameworks for setting tariffs and governing competition among service providers need to be modernized. With respect to the energy sector, regulatory frameworks should bolster the efficiency of investments and of service delivery. In the transportation sector, the areas to be addressed include: a non-competitive trucking system that keeps transportation tariffs high; poor service; disconnected linkages across different transportation modes; and significant safety gaps. Seaports too are badly in need of investment and regulatory reforms to remove bottlenecks and chronic congestion problems. Furthermore, there is the specific challenge of the 16 landlocked countries that are handicapped not only by poor logistics to the hinterland, but also by cumbersome customs regulations and lengthy delays at borders. Turning to ICT, the Africa region has witnessed dramatic progress in mobile telephony coverage. This needs to be supported by deregulation and reforms to promote intensified competition among service providers. This will reduce end-user prices and extend signal coverage further. To tackle low internet penetration rates and high tariffs, reforms should promote private sector investment in fiber-optic backbones and competitive access to submarine cables.

Less than 40% of the continent's population has access to electricity; only 33% of the rural population has access to roads; while only 5% of agriculture is under irrigation (AfDB, 2010a). According to the 2014 Millennium Development Goals (MDGs) progress report for Africa, in 2012 only 30% of the continent's population (excluding North Africa) had access to improved sanitation, and about 48% used an improved drinking water source (UNECA et al, 2015).

With respect to ICT, the situation is characterized by huge differences across specific services. In 2012, 59.3% of Sub-Saharan Africans had access to cellular mobile phones, with penetration rates growing around 25% since 2005. However, the use of the internet has recorded a slower take-up. Internet user penetration in Africa is expected to reach 9.6% by the end of 2010, compared with just 5.9% in 2008. However, this is well below the world average of 30% and the developing country average of 21%. Further efforts are also needed to improve broadband speeds. In terms of fixed telephone lines, there was little change in the number between 2000 and 2009: there were an estimated 1.6 telephone lines per 100 population in 2010, compared with 1.5 in 2008 and 2009 (AfDB et al, 2011).

Furthermore, Africa faces higher access costs for all infrastructure services compared with other developing countries. For example, the continent's road freight is about four times more expensive, power costs 14 US cents per kilowatt-hour (kWh) against 5 to 10 US cents elsewhere, and by 2012 mobile telephony sub-basket costs of US$14.6

per month compared with US$7.7 in East Asia and Pacific, and US$3.5 in South Asia.

A more cohesive approach is therefore needed to leverage the region's endowments, to integrate all these different dimensions, and improve connectivity between countries, sub-regions, and urban/rural areas. Any strategy must therefore take account of: rapid urbanization and the role of main urban areas; the linkages between major cities and the benefits from regional integration; and the spillover effects on rural productivity from regional corridors.

Challenges facing the region

Infrastructure deficits and the need for a proportionate allocation of resources

Despite some notable achievements in recent years, Africa's level of infrastructure development still lags behind other low-income regions (Figure 10.1). Access to energy records the largest comparative deficit, while total road density and access to clean water compare relatively well, though still lagging. For ICT, the increasing trend in mobile telephone subscriptions has achieved levels comparable to that of other regions, while broadband internet access seems a bigger challenge (Table 10.1). Sectoral regulatory reforms undertaken in many African countries, however, have opened up investment opportunities for the private sector as well as the donor community. These reforms have improved the business environment and enhanced efficiency in implementing and managing infrastructure investments.

A comparison on the basis of countries' income levels starkly illustrates Africa's infrastructure deficit (Figure 10.1). For example, despite the higher total road density on the continent, most roads are in a poor state and remain unusable. Africa's infrastructure endowments compared with those of other developing regions is encouraging only in terms of access to clean water for its population, mobile telephone subscriptions, and in the case of middle-income countries (MICs), electricity installed capacity.

Although Africa's infrastructure has improved during recent years, the region's infrastructure gap is more observable among its low-income countries (LICs) than MICs. For example, in terms of power generation, African LICs are 2.5 times worse off than their counterparts elsewhere (37 megawatts, or MW, per million people compared to 90 MW), while its MICs are 1.5 times better off. For road density, the MIC–LIC divide is the reverse, with African MICs almost

Figure 10.1: Infrastructure endowments for African LICs/MICs compared to other global regions

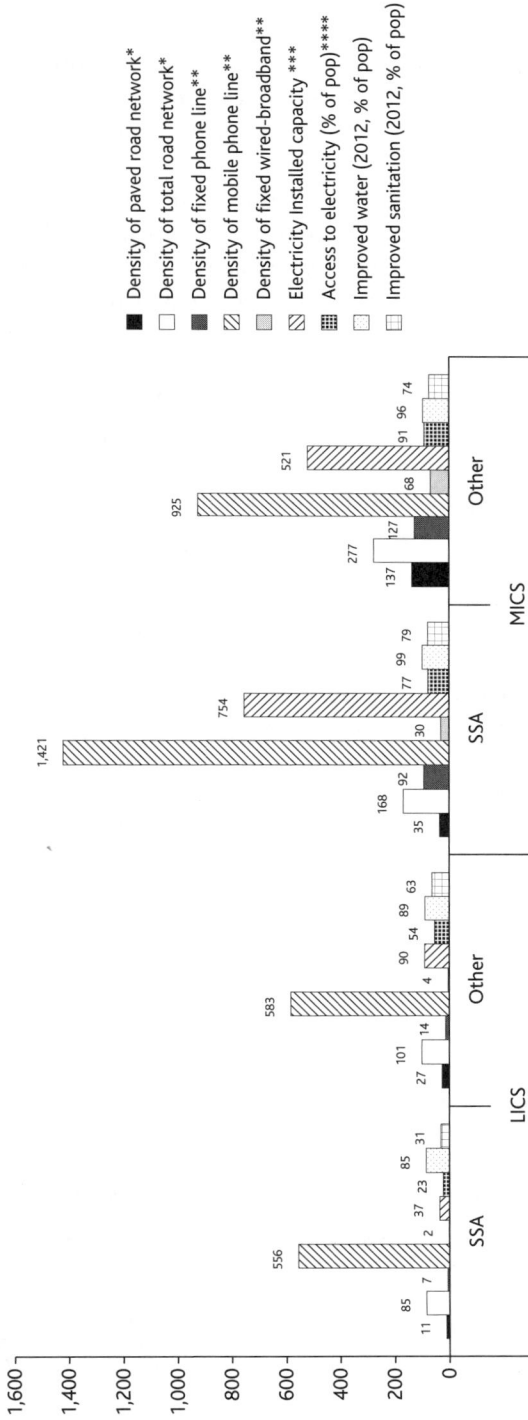

Legend:
- Density of paved road network*
- Density of total road network*
- Density of fixed phone line**
- Density of mobile phone line**
- Density of fixed wired-broadband**
- Electricity Installed capacity ***
- Access to electricity (% of pop)****
- Improved water (2012, % of pop)
- Improved sanitation (2012, % of pop)

Notes: *Km/1000 km², data from 2000-2010. ** Subscriptions per 1,000 inhabitants and fixed telephone lines per 1,000 inhabitants, 2013. *** MW per 1 million people, 2011. Ratio between the total of electricity installed capacity and total population for each region, not the average of the countries' ratios. **** Last data available is used, mostly 2008-2013.

Sources: For roads: World Development Indicators 2014; for ICT: World Bank (2014a); for electrical generation capacity: Energy Information Administration (EIA); for access to electricity: Demographic and Health Surveys, and Sustainable Energy 4 All (2013); for water and sanitation: Joint Monitoring Program (JMP) – WHO/UNICEF.

1.65 times worse off compared with their counterparts elsewhere and LICs having almost the same level of density. To sum up, the deficits in Africa's infrastructure development are most severe in the areas of paved roads, fixed telephones, and broadband internet access (Figure 10.1).

The huge initial capital outlays needed for infrastructure provision largely account for Africa's significant deficit in this area (Table 10.1). This is compounded by the extent of regulatory constraints in some African countries, which are perceived by potential private investors as increasing the level of risk. Yet we must acknowledge that significant changes are taking place across Africa, including in LICs and post-conflict countries; for example, according to the 2015 *Doing Business* report, five of the ten top improvers in 2013/14 in business reform

Table 10.1: Sub-Saharan Africa's infrastructure deficit

Aspect	SSA	South Asia	East Asia and Pacific	SSA oil exporters	SSA non-oil exporters
Transportation					
Density of paved road network*	12.5	488.4	136.7	17.6	9.1
Density of total road network*	83.1	955.6	260.9	108.0	66.1
ICT					
Density of fixed phone line**	12.4	23.9	198.6	17.8	7.1
Density of mobile phone line**	659.9	706.9	973.5	832.7	491.3
Density of fixed (wired) broadband**	3.1	10.3	121.5	4.5	1.8
Energy					
Electricity installed capacity ***	90.2	177.4	837.4	145.3	35.0
Access to electricity (% of population)****	34.1	75.2	95.7	49.5	18.9
Water and sanitation					
Improved water (2012, % of population)	83.7	95.4	97.1	82.9	84.4
Improved sanitation (2012, % of population)	37.1	60.9	78.0	42.7	31.6

Notes:
*Km/1,000 km², data from 2000-2010. ** Subscriptions per 1,000 inhabitants and fixed telephone lines per 1,000 inhabitants, 2013.
*** MW per 1 million people, 2011. Ratio between the total of electricity installed capacity and total population for each region, not the average of the countries' ratios.
**** Last data available is used, mostly 2008-2013.

Sources: For roads: World Development Indicators 2014, for ICT: World Development Indicators, 2015; for electrical generation capacity: Energy Information Administration (EIA); for access to electricity: Demographic and Health Surveys and Sustainable Energy 4 All (2013) Database.

were countries in Sub-Saharan African (SSA): Togo, Benin, Côte d'Ivoire, Senegal, and the Democratic Republic of Congo (World Bank, 2014b).

Table 10.1 demonstrates clearly that the African market is still underserved in terms of its infrastructure. However, evidence suggests that the returns to investors are potentially high. Private investors that have entered the telecommunications and finance sub-sectors, following regulatory reforms and improvements to the business environment in a number of African countries, have realized higher returns than in any other global region.

Challenges and opportunities in the energy sub-sector

In 2012, only 34% of Sub-Saharan Africans had access to electricity compared with 75% of the population for developing South Asia, 96% for East Asia and Pacific and 95% for Latin America. The comparable figure is much higher in North Africa where access to electricity is more than 99% (Energy Information Administration, nd). Furthermore, about 42 African countries endured on average 8.4 electrical outages in 2007 (Eberhard et al, 2011). The remaining high number of power outages is due largely to under-investment in maintenance and in capacity expansion to meet the growing demand, as well as to a lack of regional interconnectivity of electricity grids and shortages in affected countries. During the 2000s, regional surpluses in generation capacity were noted in all five sub-regions; however, Central Africa has been reducing its balance (Figure 10.2). The cost of power outages is significant, with Sub-Saharan Africa losing almost 7.5% of annual sales, after South Asia (11%), and followed by the Middle East and North Africa with 7% (Figure 10.3). Therefore potential productivity gains from electricity supply, together with the associated income effect, point to a market with significant growth potential.

Indeed, the emergence of independent power producers (IPPs) signals sweeping changes that are taking place in the energy sub-sector. For instance, the National Energy Regulator of South Africa has established a regulatory environment that would allow upward adjustments in tariffs and thus improve the viability of private sector suppliers. In Morocco, nearly two-thirds of electricity production is undertaken by private producers, namely the JorfLasfar Energy Company (presently Africa's largest IPP), Compagnie Eolienne de Detroit (CED), and Énergie Électrique de Tahaddart (EET). More importantly, most of the project financing for these companies was

Figure 10.2: Electricity balance in Africa; million kilowatt-hours (– deficit; +surplus)

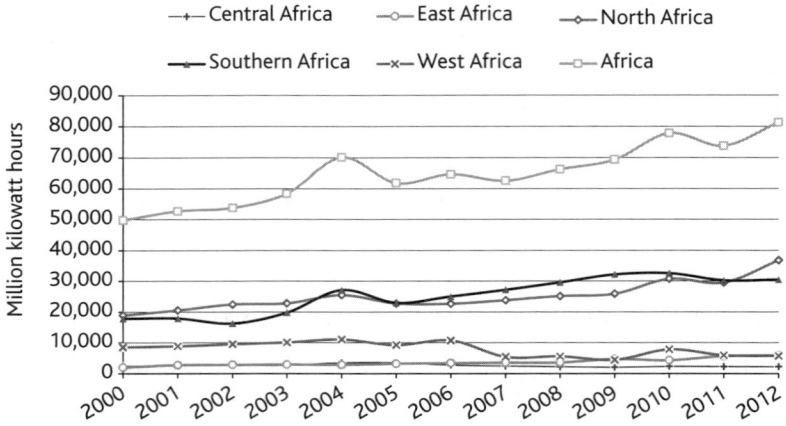

Note: Balance = electricity generation – electricity consumption.
Source: EIA (2014). AfDB region classification.

Figure 10.3: Working hours lost due to power outages, 2009

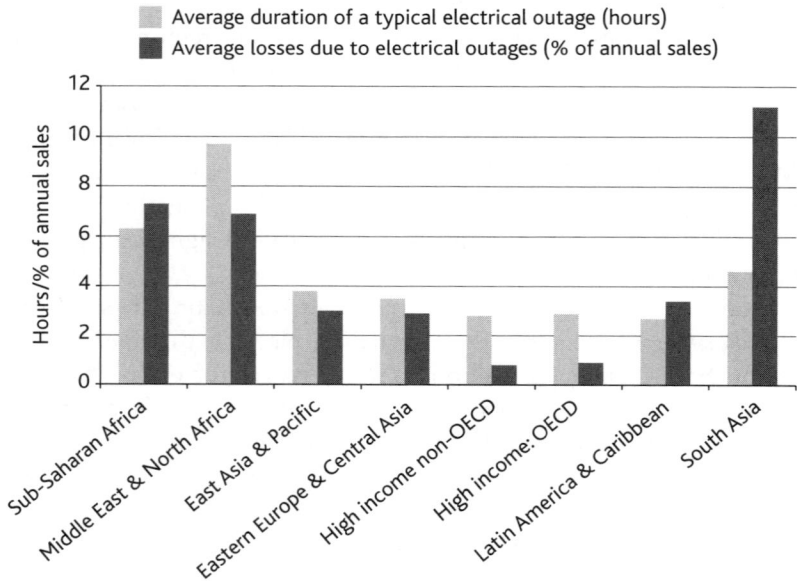

Source: World Bank (2014c)

sourced from local Moroccan banks and the sector is now diversifying into clean energy and other more efficient and cheaper forms of energy (Malgas et al, 2008). These developments clearly show opportunities for private suppliers, in a sector that is characterized by shortages.

Challenges and opportunities in the transportation sub-sector

Roads

SSA's total road network coverage is only 81.3km per 1,000km² of land area (with only about 15% paved), compared with the world average of 325km per 1,000km² of land area. This translates into 2.6km of road per 1,000 persons for the region, compared with a world average of about 6km per 1,000 persons (World Bank, 2014a). Behind these numbers, however, lie huge intra-African disparities, with the availability of rural roads ranging from 0.5km per 1,000 persons in Malawi to 35.5km per 1,000 persons in Namibia (AfDB, 2010a). To help supplement scarce public funds for road infrastructure development, Africa is moving quickly into toll roads. While the region was something of a late starter, nonetheless it has rapidly increased private sector participation in this area. Between 1990 and 1999, Africa's private investments in roads was only US$1.4 billion but this increased by more than US$21 billion between 2000 and 2005 (Rouse, 2009). The US$385 million Lekki–Epe toll road in Lagos is a recent example. Such investments are expected to increase further in the near future. For example, the Maghreb Highway in North Africa is expected to cost US$11.5 billion over a 10-year period to 2018.

Rail

Of all the transportation modes, rail networks are the least developed in Africa, with very few additions since colonial times. The 1067km long Tazara rail line, which was built in the 1970s, is a notable exception. Since the 1990s, the length of rail networks have remained unchanged in many countries and in some few cases have decreased as in Tunisia (from 2,260km in 2000 to 119km in 2011). Cross–country latest available data (from 2002 to 2011) shows that Africa had 71,334km of rail track, most of it in Southern Africa (48%) and Northern Africa (17.8%). Thirteen SSA countries have no operational rail networks, while the spatial density of operational rail ranges from one to six. The network density for most African countries ranges from 40km to 120km per million people, with a few countries (Gabon, Botswana, and South Africa) having network densities of more than 400km per million people, and others with more than 1,000km per million people because of their low population (Djibouti and Namibia). These network densities are very low compared with Europe's range of 200km to 1,000km per million people.

It is also notable that African exports are largely bulky primary commodities, which could be transported more efficiently and at lower cost by rail than by road. Rail development therefore holds some opportunities for investors. Investments in associated activities like locomotive building, logistics, and communications also exist.

Ports

Whereas Africa operates 64 ports, huge problems exist with respect to undercapacity and performance in existing facilities, as well as handling costs. Over-the-quay container-handling performance is below 20 moves per hour in the Africa region, compared with 25–30 in modern terminals worldwide. In addition, handling costs average 50% more there than in other parts of the world. With about half of the coastal countries that operate port facilities introducing sectoral legislation and regulatory reforms, new investment opportunities will present themselves. Currently, private investment in ports is low, yet there is a great need for trans-shipment facilities. Four regional hubs exist and these include Durban in Southern Africa, and Mombasa and Dar es Salaam in East Africa, with Djibouti also emerging as a new hub. In West Africa, Abidjan used to play this role but as a consequence of the civil war, it has been supplanted by the port of Malaga in Spain.

Intermodal linkage deficit

The challenge with regard to transportation infrastructure also stems from a lack of linkages between roads and rail lines, and poor connectivity to ports. This has resulted in Africa being rated the world's worst global region in the Logistics Performance Index of 2014 with an average score of 2.46, even though there exists considerable variation across countries, South Africa being the leading country with 3.43 and Somalia the lagging country with 1.77. As Africa looks at scaling up infrastructure investments in the transportation sector, the trade impact of such investments will spur growth and development. This, in turn, will have spillover effects in all other sectors, opening up further opportunities for private sector investment. Within the transportation sub-sector, there are considerable opportunities to develop systems that will improve intermodal efficiency.

Challenges and opportunities in the water and sanitation sub-sector

In the context of increasing water scarcity exacerbated by climate change, environmental degradation, rapid population growth, and urbanization, there is a pressing need to prioritize the water and sanitation sub-sector. The agricultural sector's productive capacity and its ability to feed the continent's population rely on an adequate water supply. Moreover, the resilience of this sector directly affects Africa's progress toward achievement of other MDGs, particularly those relating to gross domestic product (GDP) growth, poverty, health (including child mortality and maternal health), education, and gender.

Although Africa (excluding North Africa) increased access to improved sources of water by 16 percentage points between 1990 and 2012, this improvement is low compared with the 24 percentage points of East Asia, 19 percentage points of Southern Asia, and 18 percentage points of South-Eastern Asia. Significant progress has been made in recent years, with 16 countries having met the MDG target in 2012: Botswana, Cape Verde, Djibouti, Egypt, Gabon, Gambia, Ghana, Malawi, Mali, Mauritius, Rwanda, São Tomé and Principe, South Africa, Swaziland, Tunisia and Uganda. By contrast, in the Democratic Republic of Congo, Mozambique, Madagascar and Mauritania less than 50% of the population have access to clean water. Sanitation presents an even greater challenge, with only 30% of the region's population (excluding North Africa) having access to improved sanitation facilities in 2012, while North Africa showed an access rate of 91%. This means it has improved by only five percentage points over a period of 20 years (AfDB et al, 2011).

Challenges and opportunities in the ICT sub-sector

Access to fixed-line telephones stands at 2.4% in SSA, compared with 18% in Latin America and the Caribbean, and 16.3% in the Middle East and North Africa. Mobile phone access in Africa (66%) is lower than in South Asia (70%), in East Asia and the Pacific (97%) and Latin America and the Caribbean (114%) (World Bank, 2015).

The picture is similar for internet usage at the continental level, though North Africa is way ahead of all other African sub-regions.

However, the ICT sector witnessed investments estimated at about US$21 billion in the period 2007–2009. Expectations are that ICT investments could top US$70 billion by 2012. The International Telecommunications Union (ITU) also notes that 45 countries have implemented appropriate regulatory frameworks that are supportive of private investment in the sector (AfDB, 2010a).

Urbanization as the driving force for infrastructure provision

The population of Africa is growing faster than that of any other region in the world. By 2010 it exceeded the 1 billion mark and is projected to double by 2050 (UNFPA, 2014). Africa's urban population is also expanding rapidly at 3.6% per year, which is the highest rate in the world. If current trends continue, by 2050 more than half of the continent's population will be living in urban areas (see Figure 10.4). This means that African towns and cities will host 1.3 billion people—nearly a quarter of the world's urban population. Sub-Saharan Africa in particular is experiencing an unprecedented rate of urban growth (4.1% per year), bringing with it both opportunities and challenges for municipalities and central governments alike.

During the past 50 years, Africa's centers of economic activity have shifted markedly from agrarian to urban areas. The pull of better employment opportunities has been a significant driver of the migration, often at the cost of rural economic decline. Conflicts and civil wars in a number of African countries have accentuated this trend, as populations flee to towns in search of refuge. Each week an additional 0.23 million people joined the urban population in

Figure 10.4: Projected urban and rural population levels in Africa 2000–2050

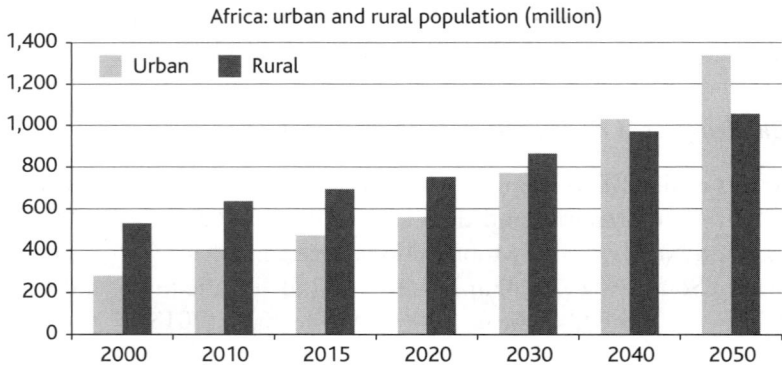

Africa: urban and rural population (million)

Source: United Nations (2014)

Sub-Saharan Africa during the last decade with the vast majority (62%) living in "informal settlements" and slums (UN-HABITAT, 2013). Indeed, according to UN-HABITAT, Sub-Saharan Africa had the largest slum population in the world by 2009, recorded at 149 million, while North Africa had the lowest prevalence of slums. These slum areas are characterized by shelter deprivations, overcrowding, little or no access to safe water and sanitation, lack of personal security, and inadequate basic social, education, and health facilities. This represents a massive challenge for municipalities and central governments alike, in their endeavors to meet the MDGs.

Despite the growth in slums on the continent, reports continue to highlight the positive links between economic development and urbanization. Indeed, cities have played a pivotal role in sustaining economic growth in the continent in recent years, contributing about 55% to total GDP. If managed properly, towns and cities in Africa could generate as much economic output as cities in other regions of the world (about 90% of GDP in the developed countries).

The expansion of cities and towns offers unique opportunities to leverage economies of scale and agglomeration effects. These include a larger manpower pool, a bigger local market, easier access to suppliers and specialized services, lower transaction costs, and an environment that encourages innovation. This means that goods can be produced more cheaply, public spending on infrastructure and services becomes cheaper per capita, and the construction of urban ICT networks becomes more financially viable. Due to these agglomeration effects, a city like Nairobi, hosting 8.4% of the national population, produces almost 20% of Kenya's GDP. Similarly, other cities and towns in Africa are more productive than rural areas. Urban centers are potential engines of growth and development that need to be harnessed.

Yet access to basic services in urban areas is still low, particularly for the very poor. UN-HABITAT recommends that building standards in urban areas should be reviewed to take into account income differentials, if affordable housing is to be provided by the private sector. In this context, urban development frameworks are being revamped jointly with regulatory reforms at national levels. This will allow greater private sector investments in housing and commercial property, including associated infrastructure and conservation of the environment. Improvements in the urban environment would have a positive impact on investment flows and generate the economic dynamism that supports growth.

Figure 10.5: Infrastructure rural–urban divide in low-income countries of Africa

Access to household services
in low income countries of Africa, by residence

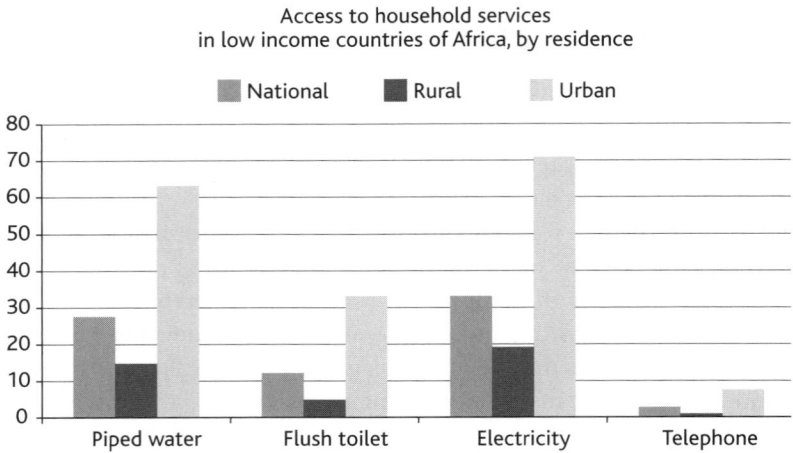

Source: Demographic and Health Surveys.
Latest available data is used (mostly 2008-2013)

The consequences of structural changes imposed by the climate change

The consequences of climate change will fall disproportionately on developing regions, especially Sub-Saharan Africa. Warming of 2°C could result in a 4–5% permanent reduction in annual income per capita for the continent as a whole. Sub-Saharan Africa suffers from natural fragility (with two-thirds of its surface area comprising desert or dry land) and high exposure to droughts and floods. Such extreme weather patterns are forecast to increase with climate change. In addition, the region's economies are highly dependent on natural resources. Evidence from Sub-Saharan Africa indicates that rainfall variability, projected to increase substantially, also reduces GDP and increases poverty. The prospects for crops and livestock in rain-fed, semi-arid lands in SSA are bleak, even before warming reaches 2–2.5°C above pre-industrial levels (World Bank, 2010).

Climate change-related events will severely impact the productivity of Africa's agriculture, increasing the region's vulnerability (World Bank, 2010). The *Climate Change 2014: Impacts Adaptation, and Vulnerability* study states that yield losses at mid-century range from 18% for southern Africa to 22% aggregated across Sub-Saharan Africa (Niang et al, 2014, p 1218). Greater rainfall variability and more severe droughts in semi-arid parts of Africa are expected. For instance, Southern Africa will suffer particularly severe drops in yields by 2030, unless adaptation measures are successfully implemented (World Bank, 2009a).

In the shorter term, the food crisis witnessed in Africa during 2011 was caused not by a supply shock but by the price shock of 2006–2008; the required policy response should therefore have been a supply stimulus. But African countries had few reserves and inadequate budgetary means to procure food at high prices (FAO, 2011). Moreover, countries in Sub-Saharan Africa are particularly vulnerable to international shocks because 45% of rice and 85% of wheat are imported (World Bank, 2011a). There is a strong need to stimulate agricultural productivity through government programs, in order to reduce vulnerability to price volatility. Over the longer term, the best way to lower food prices is to invest in agriculture. This will sustainably increase yields, reduce input costs, increase productivity, and reduce food losses and waste. It is therefore essential to encourage farmers to invest in technologies that will raise their productivity and incomes (FAO, 2011).

Addressing Africa's principal infrastructure challenge: low institutional capacity

There is no doubt that substantial investments are needed for the infrastructure agenda in Africa; however, the core issues are institutional in nature. Pouring additional funding into sectors characterized by high levels of inefficiency and low institutional capacity makes little sense. In order to promote a level of productivity among firms that is conducive to higher and sustainable economic growth, Africa needs to improve the capacity and efficiency of those institutions responsible for developing and managing infrastructure. The goal is not to reinvent existing institutions but to reform them and support their evolution.

While the challenge varies greatly across African countries, there are three general directions in which to foster institutional advancements, namely: more efficient spending; an enlarged regional approach to infrastructure investment; and an improved regulatory framework.

More efficient spending

Efficient spending is crucial to maximize the resources available for infrastructure and should inform every step of service provision. The selection of new infrastructure projects needs to be guided by a set of criteria that will secure the highest returns. When improving or expanding current infrastructure endowments, investment should make the most of the resources at hand, since any wastage will affect the development of other projects. At the other end of the process, the enterprises should charge cost-recovery tariffs and employ cost-saving technologies in order to provide a reliable and sustainable service.

One indicator of the efficiency problems in Africa is the high tariffs paid by consumers. Whether for power, water, road freight, mobile telephones, or internet services, the tariffs paid in Africa are several multiples of those paid in other developing regions. These higher prices are sometimes the result of genuinely higher costs, but sometimes stem from a demand for high profits. The lack of cost recovery has major detrimental effects on the sustainability and profitability of services. Under-priced infrastructure services are estimated to cost Africa US$4.7 billion a year in forgone revenues.

Adopting an enlarged regional approach to infrastructure investment

The challenging economic geography of Africa calls for a regional infrastructure perspective able to promote cross-country synergies and exploit economies of scale. In 2010, there were 18 African countries with fewer than five million inhabitants each; moreover, in 2009, 19 African economies recorded a GDP of less than US$5 billion. In addition, the region counts 60 international river basins and 16 landlocked countries. Therefore, what is required is a strategy that works at a regional level rather than solely within the borders of individual countries. For example, most African countries are too small to individually generate power efficiently and only a handful possess major hydropower resources. This underscores the urgency for regional transboundary planning to expand markets and reap cross-country synergies. This should help to reduce costs, improve institutional efficiency, and ensure more reliable service provision.

"Thinking regionally" means an integrated approach focusing on the following three areas: international transportation corridors that provide maritime access for landlocked countries; regional fiber-optic networks that provide access to the internet and build the competitiveness of African industries and services; and strong regional hubs for air and sea transportation that can bolster the export potential, trade, and tourism of a large number of countries.

Regional economic communities (RECs) and pan-African institutions such as the New Partnership for Africa's Development (NEPAD) continue to play a vital role in this context. For example, the newly established Program for Infrastructure Development in Africa (PIDA), which is led by the African Union Commission (AUC),

NEPAD Secretariat, and the African Development Bank (AfDB), is fully supported at national, regional, and international levels. Its aim is to develop a vision and strategic framework for the development of regional and continental infrastructure (energy, transportation, ICT, and transboundary water resources) to promote Africa's socioeconomic development and integration into the global economy. It also provides a framework for engagement with Africa's development partners willing to support continental infrastructure. A regional approach is especially relevant for investments in energy and water.

Energy

About 30 African countries face chronic blackouts and high premiums for emergency power. This represents a major obstacle to doing business, curtails the continent's competitiveness, and has a negative impact on foreign direct investment flows. In some countries in the continent, power losses last approximately 13.5 hours. As a consequence, firms in Africa lose, on average, 7.3% of their annual sales (World Bank, 2015). The 48 SSA countries, which together total 900 million in population by 2011, generate roughly the same amount of power as Spain (1.5 times), which has a population of just 48 million. Power consumption in Africa, at 124 kilowatt-hours per capita annually and falling, is only 10% of that found elsewhere in the developing world. Recent estimates suggest that given the current pace of investment, it would take Africa more than 50 years to gain universal access to a reliable source of power (AICD, 2009).

For a major turnaround in the sector, the pace of investment in Sub-Saharan Africa has to expand from about 1 to 7 gigawatts (GW) of capacity per annum. Developing cheaper energy through regional trade is one path to accelerate progress in the energy sector. Also, inefficiencies within numerous institutions have to be addressed. The direction for institutional reform should consider the international experience and a broad range of instruments including incentives, contracts, deregulation, and private sector participation. Nowadays there is substantial knowledge about what has and has not worked in the past, and this empirical knowledge should help governments to emulate successful policies, while avoiding known mistakes.

Water

In the water sector, a regional and multipurpose approach constitutes a promising way forward. Despite the fact that Africa enjoys plentiful water resources of about 5.4 trillion cubic meters a year, it is failing to harness water for development. Just 3.8% of this figure has so far been developed and 300 million Africans still lack access to safe drinking water. In addition, less than 5% of agricultural land is irrigated and less than 10% of hydropower potential is captured.

Sixty of Africa's rivers cross national boundaries, making international cooperation on water resources management essential. One example of successful transboundary cooperation for water management is the Senegal River Basin Development Organization, established in 1972. It serves as a transboundary land–water management organization, covering the Senegal River basin in Mali, Mauritania, and Senegal. Its aims include: managing water for agriculture; promoting self-sufficiency in food; improving the incomes of local populations (35 million in total, of whom 12 million live in the river basin); and preserving the natural ecosystems, inter alia. Similar organizations include the Gambia River Basin Development Organization (OMVG), the Komati Basin Water Authority, the Niger Basin Authority, Nile Basin Initiative, the Kagera Basin Authority, and the Mano River Union, among others.

Improved regulatory frameworks for cost recovery

The regulatory environment is a vital part of the business-enabling environment. Clear and transparent rules and regulations can help to attract private investment and aid. On the other hand, when rules and regulations become unwieldy and unpredictable, they can represent an obstacle and even an opportunity cost for market participants. In the African context, regulatory frameworks for setting tariffs and governing competition among service providers need to be modernized.

Energy

With respect to the energy sector, the existing regulatory frameworks need to be reformed to provide an enabling environment for increasing efficiency in investments and service delivery. In addition to a regional and coordinated investment strategy, what is required is a redesigned subsidy scheme for the energy sector, to tackle important institutional inefficiencies. Current programs use substantial resources but are ineffective in serving the poor. Another pressing requirement is to address flagrant deficiencies in the maintenance of assets.

Transportation

The regulatory frameworks governing the transportation sector in Africa are also sorely in need of reform. The focus should be on improving the quality of transportation networks and services rather than increasing physical quantities. For instance, trade facilitation measures such as one-stop border posts are as important as good-quality roads for increasing transit speed and supporting the productivity of firms. The main quality concerns in Africa include: a non-competitive trucking system that keeps transportation tariffs at too high a level; poor service; lack of linkages across different transportation modes; and significant safety gaps. Seaports too—which are vital for Africa's international trade in high-volume, low-cost commodities—are badly in need of investment and regulatory reforms to remove bottlenecks and chronic congestion problems. Ports in Africa experience institutional and regulatory constraints that create inefficiencies, hinder competition, and raise transaction costs. Furthermore, there is the specific challenge of the 16 landlocked countries that are not only handicapped by poor logistics to the hinterland, but also by cumbersome customs regulations and lengthy delays at borders. For these countries, median transportation costs are almost 50% higher than the equivalent costs for coastal economies (AfDB, 2010b).

ICT

The ICT sector has witnessed a dramatic jump in population coverage, from 5% to over 60% between 1999 and 2008, with 180 million new (prepaid) subscribers and US$28 billion in mobilized private investment. Such positive developments need to be supported by deregulation and reforms to promote intensified competition among service providers. The aim is to bring down end-user prices and extend signal coverage still further. However, the significant progress in mobile telephony has come at the expense of fixed-line telephony, which registered only modest growth between 1990 and 2007 in the vast majority of African countries. This is attributable in part to the high service charges (AfDB, 2010a). The continent also has low internet penetration rates and high tariffs, stemming mainly from a lack of high-capacity international networks. Africa relies on satellites and Very Small Aperture Terminal earth stations for most of its connectivity to the World Wide Web, which results in high access costs (AfDB and OECD, 2009). Additional reforms should seek to promote private sector investment in fiber-optic backbones and competitive access to submarine cables.

How to set a strategic vision for infrastructure provision

Investments in infrastructure should be allocated to components that will maximize the positive transformation that the region needs in terms of economic growth and improved living standards for its populations, both rural and urban. In addition to sound macroeconomic management, policies need to be synergistically aligned. This will allow firms to benefit from external cost savings derived from increased interaction and access to buyers and input markets.

To sum up, sustainable economic growth, as a means of lifting the continent out of poverty, is the principal objective of Africa's infrastructure agenda. The achievement of this goal relies on the productivity of firms and on ensuring better living conditions for individuals across the continent. Accordingly, strengthening the foundations for higher productivity in the main cities and ensuring a more even distribution of basic living standards are the two key pillars of the infrastructure agenda.

Firms concentrate in cities in order to benefit from agglomeration economies, namely lower production costs through leveraging economies of scale and network efficiencies (World Bank, 2009a). By clustering, firms increase the demand for infrastructure and reap cost savings. Roads, amenities, and services (ICT, energy, and water and sanitation) are available in greater quantity and quality in cities compared with rural locations. Consequently, securing an appropriate level of investment in infrastructure will enhance the gains to be made from urban agglomeration.

The second pillar for growth refers to a more even and equitable distribution of basic living conditions across Africa, in both rural and urban areas. A strategy to enhance living conditions in cities entails framing not only a coherent urban agenda, but also a commensurate rural agenda, able to buffer the incentives for rural–urban migration. Cities that are experiencing a growing but unmet demand for basic services from unskilled immigrants also face a long-term trend of economic deterioration, given the relatively lower contribution from those immigrants' productivity. Therefore, providing universal access to basic services across the whole urban system and its hinterland represents a macro mechanism for a healthy urbanization, as it helps to reduce the number of migrants who are in search simply of better basic services. What is needed is a broader vision of the type of technologies that can be utilized for service provision; the bundling of services wherever possible to increase effectiveness in peri–urban and rural areas; the use of land planning instruments and policies to align urban expansion with service provision; and the establishment of a complementary rural development strategy.

Framing an infrastructure agenda for Africa to address the challenges of the 21st century encompasses three dimensions of geographical aggregation: making cities more productive and better places to live ("more livable"); integrating rural areas through the spillovers of urban growth; and linking major population centers across the region.

The next three sections of this chapter analyze the dynamics of these three dimensions. It then goes on to discuss the resources and tools available to finance investment in infrastructure in Africa, and concludes by highlighting the role of the AfDB in advancing the infrastructure agenda.

Infrastructure for more livable and productive cities

African cities are growing fast. However, owing to insufficient infrastructure and poorly performing institutions, most new settlements are informal and lack access to basic services. This situation has severe consequences on health, education, incomes, market integration, and ultimately economic growth. In order to improve living conditions across Africa, it is important to develop a coherent urban agenda that provides the right incentives for migration and proper conditions for livable and productive cities.

Improving living conditions in cities implies a strong focus on institutions. A combination of land policy and planning, housing policies, and basic services coverage is key for a more equitable and inclusive urban expansion. The policy challenge is to harness market forces that encourage concentration and promote convergence in living standards between villages, towns, and cities. Policy decisions will be more effective if based on strategies for broad economic areas that integrate towns and cities with their surrounding rural hinterland.

The pull of the city, urban sprawl, and informal settlements

Africa is characterized by wide disparities in living standards across sub-regions, countries, and particularly between urban and rural areas. For household services, coverage rates in urban centers are five to 10 times higher than those in rural areas. Electricity and improved water supply (such as piped connections or standpipes) extend to the majority of the urban population, but to less than one-fifth of the rural dwellers. In addition, fewer than 40% of urban households enjoy a private water connection, a septic tank, or an improved latrine and this proportion falls to just 5% in rural areas. Rural access to ICT services remains negligible. In almost half of African countries, energy coverage barely reaches 50% of the urban population and 5% of the rural (AICD, 2009).

Such disparities boost migration toward urban settlements, where people can find better living conditions and benefit from proximity and access to bigger markets, including job markets. Between 1960 and 2006, the share of the continent's urban population increased from 15% to 35%, and this is expected to rise to around 60% by 2020. Rural migration accounts for one-quarter of that growth, with the remainder attributable to urban demographic expansion and administrative reclassifications (World Bank, 2008b). In several fragile states, civil war has contributed to urban expansion as people from the affected regions seek refuge and employment in cities.

The three main features of Africa's urbanization—high concentration of people in large cities, urban sprawl, and informality—are examined in the sections that follow.

High population density in large cities

More than one-fifth (178.5 million) of Africa's urban population is concentrated in 56 large cities (that is, cities with more than 1 million inhabitants) (see Annex, Table A10.3). Much of the remainder is spread across 232 intermediate cities of 100,000 to 1 million inhabitants and in peri-urban areas. The largest cities are growing fast, suggesting an even more concentrated urban population. However, because of insufficient infrastructure and poor institutions, most new settlements are informal and without basic services.

Ensuring access to basic services for households in both urban and rural areas can improve sustainable urbanization and social equity, enhance living conditions, and prevent disproportionate flows of rural people to cities. It should be acknowledged that labor mobility can have positive effects when it responds to the needs of market forces, rather than to a lack of security and/or basic services. Moreover, labor mobility can prompt convergence in living standards, as migration to denser and more productive areas can help to rebalance income levels and exploit the benefits of knowledge clusters. As rural and urban development is mutually dependent, economic integration is the best way to produce growth and inclusive development.

Urban sprawl

The pattern of urbanization in Africa reveals strong growth and sprawl. This is typified by moderate and patchy densification within the inner-city core, as residential areas give way to commercial users and peripheral growth occurs in an unplanned, ad-hoc manner and at low density. Built-up areas of urban sprawl are growing faster than urban populations in seven African cities, suggesting falling densities that, in turn, increase per capita infrastructure costs (Angel et al, 2005).

Increase in slum-dwellers in Sub-Saharan Africa

In addition to sprawl, slums are growing faster than cities. Slums, as defined by UN-HABITAT, feature: a lack of access to safe water and sanitation; lack of durable housing; lack of sufficient living area; and lack of security of tenure. Globally, Sub-Saharan Africa has the largest slum population at 62% of its urban population. North Africa has the lowest prevalence of slums (UN-HABITAT, 2013).

Progress on reducing slums across the continent has been highly uneven. Cities in North Africa reduced their share of slum dwellers from 20% to 13% over the decade 2000–2010, whereas in Sub-Saharan Africa, the proportion of slum dwellers decreased only by 5% (or about 17 million) over the same period. The strong performance in North Africa has been largely due to a shift in policy approach to housing strategies. Ineffective top-down housing authorities have been replaced by public–private partnerships (PPPs) to provide a greater number of both low-income and market-rate housing units to meet demand (UN-HABITAT, 2010).

Cities: the future of Africa

Cities represent the engines of growth. Their productivity is at least three times greater than that of rural areas. Rural areas contribute less than 20% of Africa's GDP, while accounting for more than 60% of its population (World Bank, 2008b). There is, though, a synergistic relationship between rural and urban areas, in that urban centers consume rural products and offer inputs for rural production, while rural areas serve as markets for goods and services produced in urban areas. The expansion of urban markets is therefore a key factor in raising rural incomes in the hinterland.

In addition, cities create growth spillovers in their hinterlands. Areas within two hours' travel time of cities of at least 100,000 people tend to diversify into non-agricultural activities (Dorosh et al, 2008). Rural areas that are located between two and eight hours' travel time from such cities account for more than 62% of the agricultural supply and generate a surplus that is sold to urban areas. In areas further than eight hours from these cities, agriculture is largely undertaken for subsistence, and less than 15% of the land's potential is realized. Similarly, farmers closer to cities tend to use more and higher-quality fertilizers and pesticides and better equipment, resulting in clear improvements in productivity.

Despite these dynamics, rural–urban links are constrained by inadequate transportation networks between products and markets, unreliable and costly sources of electricity and water provision, and limited coverage of ICT. Weak institutions exacerbate the impact of these constraints.

Resources allocation across urban and rural spaces

The African urban agenda demands a coherent resource distribution across urban and rural areas. Improving the quality and quantity of spending will maximize the complementarities between urban and rural development, counteract the failures of decentralization, and improve local authorities' revenues.

Historically, Africa has been investing around US$26 billion per annum in infrastructure. Nearly 30% of these resources have gone to productive infrastructure (energy, ports, highways, and so on) that underpins the national economy, while 50% and 20% have been used to serve urban and rural areas, respectively (Figure 10.6). Most of this investment has been targeted at the energy sector to boost industrial production and transmission. Additional spending is required to expand

Figure 10.6: Spatial split of current spending versus investment needs

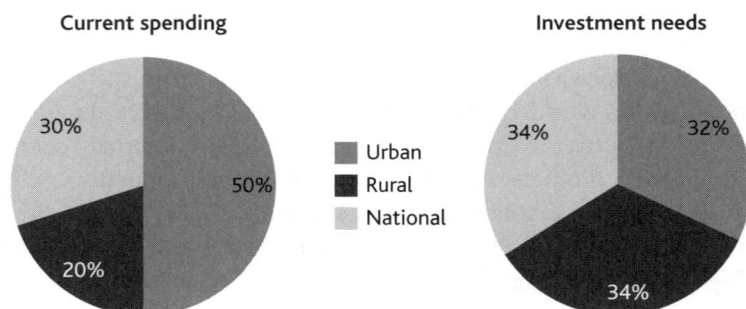

Current spending

Investment needs

- Urban
- Rural
- National

Current spending: 30%, 50%, 20%

Investment needs: 34%, 32%, 34%

Sources: AfDB Data Portal (www.afdb.org/en/knowledge/statistics/data-portal/); AICD (2009).

productive infrastructure at the national level, and to improve roads and distribution networks for basic services in rural and urban areas.

The Africa Infrastructure Country Diagnostic report (AICD, 2009) proposed a change in emphasis from urban to rural investments. To raise Africa's infrastructure endowment to a reasonable level would cost US$93 billion, split two to one between investment and maintenance. Spatially, the spending distribution would see 34% going to the productive infrastructure that underpins the national economy, 32% to urban areas, and 34% to rural areas. As presented in Figure 10.6, rebalancing the current investment from urban to rural areas does not imply a reduction in urban spending. As discussed before, there are significant externalities and complementarities between urban and rural investments. For example, growth in urban and rural coverage of network infrastructure tends to be positively correlated. It is important to maintain such connectivity to foster sustainable and balanced growth. In Figure 10.6, "national" refers to productive infrastructure underpinning the whole national economy, rather than specifically to urban or rural space (for example, the inter–urban trunk network, the national power interconnected system, major seaports, and airports). "Urban" and "rural" refer to infrastructure that is primarily oriented toward servicing the needs of urban or rural inhabitants, respectively (for example, urban or rural household services, and urban or rural roads).

The role of local government in local development

Local authorities should invest not only more, but more *wisely*. Municipal budgets are very small in relation to the total infrastructure requirements spurred by rapid urban growth. The purported benefits of decentralization have not been fully realized because policies have given cities more responsibilities (notably in social sectors), but without the additional resources needed to fund them. Accordingly, municipalities do not have sufficient funds to promote growth.

Tax revenues, hampered by undeclared informal trade and the lack of clear property titles, are insufficient to cover investment needs. In big cities where the economic base is larger, tax receipts are often sent to central agencies, creating delays and inefficiencies in the process. Political factors often hinder the use of property taxes. Although African cities generate 80% of the national tax revenues, they receive less than 20% of the resources. Consequently, they are reliant on central government for some 80% of their operating revenues. In sum, local governments lack the power and incentives to raise (and retain) their own revenue streams.

It has become clear that cities need predictable streams of revenue; they also require the flexibility to raise additional resources in order to safeguard service provision to their populations. In addition, they should try to improve their technical and managerial capacity to deal with evolving priorities in new investments, operations and maintenance, and to guide inevitable expansion. In order to achieve this, they need to attract private partners and gain a better understanding of the constituency of their neighborhoods, so that they can exploit potential synergies.

Improved and sustained revenue schemes in cities will translate into better household service coverage, which is currently quite low (as discussed earlier) and uncoordinated. Infrastructure investment continues to focus on sector-specific interventions rather than spatially synchronizing and concentrating the provision of different infrastructure services in larger "bundles". Access to multiple services leads to higher returns for beneficiary households compared with scenarios where services are provided individually.

The need for stronger institutions in main cities

In many parts of Africa, formal land institutions and related legal and regulatory frameworks are still nascent. Land ownership is made more problematic by the centralization of procedures, the high costs and complexity of registering land, and ineffective land-use policies and urban planning. These and other factors have encouraged the development of spontaneous, informal settlements. Many governments have subsidized plots, but available supply is well below demand. Governments have tried to help residents excluded from land ownership and have expanded infrastructure to new settlements, but the results have been disappointing.

The limited size of the land market and the monopoly of traditional landowners have led to shortages of urban land and high prices. The lack of land titles impedes business development and the establishment of new firms. With no access to land and living in underserved and peripheral areas, the poor suffer from low levels of connectivity and poor access to labor markets. The resistance of landowners and the lack of registries also prevent local authorities from raising revenues through taxes on urban land.

Lack of affordability and an insufficient supply of titled land make housing developments a solution restricted mostly to the middle classes. Construction costs are very high, especially in landlocked countries. Cement, iron, and other materials are imported and costly to transport, making housing unaffordable. According to estimates, only one out of every five new housing units is allocated to a needy household.

Land–use authorization procedures are characterized by long delays and high transaction costs. For example, land acquisition delays are considerable in Ethiopia and Zambia. In Mozambique, businesses pay on average US$18,000 in processing fees for land, and in Nigeria, they must register land to use it as collateral, a process that can take up to two years and cost 15% of the land value (Kessides, 2006). To rectify the situation, land management institutions should ensure a comprehensive land registry, credible mechanisms for enforcement of land transactions and conflict resolution, and flexible zoning laws. What is needed is a versatile regulation of spatial sub-divisions that help rather than hinder changes in land use according to the urban dynamics. Legislation that boosts land prices and excludes the poor should be revised. Lack of affordable serviced plots and zoning policies have often excluded the poor from integration within the urban development.

Gender equality should also be mainstreamed into any reforms relating to land ownership, as traditionally women have been excluded in many African countries. Land rights tend to be held by men or by kinship groups controlled by men. Women's access—if at all—is mainly through a male relative, usually a father or husband. Such access is tenuous and can be lost if, for example, the husband dies, leaving the widow landless and without a means of subsistence. In response, there is a need to introduce or strengthen laws to give women more secure access to land.

Urban planning is needed to guide urban expansion and the associated infrastructure needs. When implemented properly and in an integrated manner, urban planning can prevent sprawl, deter development in precarious environmental areas, and ensure optimal delivery of affordable serviced land and infrastructure. Too often, though, urban planning is not separately costed in the budgetary process, and master plans are rarely implemented. Because of a top-down approach and weak implementation, urban planning instruments have lost their relevance in many African cities. Urban dynamics are seldom foreseen, and in most cases, decisions regarding the location of infrastructure and major developments are based on the political economy rather than coherent urban planning.

To be efficient and useful, planning needs to be flexible, participatory, and indicative (with a 10- to 15-year horizon). Urban reference maps should lay out the major roads and city services, the areas for urban expansion, and the reserves for amenities. Ideally, planning should be rooted in participatory strategies and linked to local and central budgets. Without realistic projections for resource availability, urban plans often fall into discredit. The cases of Dakar, Lagos, and Maputo are recent positive examples of city development strategies as frameworks to encourage participation from the community when discussing challenges and opportunities.

Institutional development pays off substantially, even when resources for investment are lacking. A strong "city effect" also exists. Thanks to leadership, land security, ownership, and civic participation, the inhabitants of Dakar's slums have living standards far superior to those in Nairobi, even though the latter have higher incomes and education levels (Gulyani et al, 2008). Successful slum-upgrading programs should be emulated in order to improve living standards. The Accra District Rehabilitation Project in Ghana is an example of successful upgrading, as are several programs in Ethiopia, Kenya, and Uganda.

Components for a successful urban agenda

Few elements can be highlighted as central components of an agenda for action. The list is by purpose not exhaustive, as it includes only key institutional aspects.

- *Adopt a solid analytical framework to help define priorities and sequencing.* Frameworks should integrate both urban and rural needs, specific to each area. In mostly rural areas, sound land policies and the universal provision of basic services, despite adjusting for the technologies used, are critical goals. In areas where urbanization has accelerated, the emphasis should be on investments in connectivity. In heavily urbanized areas, targeted assistance to slum areas may be needed.

- *Recognize that the political economy influences the urban transition.* Local authorities do not have sufficient power to develop their cities because their budgets and responsibilities are restricted to basic services. Resources and decisions on other components crucial to the productivity of cities depend on the central government.

- *Be pragmatic.* While the long-term goal should be the achievement of well-defined property rights and land titling, some interim measures may be necessary. For example, cities need to be proactive in making land titling effective in the medium term, for example by using occupancy as a basis for land registration and taxation.

- *Focus on cities and areas important to the sub-regional economy.* Sub-regional approaches can increase the impact of individual country efforts. To maximize the benefit of such approaches, national improvement and expenditure plans should focus first on primary economic drivers and related infrastructure, which will lead to overall growth for the sub-region.

- *Improve land policies* so that markets become more flexible and responsive to the increase in demand. A lack of clarity in land-use regulation and in investment decisions across the urban space creates major uncertainties for landowners. This deters them from integrating their land into land markets, while stimulating rent-seeking behavior from those who are more influential. The aggregate effect is a market characterized by supply constraints, informality, and vacant land in the middle of dense areas.

- *Improve the fiscal environment of cities.* Improve transparency and the predictability of transfers; strengthen and simplify local taxation; change the focus of property taxes from ownership to occupancy; take advantage of cost recovery from revenue-producing services, such as markets and bus stations, as these can amount to 70% of medium-size city revenues; use municipal contracts (between central and local governments); and establish street addresses to help local governments manage their resources.

Benefits accruing to rural areas from urban and regional infrastructure

Rural activities remain highly relevant to the overall development process of Africa. The African population is still mainly located in rural areas, ranging from 78% of the population of the East African Community (EAC) to 53% in the Economic Community of Central African States (ECCAS) (based on World Bank, 2011a). Two-thirds of the labor force is engaged in agriculture-related activities, which make up a very significant share of GDP in all sub-regions, ranging from 32% in the EAC to 13% in the Southern African Development Community (SADC). Indeed, by the late 2010s, 61.7% of employment was in the agriculture sector, while only 10% was in industry and 28% in services sector (UNECA, 2010).

Rural populations face extreme poverty and a lack of access to services. In total, by 2011 831.4 million people inhabited Sub-Saharan Africa, of whom 46.8% were living on less than US$1.5

Figure 10.7: Rural activities remain highly relevant for Africa's development, 2013

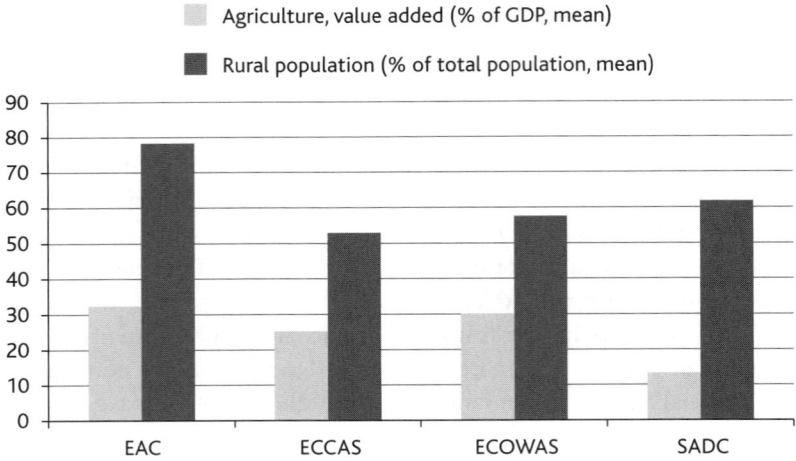

Note: EAC: East Africa Community, ECCAS: Economic Community of Central African States, ECOWAS: Economic Community of West African States, SADC: Southern Africa Development Community.

Source: World Bank (2013)

2005 Purchasing Parity Power (PPP) a day and 65% inhabit rural areas (World Bank, 2014b). For household services, coverage rates for those living in urban areas are five to 10 times higher than for those in rural areas. Electricity and improved water supply (such as piped connections or standposts) extend to the majority of the urban population, but to less than one-fifth of the rural population, with minimal differences across sub-regions. Rural access to ICT services remains negligible (AfDB, 2011b).

A vicious circle characterizes the relationship between agriculture and rural poverty. A high reliance on agriculture is not the cause of rural poverty. However, in order to fight poverty, it is essential to improve agricultural productivity. Low productivity and poverty feed each other, creating a vicious circle; this situation is known as the "Sahel-Syndrome". More accurately, this mechanism forces poor peasants on to agriculturally marginal lands for non-capital intensive exploitation. On marginal sites, an intensification of agricultural land use further degrades the environment, damages the natural production basis, and decreases yields, leading to greater impoverishment (Roehrig and Menz, 2005). Case studies analyzing agro-ecosystems in poor countries indicate that many people are caught in this vicious circle. However, breaking the circle is complex because some of the conventional solutions for rural development may in fact exacerbate the problem. For example, improving rural accessibility in some deprived areas may lead to gentrification, thereby boosting land and house prices and forcing out the poorest segments of the population.

Low productivity in Africa's rural activities

Nowhere in the world is the lack of assets greater than in Africa, where farm sizes in many of the more densely populated areas are unsustainably small and falling, land is severely degraded, investment in irrigation is negligible, and poor health and education limit productivity and access to better production options.

Rural productivity in Africa ranks among the lowest in the developing world. The agriculture sector remains largely traditional and concentrated in the hands of smallholders and pastoralists (UNECA, 2009). More than 85% of the rural poor live on land that has medium to high potential for increased productivity. However, the poorest people live in the desert or on semi-arid lands that make up almost 40% of the land base of Sub-Saharan Africa. The dominance of rain-fed agriculture throughout Sub-Saharan Africa makes production vulnerable to droughts, such as occurred during 2010 in the Sahel, with huge implications for poverty and food insecurity. Furthermore this situation has long-term impacts on ecosystems due to overgrazing and deforestation resulting from the expansion of low-productivity agricultural practices. Such outcomes can be observed currently in the Kalahari Desert. The aggregated impact is that Sub-Saharan Africa has the lowest rural productivity rate of all global developing regions (see Figure 10.8). Between 1990 and 2012, agricultural value added divided by arable land (a broad measure of productivity in agriculture) grew by only an annual average of 0.8% in ECCAS, -0.2% in SADC, and about 1.5% per annum in the Economic Community of West African States (ECOWAS) and EAC.

Logistics costs and rural infrastructure

The overall logistics costs in Sub-Saharan Africa are among the highest in the world. Cross-regional analysis of the World Bank *Doing Business* 2015 data (World Bank, 2014b) indicates that on average, exports from Sub-Saharan African countries have the second longest time to export (30.5 days) surpassed only by South Asia, the third cost to export (US$1,922.9 per container) and to import (US$2,117.8) surpassed only by South Asia and Europe Central Asia, and the major number

Figure 10.8: Productivity in the developing world, 1985 and 2012

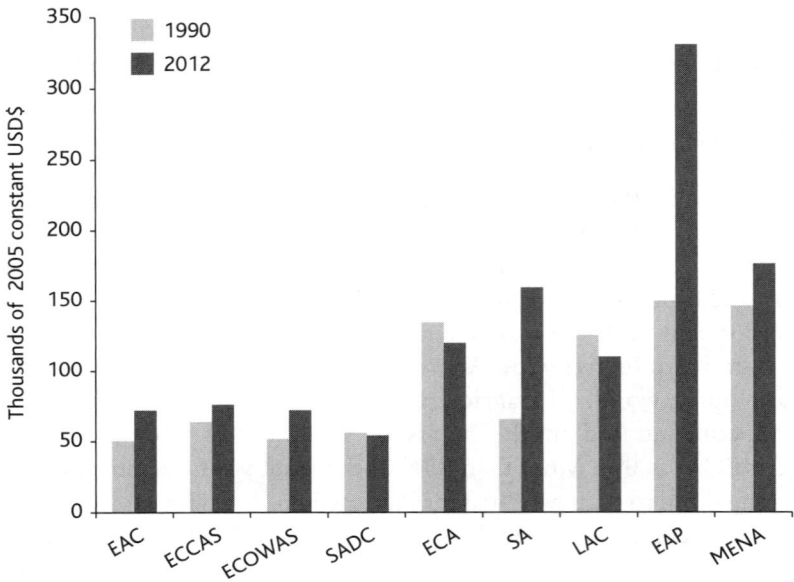

Notes: EAC: East Africa Community, ECCAS: Economic Community of Central African States, ECOWAS: Economic Community of West African States, SADC: South African Development Community, ECA: Europe and Central Asia, SA: South Asia, LAC, Latin America & Caribbean, EAP: East Asia & Pacific, MENA: Middle East & North Africa.

Source: World Development Indicators (http://data.worldbank.org/data-catalog/world-development-indicators)

of documentation requirements for export (8.1) and import (9.4) This means that exporting and importing a 20-foot dry container is more than double the cost of the leading region, East Asia and Pacific. The World Bank Logistics Performance Index of 2014 (World Bank, 2014d) reveals the extent of the problem for SSA, compared with other developing regions (see Figure 10.9).

Landlocked countries face the greatest logistical hurdles. Surface transportation costs and time delays represent a much larger share of their total export costs, and these vary substantially between the different geographic corridors within Sub-Saharan Africa. In SSA, the inland transportation cost for the median landlocked country exceeds that of the median coastal country by 328%. The landlocked countries in Central Africa (Chad and the Central African Republic) face, by far, the most costly and lengthiest constraints for their exports (Christ and Ferrantino, 2009).

However, proximity to ports does not guarantee better logistical performance. For instance, in West Africa there are shorter distances

Figure 10.9: Logistics performance in the developing world, 2014

Average logistics performance index by region, 2014

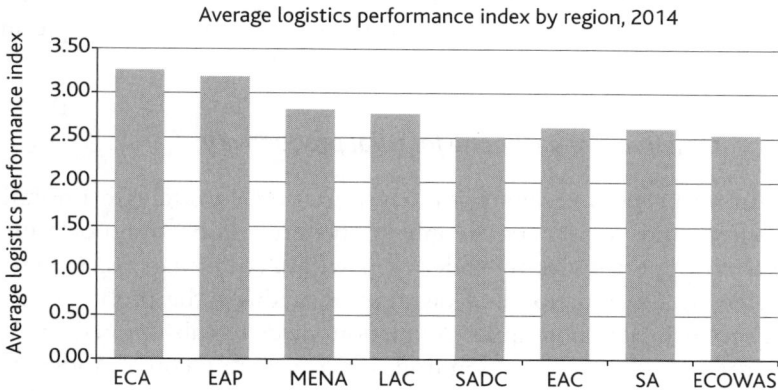

Notes: ECA: Europe and Central Asia; EAP: East Asia & Pacific; MENA: Middle East and North Africa; LAC: Latin America & Caribbean; SADC: Southern African Development Community; EAC: East African Community; SA: South Asia; ECOWAS: Economic Community of West African States.

Source: World Bank, 2014d

and a larger number of countries with ports compared to the Southern African sub-region. Nonetheless, the Southern African sub-region enjoys better regional transportation integration (Christ and Ferrantino, 2009). One apparel producer near Nairobi, Kenya, estimated that improvements in all aspects of the transportation process (including ports, roads and customs procedures) could lower his total costs by 10% to 40% and significantly improve his firm's competitiveness (cited in Christ and Ferrantino, 2009).

High logistics costs are not only due to the lack of investment in physical infrastructure—they also stem from unwieldy and lengthy regulations, delays, and informal fees. The costs that service providers face are not excessively high in Sub-Saharan Africa compared with other regions of the world; however, transportation prices or costs to the shipper (that is, the end user) *are* high, particularly in Central Africa. This mainly results from official and unofficial market regulation and structure in the trucking services, which is most noticeable in West and Central Africa. Raballand and Macchi (2008) conclude that investment in infrastructure is unlikely to reduce logistics costs unless institutional issues are also addressed.

In the SADC region, Mauritius has the best road conditions: by 2005, 100% of its road network had been paved and 95% was in good condition. Botswana ranks second best with 94% of its roads in good condition, although only 36% had been paved by 2004. At the other end of the scale, Tanzania has the lowest percentage of paved roads. In some countries, despite the low percentage of paved roads, the networks are regarded as being in good condition, for example in Namibia, South Africa, Swaziland, and Zambia.

Rural infrastructure backbone for rural productivity

Isolation perpetuated by poor transportation constrains economic progress and traps rural people in poverty. Poor transportation restricts opportunities to trade, even within local markets. It raises the costs of production and distribution, reduces the profit margin on produce sales, and limits production yields to sub-optimal levels. All this impedes the transition from subsistence to income-producing agriculture. The economic effects of better access to, from, and within rural areas can be cumulative and far-reaching. Enhanced access to markets cost-justifies the modernization of agricultural processes through mechanization, fertilizers, and the planting of high-yielding crop varieties. Such improvements increase the demand for agricultural inputs and for credit. When new roads reach remote rural areas, the economic effect can be dramatic.

Given the poor quality of the road network, it is not surprising that rural productivity in Sub-Saharan Africa is low. Poor logistics affect agriculture more than all the other sectors. Only 20% of the rural roads in Sub-Saharan Africa are in good condition and 20% in fair condition (Carruthers et al, 2008). The remaining 60% of rural roads require either rehabilitation or reconstruction, which represents both a financial and institutional challenge.

Productivity is greater in areas closer to urban centers, while better road connectivity determines higher crop production. Agricultural production and proximity (as measured by travel time) to urban markets are highly correlated in Sub-Saharan Africa, even after taking agro-ecology into account (Dorosh et al, 2010). Total crop production relative to potential production is approximately 45% for areas within four hours' travel time from a city of 100,000 people. In contrast, it is only about 5% for areas more than eight hours' travel time from a city of 100,000 people.

The impact that good rural road networks can have on rural productivity is supported by research cited in Dorosh et al (2010). This reveals that reducing travel time through road investments can significant increase the adoption of high-input/high-yield technology by farmers, thereby increasing productivity. This shift toward high-input production systems is driven by both direct and indirect channels. In the direct channel, roads increase crop production by shifting outward both the crop demand curve (through access to a larger market) and the crop supply curve (through better access to intermediate inputs and new technology). In the indirect channel, roads facilitate the adoption of high-input/high-yield crop production and therefore increase crop production by replacing low-input/low-yield crop production (Dorosh et al, 2010).

The logistics chain for buying inputs and selling produce determines the adoption of high-yield agricultural practices. Typically, costs per kilometer are higher on dirt roads than on tarmac roads. The overall impact on input prices and marketing costs for farmers located in areas with poor accessibility is substantial. Road projects, such as those funded by the AfDB, lead to higher agricultural production and land productivity, increased use of agricultural inputs and extension services, and a shift towards high-value crops and off-farm employment opportunities.

Beyond transport infrastructure: land regulations and property rights as determinants of resource allocation in rural areas

Key among the drivers of rural productivity is the issue of land regulations and property rights. This is often linked to the personal economics of land ownership. People with decision-making powers at various levels of government may have a vested interest in steering investment resources in their favor (that is, toward their own land holdings, thereby increasing their value). This may result in a conflict of interests, for example when investments that they favor do not align to the objectives of the investment agenda viewed from a broader perspective. One example is when roads are built in areas that are known to represent a challenge environmentally and that are likely to give a poor social return.

A second consideration regarding the role of land regulations in infrastructure provision is that changes in land use that can often arise from investment in roads. Moreover, investment in roads can sometimes reduce rural productivity due to weak land regulations. The main justifications for investing in rural roads is to improve accessibility and to reduce travel times and trade costs. However, poor land regulations setting the limits between urban and rural areas can result in gentrification and land speculation, which can reduce rural productivity. Land regulation should therefore enforce a limit for urban expansion, in order to safeguard the use of surrounding rural areas for agriculture. When land regulations are non-existent or weak, poor landowners may seek a change in land use from agriculture toward urban activities that offer greater returns. The result will be higher land prices that are generally inconsistent with rural productivity. The resulting landscape is of vacant rural land where road improvement has been made. Furthermore, the improved accessibility incentivizes poor households to sell their land or vacate when renting, and move further into the hinterland. In these cases, the policy instrument of road improvement works against rural productivity and strengthens the mechanisms that fuel rural poverty.

Property rights, in turn, also represent a macro mechanism that drives migration and the efficient localization of population. The rural poor barely have access to land titles due to poor institutionalization, low levels of education, informal expansion of agricultural land through deforestation, and weak government capacity. Land tenure laws remain vague and vary from one sub-region to another. Given continued restrictions on land ownership and unclear regulations on land tenure, labor mobility may be hindered. Many government controls in relation to property rights have been relaxed, which in some cases has released agricultural capital and labor for non-agricultural activities.

Land is central in promoting rural livelihoods in Africa because access to land and security of tenure are the main means through which food security and sustainable development can be realized. Issues surrounding land tenure and property rights have been on the increase in Africa over the past decade. The result has been growing poverty, landlessness, homelessness, and social distress. The last few years have witnessed increased politicization of land issues and attempts to gain land rights by some communities. Although the land question in Africa varies across the sub-regions, there are common tendencies and empirically based data that demonstrate the strong linkages between land tenure issues on the one hand, and food security and sustainable livelihoods on the other.

Sub-regional differences are substantial. In West Africa, land problems focus on the insecurity of tenure and its effect on the effective exploitation of land. Under customary law, traditional leaders (chiefs) remain the dominant and de facto landowners. It is through them that community members obtain access to land resources. Once allocated, the land comes under the control of the community member's family in most cases. In some parts of Central Africa, there is another major problem. Here the scarcity of productive land is the source of conflicts and in countries like Rwanda and Burundi, and lies at the root of much civil unrest. With a total population of 10.9 million in 2011 (AfDB, 2012), Rwanda is the most densely populated country in

Africa and its population growth rate remains very high, at 3.6%; therefore land scarcity will continue to be a critical issue for the future.

Unequal land access and low absolute levels of land per household are shown to impede poverty reduction and economic growth. This is the result of the strong linkage between access to land and household income, particularly for farm sizes below 1 hectare per capita. In Africa, households in the highest per capita quartile on average control between five and 15 times more land than the lowest quartile (FAO, 2010). Landless households or those that own less than 0.1 hectares constitute 25% of rural agricultural households. Restricted access to land prevents the poor rural population escaping poverty through agricultural productivity growth (Jayne, 2005 cited in FAO, 2010). Insufficient attention is paid to the implications of land inequality in relation to agricultural productivity and food security.

Weak or no land ownership restricts location choices and locks people into poverty. People might be better off financially if they were able to sell and move elsewhere, but this option may not be open to them if they have weak property rights. This situation is exacerbated in peri-urban areas, where land plots tend to be sub-divided among family members as housing solutions. In these areas, residents still face long travel times to urban centers; further, the potential exploitation of scale in agricultural production becomes fragmented. Clearer property rights could have the macro effect of allowing family members with better skills to move into urban areas, while leaving behind those more suited to rural activities.

The need for a strategic and integrated agenda for rural infrastructure

The challenge is how to sequence cost-effective investments in areas that have low population density and little commercial activity. One option is to focus investments geographically to foster the development of growth poles (World Bank, 2008a). The rural agenda needs to improve smallholder competitiveness in areas with high investment returns, while safeguarding the livelihoods and food security of subsistence farmers.

Improving rural productivity should not be viewed separately from the urbanization or regional integration agenda—what is needed is a holistic approach. The maximum investment returns can be obtained when the three dimensions of spatial development are considered simultaneously, given the functional relationships and synergies that exist among them. In fact, rural productivity improves when it is linked to the growth and success of neighboring cities that represent its major market, rather than relying on isolated rural areas that aim to produce, like extractive economies, for distant markets.

The best areas for rural investments are those that bring complementary benefits to urban areas and regional integration. The impact of infrastructure improvements to promote industrial development and accelerate national economic performance is greater in areas where a large market is present (Lall et al, 2009). Improving infrastructure in these places provides the highest return for public investment. Consequently, the best option for improving rural productivity is in nearby areas that will benefit from the same investment in infrastructure. For example, in Uganda the urban areas between Kampala and Jinja are most likely to boost the country's industrial development. Consequently, rural investment activities along that corridor should be prioritized in the rural productivity agenda.

It is also important to look for complementarities between on- and off-farm activities in order to reduce poverty. Poor road access in many cases coincides with other constraints, such as poor agro-ecology, low population density, and poor access to amenities. So, a well-targeted program needs to also take into account the geographic, community, and household characteristics and consider complementary investments to maximize the impacts of road construction and rehabilitation for market efficiency and social welfare. As the package required is more comprehensive than simply investing in roads, it is necessary to consider the feasibility of providing funding and implementation capacity. Otherwise, investing in road infrastructure in locations where those other components are missing will not deliver the highest returns.

Successful diversification also appears to be associated with infrastructure variables. Households that can reach fertilizer sellers, or have access to motorable roads or piped water, are more likely to diversify (World Bank, 2011b). Better access to fertilizers enables farmers to produce crops more efficiently and, therefore, to spend more time off-farm. Poor road infrastructure, particularly rural roads, raises input prices and marketing costs and creates disincentives for farmers to diversify. Advisory services can encourage farmers to introduce new technologies and raise overall farm productivity through increased commercialization. In general, the condition of roads determines the success of households in diversifying income sources, as better accessibility allows them to participate in off-farm activities.

The concept of providing rural infrastructure across the whole of Africa is not a realistic option from a financial viewpoint; moreover, it would not represent the best use of scarce resources. The challenging economic geography of Africa makes it difficult to invest in rural roads universally. Less than 40% of rural Africans live within 2km of an all-season road—this is the lowest level of rural accessibility in the developing world. Given Africa's low population density, improving rural accessibility for all would imply doubling or tripling the length of the existing network in most countries, which is financially unsustainable (Gwilliam et al, 2008).

The rural infrastructure agenda for Africa should therefore focus on improving poor-quality roads and maintaining the current service in good order, rather than extending the size of the network. Increasing the road network would result in even greater maintenance liabilities in the future. Funding and institutional arrangements need to be put in place to ensure the sustainability of road investments and maximize their long-term impact.

Community-based maintenance contracts and labor-intensive road maintenance projects can boost job creation. In addition, the cost of infrastructure provision can be reduced if labor-intensive technologies are selected instead of equipment-intensive alternatives. For example, Devereux and Solomon (2006) report that some labor-intensive programs have provided up to 30% cost savings. Other researchers have even identified savings of 50%. However, focusing solely on reducing the overall investment amount is probably not the best criterion to adopt when considering labor-intensive technologies. Their cost structure differs from that of equipment-intensive provision because it needs to include components like training and/or the development of institutional capacities. Therefore any attempt to draw comparisons by days of labor versus non-labor costs can be misleading.

Meeting the rural accessibility standard (75% of the rural population living within 2km of an all-weather road) would require a road network of more than 1.1 million km. Only a fraction of that length is currently provided by the regional and national road networks. Eleven of the 23 countries (rising to 15 under the pragmatic scenarios)[1] would not need to add any new roads to their present official road network to reach the rural accessibility standard—they would simply have to maintain their roads in good condition. In the remaining 12 countries (or eight under the pragmatic scenario), some or all of the unclassified road network would have to be upgraded to all-weather roads and maintained in good condition, while some new roads would be needed for the rural accessibility standard to be met (Carruthers et al, 2008).

Rural roads would absorb more than 53% of the requisite spending. A little more than half of that would be used to improve the existing official road network, while the remainder would be used for upgrades to the non-official network. This would add connectivity to areas that were not already connected, and would represent 20% of agricultural output potential. For Sub-Saharan Africa as a whole, the additional cost of adding the potential output would not be excessive (Carruthers et al, 2008).

Regional integration: the way forward for infrastructure provision

Regional integration and connectivity are vital to Africa because for most of its citizens, prosperity depends not only on their own efforts but also on those of their neighbors. Forty percent of Africa's population live in countries without access to the sea, compared with a global figure of about 4%. By comparison, Austria and Switzerland are landlocked countries; however, their borders are thin, people and goods pass through with few or no checks, and their ties with neighboring countries are strong. In contrast, Africa consists of 54 separate countries, each with its own borders and barriers to the movement of goods, capital, and people. The greatest barriers for accessing seaports are in central Africa, where weak regulations for the trucking industry, low investment in roads, and poor maintenance result in the highest logistics costs and longest transit times.

According to the *World Development Report* (WDR) of 2009 (World Bank, 2009b), the countries of Central, East, and West Africa face the triple challenges of internal division or thick economic borders; large distances from world markets; and low economic density due to small local economies. In order to overcome such a situation, those countries need a combination of three policy instruments conceptualized by the WDR 2009: strengthening regional institutions in countries that have thick borders; investing in regional infrastructure to improve the connectivity between countries; and providing "incentives such as preferential access to world markets, perhaps on the condition that all countries strengthen regional cooperation" (World Bank, 2009b). Adopting the same line of argument, Limão and Venables (1999) maintain that regional approaches to infrastructure provision can address the infrastructure backlog in Africa by overcoming its difficult geography.

According to the WDR 2009 framework, solving the divisions created by thick borders may not be sufficient to trigger economic growth in all countries, as other constraints will continue to affect regional development. These impediments include the scattered location of people and economic activities, and low population size along with large distances to world markets. This is especially true for the countries in ECCAS, which have a weaker infrastructure endowment compared to the rest of Sub-Saharan Africa. Although East and West African countries also face the challenge of poor connectivity, they benefit from larger local markets, bigger cities, and potential complementarities.

Sub-regional specifics

Infrastructure endowments differ substantially across sub-regions, as do institutional schemes for services provision. Tailoring an agenda for regional integration and connectivity should consider those differences to preempt and address conflicting investment priorities. The discussion on regional economic communities (RECs) later in this chapter highlights the differences in infrastructure endowments across the sub-regions. A more detailed presentation of challenges and opportunities at the intersection of sectors and sub-regions is presented in the Annex in Table A10.1, which draws on the AICD analysis.

Economic Community of Central African States

ECCAS's economic geography is complex due to the fact that economic activity takes place in isolated pockets separated by vast distances and environmentally sensitive areas. As a result, the sub-region has the poorest performing infrastructure in the continent, based on most indicators.

One third of ECCAS's regional road network is unpaved and a substantial amount is in poor condition. Coastal countries in the sub-region do not devote sufficient attention to the sea corridors; furthermore, surface transportation is the most expensive in Sub-Saharan Africa due to cartelization and restrictive regulations for the trucking industry. As a result, it also moves at a slower pace than in most other parts of Africa because of the poor road conditions, border delays, and time-consuming administrative processes. The time taken to move freight from ports to landlocked countries ranges from 26 to 71 days—the slowest in the continent. The overall cost of moving goods along Central Africa's key trade routes is in the order of US$230–US$ 650 per tonne.

Central African railroad systems do not form a network and existing lines are lightly used. Two ports in Central Africa—Douala and Pointe Noire—serve as trans-shipment hubs for the region but their performance significantly falls short of global standards. The air transportation sector in ECCAS is striking for the absence of an existing hub and the lack of connectivity between the Economic and Monetary Community of Central Africa sub-region and other ECCAS states.

Despite major hydropower potential, Central Africa has the least developed power sector on the continent. Regional power trade through the Central African Power Pool could substantially reduce power sector costs and the long-run marginal cost of energy in the sub-region but currently those opportunities are not being tapped. Compared with the other sub-regions, ECCAS's ICT infrastructure is still in its incipient stages, performs poorly on access, and has the highest prices.

Southern Africa Development Community

The SADC includes small and isolated economies, but also some of the continent's largest economies (South Africa, Angola, and the Democratic Republic of Congo [DRC]). Its varied territory is characterized by a mixture of island states and low- and middle-income countries. The economic geography of SADC reinforces the importance of adopting a regional approach to infrastructure development. However, SADC ranks consistently above other sub-regions on a range of infrastructure indicators.

SADC has a well-developed regional road network which is in relatively good condition, while almost all of the corridors (with the exception of Nacala and Lobito) are paved. Surface transportation in SADC is the cheapest in Africa (though still more expensive than in other developing countries). The overall times and costs of moving goods along Southern Africa's key trade routes are onerous. Southern Africa has an extensive railroad system with national systems forming a network centered on Durban, which offers direct competition to road transportation. In the ports sector, SADC has a very effective trans-shipment network, with Durban followed by Dar es Salaam as the key ports. The air transportation market in SADC is the largest in Africa, with Johannesburg at its center.

The power transmission network in Southern Africa is reasonably well developed, leading the rest of the continent in generation capacity and enjoying relatively low costs. The Southern African Power Pool has already established regional trade. SADC has the best record in terms of access to ICT services compared with the other sub-regions but faces very high prices.

East Africa Community

The East Africa sub-region's infrastructure ranks consistently behind that of the Southern and West African sub-regions. Its road network is in relatively good condition, though with prominent patches of poor-quality roads along some corridors and significant stretches of unpaved road. Surface transportation in East Africa is challenged by difficult border crossings and low performance logistics but faces fewer obstacles than in other sub-regions from the trucking industry, which is comparatively mature and more competitive than in some other sub-regions. However, it is still very slow when compared with SADC and global standards. Widespread delays occur in ports, at border crossings, and in other processes. The overall cost of moving a tonne of freight along East Africa's key trade routes is in the order of US$175–370 and takes between 200 and 800 hours. Apart from the Tazara railroad between Zambia and Tanzania, there are no real regional rail networks within EAC, and what does exist is very lightly used, which impedes regional integration.

East Africa has two maritime hubs that anchor the regional trans-shipment network but its ports are in need of significant improvements. With respect to air transportation, East Africa has a strong hub-and-spoke structure that centers on two regional hubs, but the region has made little progress toward market liberalization.

The power situation in EAC is constrained compared with other sub-regions. It already practices regional power trade, albeit much less actively than West and Southern Africa; however, scaling up this trade could bring substantial benefits. Compared with other regional economic communities in the continent, EAC performs poorly in terms of ICT access and prices. However, recently some countries have been able to access submarine cables, which has resulted in a drop in ICT prices and in improved access.

Economic Community of West African States

Infrastructure in the 15 countries of ECOWAS ranks consistently behind Southern Africa across a range of indicators. ECOWAS has a relatively well-developed regional road network based on seven main arteries, but coastal countries are not devoting enough attention to sea corridors. Surface transportation in West Africa is very expensive compared with the rest of Africa and the developing world. The causes are cartelization and restrictive regulation of the trucking industry. It is also very slow owing to the frequent delays associated with administrative processes. The overall times and cost of moving goods along West Africa's key trade routes are excessive, requiring in the order of 400–1,000 hours and costing between US$175 and US$310 per tonne.

There is no real regional rail network in the ECOWAS area. Existing lines are lightly used and the presence of three different rail gauges complicates integration. In the ports sector, West Africa lacks a clear maritime hub as the center for a more effective trans-shipment network and needs to improve performance across the board. In terms of air transportation, ECOWAS has made great strides on market liberalization, but safety remains a concern, and the region lacks a strong hub-and-spoke structure.

Power supply in the ECOWAS region is the most expensive and least reliable in Africa. West Africa already practices regional power trade. Deepening such trade could bring substantial benefits, but much depends on Guinea's ability to become a hydropower exporter.

Compared with other regional economic communities in Africa, ECOWAS performs reasonably well on access to ICT but faces relatively high prices for critical services.

Gains from scaling up regional integration

Transforming the current low level of collaboration among African countries would mean promoting and realizing the benefits of collective action. Among others, there are two primary sources of common benefit: the additional outcomes expected from improved accessibility to larger markets by the producers in each national market; and the efficiency gains from the joint provision of infrastructure.

Additional outcomes of improved accessibility to larger markets

Successful regional trade integration could help African countries to reap economies of scale and collectively exploit their resources, thereby expanding markets and raising their competitiveness in the global economy. A larger market is an important driver of product diversification and enables small producers to realize cost savings from larger scales of production.

The first-order objective is to make it easier for firms within Africa to reach African markets. Currently they face disadvantages compared to firms outside Africa. Ironically, firms abroad often can trade more cheaply with local African markets than can home-grown firms. For instance, there are onerous trading costs for businesses seeking to trade between East and West Africa.

Notably, infrastructure plays a central role in improving regional competitiveness, facilitating domestic and international trade, and enhancing integration into the global economy. For firms, infrastructure development is critical for creating wealth as it can reduce costs and enlarge markets. Firms are more willing to invest in intra-firm productive assets when the complementary investment in extra-firm assets is in place and quality services are available at low cost. Without reliable and competitively priced freight transportation facilitated by sturdy infrastructure, nations have little hope of trading goods on advantageous terms. Alongside these benefits for all participants, cooperation with neighbors is vital for the landlocked economies that have limited access to ports and markets.

Investment in physical infrastructure (such as roads, power plants, and ICT) is likely to generate the largest impacts on regional trade. In addition, political commitment to enhancing critical regional integration has been demonstrated in recent times through fuller implementation of tariff liberalization schedules, concerted efforts to tackle non-tariff barriers, and the development of longer-term strategies to address export supply capacity constraints at the national level. These are all welcome initiatives but investment in regional infrastructure needs to take precedence over all other efforts, as its benefits will be greater in terms of productivity than any other collective action by African governments.

Studies prepared for the *World Development Report* of 1994 (World Bank, 1994) estimated that, on average, a 1% increase in infrastructure stock is associated with a 1% increase in GDP. More recent studies (for example, Esfahani and Ramirez, 2003) show that the contribution of infrastructure services to growth is substantial and in general exceeds the cost of the provision of those services. Easterly and Rebelo (1993) found that public expenditure on transportation and communications has a positive effect on growth. A more recent study by Calderón (2009) demonstrated that the growth payoff of achieving the infrastructure development of the African leader (Mauritius) is 1.1% per year in North Africa and 2.3% in Sub-Saharan Africa, with most of the contribution coming from larger stocks. The same study also found that across Africa, infrastructure contributed 99 basis points to per capita economic growth, compared with 68 basis points for other structural policies.

Investments in regional infrastructure are expected to deliver high rates of return, with intra-regional trade potentially tripling and international trade doubling. For example, it is estimated that upgrading the major corridors linking the 16 landlocked countries to the major seaports serving the region's international trade would cost US$1.5 billion, with a further US$1.0 billion annually for maintenance (Teravaninthorn and Raballand, 2008). However, the East Africa Northern Corridor alone could yield an internal rate of return of 20–60%. Another example is the Trans-African Highway, which requires a total investment of US$20 billion and an ongoing maintenance cost of US$1 billion a year. However, these huge costs need to be set against the ensuing benefits, with intra-regional trade alone expected to triple to US$30 billion per year, not to mention the gains to international trade, which currently stands at US$200 billion per year (Buys et al, 2006).

Efficiency gains of shared provision/linking of infrastructure

The benefits of regional integration are visible across all aspects of infrastructure networks. For ICT and energy, regional infrastructure provides scale economies that substantially reduce the costs of production. For example, big hydropower projects that would not be economically viable for a single country make sense when neighbors can share the benefits. And in the area of ICT, linking to continental fiber-optic submarine cables could reduce internet and international call charges by one-half. Similarly, regional power pools that allow countries to share the most cost-effective energy resources can reduce electricity costs substantially. Infrastructure sharing has many benefits: it addresses the problems of small-scale and adverse location; it permits a scaling-up of infrastructure construction, operation, and maintenance; it reduces costs; it pools scarce technical and managerial capacity; and creates a larger market (Lederman et al, 2005).

There are significant economic and environmental benefits to the linking of electricity generation systems of different countries and encouraging energy trade. Regional integration proves very cost-effective, not only because economies of scale can be realized but also because power pools can make extensive use of trading possibilities. The DRC, for example, emerges as a huge exporter of electricity. Its net exports are almost four times larger than its domestic consumption, and it supplies hydropower through Zambia, Zimbabwe, and Botswana into South Africa. South Africa becomes an importer of 10% of its domestic consumption, trading with all neighboring countries: Namibia, Botswana, Zimbabwe, Mozambique, and Lesotho.

Regional collaboration also allows optimal management and the development of cross-border public goods. Road and rail corridors linking landlocked countries to the sea are an example of such a regional public good, as are regional airport and seaport hubs.

Focus on energy, transportation, and ICT

Cross-border infrastructure such as transportation, energy, and telecommunications is essential to move goods, services, people, and information between countries. Such linkages expand market access, reduce economic distance, and facilitate trade, investment and labor mobility. In Africa, poor transportation and communications infrastructure and unreliable power supplies raise trade costs and undermine competitiveness and the continent's ability to integrate regionally as well as globally. At a fundamental level, the low degree of intra-African trade is due to a lack of product diversification and poor trade complementarity among African countries. These structural constraints are compounded by inadequate and inefficient infrastructure, both hard (such as roads, transportation, and energy) and soft (such as customs systems). All this erodes the opportunities for the diversification of production, which should lead to increased scale and competitiveness at regional and global levels. An infrastructure agenda for regional integration and connectivity should therefore focus on addressing the needs of the transportation, energy, and telecommunications sectors.

Achieving functional connectivity at the regional level means focusing on a number of areas: smooth land corridor transportation between landlocked countries and ports, as well as between major cities for internal trade; the development of power supply options harnessing cost-effective generation technologies at efficient scale in the context of a well-functioning regional trading pool; and a robust communications network linking capital cities through fiber-optic access to submarine cables.

Energy

Electricity is by far Africa's largest infrastructure challenge, with investment needs estimated at US$40.6 billion per year (Rosnes and Vennemo, 2009). In 2010, only 32% of Sub-Saharan Africans had access to electricity compared with an average of 77% of the population for all low-middle income countries, 75% for South Asia, and 95% for Latin America. The figure is higher in North Africa at 99% (World Bank and International Energy Agency, 2014). Annual per capita electricity consumption in Sub-Saharan Africa is 317 kWh (225 kWh excluding South Africa). However, there are significant differences across and within regions: in Central Africa average consumption is 220 kWh, in Cameroon it is around 100 kWh and in Gabon 900 kWh; in Southern Africa Zambia, Botswana and Zimbabwe have more than 500 kWh per capita per year, but levels in Mozambique and Tanzania are below 200 kWh (IEA, 2014). Furthermore, data from Enterprises Surveys of the World Bank between 2006 and 2014 for 42 African countries show that the average duration of electricity outages is 6.2 hours, which represents annual average losses of 7.2% of total sales (World Bank, 2014b). During this period, regional surpluses in generation capacity were noted for all of the sub-regions, with the exception of East Africa, which had intermittent shortages. Some of the countries with surplus supplies like South Africa now have deficits due to increased local demand.

As an example, Sub-Saharan Africa has the world's lowest per capita consumption of electricity and the lowest rate of electricity access. Two-thirds of its population (500 million) are without access to electricity. SSA currently has inadequate generation capacity, limited electrification, low power consumption, unreliable services, and high and rising costs. But in order to develop economically and resolve the untenable access situation, massive amounts of electricity are required. For instance, from 2001 to 2005, half of the countries in Sub-Saharan Africa achieved solid GDP growth rates in excess of 4.5%. Their demand for power grew at a similar pace, yet generation capacity expanded only 1.2% annually. Refurbishing 44.3 GW and building an additional 7,000 MW of new generation capacity each year to meet demand, keep pace with projected economic growth, and provide additional capacity to support the rollout of electrification, would amount to US$40.6 billion a year. Even lowering the original projected growth rates of 5.1% to half their levels would reduce estimated power sector spending needs by only about 20% in absolute terms, lowering the required new generation capacity from just over 7,000 MW to just under 6,000 MW.

Electricity supply is also a serious infrastructure problem in terms of driving up exporters' costs. More than 30 countries experience power shortages and regular outages, which, among other things, disrupt economic activity and drive up operating costs. African firms report that frequent power cuts cause them to lose 5% of their sales. For firms in the informal sector that cannot afford backup generators—which is 3 to 5 times more expensive than electricity from the grid—the loss is even higher, at 20% (AICD, 2009).

Dealing with high electricity costs and the unreliability of supply is a priority issue in most African countries. In the majority of cases, addressing the problem will require significant investment in capacity that has lagged behind due to rapid growth in Africa's demand in recent years or, in the case of post-conflict states, due to civil unrest. The potential productivity gains from increasing electricity supply, together with the associated income effect, point to a market with significant growth potential.

Notwithstanding the size of the challenge, the development of energy markets on a regional basis offers significant benefits. Linking national petroleum and electricity industries can help mobilize private and domestic investments by expanding market size. Furthermore, regional interconnectivity can create export opportunities for countries with a comparative advantage in resource endowments. Secondary benefits, such as increased and cheaper energy supply alternatives, also become available to smaller markets and countries.

The *Regional Energy Integration in Africa* study (World Energy Council, 2005) confirms four major benefits associated with regional energy integration: improved security of supply; higher economic efficiency; enhanced environmental quality; and a wider deployment of renewable energy resources. For instance, large hydropower projects that would not be economically viable for a single country make sense when neighbors share the benefits and costs. Inadequate investment in such projects is mainly a cost problem, because, first, investment in the electricity sector is a large undertaking for a poor country— to developing a hydropower plant is for instance, extremely capital intensive—and, second, hydropower reserves are often located far from population centers, adding further to the cost.

Transportation

Roads

For many African countries, distance from their primary markets and high transportation costs inhibit participation in global trade. Poor infrastructure is the main cause of high transportation costs and, arguably, the greatest constraint to intra-African trade. Currently the cost of transporting goods in Africa is the highest in the world (Teravaninthorn and Raballand, 2008). It is estimated that poor infrastructure accounts for 40% of transportation costs for coastal countries, and up to 60% for landlocked countries (Limão and Venables, 2001). The burden of poor infrastructure on trade increases with geographic and sovereign fragmentation, as Sub-Saharan Africa is highly fragmented.

Several empirical studies document that the returns to investment in infrastructure (for example, upgrading of roads), measured in terms of trade growth, are particularly high in Africa. The real issue is improving (and preserving) the quality of that infrastructure. This can mean both improving the condition of existing infrastructure and upgrading its level of service (Carruthers et al, 2008).

In addition, regional collaboration is needed for effective infrastructure development because moving goods and people through regional borders and overseas requires corridors linking national capitals to each other, to other big cities, to international borders, and to deep-water ports. Corridors in Africa currently do not carry enough goods or people to reap benefits from more than one type of transport (in other words, multimodal transportation).[2] Improving services within modes and along the corridor is therefore key.

Roads constitute the main infrastructure serving regional connectivity, carrying at least 80% of goods and 90% of passengers. The concept of an intra-regional trunk network has existed for some time. In 1970 the Trans-African Highway was conceived as a network of all-weather roads that would provide direct routes between the capital cities. It was envisioned that it would contribute to political, economic, and social integration and cohesion in Africa, and ensure road transportation facilities between important areas of production and consumption (AfDB, 2000). The total length of the nine corridors is 54,120km. However, the Trans-African Highway is characterized by missing links and poor maintenance in key segments. About half of the network is in the 24 SSA countries. Of that half, 68% is paved, 6% has a gravel surface, and 26% has a dirt surface or no formed road. Only 27% of the network is in good condition, with a similar percentage in fair condition. This means that 46% of the network is in poor condition. Two segments of the system that remain unconnected by any sort of road are in Central Africa. There is a 200km gap between Salo in the Central African Republic and Ouésso in the Republic of Congo, and a 370km gap in Niger running from the Algerian border. As such, its potential to serve as the heart of regional connectivity remains unrealized. To provide a meaningful level of connectivity, between 60,000 and 100,000km of regional roads are required.

Design standards are important in estimating the costs of completing the system. Because international road links support high-speed traffic and heavy loads, high minimum standards for road widths are desirable. At present, the highways comprise a wide range of standards: the load limit for single axles in the countries through which the Trans-African Highway passes varies between 8.2 and 13 tonnes. This is a substantial variation, which delays border crossings; moreover, the separation of freight from truck deteriorates the quality of service in the logistics chain (AfDB, 2000). Although each country is responsible for the standards applied within its territory, there are important benefits to be gained from the application of common standards, such as avoiding operational and administrative complications at border crossings.

Railroads, air transportation, and seaports

Railroads provide significant internal links in some countries and particularly for some landlocked countries: for example, the corridors between Dakar and Bamako, Abidjan and Ouagadougou, or Maputo and East African countries.

In the SSA, rail coverage measured in terms of land area, population, and GDP per capita compares favorably with other regions of the world. However, rail density by land area in the low-income countries of SSA is somewhat lower than in LICs globally. Latest data from the AfDB data portal stands that the total rail network in SSA is around 58,671km and 12,663km in North Africa.

Air transportation is particularly important for sparsely populated and landlocked countries, and for future development of the region's significant tourism potential. Air freight is playing a growing role in the competitiveness of African goods in world markets for high-value, time-sensitive cargo (such as horticultural and floricultural products).

In shipping, the major ports in Africa still need to meet international standards and amplify their capacity in order to increase international trade and reap other benefits of better connectivity. While Sub-Saharan Africa has a proliferation of ports, few are large by world standards and most are not capable of handling the current generation of supersized container ships. Most are poorly equipped and operate at low levels of productivity. Generally, they are unprepared for the dramatic changes in trade and shipping patterns that have occurred since 1995. While they are moving slowly from publicly owned service ports to so-called landlord port structures, often with embedded container-terminal concessions, they still lag behind other global regions in the development of modern port-management structures. Additional momentum for modernization is coming from the growing presence of global shipping lines and international terminal operators in African ports.

ICT

Due to the size of investment requirements, the costs can outweigh the benefits for the private sector from the expansion of ICT services in Sub-Saharan Africa. Governments should, therefore, help to bridge costs and promote public–private partnerships. This will serve to expand opportunities for private investment in a sub-sector that has proved fundamental in recent years to the region's development.

The ICT revolution, especially in mobile telecommunications, has had enormous positive impacts on economic growth and social cohesiveness. Mobile phones have revolutionized the way people interact all over the world. The increasing use of ICT in Africa has had positive results both for economic growth and social advancement, such as education (for example, remote learning through the establishment of virtual universities). The ICT revolution in Africa is responsible for about one percentage point of the improvement in Africa's per capita economic growth rate between the mid-1990s and the mid-2000s. Moreover, it has proven to have multiplier effects, adding to employment growth and income generation. In East Africa alone, the cellphone industry provides direct and indirect employment for close to 500,000 people.

However, climbing the next step toward higher-speed, mass-market broadband access in Africa at affordable prices would involve major investments in backbone infrastructure. The revenue generated from customers would be insufficient to make this investment commercially attractive for the private sector alone. If governments wish to improve broadband internet access and speeds, significant levels of public subsidy are required. This underscores the need for a regional approach, by undertaking a strategic sequence of investments in fiber-optic links and backbones. This would pave the road toward leveraging further private sector investment.

The problem results from poor intra-regional connectivity, as well as insufficient undersea cables to connect Africa to the rest of the world and to the rich information resources of the internet. Ideally, the submarine cables surrounding the continent should ensure that all coastal countries have access to the intercontinental network. At present, West and Southern Africa have submarine cables, although they do not yet provide full access to all countries. However, there is no submarine infrastructure on the eastern side of the continent; this has led to exceptionally high costs for international communication. In addition, intra-regional backbones are needed both to ensure that landlocked countries secure access to submarine infrastructure and to facilitate communications across Africa's main economic regions.

Therefore there are two priorities for improving ICT in the continent: improving access to high-capacity, submarine fiber-optic cables for low-price international voice services and higher-speed internet access; and laying high-bandwidth backbone networks to connect towns and cities within countries, across borders and to the international submarine fiber-optic cable networks. Estimated one-time investment needs range from US$229 million for a minimum set of links to US$515 million for an extensive interregional network connecting all African capitals to one another with fiber-optic cables.

Strengthening regional institutional governance

Beyond the critical need to invest in regional physical infrastructure, there are two further aspects to be considered: strengthening the governance scheme for infrastructure service provision; and enhancing the institutional set-up to maintain an effective level of service provision.

The impact of poor governance and weak institutions can be observed in the transportation industry. In this sector, inadequate transit procedures, overregulation, bribes, multiple controls, and poor border service increase transportation times as well as the costs. The lack of standardized procedures at the borders also causes timing to be very variable and unpredictable, creating bottlenecks and making it difficult to meet schedules and international standards. The trucking sector in much of Africa is dominated by cartels that operate through a system of queuing for loads at fixed fares, in contrast to competitive best-offer practices and prices. In Central and West Africa, higher transportation costs are mainly explained by an oligopolized trucking industry with exceptionally high profit margins. While policy responses to these problems have included transit system reforms[3] and joint border posts or warehouses at ports for landlocked countries,[4] these practices have not reached all countries in the Sub-Saharan region.

For example, along the Central and Western African corridors, transportation costs are no greater than in other developing countries. However, transportation prices charged to the end user are much higher. The difference is explained by the set of informal payments and profits earned by trucking companies. The source of these high profit margins is the set of regulations in many African countries that restrict entry by new companies. When Rwanda, a landlocked country, deregulated its transportation sector, it saw a dramatic drop in transportation prices almost overnight (Teravaninthorn and Raballand, 2008).

Ensuring that maintenance of assets receives its fair share in any investment plan is critical—to give it short shrift is to squander any benefits from previous investments. This means strengthening the planning and budgetary capacity of the local political economy, so that the issue of maintenance is accorded its rightful importance. Planning and resourcing regional infrastructure also pose a challenge for Africa's integration.

Financing Africa's infrastructure in a two-tier market

Funding sources in a segmented market

Africa's substantial investment needs for infrastructure require a combination of traditional and innovative financing mechanisms, along with greater efficiency in public spending. According to the AICD estimates, Africa's total infrastructure financing needs amounted to US$93 billion a year in 2008, with only US$45 billion being financed. Even if all inefficiencies such as poor management and badly targeted subsidies or tariffs were eliminated, an annual gap of US$31 billion would remain. Other estimations situate the financing requirements even higher, at US$153 billion annually until 2020 (AfDB, 2010a). These financing requirements, even at the lower estimations, represent a huge challenge. African governments need to tap new sources to complement traditional financing alternatives. There is evidence that those countries that have invested strategically in infrastructure are reaping the benefits.[5]

Development partners and the public sector have to date been the main financing sources for Africa's infrastructure. Public financing has been most prominent in the water, sanitation, and transportation sub-sectors. For instance, in 2007 these sectors accounted for about 90% of public investments (Biau et al, 2008). Most private investment has targeted the ICT sector, which attracted 87% of private commitments in 2008 (OECD, 2010). There are also opportunities for traditional private investors to share in Africa's growth, provided that financing arrangements meet debt sustainability criteria. These include risk mitigation instruments, given the relatively high risk perception associated with infrastructure investment in Africa.

Innovative financing mechanisms for infrastructure are a promising trend to emerge across Africa. These mechanisms include local and foreign currency bonds, private equity, sovereign wealth funds, and emerging South partnerships with countries such as China. In a broader view of sustainable growth (that is, one encompassing social and environmental aspects), it is also important that Africa shift as much as possible to "clean energy financing", given its abundant natural resources. The AfDB is setting up the Africa Green Fund to receive and manage resources for climate change adaptation and mitigation. African countries can also do more to attract private and innovative funds on favorable terms. For example, public–private partnerships can be made more effective and remittances better utilized for development purposes.

Public spending efficiency has been identified as a source of financing because current inefficiencies in implementing infrastructure projects account for US$17 billion annually (Briceño-Garmendia et al, 2008). Therefore, improving the capacity of African countries will help to minimize these costs and to bridge the financing gap. Also there is a role to be played by the public sector through strengthening domestic resources and catalyzing private investments. One such avenue is to provide partial credit guarantee with concessional resources, to mitigate the impact of risk perception on availability and costs.

Despite all these alternative options to finance the infrastructure agenda, public financing coupled with private investment niches has left a substantial infrastructure deficit in African LICs. In LICs, official aid is not projected to increase in line with public investment spending (Redifer, 2010). MICs, on the other hand, have better prospects for securing their financing needs, due to their greater financial market development, lower capacity constraints, and lower perception of risk that limits private sector participation in LICs (Shah and Batley, 2009).

The fact of the matter is that there is a two-tier financing market at work, where specific countries can expect to attain better results through tailored financing mechanisms. For example, LICs will have difficulty in trying to deploy innovative financing instruments, whereas they are able to tap resources from donors as they improve public spending efficiency. By contrast, MICs will have more difficulty in accessing certain pockets of international aid but can utilize innovative financing instruments. The donor community should play a greater role in African LICs, while innovative financing mechanisms should be the focus in MICs. Notably, traditional funding sources for infrastructure development remain important but private investment is critical in closing the current gaps.

Both tiers must pay attention to the regulatory environment. Africa's infrastructure sector is still dominated by monopolistic incumbents that resist market reforms. While progress has been made in this regard, more has to be done. As an illustration, in South Africa, entry is still regarded as highly restricted in the telecommunications, rail freight, and electricity sub-sectors compared with countries in the Organisation for Economic Co-operation and Development (OECD). More generally, 20 out of 26 countries continent-wide score less than 5 out of a maximum of 10 in the services market liberalization index (OECD, 2010).

Traditional funding

Private investors and the donor community have increased financing for infrastructure projects in recent years, a trend that continued even through the 2008 global financial and economic crisis. According to the latest estimations, in 2010, more than US$55 billion was invested in new infrastructure investments across the continent. Investments by the Infrastructure Consortium for Africa (ICA) members alone rose by 45% over the 2008–2009 time span, from about US$14 billion to almost US$20 billion (AfDB, 2010b). In addition, the share of aid for infrastructure increased from 8% in 2006 to 18% in 2008 (see Figure 10.10); yet there is high dependency on aid in some countries, as detailed in the Annex in Table A10.2. It is also noteworthy that Africa currently meets about two-thirds of its infrastructure spending from domestic sources. In addition, the improved policy and business environment is attracting increasing levels of private sector participation through public–private partnerships (PPPs).

Figure 10.10: Aid dependency and aid allocations to infrastructure, 2006–2008

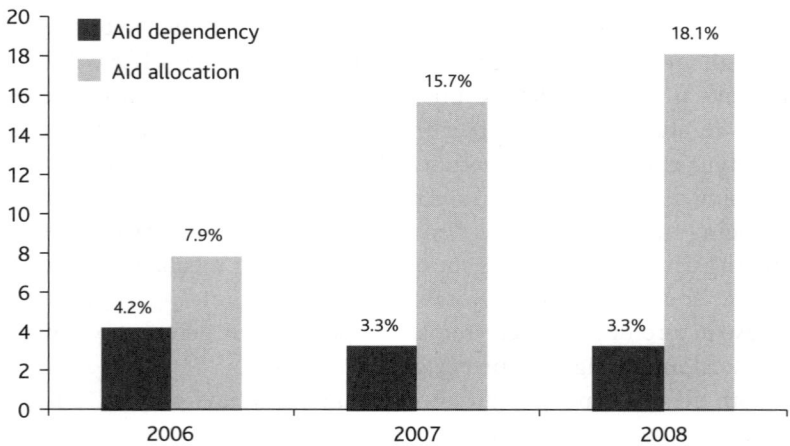

Source: AfDB Data Portal (www.afdb.org/en/knowledge/statistics/data-portal/)

The scaling up of private sector engagement in Africa's infrastructure agenda has been accompanied by changes in the lending and policy facilities of international financial institutions. The AfDB, for example, adapted its lending facilities to LICs to reflect these new developments. The new framework allows for non-concessional borrowing by countries with solid debt indicators and debt management capacity, provided such borrowing does not jeopardize fiscal and external debt sustainability.

Nonetheless, the public sector remains important, both as a direct financier and as a catalyst for private investment. It is also instrumental in addressing inefficiencies and ensuring maintenance of infrastructure assets. African policymakers are increasingly turning their attention to domestic resource mobilization amid concerns over potential decreases in official development assistance (ODA), given the global economic downturn. Hence increasing tax revenues and stimulating private and public savings are crucial measures for meeting Africa's infrastructure challenge, together with finding new and innovative financing sources.

Low tax-to-GDP ratios (below 15%) persist in many African countries, including lower-middle income economies such as Ghana. Instead of raising tax rates across the board, countries can increase revenues by removing exemptions and strengthening tax administration. In LICs, where the large informal sectors impede effective taxation collection, excises, value added tax and other indirect taxes can be relied on, provided that they are designed with consideration for poor households.

Public resource mobilization is particularly challenging in post-conflict countries, which utilize trade taxes and other simplified direct structures to reach a balance between indirect and direct taxes. Liberia is a good example of a post-conflict country that has managed to achieve high tax revenues in ratio to its GDP.

To increase public savings, government spending—including infrastructure expenditure—needs to be more efficient. Areas to be addressed include timely delivery of projects to avoid costly emergency measures; maintenance of existing infrastructure to limit expensive rehabilitation; improving efficiency of utilities; and strengthening medium-term expenditure frameworks, accounting frameworks, and auditing procedures.

African countries, especially SSA's oil importers, need to develop banking sectors, mobilize untapped private savings, and channel them into productive use. Formal financial institutions could offer long-term saving instruments, and incentivize their take-up through tax benefits. African governments could also unlock regulatory barriers that discourage institutional investors, such as pension funds, from utilizing long-term savings instruments. They could help to diversify capital markets by developing institutional frameworks that foster the participation of, for example, Islamic finance institutions and private equity funds.

Risk mitigation

In the aftermath of the 2008 financial crisis, private investors have become more risk averse. Nevertheless, the shift in investors' interests from highly leveraged products in advanced economies to real growth possibilities in selected emerging and developing countries presents an opportunity for Africa. African countries can attract private investors by promoting infrastructure projects as growth investment opportunities.

Through risk mitigation instruments, the public sector can catalyze additional private investments in infrastructure, raising the total available finance sources. These instruments need to be accompanied by reforms and institutional changes to eliminate the underlying sources of risk. The key risks are outlined below, together with the risk mitigation instruments needed to address them.

- *Commercial and political risk premiums* can be covered by both debt and equity insurance and guarantee instruments. While commercial instruments exist, concessional ones such as partial risk guarantees offered by the International Development Association and African Development Fund (and political risk insurance offered by the Multilateral Investment Guarantee Agency and the African Trade Insurance Agency are more suitable for LICs. Political risk management instruments incentivize governments to implement reforms that address performance risk. For middle-income countries, commercial risk management instruments help to develop capital markets and enable enterprises and countries to borrow externally on more competitive terms.

- *Country risk premiums* can be covered by first loss guarantees for a portfolio of transactions. For example, the First Loss Investment Portfolio Guarantee (FLPG), currently being developed by the AfDB, will facilitate the scaling-up of private sector investments in infrastructure in African LICs, by mitigating their country risk premium. The FLPG is an innovative instrument that would guarantee a portion (up to 10%) of the first loss of a defined portfolio of non-sovereign projects financed by the AfDB in LICs. This option allows African LICs to leverage at least five times the value of the guarantee in additional financing from the non-sovereign pool of lending resources.

- *Foreign exchange volatility* (prevalent in some LICs) can be addressed through currency hedging, government exchange rate guarantees, and devaluation liquidity schemes, among others. However, much greater attention needs to be paid to the affordability of these instruments in the African context.

- *Financial risks* can be mitigated through viability gap financing (for example, public subsidies in the form of partial capital cost financing for upfront investment needs). This method allows for private sector implementation of critical infrastructure projects with high economic benefits but low financial returns. By leveraging the limited public funding to attract greater private participation, governments can fast-track key infrastructure developments. Competition in the bidding process and, hence competitive pricing of the viability gap, are key to the success of this approach. In addition to subsidies, lowering financing costs for the private sector can also improve the bankability of projects.

The AfDB supports its regional member countries (RMCs) in their efforts to access long-term financing for infrastructure, including through risk-mitigating instruments. For example, the innovative Currency Exchange Fund (TCX) helps investors to hedge interest rate risks associated with infrastructure financing in local currencies, mainly through pooling market risks from different investors with geographically diversified business. Through local currency financing, TCX reduces foreign exchange rate risk. The AfDB also supports the development of local currency bond markets in RMCs with issuance of bonds in local currencies. Finally, the AfDB supports private sector-financed infrastructure through the African Legal Support Facility, which strives to improve contractual terms and legal environment for the private sector by building countries' capacity to negotiate complex commercial contracts.

Public–private partnerships

In the past decade, public–private partnerships (PPPs) have emerged as key instruments for infrastructure investment in Africa. PPPs are contractual arrangements that allow for private sector involvement in the supply of infrastructure assets and services. PPP modalities include management contract, leasing, investment concessions, divestiture, de-monopolization and new entry and build-operate-transfer (AfDB, 1999). While not innovative per se, PPPs bring innovative private funds to infrastructure. At their best, they ease budgetary constraints and raise efficiency by leveraging private sector management expertise and innovation.

PPPs are not yet common across the continent, even though in recent years African governments have increasingly used them for financing infrastructure. For example, the largest ongoing South African transport project—the Gautrain—was structured as a PPP (Deloitte, 2010). Examples of good practices emerged also at the municipal level. The Nelspruit Water and Sanitation Concession in South Africa helped raise access to water for households in Mmobela Municipality from 55% in 1999 to 94% in 2010 (Bender and Gibson, 2010).

Country experiences point to several preconditions for successful financing or executing of PPP projects, such as an adequate institutional framework (for example, political commitment and effective governance) and a transparent legislative and regulatory framework. The financial viability of a project depends on the stability of the regulatory regime responsible for its implementation. Instability acts as a deterrent to high-quality investment. Adequate risk and reward sharing between the government and the private sector is also critical for establishing effective PPPs. In particular, the pricing of infrastructure services requires careful attention, given its impact on the affordability of new services on the one hand, and the bankability of new investments on the other. In addition, the need for imported technology requires the development of local technical production sites and service centers, alongside secure and affordable supply of operating inputs.

Many African governments still lack the skills needed for the successful implementation of PPPs. In particular, sector ministries and sub-sovereign entities often lack adequate investment, financial planning, and coordination capacity. The experiences of countries that have established well-functioning PPP units in their ministries of finance (such as Senegal, Kenya, and South Africa) point to the positive impacts of such units. Developing a comprehensive and transparent list of contingent liabilities, such as implicit and explicit government debt guarantees, is also key for a realistic assessment of fiscal risks stemming from PPPs.

Reserves from "excess-savings" countries

Many Sub-Saharan African countries, especially oil importers, have low savings rates (see Figure 10.11). Overall rates are notably below the average of emerging market and developing economies, hence capital flows, especially private ones, constitute an indispensable source of financing. Key policy issues in this context are how to attract additional capital flows to Africa's infrastructure from developing Asia (for example, countries with high savings and investment rates), and how to utilize savings in African resource-rich countries, where savings rates are high but investment rates remain low. Emerging partners, especially China, have been particularly active in Africa since the mid-2000s, providing Foreign Direct Investment (FDI) in addition to official aid and non-concessional loans (discussed later).

South–South partnerships in infrastructure financing are gaining traction. Developing economies' share in Africa's annual FDI inflows increased from around 17.7% in 1999 to around 21% in 2008. South–South investment flows into Africa have been estimated at more than US$60 billion since 2003 (Freemantle and Stevens, 2010). Sovereign wealth funds (SWFs) are an important source of investment; for example, the Libyan Arab African Investment Company made investments worth US$800 million in 13 African countries in 2008 alone (Gijón, 2008). A total of 35 African countries have benefited from such inflows, with about 16% of the resources channeled into infrastructure. Over the 2001–2007 period, the electricity and transportation sub-sectors were the prime beneficiary sub-sectors (Figure 10.12).

According to the ICA, China's total commitments to Africa's infrastructure in 2009 amounted to US$5 billion. Chinese infrastructure financing in SSA is highly concentrated in resource-rich countries such as Nigeria, Angola, and Sudan, which attracted over 72% of these investments over 2001–2007. The development benefits for African nations could be enhanced by ensuring that governments negotiate equitable deals, where the appropriate economic values for resources are assigned, environmental externalities accurately valued, and the share of royalties and dividends are robust to price fluctuations. Moreover, the developed infrastructure should not be captive to the resource extraction operations. On a more positive note, only part of Chinese-financed infrastructure investments is directly linked to natural resource extraction (see Figure 10.12).

Other emerging markets have also shown interest in Africa's infrastructure projects. India has scaled up finance for infrastructure

Figure 10.11: National savings and investment rates as % of GDP, Africa versus Asia, 2000–2019

National savings and investement rates as % of GDP, Sub-Saharan Africa
vs. Emerging and Developing Asia, 2000 -2019 (e)

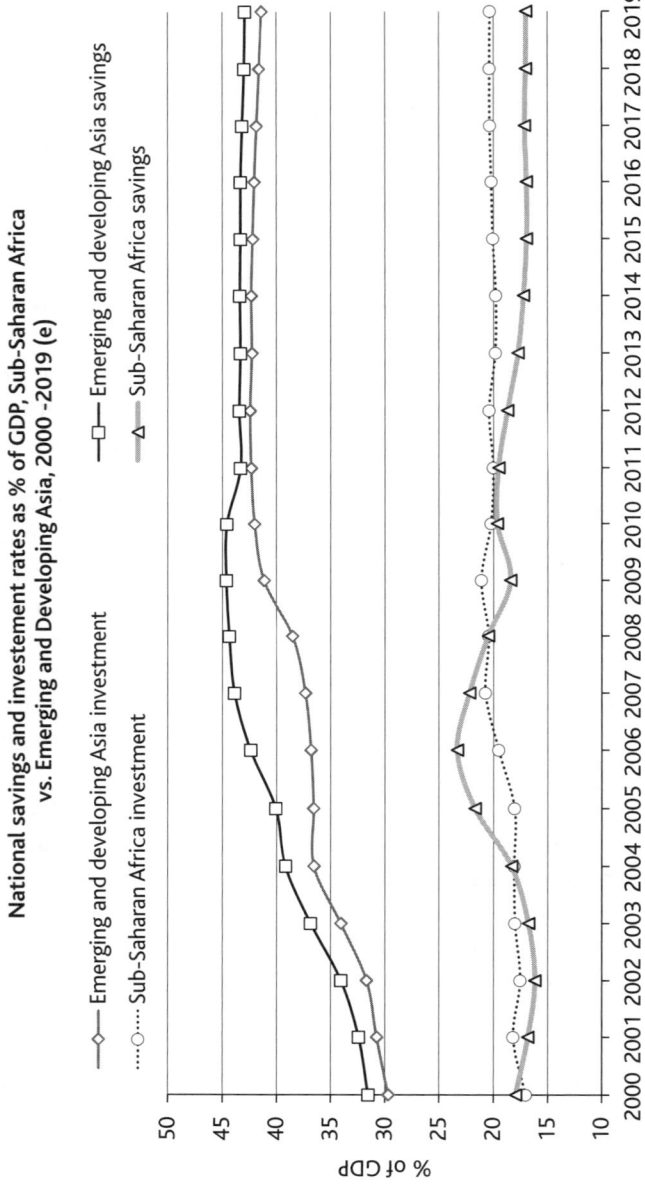

— Emerging and developing Asia investment —□— Emerging and developing Asia savings
······ Sub-Saharan Africa investment —△— Sub-Saharan Africa savings

Figure 10.12: Chinese direct investment by country and sector, 2001–2007

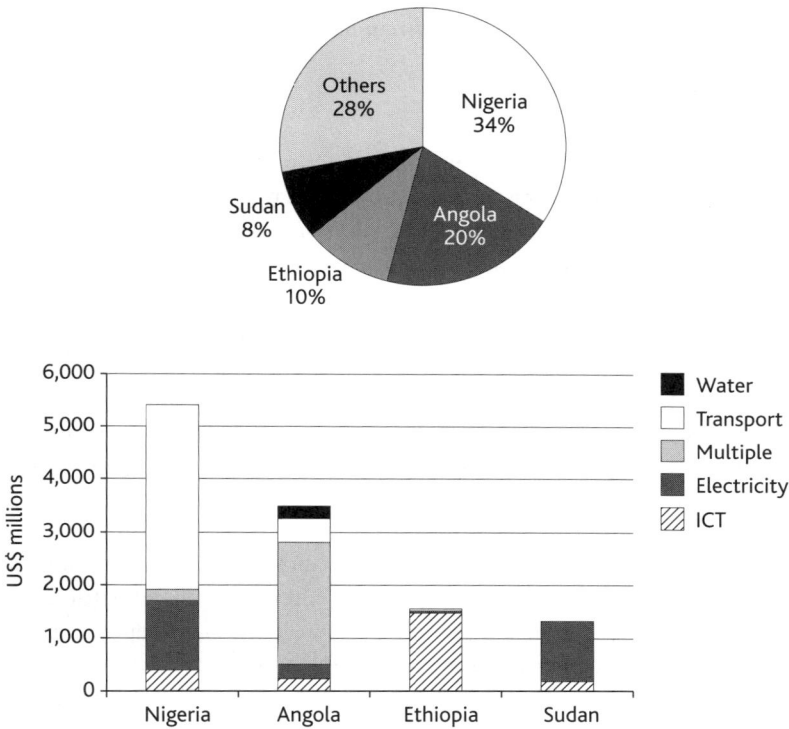

Source: Marin (2009)

projects in the region, with committed funding averaging US$0.5 billion a year during 2003–2007. Arab and Islamic funding institutions invested US$2.4 billion in 2008 and US$1.7 billion in 2009. Their coverage of recipient countries is wide (31 African countries benefiting in 2009) but there is a tendency to concentrate in the sub-regions of North Africa (60% in 2009) followed by East Africa (13%). Arab partners' finance has also been concentrated in specific sectors: 34% to road construction, 24% to the power sector, and 6% to dam construction (ICA, 2009).

Innovative financing

Several African emerging and frontier markets (such as Kenya and South Africa) have successfully adopted innovative methods utilizing domestic resources such as infrastructure and municipal bonds, pension funds, and syndicated loans. Still, given the underdeveloped local capital markets in most African LICs and some small MICs (such as Swaziland), access to international capital markets remains key for securing stable and longer-term financing.

Local currency bonds

Kenya's issuance of government infrastructure bonds (that is, longer-term bonds funding infrastructure projects in roads, water and energy) during the 2008–2009 global financial crisis is an example that other governments with sufficiently developed domestic bond markets could emulate. Besides supporting aggregate demand during the crisis, the issuance aimed at removing supply-side bottlenecks to growth. Since February 2009, Kenya has successfully issued three infrastructure bonds with a total value of US$1 billion. This paved the way for the issuance of corporate bonds by private or state-owned enterprises, for example, by the electricity utility KenGen and the mobile phone company Safaricom.

Kenya's success with infrastructure bonds is partly attributed to the use of incentives. Holders can use the bonds as collateral to acquire bank loans, while the banks can pledge them as collateral for their repo operations. To boost corporate issuance in local currency, various incentives were given, including an exemption from tax on interest for bond investors. On the innovative side, the issuance of government bonds with a sukuk (Sharia-compliant) portion facilitated participation by investors adhering to Islamic banking, such as the Gulf African Bank.

Commodity-linked bonds

Commodity-linked bonds have yet to develop in Africa. With some of the continent's export commodities being traded on the futures market, such bonds could be used to boost infrastructure investments. These bonds could help commodity exporters raise funds and hedge against unexpectedly large drops in prices. They are "capital-protected", that is, at maturity the investors are returned at least the nominal principal invested in the bond.

Commodity-linked debt instruments recently emerged in South Africa, where in August 2010 the Standard Bank Group offered investors Rand-denominated commodity-linked exchange traded notes (ETNs). ETNs are listed on the Johannesburg Stock Exchange, with a specific redemption date and returns linked to the performance of precious metals.

Sovereign external bonds

Ghana's issuance of an external sovereign bond of US$750 million in late 2007 was another innovative infrastructure financing instrument. It also set the benchmark for sovereign and private sector borrowing on the international capital market by other frontier market countries. Due to the tight credit conditions stemming from the global financial crisis, most sovereign debt issuances by SSA governments were deferred in 2009 and 2010. However, given the region's resilience during the crisis, demand for Africa's bonds is expected to rise. Ghana's experience highlights the importance of structural reforms, macroeconomic stability, credit rating and preparation before accessing international capital markets. Its debt accumulation shows the challenges to debt sustainability that may arise. Another lesson for African governments is that macroeconomic frameworks need to be robust to swings in capital flows.

Diaspora bonds

While the utilization of diaspora remittances for development has yet to be undertaken in Africa, several governments (such as Ghana and Sierra Leone) have been exploring this option. Of particular interest is the possibility of tapping into the foreign exchange component of remittances, without interrupting the actual transfer. Under securitization, inflows from foreign bank (in foreign currency) are matched with corresponding payments of the domestic bank in local currency. For remittance securitization to be feasible in Africa, several preconditions would need to be met, including supportive legislation and skills.

When it issued its Millennium Corporate Bond, Ethiopia became a pioneer in this area. The bond, which targeted Ethiopians both at home and abroad, sought to raise capital for the state-owned Ethiopian Electric Power Corporation. Across the continent, diaspora bonds present an untapped opportunity to mobilize resources in frontier markets with a large diaspora population (such as Ethiopia). The World Bank estimates that SSA countries could raise up to US$5–10 billion per year through such bonds. They are thus a potential source of longer-term financial resources for infrastructure, complementing remittance flows that are typically used for consumption or social expenditures.

Private equity funds

Private sector participation in Africa's infrastructure has also risen as a result of the increase in private equity funds (PEFs). Both multisector and specialized infrastructure funds have participated in green- and brownfield infrastructure projects, the latter being more recent and still small in number. Specialized infrastructure funds were pioneered by established infrastructure firms such as the Macquarie Group, which sponsored the South Africa Infrastructure Fund as early as 1996. To date, at least 10 specialized infrastructure funds have reached financial closure on the continent, mobilizing almost US$3 billion in direct financing. (The African Development Bank's support to such funds was outlined earlier in the chapter.)

PEFs invest in various infrastructure sectors including upstream industries, with national, regional or pan-African geographic reach. A mix of financing instruments—equity, senior debt, subordinated debt or mezzanine finance—is employed. Amounts range from US$5 million to US$120 million per project. Besides foreign currency financing, PEFs have also provided longer tenors (for example, 15 years in the SSA Emerging Africa Infrastructure Fund). Infrastructure PEFs mobilize financing both from private institutional investors (such as pension funds and insurance firms), and traditional financiers, such as development finance institution (DFIs).

Sovereign wealth funds

When well designed and implemented, SWFs can be an important source of finance for resource-rich countries. Accordingly, Nigeria has announced plans to establish a SWF of about US$1 billion (AfDB, 2011a). The investment resources will be owned and managed by the government. An infrastructure fund will be one of the three components of the SWF, which is expected to manage (that is, save and invest) the country's volatile oil revenues, and will replace the currently existing excess crude fund.

Efficiency gains from improved spending

Scaling up the current allocation of resources to infrastructure could help achieve substantial gains in the efficiency of infrastructure investments. However, in order to leverage the benefits of these and future inflows of resources, efficiency considerations must be observed when developing policies for infrastructure.

According to the AICD report of 2009, annual infrastructure investment needs in Africa amount to approximately US$93 billion, one-third of which should be allocated to operations and maintenance. African governments, infrastructure users, the private sector, and external sources together contribute about US$45 billion a year to infrastructure. The financial gap is therefore sizable and requires appropriate management to maximize the value of local and foreign investments.[6]

Spending leakages associated with poor allocation decisions amount to nearly US$17 billion. Such losses could be reversed by improving financial management and accountability. About US$7.5 billion could be saved by enhancing operational efficiency, while US$4.7 billion could be recovered by improved tariff setting aiming at cost recovery. Similarly, US$3.3 billion could be recovered through improved prioritization of public projects, and about US$1.9 billion through actual spending of resources that are regularly budgeted but not executed.

While private finance tends to be limited to certain infrastructure niches, there are significant gains to be made from more efficient management, to which the private sector could contribute. Between 2001 and 2006, Africa received substantial private investments targeted to ICT (US$28 billion), thermal power generation (US$3 billion), and ports (US$3 billion). Such preferences reflect sectors where institutions are more developed and private management has made a difference with improved, more efficient services and higher-quality delivery.

Private management without complementary investment has also helped to narrow the efficiency gap in railroads, power, and water utilities. Further private investment is needed in sectors such as alternative power technologies, water utilities, railroads, and highways, which often attract some portion of private financing in other regions of the world.

One of the most flagrant inefficiencies curbing sustainable economic growth is the failure to maintain infrastructure assets. Maintenance needs to be understood as an investment in asset preservation, which otherwise becomes more expensive to rebuild. Failure to maintain assets (such as roads) leads to deterioration in the quality of the service, deterring users from benefiting as they should. In aggregate, where infrastructure is not maintained, the expected social and economic returns from investment are severely eroded.

Institutional reform should also go beyond utilities to strengthen relevant ministries' planning functions and address serious deficiencies in the budgetary process. As underscored in the AICD report of

2009, better sector planning is needed in ministries responsible for infrastructure, to ensure that the construction of critical new assets begins early enough to come on line when needed.

Efficiency gains from strategic selection of supply technologies

One of the main issues in public resources allocation is setting the correct size and quality of the supply response to the demand for utilities. Given the topography of Africa, it is clear that piped water cannot be provided to all citizens across every African country, not even in the most developed. While the alternative of providing water via standposts for a few hours each day might be considered an inadequate response to a pressing need, nonetheless it is a compromise solution where budgets are constrained.

Just as economies of scale reduce production costs, greater population concentrations facilitate increased access to basic services at lower prices. Furthermore, urban networks ease expansion toward rural areas. Evidence shows that the cost of expanding infrastructure networks in Africa is highly sensitive to population density, supporting the argument in favor of cities. For the highest-density cities, the cost of a bundle of high-quality services per capita is US$325; for medium-density cities, it increases to US$665; for the rural hinterland US$2,837; and for isolated areas US$ 4,879 (see Table 10.2). Countries with faster expansion of urban coverage of water and electricity also tend to have faster expansion of rural coverage, suggesting that urban customers cross-subsidize rural water networks and electrification.

Increasing infrastructure coverage in rural areas should entail the building of complementarities across sectors. Bundling infrastructure services will increase the return of the investments and secure larger welfare gains for both rural and urban households. Such bundling maximizes the economic and social effect of services provision with improved access to economic opportunities, reducing the gap between the poor and non-poor. A bundling strategy would also serve to maximize coordination and complementarities across sectors beyond the infrastructure field.

Improving the quality and quantity of infrastructure spending will assist countries toward achieving their MDGs. Sub-Saharan Africa as a whole is unlikely to meet the MDGs for water supply and sanitation by the target date of 2015. Progress has been modest, with access to water increasing by only nine percentage points between 1990 and 2008, or less than one percentage point per year. Sanitation has recorded even worse progress, with only a five percentage point increase in

Table 10.2: Capital cost of infrastructure provision by density (US$ per capita, unless otherwise indicated)

Infrastructure type	Large cities						Secondary cities	Rural hinterland	Deep rural
Density (population/km²)	30,000	20,000	10,000	5,008	3,026	1,455	1,247	38	13
Water									
Private tap	104.2	124.0	168.7	231.8	293.6	416.4	448.5	1,825.2	3,156.2
Standpost	31.0	36.3	48.5	65.6	82.4	115.7	124.5	267.6	267.6
Borehole	21.1	21.1	21.1	21.1	21.1	21.1	21.1	53.0	159.7
Hand pump	8.3	8.3	8.3	8.3	8.3	8.3	8.3	16.7	50.4
Sanitation									
Septic tank	125.0	125.0	125.0	125.0	125.0	125.0	125.0	125.0	125.0
Improved latrine	57.0	57.0	57.0	57.0	57.0	57.0	57.0	57.0	57.0
Unimproved latrine	39.0	39.0	39.0	39.0	39.0	39.0	39.0	39.0	39.0
Power									
Grid	63.5	71.2	88.5	112.9	136.8	184.3	196.7	487.7	943.1
Mini-grid	87.6	95.2	112.5	136.9	160.8	208.3	220.7	485.8	704.2
Solar photovoltaic	92.3	92.3	92.3	92.3	92.3	92.3	92.3	92.3	92.3
Roads									
High quality	31.6	47.4	94.7	189.2	313.1	651.3	759.8	269.1	232.4
Low quality	23.6	35.4	70.7	141.2	233.8	486.3	567.3	224.3	193.6
ICT									
Constant capacity	1.1	1.7	3.3	6.6	10.9	22.8	26.6	39.8	129.7
Actual capacity	1.1	1.7	3.3	6.6	10.9	22.8	26.6	129.7	422.1
Total									
Variable quality*	325	369	480	665	879	1,031	1,061	940	836
Constant (high) quality**	325	369	480	665	879	1,400	1,557	2,837	4,879

Notes: * For variable quality at total, technology differs by density and location as follows: *water*: private tap in large cities, standposts in small cities, boreholes in secondary urban cities, hand pump in rural areas; *sanitation*: septic tanks in large cities, improved latrines in small and secondary urban cities, traditional latrines in rural areas; *power*: grid in urban areas, mini-grid in rural hinterland, solar in deep rural areas; *roads*: high-quality scenario; *ICT*: constant capacity in urban and rural areas. ** For constant (high) quality, the same technology – the most expensive – applies at any density except for power (grid at any level of density).

Sources: AfDB Data Portal (www.afdb.org/en/knowledge/statistics/data-portal/); World Bank (2014a)

coverage over the past 16 years. The urban–rural divide in access to improved water source continues to be a policy challenge. Access to an improved water source in rural areas increased from 40% in 1990 to 53% in 2008, while access in urban areas stagnated between 1990 and 2008 at 86% (AfDB, 2010a). Inadequate access is exacerbated by rapid urbanization, linked to the growth of informal settlements. The level of spending needed to meet the MDG target for water will require roughly 2.6% of Africa's annual GDP, while sanitation will require 0.9% of GDP per year.

For many countries, such spending levels are unaffordable, and current inefficiencies make them even more challenging. Spending in the water sector today totals about US$3.6 billion, one-quarter of the amount required to meet the water MDG. Despite such levels, nearly US$2.7 billion available to the sector is currently wasted in labor inefficiencies, under-collection of revenues, and distribution losses.

Regarding sanitation, few countries in Africa are investing in new sanitation facilities at the recommended level. Additionally, their spending on the operation and maintenance of existing facilities is inadequate.

Special challenges for infrastructure financing

Due to additional risks or externalities, the financing of regional and sustainable infrastructure projects encounters special challenges, which typically require investments by both the private and public sectors.

Regional infrastructure: innovative institutional arrangements needed

Cross-border infrastructure projects promote regional integration and spur regional trade and growth. Such projects pose special challenges, though, such as markedly higher transaction costs and complex risk factors for the private investor. Financing regional infrastructure requires effective cooperation and coordination among countries. Innovative institutional arrangements are needed, either through an expanded role for multilateral development banks (that is, taking a greater share of regional infrastructure projects), as is already the case for the AfDB, or through establishing specialized sub-regional banks/ funds. The latter would allow for drawing on the high reserves that some of the resource-rich African countries have accumulated.

To overcome the high risks and transaction costs of private investment in regional infrastructure projects, some regional economic communities (such as ECOWAS and SADC) are establishing bilateral or multilateral special purpose vehicles (SPVs). The SPVs are mandated to identify, prepare, and manage regional infrastructure projects and negotiate with private investors. A prioritized sub-regional PPP project list, as proposed by the COMESA, could help RECs to engage potential investors and leverage their efforts to mobilize infrastructure funding.

Sub-regional PPP units (as advisory centers) could be set up, especially in countries with a shallow pool of skills. The scaling-up of technical assistance to governments for project preparation activities would also help "right-size" the now disproportionately high upfront risk borne by private investors. Coordinating PPP regulatory frameworks across sub-regions would facilitate the implementation of regional infrastructure projects. The AfDB and other institutions with capacity to extend technical assistance could help in this area.

Clean technology for sustainable infrastructure

Africa, and especially SSA, is the most vulnerable region worldwide to the effects of climate change, even though it has contributed the least to carbon emissions. Nevertheless, a key challenge for the continent is to finance investment in low-carbon, climate-proof infrastructure, that is, infrastructure that would both mitigate and adapt to climate change. Given the other vast development challenges that the continent faces, resources for sustainable infrastructure financing need to be mobilized outside of national budgets. This calls for innovative forms of financing that would be additional to the existing mechanisms.

Given its abundant natural resources and the innovative financing instruments available, Africa should embark on a low-carbon, clean growth path. Carbon finance can contribute to the co-financing of sustainable infrastructure. As a market-based (and legally enforceable) mechanism, it is more predictable than budget aid and can help generate efficiency gains and bring down cost of renewable energy and other forms of sustainable infrastructure. So far though, access to carbon credits by clean energy projects in emerging markets and developing countries has met with mixed results across regions, with Africa lagging substantially behind the others.

With investments in clean energy solutions, Africa can tap into concessional financing sources and thus reduce the costs and risks of such investments. For example, the Clean Technology Fund projects will leverage at least five times their value in clean energy solutions, including energy efficiency, renewable energy, and sustainable transport investments. Private sources will play a greater role in financing clean energy projects, but low returns to private sector investors so far imply that a majority of expenditures will need to be covered from public sources (AfDB, 2010c).

Africa's perspectives must be taken into account when decisions on disbursements of global funds for climate change adaptation and mitigation are made. To help facilitate access to these funds, the AfDB is setting up the Africa Green Fund to receive and manage resources to address climate change on the continent.

The role of the African Development Bank in infrastructure

Infrastructure financing by the bank over the period 2009–2014

Infrastructure financing continues to be accorded a very high priority by the AfDB. The aim is to target high-impact projects and programs that will create an enabling environment for private sector investment, improve competitiveness and productivity in its regional member countries, enhance employment opportunities, and support sustainable economic growth.

Over the period 2009–2014, the bank's cumulative financing for infrastructure projects and programs amounted to UA 14.3 billion (US$21.9 billion, at 2012 December rate)[7] (see Table 10.3). This represents 45.2% of the total bank group's loan and grant approvals of UA 31.6 billion (US$48.4 billion) to all sectors.

The level of the amount of loans and grants approved in 2012 still indicates that the annual share of approvals to infrastructure is increasing, rising from 41.5% in 2012 and 46.7% in 2013 to 49.4% in 2014.

With respect to the sub-sectoral split, energy (43.5%) received the highest allocation over the period, 2009–2014, followed by transportation (43.4%), water supply and sanitation (11.9%), and ICT (1.1%). The lower-level allocations for ICT and water remained the same throughout the period, but transportation and energy recorded some variation. Transportation received the largest share in 2010 (49.4%), 2013 (55.9%), and 2011 (63.9%), while energy received the largest share (57.2%) in 2009. Following are some key sub-sector projects and programs approved during the period.

Regional transportation support

A focal strategic area for the AfDB during the period 2008–2012 was road transportation networks across the continent, with financing to

Table 10.3: Bank group loans and grant approvals by sector, 2009–2014 (values in UA millions unless otherwise is stated)

Sector	2009 Amount	%	2010 Amount	%	2011 Amount	%	2012 Amount	%	2013 Amount	%	2014 Amount	%	2009-2014 Amount	%
Total approvals	8,064.5		4,099.8		5,720.3		4,253.8		4,385.8		5,049.9		31,574.0	
Infrastructure	3,907.9	100.0	2,505.7	100.0	1,572.3	100.0	1,763.5	100.0	2,050.9	100.0	2,498.3	100.0	14,298.5	100.0
Transport	1,292.7	33.1	1,239.4	49.4	1,005.4	63.9	604.2	34.3	1,148.4	55.9	918.7	36.7	6,208.8	43.4
Communications	84.3	2.2	32.4	1.2	7.6	0.5	-		35.0	1.7	0.8	0.03	160.0	1.1
Water supply and sanitation	297.4	7.6	444.1	17.7	139.2	8.9	269.7	15.3	298.4	14.5	258.5	10.3	1,707.3	11.9
Power supply	2,233.5	57.2	789.8	31.5	420.1	26.7	889.7	50.4	569.1	27.7	1,320.3	52.8	6,222.4	43.5

Source: AfDB Statistics Department, Economic and Social Statistics Division (2015)

the sub-sector increasing from UA 1.29 billion in 2009, then falling slightly to UA 1.24 billion in 2010, UA 1.0 billion in 2011, and finally levels around 1 billion in 2013 and 2014 (see Table 10.3). Among the key transportation projects were the Mombasa–Nairobi Regional Corridor Phase III and the Rehabilitation of the Lomé–Cotonou Road and Transport Facilitation on the Abidjan–Lagos Corridor, Phase I. The bank also approved the financing of two major bridges to serve as regional links. These are the Kazungula Bridge linking Botswana and Zambia in Southern Africa and the Gambia Bridge linking the Gambia and Senegal in Western Africa. In addition, the bank approved a regional highway project between Tunis and Libya, which will contribute to regional economic integration for the Arab Maghreb Union countries.

Looking back to 2010, eight road projects were approved, five of which targeted rural and feeder roads. The objective for such projects is to link rural areas to urban markets, lower the cost of agricultural inputs, reduce transportation costs, and scale up food productivity and income levels. In its infrastructure programs, the bank adopts a participatory approach, in association with local communities, to improve development outcomes, particularly for roads. One key approval in 2010 was for the South Africa Transnet project, linking rail networks, ports, and pipelines (UA 271.3 million/US$417.8 million). Another key project was the Moroccan Tangiers–Marrakech Railroad Capacity Increase Project to improve the freight transportation market between Tangiers and Marrakech in partnership with Morocco's National Railway Company, ONCF.

Water and sanitation support

The bank's interventions in this sector focus mainly on sustainable water resource development and management across the continent. Over 200–2014, total loans and grant approvals for this sector cumulatively amounted to UA 1.7 billion, increasing from UA 297.4 million in 2009 to a high of UA 444.1 million in 2010, before dropping to levels around UA 250 million in 2012, 2013 and 2014. The interventions cover drinking water supply, water resources management, sanitation and hygiene, capacity building, and policy reform programs.

Urban water supply and sanitation are targeted by the bank through such interventions as rehabilitation and service expansion, reduction of high levels of water not accounted for in the billing systems, and the promotion of private sector activities to address the growing needs of the urban sector. In 2011, three new urban and peri-urban water supply and sanitation programs/projects were approved for Uganda, Egypt, and Zimbabwe for total financing of UA 38.0 million (US$58.3 million). The level of approvals was higher in 2010, when six new urban and peri-urban water supply and sanitation programs/projects were approved for Côte d'Ivoire, Kenya, Liberia, Mauritania, Morocco, and Sierra Leone in addition to one multinational project, for total financing of UA 371.3 million (US$571.8 million).

Besides the projects and programs noted here, the bank continues to host three complementary initiatives: namely, the Rural Water Supply and Sanitation Initiative (RWSSI), the African Water Facility (AWF), and the Multi-Donor Water Partnership Program (MDWPP). These initiatives jointly enhance the effectiveness of the Bank's activities and provide vital resources for scaling up access to safe water and sanitation, promoting innovative technologies, and supporting knowledge management activities (see Box 10.1).

Box 10.1: The three water initiatives

1. The Rural Water Supply and Sanitation Initiative

The overarching objective of the RWSSI is to accelerate coverage of safe water and sanitation to 80% of the rural population by 2015 at an estimated cost of US$14.2 billion. Since its inception in 2003, 31 programs and projects have benefited from RWSSI funds in 23 regional member countries, totaling US$4.8 billion. Of this amount, the bank group contributed US$1,240.5 million while the RWSSI Trust Fund contributed UA 142.8 million. The remainder was made up of contributions from other development partners, African governments, and the beneficiary communities.

In 2011, the bank group approved three RWSSI operations in Niger, Uganda, and Tunisia totaling US$191.3 million, of which US$145.1 million was provided by the AfDB, US$51.7 million by the African Development Fund, and US$10.3 million by the RWSSI Trust Fund. To date, over 33.5 million people have gained access to drinking water and nearly 21.3 million to improved sanitation as a result of the RWSSI.

2. The Multi-Donor Water Partnership Program

The Water Partnership Program (WPP), a fund managed by the AfDB at the initiative of the Netherlands in 2002, was transformed into the MDWPP in 2006, with the participation of the Canadian and Danish governments. The MDWPP was a key advocate in the establishment of the RWSSI, the AWF, the African ClimDev Program, and the Agricultural Water Management in Africa.

As of the end of 2011, a total of 61 activities, valued at US$11.4 million, had been funded under the MDWPP.

3. The African Water Facility

The AWF was established by the African Ministers' Council on Water and is managed and administered by the bank. The facility's mission is to assist African countries to mobilize and apply resources for the successful implementation of the Africa Water Vision (2025) and to meet the MDGs on water and sanitation. The current level of contribution from partners has reached EUR 135.3 million from 14 donors, including the Bank (US$15.4 million) and, as a new 2011 donor, the Bill and Melinda Gates Foundation (US$12.00 million). To date, the AWF has leveraged approximately EUR 420.0 million to finance water sector follow-on interventions (representing about 40 times the value of these projects).

By year-end 2011, the AWF portfolio had grown to US$109.8 million (EUR 82.7 million), covering 69 projects. Among these were three projects approved by the bank in 2011, amounting to US$4.5 million (EUR 3.3 million). These were for the following: a feasibility study on the Shire–Zambezi Waterway Project; a study on "Vision and Strategy for Water 2050 in Tunisia"; and a study on the establishment of a regional water observatory for the ECOWAS region.

Energy support

During the period 2009–2014, the bank approved cumulatively UA 6.2 billion for the energy sub-sector, with approvals decreasing significantly from UA 2.2 billion in 2009 to UA 789.8 million in 2010 and to UA 420.1 million in 2011, and finally rising to UA 1.3 billion in 2014. The 2011 performance covers 12 projects in the energy sub-sector and represents 26% of all approvals for infrastructure projects. Two key energy projects were: the Eskom Renewable Energy Project (US$345.7 million) in South Africa and the Menengai Geothermal Development Project (US$147.5 million) in Kenya. These projects seek to address those countries' growing energy needs and power deficits in an environmentally friendly way. Other approvals during the year included the Lom Pangar Hydroelectric Project in Cameroon to transmit electricity to an additional 150 communities; and the Rural Electrification Project in Guinea, which will bring energy to 31 more communities and 60,000 households.

During 2010, the approvals level for the energy sector was much higher, at UA 887.6 million (US$1,366.9 million) for 14 new operations. Eleven of these were public sector operations, for a total amount of UA 753.5 million (US$1,160.4 million). The remaining three were private sector projects—the Dibamba Power Project in Cameroon, the Tunisia Hasdrubal Oil and Gas Field Development Project, and the Cabeolica Wind Power Project in Cape Verde— which jointly amounted to UA 134.1 million (US$206.5 million). The Cabeolica Wind Power Project is notable for being the first renewable energy project to be approved by the bank. The two largest energy projects approved in 2010 were the Suez 650 MW Steam Cycle Thermal Power Plant in Egypt and the Semi-Urban and Rural Electrification Project in the DRC.

ICT support

The bank approved a total of UA 160.0 million to the ICT sub-sector over the period 2009 to 2012. The annual allocations were UA 84.3 million in 2009, dropping to UA 32.4 million in 2010 and to just UA 7.6 million in 2011. Although there was no allocation in 2012, in 2013 the allocation returned to 2010 levels to UA 35 million and dropped to 0.8 million in 2014. The allocation for 2011 covered the Seychelles Submarine Cable Project, which is a public–private sector project for the construction and operation of a submarine cable linking the Seychelles with other East African systems. This will help to improve communications between this island state and the rest of the continent. Previous key ICT programs co-financed by the bank include the Satellite O3B multinational project for the construction and operation of a constellation of eight middle earth orbit satellites over Africa, which attracted UA 32.1 million (US$49.4 million) from the bank in 2010. Other major ICT projects supported by the bank in earlier years include the RASCOM Telecommunications Satellite Project and the East African Submarine Cable System (EASSy) Project (both approved in 2007).

Support to private equity infrastructure funds

The bank has for several years extended long-term debt financing to private equity funds that target infrastructure development on the continent. These have included the Africa Energy Infrastructure Fund, approved for US$30 million of funding in 2008; the Emerging Africa Infrastructure Fund, which received a bank loan of US$31.25 million in 2009 and a second loan for US$45 million in 2011; the Evolution One Fund in South Africa, which targets clean technology/energy investments, and received US$12.4 million; and the Helios Investors II Fund, which includes infrastructure as one of its key areas.

The AfDB's partnerships for infrastructure development

Given the criticality of infrastructure development to the continent's economic growth and social advancement, the bank has for many years positioned this sector at the top of its operational agenda, as articulated in its Medium–Term Strategy 2008–2012. However, the sector's massive financing requirements cannot be met by any one DFI alone. It is vital for all governments, DFIs, United Nations agencies, RECs, and international donor agencies, as well as the private sector, to work together to maximize resources, catalyze additional funds, and leverage synergies. In this respect, the bank has long been supportive of strong partnerships with global and regional institutions.

The AfDB has been actively involved in a number of partnerships that specifically target infrastructure development. These include the NEPAD Short-Term Action Plan, the NEPAD Medium-to-Long-Term Strategic Framework (MLTSF), the African Union Infrastructure Master Plan Initiative, the NEPAD Infrastructure Project Preparation Fund (NEPAD-IPPF), the ICA, the EU–Africa Infrastructure Trust Fund, PIDA, and, most recently, the Africa Infrastructure Knowledge Program (AIKP). The bank also hosts three water initiatives for the continent that involve multiple stakeholders: namely, the RWSSI, the AWF, and the MDWPP (see Box 10.1).

NEPAD Infrastructure Project Preparation Fund

The NEPAD-IPFF provides grant resources for: preparing high-quality and viable regional/continental infrastructure projects with a view to requesting financing from public and private sources; (ii) developing a consensus and partnership for project implementation; and promoting infrastructure projects and programs aimed at enhancing regional integration and trade.

The NEPAD-IPPF supports regional infrastructure development projects in the following sectors: transportation, energy, ICT, and water resources management. The activities eligible for financing under the fund are: pre-feasibility studies; feasibility studies; project structuring; capacity building for infrastructure development; and facilitation and creation of an enabling environment for regional infrastructure development.

At the end of May 2010, IPPF had an active portfolio of 41 projects (53 in the pipeline until 2015) and had initiated regional infrastructure projects worth around US$4.7 billion, representing a huge leveraging potential. An Africa Action Plan priority projects list, worth about US$32 billion, has also been drawn up, with energy the dominant sub-sector. The major projects in this list include the US$20 billion Nigeria–Algeria gas connection project, and the Sambangalou Kaleta Hydropower and Kenya-Ethiopia Interconnection, both of which are worth more than US$1 billion.

Key achievements of the IPPF to date include work on the Benin–Togo–Ghana Electricity Interconnection Project, Kenya–Uganda Oil Pipeline Project, Zambia–Tanzania–Kenya Power Interconnection Project, EASSy Project, OMVG Electricity Project, and Ghana–Burkina power interconnection project.

Due to this success, new donors have joined the fund, which now counts among its members Canada, Denmark, Norway, the UK's Department for International Development (DFID), Germany and Spain in addition to AfDB. The total capital of the fund has reached US$46 million. The NEPAD-IPPF is hosted by the African Development Bank.

Infrastructure Consortium for Africa

The ICA was launched at the G8 Summit in Gleneagles in 2005. It is not a financing agency as such but acts as a catalyst to accelerate the development of Africa's infrastructure. ICA also works to help remove some of the technical and policy challenges and barriers to building more infrastructure facilities and to better coordinate the activities of its members and other significant sources of infrastructure finance, such as China, India and Arab partners.

ICA members include (in addition to the AfDB), the G8 countries, the World Bank Group, the European Commission, the European Investment Bank, and the Development Bank of Southern Africa. ICA is supported by a small secretariat that is hosted by the AfDB in Tunis, Tunisia.

The bank committed more than US$4 billion to the ICA over two years (2007–08), representing about 24% of total contributions to the initiative.

EU–Africa Infrastructure Trust Fund

The EU–Africa Infrastructure Trust Fund was launched in 2007 to catalyze financing for infrastructure programs that facilitate interconnectivity and regional integration on the African continent. It supports synergies between European development agencies for the benefit of Africa, leveraging additional funds by blending grants from the European Commission and EU member states with long-term loan finance made available by eligible financiers.

It counts among its major stakeholders the AfDB, the African Union, the European Investment Bank, the European Union, the European Commission, NEPAD, ICA, RECs and the World Bank's Public–Private Infrastructure Advisory Facility (PPIAF).

Program for Infrastructure Development in Africa

The AfDB is the executing agency for the PIDA, which was launched in July 2010 as successor to the NEPAD MLTSF. PIDA's objective is to develop a vision and strategic framework for the development of regional and continental infrastructure, including transboundary water resources. The PIDA initiative is led by the AUC, the NEPAD Secretariat, and the AfDB. The bank's role as executing agency covers the responsibility for contractual, financial, technical and administrative management of the program.

Africa Infrastructure Knowledge Program

AIKP is a recent initiative, launched as a successor program to the AICD, which grew out of the pledge made at the G8 Summit of 2005 at Gleneagles to scale up ODA assistance to Africa, particularly the infrastructure sector. The AIKP builds on the AICD flagship report commissioned by the World Bank, *Africa's Infrastructure: A Time for Transformation* (AICD, 2009), which produced a wealth of analytical products hosted through the AICD web portal.

The AIKP adopts a longer-term perspective than the AICD and provides a framework for generating knowledge on infrastructure on a more sustainable basis. The AfDB is the central actor in the AIKP process but works in close partnership with the World Bank. It takes the lead in the regular collection and assessment of infrastructure indicators; the management of the dissemination of infrastructure data via its data portal (including AICD data that have now been transferred to its database); the production of knowledge products such as the newly launched *Handbook on Infrastructure Statistics* (AfDB, 2011b) and the timely policy analysis of emerging infrastructure trends on the continent to guide future policy and funding decisions. The bank also assists through the AIKP and in partnership with organizations such as the World Bank in the training of personnel at African National Statistical Agencies to help boost statistical capacity at the national level and ensure the quality of the infrastructure data that are collected.

AfDB's Urban Development Strategy

In 2011 the AfDB adopted a new Urban Development Strategy, with the vision of making African cities and towns healthy environments for citizens to work and live in, competitive and bankable with a strong development base, and well governed. The three pillars of the AfDB's Urban Development Strategy (AfDB, 2011c) are founded on the institution's strengths and established track record in providing support in the following areas:

- *Infrastructure delivery and maintenance.* This involves a twin-track approach. The first targets improvements to the physical infrastructure, namely water supply and sanitation; transportation systems; energy supplies; broadband connectivity and ICT; and social infrastructure, including education establishments and health centers/hospitals. The second approach is to build capacity in the development and management of infrastructure, by helping municipal authorities to: implement sound urban planning schemes; maintain municipal physical infrastructure assets; tap financial markets, facilitate public–private partnerships in financing urban projects; and build appropriate regulatory institutions at national and municipal levels to improve services and scale up social protection programs.

- *Urban governance.* The objective in this area is building good governance systems and strengthening the capacity of municipal authorities to promote a culture of transparency, instigate anticorruption strategies and systems, and implement reforms targeted at fiscal decentralization, self-sufficiency, and the sustainability of public investment. The bank also provides assistance to municipalities to improve their systems of revenue collection and tax administration to supplement their budgets.

- *Private sector development.* The bank supports private enterprises and PPPs to help finance urban development programs. One way it does this is by improving the business-enabling environment through improvements to infrastructure (for example, improving ICT networks, more reliable electricity supply, and better transportation linkages). Helping municipalities and local authorities reform their legal and regulatory frameworks may also spur new investments.

In order to scale up its support for urban development, the bank group engages in partnerships with other major players (such as the World Bank, Cities Alliance, UN-HABITAT, and the Millennium Challenge Corporation), financial development banks, and bilateral donor partners (such Agence Française de Développement (AFD), German Corporation for International Cooperation (GIZ), DFID, and Swedish International Development Cooperation Agency (SIDA)). The objective is not only to leverage additional resources, but also to promote coordination and harmonization of activities, programs, and projects.

Conclusion

Investment in infrastructure should be allocated to components that will maximize the positive transformation that Africa needs. Sustainable economic growth, as a means of lifting the continent out of poverty, should be the principal objective of the agenda with two main pillars: strengthen the foundations for higher productivity in the main cities; and ensure a more even distribution of basic living standards.

The first pillar for growth refers to securing an appropriate level of investment in *urban infrastructure*. Firms concentrate in cities in order to lower production costs by leveraging economies of scale and network efficiencies. By clustering, firms increase the demand for infrastructure, thereby reaping cost savings from agglomeration. Providing them with needed infrastructure is central to their creation of jobs and its spillovers across income groups.

The second pillar for growth refers to a more even distribution of basic living conditions *in both rural and urban areas*. This entails framing not only a coherent urban agenda, but also a commensurate rural agenda, to counter the incentives for rural–urban migration. Cities that are experiencing a growing but unmet demand for basic services from unskilled immigrants also face a long-term trend of economic deterioration, given the relatively lower contribution from those immigrants to the overall productivity. What is needed is a broader vision of the technologies that can be deployed for service provision; the bundling of services wherever possible to increase effectiveness in peri–urban and rural areas; making use of land planning instruments and policies to align urban expansion with service provision; and a complementary rural development strategy.

An infrastructure agenda for Africa has to fully address the challenges of the 21st century by: making cities more productive and better places to live ("more livable"); integrating rural areas through the spillovers of urban growth; and finally, linking major population centers across the region with an strategic approach.

Infrastructure for more livable and productive cities

Cities represent the engine of a nation's growth given the increasing urbanization that Africa, as all other regions, observes. Their productivity is at least three times greater than that of rural areas. Rural areas contribute less than 20% of Africa's GDP while accounting for more than 60% of its population (World Bank, 2008b). There is, though, a symbiotic relationship between rural and urban areas, as urban centers consume rural products and provide inputs for rural production, while rural areas serve as markets for goods and services produced in urban areas. The expansion of urban markets is a key factor in raising the rural incomes in the hinterland. In addition, cities create growth spillovers in their rural hinterlands.

Despite these dynamics, rural–urban links are hampered by inadequate transportation networks between products and markets, unreliable and costly sources of electricity and water provision, and limited coverage of ICT. Weak institutions exacerbate these constraints. Further, the wide disparities in living standards across sub-regions, countries, and urban and rural areas, encourage migration toward urban settlements. This results in a high concentration of people in large cities, urban sprawl, and "informal" or slum settlements, which are the three main features of Africa's urbanization.

The policy challenge is to harness market forces that will encourage concentration and promote convergence in living standards between villages, towns, and cities. Policy decisions are more effective when they are strategized according to broad economic areas that integrate towns and cities with their surrounding rural hinterland.

Ensuring access to basic services for households in both urban and rural areas can improve sustainable urbanization and social equity, enhance living conditions, and prevent disproportionate flows of rural people to cities. It should be acknowledged, however, that labor mobility can be a positive force when it responds to the needs of market forces, rather than to a lack of security and/or basic services. Moreover, labor mobility can prompt convergence in living standards, as migration to denser and more productive areas balances income levels and exploits the benefits of knowledge clusters in both rural and urban locations. As rural and urban development are mutually dependent, the economic integration of rural and urban areas is the best way to produce growth and inclusive development.

The AICD report of 2009 proposed a shift in emphasis from urban to rural investments, assigning 34% to the productive infrastructure underpinning the national economy, 32% to urban areas, and 34% to rural areas. However, as outlined earlier, there are significant externalities and complementarities between urban and rural investments, so rebalancing investment from urban to rural areas should not mean a reduction in urban spending.

Improving living conditions in cities implies a strong focus on institutions. A combination of land policy and planning, housing policies, and basic services coverage is key for a more equitable and inclusive urban expansion. Local authorities should invest not only more, but more *wisely*. This is critical given the small size of municipal budgets in relation to the total infrastructure requirements occasioned by rapid urban growth and increased responsibilities arising from decentralization. Even as in most cases there would be not additional resources for the local level out of decentralization, administering better scarce resources and the efforts of local dwellers is a central to improve living conditions.

Benefits accruing to rural areas from urban and regional infrastructure development

Rural activities remain highly relevant to the overall development process of Africa, since its population is mainly located in rural areas. Two-thirds of the labor force is engaged in agriculture-related activities, which make up a very significant share of GDP in all sub-regions. The intersection of these two processes—high rural population and high levels of agricultural activity—results in agriculture serving as the main source of income for 90% of the rural population in Africa (UNECA, 2005).

However, rural productivity in Africa ranks among the lowest in the developing world, while the overall logistics costs are among the highest. Farm sizes in many of the more densely populated areas are unsustainably small, land is severely degraded, investment in irrigation is negligible, and poor health and education limit productivity and restrict access to better options. Access to basic services is very low for those living in the country; indeed, coverage rates in urban areas are five to 10 times higher than in rural areas. Electricity and improved water supply (such as piped connections or standposts) extend to the majority of the urban population, but to less than one-fifth of the rural population, with minimal differences across sub-regions. Rural access to ICT services remains insignificant (AfDB, 2011a).

Isolation perpetuated by poor transportation linkages restrains economic progress and traps rural people in poverty. Further, poor transportation restricts trade even within local markets. It raises the costs of production and distribution, reduces the profit margin on produce sales, and limits production yields to levels below their potential, impeding the transition from subsistence to income-producing agriculture. The economic effects of better access to, from, and within rural areas can be cumulative and far-reaching. Indeed, the positive impact that good rural road networks can have on rural productivity is well documented in the African sub-regions. The logistics chain for buying inputs and selling produce determines the adoption of high-yield agricultural practices.

Decisions on infrastructure investment are often linked to the personal economics of land ownership. People with decision-making powers at various government levels may have a vested interest in driving investment resources in their favor (that is, toward their own land holdings, thereby increasing their value). This may result in a conflict of interests, for example when investments that they have selected do not align to the criteria of the investment agenda viewed from a broader perspective. A second consideration is that changes in land use may arise from investment in roads, and this can sometimes hinder rural productivity due to weak land regulations.

Property rights also represent a macro mechanism that drives migration and the efficient localization of population. Given continued restrictions on land ownership and unclear regulations on land tenure, labor mobility may be hindered. Many government controls in relation to property rights have been relaxed, which in some cases has released agricultural capital and labor for non-agricultural activities. Access to land and security of tenure are the principal means by which food security and sustainable development can be realized in Africa. This paper makes the case that, despite variations across the sub-regions, there are common tendencies and empirically based data that demonstrate close linkages between land tenure relations on the one hand, and food security and sustainable livelihoods on the other.

A regional integration approach for infrastructure provision

Regional integration and connectivity in Africa are prerequisites for sustainable economic growth, bringing two main benefits:

- *Improved accessibility to larger markets* for producers in each national market, due to economies of scale and collective exploitation of their resources. Investments in regional infrastructure are expected to deliver high rates of return: intraregional trade could triple and international trade could double.

- *Efficiency gains from the joint provision of infrastructure.* This addresses the problems of small scale and poor location. Joint infrastructure provision increases the scale of infrastructure construction, operation, and maintenance; it also reduces costs and pools scarce technical and managerial capacity (Lederman et al, 2005).

According to the 2009 *World Development Report* (World Bank, 2009b), the countries of Central, East, and West Africa face the triple challenge of internal division or thick economic borders; large distances from world markets; and low economic density due to small local economies. In order to overcome such constraints, these countries need a combination of three policy instruments: strengthening regional institutions; investing in regional infrastructure to improve connectivity between countries; and providing "incentives such as preferential access to world markets, perhaps on the condition that all countries strengthen regional cooperation" (World Bank, 2009b).

An infrastructure agenda for regional integration and connectivity should focus on the energy, transportation, and telecommunications sectors. At a fundamental level, the low degree of intra-regional trade is partly due to a lack of product diversification and poor trade complementarity among African countries. These structural constraints are compounded by inadequate and inefficient infrastructure, both hard (such as roads and transportation networks, ICT networks, and energy) and soft (such as the regulatory environment and customs systems). All these act as impediments to the diversification of production, therefore improvements in these areas will increase scale and competitiveness at regional and global levels.

Electricity is Africa's greatest infrastructural challenge, characterized by low access rates, high costs, and low-quality provision. In 2010, only 32% of Sub-Saharan Africans had access to electricity compared with an average of 77% for all low middle-income countries, 75% for South Asia, and 95% for Latin America. The figure is significantly higher in North Africa, where it stands at 99% (World Bank and International Energy Agency, 2014). Furthermore, data from Enterprises Surveys between 2006 and 2014 for 42 African countries, show that the average duration of electricity outages is 6.2 hours, which represents annual average losses of 7.2% of total sales (World Bank, 2014b). The costs of power outages to the continent are significant, with Africa losing almost 12.5% of production time compared with 7% for South Asia, which is the next worst case.

The study *Regional Energy Integration in Africa* (World Energy Council, 2005) confirms four major benefits associated with regional energy integration: improved security of supply; higher economic efficiency; enhanced environmental quality; and a wider deployment of renewable energy resources.

Roads constitute the main infrastructure serving regional connectivity, carrying at least 80% of goods and 90% of passengers. The Trans-African Highway, currently the heart of regional connectivity for the continent, has a total length of 54,120km distributed along nine corridors. However, it is characterized by missing links and poor maintenance in key segments. To provide a meaningful level of continental connectivity, between 60,000 and 100,000km of regional roads are required.

Design standards are also important in estimating the costs of completing the system. Although each country is responsible for the standards applied within its territory, there are important benefits to be gained from applying common standards, such as avoiding operational and administrative complications at border crossings.

ICT: There are two priorities for providing or improving ICT in the continent: to improve access to high-capacity submarine fiber-optic for low-price international voice communications services and high-speed internet access; and to lay high-bandwidth backbone networks to connect towns and cities within countries, across borders, and to the international submarine fiber-optic cable networks. It is estimated that one-time investment needs range from US$229 million for a minimum set of links to US$515 million for an extensive interregional network connecting all African capitals to one another with fiber-optic cables.

Beyond the critical need to invest in physical regional infrastructure, there are two other aspects to be considered, namely strengthening the governance scheme for infrastructure service provision and streamlining the institutional system to maintain an effective level of service provision.

Across the continent's sub-regions, infrastructure endowments differ substantially, as do institutional schemes for services provision. In this respect, ECCAS underperforms in all sectors, whereas SADC consistently outperforms the other sub-regions. Though East and West African countries also face the challenge of poor connectivity, they benefit from larger local markets, bigger cities, and potential complementarities. Tailoring an agenda for regional integration and connectivity means taking account of such differences, while acknowledging that investment priorities may pull in opposite directions, making it difficult to set common goals.

Notes

[1] Carruthers et al (2008) consider an ideal scenario and a pragmatic scenario to estimate investment needs in roads. The pragmatic scenario aims to meet a similar degree of regional and national connectivity as the ideal scenario but at a lower cost, essentially by reducing the standards of infrastructure (for example, by substituting a single-surface-treatment road for an asphalt road) and by lowering the target condition (for example, maintaining infrastructure to at least fair condition rather than to good condition). The pragmatic scenario also reduces the level of ambition for rural and urban connectivity.

[2] Except for mineral lines, which are usually privately handled and are not included in the estimations.

[3] In Cameroon, Chad, and the Central African Republic.

[4] Between Kenya and Uganda at Malaba; between Zambia and Zimbabwe at Chirundu; between Zimbabwe and Mozambique at Forbes/Machipanda; along the Trans-Kalahari Corridor; and in West Africa on selective borders of Burkina Faso, Ghana, Mali, and Togo.

[5] The link between infrastructure and growth in African countries (South Africa, Nigeria, Uganda, and others) has been shown to be positive (AICD, 2009).

[6] Current local investments come from taxes and tariffs and account for nearly one-third of the current annual spend.

[7] Historic conversion rates for the Bank's Unit of Account (UA): in December 2010, 1 UA = US$1.52578; in December 2011, 1 UA = US$1.55156; in December 2012, 1 UA = US$1.534481; in December 2013, 1 UA = US$1.53521.

References

AfDB (African Development Bank) (1999) *African Development Report: Infrastructure in Africa.* Côte d'Ivoire, Abidjan: African Development Bank.

AfDB (2000) *African Development Report.* Tunis, Tunisia: African Development Bank.

AfDB (2010a) *Infrastructure Deficit and Opportunities in Africa.* Economic Brief, Volume 1, September. Tunis, Tunisia: African Development Bank.

AfDB (2010b) *African Development Report 2010: Ports, Logistics, and Trade in Africa.* Tunis, Tunisia: African Development Bank.

AfDB (2010c) *Financing of Sustainable Energy Solutions.* Committee of Ten Policy Brief No. 3. Tunis, Tunisia: African Development Bank.

AfDB (2010d) *6th Infrastructure Consortium for Africa (ICA) Annual Meeting: Agreement for Closer Collaboration on Regional Projects Among Stakeholders.*

AfDB (2011a) *Closing Africa's Infrastructure Gap: Innovative Financing and Risks.* Africa Economic Brief, Vol. 2, Issue 1. Tunis, Tunisia: African Development Bank.

AfDB (2011b) *Handbook on Infrastructure Statistics.* Tunis, Tunisia: African Development Bank.

AfDB (2011c) *Rapid Urbanization and Growing Demands for Urban Infrastructure in Africa.* Tunis, Tunisia: African Development Bank.

AfDB (2012) *Annual Report 2011.* Tunis, Tunisia: African Development Bank.

AfDB and OECD (2009) *African Economic Outlook, 2009.* Part II: "Innovation and ICT in Africa", pp. 81-137.

AfDB, AUC (African Union Commission), ECA (United Nations Economic Commission for Africa), and UNDP (United Nations Development Programme) (2011) *Assessing Progress in Africa toward the Millennium Development Goals, 2011.* New York, NY: United Nations Development Programme.

Angel, S., Sheppard, S.C. and Civco, D.L. (2005) *The Dynamics of Global Urban Expansion.* Washington, DC: World Bank, Transport and Urban Development Department.

Bender, P. and Gibson, S. (2010) *Case Study for the 10 years of the Mbombela (Nelspruit) Water and Sanitation Concession South Africa.* Johannesburg: World Bank and National Treasury, South Africa.

Biau, C., Dahou, K. and Homma, T. (2008) *How to Increase Sound Private Investment in Africa's Road Infrastructure: Building on country successes and OECD policy tools.* Background paper for NEPAD/OECD Africa Investment Initiative Regional Roundtable (Paris, December 2008).

Briceño-Garmendia, C., Smits, K. and Foster, V. (2008) *Financing Public Infrastructure in Sub-Saharan Africa: Patterns and Emerging Issues,* Background Paper 15, AICD. Washington, DC: World Bank.

Buys, P., Deichmann, U. and Wheeler, D. (2006) *Road Network Upgrading and Overland Trade Expansion in Sub-Saharan Africa,* Policy Research Working Paper 4097. Washington, DC: World Bank.

Calderón, C. (2009) *Infrastructure and Growth in Africa,* Policy Research Working Paper 4914. Washington, DC: World Bank.

Carruthers, R., Krishnamani, R. and Murray, S. (2008) *Improving Connectivity Investing in Transport Infrastructure in Sub-Saharan Africa,* Africa Infrastructure Country Diagnostic. Washington, DC: World Bank.

Christ, N. and Ferrantino, M. (2009) *Land Transport for Exports: The Effects of Cost, Time, and Uncertainty in Sub-Saharan Africa.* Washington, DC: US International Trade Commission.

Deloitte (2010) *Infrastructure Finance: Changing Landscape in South Africa.* Johannesburg: Deloitte.

Devereux, S. and Solomon, C. (2006) *Employment Creation Programmes: The International Experience, Issues in Employment and Poverty,* Discussion Paper No. 24. Geneva: International Labour Office.

Dorosh, P., Wang, H., You, L. and Schmidt, E. (2008) *Crop Production and Road Connectivity in Sub-Saharan Africa: A Spatial Analysis,* Policy Research Working Paper WPS 5385. Washington, DC: World Bank.

Easterly, W. and Rebelo, S. (1993) 'Fiscal policy and economic growth: an empirical investigation'. *Journal of Monetary Economics,* vol 32, no 3.

Eberhard, A., Rosnes, O., Shkaratan, M. and Vennemo, H. (2011) *Africa's Power Infrastructure – Investment, Integrity, Efficiency.* Washington, DC: World Bank. Available at www.ppiaf.org/sites/ppiaf.org/ files/ publication/Africas- Power-Infrastructure-2011.pdf

EIA (Energy Information Administration) (2014 database) International statistics, http://www.eia.gov/beta/international/data/browser

Esfahani, H.S. and Ramírez, M. (2003) Institutions, infrastructure, and economic growth', *Journal of Development Economics,* vol 70, pp 443-77.

FAO (Food and Agriculture Organization) (2010) *Africa's Changing Landscape: Securing Land Access for the Rural Poor.* Accra: FAO.

FAO (2011) *The State of Food Insecurity in the World.* Rome: FAO.

Foster, V. and Briceno-Garmendia, C. (eds) (2010) *Africa's Infrastructure: A Time for Transformation*. Africa Development Forum. Washington, DC: Agence Française de Développement and World Bank.

Freemantle, S. and Stevens, J. (2010) *BRIC and Africa: New Sources of Foreign Capital Mobilizing for Africa: Complementing and Competing with Traditional Investors*. Johannesburg: Standard Bank.

Gijón, J. (2008) 'SWF & infrastructure investment in Africa: challenges and perspectives', OECD Development Centre, available at www.oecd.org/dataoecd/31/36/41865534.pdf.

Gulyani, S., Talukda, D. and Darby, J. (2008) *A Tale of Three Cities: Understanding Differences in the Provision of Modern Services*, Working Paper No. 10, Africa Infrastructure Country Diagnostic. Washington, DC: World Bank.

Gwilliam, K., Foster, V., Archondo-Callao, R., Briceño-Garmendia, C., Nogales, A. and Sethi, K. (2008) *The Burden of Maintenance: Roads in Sub-Saharan Africa*. Washington, DC: International Bank for Reconstruction and Development/World Bank.

ICA (Investment Consortium for Africa) (2009) *Annual Report*. Tunis: ICA Secretariat (hosted by AfDB).

IEA (International Energy Agency) (2014) *World Energy Outlook 2014*. Paris: International Energy Agency.

Kessides, C. (2006) *The Urban Transition in Sub-Saharan Africa: Implications for Economic Growth and Poverty Reduction*. Washington, DC: Cities Alliance.

Lall, S., Schroeder, E. and Schmidt, E. (2009) *Identifying Spatial Efficiency-Equity Tradeoffs in Territorial Development Policy*, Policy Research Working Paper 4966. Washington, DC: World Bank.

Lederman, D., Maloney, W. and Servén, L. (2005) *Lessons from NAFTA for Latin America and the Caribbean*. Washington, DC: World Bank.

Limão, N. and Venables, A. (1999) *Infrastructure, Geographical Disadvantage, and Transportation Costs*, Policy Research Working Paper 2257. Washington, DC: World Bank.

Limão, N. and Venables, A. (2001) 'Infrastructure, geographical disadvantage, transport costs, and trade', *World Bank Economic Review*, vol 15, no 3, pp 451-79.

Malgas, I., Gratwick, K.N. and Eberhard, A. (2008) 'Moroccan Independent Power Producers – African Pioneers', *Journal of North African Studies*, vol 13, no 1, available at www.tandfonline.com/doi/abs/10.1080/13629380701642662.

Marin, P. (ed.) (2009) *Public–Private Partnerships for Urban Water Utilities: A Review of Experiences in Developing Countries*. Washington, DC: World Bank.

Niang, I., O.C. Ruppel, M.A. Abdrabo, A. Essel, C. Lennard, J. Padgham, and P. Urquhart (2014) 'Africa'. In: Barros, V.R., Field, C.B., Dokken, D.J., Mastrandrea, M.D., Mach, K.J., Bilir, T.E., Chatterjee, M., Ebi, K.L., Estrada, Y.O., Genova, R.C., Girma, B., Kissel, E.S., Levy, A.N.,MacCracken, S., Mastrandrea, P.R. and White, L.L. (eds) *Climate Change 2014: Impacts, Adaptation, and Vulnerability. Part B: Regional Aspects.* Contribution of Working Group II to the Fifth Assessment Report of the Intergovernmental Panel on Climate Change. Cambridge, UK and New York, NY: Cambridge University Press, pp 1199–265.

OECD (2010) *Infrastructure in Africa.* Policy Brief No. 2 (October). Paris: OECD.

Raballand, G. and Macchi, P. (2008) *Transport Prices and Costs: The Need to Revisit Donors' Policies in Transport in Africa.* BREAD Working Paper No. 190. Washington, DC: Bureau for Research and Economics Analysis of Development.

Redifer, L. (2010) *New Financing Sources for Africa's Infrastructure Deficit.* Washington, DC: IMF.

Roehrig, J. and Menz, G. (2005) 'The determination of natural agricultural potential in Western Africa using the fuzzy logic based marginality index', *EARSeL eProceedings*, vol 4, no 1.

Rosnes, O. and Vennemo, H. (2008) *Powering Up: Costing Power Infrastructure Spending Needs in Sub-Saharan Africa*, Background Paper 5, Africa Infrastructure Country Diagnostic. Washington, DC: World Bank.

Rouse, N. (2009) 'Infrastructure in Africa – a debt perspective', Paper presented for the Emerging Africa Infrastructure Fund and GuarantCo. at the G8 Africa Infrastructure Investment Conference, 2009.

Shah, R. and Batley, R. (2009) 'Private-sector investment in infrastructure: rationale and causality of pro-poor impacts', *Development Policy Review*, vol 27, no 4, pp 397–417.

Teravaninthorn, S. and Raballand, G. (2008) *Transport Prices and Costs in Africa: A Review of the Main International Corridors*, AICD Working Paper 14. Washington, DC: World Bank.

UNECA (United Nations Economic Commission for Africa) (2005) *Meeting the Challenges of Unemployment and Poverty in Africa*, Economic Report on Africa. Addis Ababa: UN Economic Commission for Africa.

UNECA (2009) *Developing African Agriculture through Regional Value Chains*, Economic Report on Africa. Addis Ababa: UN Economic Commission for Africa.

UNECA (2010) *Economic Report on Africa 2010. Promoting high-level sustainable growth to reduce unemployment in Africa.* Addis Ababa, Ethiopia: UNECA.

UNECA, African Union, African Development Bank and United Nations Development Programme (2015) *MDG Report 2015: Assessing Progress in Africa toward the Millennium Development Goals.* Addis Ababa, Ethiopia: Economic Commission for Africa.

UNFPA (United Nations Population Fund) (2014) *The State of World Population 2014: The power of 1.8 billion adolescents, youth and the transformation of the future.* New York, NY: UNFPA.

UN-HABITAT (2010) *State of the World's Cities, 2010/11: Bridging the Urban Divide.* Nairobi: UN-HABITAT.

UN_HABITAT (2013) *UN-HABITAT Global Activities Report 2013: our presence and partnerships.* Nairobi: UN-Habitat.

United Nations (2014) *World Urbanization Prospects: The 2014 Revision.* New York: UN.

World Bank (1994) *World Development Report: Infrastructure for Development.* Washington, DC: World Bank.

World Bank (2008a) *World Development Report: Agriculture for Development.* Washington, DC: World Bank.

World Bank (2008b) *Africa's Urbanization for Development: Understanding Africa's Urban Challenges and Opportunities.* Washington, DC: World Bank.

World Bank (2009a) *Doing Business 2010: Reforming through Difficult Times.* Washington, DC: World Bank.

World Bank (2009b) *World Development Report: Reshaping Economic Geography.* Washington, DC: World Bank.

World Bank (2010) *World Development Report: Development and Climate Change.* Washington, DC: World Bank.

World Bank (2011a) *World Development Indicators*, http://data.worldbank.org/data-catalog/world-development-indicators

World Bank (2011b) *A Bumpy Ride to Prosperity: Infrastructure for Shared Growth in Kenya. Poverty Reduction and Economic Management Unit Africa Region.* Washington, DC: World Bank.

World Bank (2011c) *The Global Monitoring Report 2011: Improving the Odds of Achieving MDGs.* Washington, DC: World Bank.

World Bank (2013) *World Development Indicators*, http://data.worldbank.org/data-catalog/world-development-indicators

World Bank (2014a) *World Development Indicators*, http://data.worldbank.org/data-catalog/world-development-indicators

World Bank (2014b) *Doing Business 2015: Going Beyond Efficiency: comparing business regulations for domestic firms in 189 economies.* Washington, DC: World Bank.

World Bank (2014c) *Enterprise Surveys*, www.enterprisesurveys.org

World Bank (2014d) *Connecting to Compete 2014: Trade Logistics in the Global Economy. The Logistics Performance Index and Its Indicators.* Washington, DC: World Bank.

World Bank (2015) *World Development Indicators*, http://data.worldbank.org/data-catalog/world-development-indicators

World Bank and International Energy Agency (2014) *Sustainable Energy for All 2013–2014: Global Tracking Framework.* Washington, DC: World Bank.

World Energy Council (2005) *Regional Energy Integration in Africa.* London: World Energy Council.

Yepes, T., Pierce, J. and Foster, V. (2008) *Making Sense of Africa's Infrastructure Endowment: A Benchmarking Approach*, Policy Research Working Paper No. 4912. Washington, DC: World Bank.

Annex

Table A10.1: Infrastructural deficits in low-income countries (LICs) in SSA and elsewhere

	SSA's LICs	Other LICs	ECOWAS	EAC	SADC	Central Africa
Transportation						
Density of paved road network*	31	134	38	8	92	41
Density of total road network*	137	211	144	105	214	132
ICT						
Density of fixed phone line**	10	78	28	6	74	13
Density of mobile phone line**	55	76	72	54	180	74
Density of internet connections**	2	3	2.4	2.1	5.5	1.7
Energy						
Electrical generating capacity***	37	326	31	24	175	44
Access to electricity****	16	41	18	7	21	18
Water and sanitation						
Water****	60	72	63	64	71	58
Sanitation ****	34	51	35	45	43	28

Notes: * km/1000km² (2001); ** Subscribers per 1,000 people (2004); *** MW per 1 million people (2003); **** % of households with access (2002-2004).

Source: Yepes *et al.* (2008).

Table A10.2: Total aid, aid to infrastructure, and aid dependency in African countries, 2008

Country name	Total aid (US$m)	Infrastructure aid (US$m)	Aid dependency (%)	Share of infrastructure in aid (%)
Algeria	250.7	28.3	0.1	11.3
Angola	674.4	42.4	0.8	6.3
Benin	606.3	137.2	9.1	22.6
Botswana	670.2	1.8	5.0	0.3
Burkina Faso	1,284.1	119.5	15.7	9.3
Burundi	647.6	54.4	58.4	8.4
Cameroon	1,185.0	239.4	5.0	20.2
Cape Verde	315.3	161.7	18.2	51.3
Central African Rep.	242.1	1.1	12.2	0.5
Chad	484.6	3.2	5.7	0.7
Comoros	33.2	0.4	6.6	1.3
Congo, Dem. Rep.	2,981.8	229.2	25.7	7.7
Congo, Rep.	505.1	0.8	4.8	0.2
Côte d'Ivoire	756.8	182.9	3.2	24.2
Djibouti	119.0	10.9	12.1	9.2

(continued)

Table A10.2: Total aid, aid to infrastructure, and aid dependency in African
countries, 2008 (continued)

Country name	Total aid (US$m)	Infrastructure aid (US$m)	Aid dependency (%)	Share of infrastructure in aid (%)
Egypt	1,696.0	930.4	1.0	54.9
Equatorial Guinea	18.1	0.0	0.1	0.2
Eritrea	98.2	19.0	6.6	19.4
Ethiopia	3,374.7	348.8	12.9	10.3
Gabon	118.4	63.5	0.8	53.6
Gambia	48.4	0.1	6.5	0.2
Ghana	2,429.0	303.7	15.1	12.5
Guinea	349.4	4.0	7.7	1.1
Guinea-Bissau	124.9	0.2	27.3	0.2
Kenya	1,432.5	17.6	4.7	1.2
Lesotho	443.3	1.3	27.8	0.3
Liberia	1,101.4	40.0	180.4	3.6
Libya	75.1	5.0	0.1	6.6
Madagascar	1,173.4	357.6	12.4	30.5
Malawi	786.9	10.7	18.4	1.4
Mali	1,266.1	431.0	14.5	34.0
Mauritania	187.7	8.1	5.3	4.3
Mauritius	167.8	21.7	1.8	12.9
Morocco	2,783.1	1,352.4	3.1	48.6
Mozambique	2,851.3	387.1	28.6	13.6
Namibia	293.0	88.4	3.3	30.2
Niger	835.8	170.8	15.6	20.4
Nigeria	2,221.8	489.1	1.1	22.0
Rwanda	1,011.4	76.6	22.7	7.6
São Tomé and Principe	53.4	1.8	30.5	3.3
Senegal	1,234.9	241.6	9.3	19.6
Seychelles	15.3	0.0	1.7	0.0
Sierra Leone	426.9	112.0	21.8	26.2
South Africa	1,315.7	201.0	0.5	15.3
Sudan	2,332.6	94.4	4.0	4.0
Swaziland	126.9	2.5	4.3	1.9
Tanzania	3,265.7	1,233.3	15.8	37.8
Togo	422.5	73.2	13.3	17.3
Tunisia	1,143.3	464.4	2.8	40.6
Uganda	2,050.0	188.1	12.4	9.2
Zambia	1,730.7	178.3	11.8	10.3
Zimbabwe	594.1	0.9	18.9	0.1
Total Africa	**50,355.8**	**9,131.6**	**3.3**	**18.1**

Source: OECD, Creditor Reporting System Database and AfDB Statistics Department

Table A10.3: African urban agglomerations of more than 1 million population in 2015

Country	Urban agglomeration	2015 (millions)
Algeria	El Djazaïr (Algiers)	2.59
Angola	Huambo	1.27
Angola	Luanda	5.51
Burkina Faso	Ouagadougou	2.74
Cameroon	Douala	2.94
Cameroon	Yaoundé	3.07
Chad	N'Djaména	1.26
Congo	Brazzaville	1.89
Côte d'Ivoire	Abidjan	4.86
Democratic Republic of the Congo	Kananga	1.17
Democratic Republic of the Congo	Kinshasa	11.59
Democratic Republic of the Congo	Kisangani	1.04
Democratic Republic of the Congo	Lubumbashi	2.02
Democratic Republic of the Congo	Mbuji-Mayi	2.01
Egypt	Al-Iskandariyah (Alexandria)	4.78
Egypt	Al-Qahirah (Cairo)	18.77
Ethiopia	Addis Ababa	3.24
Ghana	Accra	2.28
Ghana	Kumasi	2.60
Guinea	Conakry	1.94
Kenya	Mombasa	1.10
Kenya	Nairobi	3.91
Liberia	Monrovia	1.26
Libya	Tarabulus (Tripoli)	1.13
Madagascar	Antananarivo	2.61
Mali	Bamako	2.52
Morocco	Dar-el-Beida (Casablanca)	3.51
Morocco	Fès	1.17
Morocco	Marrakech	1.13
Morocco	Rabat	1.97
Mozambique	Maputo	1.19
Niger	Niamey	1.09
Nigeria	Abuja	2.44
Nigeria	Benin City	1.50
Nigeria	Ibadan	3.16
Nigeria	Kaduna	1.05
Nigeria	Kano	3.59
Nigeria	Lagos	13.12
Nigeria	Onitsha	1.11

(continued)

Table A10.3: African urban agglomerations of more than 1 million population in 2015 (continued)

Country	Urban agglomeration	2015 (millions)
Nigeria	Port Harcourt	2.34
Rwanda	Kigali	1.26
Senegal	Dakar	3.52
Sierra Leone	Freetown	1.01
Somalia	Muqdisho (Mogadishu)	2.14
South Africa	Cape Town	3.66
South Africa	Durban	2.90
South Africa	Johannesburg	9.40
South Africa	Port Elizabeth	1.18
South Africa	Pretoria	2.06
South Africa	Vereeniging	1.16
Sudan	Al-Khartum (Khartoum)	5.13
Tunisia	Tunis	1.99
Uganda	Kampala	1.94
United Republic of Tanzania	Dar es Salaam	5.12
Zambia	Lusaka	2.18
Zimbabwe	Harare	1.50
Total		174.58

Source: United Nations (2014)

ELEVEN

Regional integration and infrastructure connectivity in Africa

Maurice Mubila and Tito Yepes

Introduction

The idea that Africa's infrastructure gap is enormous and poses a threat to development has reached a consensus in the international development community and African governments alike. Less than 40% of the continent's population has access to electricity, about a third of the rural population has access to roads and only 5% of agriculture is under irrigation. In terms of key social infrastructure, the situation is no better, with only 34% of the population having access to improved sanitation and a slightly better situation for clean water, with about 65% having access. The information and communications technology (ICT) sector is characterized by huge differences across specific services. In 2008, four out of 10 Africans had access to mobile phones with penetration rates growing faster than the rest of the world. However, internet density is still only just above 80 persons per thousand (less than one in 10), and the figure for fixed telephone lines is even lower. Furthermore, Africa faces higher access costs for all infrastructure services compared with other developing countries. The continent's road freight is about four times more expensive, power costs 14 US dollar cents per kilowatt-hour against 5 US dollar cents to 10 US dollar cents elsewhere and mobile telephony costs US$12 per month compared with US$8 in other developing regions.

In addition to institutional capacity and investment requirements, Africa's economic geography, comprising many isolated economies, is particularly challenging for the infrastructure agenda for the following reasons: Africa is home to more landlocked countries than any other continent; Africa has more countries with low population densities than other developing regions; most African countries are far from major markets of high GDP concentration like Europe and the US; and within the African continent the countries differ greatly in their geographical situation and demographics: 26 countries are coastal, 15 countries are landlocked and three countries (Cape Verde, Madagascar, and Mauritius) are islands. The average population density is 70 people per square kilometer (km^2), somewhat lower than the average population density of other low- and lower-middle income countries in the world at 125 and 91 per km^2 respectively. Within the continent, population density varies widely. While some countries are very densely populated (Malawi, Ghana, Rwanda, Nigeria, Uganda, and Cape Verde), others are sparsely populate spreading over a relatively large geographical area (Chad, Niger, Namibia, Cameroon, Sudan, and Zambia).

The African Development Bank is framing its response to these challenges through a territorial approach so as to maximize a more cohesive and beneficial approach to using the region's endowments. A territorial strategy of three layers has been set, which addresses: rapid urbanization and the role of main urban areas; the linkages between major cities and the benefits from regional integration; and the cohesiveness brought in by the efficient use of rural opportunities. This chapter addresses the second layer of the territorial approach. It describes how to maximize the value obtained from investment in infrastructure by focusing on strengthening the linkages between major population centers across the continent.

Regional integration and connectivity in Africa is a must because prosperity depends, for most of its citizens, not only on their own efforts but also on those of its development partners. Forty percent of Africa's population lives in countries without access to the sea, whereas globally, about 4% of the world's population lives in such landlocked countries. In comparison Austria and Switzerland are also landlocked countries; however, their borders are thin, as people and goods pass through with few to no checking, and their ties with neighboring countries are strong. In contrast Africa consists of 53 independent countries, each with its own border and barriers to the movement of goods, capital and people. The worse conditions for accessing the sea are in central Africa where weak regulations for the trucking industry, low investment in roads and poor maintenance result in the highest logistics costs and longest transit times among all African countries.

According to the World Development Report (WDR) of 2009, the countries of central, east and west Africa face the triple challenge of internal division or thick economic borders between them; large distances from world markets; and low economic density due to small local economies.[1] In order to overcome such a situation those countries need a combination of three policy instruments conceptualized by the WDR 2009: strengthening regional institutions in countries that have thick borders; investing in regional infrastructure to improve the connections between countries; and providing "incentives such as preferential access to world markets, perhaps on the condition that all countries strengthen regional cooperation" (p xxiii). In the same line of argument, Limão and Venables (1999) have argued that regional approaches to infrastructure provision can address the infrastructure backlog in Africa by overcoming the region's difficult geography.[2]

This chapter focuses on investment in regional infrastructure to improve connectivity, such as better transport corridors, improved transnational use of regional energy sources and improved internet access, while touching on the need to strengthen regional institutions. However, according to the WDR 2009 framework, solving divisions created by thick borders may not be sufficient to trigger economic growth, as low economic and population density due to the scattered location of people and economic activities or just low population size, along with large distances to world markets, will also continue to impact strongly on regional development. This is especially true for the countries in the Economic Community of Central African States (ECCAS), which have weaker infrastructure endowment compared with the rest of Sub-Saharan Africa. Though East and West African countries also face the challenge of poor connectivity, they benefit from larger local markets, bigger cities and potential complementarities.

Gains from further regional integration

Transforming the current situation of poor collaboration among African countries requires envisioning the benefits of collective action. There are two primary sources of common benefit among others: the additional outcomes expected from improved accessibility to larger markets by the producers in each national market; and the efficiency gains from the joint provision of infrastructure.

Additional outcomes from improved accessibility to larger markets

Successful regional trade integration can help African countries reap economies of scale and collectively exploit their resources, thereby expanding markets and thus gradually raising their competitiveness in the global economy. A larger market is an important driver of product diversification and enables small producers to realize cost savings from larger scales of production.

The first order objective is to make it easier for firms within Africa to reach African markets. Currently African firms face great disadvantages compared with those outside Africa, and some actually find it cheaper to reach other African markets from abroad rather than, for instance, trading directly between East and West Africa.

Notably, infrastructure plays a central role in improving regional competitiveness, facilitating domestic and international trade, and enhancing integration into the global economy. For firms, infrastructure development is critical for creating wealth as it can reduce costs and enlarge markets. Firms are more willing and able to invest in intra-firm productive assets when the complementary investment in extra-firm assets is in place and quality services are available at low cost. Without reliable and competitively priced freight transport over sturdy infrastructure, nations have little hope of trading goods on advantageous terms. Alongside these benefits for all, participants' cooperation with neighbors is vital, especially for the landlocked economies with limited access to ports and markets.

Investment in physical infrastructure such as roads, power plants and ICT is likely to generate the largest impact on trade among policy options for regional integration. Despite the fact that political commitment to critical regional integration improvements has been demonstrated in recent times through fuller implementation of tariff liberalization schedules, concerted efforts to tackle non-tariff barriers and the development of longer-term strategies to address export supply capacity constraints at the national level, investment in regional infrastructure should precede all efforts as its benefits will be larger in terms of productivity than any other collective action among African governments.

Studies prepared for the World Development Report of 1994[3] estimated that on average a 1% increase in infrastructure stock is associated with a 1% increase in gross domestic product (GDP). More recent studies such as Esfahani and Ramirez (2003)[4] show that the contribution of infrastructure services to growth is substantial and in general exceeds the cost of provision of those services. Easterly and Rebelo (1993)[5] have found that public expenditure on transport and communications has a positive effect on growth. Infrastructure stocks and service quality help boost economic growth. A recent study by Calderón (2009) demonstrated that the growth payoff of achieving the infrastructure development of the African leader (Mauritius) is 1.1% per year in North Africa and 2.3% in Sub-Saharan Africa, with most of the contribution coming from larger stocks.[6] The same study also finds that across Africa, infrastructure contributed 99 basis points to per capita economic growth, compared with 68 basis points for other structural policies.

Investment in regional infrastructure is expected to deliver high rates of return, triple intra-regional trade and might double international trade. For example, it is estimated that upgrading the major corridors linking the 15 landlocked countries to the major seaports[7] serving the region's international trade would cost US$1.5 billion, plus US$1 billion annually for maintenance. However, the East African Northern Corridor alone would be expected to yield an internal rate of return of around 20% to 60%. Another example is the Trans-African Highway, which requires total investment of US$20 billion and has an ongoing maintenance cost of US$1 billion a year, but intra-regional trade alone would be expected to triple to US$30 billion per year, not to mention the gains to international trade of over US$200 billion per year.[8]

Efficiency gains from joint provision of infrastructure

The benefits of regional integration are visible across all aspects of infrastructure networks. For ICT and power, regional infrastructure provides scale economies that substantially reduce the costs of production. For example, big hydropower projects that would not be economically viable for a single country make sense when neighbors share the benefits. In the area of ICT, linking to continental fiber-optic submarine cables could reduce internet and international call charges by one-half. Similarly, regional power tools that allow countries to share the most cost-effective energy resources can reduce electricity costs substantially. Infrastructure sharing has many benefits: it addresses the problems of small scale and adverse location; increases the scale of infrastructure construction, operation, and maintenance through joint provision; reduces costs; pools scarce technical and managerial capacity; and creates a larger market.[9]

There are significant economic and environmental benefits for linking electricity generation systems of different countries and encouraging energy trade. Regional integration turns out to be very cost-effective, not only because of the economies of scale that can be realized but also because the power tools can make extensive use of trading possibilities. The Democratic Republic of the Congo (DRC), for example, emerges as a huge exporter of electricity. Its net exports are almost four times greater than its domestic consumption, and it supplies hydropower through Zambia, Zimbabwe and Botswana into South Africa. South Africa becomes an importer of 10% of its domestic consumption, trading with all neighboring countries: Namibia, Botswana, Zimbabwe, Mozambique and Lesotho.

Regional collaboration also allows optimal management and the development of cross-border public goods. Road and rail corridors linking landlocked countries to port cities are examples of such regional public goods, as are regional airports and seaports hubs.

Regional integration agenda: a focus on energy, transport and telecommunication

Cross-border infrastructure such as transport, energy and telecommunications are essential to move goods, services, people and information between countries. Such linkages expand market access, reduce economic distance and facilitate trade, investment and labor mobility. In Africa, poor transport and communications infrastructure and unreliable power increase trading costs and undermine competitiveness and the continent's ability to integrate regionally as well as globally. At a fundamental level, the low degree of intra-African trade is due to a lack of product diversification and poor trade complementarity among African countries. These structural constraints, however, are compounded by inadequate and inefficient infrastructure, both hard (such as roads, transportation and energy) and soft (such as ICT and customs systems), that reduce the opportunities for diversification of production that should lead to increased scale and competitiveness at regional and global levels. An infrastructure agenda for regional integration and connectivity should, therefore, focus on addressing the needs of the transport, energy, and telecommunications sectors.

Achieving functional connectivity at the regional level entails ensuring: smooth land corridor transportation between landlocked countries and ports, as well as between major cities for internal trade; the development of power supply options harnessing cost-effective generation technologies at an efficient scale in the context of a well-functioning regional trading pool; and a robust communications network inter-linking capital cities through fiber-optic access to submarine cables.

Electricity, the main bottleneck

Electricity is by far Africa's largest infrastructure challenge. In 2008, only 38% of Africans had access to electricity compared with an average of 68% for all developing countries, 53% for South Asia and 80%–90% for Latin America. The figure is even lower for Sub-Saharan Africa, currently at 26%. Annual per capita electricity consumption in

Africa is 518 kilowatts per hour (kWh), equal to 25 days of electricity consumption in countries in the Organisation for Economic Co-operation and Development (OECD) (IEA, 2008).[10] Furthermore, in 2007, about 30 African countries endured on average 11.5 power outages due largely to the lack of regional interconnectivity of the electricity grids and shortages in affected countries. During this period, regional surpluses in generation capacity were noted for all of the five sub-regions except for East Africa, which had intermittent shortages. Some of the countries with surplus supplies like South Africa now have deficits due to increases in local demand.

As an example, Sub-Saharan Africa (SSA) has the world's lowest per capita consumption of electricity and the lowest rate of electricity access. About 500 million of its people (or two-thirds of the population) are without access to electricity. SSA currently has inadequate generation capacity, limited electrification, low power consumption, unreliable services and high and rising costs. But in order to develop economically and end the untenable access situation, it will demand large amounts of electricity. For instance, from 2001 to 2005, half of the countries in Sub-Saharan Africa achieved solid GDP growth rates in excess of 4.5%. Their demand for power grew at a similar pace, yet generation capacity expanded only 1.2% annually. Refurbishing 44.3 gigawatts and building an additional 7,000 megawatts of new generation capacity each year to meet suppressed demand, keep pace with projected economic growth, and provide additional capacity to support the roll-out of electrification will amount to US$40.6 billion a year. Even lowering the original projected growth rates of 5.1% to half their levels would reduce estimated power sector spending needs by only about 20% in absolute terms, lowering required new generation capacity from just over 7,000 megawatts to just under 6,000 megawatts.

Overall, the costs of power outages to the continent are significant, with Africa losing almost 12.5% of production time compared with 7% for South Asia, the next worst case. Electricity supply is also a serious infrastructure problem driving up exporters' costs. More than 30 countries experience power shortages and regular outages, which, among other things, disrupt economic activity and drive up firms' operating costs. African firms report that frequent power cuts cause them to lose 5% of their sales. For firms in the informal sector that cannot afford backup generators—which is three to five times more expensive than electricity from the grid—the loss is even higher, at 20%.[11]

Dealing with high electricity costs and reliability of supply is thus a priority issue in most countries. Addressing the problem in most cases will require significant investment in capacity, which has lagged behind demand due to rapid growth in Africa in recent years or as a result of conflicts in fragile states. The potential productivity gains from increasing electricity supply, together with the associated income effect, point to a market with significant growth potential. Notwithstanding the size of the challenge, the development of energy markets on a regional basis offers significant benefits. Linking national petroleum and electricity industries can help mobilize private and domestic investments by expanding market size while interconnection can create export opportunities for countries with comparative advantage in endowments of resources. Secondary benefits such as increased and cheaper energy supply alternatives also become available to smaller markets and countries.

The study *Regional Energy Integration in Africa*[12] confirms four major benefits associated with regional energy integration: improved security of supply; higher economic efficiency; enhanced environmental quality; and a wider deployment of renewable energy resources. For instance a large hydropower project that would not be economically viable for a single country would make sense when neighbors share their costs as well as benefits. Inadequate investment in such projects and therefore electricity supply is mainly a cost problem because investment in the electricity sector is a large undertaking for a poor country (to develop a hydropower plant is, for instance, extremely capital intensive), and because hydropower reserves are often located far from population centers, adding further to the cost.

Smoother land corridors a must

For most African countries distance from their primary markets and high transport costs of their products inhibit their participation in the global economy. Poor transport infrastructure is the main cause of high transport costs and therefore, arguably, the most binding constraint to intra-African trade. Currently the cost of transporting goods in Africa is the highest in the world.[13] It is estimated that poor infrastructure accounts for 40% of predicted transport costs for coastal countries, and up to 60% for landlocked countries.[14] The burden of poor infrastructure on trade increases with geographic and sovereign fragmentation, as Sub-Saharan Africa is uncharacteristically highly fragmented.

Several empirical studies document that the returns to investment in infrastructure (for example, upgrading of roads), measured in terms of trade growth, are particularly high in Africa. However, there are findings that state that, with a few important exceptions, Sub-Saharan Africa has almost as much transport infrastructure as it needs. The real issue there is improving and preserving the quality of that infrastructure, which can mean both improving the condition of existing infrastructure and upgrading its level of service.[15]

In addition, regional collaboration is needed for effective infrastructure development because moving goods and people through regional borders and overseas requires corridors linking national capitals to each other, to other big cities, to international borders and to deep-water ports. Corridors in Africa currently do not carry enough goods nor people to obtain benefits from more than one type of transport (that is, multimodal transportation);[16] therefore, ensuring that the service is improved within modes and along the corridor is essential.

Roads constitute the main infrastructure serving regional connectivity and through them at least 80% of goods and 90% of passengers are carried. The concept of an intra-regional trunk network has existed for some time. In 1970 the Trans-African Highway system, currently the heart of regional connectivity on the continent, was conceived as a network of all-weather roads that would provide direct routes between the capitals, contribute to political, economic, and social integration and cohesion in Africa, and ensure road transport facilities between important areas of production and consumption. The total length of the nine corridors is 54,120 kilometers (km).[17]

But it is characterized by missing links and poor maintenance in key segments. About half of the network is in the 24 Sub-Saharan Africa countries of that half, 68% of the roads are paved, 6% have a gravel surface and 26% have a dirt surface or no formed road. Only 27% of the network is in good condition, with a similar percentage in fair condition. However, 46% of the road network is in poor condition. The two segments of the system that remain unconnected by any sort of road are in Central Africa, where there is a 200km gap between Salo in the Central African Republic and Ouésso in the Republic of Congo and a 370km gap in Niger from the Algerian border. As such, its potential to connect the continent remains unrealized. To provide a meaningful level of continental connectivity, between 60,000 and 100,000km of regional roads are required.

Design standards are important in estimating the costs of completing the system, because international road links support high-speed traffic and heavy loads; high minimum standards for road widths are therefore desirable. At present the highways comprise a wide range of standards; for example, the load limit for single axles in the countries through which the Trans-African Highway passes varies between 8.2 and 13 tonnes—a substantial variation, which results in delays at border crossings and separation of freight from truck, and thus a deterioration in quality of service in the logistics chain.[18] Although each country is responsible for the standards applied within its territory, there are important benefits to be gained from applying common standards, such as avoiding operational and administrative complications at border crossings.

Contemporary action in other transport modes

Railways provide significant internal links in some countries and particularly for some landlocked countries that connect to the ports of coastal cities through rail transport—for example, the corridors between Dakar and Bamako, Abidjan and Ouagadougou or Maputo and East Africa countries.

In SSA countries rail coverage measured in terms of land area, population and GDP per capita compares favorably with coverage in other countries of the world. Though rail density by land area in low-income countries of SSA is somewhat lower than in other low-income countries of the world, the total network in SSA is around 70,000km, of which about 55,000km is currently operational.

Air transport is particularly important for sparsely populated and landlocked countries and for future development of the region's significant tourism potential. Air freight is playing a growing role in the competitiveness of African goods in world markets for high-value, time-sensitive cargo such as horticultural and floricultural products.

In shipping, main ports still need to meet international standards and amplify their capacity in order for the region to increase international trade and reap other benefits of better connectivity. While Sub-Saharan Africa has a proliferation of ports, few are large by world standards. Few are capable of handling the largest of the current generation of ships and most are poorly equipped and operate at low levels of productivity. Generally, they are unprepared for the dramatic changes in trade and shipping patterns that are now occurring. While they are moving slowly from publicly owned service ports to the so-called "landlord port structures", often with embedded container-terminal concessions, they are still behind other regions in the development of modern port-management structures. Additional momentum for modernization is coming from the growing presence of global shipping lines and international terminal operators in African ports.

Enhancing ICT by targeting public investment

Due to the size of investment requirements, costs can outpost the benefits for the private sector from the expansion of ICT services in Sub-Saharan Africa. Governments should, therefore, fill in the gap in costs so as to open up opportunities for further private investment that will secure the expansion of these services, which have proven fundamental to the region's recent development.

The ICT revolution, especially in mobile telecommunications, has had enormous positive impacts on economic growth and social cohesiveness. Mobile phones have revolutionized the way African people interact, as has been the case in most developing countries. The increasing use of ICT in Africa has shown to have positive results for economic growth. The ICT revolution in Africa is responsible for about 1 percentage point of the improvement in Africa's per capita economic growth rate between the mid-1990s and the mid-2000s.[19] Moreover, it has proven to have multiplier effects, adding to employment growth and income generation. In East Africa alone, the mobile industry directly and indirectly provides employment for close to 500,000 people.[20]

However, climbing the next step towards high-speed mass-market broadband internet access in Africa at prices that would be affordable for a significant proportion of the population would involve major investment in backbone infrastructure. The revenue generated from customers would be insufficient to make this investment commercially attractive. If governments wish to achieve this level of broadband internet access, significant levels of public subsidy will likely be required, as this next step in the ladder of ICT service provision requires a level of investment that can be hardly funded by the private sector as has been the case so far. As such, there is need for a regional action to undertake a strategic sequence of investments in fiber links and backbones that would pave the way to leveraging further private sector involvement.

The problem results from both poor intra-regional connectivity and insufficient undersea cables connecting Africa to other parts of the world and to the rich information resources of the global internet. Ideally, the network of submarine cables surrounding the continent should be built in such a way that it ensures all coastal countries have access to the intercontinental network. At present, Western and Southern Africa have submarine cables, although they do not yet provide full access to all countries. However, there is no submarine infrastructure on the Eastern side of the continent, leading to exceptionally high costs of international communication. In addition, intra-regional backbones are needed both to ensure that landlocked countries secure access to submarine infrastructure and to facilitate communications across Africa's main economic regions.

Therefore there are two priorities for providing or improving the ICT in the continent: improve access to high-capacity submarine fiber-optic cables for low-price international voice communication services and higher-speed internet access; and lay high-bandwidth backbone networks to connect towns and cities within countries, across borders and to the international submarine fiber-optic cable networks. It is estimated that a one-time investment would range from US$229 million for a minimum set of links to US$515 million for an extensive interregional network connecting all African capitals to one another with fiber-optic cables.

Calibrating to respond to sub-regional specifics

Sub-Saharan Africa is not homogenous across its sub-regions regarding most aspects of development, and infrastructure provision is no exception. Infrastructure endowments differ substantially across sub-regions, as do institutional schemes for services provision. Tailoring an agenda for regional integration and connectivity should consider these differences because investment priorities may pull in opposite directions making it difficult to set common goals. The next section offers a brief picture of the differences in infrastructure endowments across the sub-regions. A more detailed presentation of challenges and opportunities at the intersection of sectors and sub-regions is presented in the Annex to this chapter using the analysis made by the Africa Infrastructure Country Diagnostics.

Economic Community of Central African States

ECCAS's economic geography is complex, due to the fact that economic activity takes place in isolated pockets separated by vast distances and environmentally sensitive areas. As a result, the sub-region has the poorest performing infrastructure of Africa on most indicators.

One-third of ECCAS's regional road network is unpaved and a substantial amount of it is in poor condition. Coastal countries do not devote sufficient attention to the sea corridors and surface transport is the most expensive in Sub-Saharan Africa, due to cartelization and restrictive regulations for the trucking industry. As a result, it also moves slower than in most other parts of Africa because of the poor road conditions, border delays and time-consuming administrative processes. The time taken to move freight from ports to landlocked countries has ranged from 26 to 71 days, among the longest durations on the continent. The overall cost of moving goods along Central Africa's key trade routes is in the order of US$230–US$650 per tonne.

Central African railway systems do not form a network and existing lines are lightly used. Two ports in Central Africa, Douala and Pointe Noire, serve as trans-shipment hubs for the region but the performance of these ports significantly lags behind global standards. The air transport sector in ECCAS is striking for the absence of an air transport hub and the lack of connectivity between the Economic and Monetary Community of Central Africa (CEMAC) and other ECCAS states.

Despite major hydropower potential, Central Africa has the least developed power sector on the continent. Regional power trade through the Central African Power Pool could substantially reduce power sector costs and the long-run marginal cost of energy in the region, but currently these opportunities are untapped. Compared with the other sub-regions of Africa, ECCAS's ICT infrastructure is still in its incipient stages, performs poorly on access and has the highest prices.

Southern Africa Development Community (SADC)

The Southern Africa Development Community (SADC) is characterized by small and isolated economies including island states and a mix of low- and middle-income countries. The economic geography of SADC reinforces the importance of adopting a regional approach to infrastructure development. However, the sub-region ranks consistently above other Africa's sub-regions on a range of infrastructure indicators.

SADC has a well-developed regional road network that is in relatively good condition and almost all of the corridors with the exception of Nacala and Lobito are paved. Surface transport in SADC is the cheapest in Africa, albeit still more expensive than in other developing countries. The overall times and costs of moving goods along Southern Africa's key trade routes is time-consuming and expensive. Southern Africa has an extensive railway system with national systems forming a network centered in Durban and offering direct competition to road transport. In the ports sector, SADC has a center for a very effective trans-shipment network with Durban followed by Dar es Salaam providing the key ports. The air transport market in SADC is the largest in Africa with a clear hub and spoke structure with Johannesburg at the center.

The power transmission network in Southern Africa is reasonably well developed, leading the rest of the continent in generation capacity and enjoying relatively low costs for power. The Southern African Power Pool has already established regional trade. SADC has the best record in terms of access to ICT services compared with the other sub-regions but faces very high prices for ICT services.

East African Community

East African Community (EAC) infrastructure ranks consistently behind that of Southern and Western Africa across infrastructure indicators. Its road network is in relatively good condition, with prominent patches of poor-quality roads along some corridors and significant stretches of unpaved road. Surface transport in East Africa is challenged by difficult border crossings and low performance logistics, but faces fewer obstacles from the trucking industry, which is comparatively mature and more competitive than in other sub-regions. However, it is still very slow when viewed against SADC and global standards. Widespread delays occur in ports, at border crossings and in other processes. The overall cost of moving a tonne of freight along East Africa's key trade routes is in the order of US$175–US$370 and takes between 200 and 800 hours. Apart from the Tazara Railway between Zambia and Tanzania, there is no real regional rail networks within the EAC and the existing rail networks are very lightly used, which complicates further regional integration.

In the ports sector, East Africa has two maritime hubs that anchor the regional trans-shipment network but the ports need significant improvement in performance across the board. With regards to air transport, East Africa has a strong hub-and-spoke structure that centers on two regional hubs, but the region has made little progress toward market liberalization.

The power situation in EAC is severe compared with that in other regions of Africa. It already practises regional power trade, albeit much less actively than Western and Southern Africa; however, greater trade could bring substantial benefits. Compared with the continent's other regional economic communities, EAC has performed poorly in terms of ICT access, and in 2007 faced relatively high prices for critical ICT services. Some countries have recently been able to access submarine cable and therefore ICT prices have dropped significantly and access has improved.

Economic Community of West African States

Infrastructure in the 15 countries of the Economic Community of West African States (ECOWAS) ranks consistently behind Southern Africa across a range of infrastructure indicators. ECOWAS has a relatively well-developed regional road network based on seven main arteries, but coastal countries are not devoting enough attention to sea corridors. Surface transport in West Africa is very expensive compared with that in the rest of Africa and the developing world. The causes are cartelization and restrictive regulation of the trucking industry. It is also very slow compared with the rest of Africa and the developing world because of frequent delays associated with administrative processes. The overall time and cost of moving goods along West Africa's key trade routes are time-consuming and expensive, requiring in the order of 400–1,000 hours and costing between US$175 and US$310 per tonne. There is no real regional rail network in the ECOWAS area. Existing lines are lightly used and the presence of three different rail gauges complicates integration. In the port sector, West Africa lacks a clear maritime hub as the center for a more effective trans-shipment network and needs to improve performance across the board. On air transport, ECOWAS has made great strides on market liberalization, but safety remains a concern and the region lacks a strong hub-and-spoke structure.

However, power supply in the ECOWAS region is the most expensive and the least reliable in Africa. West Africa already practises regional power trade. Further pursuit of such trade could bring substantial benefits, but much depends on Guinea's ability to become a hydropower exporter.

Compared with other regional economic communities in Africa, ECOWAS performs relatively well on access to ICT facilities but faces relatively high prices for critical services.

Non-physical components of the agenda

Beyond the critical need to invest in regional infrastructure, there are two aspects to be considered alongside the physical investment agenda: strengthening the governance scheme for infrastructure service provision, and the institutional set-up required to maintain an effective level of service provision.

The impact of lack of good governance and weak institutions can be observed mainly in the transport industry, such as inadequate transit procedures, overregulation, bribes, multiple controls and poor border service, which increase the time the goods take to reach their destination, as well as the costs. Also, the lack of standardized procedures at border posts causes time variability, hence making it difficult to meet planned schedules and international standards.

The trucking sector in much of Africa is dominated by transport cartels that operate through a system of queuing for loads at fixed fares as opposed to competitive best-offer practices and prices. In Central and Western Africa, higher transport costs are mainly explained by oligopolies in the trucking industry with exceptionally high profit margins. While policy responses to these problems have included transit system reforms,[21] joint border posts or warehouses at ports for landlocked countries among others,[22] these practices have not reached all countries in the Sub-Saharan region. This type of structure in an industry, in addition to the lack of regulation of the sector due to vested interests, results in very high operating costs and prices.

For example, along the Central and Western African Corridors, Africa's transportation costs are no higher than in other developing countries such as China, but transportation prices are much higher. The difference is the set of informal payments and profits earned by trucking companies. The source of these high profit margins is the set of regulations in many African countries that restrict entry of new companies, enabling incumbents to earn large profits. Rwanda, a landlocked country, deregulated its transport sector and saw a dramatic drop in transport prices almost overnight.[23]

Regarding the latter critical institutional need, ensuring maintenance receives its fair share in any investment plan is critical—to give it short shrift is to squander any benefits of previous investments. This relates to the need to break the vicious circles of the local political economy that delay maintenance and drag competitiveness down.

Conclusion

Regional integration in Africa is a must because prosperity depends, for most of its citizens, not only on their own efforts but also on those of its development partners.

Electricity is by far Africa's largest infrastructure bottleneck. The region currently has inadequate generation capacity, limited electrification, low power consumption, unreliable services and high and rising costs. Refurbishing and building additional generation capacity to meet suppressed demand, keep pace with economic growth, and provide additional capacity to support the roll-out of electrification will amount to resources beyond any individual country's capacity. Cooperation either binational, sub-regional or at any level is the only alternative is the region is see significant progress over the next years.

In contrast, but not without important exceptions, Sub-Saharan Africa has almost as much transport infrastructure as it needs. The real issue there is improving and preserving the quality of that infrastructure, which can mean both improving the condition of existing infrastructure and upgrading its level of service. The impact of lack of good governance and weak institutions can be observed mainly in the transport industry, such as inadequate transit procedures, overregulation, bribes, multiple controls and poor border service, which increase the time the goods take to reach their destination, as well as the costs. Also, the lack of standardized procedures at border posts causes time variability, hence making it difficult to meet planned schedules and international standards. A critical institutional need is ensuring that maintenance receives its fair share in any investment plan is critical. This relates to the need to break the vicious circles of the local political economy that delay maintenance and drag competitiveness down.

Finally, ICT in the third unavoidable component of a cooperation agenda of a regional approach. Includes two aspects: improve access to high-capacity submarine fiber-optic cables for low-price international voice communication services and higher-speed internet access; and lay high-bandwidth backbone networks to connect towns and cities within countries, across borders and to the international submarine fiber-optic cable networks.

Notes

[1] World Bank (2009a)

[2] Limão and Venables (1999)

[3] World Bank (1994)

[4] Esfahani and Ramirez (2003)

[5] Easterly and Rebelo (1993)

[6] Calderón (2009)

[7] Teravaninthorn and Raballand (2008)

[8] Buys et al (2006)

[9] Lederman et al (2005)

[10] IEA (2008)

[11] Rosnes and Vennemo (2008)

[12] World Energy Council (2005)

[13] World Bank (2009b)

[14] Limão and Venables (2001)

[15] Carruthers et al (2008)

[16] Except for mineral lines, which are usually privately handled and are not included in the estimations (AfDB, 2013)

[17] AfDB (2000).

[18] AfDB (2000).

[19] Foster and Briceno-Garmendia (eds) (2010)

[20] Foster and Briceno-Garmendia (eds) (2010)

[21] In Cameroon, Chad and the Central African Republic.

[22] Between Kenya and Uganda at Malaba; between Zambia and Zimbabwe at Chirundu; between Zimbabwe and Mozambique at Forbes/Machipanda; along the Trans-Kalahari Corridor; and in West Africa on selective borders of Burkina Faso, Ghana, Mali, and Togo.

[23] Teravaninthorn and Raballand (2008)

References

AfDB (2000) *African Development Report*. Tunis, Tunisia: African Development Bank.

AfDB (2013) *An Integrated Approach to Infrastructure Provision in Africa*. Statistics Department, Africa Infrastructure Knowledge Program, April. Tunis: African Development Bank.

Buys, P., Deichmann, U. and Wheeler, D. (2006. *Road Network Upgrading and Overland Trade Expansion in Sub-Saharan Africa*, Policy Research Working Paper 4097. Washington, DC: World Bank.

Calderón, C. (2009) *Infrastructure and Growth in Africa*, Policy Research Working Paper 4914. Washington, DC: World Bank.

Carruthers, R., Krishnamani, R. and Murray, S. (2008) *Improving Connectivity Investing in Transport Infrastructure in Sub-Saharan Africa.* Summary to Background Paper 7, Africa Infrastructure Country Diagnostic. Washington, DC: World Bank.

Easterly, W. and Rebelo, S. (1993) 'Fiscal policy and economic growth: an empirical investigation', *Journal of Monetary Economics*, vol 32, no 3.

Esfahani, H.S. and Ramírez, M. (2003) 'Institutions, infrastructure, and economic growth', *Journal of Development Economics*, vol 70, pp 443–77.

Foster, V. and Briceno–Garmendia, C. (eds) (2010) *Africa's Infrastructure: A Time for Transformation.* Africa Development Forum. Washington, DC: Agence Française de Développement and World Bank.

IEA (International Energy Agency) (2008) *World Energy Outlook.* Paris: International Energy Agency.

Lederman, D., Maloney, W. and Servén, L. (2005) *Lessons from NAFTA for Latin America and the Caribbean.* Washington, DC: World Bank.

Limão, N. and Venables, A. (1999) *Infrastructure, Geographical Disadvantage, and Transportation Costs*, Policy Research Working Paper 2257. Washington, DC: World Bank.

Limão, N. and Venables, A. (2001) 'Infrastructure, geographical disadvantage, transport costs, and trade', *World Bank Economic Review*, vol 15, no 3, pp 451–79.

Rosnes, O. and Vennemo, H. (2008) *Powering Up: Costing Power Infrastructure Spending Needs in Sub-Saharan Africa*, Background Paper 5, Africa Infrastructure Country Diagnostic. Washington, DC: World Bank.

Teravaninthorn, S. and Raballand, G. (2008) *Transport Prices and Costs in Africa: A Review of the Main International Corridors.* Working Paper 14, Africa Infrastructure Country Diagnostic. Washington, DC: World Bank.

World Bank (1994) *World Development Report: Infrastructure for Development.* Washinton, DC: World Bank.

World Bank (2009a) *World Development Report: Reshaping Economic Geography.* Washington, DC: World Bank.

World Bank (2009b) *Transport Prices and Costs in Africa: A Review of the Main International Corridors.* Washington, DC: World Bank.

World Energy Council (2005) *Regional Energy Integration in Africa.* London: World Energy Council.

Annex

See tables below.

Table A11.1: Progress and challenges for regional integration

	East Africa		ECCAS		ECOWAS		SADC	
	Achievements	Challenges	Achievements	Challenges	Achievements	Challenges	Achievements	Challenges
Road transport	Several gateways facilitate intraregional trade. The Northern Corridor is the most important corridor and has roads of good quality. The trucking industry is deregulated and performs relatively well.	Cumbersome trade logistics systems. Lengthy delays and inadequate infrastructure at borders.	Several gateways are being developed	High trucking charges and lengthy delays due to trade facilitation issues. Traffic on regional corridors do not justify paving. Low quality along key corridors. No connectivity between CEMAC countries and DRC and Angola.	Several major international gateways in West Africa that facilitate trade.	High trucking charges and lengthy delays due to trade facilitation issues. Coastal countries appear to neglect maintenance of regional corridors.	Several major international gateways in southern Africa that facilitate trade within the region and with East Africa.	Lengthy delays due to trade facilitation issues. Portions of major international corridors are in disrepair.
Railways	Three bi-national railways offer tremendous potential for regional integration.	Low levels of passenger and freight traffic. Poor operational performance of most railways. Stiff intermodal competition.	Two relatively successful bi-national concessions. The concessions have improved productivity of individual railways.	Low levels of passenger and freight traffic, poor operational performance of railways.	Two relatively successful bi-national concessions.	Low levels of passenger and freight traffic, poor operational performance of railways. Railways facing stiff competition from other modes of transport. Incompatible rail gauges.	Extensive and well-developed railways network extending from the DRC to Durban with compatible gauges.	Low levels of passenger and freight traffic, poor operational performance of railways outside South Africa. Railways facing stiff competition from other modes. Lengthy delays.

(continued)

	East Africa		ECCAS		ECOWAS		SADC	
	Achievements	Challenges	Achievements	Challenges	Achievements	Challenges	Achievements	Challenges
Ports	Growing container traffic. Some ports perform well in key parameters.	The ports of Dar es Salaam and Mombasa face major capacity constraints.	Douala acts as main gateway for landlocked countries. Pointe-Noire has good deep-water characteristics.	Douala and Pointe-Noire face capacity constraints. Port charges are exceedingly high.	Burgeoning container and general cargo traffic.	Poor operational performance and absence of a transshipment hub.	Growing container and general-cargo traffic. Strong trans-shipment hub in Durban (highly efficient) and in Dar es Salam (moderately efficient).	Port capacity is stretched by traffic. Handling charges are very high. Other ports in the western are not very competitive. Extensive delays at ports hinders movement of freight to landlocked countries.
Air transport	Good regional connectivity. Nairobi and Addis Ababa are strong regional hubs. Air traffic has grown steadily. Most countries progressing towards safety standards. Significant fleet modernization.	Few flights flown under fifth freedom arrangements.	CEMAC has made good progress in achieving liberalization.	Air transport market is decreasing. Very low levels of air connectivity. There is no connectivity between CEMAC countries and DRC and Angola. Air safety among the worst in the world.	Reasonable levels of interregional connectivity. WAEMU and BAG are most liberalized markets in Africa.	Low levels of connectivity within ECOWAS. Lack of a strong regional hub. Aging fleet and poor record with respect to air traffic safety.	Best regional connectivity. Steady growth in air traffic. Strong hub-and-spoke structure centered on Johannesburg. Fleet has been upgraded.	Very low level of progress toward liberalization of the sector. Air safety standards across the region are highly variable.

(continued)

Table A11.1: Progress and challenges for regional integration (continued)

	East Africa		ECCAS		ECOWAS		SADC	
	Achievements	Challenges	Achievements	Challenges	Achievements	Challenges	Achievements	Challenges
Power	Performance of power utilities is encouraging, particularly on cost recovery. Principle of regional trade already well established.	Per capita generation capacity and access to electricity are lowest in Africa.	Significant availability of cost-effective hydro resources.	Very low access and generation capacity. Utilities highly inefficient with regard to distribution losses and revenue collection.	High electrification rates. Cost recovery is better than in other regions. Principle of regional trade already well established.	Lack of generation capacity leads to unreliable service, with only 70 percent of demand being satisfied. Utilities highly inefficient with regard to distribution losses and revenue collection.	High level of existing capacity. Demand is generally being met. High electrification rates. Principles of regional trade already well established.	Cost-recovery relatively low. Low levels of access outside South Africa.
ICT	Recent initiatives to connect to submarine cables have pushed prices down. Plans to connect all countries to the cable underway.	Low access and high prices. Behind other Africa sub-regions on intraregional roaming arrangements.	Some countries connected to submarine cables, resulting in lower tariffs. Some international operators are developing regional presence.	Very low levels of access to ICT services and very high prices in ECCAS. Roaming far less developed than other parts of Africa.	Highest access in Africa. Cheaper calls to landlines within ECOWAS. Advanced roaming arrangements. Active promotion of harmonization of regulations. Well endowed with submarine cables.	High prices. Many countries not connected to the submarine cable. Those connected face high costs due to lack of competition.	Access to ICT services among the highest in Africa. Significantly cheaper to call on landline within SADC than outside the region.	Countries pay high prices for critical ICT services. Landlocked countries and Namibia along the coast are not connected to the submarine cable. Roaming arrangements are not as advanced.

Part 4: Financing issues

TWELVE

Infrastructure deficit and opportunities in Africa

*Albert Mafusire, Zuzana Brixiova, John Anyanwu
and Qingwei Meng*

Introduction

There are huge investment opportunities in Africa, especially in infrastructure, where the benefits are expected to be high. In particular, Africa's absolute and relative lack of infrastructure points to the existence of untapped productive potential could be unlocked through scaling up investments in the sector. Notably, infrastructure plays a central role in improving competitiveness, facilitating domestic and international trade, and enhancing the continent's integration into the global economy. Coupled with better human development outcomes that improve infrastructure promises, the spillover effects and the dynamism that would be generated could support the continent's economic growth and poverty reduction efforts. Similarly, improved infrastructure could help eliminate some of the binding constraints to the realization of the benefits of globalization.

The estimated financing requirement to close Africa's infrastructure deficit amounts to US$93 billion annually until 2020.[1] In as much as this financing requirement is a challenge, African governments have a wide range of policy options that could open new sources of finance. The good news is governments have started exploring opportunities for tapping into private financing, creating new partnerships and reducing wastage in such investments. This strategic shift has come about on the realization that scaling up financing from traditional sources alone would not be adequate to close the infrastructure gap. Also, there is evidence that those countries that have invested strategically in infrastructure are reaping the benefits.[2] It is therefore crucial to open up opportunities to attract new investors as well as exploring new mechanisms for financing infrastructure in Africa.

It is in this context that this chapter attempts to assess Africa's infrastructure gaps and financing requirements to close such gaps. It also identifies financing sources and suggests new sources and financing instruments. This is followed by a brief narrative of the role of the African Development Bank (AfDB) in infrastructure. In concluding, the main message is that efforts by African governments to close the gaps present huge investment opportunities to all types of investors, especially the private sector.

The state of infrastructure supply in Africa

Infrastructure investments in Africa have not kept pace with growth in demand, creating a huge deficit. Less than 45% of the continent's population has access to electricity, less than half of rural population has access to an all-season road and only 5% of agriculture is under irrigation. The situation is no better for social infrastructure, with only 34% of the population having access to improved sanitation and a slightly better situation for clean water at about 65%. On the other hand, the information and communications technology (ICT) sub-sector is characterized by huge differences across specific services. In 2014, seven out of 10 Africans had access to mobile phones, with penetration rates growing fastest compared with the rest of the world. However, internet density is just above 200 persons per thousand (around two in 10), while the figure for fixed telephones is even lower.

Furthermore, Africa faces higher access costs compared with other developing countries. The continent's road freight is about four times more expensive, power costs 14 US cents per kilowatt-hour against 5–10 US cents and mobile telephony costs US$12 per month compared with US$8 elsewhere. There is no doubt that the African market is still underserved and the returns to investors are high. Investors that have gone into the telecommunications and finance sub-sectors, following improved regulatory conditions, have realized higher returns compared with any other region in the world. The United Nations Conference on Trade and Development reports that since 1990, the rate of return on foreign direct investment (FDI) in Africa has averaged 29%, and since 1991 it has been higher than in all other regions, in many years by a factor of two.[3]

Where do the opportunities lie?

Electricity

In 2013, only 43% of Africans had access to electricity compared with an average of 78% for all developing countries, 86% for developing

Asia and 95% for Latin America. The figure is even lower for Sub-Saharan Africa (SSA), currently at 32%. Furthermore, firms in Sub-Saharan African countries endured on average 8.5 power outages per month in 2015. The power outages were due largely to lack of regional interconnectivity of the electricity grids and shortages in affected countries (see Annex, Figure A12.1). During this period, regional surpluses in generation capacity were noted for all the five sub-regions (Figure 12.1). Some of the surplus countries like Morocco now have deficits due to increases in demand. The costs of power outages are significant, with Africa losing almost 7% of total sales due to power outages compared with around 3% in the other developing regions except for South Asia.(Figure 12.2). Therefore potential productivity gains from electricity supply, together with the associated income effect point to a market with significant growth potential.

Indeed the emergence of independent power producers (IPPs) signals sweeping changes in the power sector. For instance, the National Energy Regulator of South Africa has established a regulatory environment that would allow upward adjustments in tariffs and thus improve the viability of private sector suppliers. In Morocco, nearly two-thirds of electricity production is by private producers, the Jorf Lasfar Energy Company (presently Africa's largest IPP), Compagnie Eolienne de Detroit and Energie Electrique de Tahaddart.

More importantly, the majority of project financing for these companies was sourced from local Moroccan banks and the sector is now diversifying into clean energy and other more efficient and cheaper forms of energy.[4] These developments clearly show opportunities for private suppliers, in a sector that is characterized by shortages.

Transport infrastructure

Roads

SSA's total road network is only 204km per 1,000km^2 of land area, of which only about 25% is paved, compared with the world average of 944km per 1000km^2 of land area. This translates into 3.6km of road per 1,000 persons for the region, relative to a world average of about 7km per 1,000 persons. Behind these numbers, however, lie huge intra-African disparities (regional and trans-African links are missing; see Annex, Figure A12.2), with the availability of rural roads ranging from 0.5km per thousand of persons in Malawi to 35.5km in Namibia. Having realized the inadequacy of public funds in developing

Figure 12.1: Electricity balance in Africa; million kilowatt-hours (– deficit; + surplus)

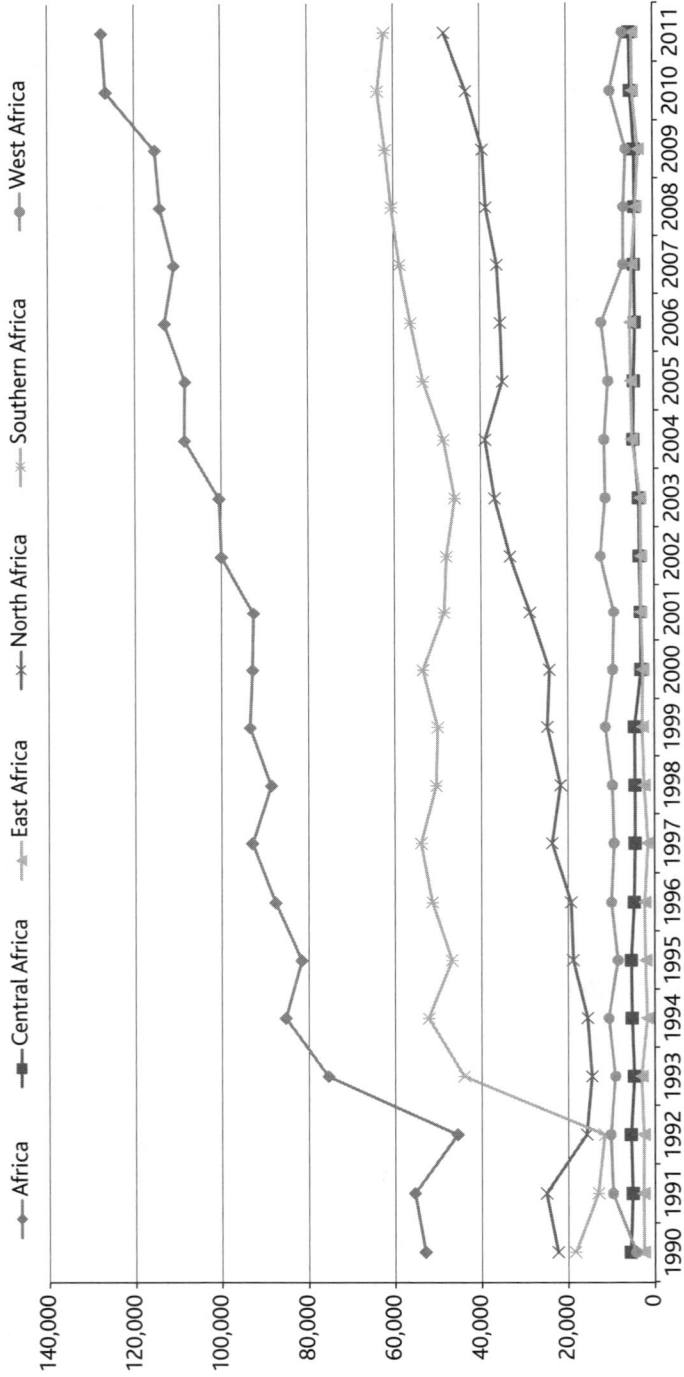

Source: UNdata, Energy Statistics Database

Figure 12.2: Value lost due to electricity outage (% of sales), 2003–2014

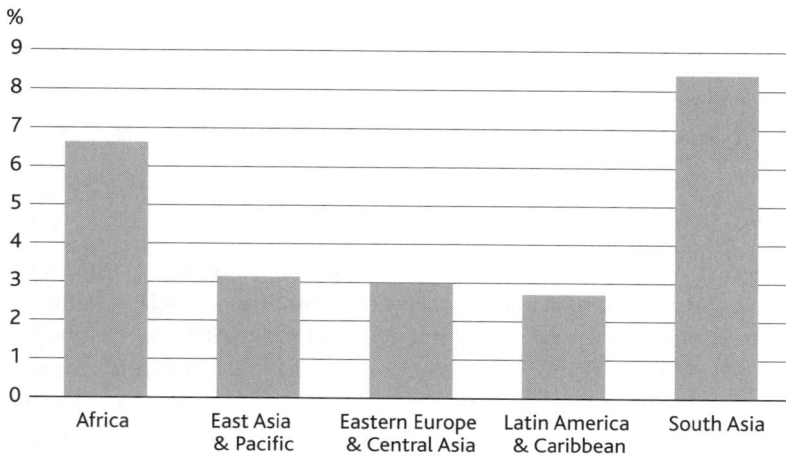

Source: World Development Indicators

road infrastructure, Africa is moving quickly into toll roads. While Africa was a late starter, it has increased private sector participation in roads. Between 1990 and 1999 Africa's private investments in roads was only US$1.4 billion, these investments increased by more than US$21 billion between 2000 and 2005.[5] The US$385 million Lekki-Epe toll road in Lagos is a recent example.

Such investments are expected to be even bigger in the near future, given the existing gaps in major road links. For example, the Maghreb Highway in North Africa is expected to cost US$11.5 billion over a 10-year period to 2018.

Rail

Rail networks are the least developed in Africa, with very little additions to the systems developed in the colonial period. The 1,067km long Tazara rail line developed in the 1970s is a notable exception. Since the 1990s, the lengths of rails have remained unchanged in many countries. Currently, Africa has 84,000km of rail track, for a surface of about 30 million square kilometers, most of it in Southern and Northern Africa. Thirteen SSA countries have no operational rail networks, while spatial density of operational rail ranges from 1 to 6. The network density for most African countries range from 30 to 50 per million people with a few countries (Gabon, Botswana and South Africa) having network densities of more than 400. These network densities are very low compared with Europe's range of 200 to 1,000. It is also notable that African exports are largely bulky primary commodities that can be moved more efficiently and at lower costs through rail than road transport. Rail development therefore holds some opportunities for investors. Investments in associated activities like locomotive building, logistics, and communications also exist.

Ports

Whereas Africa operates 64 ports, huge problems remain with respect to capacity and performance of existing facilities as well as handling costs. Over-the-quay container-handling performance is below 20 moves/hour, compared with 25–30 in modern terminals around the world. In addition, handling costs average 50% more than in other parts of the world. With about half of the coastal countries operating port facilities introducing sectoral legislation and regulatory reforms, new investment opportunities will come onboard. Currently, private investments in ports are low, yet there is a great need for transshipment facilities. Four regional hubs exist and these include Durban in Southern Africa, Mombasa and Dar-es-Salaam in East Africa, with Djibouti also emerging as a new hub. In West Africa, Abidjan used to play this role but has since lost it to Spain's Malaga due to civil war.

The challenge with regards to transport infrastructure is not only limited to the physical deficit but also suffers lack of linkages between roads and rail lines, and poor connectivity to ports. This has resulted in Africa being the world's worst rated region in the Logistics Performance Index in 2016, even though the picture varies considerably across countries. As Africa looks at scaling up infrastructure investments in the transport sector, the trade impact of such investments will spur growth and development.

This in turn will have spillover effects in all other sectors that open further opportunities for private sector investments. Within the transport subsector, investors have great opportunities in developing systems that improve intermodal efficiency.

Water and sanitation

Only 67% of Africans have access to clean water compared with 94% for East Asia and Pacific, and 95% for Latin America and the Caribbean. Significant progress has been made in this respect, with almost half of African countries (including Burkina Faso, Ghana, Malawi, Namibia and South Africa) having met the Millennium

Table 12.1: International Telecommunications Union ICT Development Index (IDI) 2013, top five per region

Regional IDI rank	Europe	Global IDI rank	Asia & Pacific	Global IDI rank	The Americas
1	Denmark	1	Korea (Rep.)	2	United States
2	Sweden	3	Hong Kong, China	9	Canada
3	Iceland	4	Japan	11	Barbados
4	United Kingdom	5	Australia	12	Uruguay
5	Norway	6	Singapore	16	St. Kitts and Nevis

Regional IDI rank	Arab States	Global IDI rank	CIS	Global IDI rank	Africa
1	Bahrain	27	Belarus	38	Mauritius
2	United Arab Emirates	32	Russian Federation	42	Seychelles
3	Qatar	34	Kazakhstan	53	South Africa
4	Saudi Arabia	47	Moldova	61	Cape Verde
5	Oman	52	Azerbaijan	64	Botswana

Source: International Telecommunications Union ICT Development Index 2013

Development Goal (MDG) target as of 2015. However, countries like Angola and Democratic Republic of the Congo are far from meeting the MDG target for clean water.

ICT

Access to fixed-line telephones is below 2% in SSA, compared with 17% in Latin America and the Caribbean, and 15% in the Middle East and North Africa. Mobile phone access in Africa (76%) is comparable to that in South Asia (78%) but trails East Asia and the Pacific (104%) and Latin America and the Caribbean (110%).

A similar situation holds for internet usage at the continental level, though North Africa is way ahead of all other African sub-regions (Figure 12.3). However, the ICT sector has seen increased investments in recent years, estimated at about US$21 billion in two years from 2007. The International Telecommunications Union (ITU) also notes that 45 countries have implemented appropriate regulatory frameworks that are supportive of private investment.

Despite some notable achievements in recent years, Africa's level of infrastructure development is still lower than other low-income

Figure 12.3: Regional internet users per 1,000 persons

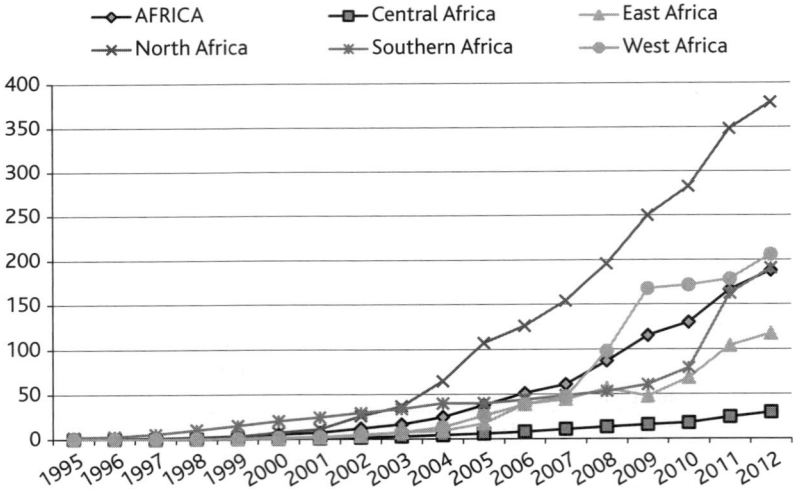

Source: International Telecommunication Union (2009, http://www.itu.int/en/ITU-D/
Statistics/Pages/definitions/regions.aspx)

regions (Figure 12.4). In particular, the energy sub-sector has the largest comparative deficit while total road density and access to clean water compare relatively well, though still lagging. For ICT, even the top five African countries are only ranked 70th to 104th on a global scale (Table 12.1). Sectoral regulatory reforms, however, have opened up opportunities for private sector investors as well as the donor community; such reforms have improved the business environment and enhanced efficiency in implementing and managing infrastructure investments.

International infrastructure comparison based on income levels

A comparison with other developing countries on the basis of income levels reveals a more severe picture of Africa's infrastructure deficit (Figure 12.4). Except for the higher road density in Africa, all other infrastructure indicators show the continent lagging. In spite of the higher total road density on the continent, however, most roads are in a poor state and remain unusable. Africa's position compared with other regions is only encouraging in the supply of clean water and sanitation facilities.

Africa's infrastructure deficit is more acute among its low-incomes countries (LICs) compared with middle-income countries (MICs). In this context, African LICs are for example four times worse off

Figure 12.4: International comparisons of infrastructure supply conditions

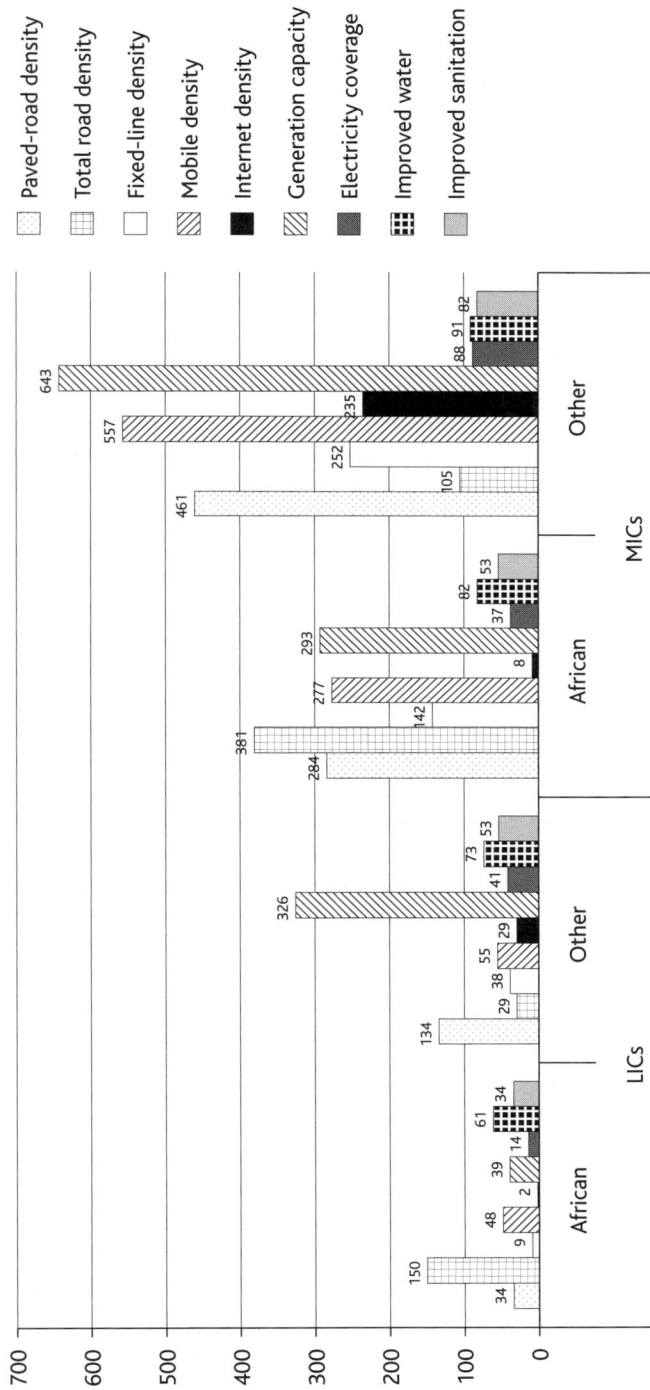

Source: Based on Foster and Briceño-Garmendia (2010).

compared with LICs from elsewhere in terms of paved-road density, while African MICs are less than twice as worse off relative to their peers in other regions.

For power generation, the figures are no better, with African LICs being eight times worse off (39 megawatts [MW] per million people compared with 326 MW) and MICs three times worse off compared with their counterparts elsewhere. For internet access, the situation is the reverse, with African MICs almost 30 times worse off compared with their peers elsewhere and LICs only 14 times (Figure 12.4). Overall disparities in infrastructure development are more pronounced for paved roads, fixed telephones, and internet access and power generation.

While the huge initial capital outlays requirements go a long a way in explaining these differences in infrastructure services, this is compounded by the extent of regulatory constraints in some of the countries, all of which impact on the level of risk faced by investors. Yet we acknowledge the significant changes that are taking place across Africa, including in LICs and post-conflict countries. For example, Rwanda was ranked as the best reformer in the 2010 *Doing Business* report.[6]

Rural–urban divide

There is a wide rural–urban divide in infrastructure supply, which is partly explained by rapid urbanization (about 4%) that Africa has been experiencing in recent years (Figure 12.5). Rural–urban migration, which accounts for about half of the urbanization rate, has taken place in spite of capacity constraints for local urban authorities to investment in infrastructure.

With about 65% of Africa's population living in rural areas, governments will need to invest more in rural infrastructure to ensure shared growth. This is because private sector investments will be extremely limited due to commercial viability problems especially in sparsely populated areas. Again, African cities are ranked at the bottom of developing cities worldwide with regards to urban infrastructure.[8] Intra-African differences are also large, with Dakar having more than 1,500 meters of paved road per thousand inhabitants, which is about four times higher than the next best case (Lagos). At the other extreme, Kinshasa has just 63 meters of paved road per thousand inhabitants, barely half that of the next worst city (Dar-es-Salaam).

The quality and access to basic services in urban areas are both poor. Yet urban centers present the greatest opportunity for infrastructure

Figure 12.5: International infrastructure: rural-urban divide[7]

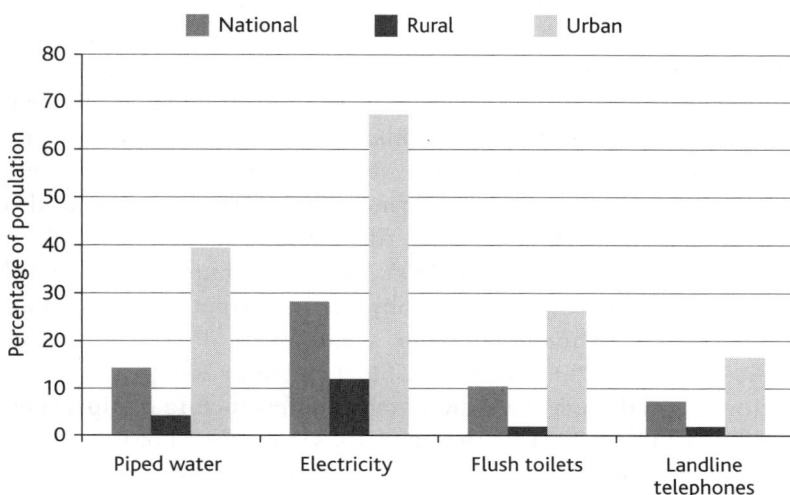

development due to the high population densities. UN-Habitat recommends that building standards in urban areas would need to be reviewed to take into account income differentials if affordable housing is to be provided by the private sector. In this context, urban development by-laws are being revamped in concert with regulatory reforms at the national levels. This will allow greater private sector investments in the housing and the commercial property sector, including the associated social infrastructure and conservation of the environment. Improvements in the urban environment would have a positive impact on investment flows and the potential for cities to generate the necessary economic dynamism that supports growth.

Africa's infrastructure financing requirements

Infrastructure financing requirements in Africa's MICs are estimated at about 10% of GDP per year until 2020.[9] While in absolute terms LICs will require a smaller amount than MICs, their investment needs are even higher, at about 15% of GDP per year. This implies overall investments of between US$93 billion per year over the next decade, depending on the realized level of GDP growth. This estimate is well above that of the United Nations (US$52 billion) in 2008,[10] about 75% of which is to go to MICs. The required investments in infrastructure are therefore about twice the current level that has been realized to date. It is almost certain that it will be impossible to scale up investments from current financing sources alone if the demand is to be met. New sources of financing have to be identified and developed while at the same time making greater efforts to maximize the potential of existing infrastructure financing mechanisms.

Though daunting, this challenge is not insurmountable. Indeed, private investors and the donor community have increased financing for infrastructure projects in recent years, a trend that continued even through the recent global financial and economic crisis. In this context, infrastructure financing in Africa rose to about US$42 billion in 2007 from US$40 billion in 2006. Despite the impact of the global economic downturn, investments by the Infrastructure Consortium for Africa (ICA) members alone went up by 45%, from about US$14 billion in 2008 to almost US$20 billion in 2009.[11]

However, although the share of aid in infrastructure has increased (e.g. from 11% in 2004 to 19% in 2013, see Figure 12.6) it has been less consistent and unpredictable; yet there is high dependency on aid in some countries (see Annex, Table A12.1). It is also noteworthy that Africa currently meets about two-thirds of its infrastructure spending from domestic sources. In addition, the improved policy and business environment is attracting increasing levels of private sector participation through public–private partnerships.

Figure 12.6: Aid dependency and aid allocations to infrastructure

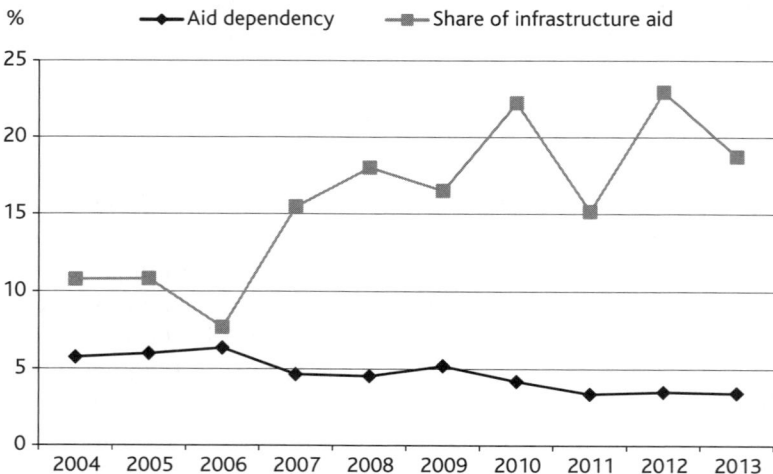

Mobilizing financing for infrastructure in Africa

Public infrastructure financing across Africa falls far short of its infrastructure needs and aid alone cannot close this gap. In fact, in several African LICs, official aid is not projected to increase in line with public investment spending.[12] Therefore financing options for closing Africa's infrastructure gaps should focus on broadening the sources of finance and a better allocation of public resources (both domestic and donor funds). This is particularly important given the capital intensity of infrastructure projects. In Nigeria, for instance, a ball-park estimation of the amount of investment required to expand energy generation capacity from 10,000 MW to 30,000 MW is between US$25 and US$30 billion.[13]

MICs have better prospects in securing such amounts of financing compared with LICs due to the latter's low levels of financial market development, capacity constraints and perceptions of high risk that limit private sector participation.[14] However, both categories of countries must pay particular attention to the regulatory environment. Africa's infrastructure sector is still dominated by monopolistic incumbents that resist market reforms. While progress has been made in this regard, more still has to be done. For instance, in South Africa entry is still regarded as highly restricted in telecommunications, rail freight and electricity sub-sectors compared countries in the Organisation for Economic Co-operation and Development. Continent-wide, 20 out of 26 countries score less than 5 out of a possible maximum of 10 on the services market liberalization index.[15]

In this context, greater efforts in identifying alternative and innovative financing mechanisms for infrastructure should be directed towards enhancing private sector participation. Such efforts will have to be complemented with greater efficiency in the allocation of public resources.

Mobilizing foreign private capital flows to co-finance infrastructure

South–South partnerships in infrastructure financing are gaining traction, with developing economies' share in Africa's annual FDI inflows having increased from around 17.7% in 1999 to around 21% in 2008. South–South FDI investment flows into Africa are estimated at more than US$60 billion since 2003.[16]

For instance, Chinese investments have increased markedly in recent years, rising from less than US$1 billion in 2003 to over US$30 billion in 2014. A total of 40 African countries have particularly benefited, with about 16% of the resources flowing into infrastructure. Average allocations of these flows over the 2001–2007 period show that the electricity and transport sub-sectors have benefited most (Figures 12.7 and 12.8). It is also noted that the largest recipients of Chinese FDI into infrastructure in Africa are Nigeria, Angola, Sudan and Ethiopia. China has also invested in the transport sub-sector in Nigeria, Gabon and Mauritania.

Alternative domestic and regional private sources of financing infrastructure

Infrastructure bonds

Kenya, for example, has successfully issued domestic infrastructure bonds, raising almost KSH 30 billion (US$370 million). However, financial markets are small in some of Africa's economies such that

Figure 12.7: Chinese investments by country, 2001–2007

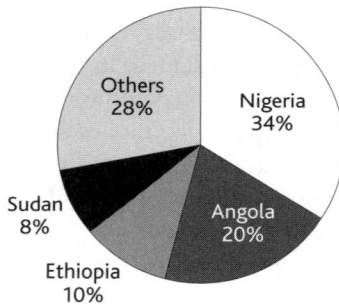

Figure 12.8: Chinese investments by sector, 2001–2007

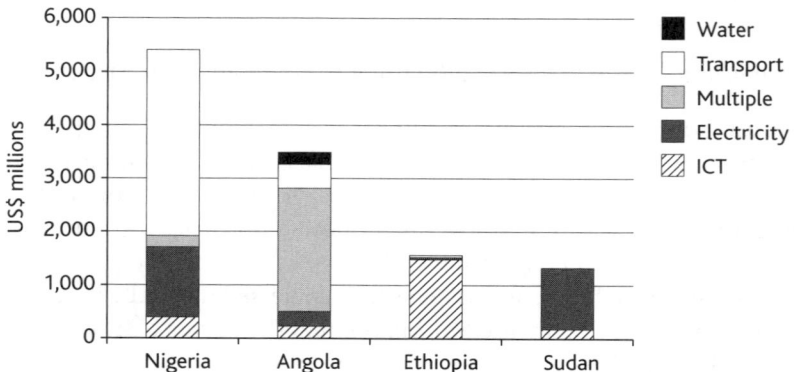

a regional approach to raising financing through similar instruments would be required.

Sovereign wealth funds

Sovereign wealth funds are another important source of investment funds, with the Libyan Arab African Investment Company (for instance) making investments worth US$800 million in 13 African countries in 2008 alone.[17]

Commodity-linked bonds

Commodity-linked bonds are yet to be explored in Africa. With some of the continent's export commodities being traded on the futures market, there are possibilities to issue commodity-linked bonds whose proceeds could be used to boost infrastructure investments.

If LDCs had issued debt contracts that were tied to their main export commodities, their debt burden would decline along with plummeting export prices.[18] Such commodity-linked bonds can therefore help hedge against fluctuations in commodity export earnings and minimize the risk of debt distress when commodity prices fall.

The role of the African Development Bank in infrastructure development

Increased focus by the AfDB is aimed at catalyzing and leveraging larger resources flows, promoting regional infrastructure connectivity, narrowing the development gaps among African economies, promoting efficient use of regional infrastructure and reducing the costs to users, and addressing country specific infrastructure capacity constraints.

Infrastructure financing by the AfDB

In line with the bank's Ten-Year Strategy 2013-2022, infrastructure financing alone accounts for more than half of bank operations. More than US$3.6 billion in 2014 out of total operations worth USD6.6 billion was invested in infrastructure of all types. Infrastructure financing currently accounts for more than half of the bank's portfolio. The energy sub-sector received the largest share of 53% (Figure 12.9). This was mainly in response to power outages and the energy shortage in many countries. The overall approval for infrastructure in 2014 represents an increase of 22% compared with 2013.[19]

Figure 12.9: Sectoral distribution of AfDB approvals for infrastructure, 2014

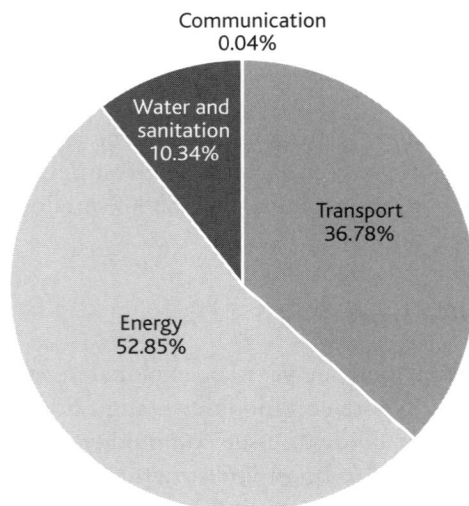

Source: African Development Bank Annual Report 2014

African leaders' aspirations, as expressed in the creation of the New Economic Partnership for Africa's Development (NEPAD) in 2001, are supportive of strong partnerships with global and regional institutions. In this context, the bank has been involved in the NEPAD Short-Term Action Plan, the NEPAD Medium-to-Long-Term Strategic Framework, the African Union Infrastructure Master Plan Initiative, and the Program for Infrastructure Development in Africa, which was launched in July 2010. Other initiatives targeting the infrastructure sector include the NEPAD Infrastructure Project Preparation Fund (IPPF),[20] the ICA and the EU-Africa Partnership on Infrastructure. At the end of May 2010, IPPF had an active portfolio of 41 projects (53 in the pipeline until 2015) and has initiated regional infrastructure projects worth around US$4.7 billion, representing a huge leveraging potential.[21]

An Africa Action Plan priority projects list, worth about US$32 billion, has also been drawn up. Main target projects on this list reflect the magnitude of infrastructure gaps as discussed earlier, with energy being the dominant sub-sector. The major projects include the US$20 billion Nigeria–Algeria gas connection project, and the Sambangalou Kaleta Hydropower and Kenya–Ethiopia Interconnection, both of which are worth more than US$1 billion.

The African Development Bank also committed more than US$4 billion to ICA in two years (2007–2008), representing about

24% of total contributions to the initiative. The EU Africa Partnership on Infrastructure's strategy aims at enhancing good governance, peace and security, economic growth, trade, regional integration and interconnectivity, health, education, and a safe environment. With this focus, this partnership seeks to reduce wastage through improved efficiency and environment friendly development. With this focus, the partnership seeks to reduce wastage through improved efficiency and environmentally friendly development.

Improvements in physical infrastructure have been complemented with "soft" infrastructure development, through capacity building and partnerships; harmonization of legislation, regulations, and technical standards; and trade facilitation activities in collaboration with national and regional agencies to drive regional integration on the continent.

Conclusion

Private sector investment opportunities in Africa's infrastructure are huge and work to identify the projects is underway. Regulatory reforms in both LICs and MICs have also been identified as critical to the realization of the expected investment flows. It has been clearly noted there are infrastructure deficiencies in all subsectors, with LICs facing the greatest challenge. Inefficiencies in implementing infrastructure projects account for US$17 billion annually and improving the capacity of African countries will help minimize these costs. In this regard, the donor community should play a greater role in African LICs, while innovative financing mechanisms must be the focus in MICs. Notably, traditional sources of financing infrastructure development remain important but private investment is critical in closing the current gaps and meeting future infrastructure demand in Africa.

Notes

[1] Foster, V. and Briceño-Garmendia, C. (2010) *Africa's Infrastructure: A Time for Transformation.* Washington, DC: The World Bank. ISBN 978-0-8213-8041-3

[2] The link between infrastructure and growth in African countries (South Africa, Nigeria, Uganda and others) has been shown to be positive (Foster and Briceño-Garmendia, 2010).

[3] www.un.org/ecosocdev/geninfo/afrec/subjindx/132inves.htm

[4] www.informaworld.com/smpp/content~db=all~ content=a789690695

[5] www.emergingafricafund.com/Files/MediaFiles/G8%20Africa%20 Infrastructure%20Conf%20June%2009.ppt.

[6] The World Bank (2010). *Doing Business 2010: Reforming through difficult times*. http://www.doingbusiness.org/~/media/GIAWB/Doing%20Business/Documents/Annual-Reports/English/DB10-FullReport.pdf

[7] Foster, V. and Briceño-Garmendia, C. (2010) Op. cit.

[8] Mercer (2010) 'Quality of Living Survey', available at www.mercer.com/qualityoflivingpr. Most of the region's cities rank below 100 in the eco-index. The highest-ranking cities are Cape Town (30), Victoria (38) and Johannesburg (54). Antananarivo in Madagascar (217) is at the bottom of the list.

[9] Africa Infrastructure Country Diagnostic (2009), World Bank, African Development Bank, African Union, Agence Française de Développement, European Union, New Economic Partnership for Africa's Development, Public–Private Infrastructure Advisory Facility, and UK Department for International Development (DfID).

[10] Foster, V. and Briceño-Garmendia, C. (2010) Op. cit.

[11] www.afdb.org/en/newsevents/article/6th-infrastructure-consortiumfor-africa-ica-annual-meeting-agreement-forcloser-collaboration-on-regional-projectsamong-stakeholders-6689/

[12] Redifer, L. (2010) *New Financing Sources for Africa's Infrastructure Deficit*, IMF Survey, July. Washington DC: International Monetary Fund. Available at http://www.imf.org/external/pubs/ft/survey/so/2010/car072110b.htm

[13] Anyanwu, J.C. (2009) 'Public–private partnerships in the Nigerian energy sector: banks' roles and lessons of experience,' in J.B. Tobin and L.R. Parker (eds) *Joint Ventures, Mergers and Acquisitions, and Capital Flow*. New York, Nya; Nova Science Publishers.

[14] Shah, R. and Batley, R. (2009) 'Private-sector investment in infrastructure: rationale and causality of pro-poor impacts', *Development Policy Review*, vol 27, no 4, pp 397-417.

[15] OECD (Organisation for Economic Co-operation and Development) (2010) 'Going for growth in Brazil, China, India, Indonesia and South Africa,' in *Economic Policy Reforms: Going for Growth*, May. OECD Publishing. Available at www.oecd.org/eco/growth/economicpolicyreformsgoingforgrowth2010.htm

[16] Stevens, J. and Freemantle, S. (2010) 'BRIC and Africa: new sources of foreign capital mobilizing for Africa complementing and competing with traditional investors', Standard Bank, South Africa.

[17] www.oecd.org/dataoecd/31/36/41865534.pdf

[18] Atta-Mensah, J. (2004) *Commodity-Linked Bonds: A Potential Means for Less-Developed Countries to Raise Foreign Capital*, Bank of Canada Working Paper 2004-20. Bank of Canada.

[19] The key infrastructure projects approved by the bank in 2014 included a multinational road development and transport facilitation Program in the Mano River Union in West Africa, Cameroon's Batschenga-Ntui-Yoko-Tibati-Ngaoundere road project, a corporate loan to Transnet, South Africa's national rail transport company, for its modernization program. The African Development Bank Group (African Development Fund and the African Development Bank) also approved power projects in Angola, Kenya, Mauritius, Morocco, Nigeria and South Africa.

[20] The bank's commitment to this fund at the end of 2007/08 was US$18 million, with US$22.5 million committed by UK's DfID, Germany and Norway. Other countries have shown interest to contribute to the fund.

[21] The World Bank's Multilateral Investment Guarantee Agency is also providing information on infrastructure investment opportunities in Africa where it has identified 162 projects in all sub-sectors.

Annex

Figure A12.1: Africa's power networks: missing links and AfDB Group-financed projects

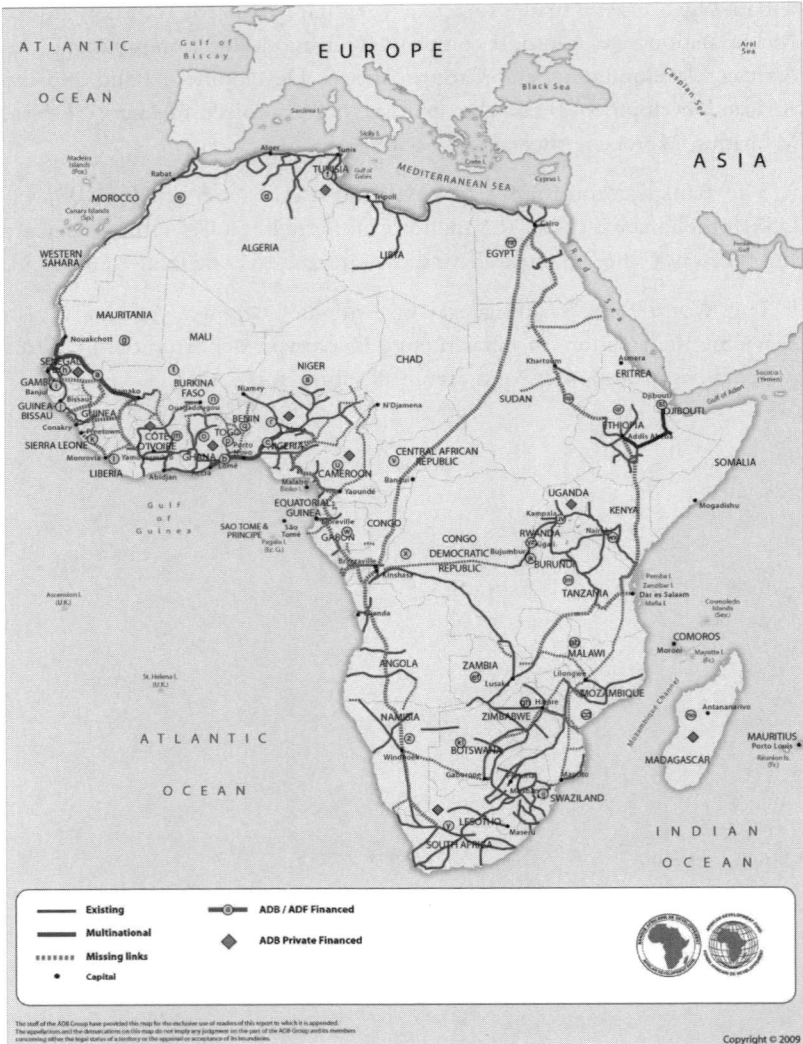

Figure A12.2: Africa's main road corridors: missing links and AfDB Group-financed projects

Table A12.1: Aid, aid allocations to infrastructure and aid dependency in African countries, 2013

Country name	Total aid (US$m)	Infrastructure aid (US$m)	Aid dependency (%)	Share of infrastructure aid (%)
Algeria	574.51	6.95	0.27	1.21
Angola	446.00	5.31	0.36	1.19
Benin	645.00	83.77	7.66	12.99
Botswana	110.75	1.74	0.78	1.57
Burkina Faso	1,140.91	311.27	8.89	27.28
Burundi	611.55	173.96	24.51	28.45
Cameroon	869.23	166.25	2.98	19.13
Cape Verde	400.32	38.46	21.80	9.61
Central African Rep.	241.85	7.34	15.28	3.03
Chad	442.49	20.60	3.29	4.66
Comoros	124.95	48.72	21.23	38.99
Congo, Dem. Rep.	2,184.38	305.33	5.88	13.98
Congo, Rep.	120.61	17.73	0.85	14.70
Côte d'Ivoire	1,582.54	79.97	5.68	5.05
Djibouti	332.18	75.05	23.20	22.59
Egypt	7,628.61	1,273.94	3.10	16.70
Equatorial Guinea	13.18	3.73	0.07	28.25
Eritrea	35.19	0.02	1.02	0.07
Ethiopia	3,137.62	502.94	6.42	16.03
Gabon	59.82	0.08	0.31	0.14
Gambia	146.28	51.48	14.61	35.19
Ghana	1,210.67	157.14	2.93	12.98
Guinea	788.24	164.32	11.91	20.85
Guinea-Bissau	92.13	2.06	8.78	2.24
Kenya	2,974.74	392.30	6.63	13.19
Lesotho	199.27	15.95	11.64	8.01
Liberia	794.07	361.74	35.33	45.56
Libya	187.07	14.84	0.23	7.94
Madagascar	591.84	168.95	5.68	28.55
Malawi	1,468.02	363.54	37.44	24.76
Mali	2,455.85	154.34	22.23	6.28
Mauritania	696.84	211.22	15.38	30.31
Mauritius	267.26	149.25	2.03	55.84
Morocco	2,885.27	961.12	2.68	33.31
Mozambique	2,766.05	675.06	16.99	24.41
Namibia	336.56	19.79	2.85	5.88
Niger	1,070.84	145.50	14.87	13.59

(continued)

Table A12.1: Aid, aid allocations to infrastructure and aid dependency in African countries, 2013 (continued)

Country name	Total aid (US$m)	Infrastructure aid (US$m)	Aid dependency (%)	Share of infrastructure aid (%)
Nigeria	2,837.78	377.86	0.55	13.32
Rwanda	1,411.36	325.28	21.22	23.05
Sao Tome and Principe	54.88	10.04	16.92	18.30
Senegal	1,238.60	93.07	9.08	7.51
Seychelles	52.96	0.00	3.68	0.00
Sierra Leone	607.42	230.27	11.87	37.91
South Africa	1,840.44	309.05	0.55	16.79
South Sudan	1,936.44	153.40	16.45	7.92
Sudan	1,286.22	292.40	1.83	22.73
Swaziland	80.62	0.03	2.44	0.04
Tanzania	3,390.45	1,307.22	10.78	38.56
Togo	304.89	87.20	7.88	28.60
Tunisia	1,463.45	612.41	3.25	41.85
Uganda	1,894.25	258.18	8.07	13.63
Zambia	1,449.41	126.76	5.66	8.75
Zimbabwe	519.34	12.28	5.01	2.36
Total Africa	60,001.18	11,327.22	3.48	18.74

Comparative analysis of costs of some selected infrastructure components across Africa

Oliver Chinganya, Abdoulaye Adam and Marc Kouakou

Introduction

The incentive to invest in an economic activity is affected by factors such as the cost of labor, the available infrastructure such as transportation and information and communications technology (ICT), and the regulatory and fiscal environment. A potential investor will be drawn to regions or countries that promise to deliver the greatest economic gains. A measure for making such comparisons is the Price Level Index (PLI), which is derived by dividing the purchasing power parity (PPP) index by the corresponding exchange rate. A PLI represents the average percentage by which the prices of goods and services in country X, when converted into country Z's currency at the current exchange rate, exceed or fall below the prices of the same goods and services in country Z. Because the PLI is usually measured in percentages, a PLI of 100 denotes that the price levels in both countries are the same. A higher or lower PLI indicates higher or lower costs, respectively. When currencies are converted using market exchange rates, they provide a comparison at a single point in time of relative purchasing power of one currency over another. However, this is a somewhat distorted picture, since exchange rates are volatile and the comparison does not take the price levels into account. Price level indices are better determinants. They can be used to make investment decisions, for example, whether to transfer capital from one country to another, or whether to alter the composition of an investment portfolio by switching economic activities, depending on the comparative advantage and economies of scale in one country over another.

According to the Africa Infrastructure Country Diagnostic (AICD) report *Overhauling the Engine of Growth: Infrastructure in Africa* (Foster, 2008), African countries devote 6% to 8% of their gross domestic product (GDP) to infrastructure. Calderón and Servén (2008) argue that across Africa, infrastructure contributed 99 basis points to per capita economic growth over the 1990 to 2005 period, whereas the contribution of structural policies represented 68 basis points. This infrastructural contribution is almost entirely attributable to advances in the telecommunications sector. Foster notes that deterioration in the energy infrastructure over the same period has had a significant lagging effect on economic growth in a number of African countries.

An article by Olu Ajakaiye and Mthuli Ncube (2010) argues that the cost of doing business in Sub-Saharan Africa is higher than in any other global region, with infrastructure services making up a disproportionately large part of production and trade costs. This viewpoint is supported by the World Economic Forum's *Global Competitiveness Report 2010-2011* (WEF 2013), which points out that although some African countries such as South Africa and Mauritius have made great strides, Sub-Saharan Africa as a whole lags behind the rest of the world in terms of competitiveness. This is largely attributable to a severe deficit in the quality, quantity, and ease of access to infrastructure services. Although some schools of thought suggest that the relationship between infrastructure development and economic development is far from clear-cut, evidence from other studies indicates that good infrastructure is making a major contribution to reducing inequality and improving growth in all regions of the world except Africa. The poor quality and low level of accessibility of Africa's infrastructure has a negative impact on the continent's productivity and growth, and acts as a major disincentive to foreign direct investment and domestic investment, as well as curtailing international trade.

A working paper by the African Development Bank (AfDB, 2010),[1] highlights the role of infrastructure in improving a nations' competitiveness and in facilitating domestic and international trade. Poor infrastructure means higher delivery costs, which, in turn, increase the price of goods in domestic and export markets. Moreover, this must be set against the background of the recent fuel and food crises, which led to hikes and volatility in commodity prices, rendering Africa more vulnerable to exogenous shocks and further weakening its competitiveness.

Methodology

This chapter provides a cost comparison for selected infrastructure components across countries using PLIs. It defines the PLI as the ratio of PPP to a corresponding market exchange rate. The PPPs were calculated using the African average as the base, that is, they were normalized with the average for Africa = 1.0. The PLI is not designed to measure inflation from one year to the next; rather, it is used to compare the cost of six selected infrastructure components—housing, water, electricity, transportation, communication, and construction—among 48 African countries, using price data collected from the International Comparison Program (ICP) round of 2005. The infrastructure components selected represent major drivers of an economy's development. A descriptive analysis of each of the six infrastructure components is provided.

A principal component analysis (PCA) is performed to explain the variation of a few uncorrelated linear combinations of the original variables. This was undertaken to shed light on the multivariate nature of the infrastructure components and to identify similarities among countries. However, because PCA is an exploratory method, the question of whether these objectives can be achieved through the use of principal components cannot be ascertained in advance of the analysis of the numerical results. The chapter concludes with a summary of results.

Price Level Indices results

The Price Level Indices for the six selected infrastructure components are presented in Table 13.1.

Infrastructure components

Transportation

This component includes passenger transportation by rail, road, air, sea and inland waterways, and other purchased transport services. Table 13.1 shows a ranking of countries from the most to the least expensive transportation price levels. The distribution of PLI varies widely, resulting in a relative variation (coefficient of variation) of 39.4%. This could be attributed to the high cost of air travel on the continent. Poor road and rail networks in many parts of Africa, and between ports and the hinterland, also contribute to high transport costs, and therefore, high PLIs. In 22 of 48 countries (nearly half), the transport PLIs are less than 1.0, ranging from 0.4 (Egypt) to 0.99 (Senegal).

Costs were highest in Zimbabwe, followed by Angola, Comoros, and the Central African Republic. The countries with the lowest costs

Table 13.1: Price Level Indices for the six selected infrastructure components

Country	Housing	Water	Electricity	Gas	Other fuels	Transport	Communication	Construction
Angola	0.66	4.44	1.2	0.82	2.43	1.47	1.72	1.24
Benin	0.76	0.97	0.59	0.78	0.61	0.87	1.62	0.7
Botswana	1.17	1.51	1.27	1.67	1.34	1.07	0.82	0.94
Burkina Faso	0.7	0.82	0.62	0.69	0.76	1.12	1.25	0.89
Burundi	0.74	0.38	1.05	2.49	0.61	0.89	0.38	0.6
Cameroon	1.02	0.89	0.82	0.9	1.03	0.87	1.54	1.13
Cape Verde	4.47	4.19	1.13	1.24	1.42	1.12	1.02	1.3
Central African Republic	0.35	0.86	1.01	2.17	0.65	1.35	1.3	1.19
Chad	0.34	1.24	1	1.51	0.91	1.1	1.6	1.3
Comoros	1.73	1.22	1.73	2.22	...	1.37	1.2	0.82
Congo	1.31	1.61	0.83	0.88	1.08	1.24	1.63	1.98
Côte d'Ivoire	1.08	1.17	0.7	0.65	1.04	1.17	1.5	3.03
Djibouti	1.13	0.83	1.51	1.69	1.85	1.16	0.94	0.91
Egypt	0.92	0.66	2.44	3.19	2.57	0.4	0.65	0.54
Equatorial Guinea	1.69	...	1.42	1.22	2.3	1.29	2.06	2.24
Ethiopia	0.65	0.36	0.93	1.11	1.08	0.49	0.5	0.57
Gabon	2.02	1.99	1.21	1.1	1.84	1.27	1.62	1.04
Gambia	0.19	0.68	1.03	1.77	0.83	0.82	0.57	0.83
Ghana	0.15	1.19	0.66	0.59	1.01	0.86	0.99	0.83
Guinea	0.47	0.77	0.87	2.56	0.41	0.81	0.79	0.78
Guinea-Bissau	0.58	1.26	1.17	1.78	1.06	1.06	2.34	0.78
Kenya	0.45	1.39	0.98	1.63	0.81	0.94	1.34	0.93
Lesotho	0.78	1.47	0.95	1.44	0.87	1.01	1.34	1.53
Liberia	1.53	3.68	1.2	2.52	0.79	1.24	1.24	1.22
Madagascar	1.02	0.36	0.69	1.43	0.46	0.83	0.71	0.67
Mali	1.08	0.81	0.82	1.24	0.76	0.95	1.17	1.09
Mauritania	0.32	1.68	0.95	0.78	1.59	0.88	1.15	0.84
Mauritius	2.06	0.67	0.54	0.7	0.57	1.19	0.49	1.09
Morocco	1.63	2.35	0.73	0.41	1.78	1	0.97	1.32
Mozambique	0.49	0.92	0.67	1.03	0.61	1.16	1.28	1.54
Namibia	1.95	2.27	1.99	2.27	2.4	1.13	1.21	1.51
Niger	0.66	1.08	0.91	1.26	0.9	1.02	1.2	0.84
Nigeria	0.52	1.15	1.26	1.78	1.23	0.79	1.14	1.1
Rwanda	1.31	0.59	0.72	0.94	0.76	0.88	0.95	0.8
São Tomé and Principe	0.87	1.74	1.51	2.26	1.4	0.96	1.22	1.18

(continued)

Table 13.1: Price level indices for the six selected infrastructure components (continued)

Country	Housing	Water	Electricity	Gas	Other fuels	Transport	Communication	Construction
Senegal	0.73	1.52	1.2	1.42	1.4	0.99	0.74	0.92
Sierra Leone	0.34	1.97	0.86	1.97	0.52	0.89	1.47	0.61
South Africa	1.78	1.21	1.57	2.06	1.66	1.08	0.99	1.56
Sudan	0.78	2.45	0.9	0.54	2.04	0.79	1.03	1.33
Swaziland	1.74	1.8	1.95	1.58	3.32	1	1.13	1.34
Tanzania	0.76	1.75	1.1	2.05	0.81	0.82	1.21	0.76
Togo	0.45	1.19	0.52	0.55	0.68	0.99	1.62	1.26
Tunisia	1.57	0.4	0.82	0.37	2.52	0.98	0.69	0.9
Uganda	0.9	1.36	0.84	1.95	0.5	0.93	1.37	0.88
Zambia	2.65	0.42	1.13	1.93	0.91	1.3	2.28	1.09
Zimbabwe	4.85	n.a.	5.54	n.a.	5.83	3.56	2.28	1.28
Average	1.00	1.00	1.00	1.00	1.00	1.00	1.00	1.00
Standard deviation	0.93	0.91	0.77	0.75	0.95	0.42	0.46	0.46
Coefficient of variation (%)	93	91	77	75	95	42	46	46

Note: n.a.=not available

were Egypt, Ethiopia, and Nigeria. The transport PLI for Zimbabwe—more than 250% above the African average—is an outlier, and, in part, reflects the massive inflation the country was experiencing as a result of its economic crisis. As well, the economic embargo imposed on the country would likely have contributed to deterioration in its infrastructure.

As indicated earlier, PLIs are not intended to rank countries in a strict hierarchy, but rather, to indicate the magnitude of price levels in one country relative to others. A counter-intuitive finding is that price levels of neighboring countries are not always of the same order of magnitude.

Communication

Communication includes postal services, telephone (cell phones and landlines), internet, and so on. These services facilitate communication for public and private enterprises within and between countries. As shown in Table 13.1, Guinea-Bissau, Zimbabwe, and Zambia have the highest communication PLIs, and Burundi, Mauritius, Ethiopia, the Gambia and Egypt, the lowest. Guinea-Bissau, the most expensive, has a communication PLI of 2.34, while Burundi is the cheapest at 0.38. The coefficient of variation is about 37%, indicating relatively high price variation among countries.

Thirty-four countries (71%) record PLIs for communication above the African average, ranging from 1.02 in Cape Verde to 2.34 in Guinea-Bissau. Intuitively, the cost of telecommunication services between neighboring countries or those located in regional economic communities (RECs) might be expected to be roughly equivalent. However, based on the price data collected from the ICP 2005 round, this is not the case. Provision of communication services, particularly for telephones, seems to be differentiated and fragmented across countries. And even when countries share the same service provider, the cost of the service often varies widely, for instance, for mobile telephony.

Construction

This includes construction of residential buildings, non-residential buildings, and civil engineering works. PLIs vary widely among countries, with a coefficient of variation of 42.5%. PLIs for construction were lowest in Malawi, Egypt, Ethiopia, and Burundi—Malawi was the cheapest at 0.35. The highest PLIs were in Côte d'Ivoire, Equatorial Guinea, Congo Republic, South Africa, and Lesotho. Côte d'Ivoire recorded the highest costs, at 50% above the African average.

Housing

This component includes actual and imputed rentals for housing and maintenance, plus the cost of repair for dwellings. The distribution of the PLIs for housing in Table 13.1 shows that Zimbabwe is, by far, the most expensive country, followed by Cape Verde, Zambia, and Mauritius. At the other end of the scale, Ghana enjoys the lowest housing costs, followed by the Gambia and Mauritania. The coefficient of variation for the housing PLI is 81.4%, revealing significantly high variation among countries.

This includes water supply and miscellaneous services, such as sanitation and sewage. Also included are associated costs such as the hire of meters, the reading of meters, and standing charges. The cost excludes drinking water sold in bottles or containers, and hot water or steam supplied by distinct heating plants. The distribution of water PLIs in Table 13.1 shows high price dispersion across countries, indicated by a coefficient of variation of 64.7%. Water is most expensive in Angola, followed by Cape Verde and Liberia, while it is cheapest in Ethiopia, Madagascar, Burundi, Tunisia, and Zambia.

Electricity

The PLI for electricity includes associated costs, such as the hire and reading of meters and standing charges. Table 13.1 also shows substantial electricity price variation across countries, indicated by a coefficient variation of 64.9%. The cost of electricity in Zimbabwe is, by, far the highest, with prices 454% above the African average. The two countries with the next highest costs (though far below Zimbabwe) are Egypt and the Democratic Republic of Congo. Prices in the latter might be expected to be lower, given the country's production potential, but the 2005 ICP data refute this. The lowest electricity costs are in Togo, Mauritius, and Benin.

Principal component analysis and scatter plot

A PCA for all the infrastructure components under study (housing, water, electricity, transportation, communication, and construction) was performed to explain the total variation with a few uncorrelated linear combinations of the original variables, called *principal components*. The number of principal components in the analysis is less than or equal to the number of original variables. This transformation is defined so that the first principal component has the highest possible variance among all linear combinations of the original variables, while each succeeding component has the next highest variance possible under the constraint that it be uncorrelated with the preceding components.

The PCA in Table 13.2 shows that most of the total variation is explained by the first four principal components (83%), with the first two accounting for 57%. The correlation coefficients of these components with variables used in the analysis are presented in Table 13.3. The first number is the correlation coefficient and the second number in parentheses is the observed significance level of the null hypothesis of a zero correlation coefficient.

The first component, which accounts for about 36% of the total variation, is correlated with housing (0.57), water (0.66), transportation (0.81), communication (0.59), and construction (0.61). It may be

Table 13.2: Proportion of variation explained by first four components

Component	Eigenvalue	Difference	Proportion (%)	Cumulative (%)
Component 1	2.182	0.942	36	36
Component 2	1.240	0.351	21	57
Component 3	0.889	0.208	15	72
Component 4	0.684	–	11	83

Source: Computed from International Comparison Program – Africa, 2005 database.

Table 13.3: Correlation coefficients of the three principal components with variables

Infrastructure components	Component 1	Component 2	Component 3	Component 4
Housing	0.57 (<0.0001)	0.52 (0.0002)	−0.39 (0.006)	0.09 (0.527)
Water	0.66 (<0.0001)	0.24 (0.097)	−0.005 (0.973)	−0.66 (<0.0001)
Electricity	0.17 (0.247)	0.76 (<0.0001)	0.45 (0.002)	0.33 (0.023)
Transportation	0.81 (<0.0001)	−0.17 (0.254)	0.13 (0.380)	0.11 (0.468)
Communication	0.59 (<0.0001)	−0.45 (0.001)	0.55 (<0.0001)	0.045 (0.767)
Construction	0.61 (<0.0001)	−0.302 (0.041)	−0.46 (0.0013)	0.34 (0.022)

Source: Computed from International Comparison Program – Africa, 2005 database.

interpreted as a measure of price levels on all infrastructure components except electricity. Countries with relatively high costs for housing, water, transport, communication, and construction will have large values for this component.

The second component is positively correlated with housing (0.52) and electricity (0.76), and negatively correlated with communication (−0.45) and construction (−0.30). Countries that have a high value for this component are characterized by high costs for electricity and housing and low costs for communication and construction.

The third component is positively correlated with electricity (0.45) and communication (0.55), and negatively correlated with housing (−0.39) and construction (−0.46). Countries with high values for these components will have high PLIs for electricity and communication, and low PLIs for construction and housing.

The fourth component is positively correlated with electricity (0.33) and construction (0.34), and negatively correlated with water (−0.66). Countries with high values for these components will have relatively high PLIs for electricity and construction and low PLIs for water.

A scatter plot of countries in the plane of the first two principal components is presented in Figure 13.1. From left to right, the plot

Figure 13.1: Countries' projections in the plan of principal components 1 and 2

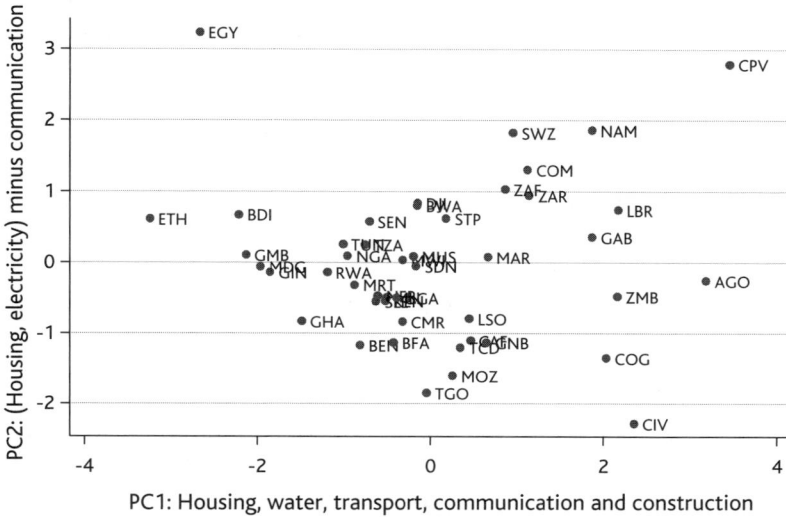

PC1: Housing, water, transport, communication and construction

Source: Computed from International Comparison Program – Africa, 2005 database.

shows the least expensive to the most expensive countries in terms of all infrastructure components except electricity. From the top down, it presents the most expensive countries for electricity and the cheapest for communication to the cheapest for electricity and the most expensive for communication. When the two dimensions are cross-tabulated, a possible grouping of countries into 15 clusters emerges. Some countries like Egypt, Cape Verde, Angola, and Zambia stand out and constitute single-element clusters. Within clusters, countries might be expected to exhibit similarities with respect to all components, but in some clusters, countries differ for one or two components. Country codes are presented in the Annex.

The 15 possible clusters are as follows.

Cluster 1: Egypt has the lowest costs for communication, construction and transportation; the third lowest cost for water; a low cost for housing; and the highest cost for electricity.

Cluster 2: Cape Verde is the most expensive for housing; the second most expensive for water; 30% above the African average for construction; 13% above the average for electricity; 12% above the average for transportation; and has an average cost for communication.

Cluster 3: Angola has the highest costs for water and transportation; 20% above the average cost for electricity; 23% above the average for construction; 72% above the average for communication; and a low cost of housing (35% below the average).

Cluster 4: Zambia has the highest cost for communication; the second highest costs for transportation and housing; an above-average cost for electricity, the lowest cost for water; and an average cost for construction.

Cluster 5: Namibia and Swaziland have 84%, 103%, 96% and 42.5% above-average costs for housing, water, electricity and construction, respectively; an above-average cost for communication; and an average cost for transportation.

Cluster 6: Côte d'Ivoire and Congo Republic have the highest cost for construction (150% above average); the second lowest cost for electricity; and above-average costs for housing (19%), water (39%), transportation (21%), and communication (56%).

Cluster 7: Gabon and Liberia have above-average costs for all components, varying from 13% above average for construction to 183% above average for water. This cluster has 20%, 25%, 43% and 78% above-average costs for electricity, transportation, communication, and housing, respectively. The costs of water are higher in Liberia.

Cluster 8: Comoros, the Democratic Republic of Congo, and South Africa have average costs for construction, above-average costs for water (16%), and high to very high costs for transportation (26%), communication (29%), housing (52%), and electricity (77%).

Cluster 9: The cluster made up of Botswana, Djibouti, and São Tomé and Príncipe is characterized by average costs for housing, transportation, communication, and construction, but above-average costs for water (35%) and electricity (43%). Djibouti differs from the other cluster members in the cost of water.

Cluster 10: Burundi, Ethiopia, the Gambia, Guinea, and Madagascar make up this cluster, which has the lowest cost of communication, the second lowest costs for housing, water, transportation, and construction, and a cost of electricity about 10% below average. The cost of housing in the Gambia is far below the cluster average, while the costs of water in the Gambia and Guinea are above the average.

Cluster 11: The cluster consisting of Central African Republic, Chad, Guinea-Bissau, Lesotho, Mozambique, and Togo has the lowest cost of housing; a below-average cost of electricity; and above-average costs of transportation (11%), water (15%), construction (26%), and communication (58%).

Cluster 12: The cluster made up of Kenya, Mali, Mauritania, Niger, Rwanda, Sierra Leone, and Uganda has below-average costs of housing (28%), electricity (14%), construction (15%), and transport (8%). It has above-average costs of water (26%) and communication (23%). In Rwanda, the cost of housing is far above the cluster average, and in Mauritania and Sierra Leone, the cost of water is also above the cluster average.

Cluster 13: Benin, Burkina Faso, Cameroon, and Ghana constitute this cluster, which has the lowest cost of electricity, below the regional average costs for housing (35%) and construction (12%); average regional costs for water and transportation; and an above-average cost for communication (35%). Within the cluster, the price of housing in Cameroon is 37% above the cluster average, and in Ghana, it is 50% below the average.

Cluster 14: Nigeria, Senegal, Tanzania, and Tunisia make up this cluster, which has below the regional average costs for housing and transportation (11%), communication (6%) and construction (8%). It has above the regional average costs for electricity (9%) and water (20%). Tunisia's cost of housing is far above (68%) the cluster average, while the cost of water is far below (80%) the cluster average.

Cluster 15: The cluster consisting of Malawi, Morocco, Mauritius, and Sudan is characterized by below-the regional average costs for electricity (21%) and communication (6%); average costs for transportation and construction, and above-the regional average costs of housing (24%) and water (87%). The cost of housing in Mauritius and Morocco is above the cluster average, while the cost of water in Mauritius is 120% below the cluster average.

Conclusion

The costs of the infrastructure components examined in this study (housing, water, electricity, transport, communication, and construction) vary substantially among countries. And while it might be expected that the price levels of these infrastructure components in neighboring countries, or countries within the same RECs, would be roughly similar, the price data collected from the ICP 2005 round show that this is not the case.

The variation in price levels suggests that policy frameworks in different countries, even those within the same RECs, are not fully integrated, and so seem to be out of alignment with the prevailing climate of support for integration at sub-regional and regional levels. Policy frameworks should aim to channel investment toward economic drivers that will accelerate economic transformation, and thus, productivity. According to the World Economic Forum (WEF, 2010), the level of productivity determines the rates of return to investments in an economy. By extension, an improvement in productivity should increase trade and foster sub-regional and regional integration. Some studies have shown that infrastructure is key to creating an environment that attracts foreign direct investment, which should translate into sustainable economic development. This is more likely to occur in countries with policies support infrastructure development.

Country projections of the costs of infrastructure components indicate possible clustering on the basis of similarities. The results suggest that the costs of some components are unexpectedly cheaper in some clusters than in others. Further research is needed to better understand the dynamics that could improve the restructuring and to formulate evidenced-based policy and economic decisions.

The variation in the price levels of items such energy, communication, and transportation—essential to a country's competitiveness—should prompt African governments to direct more investment toward infrastructure. International and multilateral development agencies such as the African Development Bank should continue to prioritize and increase development funding for sub-regional and regional infrastructure projects.

There is also a need to define strategies and mechanisms for mobilizing resources and financing infrastructure. Various instruments for financing infrastructure within the framework of public–private partnerships have been considered by Mthuli Ncube in an article on financing and managing infrastructure in Africa (Ncube, 2010). He analyzes various options, which include build-operate-transfer, build-own-operate-transfer, design-bid-build, design-build-operate-maintain, and design-build-finance-operate models. These proposals should be reviewed and implemented at national, sub-regional, and regional levels.

This chapter reveals differences in price levels among countries, which, in part, may reflect current policies. It also argues for a better clustering or grouping approach for countries with similar attributes, to allow comparison on the basis of economic similarities within and outside the regional economic communities. It is recommended that this study be repeated by calculating price level indices for the 2006 to 2011 period, and be expanded to include other economic variables. The objective is to gain a clearer understanding of the relationships between the variations in price levels of infrastructure services. Such an analysis would shed light not only on the relationship between the costs of infrastructure services in different countries, but also on the distortion in prices. Further, it would be an indication of the pace and direction of regional integration efforts aimed at enhancing investment and expanding trade.

Note

[1] A revised version of this paper is published in the current volume as Chapter 12.

References

AfDB (African Development Bank) (2010) 'Infrastructure deficit and opportunities in Africa', *Economic Brief*, vol 1, September, pp 2-15.

Ajakaiye, O. and Ncube, M. (2010) 'Infrastructure and economic development in Africa: an overview', *Journal of African Economies*, vol 19, suppl 1, pp i3-i12, available at http://ssrn.com/abstract=1601765 or doi:ejq003.

Calderón, C. and Servén, L. (2008) *Infrastructure and Economic Development in Sub-Saharan Africa*, World Bank Policy Report Working Paper Series 4712. Washington, DC: World Bank.

Foster, V. (2008) *Overhauling the Engine of Growth: Infrastructure in Africa*, Africa Infrastructure Country Diagnostic. Washington, DC: World Bank.

Ncube, M. (2010) 'Financing and managing infrastructure in Africa', *Journal of African Economies*, vol 19, suppl 1, pp i114-i164. doi:10.1093/jae/ejp020.

WEF (World Economic Forum) (2010) *Global Competitiveness Report 2010-2011*. Geneva: World Economic Forum.

Annex

Table A13.1: Country codes

Country	Code	Country	Code
Algeria	DZA	Libya	LBY
Angola	AGO	Madagascar	MDG
Benin	BEN	Malawi	MWI
Botswana	BWA	Mali	MLI
Burkina Faso	BFA	Mauritania	MRT
Burundi	BDI	Mauritius	MUS
Cameroon	CMR	Morocco	MAR
Cape Verde	CPV	Mozambique	MOZ
Central African Republic	CAF	Namibia	NAM
Chad	TCD	Niger	NER
Comoros	COM	Nigeria	NGA
Congo	COG	Rwanda	RWA
Congo, Democratic Republic	ZAR	São Tomé and Príncipe	STP
Côte d'Ivoire	CIV	Senegal	SEN
Djibouti	DJI	Seychelles	SYC
Egypt	EGY	Sierra Leone	SLE
Equatorial Guinea	GNQ	Somalia	SOM
Eritrea	ERI	South Africa	ZAF
Ethiopia	ETH	Sudan	SDN
Gabon	GAB	Swaziland	SWZ
Gambia	GMB	Tanzania	TZA
Ghana	GHA	Togo	TGO
Guinea	GIN	Tunisia	TUN
Guinea-Bissau	GNB	Uganda	UGA
Kenya	KEN	Zambia	ZMB
Lesotho	LSO	Zimbabwe	ZWE
Liberia	LBR		

Source: Computed from International Comparison Program – Africa, 2005 database.

FOURTEEN

Infrastructure deficit and financing needs in Africa

Mthuli Ncube

Introduction

Infrastructure development contributes to economic activity by lowering the costs of doing business, improving the competitiveness of local production, and facilitating trade and foreign direct investment. Firms with reliable power supply are able to produce more. Those with access to a world-class highway network can reach their customers faster and cheaper, while those with easy port access are able to source their inputs and export their finished products at a lower cost. Construction of infrastructure has the added benefit of directly contributing to economic output. Hence, in addition to being a factor of production that influences a firm's production and location decisions, infrastructure contributes to the development of both upstream and downstream industries as well as financial markets.

This positive relationship is supported empirically.[1] African countries with the most advanced manufacturing export industries, such as South Africa and Mauritius, have benefited from world-class infrastructure to support their industries.[2] Several studies find a positive correlation between foreign direct investment in Africa (other than investments in extractive industries) and a critical mass of favorable factors, including good-quality infrastructure in particular.[3] Both volume and quality of infrastructure also appear to be positively correlated with marginal productivity of capital and with private sector investments.[4] With adequate infrastructure, African firms could achieve productivity gains of up to 40%.[5] And bringing Africa's infrastructure stock to the level of that for Mauritius could enhance Africa's gross domestic product (GDP) growth by as much as 2.2% per year.[6]

This chapter examines the access to sources of local market finance for infrastructure development in Africa. The first section examines the state of infrastructure access in the continent. The second section presents a snapshot view of the constraints to infrastructure

583

development in Africa. The third section discusses innovative local sources of infrastructure finance in the continent while the fourth examines some of the constraints and solutions to a major source that the African Development Bank (AfDB) has emphasized lately—infrastructure bond. The final section concludes with a discussion of the role of the AfDB.

State of infrastructure access in Africa[7]

Africa suffers from a critical shortage of infrastructure. Its infrastructure coverage lags behind that of other developing countries, particularly regarding access to electricity, transport networks, water and sanitation, irrigation, and information and communications technology (ICT) (Figure 14.1). Power deficits are the continent's biggest infrastructure challenge: per capita power generation is less than half the rest of the developing world's and declining. Not only has electricity access stagnated, but supply has also become less stable, with regular outages reported in at least 30 countries by 2007. Power outages are estimated to cost Africa between 1% and 2% of GDP.

Figure 14.1: Africa's infrastructure stock

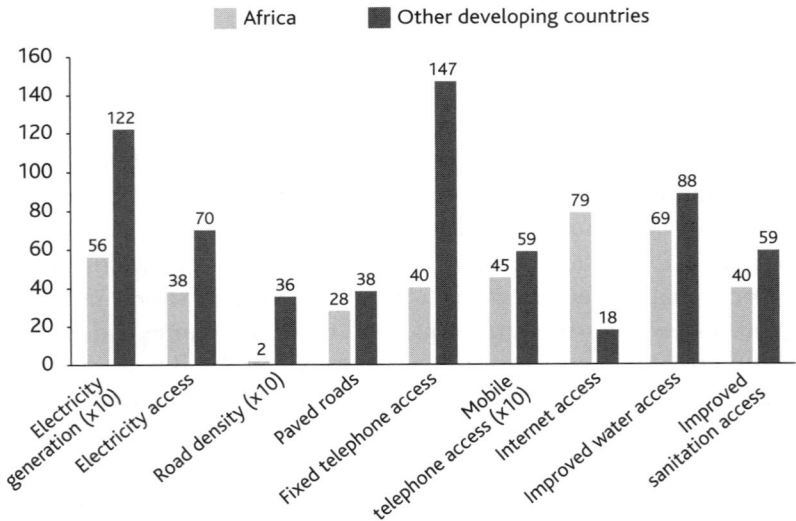

Notes: Electricity generation is measured in kilowatt hours per capita; road density in kilometers per 100 square kilometers of land; paved roads in percentage of total roads; electricity, improved water and improved sanitation access in population percentage; fixed telephone, mobile telephone and internet access in users per 1,000 people.

Source: AICD (2010); AfDB (2011b).

Transportation bottlenecks are equally critical. While Africa's road kilometers per capita have been on the rise thanks to the traditionally extensive public investments into the sector, the continent's highways remain largely fragmented. In addition, road infrastructure in African low-income countries is still plagued by poor quality, as well as low connectivity to ports and international commercial centers. Paved roads account for as little as 5% or less of total roads in some of the least developed countries and fragile states. In these markets, poor road infrastructure forces some firms to serve only the local market.[8]

Rail infrastructure is, by comparison, far less developed. Only 33 countries have operational rail networks, which are geared toward long-haul general freight, mineral freight, and non-urban passenger services. Most of these countries operate single track, un-electrified systems. Decades of under-capitalization, poor management and general neglect of railways on the continent has rendered some networks defunct, while the majority of operational networks experience a variety of capacity, efficiency and safety problems. When they exist, however, railways tend to be linked to ports and carry lower long-haul costs per unit of freight relative to roads.

Maritime transport in Africa suffers from limited berth and storage capacity. African ports struggle to efficiently handle vessels exceeding 2,000 twenty-foot equivalent units (TEUs), compared with East Asian ports, which have enough capacity to handle vessels of up to 11,000 TEUs. In 2007, African vessels accounted for less than 0.6% of the world's merchant fleet. In the same year, Port Said (Egypt) and the Port of Durban (South Africa) were the only African ports ranked in the top 50 for container traffic, and the continent's containerized cargo throughput was half the volumes handled by large ports in China and Singapore. Africa's ports are also running out of capacity. While port throughput has grown by about 10% annually since 2007, reflecting growing interest from emerging market economies in Africa's natural resources, capacity expansions have not grown as fast.

Air transport services also remain largely inefficient and expensive. Most African airlines' fleets are aging, airports struggle to meet international security standards, and air travel within the continent is among the most costly in the world. The air transport industry, however, is making significant strides. The sector is estimated to have grown by 5.8% per year between 2001 and 2007. Three major hubs have emerged in Sub-Saharan Africa—Johannesburg, Nairobi, and Addis Ababa—dominating both international and domestic markets. New budget airlines are also gaining ground in deregulated markets such as Nigeria, Kenya, the Democratic Republic of Congo (DRC) and South Africa, improving service and reducing prices.[9]

Access to clean water has improved over the past two decades. While only 49% of Sub-Saharan Africans had access to clean water in 1990, the rate had improved to 67% by 2009. Africa still lags behind other developing regions, however. Access to improved water sources is significantly higher in Latin America and the Caribbean (91%) and in South Asia (87%) than in Africa (69%). In addition, 60% of the population has no access to improved sanitation, and only 5% of agriculture is under irrigation.

Access to ICTs, on the other hand, has not only dramatically improved in the past decade, but also exceeds levels observed in some other developing regions. The proportion of Africans with access to mobile telephones has risen from about 1% in 2000, to over 40% by 2009, well above the access rates for South Asia (33%). Access to internet services is also higher in Africa (11%) than in Latin America (3%), East Asia (2%), and South Asia (less than 1%).

These measures mask significant regional and cross-country differences. The AfDB's Africa Infrastructure Index, which ranks countries on the basis of electricity generation per capita, share of population with access to mobile or fixed phone line, percentage of roads paved and share of population with access to improved water and sanitation, illustrates this diversity (Table 14.1).

There is wide variability in performance across 18 access, quality, and cost dimensions. As may be expected, the infrastructure deficit in low-income countries is worse than in middle-income ones, and fragility further weighs on most dimensions. Differences are particularly marked with regard to power generation, the density of paved roads and access to landline and mobile telephones as well as the internet, but less so for access to improved water and sanitation (Figure 14.2). Low-income countries perform better than middle-income ones only on two cost dimensions: charges for general cargo handling and for fixed telephone. This is due to high business telephone prices in South Africa, Morocco and Botswana and to the high cargo-handling charges in South African ports.

The divide between rural and urban areas is generally even more pronounced. Access to improved water, for example, is almost twice as high in cities compared with rural areas.[10] Only one in 10 Africans living in rural areas has access to grid electricity, compared with well over 50% of the urban population. Mobile phones, on the other hand, are shattering the isolation of rural areas, with one out of every two rural Africans now in range of a mobile signal. However, the cost

Table 14.1: Africa infrastructure development index

Rank	Country	Index	Rank	Country	Index
1	Seychelles	100	28	Côte d'Ivoire	27
2	Mauritius	90	29	Uganda	26
3	South Africa	81	30	Rwanda	25
4	Libya	80	31	Burundi	24
5	Egypt	80	32	Angola	24
6	Tunisia	77	33	Sudan	21
7	Algeria	71	34	Benin	21
8	Morocco	59	35	Guinea-Bissau	21
9	Cape Verde	58	36	Kenya	20
10	Botswana	57	37	Nigeria	20
11	Gambia, the	49	38	Equatorial Guinea	19
12	Gabon	45	39	Mali	18
13	São Tomé and Principe	43	40	Burkina Faso	18
14	Comoros	43	41	Togo	17
15	Swaziland	39	42	Mozambique	14
16	Namibia	38	43	Liberia	13
17	Djibouti	37	44	Tanzania	12
18	Senegal	34	45	Central Africa Republic	12
19	Malawi	31	46	Eritrea	11
20	Zimbabwe	30	47	Madagascar	7
21	Guinea	29	48	Niger	6
22	Mauritania	29.4	49	Chad	5
23	Zambia	28.6	50	Sierra Leone	5
24	Republic of Congo	28.6	51	DRC	5
25	Lesotho	28.5	52	Ethiopia	4
26	Cameroon	28.0	53	Somalia	–
27	Ghana	28			

Source: AfDB (2011c)

of ICT services, including mobile telephony, remains high in Africa relative to other developing regions.

Performance across African sub-regions is less variable, although some patterns are noteworthy (Figure 14.3). North African countries lead in overall performance, but are out-ranked by Southern African countries on density and quality of rail infrastructure. This is principally due to South Africa's extensive rail system, which accounts for 32% of the continent's total rail infrastructure. South Africa is also the only country with a dual track for part of its network and an operating inner-city fast train passenger service. North Africa's rail network, on the other hand, is largely electrified, while only part of Southern

Figure 14.2: Access to infrastructure by income level and fragility

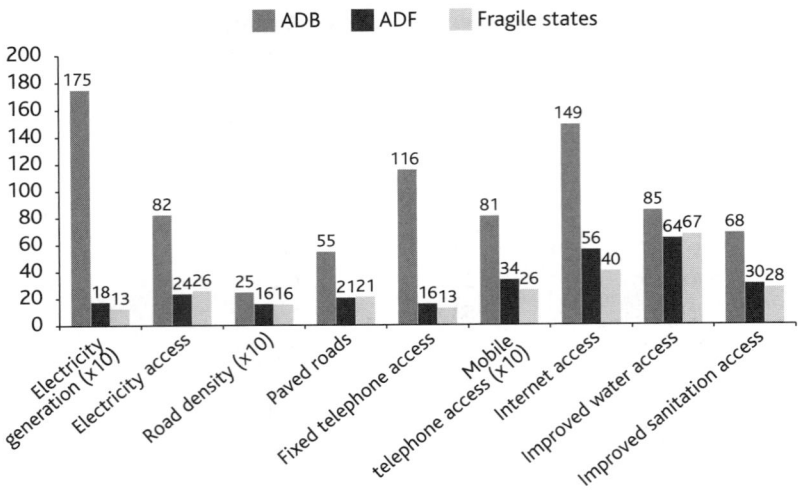

Notes: Electricity generation is measured in kilowatt hours per capita; road density in kilometers per 100 square kilometers of land; paved roads in percentage of total roads; electricity, improved water and improved sanitation access in population percentage; fixed telephone, mobile telephone and internet access in users per 1,000 people

Source: AICD (2010); AfDB (2011c).

Africa's network—including in South Africa, DRC, and Zimbabwe—is so.

Southern Africa outperforms the rest of Sub-Saharan Africa except when it comes to the quality of roads, mobile phone and internet user fees, as well as general cargo-handling fees, which are the highest on the continent. The latter is explained by South Africa's relatively high cargo-handling fees, which are based on cost recovery.[11] Central Africa, on the other hand, trails other regions on most measures.

Performance in landlocked countries is below Africa's average on all measures. Coastal countries outperform landlocked countries by a factor of three or more on measures such as electricity generation, fixed telephone line access, and airport connectivity. Broadband tariffs in landlocked countries are four times those in coastal countries on average (Figure 14.4a). Infrastructure stock in oil importing countries, while mostly worse than in oil exporting ones, is on par with the continent's average on measures such as access to clean water, quality of road infrastructure, and access to fixed and mobile telephony (Figure 14.4b).

Figure 14.3: Access to infrastructure by region

Infrastructure deficit and financing needs in Africa

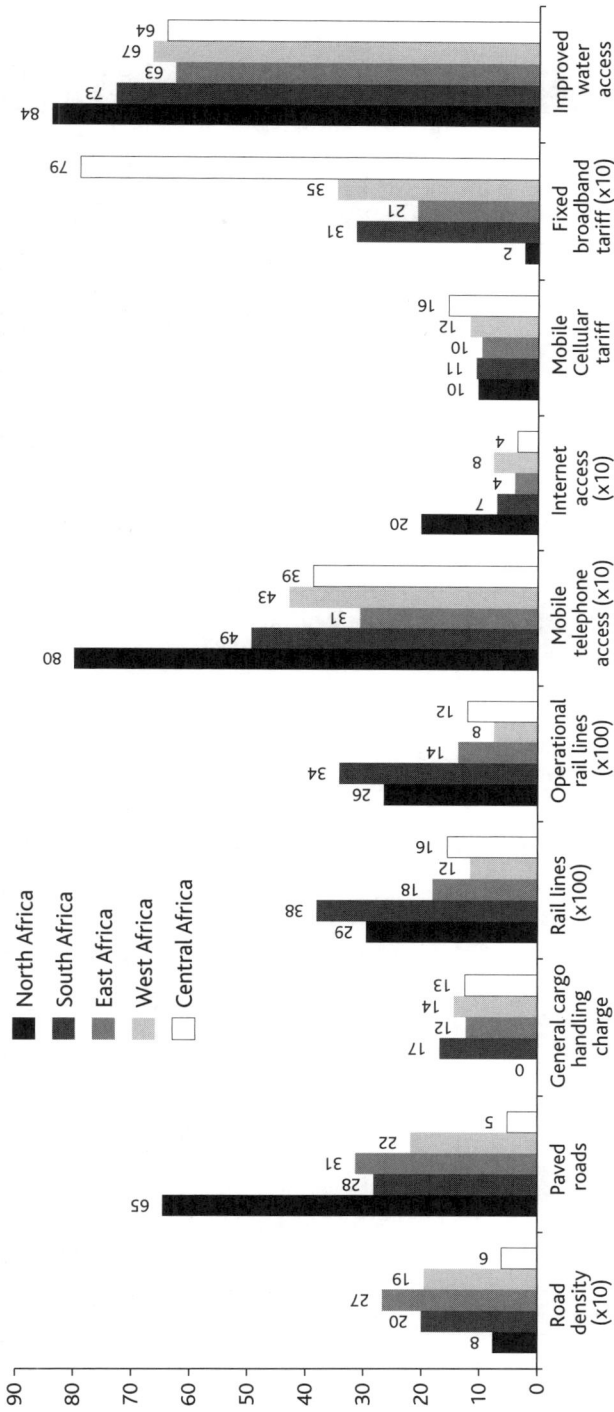

Legend:
- North Africa
- South Africa
- East Africa
- West Africa
- Central Africa

Improved water access:
- 64
- 67
- 63
- 73
- 84

Fixed broadband tariff (x10):
- 79
- 35
- 21
- 31
- 2

Mobile Cellular tariff:
- 16
- 12
- 10
- 11
- 10

Internet access (x10):
- 4
- 8
- 4
- 7
- 20

Mobile telephone access (x10):
- 39
- 43
- 31
- 49
- 80

Operational rail lines (x100):
- 12
- 8
- 14
- 34
- 26

Rail lines (x100):
- 16
- 12
- 18
- 38
- 29

General cargo handling charge:
- 13
- 14
- 12
- 17
- 0

Paved roads:
- 5
- 22
- 31
- 28
- 65

Road density (x10):
- 6
- 19
- 27
- 20
- 8

Note: Road density is measured in kilometers per 100 square kilometers of land; paved roads in percentage of total roads; general cargo handling charges in US dollars per tonne; rail lines in kilometers; improved water and sanitation access in population percentage; mobile telephone and internet access in users per 1,000 people; mobile cellular and fixed broadband tariffs in US dollars per month

Source: AICD (2010); AfDB (2011d).

589

Figure 14.4: Access to infrastructure by (a) location and (b) oil resources

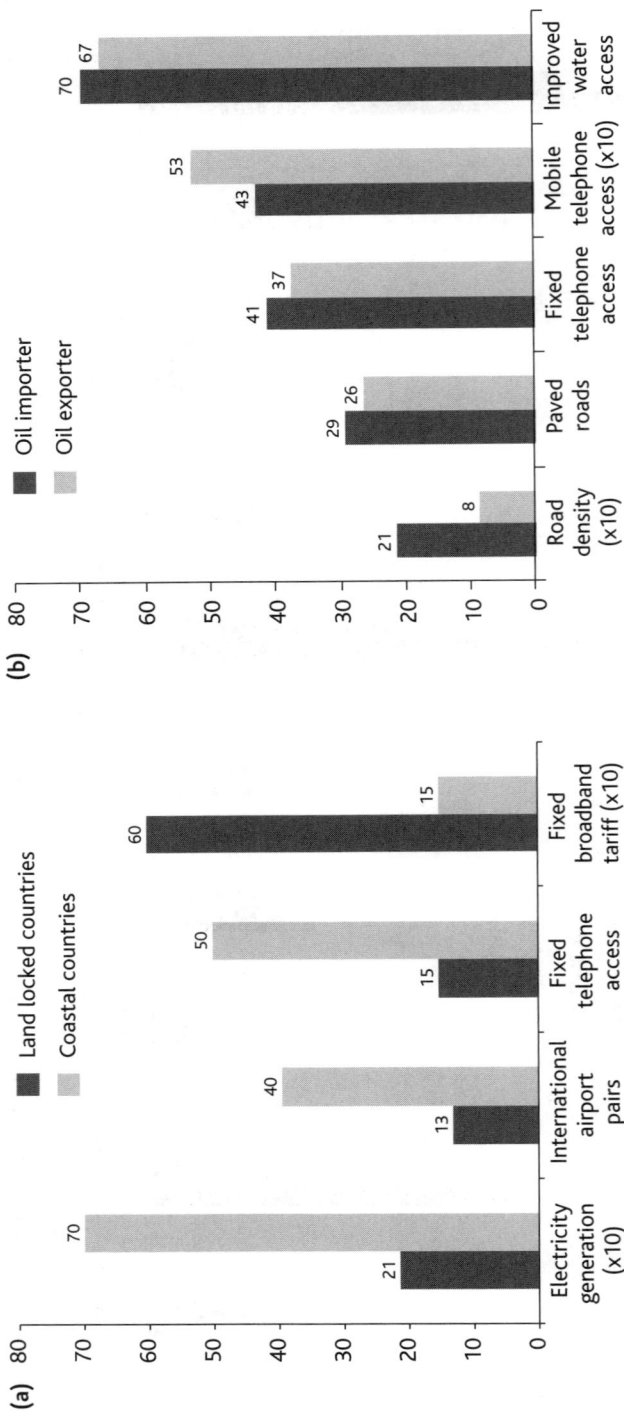

Notes: Electricity generation is measured in kilowatt hours per capita; road density in kilometers per 100 square kilometers of land; paved roads in percentage of total roads; fixed telephone mobile telephone and internet access in users per 1,000 people; business telephone, mobile cellular and fixed broadband tariffs in US dollars per month; water outages in hours.

Source: AICD (2010); AfDB (2011d).

Constraints to infrastructure development

The infrastructure deficit condemns Africa to perform below its economic potential. Power shortages, for example, cost the region 12.5% in lost production time, compared with 7% in South Asia (Figure 14.5). The shortage and poor quality of infrastructure, added to the lack of competition in service delivery, have also resulted in exorbitant connection and user costs when compared with other developing countries. Infrastructure services in Africa cost twice as much on average as in other developing regions and are exceptionally high by global standards. In the transport sector, for example, East Asia, South Asia and Latin America enjoy a significant comparative advantage, with East Asian firms saving close to 70% in transportation costs, while Latin America and South Asian firms save approximately 50% relative to their African counterparts (Figure 14.6). These costs weigh heavily on Africa's competitiveness.

African countries face several constraints regarding infrastructure development and maintenance, including geographical constraints, deficiencies in planning, poor management of existing infrastructure assets, institutional inefficiencies and regulatory bottlenecks, demand-side constraints, and inadequate financing for project preparation and implementation.

Addressing the deficiencies in Sub-Saharan Africa's infrastructure will require investments of about US$93 billion per year.[12] In most countries, infrastructure investment needs far exceed available public resources. Fragile States would require the equivalent of 37% of their GDP per year, stable low-income countries 23% of their GDP, and sub-Saharan middle-income countries the equivalent of 10% of

Figure 14.5: Productivity loss from power outages

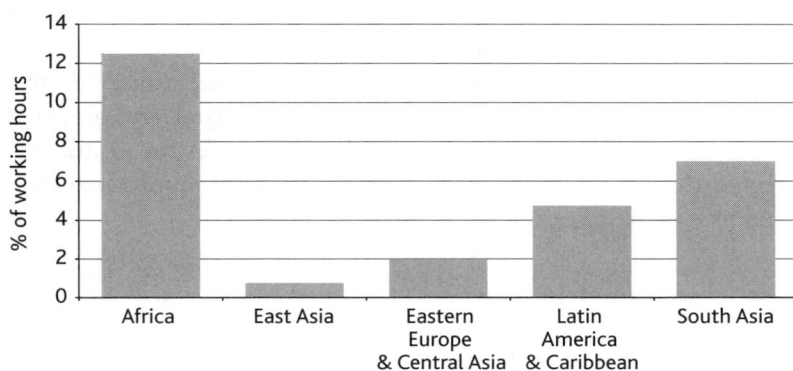

Source: Iarossi (2009)

Figure 14.6: Inland transport costs

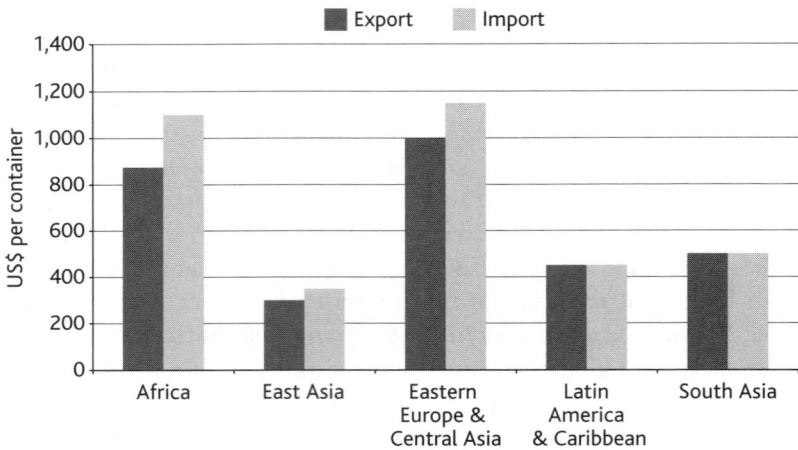

Source: Iarossi (2009)

their GDP. While spending on Africa's infrastructure had swelled to US$ 45 billion a year in 2008, the financing burden still falls disproportionately on government budgets, which shoulder 66% of the expenditures, while the private sector covers 20% and traditional development partners and emerging markets (that is, fast-growing economies outside of the Organization for Economic Co-operation and Development) another 14%.

Doubling existing investment levels will be a significant challenge. Domestic resources are constrained by low savings rates in most African countries, especially oil importers, a narrow tax base, ineffective budget administration, and underdeveloped capital markets. Traditional official development assistance remains low relative to the continent's extensive needs, is pro-cyclical, and tends to fluctuate in response to changes in donors' development aid agendas. Infrastructure financing from emerging markets is growing, but remains largely unpredictable. Private investments in infrastructure, on the other hand, are hampered by regulation and a dearth of bankable projects on the continent. Meeting Africa's infrastructure financing needs will require innovation to address these barriers.

Financing infrastructure

Developing Africa's economic infrastructure at the pace necessary to realize its economic potential will require, among other things, access to large-scale and innovative financing, local and foreign. In this chapter, our focus is on local financing.

Financing for Africa's infrastructure has been predominantly from public resources. The public sector has been most prominent in water, sanitation and transport, where it contributed above 50% of capital investments in the sector in 2001–2006. Private investment, on the other hand, accounted for over 75% of capital investments in ICT over the same period. Infrastructure financing in Africa, however, has been changing in recent years, and a new mix of sources—including increasingly private and innovative ones—is emerging. There is no "one size fits all" solution. The right financing mix will depend on a number of factors, including the country's level of financial sector development, indebtedness and business environment. As traditional strategies and sources of finance are not enough, closing Africa's infrastructure gap requires innovations on the part of the public sector, development partners, and the private sector.

Domestically, African governments can increase and channel private savings to productive uses by facilitating the development of local capital markets. Instruments such as corporate bonds or government infrastructure bonds are limited to countries with sufficiently developed domestic bond markets. Other schemes such as sovereign wealth funds and resource-backed infrastructure financing are better tailored for resource-exporting countries (Box 14.1).

Box 14.1: Local innovative instruments for infrastructure financing

Innovative government financing instruments

Government infrastructure bonds: These are government bonds issued on the domestic market to finance public infrastructure projects. Since February 2009, Kenya has issued three such bonds with a total value of US$1 billion, which, in turn, paved the way for corporate bond issues by private and state-owned companies. Kenya's success is partially attributed to its use of incentives, such as allowing the bonds to be used as collateral for bank loans and exempting bond holders from tax on the interest earned.

Sovereign wealth funds (SWFs): These are government investment funds capitalized from the proceeds of resource exports. When well designed and implemented, these funds can be a significant source of finance for both domestic and foreign projects. The Libyan Arab African Investment Company, which invested US$800 million in 13 African countries in 2008, is a best-practice example. Indeed, SWFs are another important source of investment funds for infrastructure development in Africa. The oldest African SWF is Botswana's Pula Fund, started 1994 and whose resources stands at US$6.9 billion. Though African SWFs account for less than 2% of all SWFs in the world, more African countries have since created SWFs. SWF funds include US$65 billion for Libya, US$56.7 billion for Algeria, US$5 billion for Angola, and US$1 billion for Nigeria, among others. The abundance of natural wealth on the African continent provides an opportunity for African countries to diversify the use of their revenues with SWFs, including infrastructure investment.

Diaspora bonds: These are government bonds targeted at a country's diaspora, but can also be offered to the local population. Ethiopia pioneered diaspora bonds with its Millennium Corporate Bond in 2007. The bond raised capital for the state-owned Ethiopian Electric Power Corporation. Other Sub-Saharan African countries with large diaspora could raise up to US$5–10 billion per year through the issuance of such bonds.

Resource-backed infrastructure financing: These are loans for infrastructure backed by natural resources. For example, Chinese investments in Angola, Nigeria, and Sudan are backed by oil, in Gabon by iron, in Ghana by cocoa, and in the Democratic Republic of the Congo by copper. It is critical that African governments negotiate equitable deals that correctly value the resources assigned and environmental externalities. The share of royalties and dividends should also be robust to fluctuations in world commodity prices. This form of financing can be reconfigured for local investors.

Innovative private financing instruments
Corporate bonds: These are domestic bonds issued by private firms. South Africa's private sector has been able to tap local capital markets to finance infrastructure projects in water, transportation, and power. The country's capital markets are well developed and long-term credit is available, as well as expertise to arrange more complex transactions such as the EUR 2.5 billion Gautrain project.

Specialized infrastructure funds: These are funds created by established infrastructure firms, including upstream industries, that invest in various infrastructure projects. They provide a mix of financing instruments, such as equity, senior debt, subordinated debt, or mezzanine finance with exposure ranging from about US$5–120 million per project and longer tenors (up to 15 years). The Emerging Africa Infrastructure Fund is an example.

Private sector local currency infrastructure bonds: The issuance of public local infrastructure bonds has paved the way for corporate bonds issues by the private or state-owned companies, for example the electricity utility KenGen and mobile phone company Safaricom. Kenya's success with infrastructure bonds is partially attributed to the use of incentives. For example, to boost corporate issuance in local currency, incentives including an exemption of bond investors from tax on interest were adopted. In addition, the issuance of government bonds with a sukuk (Sharia-compliant) portion facilitated participation by investors adhering to Islamic banking such as the Gulf African Bank. Also, holders of the bonds can use them as collateral to acquire bank loans while the banks can pledge them as collateral for their repo operations. Other private sector telecommunications companies that have successfully used local currency bonds in Africa include Uganda MTN Pty Limited, Uganda Telecom, Orange Cameroon, and Nigeria's MTN Pty Limited.

Private equity funds: These funds mobilize financing primarily from both international and local institutional investors and traditional financiers, such as development finance institutions. The Africa Infrastructure Investment Fund, for example, was able to mobilize US$5 billion in additional financing in addition to its initial fund of US$500 million.

Commodity-linked debt instruments: These are domestic notes linked to specific commodities that can be traded on local exchanges. In August 2010, for example, South Africa's Standard Bank Group offered Rand-denominated notes traded on the Johannesburg Stock Exchange whose returns were linked to the performance of precious metals. The capital was protected and the notes had specific redemption dates. Commodity exporters across Africa could potentially use such instruments to raise funds and hedge against commodity price fluctuations.

Source: Updated from Brixiova et al (2011).

In addition to large institutional investors, local infrastructure investment increasingly includes investors with a stake in the developed asset, such as extractive industries companies that need infrastructure to conduct their operations. The benefits of investments tied to mining can be enhanced if access to developed infrastructure is not limited to the resource extraction operations. New private investors are also emerging in sectors where infrastructure-related revenue streams from off-take agreements are not the only source of revenues. This includes co-generation in the power sector, where electricity is generated as a by-product of sugar and ethanol production in countries like Tanzania, Kenya, and Mozambique, and oil sector gas-powered electricity in Nigeria and Tanzania.

Given the abundance of natural resources, African countries can tap carbon finance markets to finance low-carbon infrastructure (Box 14.2). So far, though, access to carbon credits by clean technology projects in emerging markets and developing countries has had mixed results across regions, with Africa lagging substantially behind.

Box 14.2: Tapping carbon finance markets

Africa's reserves of renewable energy—solar, hydro, wind and geothermal—are the highest in world. On a global ranking of countries by renewable energy reserves, 17 out of the top 35 countries are African. Given its abundant natural resources, Africa is able to embark on a low-carbon infrastructure development path. This would unlock financing from carbon-credit markets through the Clean Development Mechanism and other clean technology funds. The former has the advantages of being market-based, legally enforceable and generally more predictable than concessional financing sources. The latter are crucial to reduce the costs and risks of such investments. Examples include the Clean Technology Fund, which supports the adoption of low-carbon technologies in middle-income countries. It is expected to leverage at least five times its value in clean energy solutions, including energy efficiency, renewable energy, and sustainable transport investments. The Global Environment Facility provides grants to low-income countries for projects that promote sustainable development. The challenge for African countries is poor capacity to tap these global funds to adapt to, and mitigate, climate change. To facilitate access, the AfDB is leading resource mobilization into the Africa Green Fund, which will provide direct financing towards qualifying projects on the continent.

Source: Duarte et al (2010); Buys et al (2007)

In playing its role as financier, the public sector should seek to improve efficiency in the delivery of infrastructure finance. Public savings from efficiency gains can be achieved in part by planning for timely delivery of projects to avoid costly emergency measures, maintaining existing infrastructure to limit expensive rehabilitation, improving efficiency of utilities, and strengthening medium-term expenditure frameworks, accounting frameworks and auditing procedures.

African governments should also mobilize other domestic resources. Removing exemptions and strengthening tax administration would increase public tax revenues. In low-income countries, where the large informal sectors impede effective direct taxation, excises, value-added taxes, and other indirect taxes can be relied on. Post-conflict countries may consider utilizing trade taxes and other simplified direct tax structures, before a balance between indirect and direct taxes can be reached.

To mobilize private savings, formal financial institutions could offer long-term saving instruments, and governments could provide corresponding tax incentives. African governments can also remove regulatory barriers that discourage institutional investors such as pension funds from relying on long-term savings instruments. Moreover, they can help diversify capital markets by developing institutional frameworks encouraging Islamic finance institutions and private equity funds.

African governments also have a critical role to play in providing incentives for private investment in infrastructure projects.[13] Such incentives could include risk mitigation instruments, such as viability gap financing,[14] among others. Adding "sweeteners" to risky partnerships, such as guaranteed floor returns and tax holidays, could also increase the private investors' appetite in infrastructure transactions. Such a strategy was recently employed in the Dakar Toll Road project.[15]

To unlock private infrastructure finance, Africa needs to increase the number of bankable projects. In addition to project preparation championed by multi-lateral development banks (MDBs) and donors, private investors should develop and bring projects to the market. In most African countries, however, this is constrained by the absence of relevant procurement processes, rules for handling unsolicited proposals, or mechanisms for competitive bidding. In such an environment, the risk that private investors who bring forth proposals lose proprietorship is high. MDBs and the donor community should consider supporting the development of an enabling environment for project identification and development by private partners.

Aside from reforming procurement rules, consolidating project preparation financing from grant facilities could generate immediate gains. Combining official development assistance in upstream project preparation activities with private finance in project preparation can also be seen in the case of Infraco (Box 14.3); development assistance is channeled through a commercial vehicle that, because of its higher risk tolerance, is able to absorb project preparation costs and risks.

Box 14.3: InfraCo: innovation in project preparation finance

InfraCo is a donor-funded infrastructure development company that acts as an 'honest broker' to link finance providers, the private sector, and host governments in low-income developing countries. InfraCo is mostly involved in early stage project development activities and, hence, shoulders much of the upfront costs and reduces entry costs for private sector infrastructure developers. After securing in-principle commitments from providers of finance to support an investment, InfraCo will offer the structured investment opportunity to the private sector through a competitive bidding process and in return will get compensated for its time, effort, and cost in the form of a minority carried interest in the venture. Over time, InfraCo may sell its interest to national, institutional, and public investors. InfraCo is managed as a private sector infrastructure development company with its capital provided by way of share subscription by the Private Infrastructure Development Group which is made up of the development agencies of Austria, Ireland, the Netherlands, Sweden, Switzerland, and the UK, and the World Bank.

Source: www.infracoafrica.com

With improvements in investment climate and project processes, private investments are scaling up, including in sectors traditionally dominated by the public sector, such as roads. Total private investment into African roads grew from a cumulative US$1.4 billion in 1990–1999, to more than US$21 billion between 2000 and 2005. A new wave of private road projects in South Africa, Mozambique, Kenya, Senegal, and Côte d'Ivoire adds to the list. The toll road model in particular has now been successful on the continent under both public (South Africa, Tunisia, Morocco, and recently, Zimbabwe) and private systems (South Africa).[16] The strongest recent growth in private investment, however, has been in electricity generation through independent power producers (IPPs) (Box 14.4).

Box 14.4: Private sector participation in power generation

The evolution of IPPs demonstrates opportunities for the private sector to participate both as financiers and as developers of infrastructure on the continent. Côte d'Ivoire was among the first African countries to attract foreign investors via IPP concessions (the Build-Own-Operate-Transfer model), soon followed by Egypt, and later Ghana, Morocco, Kenya, Tanzania, Tunisia and Uganda, among others. IPP funding on the continent peaked in 1997 with US$1.8 billion worth of private investment. IPPs contributed US$5.6 billion, or 75% of cumulative investments, in greenfield power sector projects in Sub-Saharan Africa, over the period 1990–2008. The trend parallels the power sector reforms implemented across Africa in the past two decades, which liberalized power generation and facilitated regulated competition in the sector.

Private sector participation in the power sector, while offering encouraging potential, also carries some risks, however. The expected benefits of private participation (competition, efficiency, cost recovery, innovation) are not always realized, and competitive bidding processes, competitive pricing and protection of intellectual property rights are necessary. In Cameroon, for example, private participation has not fostered competition; instead market power is concentrated in one public–private entity, AES-Sonel, which limits the potential benefits of regulated competition.

Source: Mutambatsere and Mukasa (2011)

Fostering a regional approach to infrastructure is another source of infrastructure financing through efficiency gains. Indeed, Africa's geography demands a regional approach to regional infrastructure development to ensure efficiency in service provision and maximize resources. The continent could save US$2 billion a year in energy costs by utilizing the existing regional power pools to their full potential.[17] Developing the continent's largely untapped hydropower potential through investments in regional infrastructure such as the Grand Inga Project (Box 14.5) would generate financial returns for Africa's power pools of 20% to 30%, and as high as 120% for the Southern African Power Pool. Similarly, developing a transnational highway network linking all capitals in Sub-Saharan Africa could result in trade gains of up to US$250 billion over 15 years.[18] Developing regional hubs, particularly in maritime and air transport infrastructure (Box 14.6), would also boost efficiency.

Box 14.5: The Grand Inga Project

The ambitious Grand Inga Project, worth US$80 billion, will develop 39,000 MW of hydropower capacity on the Congo River in the Democratic Republic of Congo. The Inga Falls' power-generation potential are second only to the Amazon's. The project's target power generation capacity is equivalent to a third of Africa's total electricity generation capacity in 2009; it also exceeds the capacity of the largest hydropower project in the world, the 18,000 MW Three Gorges Dam in China, which became operational in 2009. The project has been identified as a priority by the Southern African Development Community (SADC) and the New Economic Partnership for Africa's Development (NEPAD). At completion, the dam is expected to supply power to African consumers in Angola, Egypt, Nigeria and South Africa. While the project is far from reaching financial closing, it has drawn considerable interest from leading players in the energy industry, including power companies and development finance institutions such as the World Energy Council and the World Bank, which are leading project development. Issues surrounding the environmental and social impact of the project, as well as the potential exclusion of poor local households, still have to be addressed, however.

Source: http://www.internationalrivers.org/en/africa/grand-inga-dam

Box 14.6: Ethiopian Airlines: developing regional hubs

Regional hubs improve efficiency not only in capital investments, but also in operation and asset maintenance. In air transport, Ethiopian Airlines has emerged as a hub on the east coast and a major African carrier dominating international and domestic markets. In Sub-Saharan Africa (SSA), Ethiopian Airlines shares intercontinental and intra-African traffic with two other carriers: South African Airways and Kenya Airways. Its intra-African network already spanned more than 20 cities in 18 African countries in 1991, and the company has added new destinations to its portfolio, such as Brazzaville in Congo and Kano in Nigeria. As of 2008, Ethiopian Airlines had the highest number of destinations, serving 35 African cities in 26 countries, and accounted for 45% of the traffic. Ethiopian Airlines' aviation training center, established in 1956 to train domestic technicians and pilots, has become a regional hub servicing numerous African carriers. Ethiopian Airlines is currently increasing and modernizing its fleet to increase passenger traffic by about 175% by 2018.

Source: Mutambatsere and Mukasa (2011); AfDB (2011d)

While cross-border infrastructure projects are transformative, they are also challenging relative to single-country projects. Differing priorities across borders and poor coordination of national projects with a regional dimension, among other factors, explain the slow progress in completing strategic investments such as the Trans-African Highway initiative. Inadequacies in project preparation are also particularly evident in regional projects. In addition, these projects have markedly higher transaction costs and complex risk factors for potential financiers. Given their financial scale, they involve multiple financiers, requiring careful coordination to ensure that transactions are efficient and effective. Moreover, execution of multinational projects requires full, effective cooperation among countries and in some cases, harmonization of policies, rules and regulations.

Regional infrastructure operations thus require innovative planning, procurement, and financing. Initiatives such as the Presidential Infrastructure Champion Initiative (also known as the "Zuma initiative") and the Program for Infrastructure Development in Africa (PIDA) have taken significant steps towards spotlighting regional integration projects and national projects with regional significance. Success of such regional planning instruments will depend primarily on political commitment and buy-in at multiple levels of government. It will also depend on the extent to which regional plans are harmonized with national ones in terms of funding priorities, and balancing growth and pro-poor infrastructure investments.

Support for project preparation is making notable progress, thanks to technical assistance funds such as the NEPAD-sponsored Infrastructure Project Preparation Facility (IPPF) (Box 14.7). In addition, the Infrastructure Consortium for Africa (ICA), in partnership with IPPF, EU-Africa Infrastructure Trust Fund, and the Development Bank of Southern Africa, is developing the "Tunnel of Funds" concept, whereby project preparation activities and costs necessary to advance priority regional projects from concept to bankable prospect are identified, and financing packages assembled. The concept is still at a nascent stage, however, and its effectiveness yet to be proven. Facilities to support regional infrastructure projects are also increasingly being established by regional economic communities including the Economic Community of West African States and the SADC.

Box 14.7: Infrastructure Project Preparation Facility

The IPPF is a multi-donor fund established to assist African countries, regional economic communities and their specialized institutions to prepare high-quality and viable regional infrastructure projects, and develop consensus and broker partnerships for their implementation through public, private or other sources of finance. IPPF is a NEPAD initiative managed by the AfDB with project preparation financing of up to US$15 million per year. The facility supports regional infrastructure development in the energy, transport, water resources and ICT sectors. In 2010, IPPF contributed about US$9 million toward the development of 10 projects, including two in the energy sector, three in transport and three in capacity building. IPPF prepared regional infrastructure projects worth around US$4.7 billion between 2005 and 2010. While the facility is a step in the right direction, committed resources—currently standing at US$42 million—are not nearly enough to meet the regional project preparation for the continent.

Source: AfDB (2010e)

Innovation in funding regional infrastructure is also required to ensure an equitable allocation of risks and rewards among partnering countries. Investing in regional infrastructure may represent a disproportionately high, even prohibitive, cost for small economies, while geography often dictates that investments be concentrated in one country.

Challenges to the development of regional infrastructure can be addressed by MDBs providing a higher proportion of their financing towards cross-border projects. Progress at the country level includes the creation of national units in Kenya, Malawi, Mozambique, Nigeria, and Tanzania to help develop multinational projects involving private operators and investors. Such projects are inherently more complex, and often require instruments to help "right-size" the high upfront risk borne disproportionately by private investors. Coordinating public–private partnership (PPP) regulatory frameworks across sub-regions would facilitate the implementation of such projects.

Countries such as the Central African Republic are experimenting with innovative PPP models to improve access to clean water in small towns on cost-recovery basis. Overall, infrastructure development strategies must seek to balance pro-growth with pro-poor investments if the current bias in access is to be redressed.

Africa50 Fund for infrastructure

The African Development Bank Group plans to launch a pan-African infrastructure investment vehicle (Africa50 Fund)[19] to accelerate infrastructure development in Africa. The fund will have both an equity and bond elements. The aim of the Africa50 Fund is to unlock private financing sources and to accelerate the speed of infrastructure delivery in Africa, thereby creating a new platform for Africa's growth and prosperity. The Africa50 Fund will focus on high-impact national and regional projects in the energy, transport, ICT and water sectors.

Increasing the rate of infrastructure delivery in Africa implies a greater focus on project preparation and project development. In addition, Africa's project finance landscape lacks specialized financial tools to address specific market challenges. This demands financial innovation and deep-rooted knowledge of the local context.

The Africa50 Fund will establish two business lines:

- *project development*, increasing the number of bankable infrastructure projects in Africa;
- *project finance*, delivering the financial instruments required to attract additional infrastructure financing to the continent, including credit enhancement and other risk mitigation measures.

In addition, the Africa50 Fund will aim to reduce the timeline from project idea to financial close from a current average of seven years to an intended three years, thus accelerating the pace of infrastructure delivery in the continent.

The African Development Bank Group has already identified infrastructure projects worth US$150 billion, including the PIDA pipeline. The Africa50 Fund aims at attracting at least US$100 billion worth of local and global capital to deliver this pipeline. The African Development Bank Group has shown that for every dollar in equity, it can deliver 10 dollars in total infrastructure investment. As such, to deliver on its aim, the Africa50 Fund will need an equity investment of US$10 billion.

Through an immediate drawdown of US$3 billion, the Africa50 Fund will begin operations, bringing already-advanced projects to financial close, and building credibility within three years. The US$3 billion equity drawdown, along with its early investment operations, will position the Africa50 Fund to seek an investment-grade rating. This will enable the Africa50 Fund to issue bonds in the capital markets to mobilize a significant portion of debt from institutional investors requiring comparatively more secure returns. It is expected that the debt amount will exceed that of the equity. The remaining equity of US$7 billion will be drawn as the fund's operations grow, and will be used to raise a proportional volume of additional debt to respond to growing infrastructure needs.

The primary investors will be African governments, drawing on their internal resources, as well as the African Development Bank Group. First, lower-income African countries could opt to pay for their investments by using their country or regional operations allocation from the African Development Fund (ADF). The target is to raise US$1 billion from the ADF resources of African countries. Second, middle-income African countries will also have the opportunity to invest in this core equity base. Third, subject to the approval of its board of directors, the African Development Bank Group will participate in the equity of the Africa50 Fund with up to US$100 million per annum. This would represent up to US$1 billion over 10 years. These initial equity investors will play prominent roles in the governance of the fund, commensurate with the risk assumed. Fourth, the initial equity investments will enable the Africa50 Fund to raise additional equity-type funding from more risk-averse investors with large pools of capital, including pension funds, sovereign wealth funds and central banks.

The role of the African Development Bank

In addition to financing infrastructure and supporting capacity building on the continent, MDBs like the African Development Bank have refined their instruments to enhance involvement in areas of comparative advantage and unlock restrictions to individual country's borrowing. This includes provision of blended financing packages and risk management instruments to catalyze private finance, building capacity and country systems, and brokering complex regional projects.

Indeed, the AfDB is involved in financing infrastructure and catalyzing funds through traditional and innovative methods for both the public and private sectors in order to facilitate private sector development (Box 14.8). Over the past six years, the bank has increased the volume of financing for infrastructure projects, as well as the proportion of financing that goes to regional projects. The bank has also been utilizing blended financing packages and risk management instruments to attract private finance, build capacity in African countries, and broker complex regional projects. In addition to providing loans for infrastructure development projects, the bank has also introduced the use of quasi-equity instruments, such as subordinated loans, to raise the overall return on investment, and/ or to enhance credit structures to acceptable risk levels. To address exchange rate risk, the bank has developed the innovative Currency Exchange Fund. This fund helps investors hedge against interest rate risks associated with infrastructure financing in local currencies. The bank has also become increasingly more involved in issuing bonds in local currencies, providing guarantees, and participating in currency swaps markets. In addition, it is promoting capacity building in African countries to build efficient and sustainable institutions and regulatory frameworks that are robust enough to develop even the most complex projects. The bank is also working closely with the AU through the recently launched PIDA, and is developing a road map for the execution of a priority set of regional integration infrastructure projects.

Box 14.8: AfDB's infrastructure development activities

Lending
- US$3.7 billion to infrastructure projects in 2010 (60% approvals)
- US$1.9 billion for transport
- US$1.2 billion for energy
- US$650 million for water and sanitation
- US$50 million for communication
- US$1.7 billion earmarked for regional operations for the period 2011 to 2013

Technical assistance
- Fund for African Private Sector Assistance (US$16 million per year for private operations)
- NEPAD Infrastructure Project Preparation Facility (US$15 million per year for regional projects)
- Middle Income Countries (MICs) Technical Assistance Fund (US$16 million for operations in middle income countries)
- Technical Assistant for bond issues in RMCs

Risk management instruments
- Guarantees
- Partial credit guarantee
- Partial risk guarantee
- Hedging products

- Currency swaps
- Interest rate swaps, caps, collars
- Commodity/index swaps
- Indexed loans

Support to access climate finance
- Setting up the Africa Green Fund to mobilize resources
- Supporting pioneer development of clean energy projects at commercial scale (for example, Cabeolica wind farm in Cape Verde)
- Financing energy efficiency projects (reached US$5 billion for MDBs collectively in 2009)
- Improving uptake from existing facilities (Climate Investment Funds, Global Environment Facility)

Source: AfDB (2010f)

Between 2008 and 2011, total sovereign and non–sovereign approved investments in infrastructure operations represented 60.4% of the bank's total investment in the four core areas. Energy and power received the largest share (47%), followed by transportation (39%), water supply and sanitation (12%), communications (1%) and other infrastructure (2%). In 2011 the bank committed UA (Units of Account) 5.72 billion toward its operations in all sectors. The largest share of the Bank's resources interventions was targeted at building infrastructure, which comprises transportation, water supply and sanitation, energy, and information and communications technology. This amounted to UA 1.57 billion, representing 38.1% of total Bank's loan and grant approvals for the year. The African Development Bank seeks to contribute to the development of sound domestic debt markets in Africa through the creation of the African Domestic Bond Fund. The Bank has therefore announced a plan to launch the first pan–African infrastructure bond to member nations in order to raise up to US$22 billion for investments in infrastructure projects across Africa. The project will require African Central Banks to commit 5% of their foreign exchange reserves to contribute to infrastructure investments. The bond will be guaranteed by the African Development Bank, a triple-A rated Pan-African development finance institution.

The specific objectives of this instrument are as follows:

- reduce African countries' dependency on foreign currency denominated debt;

- encourage the deepening of domestic bond markets through investments in longer dated assets; and
- contribute to enlarge the investor base in African domestic bond markets.

The project of creating an African Domestic Bond Fund is organized in two stages. Under the first stage, for the fund to be efficient, it needs to be created within a well-functioning domestic debt market. Thus, at the outset, the fund will focus on building the necessary basic conditions for domestic debt bond markets to develop. Based on the current situation of African financial markets, the following represent the priority areas to be addressed during first stage:

- strengthening of regulatory and supervisory framework;
- expansion of primary and creation of secondary bond markets;
- enhancement of payment systems;
- development of local and international credit ratings; and
- broadening of the investor base.

The first stage will also include carrying out a mapping study dedicated to domestic bond market development initiatives in Africa in order to avoid duplication of efforts among donors and to identify potential synergies between existing initiatives at a regional and country level and the African Financial Markets Initiative (AFMI) (see later in this section). Following the strengthening of domestic bond markets, the second stage will consist of the creation of an African Domestic Bond Fund invested in local currency denominated sovereign African bonds initially funded by the African Development Bank and African Central Banks. The African Domestic Bond Fund will be passively managed and its return will be closely correlated with an underlying index.

The African Domestic Bond Fund will complement the Emerging Africa Infrastructure Fund (EAIF), which is a PPP fund designed to provide long-term US dollar- or Euro-denominated debt or mezzanine finance on commercial terms to finance the construction and development of private infrastructure in 47 countries across Sub-Saharan Africa. EAIF is able to provide between US$10 million to US$36.5 million (or its equivalent in Euros) to projects across a wide range of sectors including telecommunications, transport, water and power, among others.

In addition, the AFMI, an integrated and tailored response to further the development of domestic African capital markets, was launched by the African Development Bank Group in 2008. It is funded by the African Development Bank, the Fund for African Private Sector Assistance and the Canadian International Development Agency. The objectives of the AFMI are to contribute to the development of local currency debt markets in Africa; to reduce African countries dependency on foreign currency denominated debt; to help enlarge the investor base in African domestic debt markets; and to improve availability and transparency of African fixed income markets-related data, among others.

Several instruments have emerged to improve the bankability of projects in high-risk environments. Some projects are able to attract a blend of concessional funding and private investment that either raises the overall return on investment or enhances credit structures to acceptable risk levels. Such financing is required for projects where upfront investment is high and the time until revenues are generated is long. Blended financing is also crucial to improve the bankability of complex regional projects, such as the Kenya–Uganda railways concession (Box 14.9).

Box 14.9: MDBs in the Kenya–Uganda railways concession

In 2006, the Kenyan and Uganda governments jointly concessioned their rail networks to a private operator under a 25-year concession agreement. MDBs provided most of the support to bring the projects to closure. The International Finance Corporation acted as transaction advisor and, in partnership with AfDB, KfW of Germany, FMO of Netherlands and BIO of Belgium, as a financier of the project. The IFC's early involvement catalysed additional financing from the World Bank Group. Concessional funds from the International Development Agency (IDA), and arm of the World Bank, financed the environmental and social impact management plans, including a retrenchment plan for the Kenya Railway Corporation. IDA also provided partial risk guarantees to cover the concessionaire and lender from possible failure by the two governments to fulfil their contractual obligations. IDA support to the residual railway corporations also acted to prepare them to take on regulator roles. In addition to financing, the AfDB prepared the resettlement action plans covering the full network, both of which were financed by IDA. MDBs were also able to use their convening power to draw new interest and salvage the concession when the concessionaire faced possible termination of the concession agreement in 2008 after failing to meet performance targets and to pay concession fees.

Source: Mutambatsere et al (2011)

MDBs can also ramp up risk management support. Commercial and political risk premium can be covered by both debt and equity insurance and by guarantee instruments. While commercial instruments exist, concessional ones such as partial risk guarantees (PRGs) offered by the IDA and the African Development Fund (ADF), and political risk insurance offered by the Multilateral Investment Guarantee Agency, are more suitable for ADF countries. PRGs, for example, have been shown to generate as much as 10 times the value of the guarantee in additional financing.[20] Political risk management instruments also provide governments with incentives to implement reforms that address performance risk. Partial credit guarantees (PCG) have been used to cover losses in the event of a debt service default caused by either political or commercial risk. PCGs improve the borrowers' access to financial markets by sharing the borrowers' credit risk vis-à-vis the lenders and guarantors. Full credit guarantees or wrap guarantees may also be applied to provide full debt-service cover.

The AfDB is proposing to cover country risk premiums through first-loss guarantees for a portfolio of transactions supported by the bank. A portfolio guarantee mitigates the cost of the country risk premium affecting low-income countries and fragile states. The risk capital freed up could be used exclusively for low-income countries. This option would allow these countries to leverage at least five times the value of the guarantee in additional financing from a non-sovereign pool of lending sources.

MDB-led syndications and B-loans are intended to enable project-level risk mitigation for commercial lenders, spurred by MDBs' preferred creditor status.[21] But risk capital utilization and institutional constraints may not allow these institutions to take on this role to significantly match market demand. The same holds for direct equity participation in projects. MDBs can mitigate the equity risk premium arising primarily from political uncertainties through direct or indirect equity participation in infrastructure projects. Indirect participation through equity funds focusing on infrastructure is ongoing but on a small scale so far.[22] MDB sponsorship of such specialized funds can influence geographic reach, and facilitate the adoption of international best practices.

In addition, MDBs are experimenting with participation in infrastructure projects through direct equity, although this is still uncommon. Being an equity partner allows MDBs to participate in the early stages of project preparation and attract funding from other sources to cover project development costs incurred by developers prior to financial closing. Quasi equity instruments like subordinated loans are more common. The risk of foreign exchange rate volatility can be addressed through currency hedging, government exchange rate guarantees and devaluation liquidity schemes, among others. However, much greater attention needs to be paid to affordability of these instruments in the African context. The AfDB, for example, has developed the innovative Currency Exchange Fund (TCX), which helps investors to hedge interest rate risks associated with local currency infrastructure financing, mainly through pooling market risks from different investors with geographically diversified business. Through local currency financing, TCX reduces foreign exchange risk.[23]

To address capial market bottlenecks, the AfDB has increasingly become more involved in issuing bonds in local currencies, technical support for bond issues, providing guarantees, and participating in currency swap markets. MDBs have also traditionally supported financial markets development through policy-based lending.

The AfDB, on 17 July 2012, opened books on its 125 billion Ugandan shilling medium-term note (MTN) program. The first issue of the program, which is a 10-year, 12.5 billion Ugandan shilling bond, was open for subscription through 20 July 2012. The first tranche of the program, for example, was over-subscribed by 50%—receiving 18 billion shillings. The institutions that showed most appetite for the bond included the National Social Security Fund, Standard Chartered Bank, Stanbic Bank, and Pine East Africa among others. The coupon, to be re-priced at two-year intervals, is pegged at 85% of the yield on Uganda's two-year government bond benchmark. Part of the funds raised will be used to fund the bank's projects in Uganda including infrastructure and others. The bank had already listed a local currency bond at the Ugandan Securities Exchange. It also plans to launch local currency bonds with Nairobi Securities Exchange, Dar es Salaam Stock Exchange and Ghana Stock Exchange.

Unlike previous African currencies-linked bonds issued by the bank, all coupon and principal (re)payments will be made in shillings and there will be no currency swap attached to the transaction. As part of its local currency initiative, the bank has since 2005 issued a series of bonds denominated in or linked to the Botswana pula, Ghana cedi, Kenya shilling, Tanzania shilling, Uganda shilling, Zambian kwacha and the Nigerian naira in offshore markets. It is also a regular issuer in South African rand, which is its third-largest lending currency. This is part of a larger program of helping capital markets develop on the continent and the bank believes that deep, liquid capital markets are needed to support higher and sustainable economic growth in the continent. MDBs can also provide investment services to institutional investors, who are attracted to infrastructure investments' long-horizon and steady returns, but often lack sufficient local knowledge and information of on pipeline transactions. The AfDB provides such investment services to the Japan International Cooperation Agency, and opportunities exist to extend these services to a range of similar investors.

MDBs play a critical role in assisting countries to access special envelops of financing, such as climate finance. For example, the donor-funded Clean Technology Fund will leverage at least five times their value in clean energy solutions, including energy efficiency, renewable energy, and sustainable transport investments. Africa's perspective must be taken into account when decisions on disbursements of global funds for climate change adaptation and mitigation are made. To help facilitate access to these funds, the AfDB is setting up the Africa Green Fund to receive and manage resources to address climate change on the continent.

International financial institutions, as investors in infrastructure development, can also play a role in improving maintenance particularly in low-income, low-capacity environments. This could be achieved by, among other things, establishing a sound maintenance framework as a prerequisite to major capital investments. They can also play a countercyclical role to support maintenance activities during periods of economic recession. During the recent economic downturn, for instance, MDBs including the AfDB and the World Bank targeted the preservation of strategic assets by providing soft loans or grant facilities for maintenance.

Notes

[1] Anyanwu and Erhijakpor (2009)

[2] Soderbom and Teal (2001)

[3] Basu and Srinivasan (2002); Asiedu (2002)

[4] Ayogu (2007)

[5] Escribano et al (2008)

[6] AICD (2010)

[7] Statistics are drawn from the AICD database (ACID, 2010), which covers 24 African countries, and from the African Development Bank Statistics Department (AfDB, 2010a–2010f; 2011a).

[8] Ramachandran et al (2009)

[9] *The Economist* (2011)

[10] United Nations (2011)

[11] South African ports are operated by state-owned Transnet, which operates on a cost-recovery basis (AICD, 2010).

[12] This figure pertains to an investment and maintenance program to develop the following infrastructure in Sub-Saharan Africa: (1) 7,000 megawatts (MW) a year of new power generation capacity (about half through multipurpose dams); (2) cross-border transmission lines with a capacity of 22,000 megawatts; (3) fiber-optic cable to complete the intraregional fiber-optic backbone network and continental submarine cable loop; (4) good-quality road network to interconnect capitals, ports, border crossings, and secondary cities; (5) all-season road to access high-value agricultural land; (6) irrigation infrastructure to more than double Africa's irrigated area; (7) infrastructure to meet the Millennium Development Goals for water and sanitation; (8) electricity network to raise household electrification rates by 10 percentage points; and (9) network to provide global systems mobile voice signal and public access broadband to 100% of the population (AICD, 2010).

[13] Anyanwu (2009)

[14] This is a subsidy that can be used as partial capital cost financing for upfront investment needs to encourage private operators' involvement in critical infrastructure projects with high economic benefits but low financial returns. Competitive pricing of the viability gap is crucial if such subsidies are to be utilized successfully.

[15] AfDB (2011a)

[16] Brixiova et al (2011)

[17] AICD (2010)

[18] Buys et al (2006)

[19] AfDB (2013)

[20] Ramachandaran et al (2009)

[21] Preferred creditor status protects the bank's properties and assets from requisition, confiscation, expropriation or any other form of taking or foreclosure by executive or legislative action.

[22] Brixiova et al (2011)

[23] Brixiova et al (2011)

References

AfDB (African Development Bank) (2010a) 'Ports, Logistics and Trade in Africa', *The African Development Report 2010*.

AfDB (2010b), 'Infrastructure Deficits and Opportunities in Africa', Africa Economic Brief, Volume 1, Issue 2, African Development Bank, September 2010.

AfDB (2010c), Proposal Appraisal Report for a EUR 15 million Senior Loan to Finance the Cabeolica Wind Power Project, May 2010.

AfDB (2010d), Proposal Appraisal Report for a USD 400 million Corporate Loan to Transnet Limited, June 2010.

AfDB (2010e) *2010 Annual Report*, ADB–ADF/BG/AR/2010.

AfDB (2010f) Egypt Power Sector in Brief–2010, Regional Department North I, AfDB, 2010.

AfDB (2011a) 'Solving the bankability conundrum to fill the African infrastructure investment gap', Discussion Topics with External Expert Panel, Paris, 27-28 February.

AfDB (2011b) Proposal Appraisal Report for a USD 12 million Senior Loan to Finance the Seychelles Submarine Cable Project, April 2011.

AfDB (2011c) The Africa Infrastructure Development Index. Economic Brief, April.

AfDB (2011d) Proposal Appraisal Report for a USD 40 million Senior Loan to Finance the Ethiopian Airlines Project, March.

AfDB (2013) Africa50 Fund, Concept Note, African Development Bank Group, May 2013.

AICD (Africa Infrastructure Country Diagnostic) (2010) *Africa's Infrastructure: A Time for Transformation*. Edited by V. Foster and C. Briceño-Garmendia, Agence Francaise de Developpement and World Bank, USA.

Ayogu, M. (2007) 'Infrastructure and economic development in Africa", *Journal of African Economies*, vol 16, pp 75-126.

Anyanwu, J.C. (2009) 'Public-private partnerships in the Nigerian energy sector: banks' roles and lessons of experience', in James B. Tobin and Lawrence R. Parker (eds) *Joint Ventures, Mergers and Acquisitions, And Capital Flow*, New York, NY: Nova Science Publishers, pp 75-122.

Anyanwu, J.C. and Erhijakpor A.E.O. (2009) 'The impact of road infrastructure on poverty reduction in Africa', in Thomas W. Beasley (ed) *Poverty in Africa*, New York, NY: Nova Science Publishers, pp 1-40.

Asiedu, E. (2002) 'On the determinants of foreign direct investment to developing countries: is Africa different?', *World Development*, vol 30, no 1, pp 107-19.

Basu, A. and Srinivasan, K. (2002) *Foreign Direct Investment in Africa – Some Case Studies*, Working Paper 2002-2061. Washington, DC: IMF.

Brixiova, Z., Mutambatsere, E., Ambert, C. and Etienne, D. (2011) 'Closing Africa's infrastructure gap: innovative financing and risks', *Africa Economic Brief*, vol 2, no 1.

Buys, P., Deichmann, U. and Wheeler, D. (2006) *Road Network Upgrading and Overland Trade Expansion in Sub-Saharan Africa*, Washington, DC: World Bank.

Buys, P., Deichmann, U., Meisner, C., That, T.T. and Wheeler, D. (2007) *Country Stakes in Climate Change Negotiations: Two Dimensions of Vulnerability*, Policy Research Working Paper 4300. Washington, DC: World Bank.

Duarte, M., Nagarajan, S. and Brixiova, Z. (2010) *Financing of Sustainable Energy Solution*, Committee of Ten Policy Brief No. 3. Tunis: AfDB.

Escribano, A., Guasch, J.L. and Pena, J. (2008) *Impact of Infrastructure Constraints on Firm Productivity in Africa*, Working Paper 9, Africa Infrastructure Sector Diagnostic. Washington, DC: World Bank.

Iarossi, G. (2009) 'Benchmarking Africa's Costs and Competitiveness', in *Africa Competitiveness Report 2009*. Geneva: World Economic Forum, pp 83–108.

Kamara, A., Baresa, M., Anyanwu, J.C. and Kang, G.S. (2011) 'Improving infrastructure and energy access', in K. K. Yumkella et al (eds) *Agribusiness for Africa's Prosperity*, Geneva: UNIDO.

Mutambatsere, E., Vencatachellum, D., Nalikka, A. and Pal, M. (2011) *The Rift Valley Railway Case Study: Challenges of Multi-country Private Sector Operations and DFIs Role*, African Development Bank Working Paper. Tunis: AfDB.

Mutambatsere, E. and Mukasa, A. (2011) *Infrastructure and Private Sector Development in Africa*, Background Paper for the African Development Report. Tunis: AfDB.

Ramachandran, V., Gelb, A. and Shah, M.K. (2009) *Africa's Private Sector*. Washington, DC: Center for Global Development.

Soderbom, M. and Teal, F. (2001) 'Can African manufacturing firms become successful exporters?', Paper presented at Third United Nations Conference on Least Developed Countries, May.

The Economist (2011) 'African airlines: flying in Africa is getting easier', 16 June.

United Nations (2011) *The Millennium Development Goals Report 2011*. New York: United Nations.

FIFTEEN

Innovative financing for infrastructure: Africa50 Fund issues

George Kararach

Introduction

The role of infrastructure in Africa's sustainable development is well documented and accepted. The intriguing question that needs urgent answering is: why has the infrastructure financing gap remained relatively large and persistent? Why has the private sector not played a more active role in providing the necessary funding? Why are less as opposed to more infrastructure projects being successfully implemented in a continent desperate for transformation while world financial markets are awash with capital? Ehlers (2014) argues that the persistent funding gap is an outcome of the failures of countries to reconcile available finance with bankable projects.

There are a number of efforts that have been undertaken to rethink how additional resources can be mobilized and private sector participation increased. These efforts include policy and institutional reforms that seek to reduce risks to ramp up both short- and long-term finance. There have been attempts by countries to enhance project designs and ensure contracts are respected and adequately enforced in ways such that infrastructure investments deliver the anticipated outcomes. A balance needs to be achieved to get a win–win situation for both private gains and social outcomes. The challenge for both private and public sector participants is to design contracts where the risks and returns are distributed in an incentive-compatible way (Ehlers, 2014). There is need to broaden the spectrum of participants in infrastructure investments by identifying new sources and vehicles for finance suitable for various stages of given projects. For example, infrastructure bonds are more suitable instruments for large institutional investors, such as pension funds and insurance companies, while project finance and other structured instruments may be more suitable for banks.

Since 2009, the African Development Bank (AfDB) and other development partners such as the World Bank and the African Union have embarked on more aggressively tackling the infrastructure challenges of the continent. In 2009 the World Bank and major donors supported the African Infrastructure Country Diagnostic (AICD) study. This study, which formed the baseline against improvements in infrastructure services, has since been costed and priority investments and policy reforms around the Program for Infrastructure Development in Africa (PIDA) developed. The subsequent Africa Infrastructure Knowledge Program being spearheaded by AfDB builds on the AICD. The AfDB has also led efforts to mobilize the requisite resources needed to fund the US$93 billion per year infrastructure gap. The Africa50 Fund is part of this resource mobilization effort. The purpose of this chapter is to explore some of the issues that need to be in place to ensure that such a fund is delivered and functions effectively. For examples, how will "orphan" sectors be catered for or countries targeted be emphasized? What are the governance issues to ensure strategic coordination, and increased efficiency and sustainability? As noted by Gutman et al (2015), there are needs for political, technical, and financial synergies to address the infrastructure gap and thus consider the fund to be successful as a funding instrument.

The chapter is divided into five sections of which this is the first. The next section discusses theoretical issues on how private sector organizations makes decisions to finance their operations. The third section highlights the major issues when discussing the financing of infrastructure and what the key realities in Africa are. The next section then illustrates the significance of the infrastructure gap and argues for several key issues for the public sector to consider around the Africa50 Fund, such as development of a predictable pipeline of well-structured projects, greater ownership, and governance. The final section forms our conclusion.

Theories of infrastructure and corporate finance

Attempts to understand how firms make investment decisions have evolved over the years (see Weston [1955] for earlier analysis of these issues). Frank and Goyal (2005) provides an excellent review of the various theories of corporate finance. Our discussions draw on their contribution, which sought to explore critical questions in financial economics. How do firms finance their operations? How should firms finance their operations? What factors influence these choices? How do these choices affect the rest of the economy? Myers (1984) outlines two contrasting propositions on corporate debt and financing decisions: that of trade-off and pecking order. Under the trade-off hypothesis, firms balance tax savings from debt against deadweight bankruptcy costs. On the other hand, due to adverse selection, firms first look to retained earnings, then to debt, and only in extreme circumstances to equity for financing. This is the pecking-order theory (Frank and Goyal, 2005). With respect to the trade-off theory, the suggestion is that a firm will seek to structure its finances in ways that result in some optimal leverage in the long term. While under the pecking-order scenario, firms organize financing in a strict order. However, leverage target adjustment is neither necessary nor sufficient for the firm to be balancing tax savings against bankruptcy costs. Instead, target adjustment is arguably better viewed as being a separate hypothesis (ibid). Arguably this attempt to understand how firms make investments is equally applicable to less developed countries (LDCs). However, some variability might occur due to African specificities such as the small and medium-sized nature of firms therein.

The Frank-Goyal generalizations of 'kinds of theories'

Disagreements over the merits of financial theories stem, in part, from different views of the role that theory plays. It is, therefore, helpful to recognize the different kinds of theory. In their review, Frank and Goyal (2005) argued that different positions taken by commentators on the merits of financial theories are resultant from the intended roles of any given theory in explaining firm behavior. They outlined four broad types of theories or 'kinds of theories'. First is what they called "a point of view theory"—a type that outlines a series of principles necessary for the development of specific models and tests without being tied to a specific model formulation. The authors give the pecking order and the trade-off theories as examples of "point of view theories". The second type is an illustrative theory. An illustrative theory demonstrates that a certain idea can be expressed in a coherent and simple manner. Strong assumptions tend to be made to solve specific models in closed form. Third is a unifying model designed to tie together a variety of observations in a coherent manner by integrating underlying facts to a common structure. Often unifying models do not have closed-form solutions and so numerical calibrations are required to solve them. Fourth and finally is normative theory. Normative theory provides advice to chief executive officers on the nature of debt structure their firms should and could take. For example, Graham (2000) argues that many firms could increase value by levering up—clearly a normative proposition.

Modigliani-Miller theorem

It is arguable that to devise the correct investment vehicle, one must understand how a firm decides on the effort to maximize future investments. The question therefore is whether corporate debt policy matters (Chen and Kim, 1979). Modigliani and Miller's (1958) capital structure irrelevance proposition is seminal in the theory of corporate finance. Given a firm's particular set of expected cash flows, it chooses a certain proportion of debt and equity to finance its assets by dividing up the cash flows among investors in some specified strategic proportions. It is further assumed by the authors that investors and firms have equal access to financial markets, thus allowing homemade leverage. Frank and Goyal (2005) note that both the investor and firm can create a leverage or get rid of it. Such a leverage may not be wanted or offered, or the investor may get rid of any leverage that the firm took affecting each other's positions, leaving the market value of the firm unchanged.

The Modigliani-Miller paper led to burgeoning literature in corporate finance and how debt policy gets to be made (Chen and Kim, 1979). Theoretically, capital structure irrelevance can be proven under a range of circumstances (Frank and Goyal, 2005). Two immediately come to mind: first, arbitrage by investors keeps the value of the firm independent of its leverage (see Hirshleifer [1966] and Stiglitz [1969]), and second, capital structure irrelevance may be associated with multiple equilibria whereby equilibrium conditions determine the aggregate amount of debt and equity in the market, as in Miller (1977) and Auerbach and King (1983). Unfortunately these models do not specify how the aggregate debt quantities get divided up among firms. Equally, the notion of perfectly competitive financial market conditions raise some doubts and may explain real experiences of firms in both developed and developed economies.

Frank and Goyal (2005) note that the Modigliani-Miller theorem fails under a variety of circumstances including consideration of taxes, transaction costs, bankruptcy costs, agency conflicts, adverse selection, lack of separability between financing and operations, time varying financial market opportunities, and investor clientele effects. Indeed, these market factors are important, influencing investor decisions to finance given projects. There are also concerns that the theory does not present itself to ease of testability. For example, both debt and firm value are endogenous variables and driven by other factors such as profits, collateral, growth opportunities, corporate governance, and so on. In this regard, one will have econometric difficulties of getting a structural test of the theory by regressing value on debt. So what is the merit of the theory? It is arguable that although the Modigliani–Miller theorem does not provide a realistic description of how firms finance their operations, it provides a means of finding reasons why financing may matter (Frank and Goyal, 2005). Indeed, this argument applies to much of the theory of corporate finance including the trade-off and pecking-order theories.

Trade-off

We have noted that the trade-off theory seeks to describe how a decision maker evaluates the various costs and benefits of alternative firm's leverage plans. There is a general assumption that an interior solution is obtained so that marginal costs and marginal benefits are balanced (Frank and Goyal, 2005).

The trade-off theory is a variant or off-shoot of the Modigliani–Miller theorem whereby corporate income tax is 'added' to the original irrelevance proposition (see Modigliani and Miller, 1963) resulting in a benefit for debt as it shields earnings from taxes (ibid.). With no offsetting cost of debt, the firm thus has 100% debt financing. Kraus and Litzenberger (1973) argue that optimal leverage reflects a trade-off between the tax benefits of debt and the deadweight costs of bankruptcy. Myers (1984) notes that a firm following the trade-off theory sets a target debt-to-value ratio and then gradually moves towards the target. The target is determined by balancing debt tax shields against costs of bankruptcy (Frank and Goyal, 2005).

Myers' notion of trade-off can be critiqued in a number of ways. First, the leverage target is not directly observable. It may be imputed from evidence, but that depends on adding a structure. Different papers add that structure in different ways. Second, the tax code in most economies is more complex than that assumed by the theory and influenced by a wide number of variables readily noted by the proponents of the theory. Depending on which features of the tax code are included, different conclusions regarding the target can be reached. Graham (2003) provides a useful review of the literature on tax effects on corporate finance. In fact, appropriate tax regimes plays a critical role in shaping private sector participation in the financing of investments projects including infrastructure. Third, bankruptcy costs must be deadweight costs rather than transfers from one claimant to another, allowing firms to undertake efficiency measures when making investment decisions (see Haugen and Senbet [1978] discussion of bankruptcy costs). Finally, transactions costs must take a specific form of behavior—in particular, the adjustment has to be gradual rather than abrupt, in turn requiring that the marginal cost of adjusting increases when the adjustment is larger (see implications of alternative adjustment cost assumptions).

The models described in this section largely lean towards competitive general equilibriums in the financial markets and wider economy. These assumptions are generally difficult to discern in the real world and more so in the 'investment' market for infrastructure. We turn to that discussion in the next section with specific reference to Africa.

Debating infrastructure financing in African development

As we noted in the introduction, there is a real concern about the infrastructure gap and its stranglehold on African development. As we show, African countries and governments have made a number of attempts in recent years to put infrastructure of the continent's transformational agenda as evidenced by PIDA and the setting up of innovative financial vehicles such as the Africa50 Fund and increased use of public–private partnerships (PPPs) and regulated assets bases. As Figure 15.1 shows, there has been varied success in mobilizing infrastructure finance—especially from development partners.

From the discussions in the previous section, it is clear that infrastructure financing suffers from multiple market and government failures. Most of these failures are associated with public goods properties, sunk costs, market power and externalities as well as the lumpy nature of investments in infrastructure (Ehlers, 2014, p 4).

Figure 15.1: Trends in Infrastructure Consortium for Africa (ICA) financing of infrastructure in Africa, 2009–2013

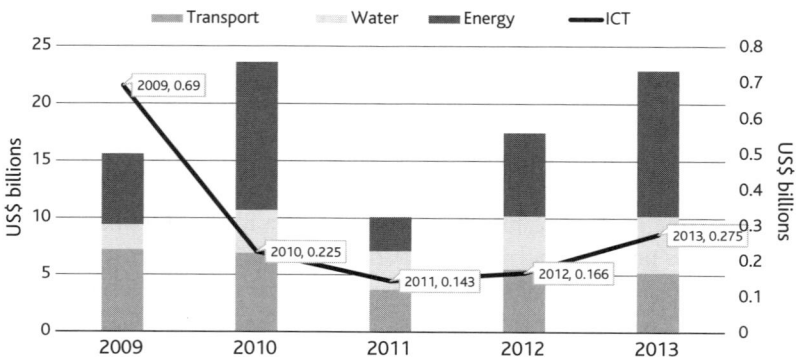

Source: Computed from ICA (2014) data

First, generally infrastructures tend to be part of networks and systems with public goods characteristics. Essentially, the marginal costs of adding on another consumer tend towards zero once the project is completed. In this regard, economic welfare is maximized by providing the public good to as many consumers as possible, with marginal incentives reflecting the marginal as opposed to the average costs. The main public goods problem, however, is the framework for recovery of the fixed (and sunk) costs without creating distortions to consumption. It is hard to set tariff regimes and guarantee them and their formula for adjustment across political cycles, leading to political risks of recovery of fixed and sunk costs.

Second, there are economic characteristics that differentiate infrastructure assets from other asset classes frequently resulting in mismatches in investment demand and financing supply: there are non-exclusion problems, benefits measurement issues and indirect spillover effects; infrastructure projects tend to be complex, natural monopolies and involve a large number of parties, thus requiring complex legal arrangements to ensure proper distribution of payoffs, and require risk-sharing to align the incentives of all parties involved; many infrastructure investments are lumpy, have long gestation periods and the initial phase of an infrastructure project is subject to high risks. These three elements—the time profile of cash flows, high initial risks and illiquidity—make purely private investment difficult and costly. Consequently, infrastructure investment from the private sector in many cases requires public support, be it direct financial support or some form of insurance, guarantees or subsidies. Equally, the quality of institutions and the rule of law are often determining factors in the supply of infrastructure finance, even when a project by itself appears to be financially viable. Infrastructure projects are also subject to electoral myopia where voters see the benefits of large-scale projects at completion, are very wary of price and tariff increases, and do not see the benefits of maintenance and upkeep (Leautier, 2014).

A number of "solutions" to the above cost recovery problem have been proposed and many have been tried in practice. Among these there is an inherent tension between economically efficient mechanisms which relate the fixed costs to the (inverse of) demand elasticities and those which take account of distributional consideration (ibid.). In theory, the "correct" solution is to price each and every externality. In practice, this is impractical and politically impossible. The result is that decisions are based on politics and planning, and very much open to political and regulatory failures.

As noted by commentators on cultural anthropology, the social aspects of infrastructure arise not only in the allocation of the fixed costs between the customer groups mentioned, but also over concerns linked to inclusion and access issues. As noted in Chapter One of this volume, infrastructure is critical for the provision of basic social goods, which in turn are essential for participating in society. Infrastructure lies behind the provision of life essentials such as health, education, heating, lighting, transport and communications. For these reasons, it is inevitable that governments will want to influence the design, provision and pricing of infrastructure.

Given the inherent market failures, the role of government is critical for the success of infrastructure policy, and its finance depends on how that role is designed and implemented. However, government interventions may bring in their wake other sets of problems. Government "failures" may raise the costs of provision and finance, and in particular affect the cost of capital and the optimal mix of debt and equity. The role of government in this regard may be circumscribed to the provision of an over-arching choice of networks and infrastructure; to facilitate planning and licensing; and to provide a credible commitment to the efficient sunk costs of the investment, while ensuring that any market power is not exploited to the detriment of the wider economy. Over time the private sector has emerged in history as a contractor as opposed to investor in infrastructure projects. With governments faced with significant fiscal constraints, and with little practical differentiation between capital and current spending, some governments will be tempted to reduce capital expenditure to protect operating expenditure while others tend to short-change maintenance by focusing on new construction as responses to short-term macroeconomic constraints. Taxpayers and customers share the risks, and governments can typically borrow at lower rates than the private sector. However, the failure to disaggregate the various types of risk, and the failure to take account of the incentive structure of the public sector, can and has also lead to sub-optimal outcomes.

Infrastructure bonds are an alternative source of financing for infrastructure projects. A debt instrument is issued by either governments or private companies to raise funds from capital markets for infrastructure projects (Mbeng-Mezui and Hundal, 2013). These bonds provide the coupon payments that are linked to cash flows generated from the underlying project. Infrastructure bonds hold several advantages compared with traditional loans: they are a cheaper financing method, and can be tailored to have longer maturity dates and wider market participation.

The African market is yet to fully develop to support classic infrastructure bonds as opposed to ordinary government bonds. Although a legal and regulatory framework exists for infrastructure bond issuance, African countries require a clear methodology and capacities to assess if particular infrastructure projects are suited to the bond market, paying attention to issues such as credit risk, execution cost and demand and supply conditions in the market (AfDB, 2013).

Since 2009, the AfDB has led the way in promoting the infrastructure bond model to infrastructure finance through the Africa50 initiative. The idea is to create a commercially oriented financial institution with the mandate to reduce Africa's infrastructure financing gap. The proposed institution is to support the funding of high-impact national and regional infrastructure projects across the continent. As of early 2015, the AfDB and partners have identified "transformative" infrastructure projects totaling US$150 billion—including the PIDA pipeline—primarily with significant regional benefits. We shall return to the Africa50 Fund issues later in the chapter.

The realities of infrastructure financing in Africa

The birth of the Africa50 Fund is part of an ever-changing picture of infrastructure finance in Africa. Gutman et al (2015) outline a number of important trends to be kept in mind when discussing the issues of infrastructure finance in Africa. We draw on the contribution and outline the major trends below:

a. Composition of external financing is changing. Overall financing for infrastructure in Africa has increased in recent years (ICA, 2014) with a large chunk coming from multilateral agencies such as the AfDB and the World Bank. Equally, private investment has surpassed official financing and surged to over 50% of external financing. On the bilateral front, China has become a major source. The change is also in line with the evolving global financial architecture with a shift in funding from traditional to non-traditional partners and private sector sources. As some countries get more and some less, the fund will play a critical role in ensuring there are no "aid" orphans.

b. There have been no clear "orphans" except for a limited number of fragile states facing serious governance issues (Gutman et al, 2015). In sectoral terms, the distribution of external finance has also been uneven. The energy sector has had the fastest growth across all external financing sources since 2009: it now attracts 45% of the total external finance,e presumably because of initiatives such as PowerAfrica. However, private investment has historically been concentrated in the telecommunications (or information and communications technology) sector. Equally, official Chinese investment has been expanding beyond the earlier focus on resource-rich economies and is reaching sectors in which it has particular technical expertise—such as hydropower—and those that are not as amenable to the private sector—such as transport (especially road and rail (ibid.).

c. Public sector budgets remain dominant. Despite the focus on external financing given by donors, the primary source of funding for infrastructure in Africa, as elsewhere in the world, continues to be public sector budgets. Public sector budgets remain critical as they establish the strategic framework within which support through external financing should be coordinated. The International Monetary Fund (IMF) estimates that countries in Sub-Saharan Africa finance about 65% of their infrastructure expenditures (IMF, 2014)—almost US$60 billion (about 4% of sub-Saharan Africa's gross domestic product [GDP])—from their public sector budgets (this amount excludes financing from multilateral institutions). This amount is under the 5–6% of GDP for infrastructure financing to sustain growth benchmark advocated by development practitioners (Fay et al, 2011). The ratio varies by country needs and level of existing infrastructure. The key message is that African countries need to keep up the progress in raising fiscal revenues by widening the fiscal space to meet the infrastructure gap through enhance domestic resource mobilization. The domestic resource mobilisation (DRM) efforts and outcomes vary across countries. For example, tax revenue to GDP varies across the board—ranging from 25% in South Africa to 2.8% in the Democratic Republic of the Congo. African countries also have to increase efforts to access international capital markets—about 13 countries as of end of 2014 had issued US$15 billion worth of international sovereign bonds since 2006 (Gutman et al, 2015, p 44). Sub-national/urban infrastructure is ignored: rising urbanization is putting pressure on the continent to have smart and livable cities. As noted in this volume by Mubila et al in Chapter Ten, there is growing pressure for investments in urban infrastructure. Comparatively, Sub-Saharan Africa remains predominantly rural, but that is changing rapidly, with some estimates noting that by 2035 50% of the population will be urban (UN-Habitat, 2014, p 23). In many cities, the challenge of urbanization and the need for critical infrastructure is already evident. Currently, one-third of urban residents in Sub-Saharan Africa are located in 36 mega cities (with more than a million inhabitants each) (World Bank, 2013, p 13). There is a need for better and strategic planning to integrate land use and infrastructure to avoid an otherwise pending irreversible deleterious effect in terms of economic growth, social progress, and environmental preparedness consequent of urbanization. Indeed, decentralization will put greater pressure on local authorities and test their capacity to raise revenues as well as explore new forms of financing to have sustainable development including decentralized infrastructure services (Gutman et al, 2015, p 48). However, experiences from many African countries show that local services and investment still depend heavily on national government transfers, instead of permitting local governments to raise sufficient revenues. Clarity need to be enhanced in relations to the level of autonomy and the uncertainties of annual budget approvals to allow explorations of alternative and innovative financing.

d. The emergence of innovative regional financiers. Another important trend is the increasing role played by regional financial players such as Afrexim Bank, the PTA Bank and Development Bank of Southern Africa (DBSA). The Afrexim Bank, for example, has a Suppliers and Buyers Credit Program. This program supports African manufacturers and importers of engineering equipment, and capital goods, as well as promoters of turn-key projects. It is designed to serve the following purposes: enable African equipment manufacturers to compete for export markets on a near equal footing with other competitors; support African users of heavy equipment manufactured competitively in Africa to source such equipment from Africa; and assist African importers of heavy equipment for export, promoting infrastructure projects to obtain such equipment from overseas at reduced costs since the bank's guarantee may reduce the fees for export credit cover required by the overseas shippers. Essentially, the bank's supplier credit facility permits African exporters of goods and equipment to give credit to their buyers for a period ranging from six months to seven years. The exporter is financed by the bank against appropriate guarantees. While under the bank's buyer credit facility, the exporter of the heavy equipment is paid while the bank receives payment in due course from the buyer. This is also provided against appropriate guarantees where necessary. The program is focused, but not limited to, encouraging intra-African trade in engineering machinery and equipment and infrastructural services. On the hand, the PTA Bank, also known as Preferential Trade Area Bank, is a trade and development financial institution in Africa. The PTA Bank is the financial arm of Common Market for Eastern and Southern Africa (COMESA), but membership is open to non-COMESA states and other institutional shareholders. As of December 2014, the bank was a large financial institution with an asset base in excess of US$2.53 billion. The bank had 20 shareholders, with shareholders' funds of nearly US$477 million. The bank provides a range of financial products including project and infrastructure finance. The PTA Bank provides medium- and long-term financing on commercial terms. Target sectors are those considered as high impact such as agribusiness and infrastructure that is a catalyst for development in member states. The range of financing solutions offered includes project finance, corporate finance, leasing and guarantees among others. PTA Bank provides funding to both public and private enterprises, covering almost all sectors of economy. The bank employs either one or a combination of modes of financing, which are direct financing (senior and mezzanine debt or equity), co-financing with local and/or foreign lenders, loan guarantees and syndications. Like the other two banks, DBSA was established in September 1983 with the objective of performing a broad economic development function within the "homeland" constitutional dispensation that prevailed at the time in South Africa. In April 1997, DBSA was reconstituted as a development finance institution under the Development Bank of Southern Africa (DBSA) Act of 1997. By 2006, new project approvals had increased from 63 to 145, and the number of households benefitting from new or improved basic services thanks to DBSA operations exceeded 1 million. After an organizational review, DBSA activities were refocused on infrastructure funding and delivery, and the same year DBSA approved loans worth Rand 9.6 billion for renewable energy projects. In 2013 the National Treasury approved a South African Rand 7.9 billion capital injection for DBSA over a three-year period from April 2013 to March 2016. The aim of the intervention was to support the DBSA's refocused mandate of driving its infrastructure funding by supporting municipal lending, the infrastructure plans of state-owned enterprises, regional lending and funding for public–private partnerships. In 2014 the South African parliament expanded the DBSA mandate into selected African countries outside the South African Development Community (SADC) area.

e. The emergent role of the Chinese in infrastructure financing. As we argued elsewhere, it is unrealistic to suppose that the infrastructure gap in Africa can only be financed by China, because of the huge amounts of money required (about UD\$93 billion per year) (Kararach, 2015). Infrastructure projects undertaken by Chinese companies are often financed by soft loans from the state, on the condition that they are carried out by Chinese companies. This accords with the Chinese "go out" strategy intended to promote the international expansion of Chinese companies (Corkin, 2006). Chinese state concessional loans are disbursed by China Exim Bank, one of the largest such institutions in the world (Moss and Rose, 2006). It is estimated that China Exim Bank has disbursed over US\$12.5 billion for large-scale infrastructural projects in Sub-Saharan African alone since 1994 (its inception date), although China Exim Bank's official reported figures are much lower (Bossard, 2007; Bräutigam, 2011a). Over 80% of these disbursements were made to resource-rich African countries, such as Angola, Nigeria, Zimbabwe and Sudan (Broadman, 2007). The major difference between China and traditional donors to Africa is that the Chinese are perceived as not interfering in the internal affairs of recipient countries—especially on issues relating to politics and human rights (Bräutigam, 2010, 2011b). Chinese investments tend to be made through bilateral engagements with individual African countries, and often lack a regional perspective. There is a large untapped potential to use China's investments for regional infrastructure projects.

Generally the discussion on Chinese cooperation has tended to focus on physical infrastructure investment (Turner et al, 2011). Analysis of the African infrastructure sector highlights gaps in both infrastructure services and technical and managerial capacity, two areas where the role and potential of South-South cooperation needs better understanding.

The role of Chinese financiers in developing technical capacity is not well documented or measured. It may be that these financiers, coming from a similar socioeconomic context to the recipient nation, have valuable and appropriate skills and technical solutions to transfer. A number of commentators, however, question the impact of China on local skills development and labor markets. Moreover, there has been much discussion of the quality of infrastructure delivery and the role that technical capacity plays in infrastructure implementation, particularly in the case of Chinese construction contractors, where there is a widespread perception that the quality of work by Chinese construction companies is inferior. However, Caulkin et al (2008) argue that very little distinguishes the quality and standards of Chinese construction companies from other firms, whether local or foreign.

Recently China changed the way it channels development assistance to Africa when it launched the Africa Growing Together Fund (AGTF), managed by the African Development Bank, and valued at US$2 billion. The new fund is intended to open development contracts to the most competitive bidder, rather than a handful of favored Chinese companies. The United States and European Union countries have criticised Beijing's "cheque book" policy, arguing that Chinese financing has benefited its own construction groups, which have built everything from roads to hospitals on the continent. African officials have also criticized the poor quality of much Chinese-built infrastructure that has relied on migrant labor from China, rather than using local workers. Bilateral trade between China and Africa was less than US$11 billion in 2000; by 2006 it had risen to nearly US$60 billion, and by 2014 trade exceeded US$210 billion. Chinese investments in African countries have risen by 3,000% in the past decade. Foreign direct investment went from US$500 million in 2003 to almost US$15 billion by 2012. In 2014 China pledged US$20 billion for infrastructure development—almost 25% of all foreign direct investment.

The Africa50 Fund: issues for consideration

The Africa50 initiative, although still in its formative and set-up stage, is being hailed as an innovative approach to financing infrastructure in Africa for several reasons. First, it will give the continent greater operational flexibility given that it is a commercially, legally and financially independent entity. Second, it has potential to raise significant resources by targeting an investment-grade rating for capital raising, designing innovative financing instruments, and crowding in new sources of capital. Third, it is focused on enhancing the commercial nature (particularly bankability and risk allocation) of transformative and regional infrastructure projects.

A key question we seek to address in this section is how infrastructure bonds can be promoted, especially in emerging markets like Africa.

What are some of the necessary conditions for the Africa50 Fund to succeed? Let us review them.

Project selection and preparation

It is critical that policymakers understand the bottleneck of channeling funds of long-term investors into infrastructure projects. What explains the apparent mismatch between infrastructure investment demand and the supply of infrastructure finance? The lack of a pipeline of properly structured projects seems to be answer to the question (Meaney and Hope, 2012). As we noted earlier, infrastructure investments entail complex legal and financial arrangements demanding a lot of expertise and capacity for efficient and effective closures. Building such capacities and expertise is usually costly. Investors are inclined to incur these fixed costs if there is a sufficient and predictable project pipelines. In the absence of good pipelines, the costs can easily outweigh the potential benefits of investing into infrastructure over other, less complex, asset classes. A coherent and trusted legal framework for infrastructure projects is necessary for the development of good pipelines. In some African countries, those frameworks do not exist or are extremely weak. Political risk is among the greatest concerns of private investors (OECD, 2014). Arbitrary political influence can take many forms: sudden capping of the prices private infrastructure operators are allowed to charge; new regulations; or unilateral renegotiation of existing contracts by new governments. Sometimes even where solid legal frameworks exist, governments can still fall short of best practices. Positive efforts are needed to adopt best practices. We must bear in mind that building such practices and institutions take time, but their development can help to realize enormous efficiency gains and enable governments to successfully undertake a much larger number of projects. Understanding the economics of infrastructure projects and the unique challenges involved in infrastructure finance is pertinent to addressing these inherent problems. For example, African countries undertaking project development must impute the social and environmental risks such as resettling communities when land is acquired for infrastructure. The environmental damage from construction and at times operation of infrastructure requires many studies to be done and these are costly in time and money.

Essentially, project selection and development significantly influence whether infrastructure delivery is efficient. As a guiding principle, projects should be undertaken when their net present value (NPV) is positive. This is a 'private sector approach' to financing which can potentially lead to more efficient decisions being made at the project selection stage. Because of political economy considerations, the public sector may deliver NPV-negative investments especially when politicians choose to undertake "vanity" or "pet" projects, or if there is a general political bias towards the short term. The hard budget constraint could in theory ensure that projects are undertaken only if they are likely to perform well (Grimsey and Lewis, 2004). Subjecting potential projects to private sector risk assessment can be beneficial if the private sector has a comparative advantage in such assessments (Jenkinson, 2003).

Berger and Udell (1998) note that financial markets and intermediaries play a critical role in market formation by acting as information producers that can assess project quality and address information problems through the activities of screening, contracting , and monitoring. These intermediaries can also screen potential customers/investors by conducting due diligence on a wide range of issues including the collection of information about the project, the market in which it will operate, any collateral that may be pledged, and the credibility of the entrepreneur or start-up team, and ensuring clear contract terms at origination (price, fraction of ownership, collateral, restrictive covenants, maturity, and so on). In this regard, African countries need to deepen their financial markets to allow for the Africa50 Fund to thrive. Greater focus should also be given to issues of project selection and development to ensure a good number and quality of pipelines.

Maximizing the fund returns

Generally, risk transfers in infrastructure projects are often ill-structured, resulting in cost overruns or even failures. An example is the provisioning of credit or cash flow guarantees by governments. Full insurance against any potential losses may distort the incentives for cost minimization and quality maintenance. Guarantees tend to result in costs which are much higher than planned. Pure government procurement is more effective and preferred as funding costs are lower while incentive structures remain the same, or may even improve. In this regard, the lack of government guarantees may not seem to be a barrier to investment in infrastructure by the private sector (Gatti, 2014). However, guarantees are needed for risks that cannot be addressed by the executive branch of government as governments change and ensuring policy and contract stability is one of the major risks of large-scale infrastructure provision. In the institutionalization of the Africa50 Fund, African countries must avoid transferring too much risk to the private sector as this may lead to wrong incentives and therefore inefficiencies. Transferring to the private sector those risks that are easily insured against (for example, political risks) may either significantly increase funding costs or even lead to a failure to attract private investment at all. It has to be noted that equity sponsors willing to take on high risks are usually those that are also involved in the construction or operating process. High-risk exposure prompts such companies to seek higher returns by charging higher construction or maintenance costs. As we noted earlier, investors and firms prefer to have predicable cost structures.

Strengthening African ownership

Africa needs to take even greater control of its infrastructure development as part and parcel of the structural transformation agenda. As indicated by a number of the chapters in this volume, current spending on infrastructure in Africa is higher than previously thought—roughly, US$45 billion a year when budget and off-budget spending (including state-owned enterprises and extra-budgetary funds) and external financing are taken into account. The external financing includes the private sector, official development assistance, and financiers that are not from the Organisation for Economic Co-operation and Development (OECD). As noted earlier most of this spending (about two-thirds annually) is domestically sourced: US$30 billion financed by the African taxpayer and infrastructure user, and a further US$15 billion from external sources. The public sector remains the dominant source of finance for water, energy, and transport in all but the fragile states. Currently, public investment is largely tax financed and executed through central government budgets, whereas the operating and maintenance expenditure is largely financed from user charges and executed through state-owned enterprises; hence the need to speed efforts towards domestic resource mobilization. As expected from theory, public financing of infrastructure is substantially higher relative to GDP in the low-income states due to underdeveloped alternative funding sources such as the financial markets, typically absorbing 5–6% percent of total GDP. In absolute terms, however, spending remains very low, no more than US$20–30 per capita a year. In this regard, securitization of government debt as a mechanism for widening the fiscal space for infrastructure financing becomes critical. For the Africa50 Fund to be an effective driver of infrastructure investment, African countries need to a high level of pro-activeness, engagement and ownership of the fund.

Developing the financial architecture and markets

African countries need to develop their financial markets to support the usage of bond finance. Ehlers et al (2014) note that infrastructure bonds should be issued in local currencies to minimize potential currency mismatches. For Africa, the development of local bond markets is a prerequisite for issuing infrastructure bonds as envisaged by the Africa50 Fund. As onshore local currency bond markets develop rapidly, the potential of infrastructure bonds on the continent will rise in tandem. A number of key enabling factors such as supportive legal frameworks, bureaucratic efficiency and contract enforceability must be in place as they strongly affect the rating of infrastructure bonds and therefore the attractiveness for investors and the costs of financing. Equally, innovative policy initiatives such as the Africa50 Fund are going to be critical in establishing the first infrastructure bonds with public support. The success of the fund will very much also depend on the emergence of a strong domestic institutional investor base to catalyze the development of infrastructure bond markets (McKinsey, 2013). Africa50 should retain the incentives for investors and insurance providers to push for the effective execution of infrastructure projects. The fund should also consider issuing infrastructure bonds off-shore to tap into international capital markets. In this context, several issues regarding legal and disclosure frameworks arise in many African countries with weak legal capacities. Compliance with more complex disclosure standards tends to be more costly in emerging markets (Ehlers et al, 2014). Strengthening disclosure capacity has a high potential for having a substantial impact on the availability of infrastructure finance. Finally, harmonizing the rules and assistance for infrastructure projects across donors may help to reduce compliance costs and encourage international issuance to access a wider investor base.

Balancing the interests of investors and consumers

The lack of cost-reflective tariffs has been put forward by a number of investors as one of the most widespread causes of poor infrastructure finance. Some investors argue that in most African countries, the tariffs paid by consumers for basic services are not sufficient to enable the utility or service providers to recover the costs incurred to provide such services (Ketchum, 2013). It is known to be politically difficult for governments to increase tariffs to cost-reflective rates as the case of post-Apartheid South Africa showed. Since the 1980s, many African governments have established independent regulatory authorities to de-politicize tariffs. However, these actions introduce a new problem—the newly established independent regulator has no proven track record of successfully balancing the interests of investors and consumers. This is particularly difficult to achieve with large and complex infrastructure projects as it may not be feasible for investors to bid a fixed price. The Bujagali Hydroelectric Dam project in Uganda is a good example, whereby tariffs had to be de-politicized before utilities could charge cost-effective rates. In January 2004, the government of Uganda published a request for proposals (an RfP) seeking investors to develop the Bujagali Hydroelectric Project. The RfP outlined a detailed tariff methodology as part of the Power Purchase Agreement (ibid.). The tariff methodology contained cost openers for the capital cost of the project and for costs associated with the servicing of the project loans. The bid evaluation criteria included an explicit internal rate of return on the equity invested in the project, a cap on the development costs the sponsors would seek to recover, and a fixed monthly operations and maintenance charge. The Bujagali Hydroelectric Project has demonstrated that regulation by contract can be successfully applied to independent power projects. Uganda has been hailed by the likes of the World Bank to have successfully avoided the trap into which many countries with newly established regulators fall. The Africa50 Fund needs to develop appropriate formulas for infrastructure service pricing.

Political instability and fragility

Historically, Africa has been known to suffer political instability and conflict at both the national and the regional levels. Protracted conflict made a number countries such as the Democratic Republic of Congo (DRC), Burundi, Central Africa Republic (CAR), Sudan and Somalia fragile. Investors and debt financiers avoid projects located in such regions. However, it is not impossible—there are tools to address these issues. A regional approach to conflict management and resolution is one way to restore stability. For example, the Ruzizi III Regional Hydroelectric Project promoted by Energie des Grands Lacs (EGL) to foster regional cooperation in energy projects is one such success story (Ketchum, 2013). The project is located on the border between the DRC and Rwanda. The major shareholders are the parastatal utilities of Burundi, the DRC, and Rwanda—three nations with a long history of conflict and instability. The Ruzizi III has benefited tremendously from EGL's cross-border facilitation of the project and regional approach to engagement on politically sensitive issues by encouraging transparency, consultation, and an unwavering focus on the technical, legal, and economic problems that must be overcome. The project has also benefited tremendously from the support of a broad range of bilateral and multilateral development finance institutions with a promise of political risk insurance and guarantees. The experience of the Ruzizi III project could be emulated by others to be finance in future by Africa50 whereby African countries priorities peace and security through a regional framework.

The capacity of the public sector to manage complex arrangements such as PPPs

The other area that the Africa50 Fund should attention to related to the popularity of PPPs as a mechanism for financing infrastructure. A successful PPP program requires governments to find the political will to make a number of decisions of critical importance quickly and transparently—especially those that may be politically difficult. This challenge more often than not gets compounded by a lack of experience and capacity gaps among the civil servants who are responsible for advising political decision-makers and implementing the PPP undertaking (Ketchum, 2013). These problems can be overcome by investing in quality advisors and project managers. Increasing, bilateral and multilateral development finance institutions and experienced investors alike have come to understand this problem and often step in to fill the gap by investing in requisite technical capacities. Of great importance is the need for Africa to invest in the culture of project maintenance.

Focusing on the governance of transactions

The dominant discourse among public officials and donors is currently on filling the infrastructure financing gap and the need to move projects from the design phase to their implementation as exemplified by PIDA. This project/transaction-oriented perspective focuses on facilitating projects closures. This trend has biased attention to supporting project preparation funding and public procurement reform to foster new forms of financing such as PPPs. While these initiatives are helpful and will most likely contribute to facilitating investments, they ignore the problem of monitoring the quality of contract/project implementation. Infrastructure has been known to face a high risk of corruption. Unfortunately, weaknesses during implementation, whether due to construction uncertainties or corruption, have substantial impact on the quality of outcomes. African countries and the multilaterals, in their ongoing discussion of procurement reform, need to focus on the downstream issues of contract management and implementation. Strengthening governance of project transactions must be at the core of the institutionalization of the Africa50 Fund.

Increasing attention to sectoral governance

Strengthening sectoral governance and overcoming inefficiencies by ensuring better maintenance of existing infrastructure, institutional reform of utilities and regulating service providers, administrative reform, and improved pricing/tariff policies and practices are now broadly accepted by most partners engaged in infrastructural development in Africa (see for example, World Bank, 2009). The World Bank (ibid.) estimated that resolving these issues could save US$17 billion of the estimated US$93 billion per year infrastructure gap. Unfortunately, sectoral governance issues have not been given equivalent effort/attention in Sub-Saharan Africa as compared with the efforts on mobilizing financing. Resolving the infrastructure gap requires more than just building infrastructure as there is a wide range of governance issues such as pricing, service quality, institutional and legal frameworks, access and maintenance among others to be resolved. The multilaterals' approach to investment has evolved over time, recognizing that the interaction of sectoral governance issues is critical to a successful outcome and recognizing that each sector and sub-sector raises particular governance issues. As the Africa50 Fund contributes to widening financial space, it is important that sector-specific impediments to financing are addressed.

Adapting global governance standards to an evolving world of finance

As the sources of infrastructure financing continue to evolve in complexity (involving both traditional and non-traditional sources; Bhushan et al, 2013) and countries are faced with a widening range of public finance options, the current institutional governance structures on aid flows, globally and regionally, must be made fit for purpose. Although infrastructure financing is pretty well distributed across countries and sectors overall with a complementarity among the sources, this has been serendipitous and not due to any strategic coordination or collaboration. While the multilateral development banks' role has been and remains substantial in the context of infrastructure in Sub-Saharan Africa, this requires adapting to the changing context of Africa and the global financial architecture. The multilateral development banks must step up their important role of setting standards for economic and social evaluation of investments, environmental sustainability, and integrity. Finally, they must strengthen coordination and monitoring of infrastructure financing. Non-traditional sources of financing such as China and other emerging economies will continue to grow, and new institutions, such as the Brazil, Russia, India, China and South Africa (BRICS) New Development Bank, or Chinese infrastructure initiatives, such as the recently established China-led AGTF. The Africa50 Fund and such related initiatives should be seen as a positive contribution to African wider structural transformation and sustainable development.

Strengthening implementation and solutions that work

It is critical that countries and stakeholders ensure the speedy implementation of the Africa50 Fund initiative. It is equally critical that countries put forwards solutions that work. Such a solution includes the South African Invoice Processing Platform (IPP)—a web-based system that provides one integrated, secure system to simplify the management of vendor invoices and intra-governmental transactions. It is offered at no charge to government agencies and their vendors. Such a platform is important for project implementation as it helps such agencies avoid prompt payment penalties by supporting more efficient procurement and invoice processing while automating invoice collection, validation and approval workflows. Vendors can manage their receivables more easily using one system to transact with multiple agencies. All of these flexibilities and benefits offered by an IPP are critical in enhancing operations in infrastructure financing and development. IPPs can help enhance PPs for infrastructure financing through better information system and financial management solutions.

Conclusion

There are considerable efforts by African countries to mobilize the necessary resources to fund their infrastructure development. The Africa50 Fund is evidence of such effort at a continental level. For the fund to be effective, there are a number of institutional and governance issues to be resolved. The supply of properly structured projects needs to be assured to enable the channeling of available finance into infrastructure. Overcoming these constraints requires substantial expertise. Without a predictable pipeline of investable projects, the costs of screening may be too high for potential investors. In this regard, governments have a critical role in setting up a pipeline of investable projects and the relevant binding legal frameworks for closing infrastructure projects. We have noted that the success of infrastructure finance hinges on a sensible transfer of risks and returns. Equally, the involvement of the private sector can be more than a source of funding and lift operational efficiency. Given the long gestation of infrastructure projects, the focus needs to turn more to the operational aspects of infrastructure such as maintenance and not merely its construction.

The Africa50 Fund may be seen as a means to boost infrastructure finance by broadening the potential group of investors and tapping into the vast financial resources of capital markets. Financial market development, trusted legal frameworks, and the development of a long-term investor base are pertinent issues for African countries to address in order to exploit the opportunities offered by the fund. Development banks and export credit agencies will all play a key role in promoting infrastructure finance in Africa. Governments need to build up regulatory and implementation capacity and also build a track record of credible commitments in order to attract the right private sector partners.

References

AfDB (2013) *Annual Report*. Tunis: AfDB. Available at: www.afdb. org/fileadmin/uploads/afdb/Documents/Publications/Annual_ Report_2013.pdf

Auerbach, A.J. and King, M.A. (1983) 'Taxation, portfolio choice, and debt–equity ratios: a general equilibrium model', *Quarterly Journal of Economics*, vol 98, no 4, pp 587-609.

Berger, A.N. and Udell, G.F. (1998) 'The economics of small business finance: the roles of private equity and debt markets in the financial growth cycle', *Journal of Banking and Finance*, vol 22, no 6-9, pp 613-73

Bhushan, A., Yiagadeesen, S. and Medu, K. (2013) *Financing the Post-2015 Development Agenda: Domestic Revenue Mobilization in Africa*, Research Report. Ottawa: North-South Institute, available at www.nsi-ins.ca/wp-content/uploads/2013/09/2013-Financing-the-Post-2015-Africa.pdf.

Bossard, P. (2007) *China's Role in Financing African Infrastructure.* Berkeley, CA: International Rivers Network.

Broadman, H.G. (2007) *Africa's Silk Road: China and India's New Economic Frontier*, Washington, DC: World Bank.

Bräutigam, D. (2010) *China, Africa and the International Aid Architecture*, AfDB Working Paper No. 107. Tunis, Tunisia: AfDB.

Bräutigam, D. (2011a) Chinese development aid in Africa: what, where, why, and how much?', in J. Golley and L. Song (eds) *Rising China: Global Challenges and Opportunities*. Canberra: Australia National University Press.

Bräutigam, D. (2011b) 'Aid "with Chinese characteristics": Chinese foreign aid and development finance meet the OECD-DAC aid regime', *Journal of International Development*, vol 23, no 5, pp 752-64.

Caulkin, L., Burke, C. and Davies, M. (2008) *China's Role in the Development of Africa's Infrastructure*, Working Papers in African Studies, John Hopkins University, available at www.saisjhu.edu/academics/regional-studies/africa.

Chen, A.H. and Kim, E.H. (1979) 'Theories of corporate debt policy: a synthesis', *Journal of Finance*, vol 34, no 2, pp 371-84.

Corkin, L. (2006) 'Chinese multinational corporations in Africa'. *Inside AISA*, October–December, pp 10-14.

Ehlers, T. (2014) *Understanding the Challenges for Infrastructure Finance*, Bank for International Settlements Working Papers No 454, August. Basel, Switzerland: IBS.

Fay, M., Toman, M., Benitez, D. and Csordas, S. (2011) 'Infrastructure and sustainable development', in S. Fardoust, Y. Kim and C. Sepulveda (eds) *Post-crisis Growth and Development*. Washington, DC: World Bank, available at http://siteresources.worldbank.org/DEC/Resources/PCGD_Consolidated.pdf.

Frank, M.Z. and Goyal, V.K. (2005) "Tradeoff and pecking order theories of debt", in B. Espen Eckbo (ed) *Handbook of Corporate Finance: Empirical Corporate Finance* (Handbooks in Finance Series). Oxford: North Holland.

Gatti, S. (2014) *Government and market based instruments and incentives to stimulate long-term investment finance in infrastructure*, OECD Working Papers on Finance, Insurance and Private Pensions, Paris: OECD.

Graham, J.R. (2000) 'How big are the tax benefits of debt?', *Journal of Finance*, vol 55, no 5, pp 1901-41.

Graham, J.R. (2003) 'Taxes and corporate finance: a review', *Review of Financial Studies*, vol 16, no 4, pp 1075-1129.

Grimsey, D. and Lewis, M.K. (2004) *Public Private Partnerships: The Worldwide Revolution of Infrastructure Provision and Project Finance.* Cheltenham: Edward Elgar.

Gutman, J., Sy, A. and Chattopadhyay, S. (2015) *Financing African infrastructure: can the world deliver?*, Washington DC: Global Economy and Development at Brookings.

Haugen, R.A., and Senbet, L.W. (1978) 'The insignificance of bankruptcy costs to the theory of optimal capital structure', *Journal of Finance*, vol 33, no 2, pp 383-93.

Hirshleifer, J. (1966) 'Investment decision under uncertainty: applications of the state-preference approach', *Quarterly Journal of Economics*, vol 80, no 2, pp 252-77.

ICA (Infrastructure Consortium for Africa) (2014) 'Infrastructure financing trends in Africa: ICA report', available at www.icafrica. org/fileadmin/documents/Annual_Reports/ICA-2013-INFRA-FIN-TRENDS-AFRICA-2013-FINAL-WEB.pdf.

IMF (International Monetary Fund) (2014) *The World Bank and IMF Annual Meetings Communiques*, October. Washington, DC: IMF, available at www.imf.org/external/np/sec/pr/2014/pr14466.htm.

Jenkinson, T. (2003) 'Private finance', *Oxford Review of Economic Policy*, vol 19, no 2, pp 323-33.

Kararach, G. (2015) 'Infrastructure, China and African Development' in G. Shelton, F.Y. April, and L. Anshan (eds) *FOCAC 2015: A new beginning of China-Africa Relations*, Pretoria: HSRC.

Ketchum, R. (2013) 'The challenges of funding Sub-Saharan infrastructure. Sub-Saharan Africa: the challenges, misconceptions and financing involved in infrastructure projects in the region', *Gateway To Africa*, 4 June.

Kraus, A. and Litzenberger, R.H. (1973) 'A state-preference model of optimal financial leverage', *Journal of Finance*, vol 28, no 4, pp 911-22.

Leautier, F. (2014) *Leadership in a Globalised World.* Basingstoke: Palgrave Macmillan.

Mbeng Mezui, C.A, and Hundal, B. (2013) *Structured Finance – Conditions for infrastructure project bonds in African markets*, Tunis, Tunisia: AfDB.

McKinsey (2013) 'Infrastructure productivity: how to save $1 trillion a year', McKinsey Infrastructure Practice, McKinsey Global Institute, January. Available at www.mckinsey.com/insights/engineering_construction/infrastructure_productivity.

Meaney, A. and Hope, P. (2012) 'Alternative ways of financing infrastructure investment: potential for "novel" financing models', International Transport Forum at the OECD, Discussion Paper No. 2012-7, available at www.internationaltransportforum.org/jtrc/DiscussionPapers/DP201207.pdf.

Miller, M.H. (1977) 'Debt and taxes', *Journal of Finance*, vol 32, no 2, pp 261-76.

Modigliani, F. and Miller, M.H. (1958) 'The cost of capital, corporate finance and the theory of investment', *American Economic Review*, vol 48, no 3, pp 261-97.

Moss, T. and Rose, S., 2006. *China Exim Bank and Africa: New Lending, New Challenges*. Washington DC: Centre for Global Development.

Myers, S.C. (1984) "The capital structure puzzle", Journal of Finance 39, 575-592.

OECD (Organisation for Economic Co-operation and Development) (2014) *Pooling of Institutional Investors Capital: Selected Case Studies in Unlisted Equity Infrastructure*. Paris: OECD.

Stiglitz, J.E. (1969) 'A re-examination of the Modigliani-Miller theorem', *American Economic Review*, vol 59, no 5, pp 784-93.

Turner, J., Hodgson, F., Porter, G., Mawdsley, E. and McCann, G. (2011) 'Changing the game for Africa's infrastructure: what role for South-South cooperation?', Paper presented at AEGIS conference, Uppsala, June.

UN-Habitat (United Nations Human Settlements Programme) (2014) *The State of African Cities 2014: Re-imagining Sustainable Urban Transitions*. Nairobi:UN-Habitat. Available at http://unhabitat.org/the-state-of-african-cities-2014.

Weston, J.F. (1955) 'Toward theories of financial policy', *Journal of Finance*, vol 10, no 2, pp 130-43.

World Bank (2009) *Africa Infrastructure Country Diagnostic Study*, Washington DC: World Bank.

World Bank (2013) 'Harnessing urbanization to end poverty and boost prosperity in Africa: an action agenda for transformation", available at http://documents.worldbank.org/curated/en/2013/09/18417628/harnessing-urbanization-end-poverty-boost-prosperity-africa-action-agenda-transformation.

Part 5: Concluding remarks

SIXTEEN

Infrastructure, political economy and Africa's transformational agenda

*Mthuli Ncube, Charles Leyeka Lufumpa
and George Kararach*

Introduction

Infrastructure has been highlighted by many commentators as a major constraint on Africa's transformation (Ayogu, 2007; AfDB, 2010a, 2010b, 2010c; Lin, 2012; IMF, 2014). Two argumentations come to the fore: good infrastructure and connectivity, which is critical for spurring supply responses and economic growth; and enhancing diversification and structural transformation by speeding up intersectoral linkages and the transitioning of economies from low to high productivity thresholds (Banerjee et al, 2009; IMF, 2014). Output from infrastructure is both a final good, providing services directly to consumers (such as power for television sets), and an intermediate input that enters into the production of other sectors, in turn raising their productivity (for example, power as an input into manufacturing), as well as a mechanism that may define institutional and governance arrangements (Herbst, 2000). The availability of an efficient infrastructure network/framework can stimulate new investment in other sectors or even strengthen state legitimacy, as infrastructural services are seen as fulfilment of the social contract. Conversely, shortage of infrastructure or its over-expansion in certain areas can raise costs and create disincentives to investment, as well as socio–political disharmony.

As national income grows, the share of infrastructure investments in gross domestic product (GDP) rises, although beyond a certain point the relative importance of particular types of infrastructure declines. Ndulu et al (2005, pp 103-4) argued that during "… the ratio of investment to GDP in sub-Saharan Africa (in 1985 international prices) averaged 9.5 percent of GDP compared to nearly 15.6 percent in other developing countries….African countries have also largely under-invested in infrastructure against the wisdom that countries which

643

typically manage to invest more, do so particularly in infrastructure sectors." This chapter seeks to analyse the role of infrastructure in accelerating Africa's development. This requires policymakers to take tangible measures to address issues of infrastructural development for socioeconomic transformation. How should African countries deal with their infrastructure deficiencies? What are some of the practical actions that need to be taken to build both physical and soft (financial) infrastructure?

Infrastructure involves both the public and private sectors. Examples of infrastructure are: water supply, sanitation, transportation, electricity, telecommunications, irrigation dams and banks. Agricultural infrastructure includes all of the basic services, facilities, equipment, and institutions needed for the economic growth and efficient functioning of the food and broader agricultural markets. Investment in agriculture-related infrastructure requires a research and cooperative extension system that enhances production, marketing, food safety, nutrition and natural resource conservation. Infrastructure reduces costs and enlarges markets for farmers (Ndulu et al, 2005, p 109). New opportunities are emerging, for example, through information technology such as mobile phones, that will allow the continent to "leapfrog" in its development. The major constraints on infrastructural development are often not technical but managerial, political, cultural, and include the lack of innovative financing.

We explore the political economy of infrastructure services in Africa, highlighting some of the dynamics that have defined availability and access. There is need to change the current configuration of access to ensure meaningful physical and socioeconomic integration. This requires a number of changes in the character of public policy. Countries need to find creative ways to overcome financing constraints given the realities of current development finance. Developing infrastructure alone is not sufficient, and the continent needs to adopt a culture of maintenance and upgrade (Kararach, 2014). Our core argument is that because of poor infrastructure, Africa's economic transformation remains constrained. It is our view that this constraint is underpinned by limited implementation capacity, weak project design and development, and limited infrastructure investment. Although we urge countries to tap into the emerging financial architecture, outside financing such as from the Chinese and Indians is not a panacea, for lack of willing lenders at reasonable terms or underhand agenda including disproportionate access to Africa's natural resources in exchange for infrastructure. Finally, weak regulatory environments that breed bad practices in procurements continue to do damage across the continent.

Political economy and status of Africa's infrastructure

Africa's infrastructure deficit is enormous and poses a severe constraint on development. It is estimated that less than 40% of the continent's population has access to electricity; only 33% of the rural population has access to roads; while only 5% of agriculture is under irrigation (AfDB, 2010a). According to the MDGs Progress Report for Africa 2011, in 2008 only 41% of the continent's population had access to improved sanitation, and about 65% to safe water (AfDB et al, 2011); and the figures declined to 39% by 2012 and improved slightly to 67% by 2012 respectively (AfDB, 2015). The information and communications technology (ICT) situation is characterized by huge differences across specific services. In 2009, 37.6% of Africans had access to cellular mobile phones, with penetration rates growing faster than in the rest of the world. However, internet user penetration in Africa was about 9.6% by the end of 2010, compared with just 5.9% in 2008. This is well below the world average of 30% and the developing country average of 21%. Further efforts are needed to improve broadband speeds. The number of fixed telephone lines changed little between 2000 and 2009. There were an estimated 1.6 telephone lines per 100 persons in 2010, compared with 1.5 in 2008 and 2009 (AfDB et al, 2011). This figure stood at 2.28 in 2013 (AfDB, 2015; see also Appendix 17.1 for more details ?? on access for infrastructure services between 2006 and 2013 and between country variations).

Africa has higher access costs for all infrastructure services compared with other developing countries. The continent's road freight is about four times more expensive, power costs 14 US cents per kilowatt-hour (kWh) against 5 to 10 US cents elsewhere, and mobile telephony costs US$12 per month compared with US$8 in other developing regions. In addition to low institutional capacity and high investment requirements, Africa's infrastructure development agenda is impeded by the region's economic geography. Specifically, Africa is home to more landlocked countries (16 in total) than any other continent; Africa has more countries with low population densities than other developing regions; most African countries are far from major markets of high GDP concentration like Europe and the US (see Manners and Behar, 2007); and African countries vary greatly in their geographical situation and demographics—32 are coastal, 16 are landlocked and six (Cape Verde, Comoros, Madagascar, Mauritius, São Tomé and Príncipe, and Seychelles) are islands. The average population density is 70 people per kilometer squared (km²), which is somewhat lower than that of other low and lower-middle income countries in the world (at 125 and 91 per km² respectively) (AfDB, 2013).

Population density varies widely. While some countries are very densely populated (Cape Verde, Ghana, Malawi, Nigeria, Rwanda, and Uganda), others have a sparse population spread over a relatively large geographical area (Botswana, Cameroon, Chad, Namibia, Niger, Sudan, and Zambia). A more cohesive approach is therefore needed to leverage the region's endowments and improve connectivity between countries, sub-regions, and urban/rural areas. Any strategy must therefore take account of: rapid urbanisation and the role of main urban areas; urban networks and the benefits from regional integration; and the spillover effects on rural productivity from regional corridors.

The energy sub-sector records the largest deficit, while total road density and access to clean water still lag behind other developing countries. In ICT, even the top five African countries ranked only 66th to 109th on a global index (Table 16.1). Sectoral regulatory reforms undertaken in many African countries, however, have opened up investment opportunities for the private sector as well as the donor community. These reforms have improved the business environment and enhanced efficiency in implementing and managing infrastructure investments. Table 16.2 provides the road and air transport configurations for the continent.

Table 16.1: Infrastructure deficit in Sub-Saharan Africa (SSA)

	SSA	South Asia	East Asia	SSA oil exporters	SSA oil importers
Transportation					
Density of paved road network*	49	149	59	14	57
Density of total road network *	152	306	237	70	173
ICT					
Density of fixed phone line**	33	39	16	16	38
Density of mobile phone line**	101	86	208	118	97
Density of internet connections **	2.8	1.7	6.6	1.7	3.1
Energy					
Electrical generating capacity ***	70	154	231	66	71
Access to electricity ****	18	44	57	26	16
Water and sanitation					
Water ****	63	72	75	59	64
Sanitation****	35	48	60	34	35

Notes: * Km/1,000km² (2001); ** Subscribers per 1,000 people (2004); ***MW per 1 million people (2003). ****% of households with access (2002-2004).

Source: Yepes et al (2008).

Table 16.2: Road and air infrastructure and transport indicators

Road infrastructure indicators	Roads, paved (% of total roads)			Road density (km of road per 100km² of land area)		
	2000-04	2005-09	2010-14	2000-04	2005-09	2010-14
Algeria	70.2	74.0	77.1	4.5	4.7	4.8
Egypt	81.0	89.4	92.2	9.3	10.1	13.8
Libya	57.2	–	–	–	–	–
Morocco	56.9	70.3	70.4	12.9	13.0	13.1
Tunisia	65.8	75.2	76.0	12.4	12.5	12.5
Sub-Saharan Africa	18.1	18.7	16.3	7.9	5.5	6.8

Air transport indicators	Air transport, freight (million ton-km, on year average)			Air transport, passengers carried (million, on year average)		
	2000-04	2005-09	2010-14	2000-04	2005-09	2010-14
Algeria	17.9	18.6	14.9	3.2	3.2	4.1
Egypt	249.4	235.8	345.2	4.4	5.7	8.4
Libya	0.3	0.3	0.1	0.6	0.9	1.3
Morocco	58.2	54.9	42.1	3.2	4.4	7.0
Tunisia	19.9	16.3	19.1	1.9	2.1	3.3
Sub-Saharan Africa	1,672.2	1,926.5	2,618.2	17.9	26.5	43.7

Source: AfDB based on World Bank World Development Indicators (WDI) database, and Africa Infrastructure Knowledge Programme (AIKP) database

The deficit is more acute among low-income countries (LICs) than middle-income countries (MICs). African LICs are four times worse off compared with LICs elsewhere in the world in terms of paved-road density, whereas its MICs are only twice as badly off. In terms of power generation, the figures are no better, with African LICs eight times worse off than their counterparts elsewhere (39 megawatts [MW] per million people compared with 326 MW), while its MICs are three times worse off. For internet access, the MIC–LIC divide is the reverse, with African MICs almost 30 times worse off compared with their counterparts elsewhere and LICs only 14 times poorer. To sum up, the deficits in Africa's infrastructure development are most severe in the areas of paved roads, fixed telephones and internet access, and power generation.

The huge initial capital outlays required largely account for Africa's significant deficit in this area (Table 16.1). This is compounded by the extent of regulatory constraints in some African countries, which are perceived by potential private investors as increasing the level of risk. Yet significant changes are taking place across Africa; for example,

Rwanda was ranked as the best reformer in the *Doing Business 2010* report (World Bank, 2009).

So whose need does the current infrastructure architecture serve? There have been a number of attempts to explain the distribution of infrastructure services. One of these is based on the notion of political economy and driven by public policy. Robinson (2009) argued that "[A]t the root, modern inequality and the distribution of income is related to three things: the distribution of assets, the returns on those assets and the incidence of public policy". Public policy is a significant source of inequality. As Robinson put it:

> A country will tend to be relatively equal if the distribution of assets is relatively equal, if the distribution of the rates of return is relatively equal and if public policy is egalitarian. Of course, there can be offsetting effects. Public policy may counteract the impact of highly unequal returns on assets.... political factors lie behind [all three of] the building blocks of inequality.... (2009, pp 2-3)

Herbst (2000) argued that infrastructure development is an institutional tool for state control. Njoh (2000) examines the role of transport infrastructure in shaping the evolution of modern Africa. He argues that by the time the first European explorers arrived in Africa in the 1400s, there was a relatively advanced transportation system as "Africans had domesticated some animals to help address the growing need to move people, goods and services over land. At the same time, there existed a number of innovations, such as the construction of rafts and canoes capable of providing water-based transportation services. The transport infrastructure in Africa at that time consisted largely, but not exclusively, of tracks for pedestrian and animal traffic, and natural navigable waterways" (p 47). The extensive series of roads, footpaths and waterways later served to facilitate the transportation of slaves during the infamous trans-Atlantic slave trade era.

In the colonial era, the authorities were interested in penetrating the hinterland primarily to extract and transport raw materials to the seaports for onward transmission to the master nations. To this end, the cost of developing rail transportation facilities was far less than that associated with road transportation. It was also easier and cheaper to freight heavy and/or bulky goods by rail than by road.

A significant portion of investments in transportation also went into the development of seaports. These were extremely important in evacuating resources and exporting them to the colonial nations.

Seaports constitute the terminuses for all the railways that were constructed during this period. Colonial efforts to develop railways and other transportation infrastructure did not attempt to link the colonies, especially when two colonial territories were under the auspices of different colonial powers. It is noteworthy that the heyday of European colonialism in Africa coincided with a period when there was extreme rivalry between European countries.

There are only two known cases of an attempt to link territories under different European colonial powers. The Germans decided in 1916 to link the Tanga rail line in German East Africa (Tanganyika, now Tanzania) to the Mombasa rail line in British-controlled Kenya. They also resolved to extend the railway from the Cape (South Africa) into German South-West Africa (Namibia).

These projects were propelled by military strategic reasons, rather than the socioeconomic development of the colonies. The Germans were interested in averting the impending danger of expulsion from the region, especially by South African forces. The construction of the Kenya–Uganda railway, which was started in 1896 and reached Lake Victoria in 1902, cannot be considered an effort to establish a veritable interregional linkage because Uganda and Kenya were colonies of one European power, namely England.

The French controlled most of the colonial territories of West Africa, which explains the fact that railway lines link Senegal and Mali; and Côte d'Ivoire and Burkina Faso. The Germans constructed two rail lines, one from agriculture-rich Mount Kilimanjaro to the Port of Tanga, and the other from Dar es Salaam to Kigoma on Lake Tanganyika. These railway projects had the purpose of facilitating the rapid movement of troops to defend the borders of Tanganyika from the English. The British construction of a railway from Kisumu (Port Florence) on Lake Victoria to Uganda was also driven by military concerns (Njoh, 1999).

Thus, in colonial Africa, the railway was not only an "instrument of occupation" (Mabogunje, 1981), but also a tool of exploitation and military defence. For example, the need to exploit the vast hinterland regions of Nigeria led the British colonial authorities to embark on the construction of one of the most elaborate railway systems in Africa. The project, which began in Lagos in 1895, reached Ibadan in 1900, was extended to Illorin in 1908 and reached Kano in the northern part of the country in 1912 (Njoh, 2008).

The literature relates economic outcomes today to the duration of colonisation (Feyrer and Sacerdote, 2009), the type of colonisation: extraction versus settlement (Engerman and Sokoloff, 2000;

Acemoglu, et al, 2001, 2002; Dell, 2010; Bruhn and Gallego, 2012); direct versus indirect rule (Banerjee and Iyer, 2005; Iyer, 2010) or the identity of the coloniser (La Porta et al, 1998; Bertocchi and Canova, 2002). Banerjee and Iyer (2005) and Dell (2010) show that colonial institutions influenced public investments, but they either look at current investments or they use proxies for colonial investments such as literacy and schooling, as in Dell (2010).

Stein (2001) characterises the colonial railroad system as "dendritic"—a leaf-like system originating from the main outlets of international trade into the African interior with few if any links between the interior regions (for example, Austen, 1987, p 127). The pattern of railways inherited from the colonial period clearly illustrates this, with the exception of South Africa. For instance, the railway running from Lobito into Angola (built in 1928), was built along a single line running into the Belgian Congo, which had the sole purpose of gaining access into the copper producing region of Katanga. The domination of railways had a number of consequences. First, much of the rail development was undertaken by the state, with the consequent (mostly foreign exchange) debt paid for by taxing the local population and encouraging the production of cash crops to earn foreign exchange, and precluded other possibly more developmental economic activities.

Second, it involved minimal direct participation by Africans. The backward linkages for the local economy were tiny. Locomotives, rolling stock, rails and associated equipment were all manufactured in Europe. Skilled workers and engineering firms were all imported. One of the motivations for building railroads was to increase employment in capital–intensive industries in the home country while conveniently leaving the debt burden with the colonies. Unskilled labour was often coercively recruited from the local population with little regard to its impact on agricultural production, and workers were frequently subjected to brutal conditions. Worst of these was the French Equatorial Congo-Ocean line, which took 12 years to build (1922 to 1934). Workers were kept in camps where conditions led to death rates of epidemic proportions (Austen, 1987, pp 128-9).

Varied levels of access to infrastructure services characterize Africa more than any other part of the world. Large infrastructure projects suffer from excessive corruption (Tanzi and Davoodi, 1998; Kenny, 2006; Transparency International, 2008). Project placements can be influenced in attempts to disproportionately favour specific regions or ethnicities (Minten, 1999; Miguel and Zaidi, 2003; Finan, 2005; Miguel and Gugerty, 2005; Cadot et al, 2006; Bates, 2008). This can lead to high regional inequalities and political instability, with long-term consequences including civil conflicts (Easterly and Levine, 1997; Alesina and La Ferrara, 2005; Montalvo and Reynal-Querol, 2005). Yet there is nothing inherently African in such behaviour, as lumpy investments are in general vulnerable to rent seeking or false accounting, as demonstrated by the reports of endemic corruption in infrastructure projects financed by the European Union (EU), estimated at US$160 billion annually (EU, 2014).

Public choice models have also been used to explain the character and beneficiation of investments in infrastructure. These seek to examine the effect of democratic elections on public goods provision (Schady, 1999). Mobarak et al (2011) find that provinces in Brazil with a high percentage of voters using health services are more likely to receive such services. Foster and Rosenzweig (2001) find that democratization at the local level increases some types of pro-poor projects. Moser (2008), using data from Madagascar, presents a common agency model in which district leaders promise votes to a national leader in return for public investment projects in their districts. Moser compares three variant models and tests them against the competing explanations of social welfare maximisation and political patronage. Model 1 considers the allocation of public projects using social welfare maximisation criteria. In Model 2 the incumbent politician is concerned only with rewarding his political base. In Model 3 the politician cares only about winning an upcoming election and uses central government-funded projects to reward local leaders who promise to deliver votes. Moser concludes that poverty did not affect the allocation of public projects. Even FID (Fonds d'Intervention pour le Développement) projects seem to have been vulnerable to political influence, and display evidence of both patronage and vote-buying behaviour. This finding does not augur well for small, isolated districts with limited access to national government and outside information, and little capacity to lobby or apply for projects. Moser's conclusions are congruent with those of the Burgess et al (2010) study of Kenya.

Infrastructure and poverty

Absolute poverty elimination is the single most important policy issue in all African countries and that proportion has somewhat been declining due to the emergence of the middle class (Ncube and Lufumpa, 2015). Measures of poverty based on income show that the proportion of the population of Africa living below the minimum subsistence level has remained roughly constant since the late 1980s. But with population growth this absolute number has risen, so that in 1993 nearly 220 million people in Africa were living on an income of less than one US dollar a day (World Bank 1996, p 4). Some social indicators, such as infant mortality and illiteracy rates, have shown an improvement, but the total number has also risen (White, 1998; White et al, 2001). Another bleak trend is the rise in inequality (measured by a rise in the Gini coefficient) (Kararach, 2011). Others have argued that this evidence is not necessarily conclusive since the data are not available for all countries. Further, there are substantial variations around the average. While the regional Gini coefficient averaged 47.0 in the 1990s (compared with 43.5 in the 1980s), it ranged from a low of 28.9 in Rwanda to 62.3 in South Africa (Deininger and Squire, 1996). Nonetheless, Africa is the second most inegalitarian region in the world in terms of income distribution (after Latin America and the Caribbean). In Sub-Saharan Africa, the bottom 20% receives only 5% of total income compared with a share of nearly 9% for the bottom 20% in South Asia.

There are two possible ways infrastructure services can help reduce poverty. First, infrastructure can positively drive economic growth if the governance architecture is socially inclusive. Insofar as infrastructure projects have rates of return above the opportunity costs of capital, they will be contributing to the growth of national income. Higher rates of economic growth are essential (Ravallion, 1997, 2001), yet this requires projects with a high return. GDP growth of somewhere between 6% and 9% annually will be required just to reduce the absolute number of the poor (White, 1998).

The second link between infrastructure activity and poverty reduction emanates from the contribution of infrastructure to pro-poor growth (World Bank, 1994). Not all infrastructure projects will benefit those living below the poverty line, but some will. The infrastructure activities most likely to be beneficial are those with positive economic and social impact assessments (AfDB, 2013).

Summarising the case for infrastructure

Reasons for investing in infrastructure include the following.

Infrastructure increases agricultural production and productivity. Gajigo and Lukoma (2011) argued that infrastructure in the agricultural sector enhances the "comparative advantage" of that region (see pp 1-2). An earlier empirical study by Binswanger et al (1993) demonstrated that increased marketing infrastructure that includes components such as road facilities enhanced the total agricultural output with the elasticity of 0.20.

Infrastructure reduces cost of production. Ahmed and Hussain (1990) demonstrated that fertiliser use in the agricultural sector increases with an improvement in the quality of roads. Gajigo and Lukoma (2011) argued that cost of infrastructure as reflected in spatial price dispersion can be substantial (Table 16.3). For example, the costs incurred by farmers in a particular region can be substantial in the absence of proper transportation facilities.

Infrastructure enhances value addition. Increased levels of infrastructure lead to "derived demand" for investment in industries that produce value added commodities. For example, increased banking or agricultural training facilities may attract new kinds of investments in areas such as food processing.

Infrastructure generates social benefits. The provision of an initial level of infrastructure, or enhancement of the existing one, may lead to a new kind of production pattern that generates indirect or "social" benefits. For example, the introduction of a new technology such as sprinkler irrigation may reduce the exploitation of groundwater in that region and this would make more groundwater available for downstream farmers some distance away. In addition, the introduction of a new technology may lead to change in cropping patterns, in favour of those that protect the soil.

Infrastructure enhances economies of scale. Economy of scale is realised when a firm's cost of production declines due to external advantages. For example, rural electrification or a rural road network may attract small–scale industrial units that also consume electricity.

Table 16.3: Cost of infrastructure as reflected in spatial commodity price dispersion in East Africa

Country	Commodity	Price dispersion* (January to June 2011) (%)
Kenya	Rice	32
	Maize	39
Tanzania	Rice	25
	Maize	37
Uganda	Rice	14
	Maize	30

Note: *The ratio of monthly price differences in major cities in a country to the monthly average price level of commodity.

Source: Regional Agricultural Trade Information Network (2011).

Infrastructure causes accelerator effects. It can be argued that a particular type of agricultural infrastructure in one region will have multiplier and accelerator effects in others, especially in urban centres. For example, additional areas of land can be brought under cultivation due to the construction of an irrigation dam.

Infrastructure enhances welfare of producers and consumers. For example, increased availability of banking operations in rural areas prevents middle-men and money lenders from appropriating substantial amounts of producer and consumer surpluses. The presence of infrastructure such as roads and regulated markets increases the efficiency of both marketing and production since they reduce transaction costs and ensure competitive pricing.

Rethinking infrastructure financing

Africa's substantial financing needs for infrastructure call for innovative mechanisms, together with greater efficiency in public spending and better project preparation/management. The continent's total infrastructure financing needs amounted to US$93 billion a year in 2008, with only US$45 billion being financed (AICD, 2009). Even if all inefficiencies such as poor management and badly targeted subsidies or tariffs were eliminated, an annual gap of US$31 billion would remain. Other estimations put the financing requirements even higher, at US$153 billion annually until 2020 (AfDB, 2010b; 2011b). Traditional development partners and the public sector have tended to be the main financing sources for Africa's infrastructure. Public financing is dominant in the water, sanitation, and transportation sub-sectors. These sectors accounted for nearly 90% of public investments in 2007 (Biau et al, 2008). Most private investment has targeted the ICT sector, which attracted 87% of private commitments in 2008 (OECD, 2010).

Innovative financing mechanisms include local and foreign currency bonds, private equity, sovereign wealth funds, and emerging South–South partners such as China, Brazil and India (Gijón, 2008). There is huge impetus for "clean energy financing," given Africa's abundant natural resources (Besada et al, 2013). African countries can also do more to attract private and innovative funds on favourable terms. Public–private partnerships can be made more effective and remittances better utilised for development financing. Public spending efficiency is another possible source of financing, as current inefficiencies in implementing infrastructure projects account for US$17 billion annually (Briceño-Garmendia et al, 2008). Equally, the public sector can strengthen domestic resource mobilization and catalyze private investment. One such avenue is to provide partial credit guarantee with concessional resources, to mitigate the impact of risk perception on availability and costs of finance.

Official aid is not projected to increase in line with public investment spending needs, due to the global financial crisis (Redifer, 2010). MICs have better prospects for securing their financing needs (Shah and Batley, 2009). Traditional funding sources for infrastructure development remain important but private investment is critical in closing the current gaps.

The call to scale up private sector engagement has been accompanied by changes in the lending and policy facilities of international financial institutions. The African Development Bank, for example, has adapted its lending facilities to LICs. The "new framework" offers non-concessional borrowing to countries with solid debt indicators and debt management capacity, provided such borrowing does not jeopardise fiscal and external debt sustainability as well as social inclusion. The public sector is important, and instrumental in addressing inefficiencies in project implementation and ensuring maintenance of assets. African policymakers are increasingly turning their attention to domestic resource mobilization. Increasing tax revenues and stimulating private and public savings are crucial policy measures for meeting Africa's infrastructure challenge, together with finding new financing sources. Public resource mobilization is particularly challenging in post-conflict and fragile countries.

To enhance public savings, government spending needs to be more efficient. Areas to be addressed include: timely delivery of projects; maintenance of existing infrastructure; improving efficiency of utilities; and strengthening medium-term expenditure and accounting frameworks (AfDB, 2013).

Formal financial institutions could offer long-term savings instruments, and incentivise their take-up through structured tax benefits. African governments could also unlock regulatory barriers that discourage institutional investors, such as pension funds, from making use of long-term instruments. They could also develop institutional frameworks that foster the participation of, for example, Islamic finance institutions and private equity funds.

Risk mitigation

Through risk mitigation instruments, the public sector can catalyze private investments in infrastructure. These instruments may be accompanied by reforms and institutional changes to eliminate the underlying sources of risk.[1] Some of the main risks are:

- commercial and political risk premiums due to commercial or political dynamics;
- country risk premiums, which can be covered by first loss guarantees for a portfolio of transactions;
- foreign exchange volatility, which provides room for currency hedging, government exchange rate guarantees, and devaluation liquidity schemes.

Financial risks can be mitigated through viability gap financing.

Public–private partnerships

Public–private partnerships (PPPs) are key instruments for infrastructure investments in Africa today. These are contractual arrangements with the state that allow for private sector involvement in the supply of infrastructure assets and services. PPP modalities include management contracts, leasing, investment concessions, divestiture, de-monopolization and new entry and build-operate-transfer (AfDB, 1999). PPPs can introduce innovative private funds to infrastructure. They may ease budgetary constraints and raise efficiency by leveraging private sector management expertise and innovation.

PPPs are not yet common across the continent. Many African governments still lack the skills needed for their successful implementation. In many instances, sector ministries and sub-sovereign entities lack adequate investment, financial planning, and regulatory and coordination capacity. The experiences of countries that have established well-functioning PPP units in their ministries of finance (including Senegal, Kenya, and South Africa) point to the positive impacts of such units.

Reserves from "excess-savings" countries

Key policy issues for consideration here are how to attract additional capital flows to Africa's infrastructure from countries with high savings and investment rates, and how to utilise savings in African resource-rich countries, where savings rates are high but investment rates remain low.

South–South investment flows into Africa have been estimated at more than US$60 billion since 2003 (Freemantle and Stevens,

2010). Sovereign wealth funds (SWFs) are an important source of investment. China's commitments to infrastructure financing in Africa in recent years have surpassed those of the World Bank (Kararach et al, 2012).

Innovative financing

Several African emerging and frontier markets (such as Kenya and South Africa) have successfully adopted innovative methods utilizing domestic resources such as infrastructure and municipal bonds, local currency bonds (holders can use the bonds as collateral to acquire bank loans), commodity-linked bonds (associated with export commodities being traded on the futures market), sovereign external bonds, diaspora bonds (utilising diaspora remittances for development), SWFs, private equities, pension funds, and syndicated loans (Deloitte, 2010; Kararach, 2014).

Regional infrastructure: innovative institutional arrangements

Well-designed cross-border infrastructure projects promote regional integration and spur regional trade and growth. Financing regional infrastructure requires effective cooperation and coordination among countries. Innovative and effective institutional arrangements are therefore necessary, either through an expanded role for multilateral development banks, or through establishing specialised sub-regional banks/funds anchored on strong transnational governance. To overcome the high risks and transaction costs of private investment in regional infrastructure projects, some regional economic communities (for examples, the Economic Community of West African States and the Southern African Development Community) have established bilateral or multilateral special purpose vehicles (SPVs) such as the West African Gas Pipeline Company. The SPVs identify, coordinate the preparation of, and manage regional infrastructure priority projects, and negotiate with private investors. Equally, coordinating PPP regulatory frameworks across sub-regions would facilitate the implementation of regional infrastructure projects.

Clean technology for sustainable infrastructure

Africa is extremely vulnerable to the effects of climate change, even though it has contributed the least to carbon emissions (Nhamo, 2013). Notwithstanding, a key challenge for the continent is to finance investment in low-carbon, climate-proof infrastructure (Besada et al, 2013). Clean Technology Fund projects will leverage at least five times their value in clean energy solutions, and private sources will play a greater role in financing these; but low returns to private sector investors so far imply that a major share of expenditures will need to be covered from public sources (AfDB, 2010c, 2010d).

Changing policies and values: capacity for maintenance and upgrade issues

Without significant improvement in its maintenance culture, mere addition of more public and private infrastructure cannot result in the anticipated improvement in Africa's economic performance and greater social inclusion.

Infrastructure delivery and maintenance.

At a policy level, operationalization of infrastructure delivery demands the following.

Inclusive governance

As Oyedele (2012) argued, infrastructure development is fundamental to measuring the performance of democratic leaders, and it is the foundation of good democratic governance. Infrastructure is the medium, the tools and techniques of a project, programme or strategy. Demand for infrastructure development is high and resources are limited. Infrastructure development in democratic governance involves identifying the right project, carrying out feasibility and viability studies and physical development of the project with sustainable social development as an end in itself (AfDB, 2013). The challenges of delivering sustainable infrastructure may also include international requirements that African countries have signed up to. The primary objective is to build good governance systems and strengthen the capacity of municipal and local authorities to promote a culture of transparency, instigating anticorruption strategies and systems, and implementing reforms targeted at fiscal decentralisation, self-sufficiency, and the sustainability of public investment. Development partners may need to provide assistance to municipalities and localities to improve their systems of revenue collection and tax administration.

Private sector development

Private enterprises and PPPs are now being encouraged to help finance urban and rural development programmes (AfDB, 2011a). Enhancing the business-enabling environment through improvements to infrastructure (for example, improving ICT networks; a more reliable electricity supply; better transportation linkages) is one practical approach. Supporting municipalities and local authorities in reforming their legal and regulatory frameworks may also spur new investments. In order to scale up its support for rural and urban development, government must form partnerships with other major international players.

The role of infrastructure in structural transformation of Africa

At least two of the chapters in this volume note the direct effects of infrastructure on production costs and profitability of agriculture, which are similar to those for industry, with profound structural changes on the rural economy. These changes have been found in various previous studies in relations to income levels, the availability of alternative sources of income, and the composition of consumption as well as the health of the population (Kessides, 1993). For example, Van Raalte et al (1979) found that improved rural roads in Colombia resulted not only in increases in agricultural production, but also greater use of credit and alternative non-farm employment as well as higher overall earnings. Binswanger (1983) also reported in a Thailand study that reduced transport costs from improved roads shifted local demand away from some cheap locally produced goods as costs of competing manufactured consumer goods were reduced; and more importantly, the improved roads contributed more non-farm jobs than were lost. We review some of the ways infrastructure influence economic transformation.

Influence of technological innovation

Information is today considered itself a factor of production, and activities involved with the processing and generation of information account for one-third to half of GDP and employment among countries in the Organisation for Economic Co-operation and Development (OECD), and a growing share of GDP in the modern sectors of less developed countries (LDCs) (Wellenius et al, 1993).

Technological change in telecommunications, which has drastically reduced the cost of communications and expanded the range of services available, has also reduced the costs of transportation and many other activities using telecommunications (Hufbauer, 1991). Infrastructure is the backbone of modern technology in practically all sectors. The "information revolution" or knowledge economy of recent decades has been based on information systems (informatics) using the technology and services of telecommunications significantly influencing production and distribution activities in secondary and tertiary sectors of the modern economy, including banking, government, and culture. Technological change in telecommunications has drastically reduced the cost of communications, transportation and expanded the range of services available to society (ibid). The emergence of modern ICT and associated innovations has had dramatic changes in cost structures, and has increased the information intensity of many activities, the globalization of trade, manufacturing, and capital flows, and contact and cultural exchange across populations (Kessides, 1993).

Changing the structure of production and consumption

As we noted in the introduction, infrastructure shapes the basic patterns of demand and supply, and to the economy's ability to respond to changes in prices or endowments of other resources. It also influences the power configuration in society. In the developed world, the expansion of service, high technology, and financial sectors relative to manufacturing and goods-producing industries has increased the demand for telecommunications, but reduced the relative requirements for transportation of manufacturing inputs and outputs, and infrastructure for industrial waste disposal (Kessides, 1993). These changes have had impacts on industrial locations and how these relate to consumers in specified markets, for example through the development of modern logistics and evolution of value-chains (Kaplinsky and Farooki, 2010).

Impacts of infrastructure on personal welfare

Infrastructure affects social welfare (and to the absence of welfare, poverty) in three broad respects: it has a basic consumption value as services; it affects labor productivity and access to employment by mediating skills and work, and thus the capacity to earn future income; and it affects real wealth for example by influencing the values of housing and real estates. As the chapters in this volume show, low-income groups generally have less access to infrastructure services, or face lower quality of such services when they are available, than higher income groups within any given population or country, with dramatic effects on the perpetuation of inequity and social exclusion. One important policy issue concerns not only the distribution of access or quality of infrastructure services among income groups, but also the incidence of net public expenditure on these services (Kessides, 1993).

Infrastructure's value in consumption

A number of the authors in this volume note that infrastructure services such as clean water, transport, and communications are important consumption benefits, and their availability is a measure of the basic welfare of the population. Arguably, individuals are poor because (insofar as) they do not have access to infrastructure services of the necessary quality. In addition, the price of infrastructure services relative to other items affects the level of overall consumption that households can achieve within a given budget constraint. Two budget constraints are relevant here—both cash income and time. With respect to the first constraint, a 1989 study of informal sector water vending in Onitsha, Nigeria found that the vast majority of households were not service by the municipal piped water distribution system, and instead were purchasing water from private vendors at prices that were 20 times those of the public utility. The authors reject the frequent assumption that households only spend 3-5% of their income on water by showing that the poor especially actually spend much larger shares of their income for water—up to 20% according to one study in Haiti (Whittington et al, 1990). This is a reflection of water's value as a basic necessity. This research shows that households incur high costs of coping with unreliability (Kessides, 1993). In relation to the second constraint—that is, time—a comparison of villages in rural Sindh, Pakistan reportedly found that women with access to improved water supply spent 70 to 80% less time collecting water than those without. Skilled women spent the greatest amount of their time savings on income-generating activities, and to a lesser extent on leisure; meanwhile unskilled women spend their extra available time mainly on domestic activities (Read and Kudat, 1992). Essentially, being disadvantaged in access to infrastructure entails losing out on the positive externalities that are derived therefrom and resulting in limited structural changes in the economy.

Infrastructure and labour productivity

As already noted, infrastructure also has impacts on labour productivity and availability of employment by influencing not just skills but access to the labor market. As noted earlier, inadequate access to infrastructure services affects the time allocations of the poor and thus their ability to engage in activities which would have a greater impact on their livelihood systems and welfare. Poor infrastructures have multiple effects on health and education, and thereby on individuals' labor productivity as well as quality of life. It is documented in this volume that improvements in water supply and sanitation have a large measured impact in reducing morbidity from major waterborne diseases, reducing child mortality, and reducing the severity of disease when it occurs. Equally, educational infrastructures in the forms of schools and associated curriculum have drastic effects on the productivity of the wider economy as well as the living conditions of concerned individuals.

Looking beyond China: South–South technical cooperation in infrastructure development

There is need to rethink the role China has allegedly been playing in the development of African infrastructure within context of the China-Africa Cooperation Forum to allow for a redefinition of terms and conditions of Chinese investments in the sector on the continent (Schiere and Rugamba, 2011). First and foremost is the need for African countries to acknowledge their own contributions as the share of financing for infrastructure projects in the region comes from domestic resources (including tax and nontax revenues and domestic borrowing) and to a lesser degree budget support provided by development partners (IMF, 2014). Indeed, scaling up domestic resource mobilization is the most logical and durable way to speed infrastructure or any other investments on the continent.

Infrastructure projects undertaken by Chinese companies are often financed by soft loans from the state, on the condition that they are carried out by Chinese companies. This is in line with the Chinese "go out" strategy promoting internationalization of Chinese companies (Corkin, 2006). Chinese state concessional loans are disbursed by China Exim Bank, one of the largest such institutions in the world (Moss and Rose, 2006). It is estimated China Exim Bank has disbursed over US$12.5 billion for large-scale infrastructural projects in Sub-Saharan African alone since 1994 (inception date) although its official reported figures are much smaller (Bossard, 2007; Bräutigum, 2011a, 2011b). Over 80% of these were to resource-rich African countries, such as Angola, Nigeria, Zimbabwe and Sudan (Broadman, 2007). According to the concessional loan requirements, Chinese contractors must be awarded the infrastructure contract financed by the loan. The only difference between China and traditional donors to Africa is that the Chinese do not interfere in the internal affairs of recipient countries (Bräutigam, 2011a, b).

India's relations with Africa are based on the principles of non-alignment and South–South cooperation, crystalized in the first Africa-India Forum Summit in 2008 (UN, 2012). There has been an expansion of private sector-led trade and investment initiatives related to the infrastructure and resource sectors. India's infrastructural activities in Africa are concentrated in economic infrastructure, particularly power and railways. As in the case of China, Indian aid for infrastructural projects is usually tied to sourcing from Indian firms.

Historically, Brazil's economic ties have favoured North America, Europe and South America, and Brazil has lagged behind China and India in establishing a comprehensive policy towards Africa. Brazil has bilateral trade, aid and investment interactions with individual African countries such as Angola and Mozambique due to linguistic ties. Brazil's involvement in Africa's infrastructure has been driven by its private sector.

South Korea has had limited aid, trade and investment relations with Africa. Most of its investment in infrastructure has focused on oil and mineral rich countries, particularly Libya, Nigeria, Angola, and South Africa. The vast majority of South Korea's infrastructure projects in Africa are aid-funded.

Infrastructure *services* refer to the delivery of services to users of the infrastructure network. This includes the provision of electricity, public transport services along roads, clean water and wastewater and mobile phone services, as well as innovations such as money transfers (World Bank, 2010). Equipment (pumps, bicycles, handcarts, motorbikes, minibuses and mobile phone handsets) is a key element of South–South cooperation.

Knowledge transfer in capacity building

A significant element of South–South cooperation involves technical assistance, capacity building and technology transfer. The Brazilian Development Co-operation Agency sees this as its main mission in

Africa. The Indian Technical and Economic Cooperation program is a long-established model of South–South collaboration.

Developing technical capacity

The role of financiers from the South in developing technical capacity is not well documented or measured. Such financiers and their contractors may come from similar socioeconomic contexts to the recipient nation and may have valuable and appropriate skills and technical solutions to transfer. A number of commentators, however, question the impact of South–South cooperation on local skills development and labor markets. Caulkin et al (2008), highlight widespread perceptions that the quality of work by Chinese construction companies is inferior, but they argue that, in some cases, very little distinguishes the quality and standards of Chinese companies from other firms, local or foreign.

Conclusion

In Africa, the demand for infrastructure services exceeds supply, and finance is still constraint by policy environmental factors at the country levels. Due to the wide gap between provision and needs, political economy considerations have tended to drive provision. The political situation is still in many circumstances not encouraging to foreign investors, and governments do not set the right priorities, thus calling for appropriate regulatory frameworks. Projects should meet development objectives, but in most cases, those embarked upon result in "white elephants".

Africa's financing needs for infrastructure are estimated at close to US$100 billion per year. Yet infrastructure investment amounts to less than half this amount. Funding the gap is thus a major development challenge. The bulk of financing still comes from domestic resources. Official development finance, as reported by the OECD, amounted to over US$10 billion in 2010 for African infrastructure alone, 80% of which qualified as official development assistance. Aid will not meet this financing gap. New energy and funding mechanisms can be found by focusing on priority investments within the framework of the Program for Infrastructure Development in Africa (PIDA). Combating current inefficiencies and creating new synergies, notably at the regional level, is a necessary starting point.

Inclusive governance is a crucial instrument that can help bridge the wide gap between demand for and availability of infrastructure services. This promotes accountability, reduces corruption and minimizes resources wasted through inefficiency. The stability brought about through greater social inclusion facilitates the mobilization of both public and private sector financing resources that are critical for infrastructure development. Building on national and regional initiatives from the bottom up, a coordinated approach can help harness energies to promote sub-regional dynamics and enhance the focus on project preparation at country and regional levels.

Capacity building is crucial in building Africa, for example to enhance budget execution, and can no longer remain one of the main constraints to development. Regional integration provides opportunities for both job creation and trade. Connecting countries through better infrastructure is fundamental to their future growth. Finding skilled labor, providing training programs and catalyzing the right investments remain top priorities for developing ambitious cross-country programs such as PIDA. It is essential to highlight and learn from best practices of transnational skills development in Africa. The University of South Africa (UNISA) approach to distance learning provides an example that can benefit universities and scientific agencies across Africa in the long term.

Apprenticeship schemes closely involve the private sector, where they will take place. Infrastructure investment can be promoted through better coordination with bilateral and multilateral lenders; increased private participation in infrastructure; and the promotion of financial deepening in order to better mobilize domestic resources. Infrastructural development is a critical tool in building African resilience to shocks and propelling its various economies to sustainable development.

Note
[1] The African Development Bank supports its regional member countries to access long-term financing for infrastructure, including through risk-mitigating instruments.

References

Acemoglu, D., Johnson, S. and Robinson, J. (2001) 'The colonial origins of comparative development: an empirical investigation', *American Economic Review*, vol 91, no 5, pp 1369-401.

Acemoglu, D., Johnson, S. and Robinson, J. (2002) "Reversal of fortune: geography and institutions in the making of the modern world income distribution', *The Quarterly Journal of Economics*, vol 117, no 4, pp 1231-94.

AfDB (African Development Bank) (1999) *African Development Report: Infrastructure in Africa.* Abidjan: African Development Bank.

AfDB (2010a) *African Development Report 2010: Ports, Logistics, and Trade in Africa.* Tunis: African Development Bank.

AfDB (2010b) *Financing of Sustainable Energy Solutions.* Committee of Ten Policy Brief, 3. Tunis: African Development Bank.

AfDB (2010c) *Infrastructure Deficit and Opportunities in Africa.* Economic Brief, Volume 1, Issue September, 2010. Tunis, Tunisia: African Development Bank.

AfDB (2010d) *Financing of Sustainable Energy Solutions.* Committee of Ten Policy Brief No. 3. Tunis: African Development Bank.

AfDB (2011a) *Rapid Urbanization and Growing Demands for Urban Infrastructure in Africa.* Tunis: African Development Bank.

AfDB (2011b) *Closing Africa's Infrastructure Gap: Innovative Financing and Risks. Africa Economic Brief,* vol 2, no 1. Tunis: African Development Bank.

AfDB (2013) *An Integrated Approach to Infrastructure Provision in Africa.* Statistics Department, Africa Infrastructure Knowledge Program, April. Tunis: African Development Bank.

AfDB (2015) *Africa Economic Outlook.* Tunis: African Development Bank.

AfDB, African Union Commission (AUC), Economic Commission for Africa (ECA), and United Nations Development Programme (UNDP) (2011) *Assessing Progress in Africa Toward the Millennium Development Goals, 2011.* MDGs Progress Report, 2011. Tunis and Addis Ababa: AfDB/AUC/ECA/UNDP.

Africa Infrastructure Country Diagnostic (AICD) (2009) *Africa's Infrastructure: A Time for Transformation.* Edited by V. Foster and C. Briceño-Garmendia. Washington DC: Agence Française de Développement and World Bank.

Ahmed, R. and Hossain, M. (1990) *Development Impact of Rural Infrastructure in Bangladesh,* International Food Policy Research Institute (IFPRI) Research Report 83. Washington, DC: IFPRI.

Alesina, A. and La Ferrara, E. (2005) 'Ethnic diversity and economic performance', *Journal of Economic Literature,* vol 63, no 9, pp 762-800.

Austen, R. (1987) *African Economic History: Internal and External Dependency.* London: James Currey.

Ayogu, M. (2007) 'Infrastructure and economic development in Africa: a review, *Journal of African Economies,* vol 16 (Supplement 1), pp 75-126.

Banerjee, A. and Iyer, L. (2005) 'History, institutions, and economic performance: the legacy of colonial land tenure systems in India', *American Economic Review,* vol 95, no 4, pp 1190-213.

Banerjee, A., Duflo, E. and Qian, N. (2009) *On the Road: Access to Transportation Infrastructure and Economic Growth in China*, Working Paper, Cambridge, MA: MIT.

Bates, R. (2008) *When Things Fell Apart: State Failure in Late Century Africa*. Cambridge: Cambridge University Press.

Bertocchi, G. and Canova, F. (2002) 'Did colonization matter for growth? An empirical exploration into the historical causes of Africa's underdevelopment', *European Economic Review*, 46, 1851–71.

Besada, H., Stevens, Y. and Olender, M. (2013) *Addressing the Economic Costs of Sustainable Energy in the Global South*. Background Research Paper Submitted to the High Level Panel on the Post-2015 Development Agenda. New York: United Nations.

Biau, C., Dahou, K. and Homma, T. (2008) *How to Increase Sound Private Investment in Africa's Road Infrastructure: Building on Country Successes and OECD Policy Tools*. NEPAD–OECD Africa Investment Initiative, Experts' Roundtable (December 2008).

Binswanger, H.P. (1983) *Growth and Employment in Rural Thailand*. Washington DC: World Bank, Report 3906

Binswanger, H.P., Khandker, S.R. and Rosenzweig, M.R. (1993) 'How infrastructure and financial institutions affect agricultural output and investment in India', *Journal of Development Economics*, vol 41, no 2, pp 337–66.

Bossard, P. (2007) *China's Role in Financing African Infrastructure*. Berkeley, CA: International Rivers Network.

Bräutigam, D. (2011a) 'Chinese development aid in Africa: what, where, why, and how much?', in J. Golley and L. Song (eds) *Rising China: Global Challenges and Opportunities*. Canberra: Australia National University Press.

Bräutigam, D. (2011b) 'Aid "with Chinese characteristics": Chinese foreign aid and development finance meet the OECD-DAC aid regime'. *Journal of International Development*, vol 23, no 5, pp 752–64.

Briceño-Garmendia, C., Smits, K. and Foster, V. (2008) *Financing Public Infrastructure in Sub-Saharan Africa: Patterns and Emerging Issues*, Background Paper 15, AICD. Washington DC: World Bank.

Broadman, H. (2007) *Africa's Silk Road: China and India's New Economic Frontier*. Washington, DC: World Bank.

Bruhn, M. and Gallego, F.A. (2012) 'Good, bad, and ugly colonial activities: do they matter for economic development?', *The Review of Economics and Statistics*, vol 94, no 2, pp 433–61.

Burgess, R., Jedwab, R., Miguel, E. and Morjaria, A. (2010) 'Our turn to eat: the political economy of roads in Kenya', 2010 NEUDC Conference paper, MIT, available at http://mitsloan.mit.edu/neudc/papers/paper_294.pdf.

Cadot, O., Roller, L.-H. and Stephan, A. (2006) 'Contribution to productivity or pork barrel? The Two faces of infrastructure investment', *Journal of Public Economics*, vol 90, no 6-7, pp 1133-53.

Caulkin, L., Burke, C. and Davies, M. (2008) *China's Role in the Development of Africa's Infrastructure*, Working Papers in African Studies, no 04-08. Baltimore, MD: John Hopkins University, available at http://www.saisjhu.edu/academics/regional-studies/africa.

Corkin, L. (2006) 'Chinese multinational corporations in Africa', *Inside AISA*, October–December, pp 10-14.

Deininger, K. and Squire, L. (1996) 'Measuring income inequality: a new database', *World Bank Economic Review*, vol 10, no 3, pp 565-91.

Dell, M. (2010) 'The persistent effects of Peru's mining mita', *Econometrica*, vol 78, no 6, pp 1863-03.

Deloitte (2010) *Infrastructure Finance: Changing Landscape in South Africa*. Johannesburg: Deloitte.

Easterly, W. and Levine, R. (1997) 'Africa's growth tragedy: policies and ethnic divisions', *Quarterly Journal of Economics*, vol 112, no 4, pp 1203-50.

Engerman, S.L. and Sokoloff, K.L. (2000) 'Factor endowments: institutions, and differential paths of growth among New World economies: a view from economic historians of the United States', *Journal of Economic Perspectives*, vol 14, no 3, pp 217-32.

EU (2014) EU *Anti-Corruption Report: Report from the Commission to the Council and the European Parliament*. Brussels: EU.

Feyrer, J.and Sacerdote, B. (2009) "Colonialism and modern income: islands as natural experiments', *The Review of Economics and Statistics*, vol 91, no 2, pp 245-62.

Finan, F. (2005) 'Political patronage and local development: a Brazilian case study', Unpublished manuscript. Department of Economics, UCLA, Los Angeles.

Foster, A.D. and Rosenzweig, M.R. (2001) *Democratisation, decentralization and the distribution of local public goods in a poor rural economy*. PIER Working Paper 01-056. Philadelphia, PA: Penn Institute for Economic Research.

Freemantle, S. and Stevens, J. (2010) *BRIC and Africa: New Sources of Foreign Capital Mobilizing for Africa: Complementing and Competing with Traditional Investors*. Johannesburg: Standard Bank.

Gajigo, O. and Lukoma, A. (2011) *Infrastructure and Agricultural Productivity in Africa*, Market Brief 23 November. Tunis: Africa Development Bank, available at www.afdb.org/fileadmin/ uploads/afdb/Documents/Publications/Infrastructure%20and%20 Agricultural%20Productivity%20in%20Africa%20FINAL.pdf.

Gijón, J. (2008) *SWF & infrastructure investment in Africa: Challenges and Perspectives*. Paris: OECD Development Centre, www.oecd.org/ investment/investmentfordevelopment/41865534.pdf.

Herbst, J. (2000) *States and Power in Africa: Comparative Lessons in Authority and Control*. Princeton, NJ: Princeton University Press.

Hufbauer, G. (1991) 'World economic integration: the long view', in *International Economic Insights*. Washington, DC: Institute of International Economics.

IMF (International Monetary Fund) (2014) *Regional Economic Outlook: Sub-Saharan Africa Staying the Course*. Washington DC: IMF.

Iyer, L. (2010) 'Direct versus indirect colonial rule in India: long-term consequences', *The Review of Economics and Statistics*, vol 92, no 4, pp 693–713.

Jedwab, R. and Moradi, A. (2013) *Colonial Investments and Long-Term Development in Africa: Evidence from Ghanaian Railways*. Dartmouth College, Department of Economics Working Paper.

Kaplinsky, R. and Farooki, M., (2010) *What are the Implications for Global Value Chains When the Market Shifts from the North to the South?*, World Bank Policy Research Working Paper Series No 5205, Washington, DC: World Bank.

Kararach, G. (2011) *Macroeconomic Policy and the Political Limits of Reform Programmes in Developing Countries*. Nairobi: African Research and Resource Forum.

Kararach, G. (2014) *Development Policy in Africa: Mastering the Future?* New York, NY: Palgrave Macmillan.

Kararach, G., Hanson, K.T. and Shaw, T. (2012) 'Africa's second half-century: enhancing capacity for sustainable human development and human security', in K. Hanson, G. Kararach, G. and T. Shaw (eds) *Rethinking Development Challenges for Public Policy: Insights from Contemporary Africa*. Basingstoke: Palgrave Macmillan.

Kenny, C. (2006) *Measuring and Reducing the Impact of Corruption in Infrastructure*. World Bank Policy Research Working Paper 4099. Washington, DC: World Bank.

Kessides, C. (1993) *The Contribution of Infrastructure to Economic Development: A Review of Experience and Policy Implications*, Discussion Paper 213. Washington, DC: World Bank

La Porta, R., Lopez-de-Silanes, F., Shleifer, A., Vishny, R. W. (1998) 'Law and Finance', *Journal of Political Economy*, vol 106, no 6, pp 1113-55.

Lin, J. (2012) 'Structural change in Africa', in E. Sryeetey, S. Devarajan, R. Kanbur, and L. Kasekende (eds) *The Oxford Companion to the Economics of Africa*. Oxford: Oxford University Press.

Mabogunje, A.L. (1981) *The Development Process. A Spatial Perspective*. New York, NY: Holmes & Meier.

Miguel, E. and Zaidi, F. (2003) 'Do politicians reward their supporters? Regression discontinuity evidence from Ghana', Unpublished manuscript, University of California, Berkeley.

Miguel, E. and Gugerty, M.K. (2005) 'Ethnic diversity, social sanctions, and public goods in Kenya', *Journal of Public Economics*, vol 89, no 12, pp 2325-68.

Minten, B (1999) *Infrastructure, Market Access, and Agricultural Prices: Evidence from Madagascar,* MSSD Discussion Paper no. 26. Washington, DC: International Food Policy Research Institute.

Mobarak, A., Rajkumar, A. and Cropper, M. (2011) 'The political economy of health services provision in Brazil', *Economic Development and Cultural Change*, vol 59, no 4, pp 723-51.

Montalvo, J. and Reynal-Querol, M. (2005) 'Ethnic diversity and economic development', *Journal of Development Economics*, vol 76, no 2, pp 293-323

Moser, C. (2008) 'Poverty reduction, patronage or vote buying? The allocation of public goods and the 2001 election in Madagascar', *Economic Development and Cultural Change*, vol 57, no 1, pp 137-62.

Moss, T. and Rose, S. (2006) *China Exim Bank and Africa: New Lending, New Challenges*. Washington, DC: Centre for Global Development.

Ncube, M. and Lufumpa, C.L. (eds) (2015) *The Emerging Middle Class in Africa*. Oxford: Routledge.

Ndulu, B. (2006) 'Infrastructure, regional integration and growth in Sub-Saharan Africa: Dealing with the disadvantages of geography and sovereign fragmentation', *Journal of African Economies*, vol 15, no 2, pp 212-44.

Ndulu, B., Niekerk, L.K., Reinikka, R. (2005) 'Infrastructure, regional integration and growth in Sub-Saharan Africa', in: Teunissen, J.J. and Akkerman, A. (eds) *Africa in the world economy – the national regional and international challenges*. The Hague: Fondad.

Nhamo, G. (2013) 'Green economy readiness in South Africa: a focus on the national sphere of government', *International Journal of African Renaissance Studies*, vol 8, no 1, pp 115-42.

Njoh, A.J. (1999) *Urban Planning, Housing and Spatial Structures in Sub-Saharan Africa: Nature, Impact and Development Implications of Exogenous Forces*. Aldershot: Ashgate.

Njoh, A.J. (2000) 'Transportation infrastructure and economic development in sub-Saharan Africa', *Public Works Management and Policy*, vol 4, no 4, pp 286-96.

Njoh, A.J. (2008) 'Implications of Africa's transportation systems for development in the era of globalization', *Review of Black Political Economy*, vol 35, pp 147-62.

OECD (2010) *Infrastructure in Africa*, Policy Brief no 2, Paris: OECD, www.un.org/en/africa/osaa/pdf/policybriefs/2010_infrastructure.pdf

Oyedele, O.A. (2012) 'The challenges of infrastructure development in democratic governance', Paper presented at FIG Working Week 2012: Knowing to Manage the Territory, Protect the Environment, Evaluate the Cultural Heritage Rome, Italy, 6-10 May.

Ravallion, M. (1997) 'Can high inequality developing countries escape absolute poverty?', *Economics Letters*, vol 56, no 1, pp 51-7.

Ravallion, M. (2001) 'Growth, inequality, and poverty: looking beyond averages', *World Development*, vol 29, no 11, pp 1803-15.

Read, G. and Kudat, A. (1992) *Why a Women in Development Component Should be Part of a Rural Water Project and What Such a Component Should Comprise: The Case of Sindh, Pakistan*. Infrastructure and Urban Development Department Infrastructure Notes No. WS-8. Washington, DC: World Bank, Infrastructure and Urban Development Department.

Redifer, L. (2010) *New Financing Sources for Africa's Infrastructure Deficit*. Washington, DC: IMF.

Robinson, J.A. (2009) *The Political Economy of Inequality*, Economic Research Forum, Working Paper 493.

Schady, N. (1999) *Seeking Votes: The Political Economy of Expenditures by the Peruvian Social Fund (FONCODES), 1991-95*, Policy Research Working Paper Series No. 2166. Washington, DC: World Bank

Schiere, R. and Rugamba, A. (2011) *Chinese Infrastructure Investments and African integration*, African Development Bank Working Paper Series No. 127. Tunis, Tunisia: AfDB.

Shah, R. and Batley, R. (2009) 'Private-sector investment in infrastructure: rationale and causality of pro-poor impacts', *Development Policy Review*, vol 27, no 4, pp 397-417.

Stein, H. (2001) *Economic Development and the Anatomy of Crisis in Africa: From Colonialism through Structural Adjustment*. Copenhagen: Centre of African Studies, University of Copenhagen.

Tanzi, V. and Davoodi, H. (1998) *Roads to Nowhere: How Corruption in Public Investment Hurts Growth*. Washington, DC: International Monetary Fund.

Transparency International. 2008. Global Corruption Report.

UN (United Nations) (2012) *The Role of Emerging Economies in Africa's Infrastructure Development*, Summary Report from the Office of the Special Adviser on Africa. New York, NY: UN.

Van Raalte, G.R. et al (1979) *Colombia: Small Farmer Market Access*. AID Project Impact Evaluation Report No. 1. Washington, DC: USAID.

Wellenius, B. et al (1993) *Telecommunications: World Bank Experience and Strategy*. World Bank Discussion Paper No. 192. Washington, DC: World Bank.

White, H. (1998) 'Dressing a wolf in sheep's clothing in the emperor's new clothes? The UK White Paper on International Development', *Journal of International Development*, vol 10, no 2, pp 151–66.

White, H., Killick, T. and Kayizzi-Mugerwa, S. (2001) *African Poverty at the Millennium: Causes, Complexities, and Challenges*. Washington, DC: World Bank.

Whittington, D., Briscoe, J., Mu, X. and Barron, W. (1990) 'Estimating the willingness to pay for water services in developing countries: A case study of the use of contingent valuation surveys in southern Haiti', *Economic Development and Cultural Change*, vol 38, no 2, pp 293–311.

World Bank (1994) *World Development Report: Infrastructure for Development*. Washington, DC: The World Bank.

World Bank (1996) *Poverty Reduction and the World Bank: Progress and Challenges in the 1990's World*. Washington, DC: World Bank.

World Bank (2009) *Doing Business 2010: Reforming through Difficult Times*. Washington, DC: World Bank.

World Bank (2010) *Global Economic Prospects: Fiscal Headwind and Recovery*. Washington, DC.: World Bank.

Yepes, T., Pierce, J. and Foster, V. (2008) *Making Sense of Africa's Infrastructure Endowment: A Benchmarking Approach*, Policy Research Working Paper No. 4912. Washington, DC: World Bank.

Index

References to tables, figures and boxes are shown in *italics*

G

Gabon
  aid *518, 566*
  AIDI rank *32, 38, 41, 44, 587*
  costs of infrastructure components
    572, 578
  electricity *57, 129*
  ICT *59, 62, 65, 68, 71, 74, 78, 354*
  transport *48, 50, 53, 284, 295, 318, 321*
  water and sanitation *80, 83, 86, 129, 171*
Gachassin, M. 10
Gajigo, O. 652, 653
Gambia, The
  aid *518, 566*
  AIDI rank *32, 38, 41, 44, 45, 587*
  costs of infrastructure components
    572, 578
  electricity *57*
  ICT *60, 63, 66, 69, 72, 75, 78, 354*
  transport *48, 51, 54, 295, 318, 321*
  water and sanitation *81, 84, 87, 171*
gas
  development opportunities 232–3, 237
  financing infrastructure 223–4
  household spending on services *125*
  infrastructure base *193*, 195–7, 208–13
  planned programs 213–15
  Price Level Index (PLI) *572–3*
  private sector 215, 223–4, 228–9
  and regional integration 187, 211, 212–13
  regulation 215–16
geothermal power 203–4
Gertler, P.J. 120
Ghana
  aid *518, 566*
  AIDI rank *32, 34, 38, 39, 42, 45, 587*
  cities *109, 183*
  costs of infrastructure components
    572, 579
  electricity *57*, 199
  hydropower 199
  ICT *60, 63, 66, 69, 72, 75, 78, 354*
  sovereign external bonds 487
  transport *48, 51, 54, 284, 318, 321*
  water and sanitation *81, 84, 87, 171*
Goyal, V.K. 616, 617, 618
Graham, J.R. 617, 619
Graham, S. 7
Grand Inga hydropower project 187, 198, 200, *600*
Guinea
  aid *518, 566*
  AIDI rank *32, 39, 40, 42, 45, 587*

costs of infrastructure components
  572, 578
electricity *57*
ICT *60, 63, 66, 69, 72, 75, 78, 354*
transport *48, 51, 54, 295, 318, 321*
water and sanitation *81, 84, 87, 171*
Guinea-Bissau
  aid *518, 566*
  AIDI rank *32, 40, 43, 46, 587*
  costs of infrastructure components
    572, 579
  electricity *57*
  ICT *60, 63, 66, 69, 72, 75, 78, 354*
  transport *48, 51, 54, 318*
  water and sanitation *81, 84, 87, 171*
Gutman, J. 616, 623–5
Gwilliam, K. 320–2

H

Hansen, N.M. 4
Herbst, J. 648
Herric, B. 4
Hirschman, A.O. 3
housing
  affordable 448–9
  costs of infrastructure components
    572–3, 576–9
  slums 98, 105–6, 114, 435, 445, 450
Hussein, M. 653
hydropower *194*, 197–201, 232, 390, 392–5, *397*, 398, *600*, 633–4

I

ICT (general)
  access to 94–5, 425, *428*, 433, *551–2, 584*, 586, *588*
  applications and services
    development 336–9, 355–7, 362–4
  benefits of 474, 659–60
  cost and population density *102, 491*
  e-government 336, 355–6, 362
  financing of 368–70, 434, *494, 495*, 499, *620*
  future investment requirements 357–68
  Infrastructure Development Index
    27–9, *59–79*
  opportunities in *551–2*
  overview of 333–42
  private sector 336, 338–9, 343–5, *347*, 348–9, 353–6, *364*, 365, 368–70
  and regional integration 370–3, 474–5, 531–2, *542*
  regulation 94–5, *367*, 341–2, 441–2
  in schools and universities 356
  tech hubs 338, *338*
  technology parks 356, *357*, 363–4
  usage of 339–40
  see also broadband; internet; phones

household spending on *123*, 124, *125*
Infrastructure Development Index *29*, *80–8*
international comparisons *553*, *584*, 586
investment needs *102*, 120, *122*, 170–3, 181
Millennium Development Goals 170, *171*
opportunities in 433
priority setting 180–1
regional approach to 92–3, 439–40
regulation 179–80
scarcity of 92–3, 178–9
sharing knowledge 180
supply and demand constraints 173–9
tariffs 173–5, 180
toilets 114, *115–16*, 116, *117*, *119*, 162, *162*, *436*, *491*, *555*
and urban population growth 166–7, *168*
and urban scale 164–6
West Africa sub-region
AIDI 35, *35–6*
airports *305*
electricity *119*, 121, *131–2*, *198*, 199–200, *392*, *393*, *430*, *548*
gas *208*, 209, 210, 213, *213*, 216
hydropower *198*, 199–200
ICT 344–7, *552*, *589*
investment in power sector *394*
logistics *142*
oil *217–19*, 218
ports *295*, *296*, *413*
power trade 393, 466
railways *281*, *285*, 466, *589*
regional integration *540–2*
roads *264*, *265*, *269*, *399*, 465–6, *589*
rural areas 137, *138*, *139*
urbanization 156, *157*, *159–60*, *183*
utility affordability *178*
water and sanitation *119*, *122*, *131–2*, *161*, *166–8*, *171–2*, *589*
Williams, E. 5
wind-powered electricity 201–2
World Bank 140, 362, *363*
world-systems theory 6

Y

Yamoussoukro Decision 309, 311, 312
Yepes, T. 127, 175

Z

Zambia
aid *518*, *567*
AIDI rank *32*, *39*, *42*, *45*, *587*
costs of infrastructure components *573*, 578
electricity *58*, *129*
ICT *61*, *64*, *67*, *70*, *73*, *76*, *79*, *354*
transport *49*, *52*, *55*, *284*, *308*, *319*, *321*
water and sanitation *82*, *85*, *88*, *129*, *171*
Zimbabwe
aid *518*, *567*
AIDI rank *32*, *38*, *39*, *41*, *44*, *587*
costs of infrastructure components *573*
electricity *58*
ICT *61*, *64*, *67*, *70*, *73*, *76*, *79*, *354*
transport *49*, *52*, *55*, *308*, *319*, *321*
water and sanitation *82*, *85*, *88*, *171*